Succession to the Throne in Early Modern Russia

This revisionist history of succession to the throne in early modern Russia, from the Moscow princes of the fifteenth century to Peter the Great, argues that legal primogeniture never existed: the monarch designated an heir that was usually the eldest son only by custom, not by law. Overturning generations of scholarship, Paul Bushkovitch persuasively demonstrates the many paths to succession to the throne, where designation of the heir and occasional elections were part of the relations of the monarch with the ruling elite, and to some extent the larger population. Exploring how the forms of designation evolved over the centuries as Russian culture changed, and in the later seventeenth century made use of Western practices, this study shows how, when Peter the Great finally formalized the custom in 1722 by enshrining the power of the tsar to designate in law, this was not a radical innovation but was in fact consistent with the experience of the previous centuries.

Paul Bushkovitch was educated at Harvard University (1970) and Columbia University (1975). He has taught at Yale University since 1975, and is the author of *Religion and Society in Russia: The Sixteenth and Seventeenth Centuries* (1992); *Peter the Great: The Struggle for Power* (Cambridge University Press, 2001); and *A Concise History of Russia* (Cambridge University Press 2011). He is a member of the American Association for Slavic, East European and Eurasian Studies, and of the editorial boards of *Cahiers du monde russe* and *Quaestio Rossica*.

Succession to the Throne in Early Modern Russia

The Transfer of Power 1450–1725

Paul Bushkovitch
Yale University, Connecticut

CAMBRIDGE
UNIVERSITY PRESS

CAMBRIDGE
UNIVERSITY PRESS

University Printing House, Cambridge CB2 8BS, United Kingdom

One Liberty Plaza, 20th Floor, New York, NY 10006, USA

477 Williamstown Road, Port Melbourne, VIC 3207, Australia

314–321, 3rd Floor, Plot 3, Splendor Forum, Jasola District Centre, New Delhi – 110025, India

79 Anson Road, #06–04/06, Singapore 079906

Cambridge University Press is part of the University of Cambridge.

It furthers the University's mission by disseminating knowledge in the pursuit of education, learning, and research at the highest international levels of excellence.

www.cambridge.org
Information on this title: www.cambridge.org/9781108479349
DOI: 10.1017/9781108783156

First published 2021

A catalogue record for this publication is available from the British Library.

Library of Congress Cataloging-in-Publication Data
Names: Bushkovitch, Paul, author.
Title: Succession to the throne in early modern Russia : the transfer of power 1450–1725 / Paul Bushkovitch.
Description: First edition. | New York : Cambridge University Press, 2021. | Includes bibliographical references and index.
Identifiers: LCCN 2020039496 (print) | LCCN 2020039497 (ebook) | ISBN 9781108479349 (hardback) | ISBN 9781108749688 (paperback) | ISBN 9781108783156 (ebook)
Subjects: LCSH: Russia – Kings and rulers – Succession – History. | Heads of state – Succession – Russia – History. | Monarchy – Russia – History. | Inheritance and succession – Russia – History. | Russkaia͡ pravoslavnaia͡ t͡serkov – Influence. | Russia – Politics and government.
Classification: LCC DK37.6 .B87 2021 (print) | LCC DK37.6 (ebook) | DDC 947/.04–dc23
LC record available at https://lccn.loc.gov/2020039496
LC ebook record available at https://lccn.loc.gov/2020039497

ISBN 978-1-108-47934-9 Hardback

Contents

Preface

> [O]n croit que chez les Rousses quand le pere est mort, et qu'il y ait un fils qui soit mineur et un oncle, ou frere du defunct père, qui soit majeur et capable de regner, ils ne regardent pas tant le droit du fils a succeder au père, que l'utilité du Roiyaume, etant gouverné par un peine en age a gouverner seul.
>
> J. G. Sparwenfeld, 9 March 1684.[1]

In 1913 the Russian government and Russian educated society celebrated the 300th anniversary of the Romanovs. The ceremonies were grand, and historians took part in the event as well: most of Russia's prominent historians participated in the publication of a six-volume history of Russia under the Romanov dynasty with the title *Tri veka: Rossiia ot Smuty do nashego vremeni*. Edited by the Russian-Ukrainian literary scholar and ethnographer V. V. Kallash, the volumes were illustrated with photographs and decorative engravings and published by the Sytin firm, one of Moscow's prestigious publishers, over 1912–13. The first volume included an account of the Smuta, the Time of Troubles, describing how the young Michael Romanov came to the throne. Written by A. E. Presniakov, one of Russia's most accomplished historians, the account virtually ignored the fact that Tsar Michael came to the throne as the result of an election by a *sobor*, an assembly of the people that included not only the boyar elite (or part of it), but also the gentry, townspeople, and even Cossacks. Presniakov, following closely the already standard account of events by his colleague S. F. Platonov, recounted the events and analyzed the social composition of the *sobor*, but never

[1] Ulla Birgegård, ed., *J. G. Sparwenfeld's Diary of a Journey to Russia 1684–87*, Kung. Vitterhets Historie och Antikvitets Akademien, Slavica Suecana, Series A, Publications, vol. 1 (Stockholm: Almquist & Wiksell, 2002), 60–61. The scholar and sometime diplomat Sparwenfeld was reporting the views of the Narva merchant Tunderfeld and his friends. Tunderfeld had a brother living in Moscow and the context was a discussion of the events of 1682. Sparwenfeld already knew that the Danish ambassador in Russia, Hildebrand von Horn, a friend of Sparwenfeld's, was in close contact with Prince Boris Golitsyn, the leader of the Naryshkin faction. Boris Golitsyn became one of the Swede's friends in Russia. Sparwenfeld's views were based on those of his contacts in Russia: *Sparwenfeld's Diary*, 228, 231.

commented on the fact that the tsar-autocrat was elected, or on the election as a form of succession to the throne.[2] Published after the 1905 revolution, the book's omissions had nothing to do with censorship and reflected the usual way of presenting Russian history at that time. On this issue little has changed since 1912. Historians have analyzed some of the better known cases of succession in great detail, but the process as a whole and the rules of succession have not found favor with scholars. They have assumed that succession to the throne was a matter of primogeniture, yet contemporaries did not see it that way. The Swedish polymath J. G. Sparwenfeld thought that the Russians decided succession by consideration of utility to the state, not by genealogy.

No state exists without a mechanism for the transfer of power from one ruler or group of rulers to another. In European history most states with powerful monarchs were hereditary. Hereditary succession by custom, tradition, and sometimes law removed the issue from the wishes and designs of great aristocrats and the populace as well. It restricted the ruling monarch to passing the throne to his eldest son (and occasionally daughter), but it kept power within the royal family. Outside of Europe some states had culture and traditions which included polygamy, such as the Ottoman Empire, the Tatar khanates, Persia, or China, and succession could be quite complicated, even when the eldest son was preferred. In Christian Europe, including Russia, monogamy radically simplified the problem, though it also meant that the chance of a ruler leaving no children at all was much higher.[3]

The throne of the monarch in Russia, the grand prince/tsar, is assumed to have been hereditary in the eldest son until Peter the Great's decree of 1722 that established testamentary succession. The practice of hereditary succession from father to eldest son, bypassing the ruler's brothers, is also supposed to have been established in the fifteenth or early sixteenth century by the conscious policy of the rulers. This is the assumption, though the only full study of succession practices after the Kievan era is the 1972 work of the German historian Peter Nitsche. The more recent account of Russell Martin is in the same vein.[4] Thus Russia seems to fit

[2] V. V. Kallash, ed. *Tri veka: Rossiia ot Smuty do nashego vremeni*, vol. 1 (Moscow: I. D. Sytin, 1912), 1–3; S. F. Platonov, *Ocherki po istorii Smuty v Moskovskom gosudarstve*, 3rd ed. (St. Petersburg: Ia. Bashmakov i Ko., 1910).

[3] Nicholas Vatin and Gilles Veinstein, *Le sérail ébranlé: Essai sur les morts, dépositions et avènements des sultans ottomans, XIVe–XIXe siècle* (Paris: Fayard, 2003), 81–258. The Ming dynasty attempted, with some success, to ensure succession of the eldest son by the emperor's principal consort: Frederick W. Mote and Dennis Twitchett, eds., *The Cambridge History of China* (Cambridge: Cambridge University Press, 1988), vol. 7, pt. 1, 192–193, 440–450, 461–465.

[4] Peter Nitsche, *Großfürst und Thronfolger: Die Nachfolgepolitik der Moskauer Herrscher bis zum Ende des Rjurikidenhauses*. Kölner historische Abhandlungen 21 (Cologne and Vienna: Böhlau, 1972); Russell Martin, "Anticipatory Association of the Heir in Early

the European pattern, but in fact the actual forms of succession and the concepts that surrounded them were not as simple as they have seemed. While historians have analyzed a few cases of succession (Vasilii III, Boris Godunov) to such an extent that it often appears that there is nothing new to find about those examples, there are many fundamental questions that remain unanswered. Was the Russian monarchy really hereditary? Or was the monarch's designation of the heir crucial? Did heredity imply primogeniture? Did the forms of succession strengthen the monarch? Did they make the state "autocratic" or "absolute" or at least point in that direction? Did these forms add an element of instability to the state, or was it strong enough to survive the changing fortunes of the ruling family? How did the instability of the early modern family influence the forms of succession? In the early modern era child mortality was enormous, and childhood diseases, not only hereditary bodily or mental anomalies, could make living children unfit to rule.

The need for an heir required the ruler to have a wife, with the result that succession was part of the issue in marriage politics. Since the rulers of Russia after 1503 married not foreign princesses, but Russian noblewomen, marriage politics are part of the succession question. The marriages of the tsars to Russian noblewomen have been analyzed by historians frequently if not systematically (Russell Martin apart), but foreign marriages did not entirely disappear from the agenda of the tsars. Boris Godunov and Tsar Michael Romanov both tried to find foreign princes to marry their daughters, the most important attempts being made with Denmark. These attempts were not irrelevant to succession, since no one could guarantee that the sons of the rulers would survive the perils of disease and accident. Boris, for example, promised Johan, his prospective Danish son-in-law, an appanage (Tver') in Russia. Boris had only one son: had the marriage taken place and the son died, Johan would have been the consort of the presumed heir, since there was nothing in law or custom that prohibited female rule, which in any case could have been a de facto regency for a child tsar. Regency was the case for the first years of the reign of Tsar Michael. Peter the Great turned to foreign princesses for a bride for his heir. As soon as he made his journey to Western Europe, the European courts began to show an interest in his

Modern Russia: Primogeniture and Succession in Russia's Ruling Dynasties." In *The Routledge History of Monarchy*, ed. Elena Woodacre, Lucinda H. S. Dean, Chris Jones, Russell E. Martin, and Zita Eva Rohr (Abingdon and New York, New York: Routledge, 2019), 420–444. Russell Martin's work on the tsars' marriages, and related to them, also contributes greatly to the topic: Russell E. Martin, *A Bride for the Tsar: Bride Shows and Marriage Politics in Early Modern Russia* (DeKalb, Illinois: Northern Illinois University Press, 2012).

son, at first for the heir's education, and ultimately tsarevich Aleksei married a German princess. All marriage negotiations involved succession. Exactly how remains largely unknown.

The presence of a potential heir meant that the tsar's sons had to be brought up to be fit rulers. The tsars also, as we shall see, presented their choices to the population, mainly but not exclusively the elites. Education and the rituals of presentation, as well as conceptions of succession, took forms that arose from Russian culture. Before the latter part of the seventeenth century, culture in Russia meant Orthodox Christianity as well as the unwritten customs of the Russian state. With the advent of various streams of Western culture after about 1660, education, presentation, and concepts began to change. Consequently, the story of the evolution of Russian culture as it touched on succession is part of the story. Again, the issue of succession has been studied in some very particular cultural forms (e.g., the court poetry of Simeon Polotskii), but as a whole has not been investigated.

As the nature of succession is a crucial part of the structure and functions of the state, it is entangled with the ideas historians use to describe the state. The terminology that historians employ to describe the past is not an abstract issue or one of mere pedantry. Aside from their pedagogical importance, these terms serve as shorthand for larger conceptions that provide a framework for analysis. Words can convey the uniqueness of the past or impose a modern framework that reflects modern ideologies. In Russian history the two fundamental organizing terms for the political history of the early modern era have been autocracy and absolutism. Both of them are essentially modern concepts, derived from late-eighteenth-, nineteenth-, and twentieth-century ideas of politics and the state. Absolutism comes from European history, though it was not a common usage in early modern Europe, coming into vogue in the time of the French Revolution and the liberal constitutional struggles of the first half of the nineteenth century. It referred to a government where the monarch was the sole source of law in the absence of any sort of legislature. Autocracy, in contrast, seems to be a more "Russian" notion, since the Russian word *samoderzhavie* has a history going far back into the Middle Ages. At the same time, its actual meaning for most scholars has been the same as absolutism, that is, unlimited rule. The problem is that this notion of Russian autocracy in the early modern era has crumbled as historians have provided more realistic accounts of the role of the boyar elite as well as the relations of the state to society as a whole. These more accurate portrayals of the operations of the state have produced a great deal of information on what the state was not (an autocracy as an "absolute" monarchy) but have not provided as much knowledge on how it actually operated. Succession to the throne was central to those operations and thus its history throws some light on the utility of these terms.

Succession to the throne in Russian history is also entangled with the notion of absolutism for a very particular reason. When Peter the Great issued his succession decree in 1722, he also had his principal spokesman, the Ukrainian Bishop Feofan Prokopovich, write a tract in its defense, *The Justice of the Monarch's Will* (*Pravda voli monarshei*). This was the first political treatise in Russian history to make use of Western juridical and political thought. In Russian historiography this tract is normally labeled as a defense of absolutism. Absolutism as a term for historians of Russia really caught on only in the middle of the twentieth century, but it had a pioneer in the person of Georgii Gurvich. It was Gurvich who argued in 1915 that bishop Feofan's little book introduced into Russian thought the Western notion of absolute monarchy. In his basic contention about the presence of "absolutist" ideas in Prokopovich's tract Gurvich was wrong (and he later changed his mind about a crucial point), but his 1915 conclusions are still present in almost all writing on Peter's time and that of his successors.[5]

In recent decades historians of early modern Europe have shown increasing skepticism toward the notion of absolutism, some disregarding it entirely. Leaving it behind is not difficult, nor is it difficult for Russian historians to adopt an interpretation of autocracy that is more consistent with the values and reality of Russia in those centuries. Nevertheless, the issue of the tsar's power remains. It does seem that the state grew in size and importance and the ruler grew (if not without interruption) more powerful as well. If we are to assess these changes correctly, we need to understand the actual mechanisms of power, and that brings us back to succession to the throne. To understand the Russian state, we need to understand how its rulers transferred power from one generation to the next, a matter of evolving custom, not written law. Finally, in order to understand that transition we need to understand not just particular events, but how the Russian court and elite conceived the transfer of power. That conception in turn reflected the larger trends in the evolution of Russian culture. Until Peter's time, that understanding was part of a religious conception of the ruler and the state, one that focused on the moral personality of the monarch, not on sovereignty, law, or the

[5] Georgii Gurvich, *"Pravda voli monarshei" Feofana Prokopovicha i ee zapadnoevropeiskie istochniki*. Uchenye zapiski imperatorskogo Iur'evskogo universiteta 11 (Iur'ev: Tipografiia K. Mattisena, 1915). For the Prokopovich text, see A. Lentin, ed. and trans., *Peter the Great: His Law on the Imperial Succession in Russia 1722 – the Official Commentary (Pravda Voli Monarshei)* (Oxford: Headstart History, 1996) and *PSZ* VII, 602–643.

Aristotelian categories. In this area as in so many, Peter and his contemporaries made more than a revolution in state structure and military affairs. They also introduced into Russian culture a revolution of ideas, and in the area of political thought the succession problem was the trigger for that revolution. Hence the need to outline the major changes in Russian culture that affected the ideas of the monarch, succession, and the presentation of these ideas at court and sometimes outside of it.

⋆

It is the argument of this book that absolutism is not a helpful concept in understanding the Russian state in the early modern era.[6] It was not the case that the tsar simply gave orders to a subject aristocracy and people. As Russian historians, in the West and Russia, have been demonstrating for decades, the boyar aristocracy and its leading clans remained at the center of power together with the Grand Prince/Tsar for several centuries.[7] Underneath that aristocracy the gradual consolidation of the lesser gentry and landholders into a nobility, and the growth of a modest but effective state administration, provided the state with a solidity that enabled it to survive social and political crises as well as the unpredictable fate of the ruling family. Russia's rulers spent much effort and time on securing succession, but they did not attempt to establish a system of automatic succession in the eldest son until 1797. Rather they strove to consolidate loyalty to the ruling family, the monarch himself, his wife, and all of his children. To secure a successor, they held to the practice of paternal designation, even though most custom would dictate that the

[6] Many Russian scholars no longer seem to need absolutism as a concept. See, for example, E. V. Anisimov, *Gosudarstvennye preobrazovaniia i samoderzhavie Petra Velikogo* (St. Petersburg: Dmitrii Bulanin, 1997); D. A. Redin, *Administrativnye struktury i biurokratiia Urala v epokhu Petrovskikh reform* (Ekaterinburg: Volot, 2007). Others have used Marc Raeff's idea of the Polizeistaat to understand Peter's reforms: D. O. Serov, *Sudebnaia reforma Petra I: Istoriko-pravovoe issledovanie* (Moscow: Zerkalo-M, 2008); Marc Raeff, *The Well-Ordered Police State: Social and Institutional Change through Law in the Germanies and Russia 1600–1800* (New Haven, Connecticut and London: Yale University Press, 1983). Western historians who still use the term have nevertheless emphasized precisely that the ruler was not unlimited in fact: John LeDonne, *Absolutism and Ruling Class: The Formation of the Russian Political Order 1700–1825* (New York, New York and Oxford: Oxford University Press, 1991).

[7] See, for example, Nancy Shields Kollmann, *Kinship and Politics: The Making of the Muscovite Political System 1345–1547* (Stanford, California: Stanford University Press, 1987); Charles J. Halperin, *Ivan the Terrible: Free to Reward and Free to Punish* (Pittsburgh, Pennsylvani: Pittsburgh University Press, 2019); and the many works of A. A. Zimin and A. P. Pavlov. The elites of medieval Western Europe were also involved, formally and informally, with the ruler in decision-making long before the emergence of parliaments and assemblies of estates. As in Russia, the recording of these decisions in chronicles and documents reflected protocol as much as reality: Gerd Althoff, *Kontrolle der Macht: Formen und Regeln politischer Beratung im Mittelalter* (Darmstadt: WBG, 2016).

eldest son was the principal heir of his father. The grand princes and tsars made their choice explicit by paternal benediction and by the inclusion of the heir in court ritual and government. All of these rituals evolved with the evolution of Russian culture in these centuries, but each new form or practice served the same goals.

The combination of all these practices was a compromise. The ruler explicitly designated his successor, usually his son, as a matter of his own will and desire. At the same time, this designation usually came on the ruler's deathbed. There is no information about the motives of the ruler in displaying the heir earlier during his reign, in political acts and ritual. In part this display accustomed the heir to the role of the monarch, if only as an observer, but it also accustomed the "public," the boyars, the court, and occasionally the people, to their next sovereign. The audience of these actions demonstrated their loyalty to the heir as well as to the ruler, as they did in the oaths of loyal service. The ruler was thereby ensuring succession in a world where he could generally count on the elite to support his family and his choice of heir, but not totally. Finally, the ruler had to think beyond his immediate successor. He needed to secure wives for all of his sons, all of them since he could not be sure which one would live to adulthood and be competent to rule. He also had to think about his daughters, unlikely as they were to rule, but who might produce sons who would rule in an exceptional case. Marriage decisions, domestic and foreign, also involved consultation with the elite. It is difficult to ignore these elements of negotiation in the process of succession. Negotiation with the elite about succession is in turn part of the larger issue of "advice" to the ruler, an important component of early modern Russian political culture.

When the monarch's family failed to produce an heir or political troubles meant a contested succession, the solution from 1598 to 1613 was to assemble the elite and people and choose a tsar. Effectively the same process, though in a much more disorderly manner, took place in 1682. These events might seem untypical or out of place, but they were not. Consultation of the population, mainly on foreign policy issues, was part of the political reality of Russia in the later sixteenth century and the first half of the seventeenth. Once elected, Tsars Boris Godunov and Michael Romanov strove to make clear their preferred successor, Boris without success and Michael without challenge. The reasons for success or failure are a story that involves elite politics. It also involved to some extent popular attitudes, but that is another story, one that makes sense only when the practices and concepts of succession in the ruling family have been clarified. It is that clarification of practices and concepts on the part of rulers and the political elite that is the aim of this work.

In short, the succession practices of the Russian state suggest that it operated by a combination of the authority of the monarch (his ability to decree), the informal consensus of the elite, repeated displays of the monarch's decision, and affirmation of its legitimacy from the elite and people. As the whole system was based on custom, not written law, there were occasional variants. Obviously the final word was normally with the Grand Prince/Tsar, who decided which of his descendants should succeed. At the same time, the explicit or implicit consent of the aristocratic elite seemed necessary to the tsar, as seen in the 1553 succession crisis and Peter's taking power in 1689. The rulers also repeatedly asked for oaths from the elite, ordinary gentry, and government servants to ratify this choice. The public demonstration of the tsar's choice of heir, especially after the 1660s, shows that the rulers thought it necessary to publicly display the choice to the elite and people. At the same time, the oaths and other evidence show that the object of loyalty was to be the entire ruling family, including the women, and not just the ruler and his chosen heir. All of these aspects of succession beyond the tsar's choice meant that the most fundamental acts of state were the result of a combination of forces and interests, not merely the autocratic choice of the ruler. The exact balance varied from case to case. It is not surprising that by custom the successor was most often the eldest son: this was the normal succession of property and land in early modern families, in Russia as elsewhere. Reality mandated the varied practices that we actually see, including on occasion bypassing the senior descent line and even electing the tsar.

All of these practices and concepts were intertwined with one another and larger developments in politics, society, and culture. It is this complex of issues around that transfer of power that is the subject of this book.

Acknowledgments

The long genesis of this book has meant that many people were involved in its creation and helped me in many ways. Maija Jansson listened for more than a decade to my ruminations and wrong turns as well as my occasional insights. Nikolai Firtich reassured me that I needed to do it at one of many moments of hesitation. Similarly, Thomas Graham reminded me that the transfer of power is still a major issue in modern politics. Nikolaos Chrissidis thoughtfully read the entire draft and was also crucial to the many parts that involved Greek actors and Greek books and manuscripts. Lidia Sazonova and Irina Podtergera provided invaluable consultation on the manuscripts of Simeon Polotskii as well as many other things. Making sense of Ivan Grozny would have been impossible without years of conversations with Charles Halperin. Andrei Ivanov was a major resource for the life and thought of Feofan Prokopovich. Danish archives and problems would have been much more difficult without Joshua Hodil. Indeed, the archivists are the colleagues to whom I have the greatest debts, primarily the staff of the Russian State Archive of Ancient Documents and its directors, Mikhail Ryzhenkov and Vladimir Arakcheev. There Evgenii Rychalovskii's contribution was immense, as always. Andrei Bulychev was crucial in tracing the book collections of the seventeenth century. My research assistants at RGADA, Aleksandra Prokof'eva and Kirill Khudin, were invaluable, as were the reading room staff, friends of many years. I could not have achieved much in the Landesarchiv Sachsen-Anhalt, Standort Wernigerode, without its graceful and efficient staff, and of course it is Friedrich von Zech to whom I have a great debt of thanks for access to the Gosseck estate papers that contain the archive of Johann Christoph von Urbich. Regina Stuber of the Leibniz edition in Hannover was also a great help with the Urbich archive and especially with Duke Anton Ulrich's handwriting. Finally, Chloe Papadopoulos provided invaluable help in the final preparation of the manuscript.

1 Succession to the Throne, Autocracy, and Absolutism

Succession to the throne was essential to the survival of the state in Russia as well as the rest of Europe in the early modern era, for all but a few states were monarchies. For all of these states, the practices of succession existed alongside conceptions about the rules of succession, a combination of custom and in some cases written law.

Succession in Western Europe

European historians have assumed that hereditary succession by primogeniture was the normal Western practice, laid down in the Middle Ages and by the early modern era, in most cases, no longer a contentious issue. The discussion of European absolutism has revolved around the relationships of kings to the various countries' elites and to institutions such as law courts and assemblies of estates.[1] Yet there obviously was also a relationship between royal power and succession practices.

Hereditary monarchy was not universal.[2] The most important of Europe's elective monarchies was the Holy Roman Empire. Elections of the kings of the Romans and emperors went back deep into the Middle Ages, but in the early modern era the basis was the Golden Bull of 1356. The imperial system placed the election in the hands of seven electors, all prelates

[1] Roland Mousnier, *Les institutions de la France sous la monarchie absolue*, 2 vols. (Paris: Presses universitaires de France, 1974–80); Bernard Barbiche, *Institutions de la monarchie française à l'époque moderne, XVIe–XVIIIe siècles* (Paris: Presses universitaires de France, 2001); Jean Barbey, *Être roi: Le roi et son* (Paris: Fayard, 1992), 34, 59–61, 64–65. One exception to the rule is Johannes Kunisch and Helmut Neuhaus, eds., *Der dynastische Fürstenstaat: Zur Bedeutung von Sukzessionsordungen für die Enstehung des frühmodernen Staates*. Historische Forschungen 21 (Berlin: Duncker & Humblot, 1982).

[2] The pioneering work on heredity and elective monarchy in the Middle Ages was Fritz Kern, *Gottesgnadentum und Widerstandsrecht im früheren Mittelalter*, 3rd ed. (Leipzig: R. F. Roehler, 1914; Darmstadt: Wissenschaftliche Buchgesellschaft, 1962), esp. 13–45. See more recently Frédérique Lachaud and Michael Penman, eds., *Making and Breaking the Rules: Succession in Medieval Europe c. 1000–c. 1600* (Turnhout: Brepols, 2008); Corinne Péneau, ed., *Élections et pouvoirs politiques du VIIe au XVIIe siècle* (Paris: Éditions Bière, 2008).

and territorial princes. The number of electors increased later, but the overall system remained until the demise of the Empire in 1806. The imperial electoral system differed from that of most other European elective monarchies in that only the electors had a voice, not the members of the Imperial Diet. The other large elective monarchy was Poland-Lithuania. The evolution of succession was somewhat different in the two parts of the kingdom, but after the death of Sigismund Augustus in 1572 the joint monarchy was fully elective and not necessarily tied to the election of the previous king's eldest son. The two elective monarchies of early modern Europe, Poland and the Holy Roman Empire, both had rulers weaker than those of their neighbors, if not powerless. The third important elective monarchy was Denmark, and it was that kingdom's weakened international position that led to the establishment of absolutism in Denmark in 1660–5. It replaced an elective monarchy with a hereditary one, in this case even using the terminology of absolutism.[3] That term was unusual. In Swedish history, the event known as the proclamation of absolutism by Charles XI in 1680 passed without the word: in the official statement the Estates (Riksdag) spoke only of the king's "sovereignty" (*överhed*).[4]

Whether primogeniture or designation, usually by testament, was more helpful to the furtherance of royal power in the West is an open question since historians have not devoted much attention to the issue. That testamentary succession existed, however, is well known: the proximate cause of the War of the Spanish Succession was the testament of King Charles II of Spain, leaving his throne to Philip, grandson of Louis XIV, rather than to any of his Habsburg relatives. Further, the king's testament was not necessarily an exercise in royal power, since the king's testament was not necessarily observed after his death. In France, the Parlement of Paris overrode the testament of Louis XIII, who was trying to set up a regency for his young son. The Parlement eliminated the aristocratic regency council in favor of the complete power of Queen Anne.[5] In 1715, the Parlement again decided to cancel the will of the deceased monarch, as the testament made Philippe, Duke of Orleans, merely the president of

[3] Knud J. V. Jesperson, *Danmarks historie*, vol. 3 (Copenhagen: Gyldendal, 1989), 174–211; Adolf Ditlev Jørgensen, ed., *Kongeloven og dens forhistorie* (Copenhagen: C. A. Reitzel, 1886).

[4] A. F. Upton, *Charles XI and Swedish Absolutism* (Cambridge: Cambridge University Press, 1998), 31–40; *Sveriges ridderskaps och adels Riksdags-Protokoll* (Stockholm: P. A. Norstedt, 1896), vols. 13 (1680), 374–377 and 14 (1682–3), 231. The new arrangement also included a ratification by the Estates of the king's views of succession and his testament: Upton, *Charles XI*, 49–50.

[5] The testament of Louis XIII in 1643 named a council to assist his widow Anne of Austria in the regency for the four-year-old Louis XIV. The Parlement rejected the testament, giving Anne discretionary power to rule, which she used to support Mazarin: François Bluche, *Louis XIV* (Paris: Fayard, 1986), 39–40.

a council. The Parlement gave full power to Philippe, as with Anne before. In both cases the king wished to restrain the power of a regent, but the Paris judiciary preferred a single ruler with royal powers.

The notion of hereditary monarchy in Western Europe is not as clear-cut as it seems. In Tudor England, for example, succession to the throne was based at one time on the testament of Henry VIII and later (de facto) on the decisions of Parliament, which ratified the accession of Elizabeth I and the enthronement of the Stuart dynasty in 1604. The statutes also specified the order, starting with the eldest male child of the king and, in cases in which sons were not available, the eldest daughter.[6] This was long before the 1688 revolution and the ensuing dynastic settlements. Election or heredity, however, was not the whole story. Even hereditary kingdoms had public ceremonies to underline the succession and the person of the heir to the court and the world. The English kings, or at least some of them, did not let matters rest with parliamentary confirmation or the simple assertion of heredity. James displayed the heir to the world initially by the installation of Prince Henry as Prince of Wales in 1610, and then, after Prince Henry's death, by the installation of Charles, the future Charles I, in 1616.[7] The patents for the two installations made clear that the purpose of the installation was to avoid strife in the future.[8] There were no obvious alternatives to the sons of James, but in each case he made it clear who was the heir. In England, heredity, royal designation, and parliamentary statute all contributed to the legal foundation of succession to the throne.

Even in the classic land of hereditary monarchy, France, succession involved other elements than simply the consultation of the genealogy of

[6] Henry: *Statutes of the Realm* (London: Record Commission, 1817), vol. 3, 471 ff. (25 H VIII, cap. 22), 955–958 (35 H VIII cap. 1); Elizabeth: *Statutes of the Realm* (London: Record Commission, 1819), vol. 4, 358–359 (1 Eliz cap. 3); James: *Statutes of the Realm* (London, Record Commission, 1819), vol. 4, 1017–1018 (1 Jac I. cap. 1); Howard Nenner, *The Right to Be King: The Succession in the Crown of England 1603–1714* (Houndsmill and London: Macmillan Press, 1995), 1–25.

[7] Roy Strong, *Henry Prince of Wales and England's Lost Renaissance* (London: Thames and Hudson,1986), 151–160; Pauline Croft, "The Parliamentary Installation of Henry, Prince of Wales," *Bulletin of the Institute of Historical Research* 65, 157 (1992), 177–193; D. M. Loades, *Princes of Wales: Royal Heirs in Waiting* (Richmond: National Archives, 2008).

[8] The patent for Prince Henry asserted that the king honored his son with the title of Prince of Wales out of the natural love of parents for children but also "because the church and state are made firm by the undoubted, of best hope, succession of princes, the flames of rivalry and conspiracies are restrained and all anxious fears about subsequent ages are entirely shattered." (ex indubitata, optimae spei, Principum Successione, tum Ecclesia tum Respublica constabilitur, Competitionis Conjurationumque Flammae restringuntur, omnesque anxii subsequentium Aetatum Metus omnino discuntiuntur): Thomas Rymer, *Foedera*, 2nd ed. (London: A. and J. Churchill, 1727), vol. 16, 688–690, 792–794 (quotation 689).

the royal family. To be sure, the French kings and their lawyers had worked out elaborate ideas and rituals that demonstrated hereditary monarchy, not least the notion of the king's two bodies.[9] Nevertheless, the existence of a tradition of hereditary monarchy did not mean that all cases of succession would be undisputed. When Henri III was assassinated in 1589, in the middle of the wars of religion, the heir by heredity was Henry of Navarre, but he was a Protestant. The leaders of the Catholic Ligue called a meeting of the Estates General in Paris in 1593 with the purpose of electing a king. The assembled delegates did not dispute the idea of electing a king. Instead, they objected to the particular candidates, especially the daughter of the king of Spain, adducing the Salic Law that prohibited women from ruling in France. The meeting came to nothing, for the news was rapidly spreading that Henry of Navarre planned to convert to Catholicism.[10] When he had completed the process, he was crowned king of France. The ceremony, like those for the recent Valois kings, placed the princes of the blood around the king, replacing the medieval practice where the great vassals surrounded the king along with the princes of the church. The family element was at the forefront. Henry IV quickly defeated his opponents, ruling until his own assassination in 1610.[11] From then on, it would seem that hereditary succession was ensured.

Yet Henry IV made a considerable public show to demonstrate to all in France and abroad just who was the heir to his throne. This was the purpose of the ceremony of baptism of the dauphin, in this case the future Louis XIII (born 1601), on September 14, 1606. Normally a Catholic child was baptized as soon as possible after birth, but in the French royal house the custom was for the presiding priest (normally a bishop) to perform only an ablution (*ondoiement*), not a full baptism, at the time of birth. The king's son thus had no name until he received the full baptism in a very public and grand ceremony. Henry IV did not invent this custom, though the delay between the birth and baptism of his son was much greater than had been the case before. Francis I had let a month elapse between the birth of his first dauphin (Francis, died 1536) and his

[9] Ernst Kantorowicz, *The King's Two Bodies: A Study in Medieval Political Theology* (Princeton, New Jersey: Princeton University Press, 1957).

[10] Richard A. Jackson, *Vive le Roi! A History of the French Coronation from Charles V to Charles X* (Chapel Hill, North Carolina and London: University of North Carolina Press,1984), 115–129; *1594: Le sacre d'Henri IV à Chartres* (Chartres: Le musée, 1994); Jean-Pierre Babelon, *Henri IV* (Paris: Fayard, 1982), 533–600; Georges Picot, *Histoire des États généraux*, 2nd ed., 5 vols. (Paris: Hachette, 1888), vol. 4, 62–108; Auguste Bernard, ed., *Procès-Verbaux des États Généraux de 1593*. Collection de documents inédits sur l'histoire de France (Paris: Imprimerie royale, 1842).

[11] Jackson, *Vive le Roi!*, 155–171; *1594*, 198, 219.

baptism, and that order of delay was typical of the last Valois.[12] After Henry IV's precedent, the long delays were normal. Louis XIV, born in 1638, was baptized only in 1643, shortly before his father's death. Louis XIV followed the same precedent with his son Louis, the "Grand Dauphin" in 1668.[13] Pierre Dan, the superior of the monastery of the Holy Spirit at Fontainebleau, explained the practice in the house of France, saying, "they reserve the ceremonies [of Baptism] for another time in order to provide the pomp worthy of their grandeur and to have the time to invite the godfathers and godmothers, who are usually some foreign princes, to be present, either in person or by their ambassadors."[14] The ceremony was, in other words, a demonstration of royal power. It was also a demonstration of the royal family, as Pierre Dan's description of the 1606 baptism shows: leading the procession and carrying the necessary accoutrements were the princes of the blood, with the young prince de Condé carrying the infant. Following them were hundreds of men and women from the royal household, the government, the orders of nobility, indeed much of the French elite. A grand banquet ensued, with fireworks and other entertainments.[15] In later years, there were other even more public means to spread the message. Louis XIV's official *Gazette* recorded both the birth and the baptism of his heir for all to read.[16] With rebellious Huguenots, nobles, and occasionally parlements, even the kings of France made sure everyone knew who was the rightful heir and how important was his undisputed succession to the throne. The public display of the heir was a form of designation, in this case to strengthen heredity and primogeniture, not to replace them.

[12] The future Henri II, the second son of Francis I, had to wait four and a half months while the English envoy made its way to France to stand for Henry VIII, the boy's godfather. Henry's oldest son, later Francis II, received baptism a few weeks after his birth in 1544, while the future Charles IX was baptized the day of his birth in 1550. Henry II's third living son, the future Henri III, also had to wait for an English envoy to represent his king in 1551. See Didier Le Fur, *Henri II* (Paris: Talandier, 2009), 23–24, 33–34, 137–138; Michel Simonin, *Charles IX* (Paris: Fayard, 1995), 15; Jean-François Solnon, *Henri III: Un désir de majesté* (Paris: Perrin, 2001), 19–20.

[13] Babelon, *Henri IV*, 880–881; Matthieu Lahaye, *Le fils de Louis XIV: Monseigneur le Grand Dauphin (1661–1711)* (Seyssel: Champ Vallon, 2013), 166–187.

[14] Pierre Dan, *Le trésor des merveilles de la maison royale de Fontainebleau* (Paris: Sebastien Cramoisy, 1642), 268, 275–284: "on reserve les ceremonies pour un autre temps, afin d'y apporter l'appareil digne de leur grandeur, et avoir loisir d'inviter les Parrains et les Marrains, qui sont d'ordinaire quelques Princes Estrangers, pour s'y trouver, ou en personne ou par leurs Ambassadeurs" (277). The ceremony in 1606 took place on September 14, the festival of the Elevation of the Cross, which Dan thought appropriate as Louis XIII later showed his piety in opposing the Huguenots and returning them to their duty of obedience after a series of revolts.

[15] Dan, *Le trésor*, 280–283.

[16] *Gazette* [*de France*], 1661, no. 132, 1179; 1668, no. 39, 311.

Autocracy and Absolutism in Russia

In Russia, the assumption of historians seems to be that Peter's 1722 law strengthened the power of the monarch by introducing something new into the system that gave him greater control over the future of the state.[17] That assumption rests on a further assumption that Russia had a clearly defined system of primogeniture before 1722. Historians have assumed that the election of tsars in 1598, 1607, and 1613 (and de facto 1682) was merely an aberration caused by the extinction of the Riurikovich dynasty at the death of Tsar Fyodor and the ensuing chaos. My contention is that this assumption is wrong. The procedure of succession in the ruling family of the Moscow principality and the Russian state, from at least 1450, relied on the public designation of the successor, not on automatic primogeniture. Peter was not introducing anything new in practice. The change that he did make was to convert a custom into a written law and to extend it to include heirs not from the imperial family: in theory, though never in practice. The real innovation was Emperor Paul's 1797 succession law, which established automatic primogeniture and thus rendered the specific designation of the heir by the ruler unnecessary. In the centuries before Peter, formal designation was necessary because the succession was not fully defined even in custom, hence, when the ruler died without children in 1598, the only possibility was an election. These are conclusions that arise from the survey of succession practices in the ensuing chapters, but first a brief account of conceptions of the state and succession in modern times is in order.

In 1832, M. M. Speranskii finished the task assigned him by Tsar Nicholas I, the production of a digest of the laws of the Russian Empire, the *Svod zakonov Rossiiskoi Imperii*. His task was not to compile a code, which Speranskii and Nicholas understood to mean a creation of new law such as the French Code Napoléon. Instead, it was to represent the traditional law of Russia, but now systematized and readily accessible for the first time. As historians of law pointed out long ago, Speranskii did not merely systematize existing law, for that law had many gaps. There were areas covered inadequately or not at all. He had already produced a chronological record of all laws known to him in the *Polnoe sobranie zakonov Rossiiskoi Imperii* in 145 volumes running from 1649 to his own time, so he knew what the legislation had been over the years. To fill the gaps, Nicholas and he produced new laws while claiming that they were merely putting the old ones in order.[18]

17 V. O. Kliuchevskii, *Sochineniia*, 8 vols. (Moscow: Izdatel'stvo sotsial'no-ekonomicheskoi literatury, 1956–9), vol. 4, 256–258; Reinhard Wittram, *Peter I Czar und Kaiser*, 2 vols. (Göttingen: Vandenhoeck und Ruprecht, 1964), vol. 2, 119–120.

18 *Svod zakonov Rossiiskoi Imperii* (St. Petersburg: Tipografiia Vtorogo otdeleniia sobstvennoi E.I.V. Kantseliarii, 1857), vol. 1, 1. On the Digest, see Marc Raeff, *Michael Speransky, Statesman of Imperial Russia, 1772–1839*, 2nd rev. ed. (The Hague: Martinus

In discussing Speranskii's innovation, the sparse literature has concentrated on civil law, but in fact the first innovation was in the first line of the entire digest. The first section of volume 1 was "laws of state" and the first article read: "The Emperor of all Russia is an autocratic and unlimited monarch" (*Imperator Vserossiiskii est' Monarkh samoderzhavnyi i neogranichennyi*). The same paragraph cites as the sources of that principle a whole series of enactments of Peter's time[19] and Empress Anna's proclamation of autocracy of February 28, 1730.[20] None of these laws used the word "unlimited" or any equivalent. The closest was Peter's formulation in the Naval Statute that the ruler answers to no one but God, which is not the same as unlimited power.[21] It means that after the tsar does something that turns out to be harmful or wrong, he answers to God; it does not say that he is not bound to consult someone before acting.[22] This first section of the Digest then went on immediately (article 3) to repeat Paul I's law of succession. Unlimited power and primogeniture were the foundations of autocracy, at least in the minds of Speranskii and Nicholas I.

The 1832 formulations came at the end of a generation and a half of upheaval in Europe which sharply polarized the issues of state power, its sources, and its extent. The monarchist conservatives, just as much as the liberals, had to define exactly what they meant, as the vaguer traditional rules of Ancien Régime monarchies, with their complicated legal and administrative hierarchies and multiple informal networks of power, had been swept away. The monarchies that remained had to redefine their status, and the ultra-monarchist camp now began to espouse "absolutism," a word that had only then come into general

Nijhoff, 1969), 320–346; Richard S. Wortman, "The 'Fundamental State Laws' of 1832 as Symbolic Act," in *Miscellanea Slavica: Sbornik statei k 70-letiiu Borisa Andreevicha Uspenskogo* (Moscow: Indrik, 2008), 398–408; Tamara Borisova, "Russian National Legal Tradition: Svod versus Ulozhenie in Nineteenth Century Russia," *Review of Central and East European Law* 33 (2008), 295–341; Tamara Borisova, "Bor'ba za russkoe 'natsional'noe' pravo v pervoi chetverti 19 veka: Izobretenie novykh smyslov starykh slov," in *Istoricheskie poniatiia i politicheskie idei v Rossii*, ed. Nikolai Koposov (St. Petersburg: Izdatel'stvo Evropeiskogo universiteta v Sankt-Peterburge Aleteia, 2006), 123–151.

[19] Peter the Great's *Voinskii ustav* (Military Statute) of 1716 (*PSZ* 5, no. 3006, 203–453), his *Morskoi ustav* (Naval Statute) (*PSZ* 6, no. 3485, 2–116, esp. 59), the law establishing the *Dukhovnia kollegiia* (Spiritual College) in 1721 (*PSZ* 6, no. 3718, ch. 1, par. 2, 316–317).

[20] *PSZ* 7, no. 5509, 253. [21] *PSZ* 6, no. 3485, book 5, ch. 1, art. 2, *tolkovanie* 1, 59.

[22] It should also be noted that those of Peter's laws which Speranskii cited were translations or compilations of Western (mainly Swedish) law and that in none of these enactments was the definition of the power of the monarch a central issue. The passages in question were buried in the middle of other issues. In Anna's manifesto, the assertion of autocracy was the point of the document, but it remained undefined.

usage.[23] Their opponent was constitutional liberalism, so the crucial point to the Russian state, and to the supporters of "absolutism" in the West, was the unlimited power of the ruler. The Russian tsar did not share power with a legislature. What Speranskii and Nicholas did was to take this new, post-1789 conception of monarchy and combine it with the older Russian term *samoderzhavie* (autocracy) to create the appearance of continuity and tradition.

This process is interesting in itself, but for the historian of early modern Russia the problem is that the later generations of historians projected this "absolutist" formulation of autocracy back into the early modern era.[24] The point is not that the tsars before the end of the eighteenth century were not powerful, but that the anti-constitutionalism of the Digest placed the discussion in a pseudo-constitutional framework which is anachronistic. To the historians who worked from the middle of the nineteenth century onward, autocracy was supposed to have meant the unlimited power of the tsar (grand prince before 1547) over all of his subjects, including the elite. This meant the absence of a legislature or other consultative bodies. Yet historians have known for some time that in the sixteenth century Russians did not use the word *samoderzhets* (autocrat) to mean unlimited power, rather they meant a ruler independent of foreign overlordship or even just "pious ruler."[25] In spite of that discovery, it has continued to be assumed that unlimited power was the core of autocracy. Conceptions of the state that emerged in the middle of the twentieth century added new elements – the bureaucratic state – to the older concept, but unlimited power remained at the center. Even when historians, at first American Slavists, began to abandon the older conception that the tsars dominated a helpless and abject elite, they did not move on to investigate all the complex mechanics of the state. One of the basic parts of these mechanics was succession, as it was for any monarchy.

[23] The most detailed account of the rise of the political term absolutism is by Horst Dreitzel, *Monarchiebegriffe in der Fürstengesellschaft: Semantik und Theoretik der Einherrschaft in Deutschland von der Reformation bis zum Vormärz*, 2 vols. (Cologne, Weimar, and Vienna: Böhlau, 1991), vol. 1, 268–315; vol. 2, 732–785.

[24] See the pre-revolutionary classics M. D'iakonov, *Vlast' Moskovskikh gosudarei: Ocherki iz istorii politicheskikh idei drevnei Rusi do kontsa XVI veka* (St. Petersburg: I. N. Skorokhodov, 1889) and Vladimir Val'denberg, *Drevnerusskie ucheniia o predelakh tsarskoi vlasti* (Petrograd: n.p., 1916).

[25] Marc Szeftel, "The Title of the Muscovite Monarch," *Canadian–American Slavic Studies* 13, 1–2 (1979): 59–81; A. I. Filiushkin, *Tituly russkikh gosudarei* (Moscow and St. Petersburg: Al'ians-Arkheo, 2006), 55–63; Charles J. Halperin, "Ivan IV as Autocrat (Samoderzhets)," *Cahiers du monde russe* 55, 3–4 (2014): 1–18.

A further complication was the notion of absolutism in West European historiography. Starting in the 1950s, the conception of absolutism propounded by Roland Mousnier and others for Western Europe began to have an impact on Russian historiography.[26] This conception went beyond the traditional legal-constitutional idea to include the notion of the bureaucratic state as the foundation of absolutism, a form of state that allegedly emerged in the early modern era.[27] Many of the Western historians of eighteenth-century Russia began to use the term for Russian history, and Soviet historians in the 1960s adopted the same term, if with somewhat different content.[28] In the final Soviet schema, the sixteenth century saw the unification of the Russian state and the seventeenth century the preparation for European-style absolutism finally introduced by Peter the Great.

What both the Soviet and the Western conceptions of absolutism shared was the assumption inherited from the older literature that the core of the state was unlimited power of the ruler and the new notion that the basis of the state was bureaucratic administration. Originally the relations of the state and the ruling elite attracted much less attention than the evolution of administration. For the eighteenth century, that has remained the case to the present with a few exceptions, mostly Western (Ransel, LeDonne, Bushkovitch), who have described the tsar's relations with the elite.[29] Much larger changes came in the history of the sixteenth century. The main Russian historians of sixteenth-century Russia in the

[26] From the middle of the nineteenth century until the 1950s very few historians of Western Europe used the term "absolutism" or any variant to describe the states of early modern Europe. The dominant organizing principle was the rise of national states (France, Britain, Spain). Historians of law did use the term, though not universally.

[27] Roland Mousnier, *Les XVIe et XVIIe siècles: Les progrès de la civilisation européenne et le déclin de l'orient (1492–1715)*, 2nd ed. (Paris: Presses universitaires de France, 1956); Fritz Hartung and Roland Mousnier, "Quelques problèmes concernant la monarchie absolue," in *Relazioni del X Congresso Internazionale de Scienze Storiche: Storia moderna* (Florence: G. C. Sansoni, 1955), vol. IV, 3–55. Mousnier's view of absolutism covered much more than the growth of bureaucracy, but his insistence on situating administration in the surrounding society came at the time of great interest in bureaucracy among sociologists, a coincidence that reinforced that aspect of his work.

[28] Soviet historians of Western Europe had begun to use the term earlier: S. V. Kondrat'ev and T. N. Kondrat'eva, *"Nauka ubezhdat'" ili Spory sovetskikh istorikov o frantsuzkom absoliutizme i klassovoi bor'be: 20-e–nachalo 50-kh godov* (Tiumen': Mandr i ko., 2003).

[29] David Ransel, *The Politics of Catherinian Russia: The Panin Party* (New Haven, Connecticut: Yale University Press, 1975); John LeDonne, *Absolutism and Ruling Class: The Formation of the Russian Political Order 1700–1825* (New York, New York and Oxford: Oxford University Press, 1991); Paul Bushkovitch, *Peter the Great: The Struggle for Power 1671–1725* (Cambridge: Cambridge University Press, 2001). Some Russian historians have begun to investigate the gentry elite and its politics: I. V. Kurukin, *Epokha "dvortsovykh bur'": Ocherki politicheskoi istorii poslepetrovskoi Rossii* (Riazan': NRIID, 2003); I. V. Babich and M. V. Babich, *Oblastnye praviteli Rossii 1719–1739 gg.* (Moscow: ROSSPEN, 2008).

Soviet era, A. A. Zimin and R. G. Skrynnikov, insisted that the final stage of state unification, which they called centralization, was the main issue. Concretely this meant, especially for Zimin, concentrating on the alleged extinction of the appanage (*udel*) system, a traditional concern of Russian historians. The course of the century was the victory of the autocratic tsar, the incarnation of centralization. At the same time they were also interested in the role of the ruling elite, essentially the boyars, and their narrative brought that elite into the limelight. Skrynnikov emphasized Ivan the Terrible's relations with that elite as a whole, and saw his reign as an attempt, not entirely successful, to increase his power over the boyar aristocracy.[30] In practice, most of their narrative was taken up with the competition between boyar clans and the personal relations of those clans and individuals within them to the tsar. Much the same story provided material for different conclusions. Nancy Kollmann demonstrated that the Russian state and its politics were really about those boyar clans, and the tsar did not have the power or resources to dominate them. Robert Crummey drew the same conclusion for the seventeenth century, as did Paul Bushkovitch for the reign of Peter the Great. Recent work by M. M. Krom and P. S. Sedov in Russia reveals the same picture. The tsar ruled by balancing boyar factions among each other and balancing all the boyars with his personal favorites.[31] The tsar was certainly the ruler, but to label him "unlimited" in the constitutional sense is anachronistic and fails to capture the mutual dependencies and varied lines of power. The "bureaucracy," if that is really the right word, was not absent but developed rather late. Still largely the grand prince's household at the end of the fifteenth century, the state's administration had become quite sophisticated by the late seventeenth. Nevertheless, it was still quite small by West European standards and remained under the command of aristocratic office holders.

The situation is complicated by the decline of the notion of absolutism among historians of Western Europe. Though there are some exceptions among historians (Joel Cornette in France) and historians of law, most

[30] A. A. Zimin, *Reformy Ivana Groznogo* (Moscow: Izdatel'stvo sotsial'no-ekonomicheskoi literatury, 1960); A. A. Zimin, *Oprichnina Ivana Groznogo* (Moscow: Mysl', 1964), 2nd ed. as *Oprichnina* (Moscow: Territoriia, 2001); R. G. Skrynnikov, *Tsarstvo terrora* (St. Petersburg: Nauka, 1992), and other works by the same authors.

[31] Nancy Shields Kollmann, *Kinship and Politics: The Making of the Muscovite Political System 1345–1547* (Stanford, California: Stanford University Press, 1987); Robert O. Crummey, *Aristocrats and Servitors: The Boyar Elite in Russia 1613–1689* (Princeton, New Jersey: Princeton University Press, 1983); Paul Bushkovitch, *Peter the Great*; M. M. Krom, *"Vdovstvuiushchee tsarstvo": Politicheskii krizis v Rossii 30–40-kh godakh XVI veka* (St. Petersburg: Novoe literaturnoe obozrenie, 2010); P. V. Sedov, *Zakat moskovskogo tsarstva: Tsarskii dvor kontsa XVII veka* (St. Petersburg: Dmitrii Bulanin, 2007).

historians of the early modern era have come either to drop the term entirely or to redefine it to the point that it is really something else.[32] Yves-Marie Bercé has recently returned to the original meaning from the early modern era: a state not dependent on pope or emperor, and notes that the king of France ruled, on the whole, with the parlements and the local estates.[33] The basic insight has been the importance of non-bureaucratic elements in the state: the court, aristocratic clans, networks of patrons and clients inside the various elites, central and local, the importance of material rewards and bribery. The nascent Weberian bureaucrats have not disappeared but have come to occupy a much more modest place in the work of historians. No European state of the period, even France, looks like the proto-modern structure familiar from historical writings of the 1950s and 1960s.

Trying to reconstruct the operations of the early modern state in Europe, East or West, requires the historian to confront monarchy as it actually worked in the period. Was it an institution? Or is it better to see it as a family ruling the state? Institution or not, it was certainly a family as well, and the historian is obliged to investigate areas that have largely been ignored or left to the antiquarian and the historical novelist. To start with, the personal details of the family and its life history are important. It is not trivial that the descendants of Michael Romanov to 1762 consisted of a large number of healthy women and a smaller number of males, most of whom were quite unhealthy (Peter was an exception) and died young. The women of any ruling family, even if their political role was small (which it usually was not), are essential to any analysis. They did more than give birth to children. The births of children also imply their upbringing, so the practices of the ruling family in educating their children and preparing them to take over the reins of power form a crucial part of the story.

[32] Fanney Cosandey and Robert Descimon, *L'absolutisme en France: Histoire et historiographie* (Paris: Éditions du Seuil, 2002); William Beik, *Absolutism and Society in Seventeenth Century France: State Power and Provincial Aristocracy in Languedoc* (Cambridge: Cambridge University Press, 1985); Nicholas Henshall, *The Myth of Absolutism: Change and Continuity in Early Modern Monarchy* (London: Longman, 1992); James B. Collins, *The State in Early Modern France* (Cambridge: Cambridge University Press, 2009;) Roland G. Asch and Heinz Duchhardt, eds., *Der Absolutismus – ein Mythos? Strukturwandel monarchischer Herrschaft in West- und Mitteleuropa (ca. 1550–1700)*. Münstersche historische Forschungen 9 (Cologne, Weimar, and Vienna: Böhlau, 1996); Lothar Schilling, ed., *Absolutismus, ein unersetzliches Forschungskonzept? Eine deutsch-französische Bilanz/L'absolutisme, un concept irremplaçable? Une mise au point franco-allemande* (Munich: Oldenbourg, 2008).

[33] Yves-Marie Bercé, *Le roi absolu: Idées reçues sur Louis XIV* (Paris: Cavalier bleu, 2013), 93–100. Bercé also notes that the normal modern conception of absolutism has its roots in the nineteenth century, not the early modern era. For a similar argument about Germany, see Dreitzel, *Monarchiebegriffe*.

Russian Ideas of the Monarch and the State to 1700

The story of succession in Russia, as we begin to see, is complicated by the radical difference between ideas of the state in Russia and in Western Europe before the time of Peter the Great. Until that time, there was no political theory or even political thought in the Western sense in Russia. There was a literature about the ruler, primarily about the question whether or not he was a good Christian. That sort of literature existed in the West, but alongside a philosophical heritage from Aristotle (including scholastic ideas of the state) and a legal tradition inherited from Roman law and its commentators. Both of the latter were lacking in Russia, which inherited only the religious side of Byzantine culture. Peter's reign introduced a fundamental cultural revolution in Russia, visible toward the end of his life in various published writings that incorporated Western political thought of the seventeenth century to varying degrees. These were only a beginning, for the assimilation and interpretation of the Western political tradition took most of the eighteenth century. It was not a simple process. To understand the centuries before Peter, some sense of the ideas and values of the Russian elite of that time is essential.

As Russia came into being out of the various medieval Rus' principalities at the end of the fifteenth century, it had three sources of tradition on matters of state. None of these included written law. First, the new Russian state certainly had inherited and further developed earlier criminal law and the law of property, as well as rules of judicial procedure, but for the structure and practices of state it relied on customs established since the beginning of the state that the scholars call Kiev Rus' in the ninth century. These customs were recorded in the many historical chronicles, and probably in oral traditions known to us only in fragments contained in those chronicles or other works. Second, the Russians had examples of Orthodox kingdoms. The most important of these was ancient Israel, known from the Old Testament, from the summary of the Old Testament called *Paleia* (discussed later in this chapter), and from the compilation of world history called the *Khronograf* and its predecessors. Of course, Israel was not Orthodox, but in the Christian interpretation of sacred history not only was it the divinely appointed and guided kingdom that preceded the appearance of Christ, but also its existence was necessary to the history of salvation. Moses, David, Solomon, and other Old Testament leaders and rulers were examples for Christians, as were the priests and prophets for the Orthodox clergy. Third, the truly Orthodox monarchy was Rome from Constantine onward, including what modern scholars call Byzantium.[34]

[34] On Rus' and Byzantium see, among others, Simon Franklin, "The Empire of the Rhomaioi as Viewed from Kievan Russia: Aspects of Byzantino-Russian Cultural

Knowledge of Byzantium, in medieval Rus' and early modern Russia, however, was limited. For medieval Rus' and later Russia, the only significant source for Roman–Byzantine history was the *Khronograf*, the principal story of world history for medieval Rus'. It summarized the story of the Bible, the four monarchies, Babylon, Persia, Alexander the Great, and Rome, continuing the last through Byzantium to 1453. The *Khronograf*'s coverage of Byzantine history, however, was extremely uneven. Quite full for the later Roman period and early Byzantium, it became more and more abbreviated for the centuries after the ninth. For the last centuries of the Greek empire the *Khronograf* often provided little more than the emperor's name and the statement that he was Orthodox.[35] Finally, the acceptance of Orthodoxy from Byzantium did not imply the reception of Byzantine secular culture, which preserved the heritage of antiquity as a culture continuously studied and commented upon. Russia thus had no acquaintance with the classical tradition of political thought beginning with Plato and Aristotle. Of the Byzantine tracts on political matters, the Russians knew only the treatise of the sixth-century deacon Agapetus. Its reception is a warning that modern historians may not read these texts the same way the Russians of the early modern era did: Agapetus seems to some modern historians a spokesman for the glory and power of the Byzantine emperor, but the main Russian text to use him extensively, the *Life of St. Fillip the Metropolitan*, quoted him to denounce tsar Ivan the Terrible. In this conception, Ivan had failed to be the powerful but virtuous ruler.[36]

Relations," *Byzantion* 53, 2 (1983): 507–537; Francis Thomson, *The Reception of Byzantine Culture in Medieval Russia* (Farnham: Ashgate, 1999). Probably the first attempt to assess the knowledge of Byzantium in medieval Rus' was Filipp Ternovskii, *Izuchenie vizantiiskoi istorii i ee tendentsioznoe prilozhenie v drevnei Rusi*, 2 vols. (Kiev: Universitetskaia tipografiia, 1875–6).

35 O. V. Tvorogov, *Drevnerusskie khronografy* (Leningrad: Nauka, 1975). Text: *PSRL* 22.

36 Paul Bushkovitch, "The *Life of Saint Filipp*: Tsar and Metropolitan in the Late Sixteenth Century," in *Medieval Russian Culture*, ed. Michael S. Flier and Daniel Rowland. California Slavic Studies XIX (Berkeley, California, Los Angeles, California, and London: University of California Press, 1994), vol. 2, 29–46; I. A. Lobakova, *Zhitie mitropolita Filippa* (St. Petersburg, Dmitrii Bulanin, 2006), 47–50, 55–61, 285–296. An interpretation of Agapetus that makes the Russian use of the text more understandable is that of Peter N. Bell, ed. and trans., *Three Political Voices from the Age of Justinian*. Translated Texts for the Historian 52 (Liverpool: Liverpool University Press, 2009): 27–49. On the Byzantines, see Otto Treitinger, *Die oströmische Kaiser- und Reichsidee*, 2nd ed. (Darmstadt: Hermann Gentner Verlag, 1956) (originally Jena: W. Biedermann, 1938); Herbert Hunger, ed., *Das byzantinische Herrscherbild* (Darmstadt: Wissenschaftliche Buchgesellschaft, 1975); Dimiter Angelov, *Imperial Ideology and Political Thought in Byzantium 1204–1330* (Cambridge: Cambridge University Press, 2006); Konstantinos D. S. Paidas, *Ta Vizantina "Katoptra hegemonos" tes hysteres periodou (1251–1403)* (Athens: Ekdoseis Gregore, 2006); and a revisionist view: Anthony Kaldellis, *The Byzantine Republic: People and Power in New Rome* (Cambridge, Massachusetts: Harvard University Press, 2015).

In the absence of philosophical or theoretical underpinning to ideas of the state, the principal form of reflection on statehood came in the texts that provided examples of good and bad monarchs. Besides the chronicles and the *Khronograf*, there were also lives of Russian saintly princes beginning with Boris and Gleb and including Alexander Nevsky, Dmitrii Donskoi, and others up to the end of the fifteenth century. The examples were not only positive, for wicked princes figured in the *Paterikon* of the Kiev Monastery of the Caves as well as in numerous chronicle stories. The reigns of Ivan III and Vasilii III formed a period of almost continuous contention in the church over matters of faith and practice, and some of these controversies had political dimensions. Out of these controversies, and independently of them, a number of writers of the time touched on the nature of princely power. Iosif Volotskii used the works of the Byzantine deacon Agapetus to express the traditional notions of the just ruler.[37] The monk Filofei of Pskov reproved the shortcomings of Vasilii III in a famous epistle that called Russia the Third Rome. Filofei asserted that Vasilii had neglected his duty as a pious Orthodox ruler by failing to allow the seat of the Archbishop of Novgorod to be filled and by tolerating homosexuality at the prince's court. God would therefore smite Russia, in Filofei's view the Third Rome, a notion that earned fame at the end of the nineteenth century. (In reality, Russian writers after 1453 understood their country as the New Israel.[38]) The few writings on rulers and rulership by Maksim Grek (Michael Trivolis), the Greek monk who came to Russia in 1518 and remained until his death in 1556, were no different. The good tsar was to be just and generous to his subjects, and the bad ruler allowed greed and avarice to flourish.[39] The occasional apocalyptic extravagance aside, all these different notions revolved around the piety and faith of the monarch and indeed of the whole Russian people, their place in the history of salvation. They said nothing about concrete forms of government, the power of the ruler, or particular practices such as primogeniture or the designation of an heir.

In addition, the Russian elites of the sixteenth century were adept at creating historical legends, the most famous being the "Tale of the

[37] Ia. S. Lur'e, *Ideologicheskaia bor'ba v russkoi publitsistike kontsa XV–nachala XVI veka* (Moscow and Leningrad: Izdatel'stvo Akademii nauk, 1960), 474–480.

[38] Daniel Rowland, "Moscow – the Third Rome or the New Israel," *Russian Review* 55 (1996): 591–614; Joel Raba, "Moscow – the Third Rome or the New Jerusalem," *Forschungen zur osteuropäischen Geschichte* 50 (1995): 297–308; N. V. Sinitsyna, *Tretii Rim: Istoki i evoliutsiia russkoi srednevekovoi kontseptsii, XV–XVII vv.* (Moscow: Indrik, 1998).

[39] Maksim Grek, *Sochineniia* (Kazan': Tipografiia gubernskogo pravlenia, 1860), vol. II, 319–337, 425–431(epistle to Ivan IV). See V. S. Ikonnikov, *Maksim Grek i ego vremia* (Kiev: Tipografiia Imperatorskogo universiteta Sv. Vladimira, 1915); and N. V. Sinitsyna, *Maksim Grek v Rossii* (Moscow: Nauka, 1977), among many other works.

Vladimir Princes" (*Skazanie o kniaz'iakh vladimirskikh*), which is the story of Riurik's descent from Caesar and the Cap of Monomakh, the tsars' crown. The "Tale of the Vladimir Princes" is about the Riurikovich clan and the regalia of monarchy, not about constitutional structures or royal power, and it only touched on the issue of succession. It vested legitimate rule in the Riurikovich clan. Finally, there were also other conceptions that were expressed in the ruler's title, in the rituals of church and state, and in the decorative schemes of the Kremlin palace, such as the notion that Russia was the new Israel, the only remaining state with the correct religion and faithful to God's commands. All of this reading provided much material for thought about princely behavior, but little about the larger issues of state structure and power, including the matter of succession to the throne.

The same was true of the account of Rome and Byzantium in the *Khronograf*. Its basis was the world chronicle of Georgios Amartolos, or Georgios the Monk, from the ninth century.[40] Georgios had told the story of the world from creation to his own time, summarizing the Bible, the story of Alexander the Great, and Roman history. He ended with the death of the emperor Theophilos in 842 and the subsequent defeat of iconoclasm. The translation of Amartolos was made into Slavic most likely in Bulgaria in the tenth or eleventh centuries and exists in several variants, but not in many copies.[41] The text of Amartolos was reworked with many additions and subtractions in the *Letopisets ellinskii i rimskii* of the later fourteenth or early fifteenth century.[42] The *Khronograf* of 1512 used the *Letopisets* but also added, among other texts, more material from Amartolos and from a Bulgarian prose translation of the twelfth-century verse chronicle of Konstantinos Manasses. That text concluded with 1081, providing an account of Byzantium from where Amartolos left off up to that year. Starting with the twelfth century, the information in the *Khronograf* became more and more laconic.[43] The resulting text did not present a very positive picture of Byzantium. Naturally the Roman

[40] Carolus de Boor, ed., *Georgii monachi chronicon*, 2 vols. (Leipzig: Teubner, 1904); Warren Treadgold, *The Middle Byzantine Historians* (London: Palgrave Macmillan, 2013), 114–119.

[41] V. M. Istrin, *Knigi vremennye i obraznye Georgiia Mnikha*, 3 vols. (Petrograd–Leningrad: Izdanie Otdeleniia Russkogo iazyka i slovesnosti Rossiiskoi Akademii nauk, 1920–30); T. V. Anisimova, *Khronika Georgiia Amartola v drevnerusskikh spiskakh* (Moscow: Indrik, 2009).

[42] O. V. Tvorogov, ed., *Letopisets ellinskii i rimskii*, 2 vols. (St. Petersburg: Dmitrii Bulanin, 1999–2001); O. V. Tvorogov, ed., "Letopisets ellinskii i rimskii," *SKKDR* 2, pt. 2, 18–20.

[43] O. V. Tvorogov, *Drevnerusskie khronografy*; E. G. Vodolazkin, *Vsemirnaia istoriia v literature drevnei Rusi*, 2nd ed. (St. Petersburg: Pushkinskii dom, 2008); Treadgold, *Byzantine Historians*, 399–403.

Empire came across as rather ambiguous, a great state but sunk in idolatry. After the conversion of Constantine, however, the story that Amartolos presented was scarcely one of rosy optimism, and the Russian compilers followed his lead. In this story, many of the emperors were sympathetic to heretics, and persecuted the fathers (John Chrysostom), and the Amartolos section concluded with the nearly 200-year reign of the iconoclastic emperors, wicked and depraved despots in his account, which was faithfully reproduced in the *Khronograf*. The Iconoclastic emperors were impious and personally depraved, persecuting faithful Orthodox Christians. Constantine Copronym was a "hateful blood-drinking wolf." Good non-Christian rulers, such as Alexander the Great, were intelligent, just, generous with gifts, and patient with those who do wrong.[44] Good Christian rulers were clearly even better, but there are not many of them in the *Khronograf*. Constantine the Great was saintly and blessed (*sviatoi blazhennyi*), a good ruler who protected the poor. The version of his life in the *Khronograf* stressed his conversion and presented him as a faithful support to the clergy against heresy as well as a victorious general.[45] The later sections from Manasses were not such unrelieved gloom, but soon came the story of the Fourth Crusade, and the very brief account of later Byzantium followed by the fall of Constantinople. The *Khronograf* for the thirteenth–fifteenth centuries devoted far more space to Serbia, Bulgaria, and the Russian principalities (mainly Moscow) than to Byzantium.

In the *Khronograf*, the historical and pseudo-historical examples of monarchs revolved around the moral character of the ruler, not his "constitutional" position. The sixteenth-century *Book of Degrees* presented the whole series of saintly Russian princes and princesses starting with Princess Ol'ga, Vladimir Sviatoslavich, and his sons Boris and Gleb. Saints Boris and Gleb, of course, were never rulers, as they were slain by their evil brother as potential rivals to the throne. A number of other princely saints were recognized as such mainly on the basis of martyrdom (Michael of Chernigov and Michael of Tver') or posthumous miracles (Fyodor of Iaroslavl' and his sons).[46] The most important ruler-saints, about whom lives were composed and widely copied, were Alexander Nevskii and Dmitrii Donskoi. The life of Alexander in the earliest version

[44] *PSRL* XX 191, 318. [45] *PSRL* XX 261–273, quotation 273.

[46] Gail Lenhoff and N. N. Pokrovskii, eds., *Stepennaia kniga tsarskogo rodosloviia po drevneishim spiskam*, vols. 1–3 (Moscow: Iazyki slavianskikh kul'tur, 2007–12). For the earlier stories of Boris and Gleb, see D. I. Abramovich, *Zhitiia sviatykh muchennikov Borisa i Gleba i sluzhby im* (Petrograd: Otdeleniia russkogo iazyka i slovesnosti Imperatorskoi akademii nauk, 1916); Gail Lenhoff, *The Martyred Princes Boris and Gleb: A Socio-cultural Study of the Cult and Its Texts*. UCLA Slavic Studies 19 (Columbus, Ohio: Slavica, 1989); Giorgetta Revelli, *Monumenti letterari su Boris e Gleb* (Genoa: La Quercia, 1993).

certainly presented him as a faithful Orthodox Christian, defending Novgorod against the Catholic Swedes and Livonian Order. He was handsome, strong-voiced, brave, wise like Solomon, and unconquerable in battle. He trusted in God for his victories, and in peacetime he built churches and towns, was not tempted by wealth and judged justly. He was also merciful, good to his servants, and generous to all. The only sense of other relations with his subjects was the brief statement that he consulted the wise when he received a letter from the Pope; presumably this meant the clergy.[47] Otherwise, he simply made decisions and gave orders, a portrait that did not coincide with the story that emerges from the chronicles. In reality, Alexander had repeated conflicts with the Novgorod boyars, whose views he had to take into consideration.[48] The princes were not always saintly: the life of St. Feodosii, hegumen of the Kiev Monastery of the Caves, records the saint's reproof to Prince Sviatoslav Iaroslavich, who had usurped his brother's throne in 1073; he refused to attend the prince's banquet, "the banquet of Beelzebub, and to take part in a meal filled with blood and murder."[49]

Alexander Nevskii was widely known, and officially proclaimed a saint in 1547, while the story with Dmitrii Donskoi is more complicated. The Orthodox Church proclaimed him a saint only in 1988, but as early as the fifteenth century (probably in the 1440s) there appeared a panegyric that found its way into several chronicles, which placed Dmitrii's sainthood under the year of his death, 1389. Less popular with scholars than the other historical tales about Dmitrii's great victory over the Horde at Kulikovo in 1380, the panegyric presented more detail than any other medieval Russian text about the relations of the ruler to his people. Dmitrii was certainly brave in battle against Mamai's Tatars, but he also loved the innocent and forgave the guilty, slept little and arose at night for prayer, and lived with his wife Evdokiia in purity (*tselomudrie*, which means purity but not complete chastity: they produced twelve children). "With a human body he lived the life of the angels (*bestelesnye*)," that is, he lived like a monk. In describing Dmitrii's death, the author of the panegyric goes into more detail. On his deathbed, Dmitrii called his wife,

[47] V. Mansikka, *Zhitie Aleksandra Nevskogo: Razbor redaktsii i tekst*. Pamiatniki drevnei pis'mennosti i iskusstva 180 (St. Petersburg: OLDP, 1913).

[48] The literature on Alexander Nevskii is extensive. See Iu. K. Begunov and A. N. Kirpichnikova, eds., *Aleksandr Nevskii i ego epokha: Issledovaniia i materialy* (St. Petersburg: Izdatel'stvo Dmitrii Bulanin, 1995); Frithjof Benjamin Schenk, *Aleksandr Nevskij, Heiliger, Fürst, Nationalheld: Eine Erinnerungsfigur im russischen kulturellen Gedächtnis* (Cologne: Böhlau, 2004); Mari Isoaho, *The Image of Alexander Nevskiy in Medieval Russia* (Leiden and Boston, Massachusetts: Brill, 2006).

[49] D. Abramovich, *Das Paterikon des Kiever Höhlenklosters*, ed. Dmitrij Tschizewskij (Munich: Eidos Verlag, 1964), 66.

sons, and boyars to him, and told his wife to guide his sons by the commands of the Lord, and his sons he ordered to obey their mother. To the boyars he said, "You know my customs and manner, I was born with you, I grew up before your eyes and with you I ruled and held the Russian land for twenty-seven years. With you I warred against many lands . . . and with God's help crushed the infidels . . . strengthened the princedom and established peace and quiet in the land. With you I preserved my inheritance [*otchina*], which God and my parents gave me; toward you I had love and honor, I kept towns and districts under you. And I loved your children, I did evil to no one, I took nothing by force, I did not annoy, or reproach, or rob anyone nor did I any misdeed, but I loved everyone and held them in honor, and was joyous with you and mourned with you. You were called not boyars, but the princes of my land." Now after his death they were to serve his widow and children with all their heart, in joy and in sorrow. Then Dmitrii called his eldest son Vasilii (aged eighteen) and gave him the Grand Princedom, the throne of his fathers, and the Russian land.[50] In reality, the succession was not quite so simple, as we shall see. The testament of Dmitrii did give the Grand Principality to his son Vasilii and put his widow in overall charge of the family and hence of the state. However, by 1389 Khan Tokhtamysh had restored the power of the Horde, and Vasilii only took the throne with his sanction.[51]

The various examples of good and bad rulers that the Russians knew from their own history as well as Byzantine history and the world history known to them did not provide them with any specific idea of the political relations between ruler and ruled, even between the monarch and the aristocracy. Instead, they had a series of portraits of pious, just, generous, and courageous rulers and the opposite. Even the panegyric of Dmitrii Donskoi, the fullest of such texts on the relations of ruler to subject, provided only a picture of moral and emotional unity, the faithful service of the boyars to the just ruler. There was neither autocracy (or absolutism) nor the opposite. The issue of succession was also left at such a general level that the tradition mandated no specific rules.

In 1547, at his coronation Ivan IV received the title tsar, the first Russian ruler to bear the title officially and permanently. In the course

[50] M. A. Salmina, ed., "Slovo o zhitii i o prestavlenii velikogo kniazia Dmitriia Ivanovicha, tsaria russkogo," *Biblioteka literatury Drevnei Rusi* (St. Petersburg: Nauka, 1999), vol. 6, 268–286, 387–388; M. A. Salmina, "Slovo o zhitii i prestavlenii velikogo kniazia Dmitriia Ivanovicha, tsaria Rus'skogo," *TODRL* 25 (1970): 81–104; *SKKDR* II, pt. 2, 403–405, II, pt. 3, 385–387; Charles J. Halperin, *The Tatar Yoke: The Image of the Mongols in Medieval Russia*, 2nd ed. (Bloomington, Indiana: Slavica, 2009), 138–142.

[51] *DDG* 33–37; Charles J. Halperin, *Russia and the Golden Horde: The Mongol Impact on Russian History* (Bloomington, Indiana: Indiana University Press, 1985), 56–57; V. V. Trepavlov, *Zolotaia Orda v XIV stoletii* (Moscow: Kvadriga, 2010).

of the sixteenth century, the official title increasingly included the term *samoderzhets*, normally translated into other languages as "autocrat," in part as the Russian word is presumably a translation of the Greek *autokrator*. As these titles were unique to Russia, much ink has been spilled in analyzing their history and meaning. The consensus of scholars has gradually emerged that in the early modern era neither of them had anything to do with absolute power, a meaning attached to *samoderzhets*/autocrat only in the nineteenth century. The term *samoderzhets* itself had become a constant part of the title only in the 1570s, perhaps even in the reign of Tsar Fyodor, and the reasons for this change are a matter of dispute. In the fifteenth century it meant only that the ruler was independent of others; by the later 1560s it may have meant no more than that the tsar was a powerful ruler or even just a pious ruler. The English merchants and diplomats translated it as "self-upholder." The title "tsar" had nothing to do with the power of the tsar; it concerned rather his status among rulers. The basis of the title was biblical, for in the Slavic Bible all the kings of Israel were called "tsar," a usage that derived from the Septuagint, which rendered their title as "basileus." The Greek usage did not distinguish king from emperor, so that "basileus" was the Greek title of Roman emperors as well as of petty Greek or barbarian kings. St. Jerome rendered the Hebrew title as "rex," so that in the Catholic world the Old Testament rulers are kings, whereas in the Orthodox Slavic world they are tsars. Similarly the Roman and Byzantine emperors in Russia were tsars, while the Holy Roman Emperor was *kesar* or later "imperator." In addition, the Ottoman Sultan and the Chingisid Tatar Khans were tsars in Russian usage. The title tsar gave the ruler of Russia equality in Russian eyes with all these monarchs, ancient and modern. It had nothing to do with his position in relationship to his subjects.[52] Needless to say, neither title, neither tsar nor *samoderzhets*, implied anything about succession to the throne.

The new title also did not change the image of the ideal ruler found in Russian historical narratives and texts in praise of the prince. The *Stepennaia kniga* of the 1560s rewrote Russian history by recasting the

[52] Filiushkin, *Tituly russkikh gosudarei*, 55–152; Halperin, "Ivan IV as Autocrat"; M. B. Pliukhanova, *Siuzhety i simvoly Moskovskogo tsarstva* (St. Petersburg: Akropol, 1995). For earlier contributions, see Michael Cherniavsky, "Khan or Basileus: An Aspect of Russian Medieval Political Theory," *Journal of the History of Ideas* 20 (1959): 3–28; Szeftel, "The Title of the Muscovite Monarch"; Helmut Neubauer, *Car und Selbstherrscher: Beiträge zur Geschichte der Autokratie in Rußland*. Veröffentlichungen der Osteuropa-Institut München 22 (Wiesbaden: Harrassowitz, 1964); Vladimir Vodoff, "Remarques sur la valeur du terme 'tsar' appliqué aux princes russes avant le milieu du XVe siècle," *Oxford Slavonic Papers* XI (1978): 1–41; Gustave Alef, "The Adoption of the Muscovite Two-Headed Eagle: A Discordant View," *Speculum* 41 (1966): 1–21.

annalistic form of the chronicles into a series of biographies of the princes and metropolitans. It had many opportunities to praise the grand princes and their ancestors, sometimes by simply incorporating earlier texts. It did not expand the notion of the ideal ruler, however, beyond what was in the older stories of Dmitrii Donskoi. In the *Stepennaia kniga*, the death of Ivan IV's father, Grand Prince Vasilii, was quite elaborate and included a section praising the prince. In this account, God had established the prince's power and was always on his side. The author quoted (apparently) Agapetus to the effect that the prince's power on earth was like God's in heaven. He was to look after men on earth, and restrain his passions. Not surprisingly, Vasilii's chief virtue was piety. He was certainly wise and clever, but he was also strong in prayer, purity, chastity, and patience. He was kind both to the laity and to the clergy, and was "humble in heart, high in his life, meek in his glance, shining with self-restraint." The portrait was close to the earlier story of Dmitrii Donskoi, which the text explicitly quoted.[53] Other compositions besides the *Stepennaia kniga* had similar themes. The famous exchange of epistles between Ivan the Terrible and Prince Andrei Kurbskii, though a different genre of composition, did not add anything new to the conception of the monarch. Kurbskii reproached Ivan that he destroyed the "mighty in Israel," presumably the boyars. Ivan's response was that his actions were just and reflected his piety, the attributes of a good Orthodox tsar. It was Kurbskii who violated justice and the commands of God.[54] Perhaps the only hint of something more specific was Ivan's claim that in Russia the autocrats rule (*vladeiut*), not the boyars and dignitaries.[55] Kurbskii, of course, did not claim that the boyars did rule or that they ought to, but this was a polemic. Maybe he thought that privately, but he did not say so. Fundamentally the framework for both Ivan and Kurbskii was the traditional Russian view of the ruler as a pious and faithful Orthodox Christian, more like a Western medieval king, not a Renaissance monarch.

The other ways in which Russian culture conveyed the essence of the monarchy included rituals, both church festivals, such as Epiphany and Palm Sunday, and coronations and other rituals in the life cycle of the

[53] Pokrovskii and Lenhoff, eds., *Stepennaia kniga*, vol. II, 321–323; vol. III, 386, 388; N. N. Rozov, "Pokhval'noe slovo velikomu kniaziu Vasiliiu III," in *Arkheograficheskii ezhegodnik za 1964 god* (Moscow: Izdatel'stvo Akademii, 1965), 278–289; D'iakonov, *Vlast' Moskovskikh gosudarei*, 105–107. Here the praise frames a longer story about the death of Vasilii III, which has been the object of much scholarly discussion. See Krom, *Vdovstuiushchee tsarstvo*, 34–55.

[54] Ia. S. Lur'e and Iu D. Rykov, eds., *Perepiska Ivana Groznogo s Andreem Kurbskim* (Leningrad: Nauka, 1979).

[55] Ibid., 16.

ruler. Both the Epiphany and Palm Sunday rituals depicted the deference paid by the tsar to the church, or more properly the metropolitan, later patriarch, of Moscow. Indeed, the ritual deference may have been greater than the reality, but the point of the ceremony was to convey an ideal, not necessarily to reflect actual relations. The nature of the monarchy also manifested itself in its visual symbols, the double-headed eagle (borrowed from the Holy Roman Empire, not Byzantium), the crowns, the tsar's "pew" in the Kremlin's Dormition cathedral, and the decoration on the walls of the Kremlin palace. Most of these in one or another way demonstrated to the viewer the notion that the tsar inherited the mantle of the ancient kings of Israel, going along with the conception voiced also in written works that Russia was the New Israel and Moscow the New Jerusalem. Russia was thus the one kingdom with the true faith, chosen by God like the people of Israel.[56] All these rituals, symbols, and historical notions said nothing specific about the power of the tsar, and none touched on succession.

Russian Ideas of Succession to 1700

The ruling dynasty of Kiev Rus' was the house of the legendary Riurik, and all princes came from that house.[57] The traditions of succession to the ruling house of Riurik were one of the mainsprings of Kievan politics and engendered repeated episodes of conflict and violence from the ninth century to the Mongol invasion. Historians are still not agreed exactly

[56] Paul Bushkovitch, "The Epiphany Ceremony of the Russian Court in the Sixteenth and Seventeenth Centuries," *Russian Review* 49, 1 (1990): 1–17; Robert Crummey, "Court Spectacles in Seventeenth Century Russia: Illusion and Reality," in *Essays in Honor of A. A. Zimin*, ed. Daniel Clarke Waugh (Columbus, Ohio: Slavica, 1985), 130–158; Michael S. Flier, "Court Ceremony in an Age of Reform: Patriarch Nikon and the Palm Sunday Ritual," in *Religion and Culture in Early Modern Russia and Ukraine*, ed. Samuel H. Baron and Nancy Shields Kollmann (DeKalb, Illinois: Northern Illinois University Press, 1997), 73–95; Daniel Rowland, "The Problem of Advice in Muscovite Tales about the Time of Troubles," *Russian History* 6, 2 (1979): 259–283; Daniel Rowland, "Did Muscovite Literary Ideology Place Limits on the Power of the Tsar (1540s–1660s)?" *Russian Review* 49 (1990): 125–155; Daniel Rowland, "Moscow – the Third Rome"; Raba, "Moscow – the Third Rome"; O. I. Podobedova, *Moskovskaia shkola zhivopisi pri Ivane IV: Rabota v moskovskoi Kremle 40kh–70kh godov XVI veka* (Moscow: Nauka, 1972); Sergei Bogatyrev, "The Battle for Divine Wisdom: The Rhetoric of Ivan IV's Campaign against Polotsk," in *The Military and Society in Russia 1450–1917*, ed. Eric Lohr and Marshall Poe (Leiden and Boston, Massachusetts: Brill, 2002), 325–363; Pliukhanova, *Siuzhety i simvoly*; B. A. Uspenskii, *Tsar' i patriarkh: Kharizma vlasti v Rossii* (Moscow: Shkola iazyki russkoi kul'tury, 1998).

[57] Kiev Rus' had one of the several ruling dynasties of the early Middle Ages in Europe with the exclusive right to rule, analogous to the Merovingians and later Carolingians of the Frankish realm, the Piasts of Poland, or the Přemyslovci of Bohemia: Kern, *Gottesgnadentum und Widerstandsrecht*, 15–25.

how to characterize those rules of succession, which combined partible inheritance – the provision that all sons of a ruler should receive some territory during his lifetime or on his death – and the differences over who was the "eldest," the eldest son or the eldest brother.[58] With the passage of time, the Kiev center became less important, and local centers in southwestern Galich and northeastern Vladimir began to battle over Kiev as well as regional power. The emergence of Novgorod with its elected princes and boyar oligarchy provided a different model, but one that was not widely imitated. The Mongol invasion that began in 1238 changed the system in fundamental ways. The destruction of Kiev removed the traditional center of the state and a main object of rivalry. The local principalities of the western parts of the Kievan state gradually fell under the rule of the Lithuanian dynasty of Gediminas, while the northeast continued to owe obedience to the Grand Prince of Vladimir and, through him, to the Khan of the Horde in Sarai. The overlordship of the Horde produced a bifurcated system of succession. The Vladimir throne was in the gift of the Khan, who bestowed it on the princes of Tver' or Moscow according to his perception of the Horde's advantage. Below that level, the various principalities of the northeast maintained the old Kievan system, with its ambiguity about the roles of eldest brother and eldest son of the ruling prince. That was the system that the Moscow princes followed from the time of Ivan I Danilovich Kalita ("Moneybag," ruled 1325–40), with the addition that they were largely successful in keeping the succession in the hands of their eldest sons. How they did that is again the subject of much historical debate. Peter Nitsche was convinced that the policy of the Moscow princes was a continuous and ultimately successful attempt to establish primogeniture.[59] Aside from Nitsche's work, however, the debate on the rise of the Moscow dynasty

[58] A. E. Presniakov, *Kniazhoe pravo v drevnei Rusi* (St. Petersburg: Nauka, 1909); B. D. Grekov, *Kievskaia Rus'* (Moscow: Gosudarstvennoe uchebno-pedagogicheskoe izdatel'stvo, 1949); M. B. Sverdlov, *Domongol'skaia Rus'* (St. Petersburg: Akademicheskii proekt, 2003); A. A. Gorskii, V. A. Kuchkin, P. V. Lukin, and P. S. Stefanovich, *Drevniaia Rus': Ocherki politicheskogo i sotsial'nogo stroia* (Moscow: Indrik, 2008); T. L. Vilkul, *Liudi i kniaz' v drevnerusskikh letopisiakh serediny XI–XIII vv.* (Moscow: Kvadriga, 2009); Christian Raffensperger, *Ties of Kinship: Genealogy and Dynastic Marriage in Kyivan Rus'* (Cambridge, Massachusetts: Harvard University Press, 2016); Yulia Mikhailova, *Property, Power, and Authority in Rus and Latin Europe, ca. 1000–1236* (Leeds: ARC Humanities Press, 2018).

[59] On the Mongols, see B. D. Grekov and A. Iu. Iakubovskii, *Zolotaia Orda i ee padenie* (Moscow and Leningrad: Izdatel'stvo Akademii nauk SSSR, 1950); George Vernadsky, *The Mongols and Russia*. A History of Russia, vol. 3 (New Haven, Connecticut: Yale University Press, 1953); Halperin, *Russia and the Golden Horde*; Iu V. Seleznev, *"A peremenit Bog Ordu": Russko-ordynskie otnosheniia v kontse XIV–pervoi treti XV vv.* (Voronezh: Voronezhskii gosudarstvennii universitet, 2006). On the Moscow principality, see A. E. Presniakov, *Obrazovanie velikorusskogo gosudarstva* (Petrograd: Tipografiia

has focused less on the character of the rules and manner of succession than on the contingent events of each moment of transition from one ruler to another or on internal conflicts in the dynasty and among the regional princes.

Since the Russian legal tradition did not include anything on princely succession, the Russian elites necessarily learned the rules either by oral transmission lost to us or through the historical records in the Russian chronicles and other historical texts.[60] The chronicles are a complicated source, produced mainly by compilation and redaction of earlier chronicle texts. They did not rely on Byzantine models. Byzantine historians produced long and complex texts with considerable literary art derived from classical Greek models, Thucydides, Polybius, and others. Russian chronicles were not as artless as they seem at first, but they were annals more like those of early medieval Western Europe than any Byzantine sources. For the northeast principalities around medieval Vladimir the Lavrentii Chronicle was the main text. It began with the earliest Russian chronicle, the so-called Primary Chronicle (*Povest' vremennykh let*) and continued the story up to 1305. Around 1400 a new compilation appeared, the Trinity Chronicle, which was lost during the French occupation of Moscow in 1812, but parts of it were incorporated into later chronicles of the fifteenth and early sixteenth centuries. These chronicles were not just the products of an individual's fancy or personal memory and reading. Some of them were more or less official statements of the history of Russia as seen at the court of the Moscow princes, though others reflected local perspectives or seem to show more the point of view of the metropolitans of Moscow. The process of compilation continued in the first half of the sixteenth century, culminating in the Nikon Chronicle of the 1560s, probably the product of the metropolitan's scriptorium.[61] In form all these chronicles were annals. In the 1550s–60s, the same metropolitan's scriptorium also produced a history of Russia rewritten as the

Ia Bashmakov i ko., 1918); L. V. Cherepnin, *Obrazovanie russkogo tsentralizovannogo gosudarstva v XIV–XV vv.: Ocherki sotsial'no-ekonomicheskoi i politicheskoi istorii Rusi* (Moscow: Izdatel'stvo sotsial'no-ekonomicheskoi literatury, 1960); Iu. G. Alekseev, *U Kormila Rossiiskogo gosudarstva: Ocherk razvitiia apparata upravleniia v XIV–XV vv.* (St. Petersburg: Izdatel'stvo Sankt-Peterburgskogo universiteta, 1998).

60 On law, see the classic M. F. Vladimirskii-Budanov, *Obzor istorii russkogo prava* (St. Petersburg: Izdatel'stvo N. Ia. Obolgina, 1905); Ferdinand Feldbrugge, *A History of Russian Law: From Ancient Times to the Council Code (Ulozhenie) of Tsar Aleksei Mikhailovich of 1649* (Leiden and Boston, Massachusetts: Brill, 2017).

61 A. A. Shakhmatov, *Razyskaniia o drevneishikh russkikh letopisnykh svodov* (St. Petersburg: Tipografiia M. A. Aleksandrova, 1908); D. S. Likhachev, *Russkie letopisi i ikh kul'turno-istoricheskoe znachenie* (Moscow and Leningrad: Izdatel'stvo Akademii nauk SSSR, 1947); Ia. S. Lur'e, *Obshcherusskie letopisi XIV–XV vv.* (Leningrad: Nauka, 1976); B. M. Kloss, *Nikonovskii svod i russkie letopisi XVI–XVII vekov* (Moscow: Nauka, 1980).

story of the dynasty, a series of biographies from Princess Ol'ga to Ivan IV (the Terrible), known as the *Book of Degrees* (*Stepennaia kniga*). The *Book of Degrees* drew on earlier texts of lives of the few Russian princely saints, but for most of the lives it simply recast the chronicle stories in the form of biography. The whole gave an aura of sanctity to the Riurikovich dynasty, though in fact only a handful of the princes were actually recognized as saints in the Orthodox Church. All these historical narratives preserved the record of succession to the throne in medieval Rus' and at the same time provided some idea of the way the events of succession were understood and justified. They provided examples, good and bad, to be imitated or avoided.

The only other potential sources of examples of succession in history were the stories of ancient Israel in the Bible and the history of the Byzantine Empire. As we have seen, the *Khronograf* was one of the main sources of Old Testament history and the unique source of Byzantine history for the Russians through the sixteenth century. However brief the accounts of the Byzantine emperors may have been, they were enough to describe the mode of succession. In fact, the mode of succession to the throne of Byzantium was not simple, and a great many cases were the object of contestation.[62] One thing was clear, however: succession to the throne was not hereditary, even if sons often succeeded fathers. "Roman and later on Byzantine imperial ideology is characterized by a refusal to accept the imperial function as hereditary."[63] The Byzantine emperors also practiced succession by designation, even in the case of eldest sons.[64] The *Khronograf* described many of these conflicts, producing a portrait of Byzantine succession that was scarcely flattering. In addition, Byzantium lacked the saintly rulers of Western Europe and Russia who provided a point of reference: of all the Byzantine emperors, only Constantine the Great attained sainthood. The result of his sainthood was a rather sanitized portrait in the *Khronograf*, but the text also made clear that even after the saint's death the succession was messy. After Constantine's death, his son Constantine "rose against his brother Constans, who was in Rome. And there were battles, and Constantine, the elder, was killed: he desired another's share and lost his own. And

[62] Angelov, *Imperial Ideology and Political Thought*, 116–133; Jean-Claude Cheynet, *Pouvoir et contestations à Byzance (963–1210)* (Paris: Publications de la Sorbonne, 1990).

[63] Gilbert Dagron, *Empereur et prêtre: Étude sur le "césaropapisme" byzantin* (Paris: Gallimard, 1996), 64; see also Peter Schreiner, *Byzanz 565–1453*, 4th ed. (Munich: Oldenbourg, 2011), 75–76.

[64] Aikaterini Christophilopoulou, *Ekloge, anagoreusis kai stepsis tou Byzantinou autokratoros*. Pragmateiai tes akademias Athenon 22/2 (Athens: Akademia Athenon, 1956), 140; Nicolas Svoronos, "Le serment de fidélité à l'empereur byzantin et sa signification constitutionelle," *Revue des études byzantines* 9 (1951): 106–142, esp. 116–125.

Constans took his territory and ruled the whole western part [of the empire] sixteen years alone."[65] For the Russian reader the Byzantine succession struggles must have seemed even worse than those of his native country, and to have no clear rules of choice among brothers, uncles, and cousins. These were the cases of succession that the Russians recorded in the *Khronograf*.

That narrative provided nothing of the reality of late Byzantine succession practices. From the recapture of Constantinople in 1261 to the end, the ruling family was the Palaiologoi, who were challenged only briefly in the middle of the fourteenth century. The late Byzantine emperors continued to practice, or tried to practice, succession by designation. The reigning emperor had his preferred heir, usually his eldest son, crowned as a co-emperor. Thus the first of the Palailogoi, Michael VIII (1259–82), made his son Andronicus II co-emperor in 1272, when he was only fourteen years old. Andronicus II (1282–1328) in turn had his son Michael IX crowned co-emperor in 1294, at age seventeen. Michael's oldest son Andronicus III became a third co-emperor in 1316 at nineteen years of age. Thus Andronicus II attempted to secure the succession for two generations after his own reign. In the event Michael IX died before his father, and Andronicus III overthrew his grandfather in 1328, ruling until his death in 1341.[66] In turn, the death of Andronicus III set off a civil war that lasted on and off for decades, for he had not designated an heir, and his son John was only nine. The result of the war was the victory of John VI Kantakuzenos (reigned 1347–54), the cousin of Andronicus III and his principal favorite. The treaty made John VI and John V Palaiologos co-emperors in 1347. As John V grew to manhood, he was not happy with the agreement and conflict soon arose. John VI had tried to guarantee succession by marrying his daughter Elena to John V and then designating his son Matthew co-emperor. This latter move was a failure, and John V deposed Kantakuzenos and eventually Matthew. The designation of heirs had not prevented civil war, and it did not in the future: Andronicus IV, the son of John V, attempted to overthrow his father during the years 1376–9, but ultimately failed. John proclaimed his second son Manuel as his heir, who succeeded to the throne on his father's death in 1391, albeit not without opposition. Manuel was able to name his son John VIII as successor before his own death in 1425.[67] John VIII (reigned 1425–48) did not name a successor, though he favored his brother Constantine IX, who was, as it happened, the last emperor of Byzantium. Constantine came to the throne largely through the efforts of Helena, the

[65] *PSRL* 22, 273.

[66] Donald M. Nicol, *The Last Centuries of Byzantium 1261–1453* (Cambridge: Cambridge University Press, 1993), 93, 151–162.

[67] Nicol, *The Last Centuries of Byzantium*, 185–251, 275–284, 330.

widow of Manuel II.[68] It is by no means clear how much of all this the Russians knew. The *Khronograf* says virtually nothing about Byzantium in those years beyond the names of the emperors.[69] The Russians must have known more than that in practice, for Manuel II's first wife was Anna Vasil'evna, the daughter of Vasilii I of Moscow; they married in 1414. Some of the Russian travelers to Constantinople, though their main interest was in relics and shrines, also show some knowledge of the Byzantine scene, but are mostly vague on these succession problems.[70] There is no evidence that Byzantium provided a precedent that the Russians knew well enough to use.

The Byzantine precedent was not necessary, since the Bible offered the Russians a much more authoritative example, the Old Testament Kingdom of Israel sanctioned and directed by God himself. The Orthodox Slavs, and in particular the Russians, were less familiar with the full text of the Old Testament, in contrast to the New, which was widely copied both for liturgy and for reading.[71] In medieval Rus', apart from the Psalms, the Old Testament was known mainly in summaries. The oldest versions seem to be the versions in the Slavonic translation of Georgios Amartolos and the *Tolkovaia Paleia* (roughly, the Interpreted Old Testament) of the thirteenth century. This text was an abridgement of the Pentateuch, Joshua, Judges, Ruth, and Kings I–IV with commentary to demonstrate the truth of Christianity over Judaism.[72] In the fifteenth century, there appeared a new version of the *Paleia* with the commentary removed; it is known to scholars as the *Kratkaia khronograficheskaia Paleia* (Short Chronographical Paleia).[73] Complete versions of

[68] Donald M. Nicol, *The Immortal Emperor: The Life and Legend of Constantine Palaiologos, Last Emperor of the Romans* (Cambridge: Cambridge University Press, 1992), 35–36.

[69] *PSRL* XXII, 401 (Michael VIII, described as a "Latin"), 402 (Andronicus II), 409–410 (Andronicus III, John V Palaiologos, John VI Kantakuzenos, Andronicus IV "ne po vole ottsa"), 419, 422 (Manuel II), 429–430 (John VIII), 435 (Constantine XI). These entries are only a few lines, with a bit more for Manuel II and John VIII. The story of Byzantium concludes with a longer account of the fall of Constantinople in 1453 (437–440). The description of the later Byzantine emperors in the *Letopisets ellinskii i rimskii* had been even briefer, just a list of names. Tvorogov, ed., *Letopisets ellinskii i rimskii*, vol. I, 506–511.

[70] George P. Majeska, *Russian Travellers to Constantinople in the Fourteenth and Fifteenth Centuries*. Dumbarton Oaks Studies XIX (Washington, D.C.: Dumbarton Oaks Research Library and Collection, 1984), 100–113 (Ignatii of Smolensk, 1389–90), 190–191 (Zosima the Deacon, noting that Manuel II had his son John crowned).

[71] A. A. Alekseev, *Tekstologiia slavianskoi Biblii* (Moscow: Dmitrii Bulanin; Cologne: Böhlau, 1999).

[72] O. V. Tvorogov, "Paleia tolkovaia," *SKKDR* I, 285–288; O. V. Tvorogov, *Paleia tolkovaia po spisku sdelannomu v g. Kolomne v 1406 g., trud uchenikov N. S. Tikhonravova*, 2 vols. (Moscow: Tipografiia i slovolitnia O. Gerbska, 1892–6); Aleksandr Kamchatnov, ed., *Paleia tolkovaia* (Moscow: Soglasie, 2002).

[73] E. G. Vodolazkin, "Redaktsii kratkoi khronograficheskoi Palei," *TODRL* 56 (2004): 164–180; E. G. Vodolazkin, "Kratkaia khronograficheskaia Paleia (tekst), vypusk I,"

most of the books of the Old Testament and the *Paleia* came to be more frequently copied in the fifteenth century and afterward in Russia, about the same time as the final form of the *Khronograf* came into begin. Thus by 1500 the Old Testament history of ancient Israel was known to the literate in some form.

The Old Testament provided the most extensive treatment of succession to the throne in the story of King David. That story begins with the election of Saul as king to replace the judges, his failure and death, and the election of David, all in accord with God's will and the prophecy of Samuel. The succession to David is one of the classic passages of the Hebrew Bible, the subject of considerable scholarly discussion. It is found in the books of Kings (2 and 3 Kings = 2 Samuel and 1 Kings), but there is also another version found in 1 Chronicles (Paralipomenon). The latter version omits the colorful details and frames the succession in David's instructions to Solomon to build the Temple in Jerusalem.[74] In the books of Kings, it is the people of Israel who desired a king from their prophet Samuel, who prayed to the Lord for instructions. His answer was that "they [the people] have not rejected thee, but they have rejected me, that I should not reign over them" (I Kings 8:7). The Lord then pointed out Saul to him and Samuel anointed him king of Israel (I Kings 9:17; 10:1). David was simply the son of a shepherd who won fame with his defeat of Goliath. Saul's troubled relationship with David takes up much of the story of his reign, and on the king's death in battle the Bible relates that the Lord told David to go to Hebron in Judah, where the "men of Judah" came and anointed him king of Judah (II Kings 2:1, 4). Later it was the "elders of Israel" who came to him, who made a league with them, and "they anointed David king over Israel" (II Kings 5:3). Struggles over succession again take up much of the history of King David, beginning with his marriage to Bathsheba and the revolt of Absalom. At the end of David's life, his eldest son Adonijah wanted to be his successor. Adonijah was "a goodly man," but the "mighty men which belonged to David" did not support him. Then the prophet Nathan successfully urged Bathsheba to persuade David to designate Solomon, who was anointed while his father still lived (III Kings I, 5–29). David said to Bathsheba: "Even as

TODRL 57 (2006): 891–915; E. G. Vodolazkin, "Kratkaia khronograficheskaia Paleia (tekst), vypusk II," *TODRL* 58 (2008): 534–556; E. G. Vodolazkin, "Kratkaia khronograficheskaia Paleia (tekst), vypusk III," *TODRL* 61 (2010): 345–374.

74 Rebecca S. Hancock, "1 and 2 Samuel," Mordecai Cogan, "1 and 2 Kings," and Isaac Kalimi, "1 and 2 Chronicles," in *The Oxford Encyclopedia of the Books of the Bible*, ed. Michael D. Coogan (New York, New York: Oxford University Press, 2011); Rolf Rendtorff, *Das alte Testament: Eine Einführung* (Neukirchen-Vluyn: Neukirchener Verlag, 1983), 30–44, 180–199, 297–303; Leonhart Rost, *Die Überlieferung von der Thronnachfolge Davids* (Stuttgart: W. Kohlhammer, 1926).

I sware unto thee by the Lord God of Israel, saying, Assuredly Solomon thy son shall reign after me, and he shall sit upon my throne in my stead." (III Kings 1, 30). On Solomon's death, his son Rehoboam succeeded him (no designation or command from the Lord was necessary), but the kingdom of Israel then split into two, leaving Rehoboam with Jerusalem and the kingdom of Judah and a separate kingdom of Israel to the north under Jeroboam (III Kings 12). Such was the story in the books of Kings, but there was another version, contained in I Chronicles, which omitted the complexities of the succession to David and merely noted that David placed his son Solomon on the throne (1 Chronicles 23, 1). Thus the Old Testament in the lives of its most authoritative monarchs provided examples of kings appointed by God, kings designated by the reigning king, kings elected by the "elders," and kings who simply succeeded to the father's throne.

The *Paleia*, though it abridged and interpreted the Biblical text in other ways, preserved these stories of succession. In the version of the establishment of kingship the choosing of Saul and David was simplified. God's reproach to the Israelites did not appear and the text merely said that "the Israelites asked for a king [*tsar'*] from the prophet Samuel" and then Samuel anointed Saul.[75] For the installation of David as king in Jerusalem, the *Paleia* followed the Bible: the "elders (*startsi*) of Israel took him to the kingdom (*tsarstvo*) in Jerusalem." Later on it quotes God's voice to the prophet Nathan saying that he, God, had placed David to rule over Israel.[76] From the succession narrative, the *Paleia tolkovaia* took the story of Bathsheba, the revolt of Absalom, and the Kings version of Solomon's succession though without mentioning Adonijah.[77] Later on the *Paleia* text inserted the version in 1 Chronicles 22, 1, 23, 1, and 29, 2–4 of the succession to David that revolved around David's command to Solomon to build the Temple. On the actual succession, 1 Chronicles stated merely: "So when David was old and full of years, he made Solomon his son king over Israel." (1 Chronicles 23, 1). The *Paleia* translated literally: "David was old, full of days, and he placed as tsar his son Solomon."[78] Then followed David's exhortation to his son, mixing the texts of 3 Kings 2, 2–4 and 1 Chronicles 2, 2–4. The result was a picture of succession uncomplicated by the attempt of Adonijah to inherit the kingdom. After the accession of Solomon, the *Paleia tolkovaia*

[75] *Paleia tolkovaia*, vol. 2, 1896, 373 (col. 745); Kamchatnov, *Paleia*, 472.
[76] *Paleia*, vol. 2, 380 (col. 759); Kamchatnov, *Paleia*, 480, 482.
[77] *Paleia*, vol 2, 381–387 (col. 762–774); Kamchatnov, *Paleia*, 482–488.
[78] "Давидъ бывъ старъ, исполнь дьни, и постави царемь сына своего Соломона," *Paleia*, vol. 2, 405–407 (cols. 809–814); Kamchatnov, *Paleia*, 513–515; quotation: 406 (col. 811); Kamchatnov, *Paleia*, 513.

went on to list his virtues and quote his wise sayings (often apocryphal) rather than to provide a narrative of the reign, and the text ends there, with no account of the succession to Solomon. In the *Paleia tolkovaia* version, succession was the result of God's designation of David and David's designation of Solomon. The *Kratkaia khronograficheskaia Paleia* simplified the story even more, combining the Kings and Chronicles versions for the succession to David. It briefly mentioned the story of Bathsheba, omitted the stories of Absalom and Adonijah, and repeated the statement from Chronicles that David placed his son on the throne.[79]

The versions of the *Paleia* were also sources for the *Khronograf*, though not necessarily for the story of the succession to David. The *Letopisets ellinskii i rimskii* had only listed the names of the Old Testament kings without comment or detail.[80] Tvorogov believed that the main source for the corresponding part of the *Khronograf* was the Bible itself, not the chronicle of Amartolos, but the stories were certainly redacted and simplified.[81] The *Khronograf* version reproduced the Old Testament: God's words are "they [the Israelites] humiliated not you but me, I am not to rule over them." Samuel then anointed Saul as in the Bible.[82] The installation of David as king in Jerusalem followed the Bible.[83] The *Khronograf* presented the Biblical version, somewhat abridged but with the crucial details about Adonijah, Nathan, and Bathsheba. David designated Solomon as his successor: "And David said to Bathsheba that your son Solomon will sit on my throne." The succeeding exhortation to Solomon follows not 1 Chronicles but 3 Kings 2, 3 in very abridged form.[84] After Solomon's death, in the *Khronograf* Rehoboam simply came to rule in Solomon's place, as in the Bible.[85] The available accounts of Old Testament kingship confirmed for the Russians the Biblical variety of forms of accession to the throne. Just like the history of the Byzantine Empire, the Bible did not offer a single method of succession vested with divine authority.

*

[79] Vodolazkin, "Kratkaia vypusk III," 365–367.

[80] Tvorogov, ed., *Letopisets ellinskii i rimskii* I, 15.

[81] Tvorogov, *Drevnerusskie khronografy*, 180. The stories of Saul, David, and Solomon in the chronicle of Amartolos were fairly detailed on the reigns but not on the appointment of Saul and David or Solomon's succession to the throne: de Boor, ed., *Georgii monachi chronicon* I, 187–188; Istrin, *Knigi vremennye* I, 137–138. Tvorogov was correct in seeing the source of the 1512 *Khronograf*'s account of these events in the Bible, not in Amartolos.

[82] *PSRL* 22, 106. [83] *PSRL* 22, 114–115.

[84] "И рече Давид Вирсавиа яко Соломон сын твой сядет на престоле моим," *PSRL* 22, 123–124.

[85] *PSRL* 22, 130.

The account of succession in Russian chronicles forms a large part of the next chapter, as they were records of recent experience of the writers, not historical tradition. The only sixteenth-century text to touch on the issue of succession was the "Tale of the Vladimir Princes."[86] As a text its importance derives not so much from its contents, interesting as they are, but rather from its use in the coronation order of Ivan IV and subsequent rulers and its role as an explanation of the history of the principal crown of the tsars, the Cap of Monomakh. In this way, the story remained part of the tradition of the Russian tsars for centuries after its appearance. Its textual history has a number of mysteries. The oldest version may be the Epistle of Spiridon-Savva, briefly metropolitan of Kiev in the 1470s, who was imprisoned in Lithuania, in Russia sent to a monastery, and nowhere recognized as metropolitan. Apparently he lived into the early years of the sixteenth century.[87] There are also two versions of the text as a tale without Spiridon's name. In brief, the account begins with the division of the earth among the sons of Noah, the story of Alexander the Great, and the Roman Empire. Emperor Augustus then placed his relatives in charge of various parts of the world, including Prus in "Marborok" (Marienburg/Małbork) and "Gdanesk" (Danzig/Gdańsk), and other lands around the Niemen River. That is, he ruled Prussia in the geographical understanding of 1500, given with the normal Polish names of places. In the tale it is here, in the lands of Prus, that the Novgorodians found Riurik, a relative of Prus and the first of the Riurikovich dynasty. The Riurikovichi were thus descendants of Caesar Augustus, or at least of his clan.

This story contradicted the genealogy of Riurik found in Russian chronicles, where he was invited to rule Novgorod from somewhere across the sea, which modern historians usually identify with Scandinavia. The story in the *Tale* after Riurik switches direction, recounting briefly the story of the conversion of Vladimir. Subsequently his descendant Prince Vladimir Vsevolodich of Kiev (ruled 1113–25) warred against the Byzantines, taking many prisoners. After that event, the reader learns that the Westerners in the time of Pope Formosus (891–6) had fallen from the true faith. Emperor Constantine Monomachos (1042–55) called a council that condemned Formosus and henceforth the Orthodox did not recognize the Pope. Then Constantine sent a variety of relics to Vladimir Vsevolodich, including a crown (*venets*). From then onward, Vladimir was called tsar with the

[86] R. P. Dmitrieva, *Skazanie o kniaziakh vladimirskikh* (Moscow and Leningrad: Izdatel'stvo Akademii nauk SSSR, 1955). Cherie Woodworth, "The Tsar's Descent from Caesar." PhD dissertation, Yale University, 2001.

[87] V. I. Ulianovs'kyi, *Mytropolyt Kyivs'kyi Spyrydon: Obraz kriz' epokhu, epokha kriz' obraz* (Kyiv: Lybid, 2004).

name Monomakh. The legend, as is clear, is not only untrue but chronologically impossible. The text concludes with the genealogy of the Lithuanian princes.[88] The other versions of the story made it a bit more logical by putting the story about Pope Formosus at the end, after Vladimir receives the cap, but all of the versions tell the same story with occasional differences in detail.

The whole story was copied many times in various sorts of miscellanies and inserted into or combined with chronicle manuscripts, but the 1547 Order of coronation only took the part about the Cap of Monomakh as the regalia of a tsar. The rest of the story about Prus and the Riurikovich dynasty was omitted. The result was that the official ceremony presented the dignity of tsar as having a precedent in the story of Vladimir Monomakh and a surviving symbol in the cap, but said nothing about inheritance or succession. The implication of the story, that Russia's ruling family was part of an imperial dynasty descended from Augustus, did not appear as part of the official ideology of the monarchy as revealed in the coronation. The story did appear, however, in the *Book of Degrees*.[89] To make matters more complicated, however, the same text appeared in the Voskresenie Chronicle (1542–4), a compilation normally understood to reflect the views of the boyar clique (or at least the Shuiskii faction) of the years of Ivan IV's minority.[90] In contrast, the more "official" Nikon Chronicle omits the story and gives a more traditional version of the calling of Riurik, who simply comes "from the Germans" (*iz Nemets*). Since the final version of the Nikon Chronicle as it comes down to us is the product of the metropolitan's scriptorium, with later input perhaps from the tsar's scribes as well, this is a bit surprising, since the same milieu produced the *Book of Degrees* at about the same time.[91] As far as we know,

[88] Dmitrieva, *Skazanie*, 159–170.

[89] Lenhoff and Pokrovskii, *Stepennaia kniga*, vol. 1, 151, 221–223; vol. 3, 32. The oldest manuscripts of the *Book of Degrees* come from the scriptorium of the Kremlin Chudov Monastery and date from 1560–5: Lenhoff and Pokrovskii, *Stepennaia kniga*, vol. 1, 6–7. See also David B. Miller, "The Velikie Minei Chet'i and the Stepennaia Kniga of Metropolitan Makarii and the Origins of Russian National Consciousness," *Forschungen zur osteuropäischen Geschichte* 26 (1979): 263–382; A. V. Sirenov, *Stepennaia kniga: Istoriia teksta* (Moscow: Iazyki Slaviaskikh kul'tur, 2007); A. S. Usachev, *Stepennaia kniga i drevnerusskaia knizhnost' vremeni mitropolita Makariia* (Moscow and St. Petersburg: Al'ians-Arkheo, 2009); and Gail Lenhoff and Ann Kleimola, eds., *The Book of Royal Degrees and the Genesis of Russian Historical Consciousness* (Bloomington, Indiana: Slavica, 2011).

[90] *PSRL* VII, 268; *SKKDR* II, pt. 2, 39–42.

[91] *PSRL* IX, 9; Kloss, *Nikonovskii svod*. In the *Primary Chronicle*, Riurik comes "from the Varangians" (*iz Variag*): V. P. Adrianova-Peretts and D. S. Likhachev, eds., *Povest' vremennykh let*, 2nd ed. (St. Petersburg: Nauka, 1999), 12. The text is not always clear about geography, but the only mention of "Prussy" places them with the Poles and seemingly in a different place around the Baltic Sea than the Varangians: Likhachev

Ivan liked the story and used it in his 1577 letter to the Lithuanian commander Prince Aleksandr Polubenskii.[92]

The story of Riurik's descent from Augustus was the only text that addressed in any way the issue of succession, and it had limits. It was essentially a genealogical legend about the Riurikovich clan that certainly glorified that clan and underscored its legitimacy but did not offer clues about the succession within that clan. The same may be said of the *Book of Degrees*. Needless to say, neither text had any implications about the nature of the monarch's power in relations to the boyar elite or society in general.[93]

The literature available to Russians about the nature of monarchy and its history recorded many examples but did not give an unambiguous ideal or pattern to follow. There was no written law on this matter, and the only guide was custom. That story of succession was also one of the evolving power of the ruler, but it was not a simple story of growing power. The ruler's power was real, but it maintained itself by a combination of personal ability and charisma, the ability to negotiate the realities of governance, and the ability to charm, persuade, and threaten the elite and occasionally the people into cooperation and obedience. As we shall see, there were moments of weakness and moments of strength. As political realities evolved, practices and ideas also evolved, and that evolution is the story of the throne in Russia from the fifteenth century onward.

and Adrianova-Peretts, *Povest'*, 8. Until the middle of the sixteenth century, the *Primary Chronicle* is the source of Russian chronicle texts about Riurik. On the milieu of the compilers of both texts, see especially Charles J. Halperin, "What is an 'Official' Muscovite Source for the Reign of Ivan IV?" in *The Book of Royal Degrees and the Genesis of Russian Historical Consciousness*, ed. Gail Lenhoff and Ann Kleimola (Bloomington, Indiana: Slavica, 2011), 81–93.

92 Adrianova-Peretts, V. P., D. S. Likhachev, and Ia. S. Lur'e, eds., *Poslaniia Ivana Groznogo* (Moscow and Leningrad: Izdatel'stvo Akademii nauk SSSR, 1951), 200–201.

93 Usachev, *Stepennaia*, 563–687. Usachev seems surprised to discover that portraits of good and bad rulers exhaust the political aspects of the text, presenting the resultant ideas as *razmyto* (perhaps "nebulous" would be the best translation), but that is exactly what Orthodox Christian ideas of rulership were. They were not political in the modern sense.

2 Designation and Heredity 1450–1533

The period from the later fifteenth century through the early part of the sixteenth was crucial to the formation of the Russian state. The most obvious changes were territorial: the Moscow grand princes started about 1450 with a congeries of territories around Moscow and Vladimir, important to be sure but only a part of the lands of the north and northeast of Kiev Rus'. Grand Princes Ivan III and his son Vasilii III made Russia into a major power in the east of Europe by including all the lands between the upper Volga and the Oka rivers (Tver' and eventually Riazan'), but also the whole of Novgorod. That meant not just the territory around the city of Novgorod, still the main trading partner of the German Hanse towns in the east Baltic, but also the enormous territories that now make up northern Russia west of the Urals. Low in population, this area was rich in fur, salt, and other goods necessary or profitable to an early modern economy. With the annexation of Pskov in 1510, the grand prince of Moscow and all Russia had under his rule the other main entrepôt of trade with the West. Russia had not expanded south and east into the steppe, but the creation of the new state altered the balance of power, and the grand princes could now contend with Kazan', Crimea, and the Great Horde in Astrakhan' on a more equal basis.

The formation of the new state was not just a matter of territory. Russia came into contact with Italy, which provided architects for the Kremlin. Ivan made the first treaties with West European powers (Denmark) in centuries, and exchanged ambassadors with the Holy Roman Empire. Doctors of medicine from the West appeared at the court of Moscow to treat the ruler and his family. The Orthodox Church, now largely separated from the Greeks, set out to form a religious culture appropriate to the new situation. In the fields and forests, thousands of peasants cut down trees and established farms. Russia had a population somewhere on the order of three to four million people, still less than Poland-Lithuania but substantial enough.

The story of the creation of the Russian state is partly one of the creation of an administrative apparatus beyond the household, but another large part is the development of the monarchy and its practices. The titles and forms of legitimation (coronation and other rituals, written panegyrics and histories) of the grand princes and tsars were among the most striking expressions of that development and are now well known, if still often controversial. The narratives of the chronicles provide vivid descriptions of interprincely feuds and court intrigues among aristocrats and relatives of the monarch, but do not go on to establish what were the norms of succession. The actual forms of transmission of power, the rituals of succession, were crucial issues, and these forms were the more important since Russia did not develop any written "constitutional" documents. Both the forms and realities of succession were changing in the period from the fourteenth century onward. The Moscow princes inherited the ambiguous custom of Kievan Rus', where collateral succession was as much an option as lineal succession to eldest sons. Indeed, this ambiguity was the origin of many of the interprincely feuds that take up so much of the chronology of events. The Moscow princes tried, ultimately successfully, to move to a system of lineal succession, which required them to develop new forms to enshrine their decisions in the practice of the state. These new forms remained, nevertheless, within the framework of the religious culture that was predominant, indeed nearly exclusive, in Russia from earliest history until the end of the seventeenth century. Thus innovations in the practice of succession required new rituals. Succession also required new formulas that appeared in the chronicles, legends, homilies, and epistles that made up the religious literature of Russia in these centuries.

The Moscow princes were one of several dynasties in the northeast of Kiev Rus' that owed obedience to the grand prince of Vladimir, the leading ruler of the area from the later twelfth century. A complicating factor from the 1230s onward was the Mongol conquest and the rule of the Golden Horde over the Rus' principalities. Succession to the Vladimir throne was in the hands of the khan of the Horde, and this relationship lasted until the second half of the fifteenth century. Even while the suzerainty of the Horde was still in force, the Moscow princes began to ensure succession by their testaments.[1] The first surviving testaments of the Moscow princes from Ivan Kalita forward, however, dealt only with

[1] L. V. Cherepnin, ed., *Dukhovnye i dogovornye gramoty velikikh i udel'nykh kniazei XIV–XVI vv.* (Moscow and Leningrad: Izdatel'stvo Akademii nauk SSSR, 1950). For the texts of the testaments, see Cherepnin, *Dukhovnye i dogovornye gramoty* (hereafter *DDG*) and Robert Craig Howe, ed. and trans., *The Testaments of the Grand Princes of Moscow* (Ithaca, New York: Cornell University Press, 1967).

the prince's domain, essentially the principality of Moscow, the personal property of the ruler, and moveable property as well. The Moscow principality of the fourteenth century was already large in area, though it was thinly populated. Its elite was small, less than a dozen boyar clans, and an administration that was essentially the few officials of the princely palace.[2] Even boyar landholding was not yet highly developed. These testaments were not just a matter of the private decision of the ruler. The princes had them written down before the elite of church and state at the time of the composition of the testaments, often by the ruler's deathbed. The metropolitan and boyars were effectively the guarantors of the testament. Starting with Dmitrii Donskoi, the Moscow princes included among the long list of villages and jewelry a brief statement that the testator blessed his son with the grand princedom, not just Moscow. The blessing was written down in the testament, but as time passed the ruler came to display his choice in a variety of other ways. From 1451, the heir often carried the same title as his father in official documents and chronicles. These chronicles were not merely narratives compiled for the edification or entertainment of the elite. They were the record of the decisions of the princes from Kievan times onward. From 1471, the grand prince placed his heir on the throne in the Dormition Cathedral in the Kremlin. As the testament and the ceremony of placement included a religious component, the church sanctified the choice well before the actual coronation. Eventually, Ivan III introduced a coronation ceremony for his heir in 1497. The testament ceased to be a means of transmission of power in the reign of Ivan the Terrible, but the blessing continued to 1584, and new forms of display of the successor to the court emerged. Succession was part of the political role of the church elite and the boyars, and until the end of the Riurikovich dynasty in 1598 it remained a matter of the ruler's family and those elites.

Succession to the throne was not a legal abstraction but a series of concrete actions that normally took place in a small area before a distinct, but not always small, group of people. The place was the Kremlin, or more specifically the ruler's palace and the Dormition Cathedral. The palace and the cathedral occupied the western tip of the Moscow Kremlin, for into the early seventeenth century aristocratic houses filled much of the Kremlin. The palace was not the present structure, which is a combination of the 1490s and the nineteenth century, but a smaller building on the same site.

[2] Nancy Kollmann Shields, *Kinship and Politics: The Making of the Muscovite Political System 1345–1547* (Stanford, California: Stanford University Press, 1987); Iu. G. Alekseev, *U kormila Rossiiskogo gosudarstva: Ocherk razvitiia apparata upravleniia v XIV–XV vv.* (St. Petersburg: Izdatel'stvo Sankt-Peterburgskogo universiteta, 1998); A. A. Iushko, *Moskovskaia zemlia IX–XIV vekov* (Moscow: Nauka, 1991).

Similarly, the Dormition Cathedral that exists now replaces an older and smaller church dedicated to the same feast of the Mother of God. Associated with the place were several monasteries, at first only the Monastery of the Savior hugging the west of the palace, whose church lasted until the 1930s, and later the Monastery of the Miracle of St. Michael the Archangel (Chudov), both connected by tradition with the princely family. Similarly the Monastery of the Ascension was a convent that served the women of the family, both as a spiritual center and as a place of burial. The men of the princely family rested after their deaths in the Archangel Cathedral. Both cathedrals were only a few hundred meters from the palace, the space between the three forming a small square. A bit farther away was the residence of the metropolitan (later patriarch). The places of burial displayed for all to see the continuity of the princely family, and the palace, the Dormition Cathedral, and the square were the sites of most of the action involving the designation and later proclamation of the heirs.

The actors in the drama of succession, besides the ruler and his heir, were the secular and church elite. The metropolitan was involved in several ways, in blessing the ruler when he made his testament and in any religious ceremonies. The hegumens of the chief monasteries usually had a role as well. The boyars witnessed the testament and were present at the ceremonies that displayed the heir. These two elites were participants, but they were also to a large extent the audience. Not all boyars signed the testament, nor did all the higher clergy, but they were present at the ceremonies. Until the end of the dynasty in 1598 it does not seem that lower ranks of the clergy and landholding class, or the urban population of Moscow, were part of the audience at any of the ceremonies. Those which took place in the Dormition Cathedral or the palace square could have been open to a larger group in theory, but the spaces were too small to accommodate more than a few hundred people.

Succession in Moscow

From 1389 to 1584, the grand princes of Vladimir, Moscow, and later of Russia ensured succession by designation of the heir by the ruler, reinforced by representation of the heir to the elite in various ways. This was not a strict primogeniture system, but custom did require succession within the ruling family of the Moscow line of Riurikovichi. Designation took two basic forms, by testament and by paternal benediction. Testamentary succession and paternal benediction began with the testament of Dmitrii Ivanovich Donskoi in 1389. In most cases the rulers designated their eldest sons, but the succession of the eldest son was not automatic. In the 1490s, Ivan III chose to leave the throne to his younger son rather than the older son's son, as was the practice in countries where primogeniture was the norm. The practices of the Moscow and Russian rulers ensured that the throne remained in the Riurikovich dynasty, and that brothers and uncles of the ruler did not take the throne, but they did not amount to strict primogeniture. Succession by testament and benediction were new practices. In Kievan times, the princes had divided the realm among their sons, giving Kiev to a favored one, usually the eldest, but the Kievan throne did not carry a formal "grand princedom" (*velikoe kniazhenie*) like the later Vladimir and Moscow thrones. Thus in 1054 Iaroslav gave the Kiev throne to Iziaslav, his eldest surviving son, and other thrones to other sons, bidding them to obey him.[3] In 1113, by contrast, at the death of Sviatopolk Iziaslavich of Kiev, the Kievans held a council and asked Vladimir Vsevolodich (Monomakh) to take "the throne of his father and grandfather" (*stol oten i deden*).[4] Sviatopolk had several living sons, but the Kievans preferred Vladimir, the son of Sviatopolk's younger brother Vsevolod, who had held the Kievan throne in 1078–93. The Kievans were correct that it was the throne of the father and grandfather of Vladimir Monomakh, but neither had succeeded their father directly. The term "throne of the father and grandfather" did not imply primogeniture, and in any case the intervention of the local elites and even the townspeople was an important part of all the Kievan succession battles. The other issue was that the contenders were not just the various sons of the ruling prince but also his brothers and uncles. In this situation, the politics of Kievan Rus', including the principalities of the northeast, were notoriously contentious, prompting extensive discussion among historians about the real basis of power and the practices of succession.[5] The Mongol conquest created a new situation, since from that moment onward the Khan of the Golden Horde was the final arbiter of succession, at least of the Vladimir throne that was most important to his control of the area. The struggles over the Vladimir throne make up much of the content of Russian history in the thirteenth and fourteenth centuries, though again the attention of historians has been on the realities of power such as the contest between Moscow and Tver' and relations with the Horde, rather than the formalities of succession to the Moscow or Vladimir thrones.[6]

[3] V. P. Adrianova-Peretts and D. S. Likhachev, eds., *Povest' vremennykh let*, 2nd ed. (St. Petersburg: Nauka, 1999), 70.

[4] Ibid., 126.

[5] A. E. Presniakov, *Kniazhoe pravo v drevnei Rusi* (St. Petersburg: Nauka, 1909); George Vernadsky, *Kievan Russia* (New Haven, Connecticut: Yale University Press, 1948); M. B. Sverdlov, *Domongol'skaia Rus'* (St. Petersburg: Akademicheskii proekt, 2003).

[6] A. E. Presniakov, *Obrazovanie velikorusskogo gosudarstva* (Petrograd: Tipografiia Ia. Bashmakov i ko., 1918); L. V. Cherepnin, *Russkie feodal'nye arkhivy XIV–XV vekov* (Moscow and Leningrad: Izdatel'stvo Akademii nauk SSSR, 1948), vol. I, 10–92;

Succession and the Historians

The Russian historians of the eighteenth century described in their narratives the many cases of succession with no preference for primogeniture. V. N. Tatishchev, writing in the 1740s, flatly asserted that there were many forms of succession in monarchies, and primogeniture was only one of them. He clearly preferred Peter's solution, the designation of the best candidate. He thought that the free disposition of property was part of natural law, and that Scripture had no mandate for primogeniture.[7] Prince M. N. Shcherbatov saw no reason for Russians to look to the lesser Riurikovichi on the death of Tsar Fyodor in 1598: there were too many of them, and they were used to their subject status. Shcherbatov saw nothing odd in the election of Boris Godunov, merely a series of concrete circumstances that gave him the throne.[8] A generation later, however, Karamzin shifted the emphasis to note the lack of a proper candidate, a situation which required an election of the tsar.[9] Karamzin, of course, was writing after the 1797 succession law, which had established primogeniture in Russian law for the first time. Thus, by the early nineteenth century the idea of primogeniture had come to be the "normal" form of succession to the throne in Russia.

The advent of more "scientific" history added a new element, for historians from S. M. Solov'ev onward saw primogeniture as teleology, the form that replaced the older tradition of collateral succession. From Solov'ev to Presniakov, Cherepnin, and Zimin, historians saw the Moscow princes as fighting for primogeniture (as part of the struggle for central power) against the older system, but they assumed that primogeniture, once established, would be automatic, and the only issue was then the existence of appanages for the brothers and uncles of the ruling

L. V. Cherepnin, *Obrazovanie russkogo tsentralizovannogo gosudarstva v XIV–XV vv.: Ocherki sotsial'no-ekonomicheskoi i politicheskoi istorii Rusi* (Moscow: Izdatel'stvo sotsial'no-ekonomicheskoi literatury, 1960); J. L. I. Fennell, *The Crisis of Medieval Russia 1200–1304* (London and New York, New York: Longman, 1983); J. L. I. Fennell, *The Emergence of Moscow 1304–1359* (Berkeley, California: University of California Press, 1968); B. D. Grekov and A. Iu. Iakubovskii, *Zolotaia Orda i ee padenie* (Moscow and Leningrad: Izdatel'stvo Akademii nauk SSSR, 1950); Bertold Spuler, *Die goldene Horde: Die Mongolen in Rußland 1223–1502*, 2nd ed. (Wiesbaden: Harrassowitz, 1965); Charles J. Halperin, *Russia and the Golden Horde: The Mongol Impact on Russian History*. Bloomington, Indiana: Indiana University Press, 1985; V. V. Trepavlov, *Stepnye imperii Evrazii: Mongoly i tatary* (Moscow: Kvadriga, 2015).

[7] V. N. Tatishchev, *Istoriia Rossiiskaia* (Moscow: Imperatorskii moskovskii universitet, 1769), vol. 1, pt. 2, 534–536.

[8] M. M. Shcherbatov, *Istoriia Rossiiskaia* (St. Petersburg: Imperatorskaia Akademiia nauk, 1790), vol. 7, pt. 1, 1–4.

[9] N. M. Karamzin, *Istoriia gosudarstva Rossiiskogo* (St. Petersburg: Eduard Prats, 1842–4; Moscow: Kniga, 1988–9), vol. 10, 131–132. Citations refer to the Eduard Prats edition.

prince. The only attempt to go beyond assumptions and actually attempt to demonstrate progress toward primogeniture was the 1972 work of the German historian Peter Nitsche.[10] Nitsche did note that testamentary succession was part of the system. This was an original insight and one of great importance, but Nitsche did not emphasize it, and furthermore he was not interested in the ceremonial details or practices such as benediction that throw so much light on the formal structure of power in the Moscow grand principality. He followed the political story that revealed the "reality" of power, or so he thought. In this he reflected the practice of his colleagues, Russians and others.[11] The conclusion was understandable, but not necessarily correct.

Inheritance and Designation 1389–1462

The founder of the Moscow branch of the Riurikovichi was Daniil Aleksandrovich (ruled 1283–1303). The main sources for the succession events in the principality are the chronicles and the testaments of the princes. The chronicles provided the annals of political events, so they included the story of succession not just to the Moscow throne but also to the Grand Principality of Vladimir, and the succession to the Khans of the Horde as well. For all these events they were extremely laconic. They described the battles between Moscow and Tver' as well as the internal strife in the Horde. In the case of Moscow, they recorded only that the Moscow princes "sat" on their princedoms, and that they went to the Horde and returned with the Grand Principality (or in some cases did not). Other than to note that the Khan awarded the grand principality, there were no specifics. It seems that they did not need the Khan's permission to take the Moscow throne; his permission was necessary only for the Grand Principality.[12] The Khans of the Horde were interested in the Grand Principality, not Moscow alone.

[10] Peter Nitsche, *Großfürst und Thronfolger: Die Nachfolgepolitik der Moskauer Herrscher bis zum Ende des Rjurikidenhauses*. Kölner historische Abhandlungen 21 (Cologne and Vienna: Böhlau, 1972). See also S. A. Mel'nikov, *Pravovyi rezhim nasledovaniia prestola v drevnei Rusi IX–nachala XVI vv.: Istoriko-pravovoe issledovanie* (Moscow: Inform-Znanie, 2009).

[11] Presniakov, *Obrazovanie velikorusskogo gosudarstva*; L. V. Cherepnin, *Obrazovanie russkogo tsentralizovannogo gosudarstva*; A. A. Zimin, *Vitiaz' na rasput'e: Feodal'naia voina v Rossii XV v.* (Moscow: Mysl', 1991); A. A. Zimin, *Rossiia na rubezhe XV–XVI stoletii* (Moscow: Mysl', 1982); Gustave Alef, *The Origins of Muscovite Autocracy: The Age of Ivan III*. Forschungen zur osteuropäischen Geschichte 39 (Berlin: Osteuropa-Institut; Wiesbaden: Harrassowitz, 1986).

[12] *PSRL* V (First Sophia Chronicle), 218, 222, 228–229. The surviving fragments of the early-fifteenth-century Trinity Chronicle suggest that the later chronicles reproduced

The other principal source for the succession to the Moscow throne in the fourteenth century and the first half of the fifteenth century is the series of testaments of the grand princes of Moscow. These were very "official" documents. The metropolitan's blessing appeared at the very beginning, except for that of Dmitrii Donskoi in 1389, as he was in conflict with Metropolitan Kiprian. The documents had as witnesses the princes' spiritual fathers and the chief boyars. One of the secretaries (*d'iaki*) physically wrote the documents. The testaments remained in the palace archive in the Kremlin until the early nineteenth century, when they were removed to a building built for the first time as a historical archive: there they now rest. The first Moscow princes, Ivan Danilovich Kalita (1325–40), Semen Ivanovich (1340–53), and Ivan Ivanovich (1353–9), left Moscow as their inheritance to their sons and brothers, dividing it into thirds.[13] Succession after Ivan Kalita was complicated by biological accidents. Semen Ivanovich died of the plague when he was only thirty-six. His sons had died as well, so the throne went to his younger brother Ivan Ivanovich, who in turn died at the age of thirty-three, leaving a regency for his nine-year-old son Dmitrii. All these testaments mentioned only Moscow, not the Grand Principality, since that was in the gift of the khan.

Grand Prince Dmitrii Ivanovich Donskoi (1359–89), writing his will in 1389, however, had a different formula: "And I bless my son, prince Vasilii, with my inheritance, the Grand Principality." Dmitrii wrote the document in the presence of his two spiritual fathers, one of whom was St. Sergii of Radonezh, and ten boyars. These included Dmitrii Mikhailovich (Bobrok-Volynskii), Timofei Vasil'evich (Vel'ianimov), Ivan Rodionovich (Kvashnin), Semen Vasil'evich (Okat'ev), Aleksandr Andreevich (Beleutov), and Fyodor Andreevich (Koshka), the ancestor of (among others) the Romanovs.[14] These boyars represented most, if not all, of the men at that rank, most of them from clans with deep roots in Moscow. The testament was composed with the full knowledge and presumed support of the elite of the church and the principality. Thus it

these earlier accounts: M. D. Priselkov, ed., *Troitskaia letopis'* (Moscow and Leningrad: Izdatel'stvo Akademii nauk SSSR, 1950), 359, 364, 366–367.

13 *DDG*, 7–11, 13–19; Cherepnin, *Russkie feodal'nye arkhivy XIV–XV vekov*, vol. I, 12–20, 27–31.

14 "А се благословляю сына своего, князя Василья, своею отчиною, великим княженьем," *DDG*, 34, 36–37. Cherepnin, *Russkie feodal'nye arkhivy XIV–XV vekov*, vol. I, 58–62. The most thorough analysis of the testament is V. A. Kuchkin, "Poslednee zaveshchanie Dmitriia Donskogo," *Srednevkovaia Rus'* 3 (2001): 106–183. For the identification of the boyars, see Kollmann, *Kinship and Politics*, 204, 211, 218, 224, 238, 239; and Kuchkin, "Poslednee zaveshchanie," 181–183, both following S. B. Veselovskii. The names seem to be listed in order of seniority in boyar rank.

was not a "private" document, but rather a statement of the prince's intentions before the boyar elite and the metropolitan. There were only some ten or eleven boyars in 1389, so the testament involved nearly all of them.[15] The composition of the testament was the closest to a public ceremony that has been recorded in the sources. If there was any other ceremony, such as a coronation or a proclamation of the heir in the main square of the Kremlin, we do not know about it.[16]

In Grand Prince Dmitrii testament, the fate of the Grand Principality after the still childless (but aged eighteen) Vasilii was not specified, but the will did state that "if God changed the Horde" Vasilii was not to pay the tribute to the khan. Presumably, if God did not change the Horde, he was to pay. His father's testament did not exempt Vasilii I from enthronement by the khan's emissary, who "seated" him on the grand principality in August 1389, according to chronicle sources.[17] In the case of the death of Vasilii Dmitrievich, the testament stated that his appanage, presumably Moscow, was to be divided by his mother, Grand Princess Evdokiia. As V. A. Kuchkin pointed out, all of Dmitrii's sons were childless in 1389, and he could not predict the future. In any case, the most important innovation in the testament was that Dmitrii "blesses" (*blagoslovliaiu*) his son with the grand princely throne. In the text, Dmitrii also "gives" (*daiu*) lands and revenues in the old Moscow principality to his sons, but "blesses" them with lands and revenues elsewhere. He also "blesses" his sons with holy icons.[18] The distinction did not seem to imply a difference in the legal status of the lands, only in the formula of transfer. The use of paternal benediction to pass on the throne would last to the end of the seventeenth century: it was a permanent addition to the repertory of means for transferring power.

The testaments of Vasilii I (1389–1425) varied, not surprisingly given the complexities of Moscow's relations with its neighbors.[19] For almost

[15] There were only some ten or eleven boyars in 1389. Kollmann, *Kinship and Politics*, 76, 104, 108.

[16] The only possible reference to such a ceremony is the phrase "sat on his princedom" or the khan "seated" him on the princedom. These are the terms that appear in the chronicles of the late fifteenth century: *PRSL* V (*posadil*), 244; *PSRL* XXV (Moscow svod of the late fifteenth century), 218: "sede na velikom kniazhen'e v Volodimeri kniaz' Vasilei Dmitreevich na stole ottsa svoego i deda i pradeda, a posazhen byst' tsarevym poslom Shikhomatom."

[17] *PSRL* XXV, 218; A. A. Gorskii, *Moskva i Orda* (Moscow: Nauka, 2000), 116.

[18] *DDG*, 33–34, 36. Nitsche attempted to prove that Dmitrii gave Iurii the grand principality in the case of the death of Vasilii, thus making a decisive step in favor of primogeniture. A careful reading of the testament does not support his interpretation: Nitsche, *Großfürst und Thronfolger*, 17–27. Kuchkin, "Poslednee zaveshchanie," 137–138, 160–166

[19] V. A. Kuchkin, "Tri zaveshchaniia Vasiliia I," *Drevniaia Rus': Voprosy medievistiki* 64, 2 (2016): 33–54; A. A. Gorskii, "Zaveshchaniia Vasiliia I Dmitrievicha: Problemy posledovatel'nosti i datirovki," *Drevniaia Rus': Voprosy medievistiki* 67, 1 (2017): 20–34;

all of the period of Vasilii's reign, the Horde was torn by internal rivalries. In addition, Vasilii married Sofiia, the daughter of Vitovt (Witowt/Vytautas), the grand duke of Lithuania, in 1391, in those decades at the height of his power.[20] Moscow had to reckon with both the Horde and Lithuania. At the moment of composition of the first testament around 1406–7, the grand prince had only the one son Ivan (then ten years old), who would receive only his father's original third of Moscow. He could not know whether God would give his son the grand principality.[21] Ivan Vasil'evich, however, died in 1417. The dates of the two later testaments are disputed. Why the Moscow prince thought he could pass on the grand principality is not clear, but the Horde had been in a state of internal disorder since 1395, when the Emir Edigei had defeated and killed Khan Tokhtamysh. In the traditionally named "third" testament from February or March 1423, Grand Prince Vasilii blessed his son with the grand princedom, but only "if God gives it to him," a highly ambiguous phrase.[22] In what is traditionally called the "second" testament (but probably from later in 1423), Vasilii blessed his second son, Vasilii Vasil'evich (born 1415) with both the third of Moscow and the Grand Principality, both called his inheritance (*votchina*). He gave the government (*riad*) to his son and widow, Sofiia Vitovtovna, and entrusted them and his other relations to his father-in-law, Vitovt.[23] The testament was again a public document. It began with the blessing of Metropolitan Photios, who signed it in Greek. Attached were five princely seals from Vasilii's brothers and others. Five boyars were witnesses, beginning with Prince Iurii Patrikeev, a Gediminovich whose father had come to Moscow in 1408. These seem to have been almost the full complement of boyars at that moment.[24] By the time of compilation of the testament Vasilii I probably had a *yarlyk*, or patent, from Khan Ulug-Mehmed (then a principal contender for the throne of the Horde for his son), so there was a legal basis for the succession.[25] The young Vasilii Vasil'evich did manage to get the throne, though not without contest.

S. V. Polekhov, "Poslednie zaveshchaniia Vasiliia I i pechati Vitovta," *Srednevekovaia Rus'* 12 (2016): 183–200.

[20] Grekov and Iakubovskii, *Zolotaia Orda*, 275–296; Donald G. Ostrowski, *Muscovy and the Mongols: Cross-Cultural Influences on the Steppe Frontier 1304–1589* (Cambridge: Cambridge University Press, 1998); Gorskii, *Moskva i Orda*, 119–140; Iu. V. Seleznev, *"A peremenit Bog Ordu": Russko-ordynskie otnosheniia v kontse XIV–pervoi treti XV vv.* (Voronezh: Voronezhskii gosudarstvennii universitet, 2006); Jarosław Nikodem, *Witołd Wielki Książe Litewski (1354 lub 1355–27 października 1430)* (Kraków: Avalon, 2013).

[21] *DDG*, 55–57.

[22] *DDG*, 61 ("A dast Bog symu moemu velikoe kniazhen'e, ino i az syna svoego blagoslovliau, kiazia Vasil'ia.").

[23] *DDG*, 57–60; Nikodem, *Witołd Wielki Książe Litewski*, 246.

[24] Kollmann, *Kinship and Politics*, 76, 225.

[25] Gorskii, *Moskva i Orda*, 136–139.

This contest was Moscow's dynastic civil war, which lasted most of the reign of Vasilii II Vasil'evich ("the Dark") from his father's death in 1425 to the death of his last rival in 1453. This bloody conflict ultimately decided who was to rule in Moscow, and in that sense laid the foundations for the formation of the Russian state in the time of Ivan III (1462–1505). Prince Vasilii Vasil'evich's rivals were first his uncle Prince Iurii Dmitrievich, until the latter's death in 1434, and then Iurii's sons, Vasilii Kosoi and Dmitrii Shemiaka.[26] In the course of the war, Vasilii Vasil'evich managed not only to hang on to the throne but also to eliminate the other branches of the Moscow ruling family from any possibility of ascent to the dignity of grand prince.

The dispute began slowly. At the death of Vasilii Dmitrievich in 1425, Prince Iurii Dmitrievich had already been in conflict with his brother. The chronicles laconically announced that Vasilii Vasil'evich, then only ten years old, "sat" on the grand princedom, and that his uncle Iurii made a truce and went off to his lands at Galich in the north.[27] In these early years, power was in the hands of Vasilii II's mother, Sofiia Vitovtovna, Metropolitan Photios, and the Moscow boyars.[28] Vasilii's ascent to the grand princedom was thus the work of his mother and the Moscow boyars, aided by the initial acquiescence of Prince Iurii. The khan of the Horde did not yet confirm the act, but then the Horde itself was the scene of its own internal struggles for the throne between Borak and Ulug-Mehmed. The latter triumphed for a time in 1427, and became the arbiter of the first round of disputes between uncle and nephew in Moscow, a round that seems to have been the result of several deaths. The first was the death of Grand Princess Sofiia's father Vitovt in 1430, after which Iurii ended the truce but did nothing. Then Metropolitan Photios died in the summer of 1431, and soon after Vasilii went to the Horde to see the khan, followed quickly by Prince Iurii. Ulug-Mehmed awarded the grand princedom to Vasilii. So much and no more is in the earliest chronicle, the First Sophia, probably compiled in the 1450s.[29]

The chronicles compiled in Moscow and other Russian centers starting in the 1470s, however, have a much more detailed story of the events at the capital of the Horde, a story that remained in Russian chronicles

[26] Presniakov, *Obrazovanie velikorusskogo gosudarstva*, 325–407; Cherepnin, *Obrazovanie russkogo tsentralizovannogo gosudarstva*, 724–810; A. A. Zimin, *Vitiaz' na rasput'e*, 31–159.

[27] *PSRL* V, 263; XXV, 246.

[28] I. G. Ponomareva, "Kto upravlial Moskovskim velikim kniazhestvom v 1425–1432 gg.?" *Srednevekovaia Rus'* 9 (2011): 167–196; I. G. Ponomareva, "Boiarskoe okruzhenie moskovskogo velikog kniazia Vasiliia Vasil'evicha v 1425–1432 gg.," *Rossiiskaia Istoriia* I (2011): 96–107.

[29] *PSRL* V, 264; Seleznev, *"A peremenit Bog Ordu,"* 79–96.

through the last great compilation of the 1560s, the Nikon Chronicle.[30] Briefly, the story is this: when the sixteen-year-old Vasilii and his uncle Iurii arrived at the Horde at the end of 1431, they found the Tatar elite divided between the two candidates, and each had to make a case. In the spring, Grand Prince Vasilii began by "seeking his throne as his father's and grandfather's" (*kniaz' velikii po otech'stvu i po ded'stvu iskashe stola svoego*). Then Prince Iurii used as his arguments "chroniclers and old documents and the testament of his father Grand Prince Dmitrii" (*leto-pistsi i starymi spiski i dukhovnoiu ottsa svoego velikogo kniazia Dmitreia*). At that point Vasilii's chief boyar, Ivan Dmitrievich Vsevolozhskii, asked to be allowed to speak and, when the Khan granted that request, said that the decision was really in the hands of the khan. The khan was free to grant the grand princedom according to his wish (*zhalovanie*) and "according to his defters and iarlyks" (*po tvoim devterem i iarlykom*), the basic documents of the Horde administration.[31] Prince Iurii, he continued, was trying to take the grand princedom "according to the dead document of his father" (*po mertvoi gramote ottsa svoego*) rather than according to the khan's grant. Finally, Ivan Dmitrievich pointed out that Vasilii's father, Grand Prince Vasilii Dmitrievich, had given (*dal*) him the grand princedom, and that Vasilii had already sat upon the throne for several years by the grant (*zhalovanie*) of the khan.[32]

This story has several peculiar features. It appeared first in chronicles compiled after the 1470s but remained in all the later compilations, forming part of the "official" history of the Moscow princely family. Yet, for the reader living after the end of the suzerainty of the Horde in 1480, it would seem rather embarrassing, as it presented Vasilii looking for the khan's decision against the "dead document" of his grandfather, although the Moscow princes, as we shall see, had continued to leave the grand princely throne to their heirs in their testaments. At the same time, Vsevolozhskii stressed that Vasilii's father had given him the throne, which was not, strictly speaking, true. Only the second testament had blessed Vasilii Vasil'evich with the throne; the third and final version had not. It only made provisions for the case in which God gave him the grand princedom. To make matters even more complicated, Vsevolozhskii was involved in the dispute over the golden belt that broke out in February,

[30] *PSRL* XII (Nikon Chronicle), 15–17. On the basis of the Nikon Chronicle, the story figured in nearly all accounts of the events from the eighteenth century, starting with Tatishchev in the 1740s: V. N. Tatishchev, *Istoriia Rossiiskaia*, 236–237.

[31] *Iarlyks* were charters from the khans and *defters* records of tax censuses: Seleznev, "*A peremenit Bog Ordu*," 93; Trepavlov, *Stepnye imperii Evrazii*, 202.

[32] *PSRL* XXV, 249. Cherepnin, *Obrazovanie russkogo tsentralizovannogo gosudarstva*, 751–754; Zimin, *Vitiaz' na rasput'e*, 45–49; Ia. S. Lur'e, *Dve istorii Rusi XV veka* (St. Petersburg: Tipografiia D. Bulanin; Paris: Institut d'études slaves, 1994), 87–88.

1434, at Grand Prince Vasilii's wedding, when Grand Princess Sofiia seized the belt from Prince Vasilii Kosoi, Prince Iurii's son. This event precipitated yet another round of disputes.[33] Ivan Dmitrievich Vsevolozhskii then went over to the side of Prince Iurii and played a major role on that side until the two princes reached a temporary compromise. At that point he disappeared from most chronicles, though the Tver' and Ermolin chronicles claim that Grand Prince Vasilii was able to capture him and have him blinded.[34] The later chroniclers kept the story, which highlighted the potential role of testaments, fatherly gift of the throne, the Horde documents, and even chronicles, though the role of the last is unspecified.[35]

The testament of Grand Prince Dmitrii Donskoi was the central document in the whole dynastic civil war for the opponents of Vasilii II, as in the statement of Iurii Dmitrievich before Khan Ulug-Mehmed in 1431 recounted above. The chronicle story does not tell us exactly what in the testament of Dmitrii Donskoi seemed to be in favor of Prince Iurii, in his opinion, but historians assume that it was the following passage:

> And if, because of my sins, God takes away my son, Prince Vasilii, then the patrimonial principality [*udel*] of Prince Vasilii [shall pass] to my son who follows him, and the patrimonial principality [*udel*] of the latter shall be divided among the others by my princess.[36]

[33] *PSRL* XXV, 250, Zimin, *Vitiaz' na rasput'e*, 52–55; Charles J. Halperin, *The Tatar Yoke: The Image of the Mongols in Medieval Russia*, 2nd ed. (Bloomington, Indiana: Slavica, 2009), 158–162; C. K. Woodworth, "Sophia and the Golden Belt: What Caused Moscow's Civil Wars of 1425–1450," *Russian Review* 68 (April, 2009): 187–198.

[34] *PSRL* XXV, 250; Zimin, *Vitiaz' na rasput'e*, 52–56, 63, 232.

[35] The Horde documents were the *defters* and *iarlyks* of the khans (according to Vasilii's spokesman Vsevolozhskii). The *iarlyks* would seem the simplest, as they were charters of grant issued by the khans of the Horde to Russian princes as well as to the church, granting them land, power, or immunities. In the existing treaties, testaments, and other documents of the Russian principalities, however, the term first appeared a year later, in the 1433 treaty between Grand Prince Vasilii II and Prince Iurii: Iurii was to surrender the khan's *yarlyk* for the town of Dmitrov to Vasilii. More interesting are the requirements in treaties of the grand prince from 1447 with lesser princes who had come over to his side from that of Dmitrii Shemiaka: Vasilii required them to surrender any *yarlyks* and *defters* that they had taken from him in the course of the fighting. A year later he required Prince Ivan Vasil'evich of Suzdal' to surrender any *yarlyks* for Suzdal' or Nizhnii Novgorod that he had received from the khan: *DDG*, 76, 78, 141, 148, 156, 158. Defters first appeared in such documents about the same time. The 1434 treaty of Vasilii II with his rivals required them to give him the Tatar tribute (*vykhod*) according to the "old defters." This was the usual formula by which the Moscow grand princes appropriated the tribute payments from their subordinate princes to themselves up until the end of the fifteenth century. The last such document was written in 1496: *DDG*, 88, 338.

[36] *DDG* 35; Howe, *The Testaments of the Grand Princes of Moscow*, 214. Zimin recognized that the grand princedom was not an *udel*. Most of the space in Dmitrii's testament went to the disposition of his lands into *udely* for his sons, and the passage that specified what

The chronicle account of the dispute before the khan is not the only source to discuss the merits of the testament of Dmitrii Donskoi. As Vasilii II grew stronger, the church came to support him openly and on December 29, 1447, the bishops led by Iona of Riazan' (the future metropolitan) sent a long epistle to Prince Dmitrii Iur'evich Shemiaka, rebuking him for his pride, a pride like that of Adam, and listing all his misdeeds. One of these misdeeds was that he wanted "to live in Moscow according to the testament of your grandfather Grand Prince Dmitrii Ivanovich." Concretely that meant that he sent letters to his steward (*tiun*) Vatazin and ordered him to call the "people" of the grand prince away to serve him, Dmitrii, so as to get at the grand princedom.[37] The terminology is vague, but it seems that they were accusing him of using the provisions of the will that gave his father an *udel* (part of which Dmitrii Shemiaka inherited) to provide a basis, through his steward, to recruit the servants (probably military servants) of the grand prince to his side. Once again, the testament served as a tool to get at the grand princedom even though it explicitly gave the throne to Vasilii II's father.

Whatever the arguments, the Moscow civil war was intense and bloody. Iurii managed to seize Moscow in 1434, but died almost immediately. His son Vasilii ("Kosoi") claimed the grand princely throne but failed to hold on to it. He was defeated by Vasilii II and blinded in 1436. From then on, the main opponent of the grand prince was Dmitrii Iur'evich Shemiaka, another of the sons of Iurii Dmitrievich. He prevailed briefly after a 1445 defeat of Vasilii II at the hands of the Tatars of Kazan', and had Vasilii blinded as well. His reign was short-lived, and in 1447 Vasilii returned to Moscow in triumph. The civil war effectively ended with the defeat of

was to happen if Vasilii I died without heir applied to the *udel*, not the grand princedom. Unfortunately, Zimin confused the issue by claiming that the absence of a son by Vasilii I in 1389 somehow meant that the heir to the *udel* would be the heir to the grand princely throne: Zimin, *Vitiaz' na rasput'e*, 7–9. This conclusion is not supported by the testament. The brief sentence blessing Vasilii Dmitrievich stands alone after many pages listing towns, villages, and districts for each *udel* and has nothing to do with it. In any case, the khan of the Horde was still supreme. Grand Prince Dmitrii Donskoi did no more than bless his eldest son with the throne in the hope that the khan would agree. Dmitrii was aware that the Horde might not be able to enforce its will. Later on in the text comes the famous phrase, "if God changes the Horde" then his children need not pay tribute. In that case, his blessing ensured that Vasilii I would inherit the grand princedom. Dmtrii said nothing about the succession to his son. In this sense, Prince Iurii was distorting the meaning of the testament, assimilating the throne to the prince's domain. Vasilii II and his spokesmen were taking the throne as separate from the domain, and correctly assumed that Dmitrii's testament had no bearing on his grandson Vasilii II. What counted in 1432 was the orally expressed designation of Vasilii and the command of Khan Ulu-Mehmed.

[37] *AI* I, 88; A. I. Pliguzov, ed., *Russkii feodal'nyi arkhiv*, 5 vols. (Moscow: Institut Istorii SSSR AN SSSR, 1986–92), vol. I, 112.

Prince Dmitrii Shemiaka before his northern stronghold at Galich in January 1450. Shemiaka tried to hold on, but died in Novgorod in 1453.

The defeat signaled the victory of the direct descent line, the sons of the grand prince of Moscow, over the claims of the uncles and cousins. This victory was effective at the moment, but it did not put an end to the claims of uncles and cousins forever in the Moscow princely family. That issue reappeared again several times in the sixteenth century, which means that it remained a possibility for all of the grand princes of Moscow and their successors, the grand princes and tsars of Russia. In some way, the rulers would have to make clear whom they designated as their successors. The testaments that had served that purpose in the fourteenth century were not enough, as the Moscow civil war had demonstrated so clearly. The end of that civil war brought some changes.

Before his death in 1462, Vasilii Vasil'evich II, called "the Dark" because of his blindness, may have made a major innovation in the history of the Moscow princely family. In the chronicles, his son Ivan Vasil'evich appeared for the first time in 1452 with the grand princely title at the age of eleven, and regularly thereafter until his father's death and his ascent to the throne in his own name. The title occurs already in the First Sophia Chronicle, at the mention of Ivan's marriage to Princess Mariia of Tver', and is repeated with different wording in the post-1471 chronicles. In the latter, the title appeared in the story of the Tatar raid in the summer of that year, but was not connected with the raid. There was no motivation for the title in the chronicles, and there is no trace of any ceremony or even a benediction.[38] In the treaties of Grand Prince Vasilii II with other Russian princes, his son Ivan is called grand prince for the first time in a treaty with Prince Ivan Vasil'evich of Suzdal', a document which historians have dated to 1448–9. In the treaty with King Kazimierz of Poland (August 13, 1449), however, the new title was absent. It appeared again in the treaties with Prince Vasilii Iaroslavich of Serpukhov, but those can only be dated generally to the early 1450s. Either the date of the treaty with Ivan of Suzdal' is wrong or Vasilii II did not want to use a new title with the king of Poland.[39] In these same years, Vasilii's coins bore the inscription "Lords of all Rus'" (*Ospodari vseia Rusi*) in the plural.[40] Finally, in his testament Vasilii II blessed his son Ivan with the grand

[38] *PSRL* V, 271; Grand Prince Vasilii left Moscow against the Tatars "s synom svoim velikim kniazem Ivanom," *PSRL* XXV, 271; Nitsche, *Großfürst und Thronfolger*, 59–61.

[39] Nitsche, *Großfürst und Thronfolger*, 62, 74–77; Zimin, *Vitiaz' na rasput'e*, 133–35, 144, 147, 251; *DDG*, 158, 179,181; *PSRL* XII, 76–77, 115. Mel'nikov's attempt to connect Ivan's grand princely title with his betrothal to Mariia of Tver' in 1446 is based on later unreliable sources. Mel'nikov, *Pravovyi rezhim nasledovaniia prestola*, 119–124.

[40] Zimin, *Vitiaz' na rasput'e*, 170.

princedom, and since Metropolitan Feodosii, in office since May 3, 1461, signed the document, it must have come from the last year of Vasilii II's life.[41] In other words, between the appearance of the grand princely title for Ivan and his father's blessing there were ten years. The chronicles recorded nothing of any ceremony, only that Ivan III "sat" on the grand princedom "according to the benediction of his father." They go on to summarize the provisions of the testament, which may have been the source for the chroniclers.[42] Thus Vasilii II added a new element to the designation of the heir beyond the testaments, and the chronicles kept the record of that element.[43]

Ivan III

Ivan III in his own time already had the reputation of the builder of the Russian state. By annexing Novgorod and subjecting it to his direct rule and by annexing Moscow's ancient rival Tver' he created a state that encompassed most of the old northeast of Kiev Rus'. Only Pskov in the far west and Riazan' to the south remained independent, if under his influence. The consolidation of Russia as a state was not just a territorial issue, for Ivan also began the development of a state apparatus out of the prince's household, and the incorporation of new territories meant the incorporation of large elements of local elites into the ranks of the Moscow boyars. Among those newcomers were several important princes from the eastern marches of Lithuania, Orthodox princes of the house of Gediminas, who brought their territories with them into the Russian state. Ivan was also a builder, for the Kremlin walls and towers, most of its churches, and the prince's palace were the work of his reign. They were also nearly all the work of Italian architects, Aristotele Fioravanti and others, part of the influx of West Europeans into Russia that was another hallmark of Ivan III's time. The greatest landmark of the

[41] *DDG*, 194. The testament had the blessing of Metropolitan Feodosii, and the witnesses were Prince Vasilii's spiritual fathers and four boyars. The first on the list of boyars was Prince Ivan Iur'evich Patrikeev, the son of the first boyar in the will of Vasilii I: *DDG*, 198, Kollmann, *Kinship and Politics*, 225.

[42] *PSRL* XXV, 278; *PSRL* VIII (Voskresenskaia Chronicle), 123; Nitsche, *Großfürst und Thronfolger*, 61–62, 89. Vasilii II not only designated his heir more clearly than ever before, but also his testament guaranteed Ivan III a much greater share of the domain and sovereign rights over his various territories than those of his brothers, by comparison with the earlier testaments of the Moscow princes: Zimin, *Vitiaz' na rasput'e*, 185–186.

[43] Russian chronicles had served as a repository of the decisions of the princes, especially interprincely diplomatic discussions and conclusions, since the time of Kiev Rus'. Simon Franklin, "Literacy and Documentation in Early Medieval Russia," *Speculum* 60, 1 (1985), 1–38; Simon Franklin, *Writing, Society, and Culture in Early Rus'* (Cambridge: Cambridge University Press, 2002), 170–173.

reign, however, was not the result of heroic or even decisive action. The end of the suzerainty of the Horde came in 1480, the outcome of a confused conflict with the Great Horde on the Volga and inside the ruling family of Moscow, but it was no less a turning point in Russian history.

That Ivan III's reign was distinctive is not simply a construction of modern historians. He had the possibly unique distinction, among Russian rulers, of finding approval among his contemporaries in Poland. Jan Długosz, Poland's greatest medieval historian, praised him in the following terms: "The elder of the princes, Ivan, was a man of great soul and activity, who set free himself together with all his principalities and lands and threw off the yoke of servitude under which all Moscow had been oppressed for a long time." Novgorod offended the spirit of the great man (*ingens vir*). It was a rich and broad land, but one whose inhabitants were woman-like and effeminate, and who removed their princes and leaders at the will of the archbishop and the people. Since King Kazimierz had abandoned them, Ivan annexed the city and its territory. The riches of the city made him so powerful that the Lithuanians could not resist him.[44] Długosz died in 1480 and his history ended in that year, but his younger contemporary, Bernard Wapowski, was no less positive. Under the year of Ivan's death he placed a summary of his accomplishments. Ivan was "worthy of praise" because he "expanded the state of the Muscovites by subjecting many princes and provinces of the Russian name" and, "as the Muscovite princes were formerly tributaries to the Scythian Tatars, he first of all threw off the yoke of servitude. So great was the virtue of the man, so great his knowledge of arms." He went on to enumerate the peoples Ivan had subjected and then came to the Lithuanian princes. "Indeed, the powerful princes of the Greek rite, mighty in horsemen, first of Mozhaisk, then of Starodub and Bel'sk, defected from the Lithuanians to the Muscovites, so great a loss of its frontiers did that people [the Lithuanians] suffer." The Swedes, Finns, and Livonians felt the "terrible assault of the Muscovite cavalry." Ivan was not just a great soldier. He removed the taverns everywhere in Russia so that "the Muscovites would study sobriety, more skillfully apply themselves to agriculture and commerce, increase their property, and be more apt for the arts of war and soldiery." He noted that Ivan left several sons, Vasilii, Iurii, Dmitrii, Simon, and Andrei. "Wishing to preserve the state of the Muscovites unshaken and whole, he gave provinces to his sons in accord with their dignity, and he put Dmitrii his nephew by his brother

[44] Jan Długosz, *Historia Polonica*. Opera omnia XIV (Kraków: Tipographia Czas F. Klurzycki, 1878), 696–698.

over them, and designated him his successor. Not long after he used better counsel and put him in prison on account of his contemptible behavior, and raised his eldest son Vasilii to Grand Prince of Moscow," who followed in his father's footsteps and expanded the Russian state, as Wapowski promised to relate in his history.[45] Wapowski, writing in Kraków in the 1520s, made some factual errors, but he grasped the essence of the succession issue as well as Ivan's achievements as a builder of the state. He understood how crucial to the success of the state was succession to the throne.

Sons and Brothers

Ivan III had come to the throne with the title of grand prince already in hand. Besides his young son Ivan Ivanovich, born in 1458, he had four brothers.[46] These were Iurii Vasil'evich (1441–73), Andrei Vasil'vich the Elder ("Goriai," 1446–93), Boris Vasil'evich (1449–94), and Andrei Vasil'evich the Younger (1452–81).[47] In the same testament in which Vasilii II had blessed Ivan with the grand princedom, he awarded appanages to his other sons. Iurii received Dmitrov, Mozhaisk, and Serpukhov; Andrei the Elder got Uglich, Bezhetskii Verkh, and Zvenigorod; Boris in turn had Volokolamsk, Rzhev, and Ruza; while Andrei the Younger found himself with distant but wealthy Vologda in the north.[48] These appanages have been the object of long discussion among historians as examples of incomplete centralization, but they were also part of the succession issue. They provided a modest provincial court and a military contingent. In 1471, as Ivan went off to Novgorod, his brothers joined him "from their inheritance," meaning they brought armed contingents along to the campaign.[49] Modest as the appanages were, they were a power base that the grand prince controlled only through the obedience of his brothers.[50]

[45] Bernard Wapowski, *Chronicorum pars posterior*. Scriptores rerum polonicarum II (Kraków: Akademia Umiejętności, 1874), 61–62.

[46] Ivan Ivanovich "the young" was born on February 15, 1458, and "narechen byst' Ivan." There is no mention of the baptism ceremony: *PSRL* 25, 275.

[47] Two sons died in infancy, Iurii and Semen: A. V. Ekzempliarskii, *Velikie i udel'nye kniazia* (Moscow: Tera-Knizhnyi klub, 1998), vol. I, 293–294.

[48] *DDG*, 194–195; *PSRL* XXV, 278; Ekzempliarskii, *Velikie i udel'nye kniazia*, vol. II, 316, 327, 347–351. Vasilii also left his widow Mariia Iaroslavovna with Rostov: *DDG*, 195–196.

[49] *PSRL* XXV, 288. On the end of Novgorod's independence, see V. N. Bernadskii, *Novgorod i novgorodskaia zemlia v XV veke* (Leningrad: Izdatel'stvo Akademii nauk SSSR, 1961); J. L. I. Fennell, *Ivan the Great of Moscow* (London: Macmillan, 1963), 29–65; Iu. G. Alekseev, *"K Moskve khotim": Zakat boiarskoi respublike v Novgorode* (St. Petersburg: Lenizdat, 1991).

[50] A. A. Zimin, "Udel'nye kniazia i ikh dvory vo vtoroi polovine XV i pervoi polovine XVI veka," in *Istoriia i genealogiia*, ed. N. I. Pavlenko (Moscow: Nauka, 1977), 161–188; Zimin, *Rossiia na rubezhe*; Nikolai Petrukhintsev, "The Duration of Integration as

Designation was the means that Ivan III chose to ensure the succession of his own son Ivan to the throne. The act was all the more important since Grand Princess Mariia Borisovna had died in 1467 at the age of twenty-five, and had given birth only to the one son. There were as yet no other children to inherit the throne. In 1471, as he marched off to subdue Novgorod, Ivan III gave the grand princely title to that son. The young Ivan Ivanovich first appeared with the title of grand prince at this moment, when his father left him, a youth of thirteen years, in Moscow during Ivan's first Novgorod campaign. Until this moment the chroniclers called him only prince, as was the case with his father during his childhood. In the First Sophia and L'vov chronicles, there is a description of the "placing" of Ivan Ivanovich on the princedom. On the eve of his departure for Novgorod, Grand Prince Ivan prayed extensively to God and His Mother, and called for the aid of the saints, the saintly Moscow metropolitans, and his princely ancestors. After the prayers, he "in the house of the most pure Mother of God and the great metropolitan and miracle-worker Peter [i.e., the Kremlin Dormition Cathedral] placed on the throne of his inheritance the grand princedom, in place of himself, his son the right believing and pious Grand Prince Ivan Ivanovich to take care of his inheritances and administer the Russian lands."[51] To guide the young heir the grand prince left in Moscow his younger brother Andrei Vasil'evich the Lesser and Tsarevich Murtaza, the son of Mustafa the Khan of Kazan'.[52] Grand Prince Ivan had not only given his son the grand princely title while he was still a minor and made him a co-ruler, but also marked the event with a ceremony in the main cathedral of Moscow.

This story about the placing of the young Ivan on the throne in 1471 does not appear in all chronicles. It is part of a story of the events called the "Selected Words" (*Slovesa izbranna*) that was included in the "unofficial" chronicles such as the First Sophia and L'vov chronicles and represented

a Factor in Russian History and Its Impact on Social and Political Development in Sixteenth-Century Russia," in *The State in Early Modern Russia: New Directions*, ed. Paul Bushkovitch (Bloomington, Indiana: Slavica, 2019), 97–132.

51 "в дому пречистые Богородицы и великого святителя и чудотворца Петра на столе его отчины великого княжения, в свое место посадил на Москве сына своего, благоверного и благочестивого великого князя Ивана Ивановича блюсти своее отчины и управляти Русские земли," *PSRL* VI, 9; *PSRL* XX, pt. 1, 290.

52 Prince Andrei Vasil'evich Men'shii was the youngest brother of Ivan III. He had Vologda as an appanage and died in 1481: Zimin, *Rossiia na rubezhe*, 55–56. The three older brothers went with the grand prince on the campaign against Novgorod. On Murtaza, see A. V. Beliakov, *Chingisidy v Rossii XV–XVII vekov: Prosopograficheskoe issledovanie* (Riazan': Mir, 2011), 55, 182, 205, 284. Ivan III had sent Nikita Beklemishev to the steppe (*v pole*) to invite Murtaza, who had lost in the feuds among the Kazan dynasty, to come to Moscow to serve him, and Murtaza came with Beklemishev to Ivan's son (*k synu velikogo kniazia*) on the eve of the Novgorod campaign. *PSRL* XXV, 291; XII, 141.

the church's versions of the events.[53] Internal evidence suggests that the story was compiled very soon after the events, for it mentions Grigorii (the Bulgarian), the originally Latin-oriented metropolitan of Kiev (1458–72/3) as "now" called metropolitan.[54] Another story appeared in the grand princely chronicles of the 1490s and in sixteenth-century chronicles derived from them such as the Voskresenie and the First Sophia Chronicle. In this version, there was only the brief sentence that "the grand prince left in Moscow his son, the grand prince Ivan, and his [Ivan III's] brother Prince Andrei the Lesser." The story of the placement of the heir on the throne in the Dormition Cathedral did not appear.[55] The same version, however, gave prominence to the chronicles as authoritative documents. As he left his son in Moscow, he called on the services of one Stefan Borodatyi, a *d'iak* in the service of his mother, Grand Princess Mariia Iaroslavna. He wanted Stefan because he could "speak according to the Russian chroniclers" and remind the grand prince to speak to the Novgorodians of their ancient treasons to the grand princes, his fathers and grandfathers, in ancient times.[56]

The grand princely chronicles continued to give Ivan Ivanovich the grand princely title in the descriptions of Ivan III's return after his victory over the Novgorodians on the Shelon' River in July 1471 and whenever he was mentioned until his death in 1490. Official documents confirmed the chronicle stories. The treaties of Ivan III with appanage princes from the 1460s mention Ivan Ivanovich only as "my son Ivan," but in the 1470s and 1480s such treaties refer to him as "grand prince."[57] In relations with

[53] For the most recent attempt to analyze the chronicles of the period roughly 1470–1510, see Lur'e, *Dve istorii Rusi XV veka*. "Unofficial" is Lur'e's term for chronicles that were not compiled in the princely court, though not necessarily in opposition to the grand prince. In the First Sophia Chronicle the text is an addition.

[54] *PSRL* VI, 6.

[55] *PSRL* XXV, 288; VI (First Sophia Chronicle), 9; VIII (Voskresenskaia), 163; XXVII (Nikanorovskaia), 132, 136; XII, 132. Cf. *PSRL* XII, 112, 119. Ia S. Lur'e, *Dve istorii Rusi XV veka*, 123–167; Ia. S. Lur'e, "Povesti o prisoedinenii Novgoroda," *SKKDR* II, pt. 2, 201–204. In the Sophia II Chronicle the grand princely title of Ivan Ivanovich is absent: *PSRL* VI (Sofiiskaia II), 192. Its text often reflected "unofficial" sources, in Lur'e's terminology: Ia S. Lur'e, "Letopis' Sofiiskaia II," *SKKDR* II, pt. 2, 60–61. The same is true of the Novgorod chronicles.

[56] Ivan III, "isprosi u materi svoei u velikoi kniaini d'iaka Stefana Borodatogo, umeiushchego govoriti po letopistsem ruskim: esli, reche, pridut, i on vospominaet emu govoriti protivu ikh izmeny davnye, kak oni izmenili velikim kniazem, v davnye vremena, ottsem ego i dedom i pradedom," *PSRL* VI (Sophia Second Chronicle), 192. Cf. Ia. S. Lur'e, "Stefan Borodatyi," *SKKDR* II, pt. 2, 416–417; Lur'e, *Dve istorii Rusi XV veka*, 82, 84, 133, 158.

[57] *PSRL* XXV, 292, 300, 304, 309, 311, 324, 326, 327, 329–331; *DDG*, 213, 215–216, 225, 247, 252. The so-called Abbreviated Chronicle compilations (*Sokrashchennyi svod*) gave him the title only from about 1480: *PSRL* XXVII (Abbreviated Chronicle of 1493), 280–285, 287, 289; (Abbreviated Chronicle of 1495), 355–360.

the Livonian order for those years, both Ivan III and his son bore the title "tsar."[58] Ivan Ivanovich seems to have begun to have some share in the government only in 1477, when the Novgorodians sent an embassy to him as well as to his father, and moreover his marriage in 1483 to Elena of Moldavia made him a full adult.[59] In 1485, Ivan III gave him Tver' as his appanage. Long before those events, however, he bore the same title as his father.[60]

The variations in the story of the acquisition of the title of grand prince by Ivan Ivanovich in 1471 are suggestive. The ceremony in the cathedral appeared only in a story that came from the church, while the grand princely chronicles ignored it. In neither of the stories did Ivan III bless his son with the throne. The reasons why are not obvious, but it may be that he did not need to. In 1451, his father Vasilii II had had four sons, Ivan Vasil'evich, the eldest, and three younger sons, Iurii, Andrei, and Boris. The grand prince made it clear, if the chronicles are accurate, whom he chose as heir by giving his son the title of grand prince while he was still a boy. In 1471, the situation was quite different. Ivan III had as yet only the one son and a young daughter, Elena, so there was no alternative to the son. Yet he felt it necessary to designate an heir. With this act he could forestall any alternative to his eldest son for the throne. These alternatives could only have been his own younger brothers.

Ivan's brother Iurii Vasil'evich died in September 1472 (only a few weeks before Ivan's second marriage, this time to Sophia Palaiologina). Iurii himself was unmarried and childless.[61] His death may have set off the first quarrel among the brothers. In any case, Iurii's appanage had to be redivided, and the result was an agreement between Ivan and his two remaining younger brothers. From Iurii's lands, the grand prince himself took Dmitrov, Mozhaisk, and Serpukhov as his own. By February 1473, he had made an agreement with Boris, who received nothing from Iurii's appanage but did receive the small town and district of Vyshgorod in addition to his original holding in Volokolamsk. Late in 1473 Andrei the Elder received Kaluga, the delay suggesting some disagreement over the shares.[62] Thus neither of the younger brothers acquired significant land

[58] A. L. Khoroshkevich, *Russkoe gosudarstvo v sisteme mezhdunarodnykh otnoshenii kontsa XV–nachala XVI vv.* (Moscow: Nauka, 1980), 102. The use of "tsar" before the coronation of Ivan IV in 1547 is a long-standing problem. See most recently A. I. Filiushkin, *Titulyrusskikh gosudarei* (Moscow and St. Petersburg: Al'ians-Arkheo, 2006).

[59] Mel'nikov asserts that Ivan and his brothers were real co-rulers, but he does not distinguish between formal titles and real actions: Mel'nikov, *Pravovyi rezhim nasledovaniia prestola*, 158–200. Ivan Ivanovich was not ruling the country in his father's absence in 1471.

[60] *PSRL* XXV, 309, 329–331; Zimin, *Rossiia na rubezhe*, 63.

[61] *PSRL* XXV, 288, 298.

[62] *DDG*, 225–249; Ekzempliarskii, *Velikie i udel'nye kniazia*, vol. II, 372–373.

from the appanage of Iurii Vasil'evich. These documents, however, were not just about the transfer of appanages. They both began with the statement that Ivan's brothers were to kiss the cross to him and his son, the Grand Prince Ivan. Boris was to obey him as a father and his son as an elder brother, and to support him, his son, and the grand princedom honorably and strongly, without offense (*derzhati chestno i grozno, bez obidy*). For Andrei the formula was the same except that he was to obey Ivan only as an elder brother, not as a father.[63] The redivision of the appanages was an opportunity to reinforce Ivan's designation of his son as his co-ruler and thus his heir, and to sanctify by oaths his younger brother's obedience.

The settlement of appanages in 1473 did not last. For the years after the settlement, relations between the brothers were quiet, and all of them supported Ivan in the final conflict that put an end to Novgorod's independence in 1478.[64] The opportunity for revision came as part of one of the great crises of Ivan's reign, the so-called Standing on the Ugra. In 1480, Khan Ahmet of the Great Horde on the southern Volga decided to make a major raid on Moscow. Months before Ahmet was even on the horizon, in the winter while Ivan was in Novgorod putting down yet another manifestation of discontent (this time by the Novgorod archbishop Feofil), he heard from his son that both Andrei the Elder and Boris had come out in revolt against him. They had left their appanages with their boyars and families and were moving toward the Lithuanian border. There they sent envoys to the king of Poland asking him to help them, but Kazimierz refused. Vassian, the archbishop of Rostov, and the boyars convinced them to come to Moscow, which they reached just before Easter. While this dispute was still unresolved, Khan Ahmet of the Great Horde appeared with his army just south of the Oka river. Grand Prince Ivan and his son Ivan went south with their forces and awaited events, forming a line watching the Tatars along the Oka and Ugra rivers. The grand prince was not sure what he should do, and he returned to Moscow to consult the clergy and the boyars. Metropolitan Gerontii and archbishop Vassian urged him to fight, the latter in a famous epistle that called on him to remember his ancestors and fight for the faith. He returned to the army, and this time his brothers Andrei and Boris joined him. No battle ensued, and finally the khan withdrew to the south. Celebrated correctly as the end of the Horde's power over Russia, it also marked a moment of weakness, and Ivan's brothers had taken

[63] *DDG*, 225, 232.

[64] *PSRL* XXV, 313. Princes Andrei and Boris commanded the right and left wings of Ivan's army.

advantage of it. In the result, Andrei got Mozhaisk and Boris a series of villages.[65] Fortunately for Ivan, both of the brothers died before the next dynastic crisis.

The Succession Crisis

Ivan managed to prevent the conflicts with his brothers from undermining his rule, but they were not the only problem for succession. A much larger issue arose after the marriage of Ivan to Sophia Palaiologina in 1472. Sophia was the daughter of Thomas, the last Despot of Morea, and thus a descendant of Byzantium's last ruling house. Ivan could not have found a more prestigious bride, at least within the Orthodox world. Modern historians and others have loaded every imaginable stereotype onto Sophia and the marriage, claiming her as the origin of Byzantine despotism in Russia or the conduit for the adoption of Byzantine culture and values. In fact, Sophia had spent most of her life in Italy, and in any case there is little evidence that she had much cultural or political impact. Russia's relations with Italy were indeed strong in those decades, but she and her Greco-Italian entourage seem to have been only one group of actors among several.[66] What is certainly true is that she gave birth to a son, Vasilii, in 1479, who became a rival for the throne to Dmitrii, born in 1483, the son of Ivan Ivanovich, Ivan III's eldest.

The fate of Dmitrii Ivanovich, the grandson of Ivan III, and the succession of Vasilii Ivanovich to the grand princely throne is one of the classic episodes of Russian history, discussed by every historian since the eighteenth century. It also served as an argument for Peter the Great in his succession decree of 1722. The story is all the more complicated because of the connections, real or imagined, between the factions at the Moscow court and the "heretics" of Novgorod and Moscow, producing a historiography of considerable complexity. Ivan III himself, after the final condemnation of the Novgorod heretics in 1503, asserted that Elena was sympathetic to the heretics.[67] Aside from this aspect, the succession story was typical of any monarchy in history, for it came from the two marriages of Ivan III, to Mariia and then

[65] *PSRL* 24, 197–201; *DDG*, 252–275; Lur'e, *Dve istorii Rusi XV veka*, 168–195; A. A. Gorskii, *Moskva i Orda*, 152–186; Paul Bushkovitch, "The Church and Russian Foreign Policy, 1480–1725," *Canadian-American Slavic Studies* 54, 1–3 (2020): 7–50 .

[66] Paul Bushkovitch, "Sofia Palaiologina in Life and Legend," *Canadian-American Slavic Studies* 52 (2018): 158–180.

[67] Lur'e, *Ideologicheskaia bor'ba v russkoi publitsistike kontsa XV–nachala XVI veka* (Moscow and Leningrad: Izdatel'stvo Akademii nauk, 1960), 143; Fennell, *Ivan the Great*, 334–355, S. M. Kashtanov, *Sotsial'no-politicheskaia istoriia Rossii kontsa pervoi poloviny XVI veka* (Moscow: Nauka, 1967), 21–69, 79–169; Nitsche, *Großfürst und Thronfolger*, 83–182; Zimin, *Rossiia na rubezhe*, 138–177; Lur'e, *Dve istorii Rusi XV veka*, 195–216.

Sophia. The story of the marriage of Ivan to Sophia Palaiologina is complicated and has some elements that defy explanation. In June 1468, Pope Paul II sent one Niccolò Gislardi and the Greek Iurii (i.e., Georgios) to Giovanni della Volpe, the master of Ivan III's mint, for unstated purposes. In February, 1469, the Greek Iurii, possibly Iurii Manuilovich Trakhaniot, arrived in Moscow with a message from Cardinal Bessarion in Rome, the former Greek metropolitan of Nicaea who had gone over to Catholicism at the Council of Florence. The Greek envoy told Ivan, so the chronicle says, that in Rome Sophia, the daughter of Thomas, the last Despot of Morea, was an Orthodox Christian and would make an appropriate bride.[68] Della Volpe and his nephew Antonio Gislardi went to Rome, to Pope Paul II in response. After their return to Moscow, Pope Paul died (July 28, 1471), and when the full Russian delegation came back to Rome they had to make arrangements with the new Pope Sixtus IV. The final result was the proxy betrothal of Ivan and the Greek princess Sophia Palaiologina in Rome in June 1472 and, after her arrival in Moscow, the wedding in November of the same year.[69] Children soon followed, but the first three were girls who died in infancy. The fourth child (born 1476) was Elena, healthy but also a girl. It was not until 1479 that a son, Vasilii, came into the world. Vasilii was born on March 25, the day of the Archangel Gabriel, and was baptized in the

[68] Paul Pierling, *La Russie et l'Orient: Mariage d'un Tsar au Vatican: Ivan III et Sophie Paléologue* (Paris: Leroux, 1891), 20–21; *PSRL* XXV (Moscow chronicle compilation of the end of the fifteenth century), 281. This chronicle, an official compilation of the late fifteenth century, gave no explanation why Bessarion would send this message. Sophia had been a ward of the Pope and would have been an unlikely Orthodox Christian. The chronicle also omitted the usual denunciations of Catholic clergy in this case, which is all the more surprising as Bessarion had himself abandoned Orthodoxy at the Council of Florence. Most historians agree that the "Greek Iurii" was the same as Ivan III's later diplomat Iurii Trakhaniot, active from about 1480 onward as a diplomat for Ivan III along with others of the same family: D. M. Bulanin, "Trakhaniot, Iurii Manuilovich," *SKKDR* II, pt. 2, 438–439.

[69] Paul Pierling, *La Russie et la Sainte-Siège* (Paris: Plon-Nourrit, 1896), vol. 1, 130–163; E. Ch. Skrzhinskaia, "Moskovskaia Rus' i Venetsiia vremen Ivan III," in *Rus', Italiia, i Vizantiia v Srednevekov'e* (St. Petersburg: Aleteiia, 2000), 180–237; Robert M. Croskey, "Byzantine Greeks in Late Fifteenth- and Early Sixteenth-Century Russia," in *The Byzantine Legacy in Eastern Europe*, ed. Lowell Clucas (New York, New York: Columbia University Press, 1988); Jonathan Harris, "A Worthless Prince? Andreas Palaeologus in Rome, 1465–1502," *Orientalia Christiana Periodica* 61 (1995): 537–554; Tat'iana Matasova, *Sof'ia Paleolog* (Moscow: Molodaia gvardiia, 2016), 76–136; Bushkovitch, "Sofia Palaiologina." Bessarion was not present for the ceremony as he was on a mission for the Pope in France, but he sent a letter to Siena asking the government to take care of the Russian embassy and Sophia on their way back to Moscow. He died on November 18, 1472, six days after the wedding of Sophia in Moscow: Pierling, *La Russie et l'Orient*, 190–191; Ludwig Mohler, *Kardinal Bessarion als Theologe, Humanist und Staatsman: Funde und Forschungen.* Quellen und Forschungen aus dem Gebiete der Geschichte, herausgegeben von der Görres-Gesellschaft 22 (Paderborn: F. Schöningh, 1923), vol. 1, 416–429.

Trinity Monastery by the archbishop of Rostov, Vassian Rylo, and hegumen Paisii of the Trinity Monastery.[70] The text is not clear about whether the two of them shared the service in some way, but it seems likely that Paisii was the godfather (the custom at that time was to have only one godparent). If so, that meant that the infant Vasilii had now a spiritual relationship with the head of the principal monastery of the Moscow principality. Four years later Ivan Ivanovich, by now twenty-five, married Elena of Moldavia ("Voloshanka").[71] Dmitrii, his son and Ivan III's grandson, appeared at the end of the same year, 1483.[72] After the death of Ivan Ivanovich the younger in 1490, his son Dmitrii had borne only the title "prince," as did Vasilii .[73]

In December 1497, the chroniclers tell us, the grand prince became angry at his wife Sofia and her son Vasilii, who was by then eighteen years old. He had six of the *deti boiarskie*, Vladimir Gusev and others, executed, presumably as her supporters. Then on February 4, 1498, Ivan III blessed the fourteen-year-old Dmitrii and placed him on the throne.[74] For the coronation of Dmitrii an entire ritual was composed, with the action prescribed and also the texts of the prayers and speeches, a *Chin venchaniia*, or Order of Coronation. It bore little resemblance to the Byzantine coronation ritual, though it borrowed some parts of the text.[75] Ivan's

[70] *PSRL* XXV, 323. Vassian was the author of the famous "Epistle to the Ugra" exhorting Ivan III to fight against the Tatars in that year: Ia. S. Lur'e, *SKKDR* II, pt. 1, 123–124; Halperin, *The Tatar Yoke*, 176–181. Paisii (Iaroslavov, died 1501) was hegumen of the Trinity-St. Sergii Monastery 1479–82 and an important monastic writer and participant in the disputes among the Russian monks at the end of the fifteenth century: G. M. Prokhorov, "Paisii Iaroslavov," *SKKDR* II, pt. 2, 156–160. On baptism and godparents, see A. I. Almazov, *Istoriia chinoposledovanii kreshcheniia i miropomazaniia* (Kazan': n.p., 1884), 605–641. On the Byzantine tradition of baptism, see Phaidon Koukoules, "Ta kata ten gennesin kai ten baptisin ethima ton Vyzantinon," *Epiteris etaireias Vyzantinon spoudon* 14 (1938): 87–146, esp. 141–146; Despoina Arianzi, *Kindheit in Byzanz* (Boston, Massachusetts and Berlin: De Gruyter, 2012), 92–118.

[71] Zimin, *Rossiia na rubezhe*, 72. The wedding took place on January 12: *PSRL* XXV, 329–330.

[72] Dmitrii was born on October 10, the feast of St. Eulampios, and "called" (baptized) Dmitrii on October 26, the feast of St. Demetrius of Salonika: *PSRL* XXV, 330. The chronicle says nothing about the officiating priest or the god-parents.

[73] Kashtanov, *Sotsial'no-politicheskaia istoriia*, 35–40; Nitsche, *Großfürst und Thronfolger*, 124–126; *PSRL* XII, 246; XXVIII (Compilation of 1487), 157, 160. In later sources about the 1490 church council concerning the Novgorod "judaizer" heretics, Vasilii Ivanovich is called grand prince, but this is clearly an anachronism: *PSRL* XII, 225 (Nikon Chronicles). The same usage is found in the later lives of Iosif Volotskii: Kashtanov, *Sotsial'no-politicheskaia istoriia*, 35; Zimin, *Rossiia na rubezhe*, 89: Lur'e, *Ideolgicheskaia bor'ba*, 236.

[74] *PSRL* VI, 43; XII, 246–248.

[75] For the Byzantine rituals, see Treitinger, *Die oströmische Kaiser- und Reichsidee*, 2nd ed. (Darmstadt: Hermann Gentner Verlag, 1956); Alexander D. Beihammer, "Comnenian Imperial Succession and the Ritual World of Niketas Choniates's Chronike Diegesis," in

Order of Coronation for Dmitrii was a completely new document, for which no Russian precedent existed. In the ceremony, Metropolitan Simon (1495–1511) took a central role, not only with prayers and liturgy but also in placing the crown (*shapka*) on the head of Dmitrii. In the Order, Ivan III bore the title of both "Grand Prince of Vladimir and Novgorod" and also "autocrat of all Rus'," one of the first instances of the latter formula.[76] The Order also included a speech from Grand Prince Ivan III himself: "by God's will from our ancestors the grand princes, our ancient custom then and until now, the grand princes, fathers, gave the grand princedom to their first sons." That is to say, he was acting on the principle of "ancient custom" (*starina*) and was therefore to pass the throne to his first son as his predecessors had. As we know, however, the grand prince was mistaken, for a number of his predecessors and ancestors had not passed the grand princely throne to their eldest sons. He continued: "And my father the grand prince already blessed me with the grand princedom in his time and I had blessed my first son Ivan in my time also with the grand princedom."[77] This part of the speech was accurate: Ivan's father had blessed him with the throne and he had in turn blessed his own eldest son, the departed Ivan Ivanovich. The blessing had now appeared in the new coronation ritual, not only in chronicles.

Court Ceremonies and Rituals of Power in Byzantium and the Medieval Mediterranean: Comparative Perspectives, ed. Alexander Beihammer, Stavroula Constantinou, and Maria G. Parani (Leiden and Boston, Massachusetts: Brill, 2013), 159–202; and Ruth Macrides, J. A. Munitiz, and Dmiter Angelov, *Pseudo-Kodinos and the Constantinopolitan Court: Offices and Ceremonies* (Farnham: Ashgate, 2013), 414–427. The Russians did have some idea of the Byzantine practice because of the account written by Ignatii of Smolensk, who witnessed the coronation of Manuel II in 1392. His account of his travels circulated in Russia, and the passage on the coronation did so even more widely: George P. Majeska, *Russian Travelers to Constantinople*. Dumbarton Oaks Studies, vol. XIX (Washington, D.C.: Dumbarton Oaks Research Library and Collection, 1984), 416–436: O. A. Belobrova, "Ignatii (Smol'nianin)," *SKKDR* II, pt. 1, 395–397. The Russians also had access to Old Slavic translations of the texts of the Byzantine ritual: E. V. Barsov, "Drevnerusskie pamiatniki sviashchennogo tsarei na tsarstvo," *ChOIDR* I (1883): 25–31.

[76] Barsov, *Drevnerusskie pamiatniki*, 32–38; "Chin postavlenie … 1498 goda," in *Russkii feodal'nyi arkhiv*, ed. A. I. Pliguzov (Moscow: Iazyski slavianskikh kul'tur, 2008), vol. 3, 608–621 (quotation 609, 615); V. I. Savva, *Moskovskie tsari i vizantiiskie vasilevsy: K voprosu o vliianii Vizantii na obrazovanie idei tsarskoi vlasti moskovskikh gosudarei* (Khar'kov: Tipografiia M. Zil'bergerg, 1901), 122–228; George P. Majeska, "The Moscow Coronation of 1498 Reconsidered," *Jahrbücher für Geschichte Osteuropas*, Neue Folge, 26, 3 (1978): 353–361; B. A. Uspenskii, "Vospriiatiia istorii v Drevnei Rusi i doktrina 'Moskva – Tretii Rim,'" in *Russkoe podvizhnichestvo*, ed. T. B. Kniazevskaia (Moskva: Nauka, 1996), 464–450, Filiushkin, *Tituly russkikh gosudarei*, 58–59.

[77] "Божиим изволением от наших прародителей великих князей, старина наша то и до сех мест отцы великие князи сыном своим первым давали великое княствою … И отец мой князь великий меня при себе еще благословил великим княжьством и аз был своего сына первого Иоанна при себе же благословил великим княжьством." Barsov, *Drevnerusskie pamiatniki*, 33.

Ivan Ivanovich had died, the grand prince concluded, but his first son Dmitrii remained, and God had given him in the place of his father. He blessed his grandson with the throne.[78]

Dmitrii did not long remain the crowned heir. Just short of a year after his coronation, in January, 1499, Ivan executed and exiled a group of important boyars; the Princes Patrikeev, Ivan Iur'evich, and his son Vasilii, as well as Princes Semen (Ivan Patrikeev's son-in-law) and Ivan Riapolovskii and others.[79] In March of the same year, Ivan granted (*pozhaloval*) his son Vasilii Novgorod and Pskov and called him (*narekl*) grand prince with the blessing of Metropolitan Simon and the bishops.[80] By early 1501, Vasilii appeared in diplomatic and other documents as grand prince as well. Thus for a short time Ivan III, his grandson, and his son all bore that title, but on April 12, 1502, Dmitrii and his mother Elena fell into disfavor (*opala*). Ivan forbad the use of the title grand prince for his grandson: "and from that day he did not allow them to be mentioned in the *okteniia* and the *litiia*, nor to be called grand prince, and he put them under guard" and put both mother and son in prison. Two days later, Ivan "favored his son Vasilii, blessed him, and placed him on the grand princedom of Vladimir and Moscow and all Rus' as an autocrat, according to the blessing of Simon, metropolitan of all Russia."[81] Now he had actually blessed Vasilii with the throne, and furthermore with the agreement of Metropolitan Simon. The word "placed" may have implied that some sort of ceremony took place, especially since Simon also blessed the new heir. Simon's blessing repeated, if less grandly, his role in the coronation of 1498.

The entire episode has many mysteries, not least its connection to the politics of the boyar duma. Some historians have advanced the hypothesis that it was related to disagreements over the attitude toward Lithuania. In this version, the Patrikeevs and their allies supported a more pacific policy, while the group around Vasilii was more

[78] Barsov, *Drevnerusskie pamiatniki*, 33–34.

[79] The chronicles did not explain the incident: *PSRL* VI, 43; XII, 248–249.

[80] *PSRL* XII (Nikon Chronicle), 249, 255; Zimin, *Rossiia na rubezhe*, 181. The mention of Simon and the bishops is also in the Vologda–Perm' Chronicle, which, according to Ia. S. Lur'e, was compiled at the time by Filofei, archbishop of Perm' and Vologda 1471–1501 and later expanded: Ia. S. Lur'e, "Letopis' Vologodsko-Permskaia," *SKKDR* II, pt. 2, 37–39.

[81] "и от того дня не велел их поминати в октениях и литиях, ни нарицати великим князем, и посади их за приставы . . . пожаловал сына своего Василья, благословил его и посадил на великое княжение Володимерское и Московское и всеа Русии самодержцем, по благословению Симона митрополита всеа Русии," *PSRL* VIII, 242; XII, 255. The omission of their names in the *ekteniia* and *litiia* meant that the priests did not pray for them in the part of the mass where the prayers were for the rulers (I owe this point to Nikolaos Chrissidis).

antagonistic.[82] Unfortunately, this is no more than a guess: the sources say nothing about the attitudes of any of the boyars on foreign policy. The sense that the Patrikeev–Riapolovskii family made a coherent group is not far-fetched, since they were related by blood and marriage. They seem to have supported Dmitrii as the heir, but no chronicle or other source assigns them any other common political views.[83] The same is true of the Gusev group that perished in 1497: it is reasonable to conclude that they in some way identified themselves with Vasilii, but the sources do not explicitly present them as the exponents of any political views. Indeed, the chronicles for the 1490s do not provide any sense of factions in the duma like those which are relatively clear for later times. All that the stories suggest is that there were groups of some sort in the elite behind the two possible candidates for the throne, perhaps only temporary coalitions or groups of clients. In other words, there was someone whom the coronation was intended to impress. The coronation of Dmitrii and the proclamation of a title for Vasilii later marked the choice of the grand prince and publicly demonstrated the rightness and legitimacy of Ivan's choice.

In any case, Vasilii was now the heir to the throne, the final end of the process that began thirty years earlier with the arrival of Sophia Palaiologina from Rome. Now it was his defeat of Dmitrii that had to be defended abroad. When the Russian ambassadors went to Lithuania early in 1503, they were instructed how to answer questions about the change in heirs. If the Lithuanians were to ask about it, the answer was to be that Vasilii now was equally the sovereign with his father. If the ambassadors were asked why Ivan preferred Vasilii, then the answer was to be: "whichever son serves his father and follows him, he is the one whom his father favors more; and the son that does not serve and follow his parents, why should the father favor him?" If Elena, the wife of King Alexander, asked where Elena Voloshanka and her son Dmitrii were, the ambassadors were to say that they lived with Ivan as before.[84] Sophia died soon after, in April 1503. Ivan III himself fell ill later the same year and never fully recovered. He did, however, compose a testament early in 1504 that put in writing the decision of two years earlier. In it, Ivan wrote "I bless my eldest son Vasilii with my inheritance (*votchina*), my grand princedoms,

[82] Zimin, *Rossiia na rubezhe*, 138–147, 160–177. Using the same sources, John Fennell came to opposite conclusions: Fennell, *Ivan the Great*, 343–352. See also M. B. Pliukhanova, "'Poslanie na Ugru' i vopros o proiskhozhdenii moskovskoi imperskoi ideologii," *TODRL* 61 (2010): 452–488.

[83] Kollmann, *Kinship and Politics*, 136–140. Kollmann argues that the Patrikeevy were dominant in the duma for the generation before their fall.

[84] *SRIO* 35, 430. The instructions on this matter were an afterthought, sent to the ambassadors already on their way to Wilno.

with which my father blessed me and which God gave to me." He commanded his younger sons to obedience to Vasilii and provided them with appanages.[85] The lion's share of the territory, of course, went to Vasilii.[86]

Sophia's rival Elena "Voloshanka" died two years later in January 1505, and Dmitrii remained in prison until his own death in 1509. It would seem that all the important decisions had been made. Perhaps not: while Dmitrii and his mother sat in prison, rumors got to Livonia that "the Russians" preferred Dmitrii to Vasilii and that the children of Ivan were not in agreement.[87] Sometime early in 1504 Ivan made his will, and in it he blessed Vasilii with the grand princedom.[88] Ivan had also begun to think about brides for Vasilii. In 1503, as he was making a truce with King Alexander of Poland-Lithuania, he had asked his daughter Elena Ivanovna, Alexander's queen, for help in finding a wife for his son Vasilii. He wanted to know about the daughters of Stefan, the despot of Serbia. Elena knew nothing about them, but provided a long list of daughters of various European ruling houses, Brandenburg, Pomerania, Bavaria, and others, a list that arrived in Moscow in February 1504.[89] The bride-show took place in the summer of 1505, and on September 4 the same year Vasilii Ivanovich, now also grand prince, married Solomoniia Saburova. This was the first time that the ruler chose his wife by means of a bride-show rather than through negotiation with other princes and rulers. Supposedly the idea came from Iurii Malyi Trakhaniotov, Vasilii's keeper of the seal (*pechatnik*), whose Greek family came to Russia with Sophia Palaiologina in 1472, if not before.[90] The Grand Prince Ivan had secured the succession for his son and removed his grandson from the competition.

A month after his son's wedding, on October 27, 1505, Ivan III died and Vasilii immediately took the throne. In the chronicles and other sources, there is not even the hint of a coronation or any other ceremony.[91] Through

[85] *DDG*, 354, 358–361.

[86] Cherepnin, *Russkie feodal'nye arkhivy XIV–XV vekov*, vol. I, 220–223; Nitsche, *Großfürst und Thronfolger*, 175–179; A. A. Zimin, *Rossiia na poroge novogo vremeni* (Moscow: Mysl', 1972), 62–66.

[87] Nitsche, *Großfürst und Thronfolger*, 184, note 7.

[88] *DDG*, 354.

[89] *SRIO* 35, 426–427, 442–443, 452–453; E. Tsereteli, *Elena Ioannovna Velikaia Kniaginia Litovskaia, russkaia, koroleva pol'skaia* (St. Petersburg: Tipografiia I. N. Skorokhodova, 1898), 282–284; Russell E. Martin, *A Bride for the Tsar: Bride Shows and Marriage Politics in Early Modern Russia* (DeKalb, Illinois: Northern Illinois University Press, 2012), 44–45. The despotate of Serbia, under the king of Hungary, was vacant in 1503. The previous despot, Jovan Brankovich, had died the previous December.

[90] A. A. Zimin, *Formirovanie boiarskoi aristokratii v Rossii vo vtoroi polovine XV–pervoi terti XVI v.* (Moscow: Nauka, 1988), 273–275; Martin, *A Bride for the Tsar*, 21–22, 43–54.

[91] *PSRL* VIII, 245; XII, 259; XIII, 1.

all the changes of mind on the part of Ivan III, he did manage to secure succession in his own descent line. This was not primogeniture in the Western sense, which would have required him to stay with Dmitrii as the eldest son of his eldest son. Instead, he designated Vasilii, his second son by a second wife, and this was his final designation. The imprisonment of Dmitrii and his mother ensured its success.

Vasilii III

Vasilii's marriage to Solomoniia Saburova showed that the Moscow grand prince was not concerned with the ancestry of his future wife. Until this moment all of the wives of the Moscow princes had been the daughters of other Russian Riurikovich princes or foreign princesses in their own right – Sofiia Vitovovna of Lithuania and Sophia Palaiologina, from the last Byzantine dynasty. Herberstein, the main source for the marriage of Vasilii to Solomoniia, claimed that Trakhaniotov argued that a foreign princess would be expensive and bring alien customs and religion, and also he secretly wanted Vasilii to marry his own daughter.[92] The Saburov clan had certainly been important for over a century, but was not a boyar clan.[93] The various sources of the time say nothing about her ancestry, indeed they seem to show total indifference to this issue.[94] Yet the Moscow princely family was clearly concerned to show its own ancestry and claims, but the male line of descent seems to have been all that was necessary to those claims.

Securing the line was all the more important since the new grand prince Vasilii had no uncles left, but he did have four younger brothers, all of whom received more or less significant appanages.[95] His nephew Dmitrii's death in 1509 removed a serious potential source of contention, but some conflicts with Vasilii's brothers did arise. In 1511, Semen Ivanovich of Kaluga tried to go to Lithuania, and escaped disgrace and punishment only because of Metropolitan Simon's intercession. He died in 1518. Around 1520, a dispute arose between the grand prince and his brother Dmitrii Ivanovich of Uglich, but nothing came of it and Dmitrii

[92] Sigismund von Herberstein, *Rerum Moscoviticarum Comentarii*, ed. Frank Kämpfer, Eva Maurer, Andreas Fülberth, and Hermann Beyer-Thoma (Munich: Osteuropa-Institut Regensburg, 2007), 77. The text is only in the German edition, not the Latin.

[93] Zimin, *Formirovanie boiarskoi aristokratii*, 191–195; Kollmann, *Kinship and Politics*, 142–144.

[94] Martin, *A Bride for the Tsar*, 46–47; *PSRL* 12, 259; Iu. K. Begunov, "Povest' o vtorom brake Vasiliia III," *TODRL* 25 (1970): 105–118; N. N. Rozov, "Pokhval'noe slovo velikomu kniaziu Vasiliiu III," in *Arkheograficheskii ezhegodnik za 1964 god* (Moscow: Izdatel'stvo Akademii, 1965), 278–289.

[95] Aleksandr Filiushkin, *Vasilii III* (Moscow: Molodaia gvardiia, 2010), 134–139.

died the next year. In Lithuania, there were rumors about the oldest of the brothers, Iurii Ivanovich of Dmitrov, but no open conflict seems to have broken out and he died only in 1536. In the case of his youngest brother, Andrei Ivanovich of Staritsa, there were not even rumors of discontent. The brothers administered their appanages, commanded parts of the army, and participated in the life of the court. None of them but Andrei married, and he married only in 1533, three years after the birth of Ivan, the first son of the grand prince. Vasilii was the one to choose Andrei's bride, Evfrosiniia Khovanskaia, probably by means of a bride-show.[96] Andrei Staritskii's marriage was the only one that Vasilii permitted, and by the time it took place Vasilii himself had an heir. This arrangement ensured that Vasilii's son, should he ever have one, would be more easily designated the successor.

Vasilii had much difficulty over the years with discontented aristocrats, and a number of them swore oaths to serve him and his children. This practice was not new, but Vasilii seems to have used it more often than his father. The oldest such text was a formulary among the documents of the metropolitanate that comes from the period 1448–71.[97] In the one such oath document from the reign of Ivan III, Prince Daniil Kholmskii had sworn to serve Ivan III and his children (unspecified), and this formula appeared again in service oaths under Vasilii III. In 1524, the Princes Bel'skii swore an oath in which they promised not to leave for another prince (presumably of Lithuania), to do only good and no evil to the grand prince and the grand princess (Solomoniia), and to serve only the grand prince himself and his as yet unborn children. This was the first time the grand princess appeared, and from then on she appeared in all such oaths. The same distinction between service as opposed to doing good and no harm appeared in 1529 when Prince F. M. Mstislavskii swore to serve Vasilii and his children, to not depart or do harm to Vasilii and his children, and to do no harm to the Grand Princess Elena. The formula "and his children" appeared in all such documents, whether Vasilii had any children at the time or not.[98] The children did not have the grand

[96] Zimin, *Rossiia na poroge novogo vremeni*, 131, 210. On Iurii Ivanovich, see Nitsche, *Großfürst und Thronfolger*, 183–202; and M. M. Bentsianov, "Sluzhilye liudi kniazia Iuriia dmitrovskogo," *Drevniaia Rus': Voprosy medievistiki* 40, 2 (2010): 41–55; 41, 3 (2010): 55–68. For Andrei Staritskii's marriage, see Martin, *A Bride for the Tsar*, 111, and *DRV* XIII, 19–29.

[97] *Russkii feodal'nyi arkhiv*, vol. 1, 175–176; vol. V, 989–991.

[98] *SGGD* I, 249–251, 401–404, 414–415, 420–427 (1524, Princes Bel'skii), 433–435 (Mstislavskii, August 23, 1529). The circumstances of the 1474 oath of Kholmskii, a minor prince from the Tver' land, are obscure: Zimin, *Rossiia na rubezhe*, 59–60; Horace W. Dewey, "Political Poruka in Muscovite Rus'," *Russian Review* 46, 2 (1987): 117–133; Kollmann, *Kinship and Politics*, 138, 209. Mstislavskii had apparently wanted to flee to Lithuania: Zimin, *Rossiia na poroge novogo vremeni*, 315–316. On oaths, see Petr

princely or any other title in these documents, and they were merely called the children of the grand prince. What was new was the appearance of the grand princess in the oaths. It was not the case that the grand princesses had played no role in the politics of court and state, but now they had become the explicit object of the subjects' loyalty.[99] The sense of a ruling family, beyond just the grand prince, was beginning to take shape, and it was to remain through the centuries to come.

Vasilii III was the sovereign of all Rus' for twenty years without an obvious heir.[100] Finally, in 1525 he divorced Solomoniia. Her inability to produce children led the grand prince to seek a new wife, in the process setting off a crisis at the court.[101] He then married Princess Elena Glinskaia, the daughter of an aristocratic Lithuanian clan of Tatar origin whose members had come to Moscow. This was a princely clan, much higher in rank than the Saburovs, but again not sovereign rulers. The Princes Glinskii had served the grand princes of Lithuania until Prince Michael rebelled against the king and went over to Vasilii in 1509.[102] He brought with him his family, including his brother Vasilii Glinskii and the brother's daughter Elena. She married Grand Prince Vasilii in 1526, but a son did not come right away, in spite of prayers in many monasteries.[103] Finally, on August 25, 1530, the needed son was born, the future Ivan the

S. Stefanovič, "Expressing Loyalty in Medieval Russia: Oath vs. Oral Formulas," in *Oralité et lien social au Moyen Âge (Occident, Byzance, Islam)*, ed. Marie-France Auzépy and Guillaume Saint-Guillain (Paris: Association des amis du Centre d'histoire et civilisation de Byzance, 2008), 147–156; and Petr S. Stefanovich, "Kniaz' i boiare: Kliatva vernosti i pravo ot"ezda," in *Drevniaia Rus': Ocherki politicheskogo i sotsial'nogo stroia*, ed. A. A. Gorskii, V. A. Kuchkin, P. V. Lukin, and P. S. Stefanovich (Moscow: Indrik, 2008), 148–269; and Nicolas Svoronos, "Le serment de fidélité à l'empereur byzantin et sa signification constitutionelle," *Revue des études byzantines* 9 (1951): 106–142.

99 The role of the grand princesses has not been systematically studied, but see Isolde Thyrêt, "The Cultural Politics of the Grand Princesses of Moscow and the Emergence of the Muscovite Dynasty," *Russian History/Histoire Russe* 33, 2–4 (2006): 333–352.

100 R. F. Iglesias, "K voprosu o predpolagaemom naslednike Vasiliia III mezhdu 1505 i 1530 gg.," *Kapterevskie chteniia* 14 (2016): 246–296; 15 (2017): 235–306. Iglesias believes that the heir was supposed to be Prince Dmitrii of Uglich until his death in 1521, then Iurii of Dmitrov until Vasilii's second marriage.

101 The crisis at court also apparently involved the condemnation of the Greek monk and theological writer Maksim Grek in the same year and some lesser events. Zimin, *Rossiia na poroge novogo vremeni*, 267–299; Martin, *A Bride for the Tsar*, 103–107; Filiushkin, *Vasilii III*, 270–288.

102 M. V. Bychkova, *Sostav klassa feodalov Rossii v XVI v.* (Moscow: Nauka, 1986), 52–63; Zimin, *Formirovanie boiarskoi aristokratii*, 142–143; Martin, *A Bride for the Tsar*, 103–107.

103 Makarii, then Archbishop of Novgorod, in giving a charter to the small Dukhov monastery in Novgorod ordered the monks to pray for children to be born to the grand prince: *AI* I, 532.

Terrible. His baptism took place in the Trinity-St. Sergii Monastery on September 4. The officiating priest was the hegumen of the monastery, Ioasaf Skripitsyn, the future metropolitan of Moscow (1539–42). The chronicle also says that three monks each "baptized him" (*krestil ego*): Kassian Bosoi of the Iosifo-Volokolamsk Monastery, Daniil of Pereiaslavl', and Iov Kurtsev of the Trinity Monastery. It did not specify who was the "receiver" (*vospriemnik*), the godfather, and the norm in the church at that time was to have only one godparent.[104] It would seem that the grand prince wanted his son to have three monks, and those among the more distinguished of their generation, as spiritual fathers.[105] Unfortunately, we know nothing of Ivan's upbringing and education, not even whether his father or later his mother appointed anyone to supervise his childhood, a role like that of the later "diad'ka" who was appointed for the sons of the ruler from the end of the sixteenth century.

The new heir immediately appeared in oaths and treaties. Only five months after the heir's birth, Prince F. M. Mstislavskii, in swearing that he would not defect to King Sigismund of Poland, kissed the cross in loyalty both to Vasilii and to "his son Ivan," as did M. A. Pleshcheev in 1532. On August 24, 1531, the grand prince's oldest brother, Iurii Ivanovich, made a new treaty with the ruler, and obligated himself to "have as his lord the grand prince, his elder brother. And to wish good in all things to your son Prince Ivan and your children." When God will take you, the grand prince, "and you will bless your son Prince Ivan with your grand princedoms, I [Iurii] will hold to your son Ivan in your place."[106] Iurii was supposed to be obedient to the grand prince for his whole life and

104 *PSRL* XIII, 48. R. P. Dmitrieva, "Ioasaf (Skripitsyn)," *SKKDR* II, pt. 1, 409–414. The Moscow metropolitans had insisted on one godparent, and the norm was repeated in the Council of the Hundred Chapters in 1551: Almazov, *Istoriia chinoposledovanii kreshcheniia i miropomazaniia*, 632–636; E. B. Emchenko, *Stoglav: Issledovanie i tekst* (Moscow: Izdatel'stvo Indrik, 2000), 281.

105 Daniil was the subject of a life by his pupil Afanasii, Metropolitan of Moscow 1564–6 and an important writer of the early reign of Ivan IV: N. N. Pokrovskii, "Afanasii," *SKKDR* II, pt. 1, 73–79; O. A. Belobrova, "Zhitie Daniila pereiaslavskogo. *SKKDR* II, pt. 1, 257–259; Bushkovitch, *Religion and Society in Russia: The Sixteenth and Seventeenth Centuries* (New York, New York: Oxford University Press, 1992), 39–40 (Kurtsevs), 79–80 (Daniil). Kassian was then very old, having been born in 1439 and a monk in the time of Iosif himself (died 1515) and one of his closest companions: A. A. Zimin, *Krupnaia feodal'naia votchina i sotsial'no-politicheskaia bor'ba v Rossii (konets XV–XVI v.)* (Moscow: Nauka, 1977), 115–116; R. P. Dmitrieva, "Zhitie Kassiana Bosogo," *SKKDR* II, pt. 1, 285–286.

106 "иметь своего господина, великого князя, братом старейшим. А сыну твоему князю Ивану, и вашим детем хотети добра во всем . . . а благословишь сына своего князя Ивана своими великими княжествы, мне [Юрию] господина держать сына твоего князя Ивана в твое место." *SGGD* 1, 439–443 (Mstislavskii, February 5, 1531), 448–450 (M. A. Pleshcheev, December 1, 1532); *DDG*, 418–419. Note that the formula implies that Vasilii would bless his son with the grand princedom(s) only on his deathbed.

to his son afterward. Once again the inheritance of the throne was the result of the blessing of the son by the grand prince with the princedom.

The mortal illness of Grand Prince Vasilii in the autumn of 1533 created a new and in many ways unprecedented situation. Until this point the eldest sons of the grand princes had been "placed" on the throne at eleven to fourteen years of age, but Ivan was only three years old, and his younger brother Iurii was only one.[107] It was necessary to decide the succession quickly, and Vasilii blessed his son Ivan with the grand princedom without placing him on the throne. According to the evidence of the Second Sophia Chronicle, the oldest version of the story, the dying sovereign blessed Ivan with the cross of St. Peter the Metropolitan, and later blessed him as he had in this testament, said Vasilii. In the course of the narrative, the chronicler began to call the infant the grand prince. Metropolitan Daniil had Vasilii's brother Iurii, the boyars, *deti boiarskie*, and princelings (*kniazhata*) kiss the cross to serve the young Ivan and his mother Elena, to do him good, to oppose his enemies the Latins and Muslims, and to seek no other ruler. In later versions of the story, the *Tsarstvennaia kniga* and the *Letopisets nachala tsarstva* (both dating from the 1550s) added more groups kissing the cross to serve Ivan and his mother. The former added *dvoriane* to the list, and the latter added a certainly anachronistic passage about the regalia of Vladimir Monomakh and said nothing about an oath. The Voskresenie Chronicles (1540s) and the Nikon Chronicle (1560s) by contrast put the initiative to kiss the cross to Ivan and his mother into the hands of the boyars, and added that they sent to the towns for all people to kiss the cross to the new rulers.[108] It is difficult to believe that this last version is accurate, and there seems to be no text of the oath or evidence of widespread kissing of the

[107] Iurii was born on October 30, 1532, Wednesday, the feast of Sts. Zenobios and Zenobia. He was called Georgii (Iurii) after the feast of the Dedication of the Church of St. George in Lydda and baptized on that feast, November 3, in the church of the Annunciation in the Trinity Monastery yard in Moscow by hegumen Ioasaf Skripitsyn and the monk Daniil of Pereiaslavl', both of whom had baptized Ivan; *PSRL* XIII, 66.

[108] *PSRL* VI (Second Sophia Chronicle), 267–276, esp. 273, 275; *PSRL* VIII (Voskresenie Chronicle), 285–286; *PSRL* XIII (Nikon Chronicle), 75–78, 409–419, esp. 418. According to Lur'e and M. M. Krom, the Sophia 2 Chronicle reflects the early redaction of the "Tale of the Death of Vasilii Ivanovich." The version of the *Letopisets nachala tsarstva* of the 1550s has obvious inaccuracies, such as the mention of the "cap of Monomakh," which was unknown before 1547: Ia. S. Lur'e, "Letopis' Sofiiaskaia II," *SKKDR* II, pt. 2, 60–61, 277–279; M. M. Krom, *"Vdovstvuiushchee tsarstvo": Politicheskii krizis v Rossii 30–40-kh godakh XVI veka* (St. Petersburg: Novoe literaturnoe obozrenie, 2010), 34–56; Nitsche, *Großfürst und Thronfolger*, 206–213. See also Isolde Thyrêt, "The *Tale of the Death of Vasilii Ivanovich* and the Evolution of the Muscovite Tsaritsa's Role in 16th Century Russia," in *Dubitando: Studies in History and Culture in Honor of Donald Ostrowski*, ed. Brian J. Boeck, Russell E. Martin, and Daniel Rowland (Bloomington, Indiana: Slavica, 2012), 209–224. The only surviving fragment of Vasilii III's testament does not mention the grand princedom: *DDG*, 415.

cross outside these two chronicles, though the court elite certainly did swear loyalty to the new ruler and his mother. Finally, there was no mention of placing the infant Ivan on the throne. To be sure, the Novgorod and Pskov chronicles did include a remark that on December 6, 1533, three days after his father's death, Ivan was "placed" (*posadili*) on the throne, but no Moscow chronicles record such an event, whatever their attitude to the events. It is hard to believe that they consciously omitted such an important ritual; it is more likely that the Novgorod and Pskov chronicles simply assumed that it took place.[109] What emerges from all these accounts is that Vasilii blessed his son with the grand princedom, and the elite (at least) swore loyalty to him.

The arguments of historians have revolved not around these procedures of succession, but around the fate and content of the lost testament of Vasilii III and the composition of the regency. It seems that very quickly Grand Princess Elena came to stand at the head of the government, and remained the most important person in it until her death in 1538. Afterward the state was in the hands of the boyars for nine years, a time filled with intrigues among aristocratic factions.[110] These began while Elena was still alive. Almost immediately she came into conflict with Ivan's uncles. In 1534, Prince Andrei Mikhailovich Shuiskii wanted to "depart" (*uekhat'*) to Dmitrov, the appanage of Prince Iurii Ivanovich. Prince Iurii was arrested, and he died in prison in 1536.[111] Even more serious disagreements appeared with Prince Andrei Ivanovich Staritskii and ended with the notorious "revolt" of 1537. The existing sources suggest that the basis of the conflict was Prince Andrei's failed request to increase the size of his appanage. His reaction was to escape from his appanage to Novgorod. Whether the appanage was the only issue or an attempt to seize the throne is unknown. The sources describe the event from various points of view, but the reasons for the "revolt" remain in the dark. According to the Voskresenie Chronicle, which is hostile to Prince Andrei, he wanted bring the grand prince's *deti boiarskie* over to his own service. More friendly accounts assert that the government of Grand Princess Elena was trying to take away his own servitors.[112] The rumor in Riga was that Prince Andrei wanted to take the

[109] Nitsche, *Großfürst und Thronfolger*, 223–224.

[110] Besides Krom, "*Vdovstvuiushchee tsarstvo*," see A. A. Zimin, *Reformy Ivana Groznogo* (Moscow: Izdatel'stvo sotsial'no-ekonomicheskoi literatury, 1960), 222–778; Nitsche, *Großfürst und Thronfolger*, 223–259; R. G. Skrynnikov, *Tsarstvo terrora* (St. Petersburg: Nauka, 1992), 81–89; and Charles J. Halperin, "The Minority of Ivan IV," in *Rude and Barbarous Kingdom Revisited: Essays in Russian History in Honor of Robert O. Crummey*, ed. Chester Dunning, Russell Martin, and Daniel Rowland (Bloomington, Indiana: Slavica, 2008), 41–52.

[111] Krom, "*Vdovstvuiushchee tsarstvo*," 83–99.

[112] *PSRL* VIII, 294; Krom, "*Vdovstvuiushchee tsarstvo*," 188.

throne, but no Russian chronicle sources confirm it.[113] Russian diplomats going to Lithuania were told to assert that Prince Andrei had tried to take the throne, but that could have been simple deception.[114] The only other source that even distantly suggests such a desire is the undated text of the oath of loyalty from Prince Andrei, in which he promised to "be honest" (*praviti*) to Grand Prince Ivan "and your mother and your children."[115] With the phrase "and your children" Prince Andrei obliged himself to serve not just Ivan and his mother but any possible successors to his nephew, excluding any possibility of taking the throne himself. Of course, the words did not necessarily imply any such plans on his part. Prince Andrei eventually surrendered, and was soon arrested and executed in December 1537.[116] Ivan himself later thought that his uncles had been the innocent victims of boyar intrigues.[117] In spite of the instability at court during the boyar regency, the question of succession did not arise after the death of Prince Andrei, and Ivan was eventually crowned tsar and married. His father's benediction seems to have triumphed. It was now for Tsar Ivan to ensure succession to this throne.

[113] Krom, *"Vdovstvuiushchee tsarstvo,"* 208; Nitsche, *Großfürst und Thronfolger*, 252; M. M. Bentsianov, "Dvor Kniazia Andreia Staritskogo i problema 'staritskogo miatezha 1537 g.,'" *Drevniaia Rus': Voprosy medievistiki* 50, 4 (2012): 64–76, 51, 1 (2013): 17–26; V. V. Shaposhnik, "Miatezh Andreia Staritskogo (osen' 1536–iun' 1537 g.)," *Studia Slavica et Balcanica Petropolitana* 1 (2013): 174–212.

[114] *SRIO* 59, 137ff. [115] *SGGD* I, 451–452; Krom, *"Vdovstvuiushchee tsarstvo,"* 177.

[116] Krom, *"Vdovstvuiushchee tsarstvo,"* 216–219.

[117] Ia. S. Lur'e and Iu. D. Rykov, *Perepiska Ivana Groznogo s Andreem Kurbskim* (Leningrad: Nauka, 1979), 27–28.

3 Benediction to Election 1533–1598

Ivan the Terrible and Fyodor Ivanovich

The second half of the sixteenth century in Russian history was a time of dramatic events.

The reign of Ivan the Terrible (1533/47–84) saw Russia's first expansion into the Volga basin, all the way to Astrakhan' at the mouth of the river and farther to foothills of the Caucasus along the Terek river. The first Russian forts were looking at the Kabarda Circassians and the Chechens in the mountains to the south. Russian peasants and noblemen began to move south and east into the new lands. Internally, Ivan and his advisors spent the 1550s on a series of measures that historians have traditionally seen as "centralizing" but are perhaps better understood as state-building. In Moscow, the system of chanceries (*prikazy*) came to maturity, including the Ambassadorial Office, whose magnificently detailed records of Russia's foreign relations are a fundamental source to this day. On the local level, the government gradually put together a system of local governors (*voevody*) combined with locally elected sheriffs (*gubnye starosty*) who tried to supervise the vast territory under the nominal rule of the tsar. The church as well was putting its house in order, with the establishment of a parish network that finally covered the Russian land, the construction of churches in most villages, and attempts at the systematization of doctrine, liturgy, and daily practice as well as the recognition of saints and the last great expansion of the monasteries. The most dramatic episode, however, was the still mysterious Oprichnina (1564–72), in which Ivan divided the country into two spheres, the Oprichnina as a sort of appanage ruled directly by him, with its own troops and tax system, and the Land (*zemshchina*), with the Boyar Duma nominally in control under his supervision. Ivan eventually turned away from the institution, which was known mostly for its torture and execution of his opponents (or seeming opponents). What it was meant to accomplish, and what it did or not, is still a matter of debate. One of the reasons for the establishment of the Oprichnina may have been Ivan's frustration at the lack of final victory in his Livonian War, which he began in 1558 in an attempt to acquire the territories of the old Livonian Order and its seacoast from Riga to Narva. That war ended in failure: indeed, Ivan even lost to Sweden the coast along the Gulf of Finland that had been Novgorodian and then Russian since the beginning of the Middle Ages. More than compensating for the failure of the Baltic expeditions, however, was the conquest of Siberia, which came at the very end of Ivan's reign. In 1583–4, the Cossack Yermak captured the Khanate of Siberia, a Tatar state small in population but huge in extent, almost the western third of Siberia. This was the beginning of Russia's conquest and settlement of northern Eurasia. Contact and trade with Western Europe expanded as well. English merchants first arrived in Russia by the northern route, over the North Cape and Archangel, in the 1550s. The Muscovy Company soon came into being, trading with the Russians through the Baltic as well. By the end of the century the Dutch had arrived in the north too, making remote Archangel an important entrepôt. Ivan's son and successor Fyodor had no such grand plans. Himself feeble in body and perhaps also in mind, his government was in the hands of the boyars and mainly his brother-in-law, Boris Godunov. Fyodor's men took back the Baltic coast from Sweden, but otherwise his reign was one of renewed rebuilding. It was also the moment of the establishment of serfdom among the peasantry, an institution that would last until 1861.[1]

In all these tumultuous events, many pregnant with profound consequences for the future, the question of succession did not seem to come into play except for two moments, the succession crisis of 1553 and the very last years of the reign of Ivan. Yet the succession question hung over the whole reign, at least from the time of the death of Tsaritsa Anastasia in 1560. She left two sons, but only the older, Ivan, was healthy, and that must have been clear by that moment. Ivan remarried six times, as far as we know, but only the last marriage to Mariia Nagaia produced a living child, his son, Dmitrii, born in 1582. In between, none of the marriages produced children that lived, and the three marriages of his son and heir,

[1] See, among others, A. A. Zimin, *Reformy Ivana Groznogo* (Moscow: Izdatel'stvo sotsial'no-ekonomicheskoi literatury, 1960); A. A. Zimin, *Oprichnina*, 2nd ed. (Moscow: Territoriia, 2001); A. A. Zimin, *V kanun groznykh potriasenii* (Moscow: Mysl', 1986); R. G. Skrynnikov, *Tsarstvo terrora* (St. Petersburg: Nauka, 1992); A. I. Filiushkin, *Istoriia odnoi mistifikatsii: Ivan Groznyi i "Izbrannaia Rada"* (Moscow: VGU, 1998); Andrey Pavlov and Maureen Perrie, *Ivan the Terrible* (London: Pearson/Longman, 2003); Charles J. Halperin, "Ivan IV as Autocrat (samoderzhets)," *Cahiers du monde russe* 55, 3–4 (2014): 1–18; and Charles J. Halperin, *Ivan the Terrible: Free to Reward and Free to Punish* (Pittsburgh, Pennsylvania: Pittsburgh University Press, 2019).

Ivan Ivanovich, were also childless. It is most likely that the absence of more than one viable heir was behind the multiple marriages, both for the father and for his son.[2] Unfortunately, the official documents and chronicles are full of facts but short on the motivations of the actors. What Ivan did can be reconstructed, but why he did it usually remains in the dark. At the same time, the sources for Ivan's reign, more abundant than for previous decades in consequence of the ongoing building of the state apparatus, make it possible to trace with much more detail than before the life and activity of the presumed heirs, Ivan's sons. The role of the heir in court and state is clear in general outlines. The paradox of the period, of course, comes at the end, in the reign of Ivan's son. In spite of many efforts, Tsar Fyodor produced no sons, and on his death the assembled elites and the people of Moscow elected Boris Godunov the tsar. Paradoxical as it may seem, the new tsar was an elected autocrat.

The Beginning of the Reign of Ivan IV

At the death of Vasilii III, his widow, Elena Glinskaia, took the reins of power as regent for her son. Grand Princess Elena guaranteed her son's succession by the arrest of Vasilii's surviving brothers, Iurii in 1534 and Andrei of Staritsa in 1537. They both died in prison, Iurii in 1536 and Andrei shortly after his arrest. After Elena's death in 1538, the boyars exercised power in the name of the young Ivan. They inevitably split into factions, warring with one another over control of the state until Ivan's coronation. During the whole period, all acts of state were in the name of the young grand prince, though in fact his mother, the Glinskiis, and the princes Shuiskii and Bel'skii made the decisions at various times.[3]

The coronation of Ivan IV as tsar on January 16, 1547, confirmed his succession to the throne and gave him the new title of tsar.[4] Carrying out the ceremony was Metropolitan Makarii (1482–1563, metropolitan 1542–63), a major figure in the early years of Ivan's

[2] Russell E. Martin, *A Bride for the Tsar: Bride Shows and Marriage Politics in Early Modern Russia* (DeKalb, Illinois: Northern Illinois University Press, 2012), 131–132.

[3] Peter Nitsche, *Großfürst und Thronfolger: Die Nachfolgepolitik der Moskauer Herrscher bis zum Ende des Rjurikidenhauses*. Kölner historische Abhandlungen 21 (Cologne and Vienna: Böhlau, 1972), 223–259; M. M. Krom, *"Vdovstvuiushchee tsarstvo": Politicheskii krizis v Rossii 30–40-kh godakh XVI veka* (St. Petersburg: Novoe literaturnoe obozrenie, 2010); Charles J. Halperin, "The Minority of Ivan IV," *Rude and Barbarous Kingdom Revisited: Essays in Russian History in Honor of Robert O. Crummey*, ed. Chester Dunning, Russell Martin, and Daniel Rowland (Bloomington, Indiana: Slavica, 2008), 41–52.

[4] *PSRL* XIII, 150–151, 451–453; B. A. Uspenskii, *Tsar i patriarkh: Kharizma vlasti v Rossii* (Moscow: Shkola iazyki russkoi kul'tury, 1998), 109–110; S. N. Bogatyrev, "Reinventing the Russian Monarchy in the 1550s: Ivan the Terrible, the Dynasty, and the Church," *Slavonic and East European Review* 85, 2 (2007): 271–293.

reign.[5] What exactly happened at the ceremony is not clear in all details, for the coronation documents exist in several versions. The earlier version of the order of coronation, contained only in chronicles, said nothing about succession one way or the other. Ivan was crowned with the "cap of Monomakh," first mentioned in the "Tale of the Vladimir Princes," with which his ancestors allegedly had been crowned.[6] Metropolitan Makarii's prayer asked God to give Ivan, whom He had blessed with the tsardom as He had King David in Israel, long life.[7] In the "Formulaic redaction" the text was different. It was clearly compiled later, for it included anachronistic mention of Tsaritsa Anastasiia and Ivan's children.[8] In this later and much longer version, there were long speeches from both Ivan and the metropolitan that presented the coronation of Ivan as the result of his father's blessing.[9] In this version, Ivan addressed Metropolitan Makarii and said that in olden times (*starina*) my "fathers the grand princes gave to their first sons the grand princedom and my father the grand prince in his lifetime blessed me with the grand princedoms of Vladimir and Novgorod and Moscow and all Rus" and added that Vasilii Ivanovich had ordered that his son be crowned with the tsar's crown (*venets*). In his reply, the metropolitan repeated the same formula. In this version of the coronation text, Grand Prince Vasilii both designated Ivan as the heir to the throne and gave him the title of tsar.[10] At the end the metropolitan wished that the Lord would allow him long life to see his grandchildren rule "for many generations and years" (*v mnogie rody i leta*).[11] The difference in texts seems to reflect not differences over what happened, but a retrospective reformulation. It was also in the second version that the anointment of the tsar appeared, a part of the ceremony for which there is no evidence that

[5] Charles J. Halperin, "Metropolitan Makarii and Muscovite Court Politics in the Reign of Ivan IV," *Russian Review* 73 (July 2014): 447–464.

[6] The tale arose in the sixteenth century and claimed that the cap was presented to the Rus' prince Vladimir Monomakh of Kiev by the Byzantine emperor Konstantinos Monomachos in the twelfth century: R. P. Dmitrieva, *Skazanie o kniaziakh vladimirskikh* (Moscow and Leningrad: Izdatel'stvo Akademii nauk SSSR, 1955). In reality, the "cap of Monomakh" was probably constructed during the reign of Vasilii III: S. N. Bogatyrev, "Shapka Monomakha i shlem naslednika: Vlasti i dinasticheskaia politika pri Vasilie III i Ivane Groznom," *Studia Slavica et Balcanica Petropolitana* 9, 1 (2011): 171–200.

[7] *PSRL* XIII, 150–151, 451–452.

[8] V. Barsov, *Drevnerusskie pamiatniki*, 42–90. Originally *ChOIDR* I (1883).

[9] Ibid., 47–49, 73–74.

[10] "отцы великие князья сыном своим первым давали великое княжество и отец мои великий князь мене при собе еще благословил великим княжеством владимирским и новгороским и московским и всеа Русии": Ibid., 47–49, 73–75.

[11] Ibid., *Drevnerusskie pamiatniki*, 55, 60, 80, 85.

it actually took place in 1547. The second version, the "Formulaic redaction," however, became the precedent for later coronations.[12]

Ivan's coronation as tsar had great implications for Russia, both internationally and domestically. It gave to the ruler a title that had before been confined to the Byzantine emperors, the khans of the Golden Horde and its successor states, and the Ottoman Empire. Most importantly, however, it was the title of the kings of ancient Israel in the Slavic text of the Bible. It reinforced the idea of Russia as the New Israel, the only place on earth with the true religion.[13] What the coronation did not do, however, was introduce any new ideas about succession to the throne. The chronicle version of the ceremony made no mention of his father's blessing, understandably as he had already inherited the grand princedom from his father and bore that title. What the coronation did was give him a new and greater title and underscore the role of the church. Already in the Chronicle version, the text made Makarii the central figure and noted that King David was chosen king by God through the instrument of the prophet Samuel, the equivalent of the metropolitan.[14] The later version, however, did introduce a notion of heredity into the text. Never used for any ceremony in Ivan's time, it introduced Ivan's children (not just the eldest son) and wished that he might see them (plural) on the throne. It did not establish primogeniture, but it did manufacture a role for the ruling family, wife and children.

The reign of Ivan the Terrible has been the object of much discussion and heated debate for at least 200 years, mostly about state policy (especially the Oprichnina) and the story of boyar intrigues and their real or imagined relations with the larger policies of the tsar. For all the interest in Ivan the question of succession has not attracted much attention, other than to the short-lived 1553 crisis during Ivan's illness and the role in those events, real or imagined, of Ivan's first cousin, Prince Vladimir

[12] Uspenskii, *Tsar' i patriarkh*, 111–112. The second version also roughly coincided with the recognition of the title of tsar by the patriarch of Constantinople: S. M. Kashtanov, ed., *Rossiia i grecheskii mir v XVI veke* (Moscow: Nauka, 2004), vol. 1, 381–388. This was the occasion for the formulaic redaction in the opinion of V. I. Savva, *Moskovskie tsari i vizantiiskie vasilevsy: K voprosu o vliianii Vizantii na obrazovanie idei tsarskoi vlasti moskovskikh gosudarei* (Khar'kov: Tipografiia M. Zil'bergerg, 1901), 146–151, and Uspenskii, *Tsar' i patriarkh*, 109, note 1. S. N. Bogatyrev believes that this second, "formulaic," version was the result of contact and competition with Sweden: Sergei Bogatyrev, "Ivan the Terrible Discovers the West: The Cultural Transformation of Autocracy during the Early Northern Wars," *Russian History* 34, 1–4 (2007): 166–168.

[13] Daniel Rowland, "Moscow – the Third Rome or the New Israel?" *Russian Review* 55 (1996): 591–614; A. I. Filiushkin, *Tituly russkikh gosudarei* (Moscow and St. Petersburg: Al'ians-Arkheo, 2006), 71–151. Vasilii III had occasionally, not regularly, used the title "tsar" in letters to other rulers: Filiushkin, *Tituly russkikh gosudarei*, 80–81.

[14] *PSRL* XIII, 150.

Staritskiii, and his relatives. For the later years of the reign the succession question has not arisen for scholars. Tsar Ivan's younger brother Iurii (1532–63) and the Tsarevichi Ivan (1554–81) and Fyodor (1557–98), for whatever reason, seem to historians to have played no important role in the dramatic and bloody events of the reign. In spite of this apparent invisibility, the Tsarevichi Ivan and (to a much lesser extent) Fyodor did participate in military campaigns, in the journeys to the tsar's villages, and in pilgrimages to monasteries and shrines as well as in court ceremonies. Ivan did not, however, carry out the ceremony of "placing" his heir on the throne during his lifetime as had most of his predecessors. Ivan Ivanovich and Fyodor bore the title, or at least the epithet, "tsarevich," but Ivan, though the elder son, had no title peculiar to himself. Ivan Grozny did, however, bless Ivan Ivanovich with the throne, the tsardom, in his testament in the 1570s and did bless Fyodor on the eve of his own death in 1584.

The 1547 coronation was quickly followed by Ivan's marriage to Anastasiia Romanovna Iur'eva-Zakhar'ina, the daughter of one of the most important of the boyars, on February 3. The choice of Anastasiia was formally the result of a bride-show, but it seems clear that the reasons were political.[15] Ivan himself, the historians tell us, was not the one who made the choice, not surprisingly as he was only sixteen years old.[16] That boyar politics were behind the choice is most probable, but the exact character of those politics is a matter of discussion.[17] At the wedding itself, the central roles went to Ivan's immediate relatives: among those at the "great table" before the ceremony were his brother Iurii (then fifteen years old), who sat in the "great chair." The place of the mother was taken by Princess Evrosiniia Staritskaia, and the *tysiatskii*, formally the leader of the ceremony, was her son, Prince Vladimir Andreevich (then fourteen years old).[18] Prince Iurii was the leader of the ceremony of departure for the church, though two boyars, Princes I. M. Shuiskii and D. D. Pronskii, spoke for him. The rest of the roles were distributed among the most

[15] Martin, *A Bride for the Tsar*, 113–117.

[16] Soviet-era historians spent almost no space on the marriage: I. I. Smirnov, *Ocherki politicheskoi istorii Russkogo gosudarstva 30–50-kh godov* (Moscow and Leningrad: Izdatel'stvo Akademii nauk SSSR, 1958), 119; Zimin, *Reformy Ivana Groznogo*, 277–278; Skrynnikov, *Tsarstvo terrora*, 97, concentrating on its role in the rise of the Iur'ev-Zakhar'in clan.

[17] Nancy Shields Kollmann, *Kinship and Politics: The Making of the Muscovite Political System 1345–1547* (Stanford, California: Stanford University Press, 1987), 127, 174.

[18] *DRV* XIII, 29–30; V. I. Buganov, ed., *Razriadnaia kniga 1475–1598* (Moscow: Nauka, 1966), 10 (hereafter *RK 1475–1598*). On the *razriad* books, see V. I. Buganov, *Razriadnye knigi poslednei chetverti XV–nachala XVII v.* (Moscow: Izdatel'stvo Akademii nauk SSSR, 1962).

prominent boyars.[19] The young tsar's relatives, his brother Iurii and his cousin Vladimir Staritskii, had important ceremonial roles even though they were still too young to make decisions.

The young tsar and his new wife did not have children right away. Their first child, a girl Anna, was born only in August 1549, after much prayer and many pilgrimages to monasteries.[20] She lived only a year. The first son of the marriage, Dmitrii, was born in October 1552, during Ivan's victorious return from Kazan'. There is no information about his baptism. The object of much contention early in 1553 at the time of his father's illness, the baby perished during a family pilgrimage, allegedly accidently dropped into a river by his nurse, in June of the same year.[21] The new heir, Ivan Ivanovich, came into the world on March 24, 1554, on the Wednesday of Bright Week, the week after Easter. He was baptized in the third week after Easter, on April 15, in the Annunciation church of the Chudov Monastery, the Kremlin monastery dedicated to the Miracle of Archangel Michael and the relics of Metropolitan Aleksii. The officiating priest was the archpriest Andrei of the Annunciation Cathedral in the Kremlin palace. Father Andrei is better known as the later Metropolitan Afanasii, but had been Tsar Ivan's spiritual father since 1550. His godfather (*prinial ego ot kupeli*) was no less than Metropolitan Makarii.[22] His younger brother Fyodor arrived on May 31, 1557, the Monday of the seventh week after Easter. He too was baptized in the Chudov Monastery, and his godfather was also Metropolitan Makarii.[23] These were the surviving sons of Ivan until the birth of the second tsarevich, Dmitrii, to the tsar's last wife, Mariia Nagaia, on October 19, 1582.[24] Tsaritsa Anastasiia's last child, Evdokiia, born on February 26, 1556, followed the precedent of her brothers for her baptism. It took place in the Chudov Monastery; the godfather (*prinial ego ot kupeli*) was Metropolitan Makarii and the officiating priest was Andrei of the Annunciation Cathedral.[25] These baptisms reinforced the relationship of the ruling family, not just the eldest son, to the church. Both of the tsar's children had the metropolitan as their spiritual father.

[19] *DRV* XIII, 30–36; *RK 1475–1598*, 10–11.

[20] Isolde Thyrêt, *Between God and Tsar: Religious Symbolism and the Royal Women of Muscovite Russia* (DeKalb, Illinois: Northern Illinois University Press, 2001), 28–29. Anna was baptized in the Novodevichii Convent near Moscow, and the officiating priest was hegumen Serapion Kurtsev of the Trinity Monastery. Both the godfathers were monks from provincial monasteries: *PSRL* XIII, 158, 459–460. Another short-lived daughter, Mariia, was born on March 17, 1551, but the chronicle reports only that she was baptized, without specifying any further details: *PSRL* XIII, 161.

[21] *PSRL* XIII, 222–223, 232.

[22] *PSRL* XIII, 239; N. N. Pokrovskii, "Afanasii (v miru Andrei)," *SKKDR* II, pt. 1, 73–79.

[23] *PSRL* XIII, 283.

[24] Ivan's second wife Mariia Temriukovna gave birth to a son Vasilii in March, 1563, but he died after living only a few weeks: *PSRL* XIII, 365–366.

[25] *PSRL* XIII, 265.

The choice of location for the baptism is revealing. The Chudov Monastery was a Kremlin institution. Though certainly a monastery, it was not famous for asceticism like the Kirillov or Solovetskii Monasteries in the north. It did house the relics of St. Aleksii the Metropolitan of Kiev (1354–78). Aleksii's Kiev title was to a certain extent honorary, and he spent his life in Moscow. By the sixteenth century, he was one of the "Moscow miracle workers," the metropolitans Petr, Aleksii, and Iona, who were the patrons of the ruling family, the city, and the country as a whole. In the seventeenth century, the tsars normally went to the monastery to pray on the days of St. Aleksii (February 12 and May 20), much more often than they did on the day of St. Michael the Archangel (September 6), to whom the monastery had been dedicated by St. Aleksii when he founded it.[26] After Ivan Ivanovich, the children of the tsars were normally baptized in the Chudov Monastery, and it looks very much as if the association was with St. Aleksii. If the tsar needed a church, the Dormition Cathedral and several others were available, but he chose the church of the Chudov Monastery. The Chudov Monastery served in place of the Trinity-St. Sergii Monastery in the earlier baptisms of Vasilii III and Tsar Ivan himself.

In 1547, no one could predict the future of Ivan's family. Anastasiia could have produced no children, like Solomoniia, or only girls. There were other men in the tsar's family, Ivan's younger brother Iurii and his cousin Vladimir Staritskii. Their weddings soon followed. The fact that they were married at all was a change from the policy of Vasilii III, who forbad or delayed the marriages of his brothers. It was also the case that they had bride-shows before their weddings, following the same practice as Ivan, his father Vasilii, and probably Andrei Staritskii as well. The first of these weddings was that of Iurii Vasil'evich. Prince Iurii was only fifteen years old in 1547, and was, it seems, deaf and dumb. The only source for his condition, however, is Prince Andrei Kurbskii's polemical history of Ivan the Terrible written about 1570. Kurbskii made the statement in the context of the claim that Vasilii III's sons were born as a result of witchcraft. Ivan was as a result wicked and murderous and "the other was strange and wondrous, without a mind and memory and unable to speak."[27] Later on Iurii often had an appointed spokesman at official occasions, so Prince Iurii seems to have had some difficulties now unidentifiable.[28] In any case, the

[26] Pavel Stroev, *Vykhody gosudarei tsarei i velikikh kniazei Mikhaila Fedorovicha, Aleksiia Mikhailovicha, Fedora Aleksievicha vseia Rusi samoderzhtsev s 1632 po 1682 god* (Moscow: Tipografiia A. Semena, 1844), index, 105.

[27] Andrei Kurbskii, *Istoriia o delakh velikogo kniazia Moskovskogo*, ed. K. Iu. Erusalimskii (Moscow: Nauka, 2015), 152.

[28] Charles J. Halperin, "Ivan the Terrible's Younger Brother: Prince Iury Vasil'evich (1533–63)," *The Court Historian* 22, 1 (2017): 1–16.

bride show took place on September 18, 1547: in the official record Ivan "ordered" his brother to be married. The two brothers went to Metropolitan Makarii, who blessed the idea of Iurii's marriage, and the young girls were brought to the Kremlin to be viewed. Both brothers inspected them, and Iurii decided on Princess Uliana Paletskaia, the daughter of the boyar Prince D. F. Paletskii. Ivan then ordered the wedding to take place on November 3. Ivan himself took the place of the father at the wedding, and the *tysiatskii* (the person in charge of the procession) was Prince Vladimir Staritskii. His mother Evfrosin'ia was also among the central group, in fact (if not explicitly) in the place of the mother. The boyar Prince M. I. Kubenskii led Prince Iurii to the ceremony.[29] Prince Vladmir Staritskii had received Ivan's command, that is, permission, to marry on September 10, 1549, but the bride-show did not take place until the next spring, and the chosen bride was Evdokiia Nagaia. Evdokiia's father was not a boyar, though she had some boyar relatives. The actual wedding took place on May 31, 1550. Again Ivan was in the place of the father, Iurii was at the head table with Ivan and Vladimir, and Evfrosin'ia sat by the bride.[30] All three weddings reveal a family circle consisting of Ivan, his brother Iurii, and his cousin Vladimir Staritskii with his mother Evfrosin'ia.[31] Princes Iurii Vasil'evich and Vladimir Staritskii were involved in all the activities of Tsar Ivan in the early years of his reign, a fact that the emphasis on boyar intrigues and the "Chosen Council" of the 1550s has overshadowed.

The years of all these weddings were also the years of the Kazan' campaigns, a local struggle with enormous consequences. The Kazan' khanate was the closest to Moscow of the Horde successor states and controlled the middle Volga and much of the Urals. The eventual capture of Kazan' and its khanate gave Russia control of the Volga river and full access to the Urals, enormously expanding its territory. It also brought Russian troops to the foothills of the Caucasus Mountains and inserted Russia for the first time in history far into the southern steppe. The records of the war with Kazan' that began in 1545 and led to Ivan's first great victory seven years later also provide another glimpse into the roles of both princes.[32] The first time that the military records record the presence of the young Ivan with the army, in 1546, his brother Iurii

29 *DRV* XIII, 36–46; *RK 1475–1598*, 11–12. At the weddings of Ivan and later Vladimir Staritskii, neither groom was led to the ceremony.

30 *DRV* XIII, 46–57; *RK 1475–1598*, 14–15; Martin, *A Bride for the Tsar*, 118–119, 291.

31 Bogatyrev, "Reinventing the Russian Monarchy," 278–280, stresses the element of family unity in the weddings.

32 For the Kazan' campaigns, see most recently A. L. Khoroshkevich, *Rossiia v sisteme mezhdunarodnykh otnoshenii XVI veka* (Moscow: Drevlekhranilishche, 2003), 96–113.

accompanied him.[33] The next summer, after Ivan's coronation and wedding, the army was again mobilized at Kolomna and with Ivan were both Iurii and Vladimir Staritskii.[34] At the end of the year into early 1548, Ivan again mobilized the army, this time against Kazan', and took Iurii with him to Vladimir. Vladimir Staritskii remained in Moscow with a group of boyars to mind the city under the supervision of Metropolitan Makarii.[35] The campaign was a failure, and later in the summer Vladimir Staritskii was in command of the army at Kolomna, the usual point for watching the south.[36] The next major attempt against Kazan' came in the autumn of 1549, after the bride-show for Vladimir Staritskii. Prince Vladimir accompanied the tsar only partway on the campaign, and remained behind to preside over the group of boyars in charge of the capital. Iurii Vasil'evich went on with the tsar. Unusually warm winter weather made a siege of Kazan' impossible, but on the way back Ivan and the boyars decided to build a fortress at Sviiazhsk, which would give the Russian army a base nearer to Kazan'. The chronicle story was that both Prince Iurii and Vladimir Staritskii participated in the decision. In July 1550, Ivan, consulting Prince Iurii and Vladimir Staritskii, reorganized the command system in the army.[37] After returning from the campaign, the court celebrated the wedding of Vladimir Staritskii.[38] The Russians built the fort at Sviiazhsk, and the pro-Moscow khan Sheikh Ali ruled briefly in Kazan'. That summer rumors of a Crimean raid caused Ivan to mobilize the army again at Kolomna, and Vladimir Staritskii accompanied him.[39] Sheikh Ali did not last long, and on his ouster early in 1552, Ivan called together his boyars, Prince Iurii, and Vladimir Staritskii and decided on a major expedition against the Tatar capital.[40] The army assembled, but troubling news of a possible Crimean raid led them to divert their path briefly south to Kolomna. The danger evaporated and the army went on to Kazan'. This was the final, ultimately victorious, campaign, and Prince Vladimir Staritskii was part of the army, again "with his own boyars and nobles."[41] For the first time, Vladimir, now nineteen years old, came with his own military unit. Prince Iurii remained behind in Moscow with seven leading boyars.[42] During the march to Kazan' and the siege, Prince

[33] The army was mobilized at Kolomna to watch the steppe frontier: *PSRL* XXIX, 48; *RK 1475–1598*, 109. It was also the occasion of the execution of several boyars: Krom, *"Vdovstvuiushchee tsarstvo,"* 301–326.

[34] *RK 1475–1598*, 112. The chronicles do not mention the army or Ivan in Kolomna that year, taken up as they are with the dramatic story of the fire in Moscow and the murder of Prince Iurii Glinskii by the mob: *PSRL* XXIX, 51–54.

[35] *RK 1475–1598*, 115; *PSRL* XXIX, 55. [36] *RK 1475–1598*, 116. [37] Ibid., 125–126.

[38] *RK 1475–1598*, 121, 124; PSRL XXIX, 57–60. [39] *RK 1475–1598*, 127, 129.

[40] *PSRL* XXIX, 61–73. [41] *RK 1475–1598*, 136; *PSRL* XXIX, 80, 82, 85–86.

[42] *RK 1475–1598*, 141.

Vladimir had both ceremonial and substantive roles, though he and his men mostly stayed close to the tsar himself. The chronicle named him first before the boyars in consultations with Ivan.[43] He participated in the fighting, but not often or in the main events. In the triumphal procession into Kazan' after it fell, Vladimir Staritskii rode immediately after the tsar, together with Sheikh Ali, and was present with Prince Iurii at the victory banquet after the army returned to Moscow in November.[44]

The roles played in the events of the last years of the boyar regency and the early years of Ivan's reign, as well as in the marriages of Princes Iurii and Vladimir Staritskii, show that the tsar's younger brother and his cousin were both part of the family inner circle. They were always mentioned in the chronicles before all boyars, they participated in the tsar's pilgrimages and court ceremonies, and they were present in the army and in important cases of consultation between the tsar and the boyar elite. There were also differences between the two. Prince Iurii after 1547 ceased to accompany Ivan with the army, and stayed back in Moscow with the boyars, ostensibly in charge of the city. From what we know of his health, he was not capable of actually carrying out any administrative duties on his own, but symbolically he remained his brother's proxy. Prince Vladimir Staritskii was another story, for he continued to participate in the military campaign, sometimes just accompanying his cousin the tsar but soon with his own command, together with older boyars, and then with his own "court" in the final conquest of Kazan'. The weddings of the two princes were more than just court ceremonies. Iurii may have been incapable of ruling, but he was not obviously incapable of fathering children.[45] In fact, Iurii had a son Vasilii, born in 1559.[46] The boy lived less than a year, but his birth means that Prince Iurii's line might have provided a successor even if he himself could not. Prince Vladimir Staritskii also had children, a son Vasilii (1552–73) and two daughters. Had Ivan not produced children with Anastasiia, as his father had not with Solomoniia, either Iurii or Vladimir, or their children, would have been next in line for the throne. Ivan, or Ivan and his advisers, had not just allowed but clearly encouraged both of them to marry, in contrast to the policy of Vasilii III. These marriages ensured that the throne would remain in the tsar's family even if Ivan were to have no sons. The tsar's family was more important than lineal succession from father to son.

[43] *PSRL* XXIX, 88–96. [44] *PSRL* XXIX, 104–105, 109, 115.

[45] Tsar Ivan V, Peter the Great's co-tsar, was equally lacking in the physical health needed to rule but produced several daughters, one of whom, Anna Ivanovna, became the Empress of Russia.

[46] Halperin, "Ivan the Terrible's Younger Brother," 6–7.

The Uncertainties of Succession

The 1553 succession crisis came about because of Ivan's sudden and threatening illness. As the historians tell it, he wrote a testament and asked the boyars to swear an oath of loyalty to his infant son Dmitrii, but some of them would not do it because of fear or anger at the prospect of the inevitable primacy of the Zakhar'ev-Iur'ev clan, the relatives of Tsaritsa Anastasiia. They also did not want an infant tsar. The alternative candidate would be Prince Vladimir Staritskii. Ivan succeeded in convincing or forcing the hesitant to swear the oath, but then he recovered and it seemed that the incident was closed, at least for the immediate future.[47]

The story is well known, not least from Sergei Eisenstein's film *Ivan the Terrible*, but the sources are not simple to interpret. The fullest version is in the vivid notations to the *Illustrated Chronicle* (*Litsevoi svod*), and the texts of the oaths sworn by Vladimir Staritskii after the conflict was over provide additional information. Other chronicles provide very sparse information, and the notations to the *Illustrated Chronicle* are late and tendentious, emphasizing that the boyars were disloyal to him and his family.[48] Prince Vladimir's three oaths are closer to the events, and in them he swore to serve the tsar faithfully and in the case of his death his eldest son, the tsaritsa, and the children, including those yet unborn. Scholars have used the oaths unsystematically and often just in passing, mainly as a source for the event, and have noted that the text generally reproduced the treaty of Vasilii III with his brother Iurii Ivanovich from 1531. The 1553 oath of Prince Vladimir contained the obligation to serve the tsar and Tsaritsa Anastasiia, her son Dmitrii, and "the children whom God gives." The phrase about the "children whom God gives" was more precise than the earlier formula in the oaths from the time of Vasilii III from 1505–30, where the princes and boyars swore to serve the grand prince "and his children" who did not yet exist.[49] Only a few months later, in June 1553, the situation suddenly changed: the infant Dmitrii's nurse dropped him while crossing a river, and he drowned, leaving no heir until the birth of Ivan Ivanovich in

[47] Zimin, Reformy *Ivana Groznogo*, 406–415; Skrynnikov, Tsarstvo *terrora*, 109–115; Sergei Bogatyrev, *The Sovereign and His Counsellors: Ritualized Consultations in Muscovite Political Culture 1350s–1570s*. Suomalaisen Tiedeakatemian Toimituksia, Sarja Humaniora 307 (Helsinki: Academia Scientiarum Fennica, 2000), 144–145; Halperin, Ivan the Terrible, 57–62.

[48] *PSRL* XIII, 523–526. The notes are in the *Tsarstvennaia kniga* portion of the *Illustrated Chronicle* and presumably date from the 1560s like the rest of the work: B. M. Kloss, "Tsarstvennaia kniga," *SKKDR* II, pt. 2, 506–508.

[49] *SGGD* I, 460–461; Zimin, *Reformy Ivana Groznogo*, 412.

March 1554.[50] Ivan, or the boyars behind him at this point, did not seem to hold a grudge.[51]

The next oaths from Vladimir Staritskii testify to the tsar's desire to insure support for his family and new heir. In all three, Vladimir swore to serve Anastasia and the tsar's children. The second and third oaths (April and May 1554) provided for the case that Ivan died without any heir. The second oath reads: "And if God should take your son Tsarevich Ivan, and there are no more children of yours, our sovereign, I will follow your order to obey (*prikaz ... ispraviti*) your tsaritsa the Grand Princess Anastasiia, according to your testament and to this oath, and you, as you are the sovereign, have written about all this in your testament." In the third oath, the text also included the name of Prince Iurii Vasil'evich together with that of Anastasiia.[52] Zimin and Nitsche believed that Ivan added this passage looking out for the possibility that Vladimir Staritskii would become tsar in the event that Ivan died childless, since Iurii's physical or psychological disabilities made him unviable as a candidate. In this interpretation, the passage is to be read as a promise to protect Anastasiia and Iurii if the Staritskii prince became the tsar.[53]

Another interpretation is also possible. Iurii Vasil'evich was married, and in 1554 was only twenty-two years old.[54] In spite of his disabilities, he might have fathered healthy children. In the oath, Prince Vladimir swore to follow the wishes of Ivan's testament (which is now unfortunately lost) and, in the case of the tsar's death without children, the closest relative would have been Prince Iurii, and Anastasiia the eldest female in the family. This may have been the meaning of the offer of Prince Iurii's father-in-law, Prince D. F. Paletskii, made at the time of the 1553 succession crisis, to serve Vladimir Staritskii if he mounted the throne.[55] The offer made sense only if there was an expectation that Iurii would succeed if Ivan were childless. Paletskii doubted that

[50] *PSRL* XIII, 222–223, 232.

[51] Later in the summer, in August 1553, Prince Vladimir Staritskii was put in charge of Serpukhov to the south on the Oka, "with his own boyars and nobles," that is, with his own court. He continued in this post the next year as well. *RK 1475–1598*, 141: "s svoimi boiary i s det'mi boiarskimi"; 143.

[52] "А возмет Бог и сына твоего царевича Ивана, а иных детей твоих государя нашего не останет же ся, и мне твой государя своего приказ весь исправити твоей царице великой княгине Анастасие, и твоему брату Юрию Васильевичу по твоей государя своего душевной грамоте и по сему крестному целованию, о всем по тому, как еси государь ей в своей душевной грамоте написал"; *SGGD* I, 464, 467.

[53] Zimin, *Reformy Ivana Groznogo*, 415–417; Nitsche, *Großfürst und Thronfolger*, 297–303; D. N. Al'shits, "Krestotseloval'nye zapisi Vladimira Andreevicha Staritskogo i nedoshedshee zaveshchanie Ivana Groznogo," *Istoriia SSSR* 4 (1959): 147–155.

[54] Martin, *A Bride for the Tsar*, 64–65, 118; A. A. Zimin, *Formirovanie boiarskoi aristokratii v Rossii vo vtoroi polovine XV–pervoi terti XVI v.* (Moscow: Nauka, 1988), 43.

[55] Skrynnikov, *Tsartsvo terrora*, 110; *PSRL* XIII, 523.

possibility, or did not like it, and wanted to cover himself with the Staritskiis. In the event it was Prince Iurii who died childless in 1563, but no one could have predicted that nine or ten years earlier.

Shaping the Family

The years after the 1553 succession crisis saw more than the swearing of oaths. These were the years of the dominance of Ivan's first circle of advisers, including informal advisers beyond the duma's highest ranks such as the priest Sil'vestr and the *okol'nichii* Aleksei Adashev. With their advice, the tsar carried out a series of state-building measures called "reforms" by modern historians, namely the consolidation and establishment of some central administrative offices such as the Ambassadorial Office to conduct Russia's foreign policy and the gradual abolition of the "feeding" system of paying local officials. A new compilation of laws, the *Sudebnik* of 1550, had already been one of the major achievements. The period of state-building came to an end in 1558, when Ivan began his long and unsuccessful war to conquer Livonia and eventually the eastern parts of Poland-Lithuania. None of the well-known enactments of the years up to the war had anything to do with succession to the throne, but other measures did.

In those years, Ivan and his government were not only building and consolidating the state but also consolidating their understanding of the ruling family. The tsar and his officials extended and put down on paper the personal history and composition of the family in genealogy and commemoration. Russia's first official genealogical register, the "Sovereign's Genealogy" (*Gosudarev rodoslovets*), came into being in 1555–6. The document was the work of the *Razriad* (the military office) secretary Ivan Elizarov Tsypliatev.[56] Several versions have been published, though not the earliest.[57] It was not the first document to include a genealogy of the ruling family of Moscow. The earliest version of the genealogy to survive came along with the princely chronicles of the 1490s,

[56] N. P. Likhachev, *Razriadnye d'iaki XVI veka* (St. Petersburg: Tipografiia V. S. Balashova, 1887), 349–440; M. E. Bychkova, *Rodoslovnye knigi XVI–XVII vv.* (Moscow: Nauka, 1975); S. B. Veselovskii, *D'iaki i pod'iachie XV–XVII vv.* (Moscow: Nauka, 1975), 560.

[57] Anon., ed., "Rodoslovnaia kniga," *Vremennik OIDR* 10, 3rd pagination (1851): I–IV, 1–286; Anon., ed., "Rodoslovnaia keleinaia kniga sviateishego gosudaria Filareta patriarkha vseia Rossii," in *Iubileinyi sbornik S.-Peterburgskogo Arkheologicheskogo Instituta 1613–1913* (St. Petersburg: Sinodalnaia Tipografiia, 1913), I–XXVII, 1–106. The 1686 version, the so-called Velvet Book (*Barkhatnaia kniga*), is found in N. I. Novikov, ed., *Rodoslovnaia kniga kiazei i dvorian rossiiskikh i vyezzhikh*, 2 vols. (Moscow: Universitetskaia Tipografiia u N. Novikova, 1787).

and was simply a list of the princes with all of their sons (no wives or daughters were included), followed by the main boyar families. Later on, probably in the 1540s, a similar text with the appanage princes of the Moscow dynasty was compiled and added on.[58] This version was the basis of the new compilation of 1555–6. Though it provided genealogical data, its purpose was to provide information for the *Razriad* to set appointments according to the precedence system (*mestnichestvo*) and to resolve disputes.[59] The result was a text that was relatively stable through the ensuing century and a half.[60] The first chapter was naturally the genealogy of the ruling family, beginning with Riurik, and the second chapter followed the line up to Ivan the Terrible. After that came the chapter with the appanage princes (*udel'nye kniazia*) of the ruling family, that is the younger sons of the Kiev, Vladimir, and Moscow princes, down to Ivan IV's brother Iurii. Following these immediate relatives of the ruler came the chapters with genealogies of the tsars of Astrakhan', Crimea, and the Great Horde back to Chingis Khan. Then the text provided in chapter 5 a genealogy of the Gediminovich princes of Lithuania, connecting them with the Riurikovich princes of Polotsk. Only then did it move to more distant Riurikovichi and then to the Moscow boyars.[61] Thus Ivan's brother Iurii appeared with him as the son of Vasilii III in the first two chapters, while the Staritskii princes came in the third chapter with the appanage princes of the Moscow line. The text gave the title of grand prince and then tsar to the actual ruler, but he appeared in the context of his brothers and uncles. The chapters on the Tatar khans and the grand dukes of Lithuania came next, separating the ruling family, all of it, not just the line of ruling fathers and sons, from the rest of the princes and boyars of the Russian state.[62] This separation was an innovation, not only presenting the tsar's family in a more prestigious context and raising it over the Russian elite, but also defining it: the ruling family was not just the direct descent line, but also the collateral lines through the Staritskii princes. What it did not do was to include the women of the family, but

[58] Bychkova, *Rodoslovnye knigi XVI–XVII vv.*, 19–21, 179; *PSRL* 27, 367.

[59] Bychkova, *Rodoslovnye knigi XVI–XVII vv.*, 16–17; Kollmann, *Kinship and Politics*, 56–57.

[60] The original version had forty-three chapters, more or less one chapter for each clan. The various later versions had more or less the same series of clans, though sometimes with omissions. Starting at the end of the sixteenth century or a bit before, other clans were added, ending in the "Velvet Book" of 1686, which took the original 43-chapter version and added another 247 clans.

[61] Likhachev, *Razriadnye d'iaki XVI veka*, 367, 374–375; Bychkova, *Rodoslovnye knigi XVI–XVII vv.*, 180–181.

[62] For these texts in later (*c.* 1584–1630) versions, see Anon., *Vremennik OIDR* 10, 131–134, 218–221; and Anon., "Rodoslovnaia keleinaia kniga," 1–4. On these texts: Bychkova, *Rodoslovnye knigi XVI–XVII vv.*, 78, 80.

that omission was the consequence of its function, which was not purely genealogical but rather to provide a work of reference for resolving precedence disputes at court and in the army.

The other document that clarified the boundaries of the ruling family was the *sinodik*, the list of the dead to be commemorated in churches. The compilation of such documents had long been a Byzantine practice.[63] The most general memorialization of the dead came in the Synodikon of Orthodoxy, a Byzantine liturgical text for the Sunday of Orthodoxy (the first Sunday of Lent), which had originally been composed to commemorate the victory over iconoclasm in 843.[64] Aside from commemorating that victory by anathemas on heretics and iconoclasts, it also included the names of the most important clergy and emperors who had fought for the icons. During the course of the history of the Byzantine empire, the Synodikon of Orthodoxy expanded, including more heretics, but also including a prayer for eternal memory to all the past Byzantine emperors and empresses, at least those who had been true to Orthodoxy. The text acquired a dual function. The dual function was also the practice in the Slavic Orthodox *sinodiki* for the Sunday of Orthodoxy.[65] The Russian version of the Synodikon of Orthodoxy, the universal *sinodik*, continued to commemorate the Byzantine emperors and empresses, but, starting in the sixteenth century, the manuscripts began by including the ruling family, the Moscow branch of the Riurikovichi.[66] In the *sinodik* of the Kremlin Dormition Cathedral, the family included the brothers and cousins of the ruler, such as Vasilii III's brothers and Andrei and Vladimir Staritskii. After

[63] Vasilieos Marinis, *Death and the Afterlife in Byzantium: The Fate of the Soul in Theology, Liturgy, and Art* (New York, New York: Cambridge University Press, 2017).

[64] Jean Gouillard, ed., *Le Synodikon de l'orthodoxie. Édition et commentaire*. Travaux et Mémoires du Centre de recherche d'histoire et civilisation byzantines 2 (Paris: E. de Boccard, 1967).

[65] V. A. Moshin, "Serbskaia redaktsiia Sinodika v Nedeliu Pravoslaviia: Analiz tekstov," *Vizantiiskii vremennik* 16 (1959): 317–394; V. A. Moshin, "Serbskaia redaktsiia Sinodika v Nedeliu Pravoslaviia: Teksty," *Vizantiiskii vremennik* 17 (1960): 278–353; Ivan Biliarski, Ivan Bozhikov, and A. Totomanova, *Borilov Sinodik: Izdanie i prevod* (Sofiia: PAM Publishing Company, 2010); Ivan Biliarski, *Paleologoviiat Sinodik v slavianski prevod* (Sofiia: Universitetsko izdatelstvo Sv. Kliment Ochridski, 2013).

[66] The oldest version, at least the oldest published, is the *sinodik* of the Kremlin Dormition Cathedral and was published by N. I. Novikov in the eighteenth century: *Drevniaia rossiiskaia vivliofika ili sobranie raznykh drevnikh sochinenii*, 20 vols., 2nd ed. (Moscow: Kompaniia tipograficheskaia, 1788–91), vol. VI, 420–506. See A. V. Gorskii and K. I. Nevostruev, *Opisanie slavianskikh rukopisei Moskovskoi sinodal'noi biblioteki* (Wiesbaden: Harrassowitz, 1964), vol. 3, pt. 2, 460; G. N. Moiseeva, "Pergamennyi sinodik Gosudarstvennogo Istoricheskogo Muzeia v izdanii N. I. Novikova," *TODRL* 26 (1971): 100–108; V. V. Dergachev, "Vselenskii sinodik v drevnei i srednevekovoi Rossii," *Drevniaia Rus': Voprosy medievistiki* 1, 3 (2001): 18–29.

the family of the grand princes and tsars came the list of appanage princes.[67]

Besides the commemoration on the Sunday of Orthodoxy, there were massive commemorations throughout the year in the larger churches and monasteries. For this hundreds, probably thousands, of documents also called *sinodiki* were compiled in the churches and especially monasteries to list those dead whose children and relatives had requested and paid for the service.[68] This sort of *sinodik* and the practices it reflects seem to have begun to be compiled toward the end of the fifteenth century. Many of them have prefaces on the soul after death that may have originated with Iosif Volotskii.[69] After the prefaces, the *sinodiki* listed the grand princes, the ruling family, including women and appanage princes, and the metropolitans, following the pattern of the commemoration on the Sunday of Orthodoxy. Only after these lists came the lists of the actual donors, including the grand princes. This is the case with the 1479 *sinodik* of the Iosifo-Volokolamskii monastery.[70] Thus some *sinodiki* have the grand princes listed twice.[71] The commemoration of the grand princes was not left to chance: Makarii, still archbishop of Novogorod, included in his charter to the Dukhov (Holy Spirit) Monastery in Novgorod a requirement to commemorate the grand princely family.[72] In 1548, Ivan IV and the now Metropolitan Makarii ordered a service for the commemoration of all dead, starting with the tsars and princes and the higher clergy, to be established and written down. The commemoration was also to include prayers for all those who died by misfortune in wars or accidents.[73]

[67] Moiseeva, "Pergamennyi sinodik," 101, 104; *Drevniaia rossiiskaia vivliofika*, 2nd ed., vol. VI, 438–445 (Moscow family), 445–447 (appanage princes); 447–481 (princely and boyar clans), 487 (Byzantine rulers).

[68] Ludwig Steindorff, *Memoria in Altrußland: Untersuchungen zu den Formen christlicher Totensorge*. Quellen und Studien zur Geschichte des östlichen Europa 38 (Stuttgart: F. Steiner, 1994); I. V. Dergacheva, *Drevnerusskii Sinodik: Issledovaniia i teksty* (Moscow: Izdatel'stvo Krug, 2011).

[69] Dergacheva, *Drevnerusskii Sinodik*, 125–126.

[70] T. I. Shablova, ed., *Sinodik Iosifo-volokolamskogo monastyria* (St. Petersburg: Dmitrii Bulanin, 2004), 69–74, 99–100.

[71] B. M. Pudalov, ed., *Sinodik Nizhegorodskogo Voznesenskogo Pecherskogo monastyria 1552 goda. Sinodik opal'nykh tsaria Ivana Groznogo* (Nizhnii Novgorod: Izdatel'stvo Otdeleniia Nizhegorodskoi Eparkhii i Vosnesenskii Pecherskii muzhskoi monastir', 2009), 45–46, 57–58. The sinodik actually carries the date 1556: Pudalov, ed., *Sinodik Nizhegorodskogo Voznesenskogo Pecherskogo monastyria*, 6, 17.

[72] *AI* I, 531–534. The charter comes from the late 1520s and commands both prayers for the health and life of the rulers (Vasilii and Elena) and also commemoration of the past grand princes.

[73] *AAE* I, 208; Dergacheva, *Drevnerusskii Sinodik*, 37; Steindorff, *Memoria in Altrußland*, 76. The decree says that the commemoration should be written down in *sobornye knigi*. It is not clear what that meant, perhaps the *sinodiki* of the main cathedrals.

In the 1550s, Tsar Ivan himself began to commemorate the tsar's family in Russia and also Constantinople. The best known example is the list of the dead and request for prayers that Ivan sent to Ioasaph II, Patriarch of Constantinople, in January 1557. Besides the ruling princes and their heirs of the Moscow family, it includes all of the brothers of the ruling princes, up to Andrei Staritskii, and all their wives and daughters. The appanage princes and collateral lines in Tver', Riazan', and other principalities were also listed. This was the family as Ivan the Terrible saw it, for, as S. M. Kashtanov noted, the *sinodik* reveals the membership of the tsar's family (*rod*).[74] From the 1550s onward, the monastery *sinodiki* also often began with a variant of this list of the princes and princesses of the family, followed by the extensive lists of all those who purchased commemoration. Two manuscripts from the library of the Trinity-St. Sergii Monastery, the most important monastery in Russia, illustrate that practice. One *sinodik*, from about 1570 with later additions, includes a chapter at the beginning, after the prefaces, listing the members of the Moscow dynasty starting with Daniil Aleksandrovich (ruled 1272–1303) and originally went up through the 1560s, including not only Ivan's brother Iurii but also Vladimir Staritskii. It encompassed all the women of the family, including Vladimir Staritskii's mother Evfrosin'ia and Ivan the Terrible's wives. The Russian tsars and their wives, sons, and daughters through Michael Romanov were added in another hand.[75] Another *sinodik* from the Kirzhach Monastery of the Annunciation, a dependency of the Trinity-St. Sergii Monastery, from before 1585, includes the same members of the family as the Trinity *sinodik*, with additions in another later hand up to Tsar Michael and Tsaritsa Evdokiia, both of whom died in 1645.[76] Given the close ties of the Trinity-St. Sergii Monastery with the tsars, the inclusion of the ruling family presumably was the result of the many donations to the monastery, and reflected how the family understood itself.

The Russian understanding of the past rulers to be commemorated on the Sunday of Orthodoxy differed from that of the Byzantines and the Slavic Orthodox states in the Balkans. In the Synodikon, the Byzantines

[74] Kashtanov, ed., *Rossiia i grecheskii mir*, vol. 1, 214–221, 388–430, esp. 393; Russell E. Martin, "Praying for the Dead in Muscovy: Kinship Awareness and Orthodox Belief in the Commemorations of Muscovite Royalty," in *The Tapestry of Russian Christianity*, ed. Nickolas Lupinin, Donald Ostrowski, and Jennifer B. Spock. Ohio Slavic Papers 10/ Eastern Christian Studies 2 (Columbus, Ohio: Ohio State University, 2016), 189–228.

[75] Rossiiskaia gosudarstvennaia biblioteka f. 304. III, Riznitsa no. 25, ll. 3–4. The list included all the children of Ivan IV, including Dmitrii and Ivan Ivanovichi, who died before they could come to the throne.

[76] Rossiiskaia gosudarstvennaia biblioteka f. 304, no. 43, ll. 7–11 (later page inserted l. 9–9v).

commemorated only the actual emperors and empresses, not other members of the family.[77] That the empresses were commemorated was understandable, as Byzantine empresses were formally crowned from very early on. They were not just the wives of the ruler.[78] In the *sinodiki* of Serbia and Bulgaria, the compilers reproduced the Greek lists, adding their own rulers and their wives.[79] In contrast, the Russian ruling family commemorated all of its dead, all the women and the princes of the Moscow appanages, not just the immediate descent line of the rulers. This practice reflected the Russian norm, for Russians in their requests for prayers for the dead usually included the extended family, at least if the donor was wealthy enough.[80]

Genealogy and commemoration of the dead were not the only means by which the tsar conveyed his understanding of the composition of the ruling family. In these years and after, his conflicts with some of the boyars resulted in oaths sworn by the boyars to serve the ruler, as in earlier reigns. The formula at first remained that of Ivan's father: the boyar swore to serve Ivan and his children and to do no harm to the tsar, his tsaritsa, or the children. Such was the formula in the oaths of Prince V. M. Glinskii

[77] Gouillard, *Le Synodikon de l'orthodoxie*, 96–102. It seems that in Byzantine churches and monasteries, however, commemoration by ordinary people who were not related to the dynasty included only the immediate family of the donor. They did not include the emperors and empresses: Rosemary Morris, *Monks and Laymen in Byzantium, 843–1118* (Cambridge and New York, New York: Cambridge University Press, 1995), 132–134. These results, however, may reflect the absence of sources for most of the great monasteries in Constantinople and its vicinity.

[78] Peter Schreiner, *Byzanz 565–1453*, 4th ed. (Munich: Oldenbourg, 2011), 77–78.

[79] Biliarski, Bozhikov, and Totomanova, *Borilov Sinodik*, 146–157; Moshin, "Serbskaia redaktsiia Sinodika … teksty," 305, 313, 329–330, 339–340, 343; Biliarski, *Paleologoviiat Sinodik*, 33–37, 95.

[80] Ludwig Steindorff, "Wer sind die Meinen? Individuum und Memorialkultur in frühneuzeitlichen Russland," in *Das Individuum und die Seinen: Individualität in der okzidentalen und in der russischen Kultur in Mittelalter und früher Neuzeit*, ed. Yuri L. Bessmertny and Otto Gerhard Oexle. Veröffentllichungen des Max-Planck-Instituts für Geschichte 163 (Göttingen: Vandenhoeck und Ruprecht, 2001), 231–258; Steindorff, "Desirable Ubiquity? Family Strategies of Donation and Commemoration in Muscovy," *Cahiers du monde russe* 57, 2–3 (2016), 641–665; David B. Miller, "Another Sort of Genealogy: The Culture of Commemoration at the Trinity-Sergius Monastery and Trinity's First *Sinodik*," in *"The Book of Royal Degrees" and the Genesis of Russian Historical Consciousness*, ed. Gail Lenhoff and Ann Kleimola (Bloomington, Indiana: Slavica, 2011), 271–286. For other examples, see Shablova, ed. *Sinodik Iosifo-volokolamskogo monastyria*, 102–103 ("Rod kniazia Semena Ivanovich Bel'skogo"); T. I. Shablova, *Kormovoe pominovanie v Uspenskom Kirillo-belozerskom Monastyre v XVI–XVII vekakh* (St. Petersburg: Renome, 2012), 289–307 (two 1604 sinodiki of the Stroganovs); Sinodik Nizhegorodskogo Voznesenskogo Pecherskogo monastyria 1595 goda: Sinodik arkhimandrita Trifona (Nizhnii Novgorod: Izdatel'skii otdel Nizhegorodskoi eparkhii pri Voznesenskom Pecherskom monastyre, 2010), 178–185 ("Rod kniazei Troekurovykh"). This sinodik is probably from the early seventeenth century.

(1561) and Prince Ivan Bel'skii (April 1562). The oath of the boyars Prince Ivan Mstislavskii, Vasilii Mikhailovich Iur'ev-Zakhar'in, Ivan Petrovich Iakovlev, Prince Petr Gorenskii, the *okol'nichii* F. Umnoi-Kolychev, and others (probably in autumn 1562) was a different story. The boyars swore to serve Tsarevich Ivan, Tsaritsa Mariia, whom he had married on August 21, 1561, and Tsarevich Fyodor (in that order). They swore to seek no other sovereign than from among Ivan's children. The oath does not explicitly say that Ivan Ivanovich was the heir, but did say that the boyars would proceed as in Ivan's testament. The oath placed the eldest son first in order before his brother and any others.[81] Thus it ensured the succession of Ivan Ivanovich, but allowed for another possibility, obviously in case of the heir's death, that kept the throne in Ivan's descent line. The later oath of boyar I. P. Iakovlia on March 28, 1565, followed this pattern. Iakovlia swore to serve not just Ivan and his sons, but also Tsaritsa Mariia.[82] Only a year later, Prince M. I. Vorotynskii swore the same oath that included Mariia, not only to do her no harm, but also to serve her as well as her husband and children.[83] Such oaths for the rest of Ivan's reign are not many, not surprisingly during the years of the Oprichnina and afterward. Two oaths from Prince Mstislavskii did not include the tsaritsa, but both occurred at moments between Ivan's many marriages.[84] More interesting is the decision of the Assembly of the Land of 1566, dated July 2, 1566. Ivan called the Sobor to discuss the continuation of the Livonian War, which the Sobor supported, and at the end they kissed the cross to serve him and his children. There was no mention of the tsaritsa, though Mariia was still alive. The Sobor has been the object of extensive scrutiny, though this element has escaped the attention of historians.[85] Perhaps the Sobor omitted Mariia because the issue at question was a narrow military and diplomatic problem in which she could not be expected to participate, not the general matter of loyal service in all circumstances. Be that as it may, there is no text of any service oaths (other than the two ambiguous Mstislavskii documents)

[81] *SGGD* I, 470–475, 484–487. Zimin believed that Mstislavskii and his fellows were to constitute a regency in case of Ivan's death: Zimin, *Oprichnina*, 86–88, 90–92.

[82] *SGGD* I, 503–506; Zimin, *Oprichnina*, 150–151.

[83] *SGGD* I, 533–537; Zimin, *Oprichnina*, 161–162.

[84] *SGGD* I, 561–565 (1570–1), 588–591 (1580–1).

[85] *SGGD* I, 545–556, and see 555; Zimin, *Oprichnina*, 159–211; L. V. Cherepnin, *Zemskie sobory Russkogo gosudarstva v XVI–XVII vv.* (Moscow: Iazyki slavianskoi kul'tury, 1978), 106–115; Skrynnikov, *Tsarstvo terrora*, 266–267; Khoroshkevich, *Rossiia v sisteme mezhdunarodnykh otnoshenii*, 434–451; A. I. Filiushkin, *Izobretaia pervuiu voinu Rossii i Evropy: Baltiiskie voiny vtoroi poloviny XVI v. glazami sovremennikov i potomkov* (St. Petersburg: Izdatel'stvo Dmitrii Bulanin, 2013), 194; A. N. Ianushkevich, *Livonskaia voina: Vil'no protiv Moskvy 1558–1570* (Moscow: Kvadriga, 2015), 106–108; Halperin, *Ivan the Terrible*, 198–201.

until 1598. When the texts appear again, they always included the tsaritsa (when there was one) along with the tsar and the children. Ivan thus continued the practice of his father's reign, exacting oaths to serve not just himself but also his tsaritsa and all of his children.

The service oaths in a society where oaths were a sacred act were not just a ceremony, though they certainly had also a symbolic element. Another symbolic association of the heirs to the throne with the tsar came with the introduction of printing into Russia. The first printed books in the 1550s contained only the text, but starting in 1564 many of them included a preface and an afterword. The first to do so was Ivan Fedorov's *Apostol* of 1564, which contained the book of Acts and the epistles from the New Testament. The afterword explained that the book was printed by the will of Tsar Ivan and at the order of Metropolitan Makarii, and that the printing was completed on March 1, 1564 in the first year of the metropolitanate of Afanasii. The next book to be dated was the 1568 *Psaltir'*, and this time the tsar's sons were included. The afterword repeated the formula that it was printed at the will of the tsar and the order of Metropolitan Afanasii, but the date was December 20, 1568, in the thirty-fourth year of the reign of Tsar Ivan Vasil'evich "and at the time of his children Ivan and Fyodor and the most holy Metropolitan Kirill of all Rus'." The 1577 *Psaltir'* also included Ivan and Fyodor in the dating notice.[86] A new way to associate the tsarevichi with their father had appeared, one that potentially circulated throughout the clergy and even among laymen.

The Fate of Vladimir Staritskii

In December 1564, Tsar Ivan suddenly left Moscow with his entire family and most of his household. He went first south to Kolomenskoe, a nearby residence of the tsars, and then circled around the city to the north to Aleksandrova Sloboda. He announced that he was abandoning his "sovereignty" because of the evil deeds of the boyars. He was not angry at the people of Moscow, just the boyars. Led by Metropolitan Afanasii, the boyars and people begged him to return to the throne. This he did, but he then divided the country, establishing a separate duma, court, household, and army directly under the tsar, the Oprichnina. The rest, the "land" (*zemlia*, *zemshchina*), he left to the remaining members of the duma. Thus began one of the most famous episodes in Russian history. At the time

[86] I. V. Pozdeeva, V. P. Pushkov, and A. V. Dadykin, *Moskovskii pechatnyi dvor – fakt i faktor russkoi kul'tury 1618–1652* (Moscow: Mosgorarkhiv, 2001), 166–171, 174 reproduces the afterwords.

both his sons were still children, ten and eight years old, and the events seem to have had nothing to do with succession.[87] Some historians have argued, however, that the first victims of Ivan's wrath were former supporters of Prince Vladimir Staritskii from the events of 1553.[88] This conclusion is entirely based, however, on a reconstruction of the factions in 1553. The Nikon Chronicle, the main Russian narrative source, has a long account of the events but does not mention either Vladimir Staritskii or any issue of succession.[89] Ivan himself, in his first epistle to Prince Andrei Kurbskii the previous July, 1564, referred to his son Dmitrii in 1553 as his heir (*naslednik*), and claimed that Kurbskii and the others wanted to put Prince Vladimir Staritskii on the throne, "though he was far from our line" (*ezhe ot nas rastoiashchasia v kolene*).[90]

The one case, and it was not minor, during the Oprichnina that involved succession came later on. That was the case of Prince Vladimir Staritskii, for he was the tsar's cousin and, should Ivan and all his descendants perish, could theoretically inherit the throne. Vladimir had figured as the alternative to Ivan's son Dmitrii in 1553. In 1563, suspicion had already fallen on him, though the charges in the surviving sources are vague. He went into exile, and his mother Evfrosinia to a convent. Metropolitan Makarii and the clergy spoke on their behalf.[91] In the intervening years (as mentioned earlier in this chapter), he was back in favor. The final case came as a result of the execution of I. P. Fedorov-Cheliadnin in September 1568. Fedorov was the tsar's *koniushii* (master of the horse) and the leading boyar in the "land" part of the country under the division of the Oprichnina era.[92] Supposedly the investigation of the Fedorov case uncovered Vladimir Staritskii's ambitions. Ivan sent him into exile in Nizhnii Novgorod, and while he was there one of the tsar's

[87] See Zimin, *Oprichnina*, and Skrynnikov, *Tsarstvo terrora*, 170–482.

[88] Zimin, *Oprichnina*, 127–141. Skrynnikov believed that Ivan's sons were to replace him in ruling the country, but he based this conclusion on his reading of the undated testament of Ivan: Skrynnikov, *Tsarstvo terrora*, 203–237.

[89] *PSRL* XIII, 391–396. Only the notes to the Litsevoi svod mention succession.

[90] Ia. S. Lur'e and Iu. D. Rykov, eds., *Perepiska Ivana Groznogo s Andreem Kurbskim* (Leningrad: Nauka, 1979), 32, 80.

[91] Skrynnikov, *Tsarstvo terrora*, 159–161; Halperin, *Ivan the Terrible*, 191–193.

[92] According to the German interpreter Albert Schlichting, Ivan believed that Fedorov-Cheliadnin was after Ivan's throne, but no Russian sources confirm that this was the allegation: Skrynnikov, *Tsarstvo terrora*, 337. I. V. Dubrovskii, "Latinskie rukopisi sochineniia Al'berta Shlikhtinga," *Russkii sbornik* 18 (2016), 74–217, esp. 106–108; A. I. Malein, ed. and trans., *Novoe izvestie o Rossii vremeni Ivana Groznogo: Skazanie Al'berta Shlikhtinga* (Leningrad: Izdatel'stvo Akademii nauk SSSR, 1934), 21–22. Another version of Schlichting's account: "Nova ex Moscovia per Albertum Schlichting," in Szujski, Józef, ed., *Diariusze sejmów koronnych 1548, 1553, 1570 r.* Scriptores rerum polonicarum I (Kraków: Komisja Historyczna Towarzystwa Naukowego Krakowskiego, 1872), 145–147.

cooks denounced him for trying to poison Ivan.[93] The *oprichniki* summoned him to Aleksandrova Sloboda, and he was executed there on October 9, 1569, together with his wife and eldest daughter. His mother, by then a nun, but whose role in the events of 1553 was apparently not forgotten, was put to death a few days later. Again the details come from the Livonian nobles Johann Taube and Elbert Kruse, though the fact of the deaths is also found in Russian sources such as the famous list of the dead to be remembered in prayers.[94] Russian diplomats to Lithuania were ordered in January 1571 to report that Prince Vladimir and his mother had wished to harm (*isportiti*) Ivan and his children.[95] Some years later, in 1577 Ivan repeated the charge in another epistle to Kurbskii, who replied that Vladimir was not worthy of the throne (*ne dostoin byl togo*).[96] In Ivan's mind, at least, Vladimir Staritskii was a potential rival and successor to the throne.

The Oprichnina ended in 1572, and it might have seemed that the family of Vladimir Staritskii was off the political scene permanently. This was not the case. His son Vasilii survived and even regained an appanage in Dmitrov, though he died in 1573/4, and was buried in the Kremlin's Archangel Cathedral with his father.[97] Even more remarkably, Vladimir's daughter Mariia played a role in Ivan's political maneuvers in Livonia by her marriage to Magnus, the "king" of Livonia. Magnus (1540–83) was the younger brother of King Frederick II of Denmark (reigned 1559–88). As a younger brother of the king, Magnus had rights to inherit part of the Duchy of Holstein, long a part of the kingdom of Denmark, but Frederick had other plans. Denmark had possessed since the Baltic crusades of the thirteenth century the lordship over the bishopric of Ösel (Saaremaa), one of the Livonian islands. The Lutheran bishop sold his rights to the Danish crown, and Frederick sent his brother Magnus to take his place, first renouncing his succession

[93] He was indeed a commander in Nizhnii Novogorod: Buganov, *Razriadnaia kniga 1475–1598*, 230.

[94] Zimin, *Oprichnina*, 288–292; Skrynnikov, *Tsarstvo terrora*, 354–356; Elert Kruse and Iohann Taube, "Zar' Iwan der Grausame," in *Beyträge zur Kenntnis Rußlands und seiner Geschichte*, ed. Gustav Ewers and Moritz von Engelhardt (Dorpat: n.p., 1816), vol. I, 185–238, esp. 213–217; M. G. Roginskii, trans., "Poslanie Ioganna Taube i Elerta Kruze kak istoricheskii istochnik," *Russkii istoricheskii zhurnal* 8 (1922): 10–59; esp. 45–47. Taube and Kruse were Livonian soldiers of the Oprichnina and thus possible eyewitnesses, but also needed to justify their flight to Poland.

[95] *SRIO* 71, 777. There was also a record of the investigation of Vladimir Staritskii that remained in the archives until the seventeenth-century fires that alleged that he want to kill the tsar: Skrynnikov, *Tsarstvo terrora*, 356.

[96] Lur'e and Rykov, *Perepiska Ivana Groznogo*, 104, 109.

[97] Skrynnikov, *Tsarstvo terrora*, 511; M. N. Tikhomirov, "Maloizvestnye letopisnye istochniki XVI v.," *Istoricheskie zapiski* 10 (1941): 92.

rights in Holstein. This act involved Magnus, and also Denmark, in the Livonian War to the point of a Russo-Danish treaty in 1562. Ivan IV guaranteed the possessions of Magnus in Livonia and the Danes allowed trade to Russian-held Narva.[98] During the next years Denmark was occupied with its major war with Sweden, and Ivan with Poland, but Ivan and Frederick had some common interests: Sweden was an enemy to both. Out of this situation came one of the stranger episodes of the Livonian War. Ivan wanted an instrument in Livonia, and agreed late in 1569 to grant Livonia, the Russian conquests and the rest, to Magnus and his descendants. The king of Denmark should not rule in Livonia. If Magnus's line ever failed, then Ivan allowed him to choose a successor from the Danish royal house, who would swear to serve Ivan.[99] In early 1570, Magnus went to Moscow and proclaimed himself the vassal of Ivan IV, who named him "king of Livonia." The substance of the agreement, according to Hans Schultz from Danzig, who witnessed the meeting of Magnus and Ivan, was that Magnus would be the hereditary ruler of "my land," the tsar said, "even though I have two sons."[100] If Ivan actually said that, the idea left no trace in the written agreements, which specified only what would happen if Magnus died, not Ivan.[101] Magnus also married the eldest surviving daughter of Vladimir Staritskii, Mariia.[102] Ivan wrote to the king of Denmark that he had married the king of Livonia to "our family and noble line Mariia, the

[98] Eckhard Hübner, "Zwischen aller Fronten: Magnus von Holstein als König von Livland," in *Zwischen Christianisierung und Europäisierung: Beiträge zur Geschichte Osteuropas in Mittelalter und Früher Neuzeit*, ed. Eckhard Hübner, Ekkehard Klug, and Jan Kusber. Quellen und Studien zur Geschichte des östlichen Europa 51 (Stuttgart: Franz Steiner, 1998), 313–334; L. Iu. Taimasova, "Diplomaticheskii etiud vremen Livonskoi voiny: Skandal'naia svad'ba v Novgorode," *Novyi istoricheskii vestnik* 3, 45 (2015): 79–126; 4, 46 (2015): 40–76; *Dansk undenrigspolitiks historie* (Copenhagen: Danmarks Nationalleksikon, 2001), vol. I, 294, 300–301, 306.

[99] Iu. N. Shcherbachev, ed., "Kopengagenskie akty, otnosiashchiesia do russkoi istorii I (1326–1569)," *ChOIDR* 255, 4 (1915): 284–288.

[100] G. V. Forsten, *Baltiiskii vopros v XVI i XVII stoletiiakh, 1544–1648.* Zapiski istoriko-filologicheskogo fakul'teta Sankt-Peterburgskogo universiteta 33 (Moscow: Tipografiia V. S. Balasheva, 1893), vol. I, 535–540, esp. 539, note 1; Forsten, *Akty i pis'ma k istorii Baltiiskogo voprosa v XVI i XVII stoletiiakh.* Zapiski istoriko-filologicheskogo fakul'teta Sankt-Peterburgskogo universiteta XXI (Moscow: Tipografiia I. N. Skorokhodova, 1889), 132–134.

[101] Martin, *A Bride for the Tsar*, 143–144. The Schultz report: Iu. N. Shcherbachev, "Kopengagenskie akty, otnosiashchiesia do russkoi istorii II (1570–1575)," *ChOIDR* 257, 2 (1916): 33–34. Forsten, *Baltiiskii vopros*, vol. I, 539, believed that "my land" was Livonia. Tsar Ivan did claim that Livonia was his patrimony.

[102] Skrynnikov, *Tsarstvo terrora*, 394–395, 421–422, 478; D. Tsvetaev, "Mariia Vladimirovna i Magnus Datskii," *Zhurnal Ministerstvo narodnogo prosveshcheniia* 196, 3 (1878): 57–85; Peder Hansen Resen, *Kong Fredericks den andens Krønicke* (Copenhagen: S. M. Jørgensøn, 1680), 272.

daughter of Vladimir Andreevich."[103] Magnus was quite aware that his bride came from the grand princely Vladimir line, the same as the tsar.[104] The wedding took place in Novgorod in early 1573, in the "sovereign's court," in the presence of Ivan himself and his son Ivan Ivanovich. From the bride's side, her brother Vasilii and his wife were there "in place of the mother." Both a Lutheran pastor and a Russian priest were present: the Russian priest married Mariia and the Lutheran Magnus, each according to his own rite. Both clergymen participated in the exchange of rings.[105] Magnus was now part of the ruling Russian family by marriage, but he did not remain long. Increasingly discontented with his position in Livonia, he made contact with King Stefan Batory of Poland late in 1577 and soon abandoned Ivan for the king.[106] He died more or less in exile in 1583. His widow Mariia returned to Russia and entered a monastery. Magnus and Mariia had only a daughter, with whom the line of Vladimir Staritskii came to an end.

The importance of this episode, other than as one of the many complications of the Livonian War, is the role that it reveals for the relatives of the ruling family. As in the case of Vladimir Staritskii's continued presence at court and in military service, his line was very much part of the ruling family. Magnus was aware that he was marrying into that family. In theory, Vladimir's son Vasilii could have continued as an alternative ruler if the main line of Ivan himself failed, but he did not live long enough. Since his parents were married in 1555, he must have been only about fourteen when his father and grandmother perished. He died himself only a few years later, and was buried in the dynastic necropolis. The Staritsa line was not just another boyar clan. They were part of the ruling family, and Ivan treated them as such, to the point that he could be afraid, in 1569 as in 1553, that someone might want to replace him with them. Only

[103] "woris slegtt och byrdtt Mariie Wladimer Andres datter," Ivan to Frederick II, Novgorod, April 1, 1573, Scherbachev, "Kopengagenskie akty ... II," 85. Frederick's reply of August 22, 1573, called Mariia Ivan's "hogeborene blutfreundin": Scherbachev, "Kopengagenskie akty ... II," 88–89.

[104] Forsten, *Akty i pis'ma k istorii Baltiiskogo voprosa*, 153–155; Danske Rigsarkiv, TKUA, Speciel del, Livland, AI 2 (letters of Magnus to Frederick II), Magnus to King Frederick II, August 20, 1573. He did not, however, stress this fact in his later defense: Frede P. Jensen, "Hertug Magnus af Holstens forsvarsskrift af 1579 om hans forhold til tsar Ivan den Grusomme," *Danske Magazin* series 8, 5 (1976): 54–83, esp. 64.

[105] *DRV* XIII, 97–103; V. I. Buganov, ed., *Razriadnaia kniga 1550–1636 gg.* (Moscow: Nauka, 1975), vol. 1, 208–212; Shcherbachev, "Kopengagenskie akty ... I," 85 (Ivan IV to Frederick II, announcing the wedding of Magnus, Novgorod, April 1, 1573); Tsvetaev, "Mariia Vladimirovna i Magnus Datskii," 65–68; Martin, *A Bride for the Tsar*, 142–145. This was the first and only interconfessional dynastic marriage in Russia before that of Tsarevich Aleksei in 1711.

[106] Zimin, *V kanun groznykh potriasenii*, 46–50, 53–54.

when they were finally gone were Ivan's sons the only contenders for the throne.

The Sons of Tsar Ivan

Ivan's sons Ivan and Fyodor did not die in childhood but grew to maturity. In the historical literature, however, they are virtually invisible almost to the end of the reign. Their births and baptism are barely noted. Tsarevich Ivan has had some notice only for the moment of his death, and his participation in the military campaigns or state affairs has been ignored to such an extent that it is difficult to say whether his participation was real, symbolic, or a combination of the two. Historians have paid virtually no attention to his three marriages. The marriage of Fyodor to Irina Godunova figures only as a step in the rise of her brother Boris. Zimin and Skrynnikov provided no more than the names of the first wives of Ivan Ivanovich, and mentioned the third only in connection with the rumors about his death.[107] The fate of the first wives is unclear: both became nuns, but exactly when and why seems to be unknown.[108] Yet Fyodor became the tsar not just because of the death of his brother but also because that brother had no children with any of his three wives.

Judging by the Nikon and other chronicles as well as the *Razriad* records, the position of Tsarevich Ivan at the court in some respects changed over the years very slowly. At his birth the chronicles reported only that a son was born, a tsarevich, and after that his title never changed.[109] This usage was the same for the short-lived Tsarevich Dmitrii as well as for Ivan's younger brother Fyodor.[110] Both tsarevichi participated in the tsar's pilgrimages, in meeting the tsar when he returned to Moscow, in church services, and in other ceremonies during the 1550s. On August 8, 1560, on the day after the death of Tsaritsa Anastasiia, both tsarevichi (and Prince Iurii Vasil'evich as well as the Kazan' tsarevich Alexander Safagireevich) received their own courts. Obviously, at their mother's death some provision had to be made for

[107] Ivan Ivanovich married Evdokiia Saburova (1571), Pelageia/Feodosiia Petrova-Solovaia (1575), and Elena Ivanovna Sheremeteva (1582): *Russkii biograficheskii slovar'*. Ibak–Kliucharev (St. Petersburg: Izdanie Imperatorskogo Russkogo istoricheskogo obshchestva, 1897), 188–189; Zimin, *Oprichnina*, 215, 278; Zimin, *V kanun groznykh potriasenii*, 14–19, 91, 265; R. G. Skrynnikov, *Rossiia posle Oprichniny* (Leningrad: Izdatel'stvo Leningradskogo universiteta, 1975), 92–94; Martin, *A Bride for the Tsar*, 133–135, 148, 158–159.

[108] Ivan Timofeev asserted that they were both compelled to enter a convent, but Timofeev wrote after the end of the Time of Troubles, nearly fifty years later. O. A. Derzhavina, ed., *Vremennik Ivana Timofeeva* (St. Petersburg: Nauka, 2004), 19.

[109] *PSRL* XIII, 239. [110] *PSRL* XIII, 222–223, 283

the two boys, six and three years old, but the historians have been interested only in the political side of the event.[111] Perhaps equally important is the subsequent appearance of the dead tsaritsa in the many prayers and appeals to the Lord for protection, along with the patron saints of the Russian land. This seems to have been increasingly the case with the wives of Russian rulers in the sixteenth century. Earlier the only female ruler regularly called on for blessings and intercession was the tenth-century princess St. Ol'ga. A new role had emerged for the mother of the successors to the throne.[112]

At the establishment of their courts, Tsar Ivan treated both boys the same, but a year later he singled out his older son Ivan Ivanovich. In September 1561, Tsar Ivan went on the now annual pilgrimage to the Trinity-St. Sergii Monastery and "ordered Tsarevich Ivan to be in his place in Moscow and ordered him to issue documents about all military affairs and the affairs of the land in his name." Thus he formally handed the state over to his seven-year-old son. When the tsar returned to Moscow on November 25, he presumably took things back into his own hands.[113] In May of the next year, 1562, he went on campaign against Lithuania and left Prince Iurii Vasil'evich, Tsarevich Ivan, and Tsarevich Fyodor back in Moscow, ordering Ivan Ivanovich "to write in his name to the commanders in all the towns about taking care of things and ordered all affairs of the land to his son Tsarevich Ivan." With Tsarevich Ivan he left three boyars from the Iur'ev-Zakhar'in clan, his mother's family, namely the uncles of the tsarevich Danilo and Nikita Romanovich Iur'ev-Zakhar'in as well as V. M. Iur'ev-Zakhar'in. Furthermore Tsar Ivan also left the boyars V. P. Iakovlev-Zakhar'in and Prince V. A. Sitskii as well as many nobles to be with his son.[114] There is no sign that these boyars were in any more permanent way exclusively attached to the persons or courts of the tsarevichi.[115] This was a particular arrangement for the absence of the tsar.

[111] *PSRL* XIII, 328–329. For example, Skrynnikov, *Tsarstvo terrora*, 142–144, but see Halperin, "Ivan the Terrible's Younger Brother," 7–8.

[112] Isolde Thyrêt, *Between God and Tsar: Religious Symbolism and the Royal Women of Muscovite Russia* (DeKalb, Illinois: Northern Illinois University Press, 2001), 55–64.

[113] *PSRL* XIII, 339; Zimin, *Oprichnina*, 86.

[114] *PSRL* XIII, 341: "по вестем во все городы о бережении к воеводам писати от себя, и всякие свои земские дела приказал сыну своему царевичу Ивану." Both Prince Iurii and Tsarevich Fyodor also had a staff of boyars and *okol'chie* with many nobles at their sides. Ivan Ivanovich also wrote to the Nogais in October of the same year asserting that he was in charge while his father was away: Zimin, *Oprichnina*, 86–89.

[115] *RK 1475–1598*, for example, Nikita Romanov: 185, 216–217. This was almost the same group that swore the oath that autumn to serve Ivan Ivanovich, Tsaritsa Mariia, and Tsarevich Fyodor: *SGGD* I, 474–475.

In the fall of 1562, the tsar returned to Moscow, and his sons met him on the Arbat together with the metropolitan.[116] During the next military campaign, which began at the end of the year and finished with the capture of Polotsk in 1563, nothing of the sort took place. The two tsarevichi stayed home and did not participate in any affairs, even formally. At the end of 1564 Ivan took the two boys with him in the famous procession to Aleksandrova Sloboda, where he would spend most of his time for the rest of the reign. This event marked the beginning of the Oprichnina, and he assigned them territories in the Oprichnina lands.[117]

Tsarevich Ivan "participated" in state affairs and returned to the usual series of formal obligations at the court. During the church councils of 1564–6 he was present along with his father. Immediately after the death of Makarii on February 9, 1564, Ivan called a church council, and among the participants of the council was the ten-year-old Tsarevich Ivan. The council also selected the new metropolitan, Ivan's former spiritual father Afanasii, and again the chronicles noted the presence of Tsarevich Ivan.[118] In 1565, the metropolitan and the two tsarevichi Ivan and Fyodor petitioned Ivan to allow some of the Polish prisoners of war to return home to collect money to ransom their fellow prisoners.[119] Two years later Metropolitan Afanasii left his office, and a new council had to find a successor. Tsarevich Ivan was present both at the council that selected the successor, Filipp, and at his consecration.[120] The presence of the tsarevich at the church councils is hard to explain, especially since he was absent from the Assembly of the Land of 1566, which took place only two weeks before the selection of Filipp.[121] After the councils, Tsarevich Ivan continued his travels with his father to monasteries and elsewhere, but he also began to play a modest role in diplomatic ceremonies.[122] Already in June 1566, the tsar had ordered him to be present for the meeting with the Lithuanian ambassadors, and the twelve-year-old Ivan Ivanovich said some polite words.[123] In the winter of 1566–7, both father and son were in Aleksandrova Sloboda. In February, emissaries arrived from King Erik IV of Sweden. Tsarevich

[116] *PSRL* XIII, 344. [117] *PSRL* XIII, 394.

[118] *PSRL* XIII, 378, 380; Ivan proposed that the Moscow metropolitans wear the white cowl (*belyi klobuk*) as did the archbishops of Novgorod. Skrynnikov, *Tsarstvo terrora*, 179, considered that the council on the White Cowl was intended to attract the clergy to the side of the tsar. That might have been the case, but it is not clear why the presence of the tsarevich was necessary for this purpose.

[119] Khoroshkevich, *Rossiia v sisteme mezhdunarodnykh otnoshenii*, 426, 429.

[120] At the consecration, Tsarevich Ivan was joined by his brother Fyodor and Prince Vladimir Staritskii: *PSRL* XIII, 403; *SGGD* I, 557–58; Zimin, *Oprichnina*, 246.

[121] *PSRL* XIII, 402–03; *SGGD* I, 545–57. [122] *PSRL* XIII, 404–407.

[123] *SRIO* 71, 364; Nitsche, *Großfürst und Thronfolger*, 320–321; Khoroshkevich, *Rossiia v sisteme mezhdunarodnykh otnoshenii*, 437.

Ivan was present for the farewell audience and made a short speech.[124] Ivan Ivanovich participated in the audience for the Polish embassy in October 1567, and in September 1569 both Ivan and Fyodor received gifts from the Polish ambassador.[125] The Nikon Chronicle ends in 1567, but precisely in that year the name of Ivan Ivanovich, then thirteen, appeared for the first time in the *razriad* records at the age. The military campaign of that year against the Poles was called "his [the tsar's] own campaign and that of his son the tsarevich Ivan," and the tsarevich actually accompanied his father. With the boy were the Oprichnina boyars V. P. Iakovlev-Zakhar'in and Prince V. A. Sitskii.[126] From that time until the death of Tsarevich Ivan in 1581, his name appeared almost every year and sometimes more often in the *razriad* books as a participant both in military campaigns and in the discussion of various political and military issues.[127] On July 25, 1570, he joined his father in declaring the guilt of some 300 boyars, secretaries, and members of their families, and was present at their execution in Moscow.[128] Did his presence imply that he participated as an adult in the Oprichnina? In 1570, he was sixteen years old. Albert Schlichting reported that he approved of the executions and was just as bloodthirsty as his father, but Schlichting is often unreliable. No other witness, Russian or foreign, reported the attitude of the tsarevich one way or the other.[129] Later in 1570, "on September 22 the tsar and grand prince Ivan Vasil'evich and his son Tsarevich Ivan Ivanovich decreed together with all the boyars and commanders in Serpukhov" to hear the news about the Crimeans. Then the tsar and tsarevich left the boyars on the frontier (*na beregu*) and returned to Aleksandrova Sloboda.[130] In some cases, the records describe decisions as made by Tsar Ivan and his son together.[131] Tsarevich Ivan also continued to participate in the reception of diplomats from abroad. In May 1572, he was present for the reception of

[124] *PSRL* XIII, 407; "En svensk beskickning til Ryssland under Erik XIV:s regering," *Historisk tidskrift* VII (1887), 325–341.

[125] *SRIO* 71, 555, 561, 613.

[126] *RK 1475–1598*, 227: Ivan ordered "pokhod svoi i syna svoego tsarevichev Ivanov" against the king of Poland on September 3, 1567. Cf. Zimin, *Oprichnina*, 361, 364.

[127] *RK 1475–1598*, 1570: 232–233, 235–237; 1571: 239–240; 1572: 243–244, 249; 1574: 254; 1576: 259–260, 263, 273; 1577: 275–276, 278–279, 281–282; 1578: 284–286; 1579: 292–293, 295; 1580: 304–305; *RK 1550–1636* I, 1570: 175, 181–182; 1572: 196, 198, 202; 1574: 223.

[128] Zimin, *Oprichnina*, 437; *Dukhovnye i dogovornye gramoty*, 481 [= Opis' Posol'skogo prikaza 1626 g.].

[129] Dubrovskii, "Latinskie rukopisi," 116; A. I. Malein, ed., *Novoe izvestie o Rossii vremeni Ivana Groznogo* (Leningrad: Izdatel'stvo Akademii nauk SSSR, 1934), 26.

[130] "сентября в 22 день царь и великий князь Иван Васильвич всеа Русии и сын его царевич Иван Иванович приговорили со всеми боярами и воеводами в Серпухове," *RK 1475–1598*, 237.

[131] *RK 1475–1598*, for example, 249 (1572), 273 (1576).

the English envoy Anthony Jenkinson.[132] In November 1575, Tsar Ivan and his son Ivan agreed to meet the Imperial ambassador Hans Kobenzl, and in early 1576 both of them received him in Mozhaisk. At the audience Ivan spoke, as did his son.[133] In 1578, Ivan Ivanovich was present at the audience for the Polish ambassador Stanisław Kryski and later the Danish ambassador Jacob Ulfeldt.[134] In 1580, decisions about embassies to the Empire again came in the name of the tsar, Tsarevich Ivan, and the boyars.[135] Tsarevich Fyodor did not play even a ceremonial role in foreign affairs, but he was the tsar's candidate for the Polish throne (besides himself) in the 1572–3 and 1574–6 interregna in Poland.[136]

There is no evidence that Ivan singled out Ivan Ivanovich with any special tutor or guardian (*diad'ka*), as became the custom later on. The tsarevich must have had teachers and a "spiritual father," but we know nothing about them. At the first campaign in which Ivan Ivanovich took part, in 1567, Iakovlev-Zakhar'in and Prince Sitskii were with him, but on the next such occasion in 1570 the group was much more elaborate. Tsarevich Ivan came with *ryndy*, who were young men who served as guards and his suite, but he again did not have an older guardian. There are two versions of the composition of the *ryndy* of the tsarevich, one of which includes the first mention of Boris Godunov.[137] The next summer campaign saw many of the same men

[132] Iurii Tolstoi, *Pervye sorok let snoshenii mezhdu Rossiei i Anglieiu 1553–1593* (St. Petersburg: Tipografiia i khromolitografiia A. Transhelia, 1875), 140.

[133] *PDS*, I, 481, 512–513, 532, 545; Fedor Verzhbovskii [Theodor Wierzbowski], *Donesenie Ioanna Kobentselia*. Materialy k istorii Moskovskogo gosudarstva v XVI i XVII stoletiiakh IV (Warsaw: Tipografiia Varshavskogo uchebnogo okruga, 1901), 35–36. Both had a gold jeweled crown next to them at the banquet: Ibid., 37–38. For Russia's relations with the Empire in these years, see most recently K. Iu. Erusalimskii and I. Shvarts [Iskra Schwarcz], "Missiia Zhdana Kvashnina v Sviashchennoi Rimskoi Imperii: K istorii rossiisko-imperskikh otnoshenii XVI veka," *Peterburgskie slaviankie i balkanskie issledovaniia* 1, 23 (2018): 71–104.

[134] Filiushkin, *Izobretaia pervuiu voinu*, 745; Jakob Ulfeldt, *Hodoeporicon Ruthenicum* (Frankfurt: Matthias Becker, Ioannis Theodoris, and Ioannis Israelis de Bry, 1608), 32–34, Russian in *ChOIDR*, 1–4 (1883) (ref. to 2, 29–31); Iakov Ul'feldt, *Puteshestvie v Rossiiu*. Translated by L. N. Godovikova (Moscow: Iazyki slavianskoi kul'tury, 2002).

[135] *PDS* I, 765, 785.

[136] Zimin, *V kanun groznykh potriasenii*, 10; B. N. Floria, *Russko-pol'skie otnosheniia i baltiiskii vopros v kontse shestnadtsatogo–nachale semnadtsatogo v.* (Moscow: Nauka, 1973), 54–56, 113–115. In 1567–71, Ivan had put out feelers about the possible candidacy of Ivan Ivanovich: Ibid., 36–38. See also V. Novodvorskii [Witold Nowodworski], *Bor'ba za Livoniiu mezhdu Moskvoiu i Rech'iu Pospolitoiu (1570–1582)*. Zapiski istoriko-filologicheskogo fakul'teta imperatorskogo Sankt-Peterburgskogo universiteta 72 (St. Petersburg: Tipografiia I. N. Skorokhodova, 1904), 8–28; and Henryk Lulewicz, *Gniewów o unię ciąg dalszy: Stosunki polsko-litewskie w latach 1569–1588* (Warsaw: Instytut Historii Polskiej Akademii Nauk, 2002), 96–114.

[137] *RK 1475–1598*, 227, 236; *RK 1550–1636*, vol. I, 180 (with Boris Godunov). The men with full *rynda* rank, P. Iu. Iur'ev, F. I. Godunov, B. F. Godunov, and V. L. Saltykov, were all the sons of Oprichnina boyars or other ranks in the Oprichnina.

with the tsarevich, including Godunov.[138] In the 1572 campaigns, his *ryndy* once more included Godunov, and Tsarevich Ivan commanded, at least in name, the Great Regiment.[139] In 1576, 1577, and 1579 again, the elder tsarevich took the field with his complement of *ryndy*, although with different men each time.[140] Boris Godunov was no longer among them. In 1575 his sister had married Tsarevich Fyodor, and Godunov disappeared from the military records in the middle of the 1570s only to reappear again in 1579 as *kravchii*, one of the court officers who followed the tsar on his campaign.[141] Ivan Ivanovich then disappeared from the *razriad* record from this point until his death, though it is not clear whether that was because he did not go on the campaigns or because there is a gap in the records. From all this evidence, it seems that there was no one appointed to bring up or supervise him at any point. He went from his mother to his father, and then to military commands under his father's eye.

In the middle of these military campaigns, Tsarevich Ivan married. The wedding took place on November 4, 1571, a week after Ivan IV's own wedding to his third wife, Marfa Sobakina, who died a few weeks later. The young Ivan's bride, Evdokiia Bogdanovna Saburova, came from the same clan as Vasilii III's first wife, Solomoniia Saburova. The marriage did not last long, for sometime before 1575 Evdokiia became a nun in the Pokrov Monastery in Suzdal', presumably not of her own choice.[142] In 1575, Ivan Ivanovich married again, this time to Pelageia Petrova-Solovaia, the daughter of a provincial nobleman from Riazan', probably a few months after his father's fifth wedding, this time to Anna Vasil'chikova. Like her predecessor, Pelageia also became a nun, though in Belozero, approximately in 1579–80.[143] Finally, in 1580, Tsarevich Ivan married Elena Sheremeteva. Exactly when is not known, but this wedding as well seems to have been coordinated with his father's seventh and last marriage in that year, to Mariia Nagaia, the mother of the ill-fated Tsarevich Dmitrii.[144] Why the first two wives of the tsarevich, Evdokiia and Pelageia, were repudiated is unknown. It could have been a failure to produce an heir, or it could have been a result of the politics of the court. In any case, Elena Ivanovna Sheremeteva came from an old boyar family

[138] *RK 1475–1598*, 240; *RK 1550–1636*, vol. I, 188. Boris Godunov has a more honorable position in the former version.

[139] *RK 1475–1598*, 244; *RK 1550–1636*, vol. I, 196–198, 202.

[140] *RK 1475–1598*, 260, 276, 293 [141] Ibid., 292, 295.

[142] Martin, *A Bride for the Tsar*, 133–137; *PSRL* 34, 228. The source is the seventeenth-century Moscow Chronicle, probably a text of 1635–45: Ia. G. Solodkin, "Moskovskii letopisets," *SKKDR* XVII, pt. 2, 1993, 252–254. Saburova's male relatives, including her father, were in the Oprichnina or soon entered it: Zimin, *Oprichnina*, 350.

[143] Zimin, *V kanun groznykh potriasenii*, 91; *PSRL* 34, 228.

[144] Martin, *A Bride for the Tsar*, 148, 158–160,

that had come into prominence around the middle of the century. One of her uncles, however, Nikita Vasil'evich Sheremetev, had been executed in 1563 or 1564, perhaps as a result of the defeat at the battle on the river Ula near Polotsk in January 1564. Her father was Ivan Vasil'evich Men'shoi Sheremetev, who had died in battle in 1577. Ivan IV had trusted neither him nor his older brother Ivan Vasil'evich Bol'shoi, a monk since early 1571, with his own history of disfavor with the tsar.[145] In the tsar's epistle to the Kirillo-Belozerskii Monastery of 1573, he not only reproached Ivan Bol'shoi for living more grandly than his monastic vows permitted, but also accused his brothers, Ivan Men'shoi and Fyodor, of encouraging the Crimeans to attack Russia.[146] The only prominent Sheremetev in the later years of Ivan's reign was the same Fyodor Vasil'evich Sheremetev, an *okol'nichii*, the uncle of Elena Ivanovna. He was one of the boyars in the "land" (*zemlia*) part of the duma, not the Oprichnina, on the eve of the death of Ivan the Terrible.[147] Normally historians view the ruling elite in the last years of Ivan's rule as divided between the more aristocratic "land" boyars and the "court" (*dvor*) boyars, the former *oprichniki*.[148] In other words, Ivan married his heir to the daughter and niece of men he suspected of treason. Was Ivan in this way trying to conciliate the *zemskie boiare*? Historians have not attempted to explain the marriage.[149]

There is little reliable information on Tsarevich Ivan as an adult. No ceremony of "placing" him on the throne took place. There is no way of knowing whether his voice was really heard in the discussions he attended on military or political matters. One thing is clear: he never got a new title and remained only the tsarevich, but that was also the title that his brothers Fyodor held. In a few documents he has a better title. In correspondence from 1564 with the Crimean khan, Ivan Ivanovich is called "autocrat" (*samoderzhets*), and later in 1565 he is even called "heir" (*naslednik*), both titles best understood as responses to the situation of

[145] Zimin, *Oprichnina*, 109–110, 439, note 7; Zimin, *V kanun groznykh potriasenii*, 11, 91. Sheremetev, however, had supported Ivan's son Dmitrii in the succession crisis of 1553: Zimin, *Reformy Ivana Groznogo*, 410.

[146] V. P. Adrianova-Peretts, D. S. Likhachev, and Ia. S. Lur'e, eds., *Poslaniia Ivana Groznogo*(Moscow and Leningrad: Izdatel'stvo Akademii nauk SSSR, 1951), 191. Returning prisoners from Crimea reported somewhat later that the Sheremetevs were in contact with the khan: Ibid., 639.

[147] Skrynnikov, *Tsarstvo terrora*, 515. Sheremetev did not attain boyar rank until after the death of Ivan: Zimin, *V kanun groznykh potriasenii*, 113.

[148] Zimin, *V kanun groznykh potriasenii*, 81–104; Skrynnikov, *Tsarstvo terrora*, 508–521.

[149] Zimin and Skrynnikov both concentrated on explaining the death of Ivan Ivanovich, noting the hostility of Ivan to the Sheremetev clan: Zimin, *V kanun groznykh potriasenii*, 91–93; Skrynnikov, *Rossiia posle Oprichniny*, 92–93. Martin noted only that it was highly unusual for the tsar or his heir to marry a woman from such an aristocratic family: Martin, *A Bride for the Tsar*, 158.

those moments.[150] Ivan the Terrible himself confirmed that his son had no new title, for in August 1581 he ordered that the papal envoy Antonio Possevino be told that Russian documents need not be written in the name of the tsar and the tsarevichi as well because "my son Ivan has not yet been honored with the name of sovereign and my son Fyodor has not attained the age when he can rule the state with us."[151] Yet Ivan's statement was somewhat disingenuous. Pope Gregory XIII had sent Possevino to Russia to negotiate a peace with Poland and make an alliance against the Turks, and supplied his envoy with letters not only to the tsar but to the tsaritsa and to the tsarevichi Ivan and Fyodor.[152] As was usual by that time, Ivan Ivanovich appeared in the record of decisions after his father and before the boyars, and he participated in the audiences.[153] Ivan Ivanovich also sent a letter to the Pope in September with Possevino as he left Russia, repeating his father's willingness to make an alliance against the Turks. In the letter, Ivan Ivanovich titled himself only as the son of Tsar Ivan Vasil'evich, followed by his father's full title.[154] Ivan's instructions explain the formulary of his son's letter to Rome. They also give a hint of his understanding of the role of his sons in the state: Fyodor was too young to rule (*praviti*) the state with him, and Ivan had not yet acquired the title of a sovereign, which implies that he could participate in ruling the state but not as a sovereign like his father.

Even though Ivan Ivanovich did not receive a sovereign title, he figured in his father's testaments, both the lost version(s) and the extant text that never came into force because of the young man's death.[155] The testament of Ivan IV survives only in an eighteenth-century copy, which most historians have dated to the 1570s. It has two parts, a long introductory passage of edifying repentance followed by the concrete testamentary provisions. Both parts are amplified versions of the surviving testaments of earlier rulers, particularly of Ivan III. In it, Ivan Grozny blessed Ivan Ivanovich with the tsardom and then apportioned out the personal domain of the tsar, with the bulk of it going to Ivan Ivanovich, including

[150] Filiushkin, *Tituly russkikh gosudarei*, 59–60, 95. I owe these observations and their interpretation to Charles Halperin, personal communication on July 5, 2012.

[151] "Иван сын еще государским именем не почтен, а Федор сын того возраста не дошел, как ему с нами государство правити." *PDS* X, 128–130; Nitsche, *Großfürst und Thronfolger*, 323.

[152] *PDS* X, 85–86, 88–90. [153] *PDS* X, 5, 39, 72–73.

[154] *Dopolneniia k aktam istoricheskim, otnosiashchimsia k Rossii* (St. Petersburg: Eduard Prats, 1848), 7 (Latin summary of the letter, dated September 7090); I. V. Dubrovskii, "Issledovaniia o diplomaticheskoi perepiske Ivana Groznogo," *Russkii sbornik* 24 (2018): 84–86 (German translation of the letter to the Pope, September 7090).

[155] Ivan seems to have had earlier testaments. In the description of the 1553 succession crisis, the *Tsarstvennaia kniga* refers to a testament naming Dmitrii Ivanovich as his heir: *PSRL* XIII, 523.

the newly acquired territories such as Kazan'. Effectively it created an *udel* for Fyodor, but none of that mattered because of the sudden death of Ivan Ivanovich on November 9, 1581.[156] The Jesuit envoy Antonio Possevino asserted in his 1586 book *Moscovia* that Ivan killed his son in a fit of rage, but Possevino told a very different story in his private correspondence with the Vatican.[157] There is actually no evidence for the story that Ivan killed his son other than Possevino and later rumors. Whatever the cause of death, the remaining sons were then Fyodor and the infant Dmitrii, son of Ivan IV and his last wife.[158] Elena, the widow of Ivan Ivanovich, became a nun in the Novodevichii Convent outside Moscow.[159]

The only hint we have of the life of Tsarevich Ivan Ivanovich beyond the brief records of his military service and court events is his redaction of the life of Antonii Siiskii, a northern Russian monastic saint. Saint Antonii (1478–1557) was one of a number of sixteenth-century monks who lived in or founded monasteries in the Russian north, in ecclesiastical terms under the Archbishop of Novgorod. In 1578, the monk Iona wrote a life of Antonii, and a year later Ivan Ivanovich produced a new redaction.[160] It was the hegumen Pitirim of the monastery, Metropolitan Antonii (1572–81), and others who persuaded Ivan Ivanovich to take on the task. He had already heard of Antonii from his father and the boyars (*velmozhi*). The text as revised by Ivan was a fairly typical life of a saintly monk, a good example of the central place of monastic spirituality in the Orthodoxy of

[156] In the document, Ivan calls his son consistently "my son Ivan" without any title. *DDG*, 426–444; For the date of the testament, see Günter Stökl, *Testament und Siegel Ivans IV* (Wiesbaden: Westdeutscher Verlag, 1972); S. B. Veselovskii, "Dukhovnoe zaveshchanie Ivana Groznogo kak istoricheskii istochnik," in S. B. Veselovskii, *Issledovaniia po istorii Oprichniny* (Moscow: Akademiia nauk SSSR, 1963), 320–322; R. G. Skrynnikov, "Dukhovnoe zaveshchaniia tsaria Ivana Groznogo," *TODRL* 21 (1965): 309–318; A. L. Iurganov, "O date napisaniia zaveshchaniia Ivana Groznogo," *Otechestvennaia istoriia* 6 (1993): 125–141; Halperin, *Ivan the Terrible*, 243–244. A recent attempt to demonstrate that the testament is a nineteenth-century forgery is unconvincing: Cornelia Soldat, *Das Testament Ivans des Schrecklichen von 1572: Eine kritische Aufklärung* (Lewiston, New York, Queenston, and Lampeter: The Edwin Mellen Press, 2013).

[157] Paul Bushkovitch, "Possevino and the Death of Tsarevich Ivan Ivanovich," *Cahiers du monde russe* 55, 1–2 (2014): 119–134; Halperin, *Ivan the Terrible*, 250–253.

[158] Zimin, *V kanun groznykh potriasenii*, 90–95.

[159] *PSRL* 34, 228. The same source reported that she received from the tsar also the town of Lukh as well as another volost', Stavrova, both apparently to the northeast of Moscow.

[160] N. Tupikov, "Literaturnaia deiatel'nost' tsarevicha Ivana Ivanovicha," *Zhurnal Ministerstva Narodnago Prosveshcheniia* 296 (December 1894): 358–374; L. A. Dmitriev, "Zhitie Antoniia Siiskogo," *SKKDR* II, pt. 1, 247–248; L. A. Dmitriev, "Ivan Ivanovich," *SKKDR* II, pt. 1, 384–386; L. A. Dmitriev, "Iona," *SKKDR* II, pt. 1, 427–430; A. S. Gerd, ed., *Zhitie Antoniia Siiskogo* (St. Petersburg: Izdatel'stvo Sankt-Peterburgskogo Universiteta, 2003) (the version of Ivan Ivanovich).

sixteenth-century Russia, for laymen as well as clergy.[161] In the text, Ivan not only glorified the saintly monk, but also described himself as "of the generation of Augustus, of the tribe of the Varangians, by birth - a Russian."[162] This was the circle of ideas from the *Tale of the Vladimir Princes* and the *Book of Degrees*. The texts seem to have had an effect, for Antonii had appeared in the official list of saints to be commemorated by 1610 at the latest.[163]

In any case, the death of Ivan Ivanovich made his younger brother Fyodor the heir. Tsarevich Fyodor seems to have lived very differently from his elder brother. As would be expected from the many accounts of his physical and perhaps mental weakness, he rarely appeared in the military or court records. He did join his brother and father for the 1572 campaign and had *ryndy* like his brother, though fewer. In May, 1577, however, the tsar left Fyodor, now twenty years old, back in Novgorod away from the fighting, with the boyar Dmitrii Ivanovich Godunov, Boris Godunov (still *kravchii*), and others with some thirty men of lesser ranks. He also left him with a tutor (*diad'ka*), Grigorii Vasil'evich Godunov. In September 1580, at the marriage of Tsar Ivan to Mariia Nagaia at Aleksandrova Sloboda, Tsarevich Fyodor stood in for the bride's father at the ceremony.[164] This is the first reference to anyone with the position of tutor in sixteenth-century Russia. In spring 1583, in the last army list of Ivan the Terrible's life, Tsarevich Fyodor accompanied the army on a campaign against rebels around Kazan'. Fyodor also had with him two *diad'ki*, G. V. Godunov again and A. P. Kleshin.[165] The two *diad'ki* were not important boyars, though of course G. V. Godunov was part of the clan of the future Tsar Boris. G. V. Godunov does not appear in any of the records other than these two times as *diad'ka*, and achieved boyar rank and the office of *dvoretskii* only in the months after Fyodor ascended the throne. Kleshin was another supporter of the Godunovs, who was raised to the status of *okol'nichii* from that of *dumnyi dvorianin* in 1586.[166]

161 Bushkovitch, *Religion and Society in Russia: The Sixteenth and Seventeenth Centuries* (New York, New York: Oxford University Press, 1992), 10–50.

162 Tupikov, "Literaturnaia deiatel'nost' tsarevicha Ivana Ivanovicha," 369; Gerd, *Zhitie Antoniia Siiskogo*: "kolena avgustova, ot plemeni variazhskogo, rodom rusina bliz vostochnyia strany, mezh predel slovenskykh i variazhskykh i agariankykh. Izhe naritsaetsia Rus' po reke Ruse," 15.

163 Bushkovitch, *Religion and Society in Russia*, 87, 209.

164 *RK 1550–1636*, vol. I, 329. Ivan Ivanovich was the *tysiatskii* for the wedding.

165 Ibid., vol. I, 254, 351. For the 1576 meeting of the tsar and Kobenzl, Fyodor accompanied the party to Mozhaisk but did not meet the ambassador: *PDS* I 481, 512–513.

166 Zimin, *V kanun groznykh potriasenii*, 112, 133–134.; A. P. Pavlov, *Gosudarev dvor i politicheskaia bor'ba pri Borise Godunove, 1584–1604* (St. Petersburg: Nauka, 1992), 33.

The appearance of a tutor for the tsarevich may have been prompted by Fyodor's disabilities, whatever they were. Information about the institution is scarce, and comes almost entirely from the period after the Time of Troubles. Furthermore, such information as there is mostly about the political role of the tutors as the tsarevichi grew to manhood and ascended the throne, not what the duties of the tutor were. These were presumably the supervision of each boy and his education, particularly during the temporary absences of his father the tsar. It was a practice in many European monarchies. In Spain the tutor of the heir was called an *ayo*, and all the heirs to Spanish monarchy had such a tutor.[167]

The Last Years of Ivan IV

The last years of Ivan IV's life were taken up with the end of the Livonian War. A truce with Poland in 1582 left Russia's western border exactly where it had been in 1558, and a year later the truce with Sweden was even worse: Ivan lost all his conquests in Livonia but also Ingria on the Gulf of Finland to the Swedes. Sweden and Poland divided up Livonia. While Ivan was digesting these defeats, the issue of succession remained, and remained the more acute after the death of Ivan Ivanovich.

It would not fit the pattern of the reign of Ivan the Terrible if there were not one final curious episode. That is Ivan's attempt to find an eighth wife in England, and his plans for the succession if that attempt were to succeed. As we know, Ivan had married his seventh and last wife, Mariia Nagaia, on September 6, 1580, and Mariia gave birth to Dmitrii on October 19, 1582, the subsequent object of so much contention in the Time of Troubles.[168] While Mariia was pregnant, Ivan sent an embassy to Queen Elizabeth of England, primarily to discuss commercial issues. The embassy left in August 1582, before the tsaritsa had given birth. Ivan's ambassador, Fyodor Andreevich Pisemskii, had before him another task besides the settlement of commercial issues. Apparently Ivan had consulted his English doctor Robert Jacob ("Roman Elizarov") about relatives of the English queen who would make suitable brides. Jacob

[167] Martha K. Hoffman, *Raised to Rule: Educating Royalty at the Court of the Spanish Habsburgs 1601–1634* (Baton Rouge, Louisiana: Louisiana State University Press, 2011). In England Henry, Prince of Wales had a chamberlain, who seems to have been more like the Spanish *ayo* or the Russian *diad'ka*, as well as a tutor who actually taught the prince languages and other subjects: Roy Strong, , *Henry Prince of Wales and England's Lost Renaissance* (London: Thames and Hudson, 1986), 27–28.

[168] Martin, *A Bride for the Tsar*, 156. In theory, the marriage to Mariia was uncanonical, since Ivan had already married six wives, well beyond the permitted number, three. Yet the church included her in prayers for the dead along with the first three wives: Ibid., 162–163.

suggested Lady Mary Hastings, the sister of Henry Hastings, third Earl of Huntingdon. Pisemskii was in England over the winter, and discussed the issue with Elizabeth on January 18, 1583. The queen told him that Hastings was not beautiful enough for the tsar, for she had suffered from smallpox (*vospitsa*) and her face was red and pockmarked. Pisemskii, however, would not be put off: the tsar had ordered him to tell the queen that Mary would have her own court, but she would have to convert. Elizabeth asked him about Ivan's plans for her, including succession. The answer was that Ivan had a son Fyodor "and his [future] children" and that if Ivan and Mary were to have sons, they would be given appanages "according to their sovereign rank" (*po ikh gosudarskomu chinu*), and Ivan would treat them "equally in degree with Fyodor" (*v rovenstve po stepeni so tsarevichem Fedorom*). Then the queen asked about possible daughters: to whom had the Russian monarchs married their daughters? Ivan's father had no daughters, but his grandfather's daughter (Elena) had married the king of Poland, was the answer. Needless to say, the Hastings plan went nowhere. Elizabeth was not enthusiastic. When Pisemskii returned to Russia in the summer of 1583, he came with Sir Jerome Bowes as the English ambassador.[169] Bowes did not press the issue, and neither did Ivan.[170] The next March Ivan died. What he had been thinking we can only guess. If Mariia Nagaia had produced a girl and no more heirs, then the only heir would have been Fyodor. Fyodor had no children and was not himself healthy, so there would have been a reason to look for another wife after Mariia. The answer to Elizabeth's question about sons suggests that any such sons of Ivan and Mary Hastings would have indeed been in line for the throne. As a ruler, it seems Ivan must have thought about these possibilities, but we can only infer that he might have.

Ivan's reign, with its wars, crises, and multiple marriages, created a series of problems for the succession, but we know very little about his intentions and plans. Only two modest conclusions are possible. The first is that Ivan and his contemporaries considered Ivan Ivanovich the heir, even if they did not use the word. The second is that the sources do not

[169] Elizabeth instructed Bowes to offer reasons why the marriage was not feasible: Tolstoi, *Pervye sorok let snoshenii mezhdu Rossiei i Anglieiu*, 204 (May 1583). A similar version of the story is given in Jerome Horsey's manuscript account of experiences with Russia: Sir Jerome Horsey, "Travels," in *Rude and Barbarous Kingdom: Russia in the Accounts of Sixteenth-Century English Voyagers*, ed. Lloyd E. Berry and Robert O. Crummey (Madison, Wisconsin: University of Wisconsin Press, 1969), 300–301.

[170] *SRIO* 38, 65–67; Isabel de Madariaga, *Ivan the Terrible: First Tsar of Russia* (New Haven, Connecticut: Yale University Press, 2005), 344–345, 348–349. Lady Mary had died by 1589: Claire Cross, *The Puritan Earl: The Life of Henry Hastings, Third Earl of Huntingdon 1536–1595* (London: Macmillan, 1966), 29–30, 286.

permit us to show a conscious policy establishing primogeniture. Both sons bore the same title, tsarevich, if the word is to be taken as a title and not just a patronymic. Around 1575 Fyodor married Irina Godunova, the sister of the increasingly influential Boris: it is characteristic of the sources of those years that the exact date is not known.[171] It would seem that the marriage had no effect on the position of Fyodor. His elder brother remained at the center of the court, if not with power, while the younger remained in the shadow. As we have seen, Ivan made clear who was to be his heir primarily by the continuous public association of his eldest son Ivan with him in the governance of the state. Although there was no public coronation or placing of Ivan Ivanovich on the throne, the eldest tsarevich appeared with his father during military campaigns (eventually receiving his own command), in diplomatic audiences, and apparently at some of the occasions when the tsar met with the boyars to decide on political affairs. From the few references to Tsarevich Fyodor in the later years of Ivan's life, including after 1581, it seems that Fyodor too was brought into the army at least to associate him with the rule of his father.

Tsar Fyodor: The End of the Riurikovich Dynasty

The last representative of the Riurikovich dynasty on the Russian throne, Tsar Fyodor Ivanovich, ascended the throne without any obstacle. This was the case in spite of the complete absence of any reference to a testament from Ivan IV.[172] The only surviving testament had become out of date with the death of Ivan Ivanovich, and there is no reference in any source to the composition of another one. After this moment, Russian tsars do not seem to have composed a testament. Historians have argued whether there was an informal regency council or not, especially since all contemporary sources report ongoing disputes and intrigues among the boyars even if they differ in details. R. G. Skrynnikov even tried to prove that an Assembly of the Land elected Fyodor tsar, while Zimin rejected this conception. Cherepnin tried to prove that an assembly did meet but did not elect Fyodor, who was already recognized as tsar by that time.[173] In part, the problem is that historians have tried make consistent all the

171 Zimin, *V kanun groznykh potriasenii*, 249.

172 Horsey did mention that Ivan on his deathbed "peruseth over his will," but obviously Horsey was not there and his manuscript account was written after 1613: Horsey, "Travels," 306.

173 Skrynnikov, *Rossiia posle Oprichniny*, 14–16; Zimin, *V kanun groznykh potriasenii*, 117–120; Cherepnin, *Zemskie sobory Russkogo gosudarstva*, 125–133; A. P. Pavlov, *Gosudarev dvor*, 219–221; Ia. G. Solodkin, *Zemskie sobory Moskovskoi Rusi kontsa XVI veka: Spornye problemy istorii i istoriografii* (Nizhnevartovsk: Izdatel'stvo Nizhnevartovskogo gosudarstvennogo gumanitarnogo universiteta, 2010), 41–62.

sources, Russian and foreign, early and late. The Russian narrative sources are all later and highly partisan, having been composed after the death of Boris Godunov, during and after the Time of Troubles. For the weeks around the accession of Tsar Fyodor the only accounts are the reports of foreign diplomats, the English emissaries, and the Polish diplomat Lew Sapieha, and the summaries of some of the latter's reports in the correspondence of the papal nuncio Alberto Bolognetti.

The emissary of Queen Elizabeth, Sir Jerome Bowes, left a description of this time in Moscow from the autumn of 1583 to the end of May 1584 that was published in 1589 by the English clergyman and writer Richard Hakluyt. Bowes did not mention a sobor and described Fyodor's succession to power as normal and unremarkable. Bowes was kept isolated immediately after the death of Ivan on March 18/19, 1584, and left Moscow on May 29, before Fyodor's coronation.[174] The basis for Skrynnikov's assertions was another English source, the description of the same weeks from Jerome Horsey, an English commercial agent in Russia at that time. Horsey said that the boyars B. F. Godunov, Prince I. F. Mstislavskii, Nikita Romanov-Iur'ev, and Prince B. Ia. Bel'skii "were appointed to settle and dispose his [Ivan the Terrible's] son Fyodor Ivanovich, having sworn one another, and all the nobility and officers whosoever." Then a "parliament" met on May 4.[175] Zimin, following a suggestion from N. N. Pavlenko, thought that this "parliament" was actually a church council. This is not likely, however, as in England an assembly of the Anglican church was already called a "convocation," not a parliament, and the ancient councils of the church were called councils. An Englishman of the sixteenth century was not likely to use the wrong terms. According to Horsey, the "parliament" included representatives of the gentry and clergy and dealt with affairs of state and the coronation, but he said nothing about an election of the tsar. Horsey later described the coronation in some detail.[176] The English reports thus support

[174] Sir Jerome Bowes, "The Ambassage of Sir Hierome Bowes to the Emperour of Muscovie 1583," in *The Principall Navigations, Voiages and Discoveries of the English Nation*, ed. Richard Hakluyt (London: George Bishop and Ralph Newberie, deputies to Christopher Barker, 1589), vol. 1, 487–500, 499 ("the newe Emperour").

[175] Jerome Horsey, "The Most Solemn and Magnificent Coronation of Pheodore Ivanowiche, Emperour of Russia," in *The Principall Navigations, Voiages and Discoveries of the English Nation*, ed. Richard Hakluyt (London: George Bishop and Ralph Newberie, deputies to Christopher Barker, 1589), vol. 1, 819–825; also in *The Principall Navigations, Voiages and Discoveries of the English Nation*, ed. Richard Hakluyt, 1599 edition, vol. 1, 466–470.

[176] Skrynnikov also further confused the situation by his assertion that Horsey dated the events by the Gregorian calendar: R. G. Skrynnikov *Rossiia nakanune "Smutnogo vremeni"* (Moscow: Mysl', 1980), 15. England adopted the Gregorian calendar in 1752. See also A. S. Sevast'ianova, ed., *Dzherom Gorsei: Zapiski o Rossii kontsa XVI–nachala*

Cherepnin's view of the events, a sobor but not an election of the tsar. The English reports, however, have one defect: they were both published fairly soon after the events and such publications were often made with omissions for political or other reasons. The originals have not survived.

In contrast, the contemporary Polish and Vatican reports do not have this defect. It is true that on the eve of Ivan the Terrible's death King Stefan Batory of Poland and the nuncio Bolognetti did expect an election of the new tsar, perhaps Stefan himself, or Prince Konstanty Wasyl Ostrogski, the Orthodox woewoda of Kiev, because of Fyodor's "madness."[177] The notion that the Russian tsar would be elected was not just based on Fyodor's incompetence to rule but was also part of the plan of Stefan Batory to expand Poland to the east.[178] The events did not follow his expectations. The letter of the Polish emissary Lew Sapieha of April 26, 1584, from Moscow to Prince Krzysztof Radziwiłł reported that the Russian conductor (*pristav*) met him "at the Moscow river" (presumably Dorogomilovo) and related the story "from the young grand prince about his father's death and that, according to the blessing of his father, he had sat upon the Moscow state."[179] The Polish envoy was then locked up in the residence for ambassadors, which did not surprise him as he had heard that the new sovereign was very ill and had little reason (*rozumu swego mało ma*). When Sapieha came to the palace, the boyars sent out the Shchelkalov brothers (Andrei, the head of the Ambassadorial Office, and Vasilii), Fyodor Borisovich (obviously Boris Fyodorovich) Godunov, and Prince F. M. Trubetskoi to talk to him. They wanted Sapieha to carry out his mission, since the new tsar was "not alien, but a born sovereign, like the first, and in addition had sat upon his father's throne according to his father's blessing during his lifetime." Then Sapieha described the attempted April revolt of Prince Bogdan Bel'skii, the last favorite of the deceased Ivan.[180] The letter reached King Stefan around May 16 (NS),

XVII veka (Moscow: Izdatel'stvo MGU, 1990), 209. Horsey's date, June 10, was not the result of the new calendar but just a mistake: Horsey, "Travels," 314, note 3.

177 *Monumenta Poloniae vaticana*, 8 vols. (Warsaw: Komisja Historyczna Akademii Umiejętności w Krakowie, 1908–48), vol. VII, 178–179 (the "pazzia" of Fyodor, also called "mentecatto"), 201.

178 B. N. Floria, *Russko-pol'skie otnosheniia i politicheskoe razvitie Vostochnoi Evropy vo vtoroi polovine XVI–nachale XVII v.* (Moscow: Nauka, 1978), 120–140.

179 "od młodego kniazia wielkiego o śmierci ojca jego, i o tem iż on za błogosławieństwem ojca swego usiadł na państwie moskiewskim," in *Archiwum domu Radziwiłłów*. Scriptores rerum polonicarum VIII (Kraków: Nakład Księcia Antoniego Radziwiłła, 1885), 174. The Polish text was clearly using Russian terminology. The letter remained in the family archive until it was published in the nineteenth century:

180 "to nie obcy, ale przyrodzony Hospodar, także jako i pierwszy, a ktemu iż za błogosławieństwem ojca swego jeszcze za żywota jego na stolicy ojcowskiej usiadł . . .," in *Archiwum domu Radziwiłłów*, 174–175.

and nuncio Bolognetti summarized it in his letter to the cardinal of Como in Rome.[181] From Grodno, on May 29 the nuncio wrote to Rome that almost at once three Russian emissaries had arrived; the first of them "had recounted the death of the grand prince and the succession of the eldest son according to the blessing of his father, as he said."[182] A month later the nuncio summarized another letter from Sapieha that he learned about from the king or his courtiers. It contained a description of the dissension between the boyars N. R. Iur'ev-Romanov and Prince I. P. Shuiskii. In Bolognetti's account, Sapieha thought that Iur'ev-Romanov was the main figure in the government. The "elected" Grand Prince Fyodor had given him the management of the most important business: "il Gran Duca eletto, subito dopo l'elettione, diede il maneggio de' negotii più importanti."[183] The letter from Sapieha himself from June 10, however, says nothing about an election.[184] It is unclear why Bolognetti wrote of Tsar Fyodor as "elected," but King Stefan in his correspondence with his chancellor Jan Zamoyski also said nothing about election, instead relating that the boyars had "put in" (*inauguratus*) Fyodor.[185]

In Sweden there were hopes similar to King Stefan's, if not plans. On April 16, 1584, Pontus De la Gardie, the viceroy of Swedish Livonia, wrote to the viceroy of Novgorod, Prince Vasilii Skopin-Shuiskii, about prolonging the truce between the two countries. He sent the letter because he had learned that Tsar Ivan had died and that "in his place they had elected as grand prince his son Fyodor to the rank of his father and crowned him."[186] The letter does not prove that there was an election, since it refers to the coronation as a fact, but was written six weeks

[181] In Moscow "il figliuolo pazzo si trova in possessione." *MPV* VII, 248.

[182] "haver conto della morte del duca vecchio et dell' esser succeduto il figliuolo maggiore, come disse per la benedittione del padre." *MPV* VII, 275

[183] *MPV* VII, 315 (June 20, 1584 NS).

[184] A. I. Turgenev, ed., *Historica Russiae monumenta* (St. Petersburg: Eduard Prats, 1842), vol. 2, 2–3.

[185] Jósef Siemieński, ed., *Archiwum Jana Zamoyskiego* (Warsaw: Komisja Historyczna Akademii Umiejętności w Krakowie, 1913), vol. 3, 310 (May 23, 1584, King Stefan to Zamoyski), 322–323 (May 29, 1584, Zamoyski to Possevino). On Sapieha's mission, see Arkadiusz Czwołek, *Piórem i Buławą: Działalność polityczna Lwa Sapiehy kanczlerza litewskiego, wojewody wileńskiego* (Toruń: Wydawnictwo Naukowe Uniwersytetu Mikołaja Kopernika, 2012), 30–36, quoting AGAD AR (Archiwum Radziwiłłów) II, nr. 134, k 1–2, letter of Lew Sapieha to Batory from Moscow, May 20, 1584. According to Czwołek, Lew Sapieha reported that Dmitrii was not eligible for the throne since he was the son of Ivan's sixth wife, so Fyodor had to be the tsar in spite of his physical problems (Czwołek, *Piórem i Buławą*, 32). See also Sapieha, July 10, 1584, *HRM* II, no. 3, 3.

[186] "на его место избрали в великие князья сына его Федора на степень отца его и коруновали," *SRIO* 129, 361–362.

before the coronation took place on May 31.[187] The Russians did not bother to correct De la Gardie's error. The answering letter merely stated that "with God's help according to the blessing of his father, his son our sovereign tsar and grand prince Fyodor Ivanovich came to rule his states."[188] Perhaps De la Gardie was influenced by the Swedish custom of referring to their kings as "chosen" before their coronation, though since 1544 Sweden was a hereditary monarchy.[189] There is no contemporary source that confirms the suggestion that there was an election of the tsar in 1584.

The few contemporary Russian sources tell the same story, that there was no election. The council decisions of the church council of 2 July, 1584, contain the statement that Tsar Fyodor ascended to the throne "according to the blessing of his father . . . having taken up the scepter of the Russian tsardom."[190] This was the now traditional formula, as in Sapieha's dispatches. The coronation text for Tsar Fyodor repeated the formula of the 1547 coronation (second version), and both Fyodor and Metropolitan Dionisii said in their speeches that the tsar father Ivan had blessed his son, the heir (*naslednik*), with the tsardom, as of old the grand princes had blessed their sons (omitting the word "first") with the princedom. Fyodor also was to have asserted that his father ordered him to have the title "Tsar and Grand Prince, *otchich i dedich i naslednik Rossiiskogo tsarstviia* (inheritor from his father and grandfather of the Russian tsardom)."[191] Thus Tsar Fyodor came to the throne by his father's blessing, but also as the heir to the Russian tsardom. Later on in the service, Metropolitan Dionisii repeated the formula from the second version of Ivan's coronation text, wishing long life to Tsar Fyodor with his Tsaritsa Irina and asking God that Fyodor might see his grandsons "in his tsardom" (*na svoem tsarstvii*).[192] At the end of his homily, the metropolitan gave his blessing and that of the clergy to the tsar, his tsaritsa, and the children given by God.[193] The element of heredity at the coronation

187 Skrynnikov did not notice the discrepancy in time: Skrynnikov, *Rossiia nakanune "Smutnogo vremeni,"* 16.

188 "з Божьею помочью по благословению отца своего сын его государь наш царь и великий князь Федор Иванович всеа Русии сел на своих государствах," *SRIO* 129, 366–367

189 Emil Hildebrand, *Svenska statsförfattningens historiska utveckling* (Stockholm: P. A. Norstedt, 1896), 220–226; see 224, note 1.

190 "по благословенью отца своего . . . взем скипетр Российского царсвия," *SGGD* I, 593; Cherepnin, *Zemskie sobory Russkogo gosudarstva*, 130–131. The July council consisted of the church (*osviashchennyi sobor*) and the Duma and discussed church lands. This was clearly a different assembly from that reported by Horsey for May 4.

191 *SGGD* II, 72–85, 75–76 (quotation). The formula seems to imply legitimate inheritor, as in land transactions: *Akty iuridicheskogo byta* (St. Petersburg: n.p., 1864), vol. II, 343 (1511).

192 *SGGD* II, 79. 193 *SGGD* II, 82.

was now no longer just on paper, as in the second version of Ivan's coronation text, but proclaimed aloud to all the clergy, boyars, and people witnessing the event. Heredity was there, but not primogeniture.

Heredity and Dynasty

The hereditary claim was not confined to the coronation ceremony. In the later years of the reign of Ivan the Terrible, the claim appeared in very different contexts, namely in certain of the letters that Ivan sent to foreign rulers and in a series of historical narratives. Most of those narratives were connected with the court or the church elite.

Heredity did not play a role in the early writings on saintly princes in the ancestry of the Moscow dynasty that were still read in the sixteenth century. The main text to touch on the issue of genealogy and succession was the *Tale of the Vladimir Princes*, attributed to Spiridon-Savva, who was briefly (in the 1470s) metropolitan of Kiev. It consisted of three parts, the story of the descent of Riurik from Augustus Caesar through the legendary Prus, the legend of the gift of the regalia (the "Cap of Monomakh") to Vladimir Monomakh from the Byzantines, and a highly embroidered genealogy of the grand dukes of Lithuania. The result was to give the Moscow dynasty a more glorious ancestor and also more dignified regalia as well as to connect it to ancient Rome and to Byzantium, but none of these stories of descent involved primogeniture. The exact relationships in the story of Augustus and Riurik were quite vague, and the Lithuanian story, which also was vague at crucial points, was irrelevant too: it was not a precedent for the rulers of Russia.[194] Though the "Tale of the Vladimir Princes" had been a source for the coronation order of Ivan IV, it did not introduce the benediction of the successor, which had arisen in Moscow long before. It presented a series of rulers, but did not mention inheritance or use the term "heir."

The first compositions to use the term "heir" (*naslednik*) appeared in the 1550s in a series of texts about Vasilii III, his birth, his second marriage, and the birth of Ivan IV.[195] The first of these brief compositions was a "Thanksgiving and Panegyric on Vasilii III" that appeared in the *Illustrated Chronicle*. The "Thanksgiving" presented "people's" (*liudi*) gratitude for Ivan's birth and, predicting his achievements, said that

[194] Dmitrieva, *Skazanie o kniaziakh vladimirskikh*, 159–181. On Spiridon, see most recently V. I. Ulianovs'kyi, *Mytropolyt Kyivs'kyi Spyrydon: Obraz kriz' epokhu, epokha kriz' obraz* (Kyiv: Lybid, 2004).

[195] The same texts also presented a much more significant role for the ruler's wife: Thyrêt, *Between God and Tsar*; Paul Bushkovitch, "Sofia Palaiologina in Life and Legend," *Canadian–American Slavic Studies* 52 (2018): 158–180.

God gave him as an heir (*naslednik*) to Vasilii's "tsardom," a clue to its post-1547 composition.[196] Two more such tales were the "Panegyric for Vasilii III"[197] and the "Tale of the Death of Vasilii III."[198] The first was an even more rhetorical story of the birth and baptism of Ivan IV, stressing Vasilii's piety and God's providence. It named Ivan the *naslednik* once, among many other epithets.[199] The second was a detailed, seemingly realistic account of the death of Vasilii III three years later, found in several versions. This tale did not use the term *naslednik*.[200] Clearly the usage was only becoming established, and these stories spread into several important compilations. The first story about Vasilii III appeared reworked in the *Book of Degrees*, the second in several chronicles as well as the *Illustrated Chronicle* and the *Book of Degrees*.[201] Both, it should be remembered, were historical works of the 1560s emanating from the palace or the metropolitan's staff or both.

The *Book of Degrees* was the first major historical work to regularly describe the successor to the throne as *naslednik*. To describe the birth of Ivan IV, it relied on the "Thanksgiving and Tale of the Death of Vasilii III," using the term *naslednik*, but not just in this case. It used this term back to Kievan times, for Iaroslav of Kiev, and also for the later Moscow princes Vasilii I and Ivan III.[202] The regular appearance of the term is hardly surprising, since the main theme and form of narrative of the book were new. In place of the yearly annals interspersed with shorter narratives, it offered a series of biographies of the princes of the Riurikovich

[196] *PSRL* XIII, 48–53, 52 (*naslednik*).

[197] N. N. Rozov, "Pokhval'noe slovo velikomu kniaziu Vasiliiu III," in *Arkheograficheskii ezhegodnik za 1964 god* (Moscow: Izdatel'stvo Akademii, 1965), 278–289.

[198] *PSRL* VI, 267–276; XIII, 409–420; *SKKDR* II, pt. 2, 277–279; Isolde Thyrêt, "The *Tale of the Death of Vasilii Ivanovich* and the Evolution of the Muscovite Tsaritsa's Role in 16th Century Russia," in *Dubitando: Studies in History and Culture in Honor of Donald Ostrowski*, ed. Brian J. Boeck, Russell E. Martin, and Daniel Rowland. (Bloomington, Indiana: Slavica, 2012), 209–224.

[199] Rozov, "Pokhval'noe slovo velikomu kniaziu Vasiliiu III," 286.

[200] In the first and second versions, the dying grand prince "gives" his sovereignty (*gosudarstvo*) that his father had "blessed" (*blagoslovil*) to his son Ivan and then said to the boyars, "you know yourselves that our sovereignty of Vladimir and Novgorod and Moscow comes from the grand prince Vladimir of Kiev; we are your born sovereigns and you are our boyars from time immemorial." (vedaete i sami, chto ot velikogo kniazia Volodimera Kievskogo vedetsia nashe gosudarstvo Vladimerskoe i Novgorodskoe i Moskovskoe; my vam gosudari prirozhenye, a vy nashi izvechnye boiare), *PSRL* VI, 270–271. In the second version, included in the Nikon Chronicle, Vasilii also blessed his son with the regalia of Vladimir Monomakh. *PSRL* XIII, 413, 415.

[201] Gail Lenhoff and N. N. Pokrovskii, eds., *Stepennaia kniga tsarskogo rodosloviia po drevneishim spiskam*, vols. 1–3 (Moscow: Iazyki slavianskikh kul'tur, 2007–12), vol. 2, 315–327; vol. 3, 386, 388.

[202] Lenhoff and Pokrovskii, eds., *Stepennaia kniga tsarskogo rodosloviia*, vol. 1, 379 (*naslednik*); vol. 2, 71(*naslednik*), 250 (*v nasledie*), 315–320, 319 (*naslednik*), 324 (*naslednik*).

dynasty, from Princess Ol'ga to Ivan IV, presented as a genealogy of the ruling clan.[203] The biographical model continued in the account (*zhitie*) by Patriarch Iov (died 1607) of the life of Tsar Fyodor. In Iov's words, Fyodor came from the "imperial root" (*tsarskii koren'*) that stretched from Augustus Caesar onward through Riurik to Tsar Fyodor, who mounted the throne by the desire and benediction of his father.[204] The patriarch also called Tsar Fyodor the "receiver" (*priemnik*) of his father's throne, which was probably a more rhetorical way of saying "heir."[205]

Beyond the writing of history, in international affairs the Moscow princes and tsars, like their fellow sovereigns, had always made hereditary claims on various territories. The lands of the Grand Duchy of Lithuania that had been part of Kiev Rus' in the early Middle Ages could be and were claimed as the patrimony (*votchina*) of the rulers in Moscow.[206] This claim was not ridiculous, for all the histories, Russian chronicles or those by Polish historians, told the story of Kiev and its Riurikovich rulers. Ivan IV also made the claim that Kazan' and Livonia were his patrimony as well, but this was a wholly spurious assertion.[207] These claims were matters of international competition, and in any case stated only that the ruler in Moscow was entitled to these lands, not who that ruler in Moscow should be.

The most elaborate exposition of notions of ancestry, inheritance, and designation of heirs came in Tsar Ivan's diplomatic and polemical epistles. Ivan's exchange of polemics with Prince Andrey Kurbskii in the 1560s revealed his view of ancestry and designation. Ivan's first epistle to Kurbskii (July 1564) started with a summary of the legend of the Vladimir princes, omitting, however, the descent of Riurik from Augustus Caesar and beginning the history of the Russian *tsarstvo* from Prince Vladimir of Kiev. Ivan saw his ancestors, Alexander

[203] David B. Miller, "The Velikie Minei Chet'i and the Stepennaia Kniga of Metropolitian Makarii and the Origins of Russian National Consciousness," *Forschungen zur osteuropäischen Geschichte* 26 (1979): 263–382; Lenhoff and Kleimola, eds., *The Book of Royal Degrees.*

[204] *PSRL* XIV, 2. The term "root" (*koren'*) is Biblical, referring to the "root of Jesse" (Isaiah, 11: 1 and 10) or "root of David" (Revelation 22: 16, "I Jesus . . . am the root and the offspring of David"). In all these cases the Greek is *riza*, the Slavic *koren'* (Ostrog Bible). The King James Bible translated it as "root," for example, Rev. 22.

[205] *PSRL* XIV, 2

[206] This was Ivan III's claim to the Lithuanians in 1504: *SRIO* 35, 460.

[207] J. L. I. Fennell, *Ivan the Great of Moscow* (London: Macmillan, 1963), 215–216, 284–285; A. L. Khoroshkevich, *Russkoe gosudarstvo v sisteme mezhdunarodnykh otnoshenii kontsa XV–nachala XVI vv.* (Moscow: Nauka, 1980), 106; Khoroshkevich, *Rossiia v sisteme mezhdunarodnykh otnoshenii*, 202–203; Jaroslav Z. Pelenskyj, *Russia and Kazan': Conquest and Imperial Ideology (1438–1560s)* (The Hague: De Gruyter Mouton, 1974); Jaroslaw Pelenski, *The Contest for the Legacy of Kievan Rus* (Boulder, Colorado: East European Monographs, 1998); Filiushkin, *Izobretaia pervuiu voinu*, 129–136.

Nevskii, Dmitrii Donskoi, and his grandfather Ivan and father Vasilii, passing on the Orthodox *tsarstvo* to him. The term *tsarstvo*, of course was an anachronism for the earlier rulers, but the account clearly emphasized the tsar's sense of dynasty and of the worthiness of the family sprung from that dynasty to rule. At the end of the story, he also emphasized that he had received the *tsarstvo* through the blessing (*blagoslovenie*) of his father. He had not unjustly taken it from anyone else.[208] Ivan explained his ascent to the throne by ancestry (but without the use of *naslednik* or any similar term) and paternal designation. In reply, Kurbskii said nothing about the issue of succession, putting his emphasis on Ivan's evil behavior. Kurbskii's comments on Ivan's ancestors, both male and female, were certainly negative as well, but he did not argue that they were not legitimate rulers. Neither did the prince laud the Polish system of elective monarchy: the only issue in his writings was the matter of the wicked and unjust actions of the tsar. Ivan, in his eyes, was simply an unworthy Orthodox ruler.[209] This was the usual conception of rulership in sixteenth-century Russia. It was not about heredity.

Ivan himself first made a claim that he was the legitimate hereditary ruler in Russia with a 1563 letter to King Sigismund Augustus of Poland. He included after the usual list of territories that he ruled or claimed the statement that he was "*mnogim zemliam vostochnym i severnym i zapadnim otchich i dedich i naslednik* (the heir from his father and grandfather of many eastern and northern and western lands)." The appearance of this phrase in this letter and later ones is difficult to explain, since it did not appear in most of his official letters. The 1563 letter followed some five or six preserved letters to the king of Poland that merely listed the names of territories and had no such phrase. The 1563 letter to Sigismund Augustus offers no clue for the innovation. It was largely a routine letter about the arrangements for negotiations.[210] Ivan's letters to the kings of Poland had included no reference to heredity in his title from the 1530s

[208] "ne voskhotekhom ni pod nim zhe tsarstva, no po Bozhiim izvoleniem i prarodotilei svoikh i roditelei blagosloveniem, iako zhe rodikhomsia v tsarstvii, tako i vospitakhomsia i vozrastokhom i votsarikhomsia Bozhiim veleniem, i praroditelei svoikh i roditelei blagosloveniem svoe vziakhom." Lur'e and Rykov, *Perepiska Ivana Groznogo*, 12–13.

[209] In his epistles, Kurbskii did not mention Ivan's ancestors; see, for example, Lur'e and Rykov, *Perepiska Ivana Groznogo*, 7–11. For comments in the history see Kurbskii, *Istoriia o delakh velikogo kniazia Moskovskogo*, 16–19, 130–133. Other editions: J. L. I. Fennell, ed. and trans., *Prince A. M. Kurbsky's History of Ivan IV* (Cambridge: Cambridge University Press, 1965); and "Istoriia o velikom kniaze Moskovskom," in *Sochineniia Kniazia Kurbskogo*. Russkaia istoricheskaia biblioteka 31, 1914.

[210] I. Danilovich and M. Obolenskii, eds., *Kniga Posol'skaia Metriki Velikogo Kniazhestva Litovskogo* (Moscow: Universitetskaia tipografiia, 1843), vol. I, 237–241 (quotation 238). The phrase does not appear in the *SRIO* 71 version of the letter (143–147) as

onward.[211] The heredity formula appeared again only in January 1578, in a letter to Stefan Batory devoted to the details of discussion of a proposed truce.[212] The 1581 letter to Stefan Batory was also full of various sorts of abuse, but the election of kings, such as that of Stefan as voivode of Transylvania in 1571 and as king of Poland in 1575, was the object of muffled irony, but no more. It was the Polish king's alleged crimes and misdeeds that were the objects of the tsar's wrath as well as his non-royal origins and the subjection of Batory's Transylvania to the Ottomans.[213] Why Ivan should include the claim of heredity in his title in this letter is no more evident than for the earlier ones, and the subsequent letters from Ivan to Stefan, to the end of the tsar's life, do not contain it.

Ivan's letters to Johan III of Sweden in 1572–3 seem to offer more material for analysis. Ivan's letters to Johan expanded on his conceptions of ancestry and fitness to rule (not the "right" to rule). The Swedish context offered him much to comment upon. In Sweden, the Vasa dynasty had come to the throne in consequence of the revolt against the Scandinavian union kingdom in 1521. Gustav Vasa was elected king in 1523, and by agreement with the estates the throne was made hereditary in the Vasa line in 1544. In accordance with this law, Erik XIV, Gustav's eldest son, succeeded his father in 1560. Erik's behavior grew increasingly erratic, until his murder of several members of the aristocratic Sture family led to his overthrow in 1568. His younger brother ascended the throne as Johan III. The Russian government took a long time to officially recognize the new Swedish kingdom as equal in rank to its neighbors, but it did not quibble about the election of Gustav Vasa and the later troubles. In 1568, the Russian embassy that happened to be in the country blandly noted that "In the Swedish land Prince Johan has become the chosen king and expelled his brother King Erik."[214]

the editor omitted the titles of the tsar and other rulers, substituting the phrase *polnyi titul.*

211 *SRIO* 59, 109, 309, 340, 374, 421, 516 (1537–56); D. Dubenskii and M. Pogodin, eds., *Kniga Posol'skaia Metriki Velikogo Kniazhestva Litovskogo* (Moscow: Universitetskaia tipografiia, 1843), vol. II, 15–17 (1576).

212 Dubenskii and Pogodin, eds., *Kniga Posol'skaia Metriki Velikogo Kniazhestva Litovskogo*, vol. II, 29, 33.

213 Adrianova-Peretts, Likhachev, and Lur'e, eds., *Poslaniia Ivana Groznogo*, 229; Filiushkin, *Izobretaia pervuiu voinu*, 172–191; A. I. Filiushkin, "Ivan the Terrible's Struggle for Recognition in the Latter Half of the Sixteenth Century," *Russian Studies in History* 53, 1 (2014): 28–41.

214 Ivan Svalenius, *Gustav Vasa* (Stockholm: Wahlstrom & Widstrand, 1963); Michael Roberts, *The Early Vasas: A History of Sweden 1623–1611* (Cambridge: Cambridge University Press, 1968); *SRIO* 129, 169 (October 3, 1568): "Uchinilsia v Sveiskoi zemle nyne izbrannym korolem Iagan korolevich, a brata svoego Irika korolia s korolevtsva zgonil." Cf. Ivan IV's letter to Johan III of February 1569: N. S. Demkova, "Gramoty Ivana Groznogo shvedskim koroliam Eriku XIV i Ioganny III (po rukopisiam Shvedskogo gosudarstvennogo arkhiva),"

The occasion for Ivan's letter was Sweden's involvement in the Livonian conflict, since 1561 expanding its rule in Estonia in competition with both Russia and Poland. In 1572, Ivan wrote to Johan on August 11, reproaching him for the behavior of his ambassador, bishop Paul of Åbo in Finland, as well as for the king's personal misdeeds. Other than its tone, the letter was just diplomatic polemic, but here Ivan also added to his title the final phrase *otchich i dedich i naslednik*.[215] This addition did not appear in earlier official letters from Ivan to the Swedish kings. The next letter, dated January 6, 1573, was also harsh and abusive. Ivan expatiated on the low origins of the Vasa dynasty. "And it is the very truth that you are a clan of peasants, not sovereigns," he wrote, ". . . we know for certain that your father Gustav came from Småland, and this is why we know that you are a peasant clan, and not a sovereign one: in the time of your father Gustav our merchants came with lard and wax and your father himself, putting on gloves and like a simple person, tested the lard and wax." Ivan did not reproach Johan that his father had been elected, only for his low origins and the fact that his letters to Moscow came not just from the king but also from his counsellors, the archbishop of Uppsala and the Swedish land. That is to say, King Johan was not really a sovereign ruler who would write only in his own name.[216] Johan could only reply that the Vasas were a high-born family and that he did not have to give any account to Ivan.[217] Johan did not comment on the phrase about heredity, though his defense of the legitimacy of his dynasty implied heredity, at least after Gustav. Ivan's later letters to Johan, whatever their content, did not contain the addition to the Russian title.

Ivan's letters with the phrase *mnogim zemliam vostochnym i severnym i zapadnim otchich i dedich i naslednik* are among the many anomalies of his reign. Why he used the phrase, especially in 1563 and 1578, is simply unexplainable. What is clear is that his polemics against both Johan and

TODRL 50 (1997): 494–495; and the contemporary Swedish translation in Harald Hjärne, "Ur brefvexlingen mellan konung Johan III och tsar Ivan Vasilevitj," *Historiskt Bibliotek* 7 (1880): 537–538, 1–3 (appendix).

215 *SRIO* 129, 228–230.

216 "A to pravda istinnaia, a ne lozh', chto ty muzhichei rod, a ne gosudar'skoi." It did not matter that your [Johan's] parents, Gustav and his queen, were both crowned. "A nam dopolna vedomo, chto otets tvoi Gustav iz Shmalot, da i potomu nam to verdomo, chto vy muzhichei rod, a ne gosudar'skoi: koli pri ottse pri tvoem pri Gustave priezzhali nashi torgovye liudi s salom i s voskom, i otets tvoi sam, v rukavitsy nariadisia, sala i vosku za prostogo cheloveka vmesto opytom pytal . . .," *SRIO* 129, 230–240 (quotation: 234); Adrianova-Peretts, Likhachev, and Lur'e, eds., *Poslaniia Ivana Groznogo*, 153–157 (quotation 153).

217 Hjärne, "Ur brefvexlingen mellan konung Johan III och tsar Ivan Vasilevitj," 553–554; Demkova, "Gramoty Ivana Groznogo shvedskim koroliam Eriku XIV i Ioganny III," 488–500.

Stefan Batory did not directly confront the issue of heredity or election. It was the lack of royal or even distinguished origins of the two kings and their wicked deeds that were the objects of the tsar's wrath. Ivan, of course, could not really challenge the Polish practice of election of kings since he himself tried to participate in it as a candidate (as well as putting forth his sons), if only for diplomatic reasons, in 1572–3 and 1575. The most significant use of the heredity phrase came in the coronation of Tsar Fyodor in 1584. During his reign, Tsar Fyodor seems to have used the phrase, but not regularly. In his correspondence with the kings of Demark, he used it only in 1590, not in the letters from other years.[218] The subsequent history, with four elected tsars to 1613, rendered the phrase useless, but it was not lost. It reappeared in the 1650s and remained in the titles of the tsars into the eighteenth century.

Tsar Fyodor and the Succession Problem

The proclamation that Fyodor was the inheritor of his father and grandfather at his coronation was all very well, but Tsar Fyodor himself had no children at all at that moment. He did have a half-brother, Dmitrii, not yet two years old and the son of the last wife of Ivan IV, Mariia Nagaia. Both were quickly sent off to Dmitrii's appanage in Uglich after Ivan's death. As Dmitrii grew up, he and his mother did not become part of the court in Moscow. They remained in Uglich until his death (or murder) in 1591. Tsaritsa Irina also began to play some sort of role in the state. It is not clear whether Irina actually had any political power alongside her weak husband the tsar and her powerful brother, but her name certainly appeared in official documents alongside that of the tsar. Three charters of grant to monasteries from 1587 to 1597 are in the name of both Tsar Fyodor and Irina.[219] This sort of official presentation of Tsaritsa Irina as co-ruler with her husband provided both a regent in case she were to bear

[218] The diplomatic records for Fyodor's reign are mostly unpublished, but it does not seem that the phrase invoking heredity was used. See, for example, the records of the negotiations with Giles Fletcher in 1588–9: "Stateinyi spisok priezda i prebyvaniia v Rossii angliiskogo posla, Elizara Fletchera," *Vremennik OIDR* VIII, 14, 45. Similarly, the letters to Emperor Rudolf in 1593: *PDS* I, 1359. The one case where it did occur was the July 1590 letter from Tsar Fyodor to Christian IV of Denmark: TKUA Rusland A I, 3, printed (without the title) in Iu. N. Shcherbachev, ed., *Russkie akty Kopengagenskogo gosudarstvennogo arkhiva*. RIB 16 (St. Petersburg: Tovarishchestvo Pechatnia S. P. Iakovleva, 1897), 239. (I owe this reference to Joshua Earl Hodil.)

[219] *AI* I, 415–16; *AAE* I, 413; DAI I, 236–237; *Sudebniki XV–XVI vv.* (Moscow and Leningrad: Izdatel'stvo Akademii nauk SSSR, 1952), 443; Zimin, *V kanun groznykh potriasenii*, 174, 281; Thyrêt, *Between God and Tsar*, 81–82.

children and a successor if she did not.[220] As we shall see, she did succeed briefly at her husband's death, but in the meantime hopes of a child were not ridiculous. The only one that appeared, however, was a girl, who thus created a new succession problem. A daughter could have either a Russian or a foreign husband, and in this case it was the foreign option that eventually arose.

As early as 1584 some of the boyars seem to have been interested in a Habsburg succession, even without a dynastic marriage. At that point Fyodor had no children, so the plan (if it existed) would have meant the election of one of Rudolf II's brothers as tsar. This, at least, was rumored at Rudolf's court and in Moscow, where the rumor was that Rudolf's brother would marry Irina Godunov on Fyodor's death. Discussions in Prague lasted until 1586, for the Habsburg court had an interest in preventing Stefan Batory, the king of Poland, from fulfilling any plans of expansion in Russia. Batory was also the ruler of Transylvania and as such the vassal of the Ottoman Sultan, the mortal enemy of the Habsburgs. In 1589, the Habsburg envoy Nicolaus Warkotsch reported that Boris Godunov wanted Emperor Rudolf's brother Archduke Maximilian, who had once been a candidate for the Polish throne, as the successor to Tsar Fyodor. In the autumn of 1593, Andrei Shchelkalov, still head of the Ambassadorial Office, made a secret proposal to Warkotsch, who was now back in Moscow. Speaking in the name of Boris Godunov as well as his own, he proposed that Fyodor's infant daughter Feodosiia (1592–4) be married to one of the Habsburg princes, perhaps one of the sons of Archduke Karl of Steiermark. After this point the issue died, perhaps simply because Tsar Fyodor's daughter had died, but it is not clear whether a marriage was the central point in these proposals or simply the election of one of the Habsburgs. In either case, these proposals ignored the last son of Ivan the Terrible, Dmitrii. Dmitrii was a factor until his mysterious death in 1591, and was certainly the son of Ivan. It might have been the case that the boyars were uncomfortable with the fact that his mother was Ivan's seventh wife, a marriage that in theory went against Orthodox practice, but we have no sources that even mention such an idea. The only other possibility is that the Habsburg plans were a means of exploring an alliance with the Habsburgs against

[220] Irina's role may have been contingent to the situation, but was in harmony with the regular inclusion of the tsaritsa in delineating the ruling family after the middle of the century. The older images of the pious wife and mother grew more elaborate, and the notion that women were the link in the dynasty and even fit to rule took on new forms: Thyrêt, *Between God and Tsar*, 80–117. The unique place of Princess Ol'ga in the *Book of Degrees* provided a template for all these notions, for it was her fitness to rule that was the core of the story. Lenhoff and Pokrovksii, eds., *Stepennaia kniga tsarskogo rodosloviia*, vol. 1, 149–196.

Poland and perhaps Sweden as well. Russia's war with Sweden resumed in 1590 and ended in victory: Russia regained Ingria at the peace in 1595, and Boris Godunov and others at the Moscow court may well have wanted allies.

Russian historians have paid little attention to these marriage feelers, as they got nowhere and contradict the conventional view of Godunov's ambition for the throne. They also contradict the notion of Russia's self-isolation from the West, since it seems that the Russian elite wanted to at least explore the possibility of a foreign sovereign. In any case, the death of the infant tsarevna Feodosiia put an end to the first plan.[221] What is not clear from the remaining records is how the succession was to be managed if any of the plans succeeded. Was Fyodor to designate his son-in-law or one of the Habsburgs the tsar, or was there to be some wider consultation, even an Assembly of the Land?[222] Perhaps all that these intrigues demonstrate about real politics was the insecurity of Boris Godunov and his allies among the boyars before about 1594. At the same time, these plans, however unlikely, also show that the Russian elite was thinking about finding a tsar outside the Riurikovich dynasty well before Tsar Fyodor's death in 1598. The idea of dynastic inheritance had its limits when the ruling family of that dynasty produced no children.

Succession in the Sixteenth Century

The basis of Russian succession practice from the fifteenth century to the end of the Riurikovich dynasty was the designation ("blessing") of the heir by his father. Normally the ruling father designated his eldest son, but in the

[221] Feodosiia was born in 1592 and died in 1594: *PSRL* XIV, 45.

[222] Joseph Fiedler, "Die Beziehungen Österreichs zu Russland in den Jahren 1584–1598," *Almanach der kaiserlichen Akademie der Wissenschaften* 16 (1866): 253–278; Hans Uebersberger, *Österreich und Russland seit dem Ende des 15. Jahrhunderts*. Veröffentlichungen der Kommission für neuere Geschichte Österreichs (Vienna: W. Braumüller, 1906), 503–509, 543–544, 558–559; "Beschreibung der Rais in die Moskau, so Herr Niclas Warkotsch ... gethan," in *Sammlung bisher noch ungedruckten kleiner Schriften zur ältern Geschichte und Kenntniss des russischen Reiches*, ed. B. von Wichmann (Berlin: Reimer, 1820), vol. 1, 123–200, esp. 186; A. Shemiakin, ed. and trans., "Opisanie puteshestviia v Moskvu posla Rimskogo Imperatora Nikolaia Varkocha s 22 iiulia 1593 g.," *ChOIDR* 4 (1874): i–xii, 1–36; Skrynnikov, *Rossiia nakanune "Smutnogo vremeni,"* 114–115; Zimin, *V kanun groznykh potriasenii*, 120. The various Polish plans to place the king of Poland on the Russian throne, a matter of continuous discussion in Warsaw, suffered from the same defect. How was the succession to be managed: by designation, by some sort of consultation (like the Polish elections of the kings), or simply by force? The problem was all the greater since there seems to have been no important Russian constituency for these plans, despite all the discontent with Boris Godunov. Floria, *Russko-pol'skie otnosheniia i politicheskoe razvitie Vostochnoi Evropy*, 130–135, 227–231, 245–248.

case of Ivan III he did not, choosing a second son over the eldest grandson. The effect of the practice of designation was to eliminate collateral succession, which had been a major issue during the whole medieval period from Kiev Rus' onward and the background to the dynastic civil war in the principality of Moscow in the second quarter of the fifteenth century. The means of this designation was at first the ruler's testament, but the last testament, Ivan IV's, ultimately had no effect. What remained were the oral designation by the ruler, reinforced by the public display of that choice in the ceremonies of the court, and the participation of the heir in warfare and politics. The use of the testaments had made sense in the small Moscow principality of the fourteenth century. Dmitrii Donskoi simply added his choice of successor to the disposition of his personal domain and property. The Russia of the later sixteenth century was too complicated a state: the personal domain (*dvortsovye zemli*) of the tsar was eventually much too extensive to easily list in a single document. Visible designation made more sense, especially since the court and military elite now comprised not hundreds but thousands of men, all of whom saw the tsar's choice on a daily basis.

The result was not primogeniture as understood (at least in theory) in Western Europe because the succession was not automatic and the custom did not mandate the eldest son unquestionably. In service oaths, boyars and others swore to serve the entire ruling family, the tsar, eventually his tsaritsa, and the children, male and female, not just the heir named as such. In a system where primogeniture was the rule, the notorious incident over the succession to Ivan IV in 1553 could not have occurred. Rather than arguing over who was the heir, the approaching death of a ruler with an infant son would have set off a dispute over the regency. This is what happened in England when Henry VIII died in 1547, leaving his son Edward aged nine, and in France when Louis XIII died in 1643, leaving a five-year-old son.

In Russia, legitimacy came from paternal designation. Claims of simple heredity did not yet play the main role in settling the succession. This system depended, however, on the existence of someone for the tsar to designate as heir. Thus, when Tsar Fyodor failed to produce children, and none of his brothers remained alive after the death of Dmitrii at Uglich in 1591, a new situation arose. The Russian elite did not search the genealogies for a distant Riurikovich relative and, supported by church and people, it moved to elect a tsar. This move was unprecedented, and needs to be explained.

4 Election and Heredity 1598–1645

Coming after a century and a half of succession by paternal designation, the events of 1598 surrounding the election of Boris Godunov are not so surprising. A purely hereditary system would have required the boyars and the church elite to search their genealogies for another Riurikovich, a move no one seems to have even contemplated. Fyodor had no sons to designate, only a wife, who did assume power for a brief moment and then blessed her brother with the throne, as we shall see. An Assembly of the Land, a sobor, then confirmed her choice by electing Boris. This decision has no explanation in the sources, but it did not come out of the blue. There had already been at least one Assembly of the Land in 1566 that confirmed Ivan the Terrible's policies in the Livonian War, so the institution was not new.[1] It was also the case that the Russians had very good examples of elective kingship in their nearest neighbors, Poland, Denmark, and to some extent Sweden, and the more distant Holy Roman Empire. These elections were part of the relations of Russia with those kingdoms, and consequently appeared in diplomatic discussions with some regularity. Finally, the Russians had the precedent of ancient Israel and the Roman–Byzantine world, where election or at least choice coexisted with heredity. They do not seem to have thought that election was in any way inferior to heredity or designation. The only issue that they occasionally raised in diplomacy was the descent of neighboring rulers from sovereign dynasties or the opposite.

Elective Monarchy and the Russians

The most important example of elective monarchy, and one of the oldest, was the Holy Roman Empire as well as some of its constituent parts, such

[1] A. A. Zimin, *Oprichnina*, 2nd ed. (Moscow: Territoriia, 2001), 159–211; L. V. Cherepnin, *Zemskie sobory Russkogo gosudarstva v XVI–XVII vv.* (Moscow: Iazyki slavianskoi kul'tury, 1978), 106–115, R. G. Skrynnikov, *Tsarstvo terrora* (St. Petersburg: Nauka, 1992), 288–298.

as the kingdom of Bohemia.[2] The other, much more relevant to the Russians, was Poland-Lithuania. The two parts of the kingdom had different traditions. The kings of Poland had originally come from the Piast dynasty, but by the fourteenth century their succession was confirmed by the nobility. The process of election was increasingly formalized in Polish practice and law through the years of the next dynasty, the Jagiellonian (1386–1572).[3] The Lithuanian story was more complicated.[4] In early Lithuania, the Gediminovich dynasty ruled the state, with much contention among the princes for supremacy. In 1377, Olgerd, the son of Gedimin, left the throne to his son Jogailo by designation.[5] When Jogailo accepted Catholic Christianity and was elected king of Poland (as Władysław Jagiełło) in 1386, the union agreements did not override the Lithuanian tradition of designation within the Gediminovich dynasty. The king's designation made Vitovt the ruler of Lithuania under Władysław Jagiełło, with some disagreement over the matter of Vitovt's legal status – viceroy or autonomous ruler. Lithuania, like the Moscow dynasty, had its civil war over succession in 1430–40.[6] The combination of designation and election persisted in the succession of Kings Kazimierz Jagiellończyk, Jan Olbracht, and Aleksander Jagiellończyk.[7] Lithuania first went over to a fully elective system as

[2] Jaroslav Panek, "Königswahl oder Königsannahme? (Thronwechsel im Königreich Böhmen an der Schwelle der Neuzeit)," *Historica: Historical Sciences in the Czech Republic* 3–4 (1996–7): 51–67.

[3] The process of election in Poland after the union with Lithuania was also immensely complicated by the evolving relations between the two parts of the joint kingdom. See Henryk Łowmiański, *Polityka Jagiellonów* (Poznań: Wydawnictwo Poznańskie, 1999); and Robert I. Frost, *The Oxford History of Poland-Lithuania. Volume I: The Making of the Polish-Lithuanian Union, 1385–1569* (Oxford: Oxford University Press, 2105).

[4] Lidia Korczak, *Monarcha i poddani: System władzy w Wielkim Księstwie Litewskim w okresie wczesnojagiellonńskim* (Kraków: Towarzystwo Wydawnicze Historia Iagellonica, 2008), 15–31.

[5] Ludwik Kolankowski, *Dzieje Wielkiego Księstwa Litewskiego za Jagiellonów* (Warsaw: Kasa im. Mianowskiego, 1930), vol. I, 11–12; Jadwiga Krzyżaniakowa and Jerzy Ochmański, *Władysław II Jagiełło* (Wrocław: Zakład Narodowy im. Ossolińskich, 1990). It may be that the designation was manufactured after Olgerd's death, but in the Lithuanian (and Russian) chronicles the designator was Olgerd: Jan Tęgowski, "O następstwie tronu na Litwie po śmierci Olgierda," *Przegląd Historyczny* 84, 2 (1993): 127–134; *PSRL* XVII, 192–193 (Letopis' Avraamki); 220–221 (Origo regis Jagyelo); Maciej Stryjkowski, *Kronika Polska, Litewska, Żmódzka, i wszystkiej Rusi* (Warsaw: Gustaw Leon Glücksberg, 1846) (from 1582 edition), vol. 2, 59–60; *PSRL* XVIII, 118 (Simeonovskaia letopis'); *PSRL* XI, 25–26 (Nikon Chronicle).

[6] Wioletta Zawitkowska, *Walka polityczno-prawna o następstwo tronu po Władysławie Jagielle w latach 1424–1434* (Rzeszów: Wydawnictwo Uniwersytetu Rzeszowskiego, 2015); Sergei Polekhov, *Nasledniki Vitovta: Dinasticheskaia voina v Velikom kniazhestve Litovskom v 30-e gody XV veka* (Moscow: Indrik, 2015).

[7] Fryderik Papée, *Jan Olbracht* (Kraków: Gebethner i Wolff, 1936); Fryderik Papée, *Aleksander Jagiellończyk* (Kraków: n.p., 1949).

a result of the 1501 Union of Mielnik, which was negotiated on the death of Jan Olbracht to allow his brother Alexander, Grand Duke of Lithuania since 1492, to succeed to the Polish throne.[8] In 1506 both parts of the kingdom elected Sigismund, although not at the same time. In fact designation was still active, for in 1522 Sigismund managed to convince the Lithuanian lords to elect his son Sigismund Augustus grand duke of Lithuania (in the process again violating the Mielnik union's provision for common elections).[9]

The Russian diplomatic records make it clear that in Moscow they took the Polish and Lithuanian elections as a matter of course, and indeed the Russians even tried to participate. The reaction in Moscow to King Aleksander's death in 1506 was to send an official messenger to encourage the widowed Queen Elena and the Polish-Lithuanian elite to support the candidacy of her half-brother, Grand Prince Vasilii III, for the Polish throne, arguing that they should "want his sovereignty" (*pokhoteli ego gosudarstva*). Elena replied that Alexander had "given" (*postupilsia*) his kingdom to his brother; in other words, Elena described the election as an act of designation. Not surprisingly, this attempt came to nothing, for both Poland and Lithuania elected Sigismund. Nevertheless, the episode shows that the Polish elections were just another part of political reality for the Russians.[10] When Sigismund arranged that the diet elect his son Sigismund August as the heir to the Polish throne *vivente rege*, and the Lithuanian rada confirmed the decision, he informed Vasilii that he had decided to "place" (*esmo ... posadili*) his son on the throne to rule "after his death" (*po nashem zhivote*). The Russians had no reaction to this, and when Sigismund I died his son came to the throne without comment. Not until Sigismund II Augustus died in 1572 did the issue arise again, this time more sharply, since the king had no sons. The result was the first open election in Polish history, an event that produced the short reign of Henry of Valois.[11] Russian diplomatic sources are fragmentary on the subject, but again Ivan IV's official reply to the news was simply to offer

[8] Frost, *The Oxford History of Poland-Lithuania*, vol. I, 327–343.

[9] Ludwik Kolankowski, *Zygmunt August Wielki Książę Litwy do roku 1548* (Lwów: Towarzystwo dla Popierania Nauki Polskiej, 1913), 11–17; Frost, *The Oxford History of Poland-Lithuania*, vol. I, 406–409.

[10] *SRIO* 35, 481–482; A. A. Zimin, *Rossiia na poroge novogo vremeni* (Moscow: Mysl', 1972), 79–80. In fact, King Alexander did designate his brother Sigismund as his successor in his testament, though both the Lithuanians and the Poles also elected him. Papée, *Aleksander Jagiellończyk*, 115; *Acta Tomiciana* I, (Poznań, Sumptibus Bibliothecae Kornicensis, 1852), additamenta, 20–21.

[11] Aleksandr Trachevskii, *Pols'koe beskorolev'e po prekrashchenii dinastii Iagiellonov* (Moscow: K. Soldatenkov, Tipografiia Gracheva i ko., 1869): Stefan Gruszecki, *Walka o władzę w Rzeczypospolitej polskiej po wygaśnięciu dynastii Jagiellonów (1572–1573)* (Warsaw: Państwowe Wydawnictwo Naukowe, 1969).

condolences and brief remarks about the ongoing Livonian War. Ivan also responded in detail to Polish-Lithuanian feelers about his own or his younger son Fyodor's candidacy for the throne, both in 1572–3 and later in 1574–6, after Henry's flight from Poland back to France to assume the French throne. These discussions are known almost entirely from Polish sources, so it is sometimes difficult to understand what Ivan was trying to accomplish, but the discussions were certainly based on acceptance of the Polish election system. At the same time, Ivan proposed that the Polish throne should henceforth be hereditary, and even advanced a complicated historical justification for the Russian candidacy that was based on the supposed blood relationship of the Riurikovich and Jagiellonian dynasties. Ivan was claiming that he had a hereditary right to at least the Lithuanian throne.[12] At the next Polish election in 1587, the Russians came forward with a candidate, this time Tsar Fyodor. The conditions they proposed through the Russian ambassadors were not accepted, and the outcome was the double election of Prince Sigismund Vasa of Sweden and the Austrian Archduke Maximilian, who lost to his Swedish rival. The Russian candidacy had considerable support in Poland-Lithuania, and the Russians certainly played the game, whatever their ultimate goals.[13]

Sweden was a more complicated story than Poland, since the Vasa dynasty came to the throne in consequence of the revolt against the Scandinavian union kingdom, and Gustav Vasa was elected king in 1523. By agreement with the estates, the throne was made hereditary in the Vasa line in 1544. Religion proved to be a sore point, such that the Catholic Sigismund Vasa's succession to the throne in 1592 (as king of both Poland and Sweden) led to revolt in 1599 under his uncle Karl, whom the riksdag then elected king in 1604. The Russian government had taken a long time to recognize the new Swedish kingdom as more than a rebellious province of Denmark, and (as we have seen) Ivan the Terrible was contemptuous of the Vasa dynasty's origins. Neither Ivan nor later Russian rulers made any comments about the election of Gustav Vasa itself, and the later troubles were not an issue. The government of Boris Godunov looked kindly on Karl's revolt against Sigismund, and

12 "'Vypiska iz posol'skikh knig' o snosheniikh Rossiiskogo gosudarstva s Pol'sko-Litovskim za 1547 [sic: 1487]–1572 gg.," in *Pamiatniki istorii Vostochnoi Evropy* II, ed. B. N. Morozov (Moscow and Warsaw: Arkheograficheskii tsentr, 1997), 272–273; B. N. Floria, *Russko-pol'skie otnosheniia i politicheskoe razvitie Vostochnoi Evropy vo vtoroi polovine XVI–nachale XVII v.* (Moscow: Nauka, 1978), 32–119. The claim to a blood relationship with the Jagiellonians also required the Russians to promote Gediminas, the first Lithuanian prince, from a servant of the Russian princes to their relative: Floria, *Russko-pol'skie otnosheniia i politicheskoe razvitie Vostochnoi Evropy*, 57.

13 Floria, *Russko-pol'skie otnosheniia i politicheskoe razvitie Vostochnoi Evropy*, 141–216.

later Tsar Vasilii Shuiskii sought his alliance.[14] The fact of election, as in Poland, was simply not an issue.

Denmark was even less an issue. Denmark's throne had been elective for centuries, but the sixteenth-century Danish kings managed to get their eldest sons elected while they themselves were still on the throne. Thus Frederick II was elected while only two years old in 1536, and ascended the throne in 1559 without difficulty. He in turn had his son Christian elected king in 1580 at age three, so that when Frederick died in 1588 a regency ruled the country until Christian IV's majority in 1596. The Russians made no issue of these elections in their generally friendly relations with Denmark. Thus in 1590 Tsar Fyodor wrote to Christian IV, primarily about the ongoing boundary issues in Lapland and the war with Sweden, but also reproaching Christian (de facto the regency) for not informing him of the death of Frederick II. Fyodor's letter noted that when Ivan IV died and he ascended the throne "with God's help and the blessing of his father," the Danish king had communicated his condolences. Yet on Frederick's death, when "it became known to us" that Frederick had died and "you, Christian, had come to be in the place of your father (*na ottsa svoego mesto uchinilsia*) as king in the Danish land," he had heard nothing.[15] There was no mention of election or the legal status of the Danish monarchy. Indeed, in Russian relations with Denmark and Sweden the Russians throughout the sixteenth century had seen the kings of Denmark as true kings, unlike the more dubious Vasas.

Russia's neighbors not only elected their kings, but had also all developed ideas about their history that explained the practice, and to some extent included them in law. Legends about the ruling dynasties and succession practices were part of notions of national history and identity in East, West, and North Europe. In the Empire, lawyers were the most active in providing an explanation and justification of its existence, and historical legends seem to have played a minor role.[16] In Hungary the idea that election of kings went back to Attila was current by the fifteenth century, and in the sixteenth such ideas made their way into the

[14] Michael Roberts, *The Early Vasas: A History of Sweden 1623–1611* (Cambridge: Cambridge University Press, 1968), 327–411; B. N. Floria, *Russko-pol'skie otnosheniia i baltiiskii vopros v kontse shestnadtsatogo–nachale semnadtsatogo v.* (Moscow: Nauka, 1973), 102–169.

[15] Iu N. Shcherbachev, ed., *Russkie akty Kopengagenskogo gosudarstvennogo arkhiva*. RIB 16 (St Petersburg: Tovarishchestvo Pechatnia S. P. Iakovleva, 1897), 240, 243; TKUA Rusland A I, 3 (July 1590). This is the same letter in which Tsar Fyodor used the title "otchich i dedich i naslednik."

[16] Robert von Friedeburg and Michael Seidler, "The Holy Roman Empire of the German Nation," in *European Political Thought 1500–1700: Religion, Law and Philosophy*, ed. Howell A. Lloyd, Glenn Burgess, and Simon Hodson (New Haven, Connecticut and London: Yale University Press, 2007), 102–175, esp. 113.

Tripartitum, the standard compilation of Hungarian law that was valid later in Transylvania as well.[17] In Poland Sarmatianism provided a similar historical justification for this and other features of state and society. In Marcin Bielski's history of Poland, the people elected Krok, or Krakus, the legendary founder of Kraków and of the second (legendary) dynasty, to be their king, just as they later on elected Piast as their king.[18] Swedish historical texts took the election of kings back to Gothic beginnings.[19] The Danish elite, in the person of the widely read Arild Huitfeldt, constructed the first history of the country in Danish, which stressed the tradition of elective kingship.[20]

These histories with their elected kings contrast strongly with the West European histories written in the sixteenth century, such as that of Polydore Vergil and Holinshed in England, whose legendary kings come to power by conquest or heredity. Historical texts were not the only means of defending succession practices. In France, jurists and antiquaries defended heredity. Claude de Seyssel argued that hereditary monarchy was better than elective, and Étienne Pasquier simply assumed that the kings of France had been hereditary, part of their glorious tradition.[21] In Poland, political writers advanced the cause of elective monarchy. In 1568 Wawrzyniec Goślicki published in Venice a book on

[17] Martyn Rady, "'They Brought in an Ox as King, They Elected and Installed Him': The Royal Succession in Later Medieval Hungary," in *Making and Breaking the Rules: Succession in Medieval Europe c. 1000–1600*, ed. Frédérique Lachaud and Michael Penman (Turnhout: Brepols, 2008), 61–70. See also László Kontler and Balázs Trencsényi, "Hungary," in *European Political Thought 1500–1700: Religion, Law and Philosophy*, ed. Howell A. Lloyd, Glenn Burgess, and Simon Hodson (New Haven, Connecticut and London: Yale University Press, 2007), 176–207.

[18] Tadeusz Ulewicz, *Sarmacja: Studium z problematyki słowiańskiej XV–XVI w.* (Kraków: Studium Słowiańskiego Uniwersytetu Jagiellońskiego, 1950); Janusz Pelc, *Barok: Epoka przeciwieństw* (Warsaw: Czytelnik, 1993), 207–269; Marcin Bielski, *Kronika*, vol. I (Sanok: Karol Pollak, 1856), 48–49, 61–63 (originally Kraków: Drukarnia Jakuba Sibeneychera, 1597).

[19] Roberts, *The Early Vasas*, 138–144, 426–445; Michael Roberts, *The Swedish Imperial Experience* (Cambridge: Cambridge University Press, 1979), 70–75; Kurt Johannesson, *Renaissance of the Goths in Sixteenth-Century Sweden* (Berkeley, California: University of California Press, 1991), 76–78.

[20] Leon Jespersen, ed., *A Revolution from Above? The Power State of Sixteenth and Seventeenth Century Scandinavia* (Odense: Odense University Press, 2000), 44–65, 162–174; Karen Skovgaard-Petersen, "'... By the Direction of the Most Noble and Distinguished Christen Friis': The Influence of the Chancellor Christen Friis (1581–1639) on the Histories of Denmark by Johannes Pontanus (1571–1639) and Johannes Meursius (1579–1639)," in *Pomp, Power, and Politics: Essays on German and Scandinavian Court Culture and Their Context*, ed. Mara R. Wade, special issue of *Daphnis: Zeitschrift für mittlere deutsche Literatur und Kultur der frühen Neuzeit (1400–1750)* 32, 1–2 (2003): 199–229.

[21] Polydore Vergil, *Historia anglica* (Oxford: Clarendon Press, 1952), books I and IV; Raphael Holinshed, *Chronicles of England, Scotland, and Ireland* (London: Iohn Harrison, 1587); Claude de Seyssel, *La grant monarchie de France* (Paris: Regnault

the duties of the senator that extolled the Polish system which, as he saw it, centered on the Senate, the great officers of state of the Kingdom of Poland. He presented the king as an executive following the advice of the Senate, and maintained that elective monarchy was the best arrangement to produce a virtuous king. States like France, with a hereditary monarchy, were the result either of barbarous customs or of a history of dissension and civil unrest.[22] In Denmark there were no political writers like Goślicki, but the documents of the elections and coronation ceremonies, as well as the oaths of king and subjects, presented an implicit conception of the virtues of elective monarchy.[23]

In contrast, Russia met the dynastic crisis that arose at the death of Tsar Fyodor with no tradition firmly for or against the election of the monarch. The only issue that had aroused comment was the dignity and status of the chosen monarch's family, an issue that arose in 1598 at the death of Tsar Fyodor.

Boris Godunov

The election of Boris Godunov is one of the classic stories of Russian history, the beginning of a reign immortalized by Pushkin and Mussorgskii. Since the time of Karamzin, Russian historians have told the story essentially the same way: Tsar Fyodor dies, and then Boris maneuvers to secure the throne. The contemporary sources are rather

Chaudière, 1519), ch. 5, ff. 6–6v; Étienne Pasquier, *Les recherches de la France* (Paris: L. Sonnivs, 1607), book 2, ch. 1. Pasquier, who believed that France was a monarchy tempered by the sovereign courts, devoted many pages to the history of French legal and other institutions and little to the monarchy per se. See Colette Beaune, *Naissance de la nation française* (Paris: Gallimard, 1985), esp. 264–290.

[22] Wawrzyniec Grzymała Goślicki, *De optimo senatore* (Venice: Apud Iordanum Zilettum, 1568); English translation: *The Counsellor* (London: Richard Bradocke, 1598). The 1733 Oldisworth translation adds material and terminology not in the original. Goślicki became a royal secretary and then a bishop, dying as bishop of Poznań in 1607. See Karin Friedrich, "Poland-Lithuania," in *European Political Thought 1500–1700: Religion, Law and Philosophy*, ed. Howell A. Lloyd, Glenn Burgess, and Simon Hodson (New Haven, Connecticut and London: Yale University Press, 2007), 208–242; Robert I. Frost, "'Ut unusquisque qui vellet, ad illum venire possit': Nobility, Citizenship, and Corporate Decision-Making in the Polish-Lithuanian Commonwealth 1454–1795," in *What Makes the Nobility Noble? Comparative Perspectives from the Sixteenth to the Twentieth Centiuries*, ed. Jörn Leonhard and Christian Wieland. Schriftenreihe der FRIAS School of History 2 (Göttingen: Vandenhoeck & Ruprecht, 2011), 146–150.

[23] Leon Jespersen, "Teokrati og kontraktlære: Et aspekt af de statsretlige brydninger ved Frederik 3.s kroning," in *Struktur og funktion: Festskrift til Erling Ladewig Petersen*, ed. Carsten Due-Nielsen, Knud J. V. Jespersen, Leon Jespersen, and Anders Monrad Møller (Odense: Odense universitetsforlag, 1994), 169–186; Sebastian Olden-Jørgensen, "Scandinavia," in *European Political Thought 1450–1700: Religion, Law and Philosophy*, ed. Howell A. Lloyd, Glenn Burgess, and Simon Hodson (New Haven, Connecticut and London: Yale University Press, 2007), 300–331.

sparse, and historians have often relied on narrative sources written or compiled later, after the end of the Time of Troubles. The maneuvers of Boris, his supporters, and his rivals are the object of much discussion, but on closer examination a number of points seem clear from contemporary or near-contemporary sources.[24] Tsar Fyodor did not leave any testament. Not only is there no surviving document, but also there is no reference to one in any source.[25] After the death of Fyodor on January 6, 1598, power passed briefly to Irina, who announced her desire not to rule and then entered the Novodevichii Convent outside the wall of Moscow on January 15, with Boris accompanying her. There she was tonsured as a nun. She refused to indicate a successor, and Boris refused to accept the throne. On February 17, the Assembly of the Land, the Sobor, met in the patriarch's palace and decided to ask Irina to bless Boris with the throne and him to accept it. They included Mariia, the wife of Boris, and their two children in their request.[26] Irina, now the nun Aleksandra, refused to designate Boris, and he refused to accept the throne for four days. The patriarch, the clergy, the boyars, the gentry, and the multitude went again on February 21 to the Novodevichii Convent, this time with crosses and miracle-working icons. Tsaritsa Irina/Aleksandra gave in after much persuasion and told Patriarch Iov and the crowd that it was God's will and they might do as they wish.[27] Boris accepted the throne. It should be noted that Irina's words were not the traditional blessing of the successor with the throne that the Sobor had requested, even as reported in the official documents. On March 9, the Duma, Iov, and the higher clergy met and decided to compile a Charter of

[24] S. F. Platonov, *Ocherki po istorii Smuty v Moskovskom gosudarstve*, 3rd ed. (St. Petersburg: Ia. Bashmakov i ko., 1910), 211–236; A. A. Zimin, *V kanun groznykh potriasenii* (Moscow: Mysl', 1986), 212–233; R. G. Skrynnikov, *Rossiia nakanune "Smutnogo vremeni"* (Moscow: Mysl', 1980), 120–150; A. P. Pavlov, *Gosudarev dvor i politicheskaia bor'ba pri Borise Godunove, 1584–1604* (St. Petersburg: Nauka, 1992), 56–60; Chester S. L. Dunning, *Russia's First Civil War* (University Park, Pennsylvania: Pensylvania State University Press, 2001), 90–94: L. E. Morozova, *Dva tsaria: Fyodor i Boris* (Moscow: Russkaia slovo 2001), 235–253; Marie-Karine Schaub, "Les élections des tsars russes durant le Temps des Troubles (1598–1613)," in *Élections et pouvoirs politiques du VIIe au XVIIe siècle*, ed. Corinne Péneau (Paris: Éditions Bière, 2008), 325–338; Isaiah Gruber, *Orthodox Russia in Crisis: Church and Nation in the Time of Troubles* (DeKalb, Illinois, Northern Illinois University Press, 2012).

[25] Patriarch Iov's *Life* of Tsar Fyodor mentions no testament and explicitly says that Fyodor on the eve of his death handed the scepter to Tsaritsa Irina: "Zhitie tsaria i velikogo kniazia Fedora Ivanovicha," *PSRL* XIV, 19. As Iov died in 1607, the text, though highly partisan, is close to the events.

[26] *AAE* II, 13, 27. In the provinces local administrators believed that Irina ruled, for they addressed petitions to her, under her monastic name Aleksandra, about *mestnichestvo* cases on January 17: V. I. Buganov, ed., *Razriadnaia kniga 1475–1598* (Moscow: Nauka, 1966) (henceforth *RK 1475–1598*), 534–539.

[27] *AAE* II, 33.

Affirmation (*Utverzhdennaia gramota*) with signatures declaring the election of Boris in the name of the Sobor. On March 15, Iov sent out a general letter (*okruzhnaia gramota*) summarizing the events, the first contemporary document describing the election.[28] The coronation of Boris took place only in September, having been delayed by the need to confront a possible Crimean Tatar raid over the summer.

The Sobor itself produced a document describing its decision.[29] It began by invoking the Trinity, and then passed to an undoubtedly mythical story that Ivan IV had commended his son Fyodor to the care of Boris Godunov and designated him the heir after Fyodor's death. The story was obviously mythical, since at Ivan's death no one knew that Fyodor would not have an heir, and in any case Dmitrii Ivanovich was still alive. Then it asserted that Fyodor had designated Boris his heir with his blessing. This story was at least possible, if not likely. Then, with complete lack of logic, it asserted that the whole people from greatest to least saw that they were without a sovereign and chose Boris to be the tsar. The patriarch rejoiced and made a speech. He said that they would all now serve Boris, his wife Mariia, their children Fyodor and Kseniia, and any other children God would give the new tsar. They did this because no one was left of the dynasty that had ruled from Riurik to Fyodor, so they searched the holy writings to see how tsars had come to the throne in Israel and among the Greeks. They found that David came from a family (*rod*) of tsars, not from one of aristocrats, while Joseph came not from a royal clan, but from the just seed of Abraham. Patriarch Iov then listed Roman and Greek emperors who did not come from the lineage of tsars but attained that rank. All the rulers he listed ruled piously and justly, and demonstrated that God looked for those good qualities, not descent from the lineage of tsars. As the Bible says, "many are called but few are chosen" (Matthew 22:14).

The Affirmation Charter of 1598 was compiled after the Sobor and included all of Patriarch Iov's speech from that Sobor, but it also added an extensive narrative of events. There were, however, two versions of the Charter. The differences between the two versions, the first from May 1598 and the second from early 1599, are largely a matter of rhetoric, and both relied heavily on the earlier circular letter of Patriarch Iov and the Sobor decision.[30] At the end of the document are the

[28] *AAE* II, 1–6.

[29] The document is undated but presumably reflects the decision of March 15: *AAE* II, 13–16.

[30] First version: *DRV* VII, 36–127; second version: *AAE* II, 16–54. See S. P. Mordovina, "K istorii utverzhdennoi gramoty 1598 g.," in *Arkheograficheskii ezhegodnik za 1968 god* (Moscow: Izdatel'stvo Akademii, 1970), 127–141; A. P. Pavlov, "Sobornaia

signatures, the object of much scholarly attention. In the course of trying to convince Boris, Patriarch Iov delivered a speech adducing the Biblical and Byzantine precedents for the election as tsar of a person not of exalted (i.e., royal) status.[31] The only other early source is the *Posol'skii Prikaz*'s reply to the Danish envoys in Moscow made on March 17, announcing that Boris was the new tsar. In all these documents Irina blessed her brother for the throne, and he accepted the requests of all ranks of people.[32]

The political realities behind this and later elections are certainly a major issue, and the ink spilled on them is worthwhile, but historians have not asked another question: why have an election and a sobor at all? And how did the elites who produced and approved the relevant documents explain the fact of election at a sobor?[33] None of the authors of the official documents seemed to find it necessary to defend the practice, though the historical sections of those documents show acute consciousness of the history of the Riurikovich dynasty. The closest to a defense of the practice of election is the speech of Patriarch Iov in the Council Decision and the Affirmation Charter of 1598. Iov's speech asserted that the pious clan (*koren'*) of tsars had extended up to Tsar Fyodor and there ended, and that God was placing the tsar's honor on Boris "like a flower chosen by God according to the kinship of the seed of tsars."[34] The element of kinship, it should be noted, was left vague, and Boris's

utverzhdennaia gramota ob izbranii Borisa Godunova na prestol," *Vspomogatel'nye istoricheskie distsipliny* 10 (1978): 206–225; Skrynnikov, *Rossiia nakanune "Smutnogo vremeni,"* 121–125.

31 Another quasi-official source also stressed Irina's role in the transfer of power: V. I. Buganov, ed., "Skazanie o smerti tsaria Fyodora Ivanovicha i votsarenii Borisa Godunova (Zapiski v Razriadnoi knige)," *Zapiski Otdela rukopisei GBL* 19 (Moscow: Kniga, 1957), 167–184. See also Gruber, *Orthodox Russia*, 80–96.

32 *AAE* II, 1–6; Shcherbachev, ed., *Russkie akty*, 309–315.

33 In part the problem is that the elections of the tsars are entangled with the larger issue of the Zemskii sobor, an endless conundrum. Most historians are committed for ideological or historiographical reasons to denying it any significance, to reducing it to a sort of Supreme Soviet of old Russia. They are so quick to reassure the reader that the Sobor had no significance that they have failed to explain why it existed at all, and why its most important occasions were the elections of the tsars. An exception was Cherepnin, *Zemskie sobory Russkogo gosudarstva*. Karamzin, who had lived through the proclamation of the 1797 decree and clearly thought that it represented some sort of norm, was perplexed by the Sobor. He noted the presence of numerous Riurikovich princes in the boyar elite. Why were they not simply chosen by working out the genealogy? His rather weak answer was that they had not been sovereign princes for a long time, but then that was true of the Shuiskiis as well, and the Romanovs had never been sovereign princes. N. M. Karamzin, *Istoriia gosudarstva Rossiiskogo* (St. Petersburg: Eduard Prats, 1842–4; Moscow: Izdatel'stvo Kniga, 1988–9), vol. X, 131–132. See also Daniel Rowland, "The Problem of Advice in Muscovite Tales about the Time of Troubles," *Russian History* 6, 2 (1979): 259–283, esp. 276.

34 *AAE* II, 21: "iako po svoistvu srodstvennomu tsarskogo semeni bogoizbrannyi tsvet."

virtues made him like those tsars of the blood of rulers. Using the examples of King David and the Byzantine emperors Constantine, Theodosius, Marcian, Justin II, and Tiberius II, he pointed to rulers who were chosen by God or by the previous rulers and were not necessarily from any sort of high position, much less from imperial or royal stock.[35] The speech did not directly pose the question of election, but it pointed out that God (and the Israelites) and the Romans had chosen monarchs, which it presented as perfectly correct, even when the chosen rulers were not the sons of kings or even of royal blood. Iov did not spell out in detail the Biblical precedents, but he was correct in what he said. In the Old Testament, God and the Israelites several times ignored heredity to choose kings, most notably King David. God had Samuel anoint David while Saul was still alive (1 Kings 16:13), but after Saul's death David did not become king right away. On God's command David went to the cities of Hebron. "And the men of Judah came, and there they anointed David king over the house of Judah" (2 Kings 2:4). Later on, when the king of Israel was murdered, "all the elders of Israel came to the king to Hebron; and King David made a league [Sept. *diatheken*] with them in Hebron before the Lord: and they anointed David king over Israel" (2 Kings 5:3). In the Bible, both God and the people chose the king. The *Khronograf* preserved this story, namely that God first anointed David, then the men of Judah anointed him king and finally "all the elders of Israel came to David in Hebron and anointed him over all Israel."[36] The four late Roman emperors were all designated by previous rulers, or, in the case of Marcian, by the previous ruler's daughter Pulcheria.[37] Byzantium certainly had long-lasting dynasties, at least after the ninth century, but it never had a formal law of succession for the throne, hereditary, or otherwise.[38] Nevertheless, neither

[35] *AAE* II, 21–23. The first to notice the importance of the speech was I. P. Medvedev, "Vizantiiskoe prestolonasledie i russkii prestol v XVI–XVII vv.," in *Sudebnik Ivana III: Stanovlenie samoderzhavnogo gosudarstva na Rusi*, ed. I. Ia. Froianov (St. Petersburg: Izdatel'stvo Sankt-Peterburgskogo universiteta, 2004), 427–435. The sources of the speech appear to be the Bible and the *Khronograf* (*PSRL* 22, pt. 1), namely the story of Joseph: Gen. 30–50 and *Khronograf* (*PSRL* 22, 50–59) and that of David: 1 Kings 16, 12–13 and *Khronograf* (*PSRL* 22, pt. 1, 108); the story of Constantine (the version in the *Zhitie* in the *Velikie Cheti Minei* is different from that in the *Khronograf*) was not a source for Iov's text.

[36] "priidosha vsi startsi Izrailevi k Davidu v Khevron i pomazasha ego nad vsem Izrailem," *PSRL* 22, 108, 114–115.

[37] For Constantine and Constans, Theodosius. Marcian, Justin II (chose Tiberius), and Mauricius: *Khronograf* (*PSRL* 22, pt. 1), 261, 279, 287–288, 299–300. Roman imperial succession was normally by cooptation or designation, if not the result of proclamation by the army.

[38] The cases of formal election in Byzantium were few and quickly forgotten, and in any case the Russians did not know about them. Dimiter Angelov, *Imperial Ideology*, 131–132; Vincent Puech, "Élections et enjeux politiques à Byzance: Patriarcat et régence imperial

the Byzantines nor the ancient Israelites had anything like a *Zemskii sobor*, and the patriarch's speech was about the origins of the kings, not about the practice of election or choice. The Affirmation Charter of 1598 was concerned with the dignity of the ruler's family or its absence, not the fact of election.[39]

The official account of the accession of Boris that Russian diplomats provided in the reign of Boris gave equal space to the blessing of Irina and Boris by Tsar Fyodor and to the election.[40] The historians who wrote in the aftermath of the Time of Troubles and formed the basis of modern historical research are a more complicated story.[41] The very official *Novyi letopisets* asserted that on his deathbed Tsar Fyodor forbad his sister to rule and refused to name a successor, saying that all was up to God. After Fyodor's death, Irina went immediately to the convent, thus concealing the role she played according to the Affirmation Charter. The text described carefully the calling of the Sobor, making it appear much more orderly than was probably the case, but it did not offer any explanation for the decision of the church, boyars, and gentry to call the Sobor. It then went directly to a description of the decision to choose Boris and the discontent of the Princes Shuiskii.[42] The monk Avraamii Palitsyn's widely copied *Tale* also merely presented the fact of the choice of Boris and his personal hypocrisy and wickedness, but did not comment on the fact of election, and the so-called Other Tale (*Inoe skazanie*) that often accompanied Palitsyn's tale in manuscripts was in this respect no

au milieu du XIIIe siècle," in *Élections et pouvoirs politiques du VIIe au XVIIe siècle*, ed. Corinne Péneau (Paris: Éditions Bière, 2008), 311–324; Gilbert Dagron, *Empereur et prêtre: Étude sur le "césaropapisme" byzantin* (Paris: Gallimard, 1996), 64. There were many times when the emperor was overthrown or installed with popular insistence or approval: Jean-Claude Cheynet, *Pouvoir et contestations à Byzance (963–1210)* (Paris: Publications de la Sorbonne, 1990), Anthony Kaldellis, *The Byzantine Republic: People and Power in New Rome* (Cambridge, Massachusetts: Harvard University Press, 2015).

39 Unfortunately, contemporary diplomatic sources reflect information only from after the 1598 election, and do not comment on the validity of the decision to elect a monarch: L. Sapiega, "Diplomaticheskoe donesenie Sigizmundu III, koroliu pol'skomu o delakh Moskovskikh," *ChOIDR* 1858, book 2, pt. 4, 1–24; Kazimierz Tyszkowski, *Poselstwo Lwa Sapiehy w Moskwie 1600 r.* Archiwum Towarzystwa Naukowego we Lwowie, section 2, vol. 4, notebook 1, (Lwów: Towarzystwo Naukowe, 1927); Arkadiusz Czwołek, *Piórem i Buławą: Działalność polityczna Lwa Sapiehy kanczlerza litewskiego, wojewody wileńskiego* (Toruń: Wydawnictwo Naukowe Uniwersytetu Mikołaja Kopernika, 2012), 139–157.

40 *SRIO* 38, 285–288 (instructions to the Mikulin embassy to England in 1600).

41 D. I. Antonov argues that the election documents amounted to a "conceptual model" of election, but he takes the defense of election of a tsar of non-royal stock for a defense of election in general. He further argues that this position was reflected in the later narratives, yet none of the documents defend election against heredity or justified the calling of the Sobor. D. I. Antonov, *Smuta v kul'ture srednevekovoi Rusi* (Moscow: RGGU, 2009), 144–157.

42 *Novyi letopisets*, *PSRL* 14, 49–50; V. G. Vovina-Lebedeva, *Novyi letopisets: Istoriia teksta* (St. Petersburg: Dmitrii Bulanin, 2004).

different.[43] Similarly, the idiosyncratic account of the secretary Ivan Timofeev also only mentioned the election and devoted most of the relevant text to a longer and more colorful description of Boris's initial hypocritical refusal to take the throne.[44] The actual election virtually disappeared in all of these accounts, with the exception of that of the most official text, the *Novyi letopisets*.

If the election did not elicit any comment or defense, Boris and Patriarch Iov took measures to ensure that it had as much validity as they could muster. In fact, there does not seem to have been much opposition to Boris from the boyars, other than from the Shuiskii and probably Romanov clans. How strong their opposition was is not clear, but the *Novyi letopisets* pointed to the Shuiskiis, and circumstantial evidence points to the Romanovs.[45] All the actual election documents ignore such possibilities and stress the unanimity of the decision. The roughly 500 signatures on the Affirmation Charter included most of the upper clergy, the Duma, including its lesser ranks, many palace officials, and the Moscow ranks of the gentry. The names of provincial gentry appeared as well, though in fewer numbers, as well as some of the Moscow merchants. Historians have concentrated on the relationship of the signatures to the actual composition of the Sobor, concluding that many or even most of them were not present, but were asked to sign later.[46] Finally, the Russian narrative sources, the election documents in general terms, and the report of the imperial envoy Michael Schiel, who was in Moscow later in the year, report that the people of Moscow played an important role in the election. The Sobor decision asserted that the petition to Boris to accept the throne came not just from the elites but "from all service people, the elite merchants, the traders, and the common people" (*ot sluzhilykh liudei, i ot gostei, i ot torgovykh liudei, i ot chernykh liudei*). The Affirmation Charter repeated the same formula. In Schiel's account, it was "the whole commons" (*die ganze Gemeindt*) that begged Irina to rule, and failing that, for her brother Boris to accept the throne.[47]

[43] L. V. Cherepnin, O. A. Derzhavina, and E. V. Kolosova, eds., *Skazanie Avraamiia Palitsyna* (Moscow and Leningrad: Izdatel'stvo Akademii nauk SSSR, 1955), 103–104, 251–252; S. F. Platonov, ed., *Inoe skazanie*. RIB 13 (St. Petersburg: Tovarishchestvo Pechatnia S. P. Iakovleva, 1893), 12–16.

[44] V. P. Adrianova-Peretts and O. A. Derzhavina, eds., *Vremennik Ivana Timofeeva* (St. Petersburg: Nauka, 2004), 51–56.

[45] *PSRL* XIV, 50; cf. Skrynnikov, *Rossiia nakanune "Smutnogo vremeni,"* 130–131, 134.

[46] Mordovina, "K istorii utverzhdennoi gramoty"; Zimin, *V kanun groznykh potriasenii*, 227–232; Skrynnikov, *Rossiia nakanune "Smutnogo vremeni,"* 120–125. Pavlov argued that there were probably more provincial gentry at the actual Sobor than were later able to sign the Affirmation Charter: Pavlov, "Sobornaia utverzhdennaia gramota," 223–225.

[47] "Relation wegen der jungsten Anno 98 von der Röm. Kay. Mayt. unsers allergn. Herrn Hofdiener Michael Spielen [sic] anbefohlenen Rais in die Moscaw," in *Sammlung bisher*

The role of wider circles of the population in these elections was new. Only the Duma ranks and the upper clergy had been the audience for the Testament and the designation by blessing of the heir back to the fourteenth century. The 1498 coronation of Dmitrii, the presence of the heir at diplomatic receptions, and other court ceremonies introduced him to a wider audience, namely the larger court circles beyond the Duma ranks, as well as a wider circle of clergy associated with the court. Perhaps some of these events involved groups of the landholding class, if only as part of the army, but not necessarily. The Moscow merchants and townspeople must have witnessed some of the court ceremonies that involved processions through the city, but the presence of provincial gentry, even in limited numbers, was completely new. It is difficult to escape the conclusion that a larger number of men were involved in the process than before. The Affirmation Charter of 1598 had around 100 signatures of the clergy, many of them from monasteries far from Moscow, who normally appeared in the capital for church councils but not for the various ceremonies involving the heir. There were also about forty men with Duma rank: boyars, *okol'nichie*, duma gentry, and duma secretaries. Some 300 men were Moscow gentry or gentry servants of the court, and the rest provincial gentry and townsmen. In the past, all but (perhaps) the metropolitan and a few boyars were passive observers of the ruler's decision to designate an heir. In 1598, virtually the whole Duma and Moscow ranks were participants in the decision, and, if we are to believe Schiel and other sources, the people of Moscow were the decisive force that brought Boris to the throne. It may certainly have been the case that Boris to a greater or lesser extent manipulated the events, which would hardly have been unique in the history of elections, but his manipulation was designed to convince all of these people to support him, not just the Duma and higher clergy. This was a radical break with earlier practice. It is less important whether the signatures actually reflected the personal composition of the Sobor on February 17 than that Boris and his entourage, especially Patriarch Iov, thought it necessary to get the participants to sign the document. By doing so, the signatories demonstrated in writing what people of their rank, if not they themselves personally, had demanded orally at the time of the election. Their acquiescence also signified their loyalty to the new tsar. The election of Boris Godunov was not the victory of the gentry in the sense that the elections in Poland or Hungary were

noch ungedruckten kleiner Schriften zur ältern Geschichte und Kenntniss des russischen Reiches, ed. B. von Wichmann (Berlin: Reimer, 1820), vol. I, 423–464, esp. 449, 450 (Volck und Gemeindt), 451–455; A. N. Shemiakin, ed. and trans. "Donesenie o poezdke v Moskvu pridvornogo rimskogo imperatora Mikhaila Shilia v 1598 godu," *ChOIDR* 2 (1875): i–ii, 1–22; *AAE* II, 14.

alleged to be. The main participants from the landholding class involved in the process, even if the signatures underrepresent the provincial gentry, were the aristocrats in the Duma and the upper layers of the landholding class represented in the Moscow ranks. What is remarkable is that the provincial gentry and the townspeople appeared at all among the signatories. Beyond the official documents, it seems that the populace of Moscow played an important role in the events, though no representatives of that group appeared officially in the Affirmation Charter, with the exception of a few elite merchants. This breadth of participation was new in Russian history.

In the European context, the election of Boris Godunov has a number of unique features. It was undoubtedly more disorderly than the norm in Poland or the Scandinavian countries. In those lands royal elections were rarely a matter of calm deliberation, but forms had evolved through legal culture that specified much of the procedure and were mostly followed. Russia had none of this, since the only real precedent for a sobor was the Assembly of the Land of 1566, which was about war and foreign policy, not the election of a monarch. In spite of this absence of precedent, the Russian elites, most probably the patriarchal chancellery or the tsar's *d'iaki*, managed to produce documents that, while rhetorical and sometimes mendacious, provided a coherent account of the events and the fact of the election, justifying at least the choice of a tsar not from a ruling clan.

The composition of the Sobor, seen not in legal terms but as social reality, was not absolutely unique. In Polish elections the Senators played the role of the Russian Duma, and the mass of the nobility was present in large numbers. Here the Russians were different, since the whole procedure in Moscow was impromptu. In Poland, the elections were announced well in advance and the *szlachta* could assemble in fields outside of Warsaw. Outside Russia the estates also participated with the aristocracy. In Poland no non-nobles were present, in Denmark their role was limited, and only in Sweden did the third (urban) estate and the fourth (the peasants) participate and vote in the proceedings. What stands out by comparison with these countries is the role of the people of Moscow. The vague terms of Schiel and the election documents certainly point to the common people of Moscow, and indeed some men with palace ranks were hardly gentry. At the end of the list of signatories are the *barashi*, the artisans who took care of the tsar's tents when he was traveling or on campaign. They were palace servants to be sure, but their place in society was closer to the common people of Moscow than to the gentry and aristocratic palace officials. The election of Tsar Boris represented a new form of succession to the throne, but also included a much wider and more active involvement of the population in that succession.

Succession to Boris

Boris clearly understood that he represented a new reality and took some measures to ensure his position and potentially his succession. Initially Boris expanded the duma considerably to reward his friends and conciliate his enemies. This policy seems to have worked, with the important exception of the Romanov clan, exiled in November 1600.[48] Succession was an issue that came up again and again. The original decision of the Sobor noted that henceforth service was to be to Tsar Boris and also to his wife and children.[49] The children were two, his son Fyodor (born 1589) and daughter Kseniia (born 1582). Soon after the election Patriarch Iov ordered prayers for the new tsar, and included in the list Boris's wife Tsaritsa Mariia, and the children. In June, at the approach of the Crimean khan, Iov again prayed for Boris and the whole family.[50] The coronation of Boris took place on September 3, 1598, following the precedent of Tsar Fyodor's coronation with some changes.[51] One of the first was a speech from Boris himself, stating that Ivan had blessed his son Fyodor with the throne, but that Tsar Fyodor had ordered the clergy and people to elect a tsar since he had no children. Thus he had been elected by God's will. Patriarch Iov repeated this story in his reply.[52] The patriarch then prayed for long life to Boris, Tsaritsa Mariia, and Tsarevich Fyodor Borisovich.[53] Later on in the homily Iov asked God's blessing "*vo mnogie rody i leta*" on Boris and Mariia, Tsarevich Fyodor and this time his sister Kseniia, and prayed that Boris would see his grandchildren, though he omitted the phrase *na svoem tsarstvii.*[54] If God was to grant long life to Tsarevich Fyodor, presumably he would be the heir, though the text does not explicitly say that. In any case, it never named him an heir and repeated the formulas of succession to the newly crowned tsar from the coronation ritual of Tsar Fyodor. The ceremony celebrated the election of the new tsar but also the formation of a new ruling family, including the tsar's children, one of them a son.[55]

Shortly after his coronation, Tsar Boris ordered provincial *voevodas*, the local governors, to perform public prayers for him and his family, "that the Lord God might multiply the years of our life and establish our

[48] Platonov, *Ocherki po istorii Smuty*, 256–271; S. F. Platonov, *Boris Godunov* (Petrograd: Knigoizdatel'stvo Ogni, 1921), 127–154; Pavlov, *Gosudarev dvor i politicheskaia bor'ba pri Borise Godunove*, 63–85.

[49] *AAE* II, 15. [50] *AAE* II, 1–9.

[51] *DAI* I, 239–249; B. A. Uspenskii, *Tsar' i patriarkh: Kharizma vlasti v Rossii* (Moscow: Shkola iazyki russkoi kul'tury, 1998), 136–139.

[52] *DAI* I, 240–241. [53] *DAI* I, 243. [54] *DAI* I, 246.

[55] The other surviving coronation speeches did not mention the family of Boris, merely repeating that he, Boris, was the chosen one. *AAE* II, 54–56.

tsar's root from generation to generation forever in health for many years."[56] The oath that the population was supposed to swear appeared the next day. They swore to serve Tsar Boris, Tsaritsa Mariia, Tsarevich Fyodor, and Tsarevna Kseniia, and those children whom God might give them in the future, since Tsaritsa Irina had, on the petition of the people of all ranks, agreed to bless Boris with the tsardom. Those who swore were not to try to harm the tsar and his family by witchcraft or poison. Oddly enough, they also swore that they would not support Tsar Semen (Bekbulatovich) or his son for the throne.[57] They were to report any plots against the throne and not go to other states to join Russia's enemies. They were to obey all the tsar's orders to find criminals, a provision which suggests that the oath was written for the provincial landholders, who were expected to assist the local governors in the suppression of crime. In all cases it was the whole family, listed each time, that was the object of faithful service.[58] As we have seen, the evidence for such an oath from all subjects in earlier decades is slim.[59] Boris demanded such an oath not just from some (possibly discontented) aristocrats, but from all the gentry, townsmen, soldiers, and presumably free peasants.[60]

[56] "chtob Gospod' Bog umnozhil let zhivota nashego i koren' nash tsarskoi ustroil v rod i rod naveki na mnogoletnoe zdravie" (September 14, 1598), *AAE* II, 56–57. The document in question went to Ivan Saburov, *voevoda* of Sol'vychegodsk.

[57] Semen Bekbulatovich, originally from the Nogai Horde, was khan of Kasimov (the vassal khanate south of Moscow 1452–1681), and in 1575 Ivan the Terrible, in one of the stranger episodes of the reign, named him grand prince of Moscow. Less than a year later, Ivan resumed the throne and relegated Semen to a provincial appanage. He lived until 1616. See Donald Ostrowski, "Simeon Bekbulatovich's Remarkable Career as Tatar Khan, Grand Prince of Rus', and Monastic Elder," *Russian History* 39, 3 (2012): 269–299; and Charles J. Halperin, "Simeon Bekbulatovich and Mongol Influence on Ivan IV's Muscovy," *Russian History* 39, 3 (2012): 306–330.

[58] *AAE* II, 57–61 (September 15, 1598).

[59] The later versions of the story of the death of Vasilii III assert that anyone beyond the court elite swore an oath to serve Ivan IV and his mother. There does not seem to have been a general oath sworn at the accession of Fyodor Ivanovich. The only surviving texts of any such service oaths involved only individual boyars and the tsar's male relatives. The oath of Mstislavskii and the others from 1562 had a formula very similar to the oath to Boris, but was not universal. The oath at the end of the 1566 Assembly of the Land covered a much larger part of the population but was still not universal. See Chapter 2.

[60] Timofeev in his *Vremennik* charged Boris with impiety in requiring the kissing of the cross to take place in churches instead of private houses so as to make the oath stronger than was the practice of earlier tsars. He also seems to imply that the order from Boris to require the oath beyond the court (or Moscow) was new. *Vremennik Ivana Timofeeva*, ed. O. A. Derzhavina (St. Petersburg: Nauka, 2004), 66–71. It is not clear whether he was referring to a general oath or those of individual boyars. In any case, Timofeev was writing during the 1620s. The First False Dmitrii also referred to an oath that everyone had sworn to his "father" Ivan IV: *SGGD* II, 201. If by that oath he meant the one allegedly sworn in 1534, there would have been no one left to contradict him. The context was his

The same summer after the election of Boris, he mobilized the army against the threat of a Crimean raid. He left his sister, Tsaritsa Irina/ Aleksandra, and his son Fyodor Borisovich back in Moscow. With Fyodor Borisovich were two men explicitly called "tutors" (*diad'ki*), Matvei Mikhailovich Godunov and Ivan Ivanovich Chemodanov.[61] The *Razriad* in this case gave no rank for either one, but in 1588–9 and 1590 M. M. Godunov was only a *stol'nik* (a court rank, roughly "table assistant"), albeit "with the sovereign," in the former year.[62] Another *razriad* notice gave his rank in the summer mobilization as *stol'nik*, but by December, 1598, M. M. Godunov was already an *okol'nichii*.[63] He received boyar rank at Christmas, 1603. During the Time of Troubles he served Tsar Vasilii Shuiskii as *voevoda* in Siberian Tiumen'. Unlike many others of the Godunov clan, he remained alive and a member of the elite under Tsar Michael, serving both at court and as governor of Tobol'sk and elsewhere until his death in 1638.[64] For Chemodanov there is no information on his rank in 1598, but he seems to have been a Moscow gentleman for most of the reign.[65] It appears that Boris chose a cousin to supervise or bring up his son and to help him a man of lesser rank. M. M. Godunov, judging from what we do know of his career at court, must have been about thirty years old. There is no mention of M. M. Godunov as *diad'ka* after the entry for summer 1598, but in the autumn Tsar Boris went on the usual pilgrimage to the Trinity-St. Sergii Monastery, and the records show that "with the tsarevich was Ivan

order to the population to swear an oath to him, "Dmitrii," in 1605, and the order made no mention of any oath to his "brother," Tsar Fyodor.

61 V. I. Buganov, ed., *Razriadnaia kniga 1550–1636 gg.* (Moscow: Nauka, 1975) (henceforth *RK 1550–1636*), vol. 2, pt. 1, 149; *RK 1475–1598*, 542–543. The two men with Aleksandra were the boyar B. Iu. Saburov and the *okol'nichii* Andrei Petrovich Kleshin, the latter being one of the then tsarevich Fyodor's *diad'ki* in 1582. Saburov, a boyar since the time of Ivan IV, was a relative of the Godunovs and seems to have died about 1598. Kleshin had been promoted from duma gentleman to *okol'nichii* in 1586, at which rank he remained in 1598. He died around 1559: Pavlov, *Gosudarev dvor i politicheskaia bor'ba pri Borise Godunove*, 33, 39, 53, 64–65, 80.

62 S. P. Mordovina and A. L. Stanislavskii, *Boiarskie spiski poslednei chetverti XVI–nachala XVII v.* (Moscow: TSGADA, 1979), 109; *RK 1475–1598*, 416.

63 *RK 1475–1598*, 542; *RK 1550–1636*, vol. 2, pt. 1, 166.

64 *RK 1550–1636*, vol. 2, pt. 1, 215 (boyar rank); vol. 2, pt. 2, 310 (1618, at court), 323 (1620, *voevoda* in Tobol'sk), 359 (1631, to Riazan' to assemble gentry cavalry); 371 (1632, *voevoda* in Kazan'); S. A. Belokurov, *Razriadnye zapisi za Smutnoe vremia, 7113–7121 gg.* (Moscow: Izdatel'stvo Imperatorskogo obshestva istorii drevnostei rossiiskikh pri Moskovskom universiteta, 1907) (first published *ChOIDR* 2–3 in 1907), 49, 85, 149, 241–242; Marshall Poe, *The Russian Elite in the Seventeenth Century* (Helsinki: Academia Scientarium Fennica, 2004), 396.

65 Pavlov, *Gosudarev dvor i politicheskaia bor'ba pri Borise Godunove*, 114–115. Tsar Michael appointed one Ivan Ivanovich Chemodanov *striapchii s kliuchom* in May 1614, but this may have been the son of the *diad'ka* of 1598: *DR* I, 130, 132.

Vasil'ev syn Morozov," who was apparently not his tutor. I. V. Morozov was not an important figure in other respects, but his son would be the tutor and favorite of Tsar Aleksei forty years later.[66] The establishment of a tutor to supervise the upbringing of the heir was apparently an innovation, and it also paralleled the European practice. From at least the sixteenth century the heirs to the kings of France had a tutor (*gouverneur*) as well, a nobleman but not of the highest aristocracy. Under his supervision were teachers (*précepteurs*) who actually taught the boy to read and write, as well as teaching Latin and many humanistic subjects.[67]

The issue of succession came up several times again in the short reign of Boris Godunov in his relations with foreign powers. Boris was often ill, and his son Fyodor was only eleven years old at the accession and not robust himself. A new reign, of course, also meant the need to announce the new tsar and renegotiate treaties that elapsed with the death of Tsar Fyodor. One of the first embassies that Boris sent abroad was to the Holy Roman Emperor Rudolf, which arrived in Hamburg in August 1599. At the ceremony in the city the *d'iak* Afanasii Vlas'ev, the head of the Russian embassy delivered a speech explaining how Boris came to the throne, listing the order (*prikaz*) of Tsar Fyodor, the blessing of Tsaritsa Irina, the wishes of the church and people, and the will of God.[68] The Russian records of the embassy are incomplete, but the Vienna records show that Vlas'ev also discussed a marriage between Tsarevna Kseniia and Maximilian Ernst, the young son of Archduke Karl of Steiermark, Rudolf's brother. In this

66 *RK 1550–1636*, 2, pt. 1, 165. I. V. Morozov was a young man, the son of Vasilii Petrovich Morozov, then an *okol'nichii*, raised to the rank of boyar by Tsar Vasilii Shuiskii in 1608, and died only in 1630. The family was prominent in the first half of the sixteenth century, but for some reason almost unknown during most of the reign of Ivan IV. Vasilii Petrovich seems to have restored the family fortunes. The father of V. P. Morozov was Peter Grigor'evich, about whom nothing is known, though his grandfather was a boyar in the 1550s: A. B. Lobanov-Rostovskii, *Russkaia rodoslovnaia kniga* (St. Petersburg: Izdatel'stvo A. S. Suvorina, 1895), vol. 1, 398–399; Nancy Shields Kollmann, *Kinship and Politics: The Making of the Muscovite Political System 1345–1547* (Stanford, California: Stanford University Press, 1987), 219–221. In 1566 Lev Grigor'evich Morozov, the brother of Petr, was one of the signatories to the *poruka* for Prince I. M. Vorotynskii, and thus part of the *zemshchina*, not the *oprichnina*: *SGGD* I, 538; Skrynnikov, *Tsarstvo terrora*, 273. I. V. Morozov attained boyar rank only in 1634 and entered a monastery twenty years later: Lobanov-Rostovskii, *Russkaia rodoslovnaia kniga*, 399.

67 Pascale Mormiche, *Devenir prince: L'école du pouvoir en France XVII ᵉ–XVIIIᵉ siècles* (Paris: Éditions CNRS, 2009), 3–20. For England, see Roy Strong, *Henry, Prince of Wales and England's Lost Renaissance* (London: Thames and Hudson, 1986); for Spain: Martha K. Hoffman, *Raised to Rule: Educating Royalty at the Court of the Spanish Habsburgs 1601–1634* (Baton Rouge, Louisiana: Louisiana State University Press, 2011).

68 *PDS* II, 664–665. Vlas'ev discussed the marriage plan both with Rudolf's advisers and with Archduke Maximilian, the former candidate for the Polish throne and Grand Master of the Teutonic Order: Heinz Noflatscher, *Maximilian der Deutschmeister (1558–1618): Glaube, Reich und Dynastie*. Quellen und Studien zur Geschichte des Deutschen Ordens 11 (Marburg: N. G. Elwert, 1987), 169–170.

arrangement, if Tsarevich Fyodor died without issue, Kseniia would inherit the throne with the Habsburg prince as her consort. The succession agreement was not, however, clear in all details, which caused the project to come to nothing.[69] A year later Grigorii Mikulin led a Russian embassy to England, and had orders how to explain there the accession of Boris. He was to say that the tsar, Fyodor, had blessed Irina and Boris with the tsardom, Irina then retired to a convent, but the church and people petitioned her to bless Boris with the throne, which she did.[70] This story was the same one that Vlas'ev had given in Hamburg the year before, but in this case there was no discussion of marriages.

Tsar Boris continued to discuss marriages for his children with foreign powers, discussions that necessarily raised the issue of succession. At the same time as the Habsburg project got nowhere, a more unusual possibility arrived in 1599 in the form of Gustav Eriksson, the son of King Erik XIV of Sweden by his mistress Karin Månsdotter. He came to the attention of Russian diplomats passing through Poland, and Boris invited him to Moscow, bestowing him with expensive gifts. Gustav was a pretender to the Swedish throne, and Boris had the plan of making him a vassal ruler in the Baltic provinces and perhaps Finland. He was also to marry Boris's daughter Kseniia. Nothing came of this, however, for it depended on the confused political situation in Sweden that would eventually clear up with the victory of Karl IX in 1604. Gustav fell out of favor with the tsar, but spent the rest of his life in Russia, dying in 1607. The sources for this episode are very incomplete, but it seems that the initiative, for the marriage at least, came from Boris.[71] It is noteworthy that Tsarevich Fyodor was already present at the reception for the Swedish prince, even though he was only ten years old, and Gustav kissed his hand as well as that of his father.[72]

[69] Hans Uebersberger, *Österreich und Russland seit dem Ende des 15. Jahrhunderts*. Veröffentlichungen der Kommission für neuere Geschichte Österreichs (Vienna: W. Braumüller, 1906), 569; "Responsus legati Mosci in negotio secreto matrimoniali," in V. N. Aleksandrenko, ed., "Materialy po Smutnomu vremeni na Rusi XVII v.," *Starina i Novizna* XIV (1911): 304–308.

[70] *SRIO* 38, 285–288. There was also some discussion in those years of an English marriage for Boris's son, but neither side seems to have been serious: Norman Evans, "The Anglo-Russian Royal Marriage Negotiations of 1600–1603," *Slavonic and East European Review* 61, 3 (1983): 363–387.

[71] Helge Almquist, *Sverge och Ryssland 1595–1911* (Uppsala: Almquist & Wiksell, 1907), 48–49; Henri Biaudet, *Gustaf Eriksson Vasa, Prince de Suède: Une énigme historique du XVIe siècle*. Suomalaisen Tiedeakatemian Toimituksia Series B, vol. 8, no. 5 (Geneva: Expédition historique finlandaise à Rome, 1913); Floria, *Russko-pol'skie otnosheniia i baltiiskii vopros*, 53, 91–101; A. V. Tolstikov, "'Reliatsiia o Gustave, syne korolia Erika' i Petr Petrei," in *Grani sotrudnichestva: Rossiia i Severnaia Evropa*, ed. I. R. Takal and I. M. Solomeshch (Petrozavodsk: Izdatel'stvo PetrGU, 2012), 104–121.

[72] Karamzin, *Istoriia gosudarstva Rossiiskogo*, vol. XI, 31, notes 14.

A new succession issue came up with the Polish embassy of 1600. Like the later Swedish embassy, the chief aim was to confirm the truce between the two countries, but Sigismund III and his ambassador Lew Sapieha, chancellor of Lithuania, had another agenda as well: they wanted to propose a union of Poland and Russia. The idea was to have a joint kingdom with two rulers, but the succession to go to one of them should the other have no heirs. The plan was clumsy, another episode of the more or less fantastic plans made in the Polish court to cement Polish hegemony in Eastern Europe. If conquest was unrealistic, perhaps a union might accomplish the same goal. The Polish embassy arrived in Moscow at the end of 1600, and was received by both Boris and his son Fyodor. Russian records of the embassy are fragmentary, but Eljasz Pielgrzymowski, secretary (*pisarz*) of the Grand Duchy of Lithuania, preserved a full record, which survives in two versions, one an incomplete prose version and the other his reworking of the narrative and much of the negotiations into verse.[73] The issue came up on December 7 at the third meeting of the Polish embassy with the Russian negotiators, Princes F. I. Mstislavskii and F. M. Trubetskoi, the head of the Ambassadorial Office V. Ia. Shchelkalov, and the *d'iak* Afanasii Vlas'ev. The boyars replied to the Polish proposals at that meeting by rejecting the union plan. The Polish plan would involve the election of the future tsar, but the boyars were against that. They asserted that the Russian throne was hereditary. They said:

> The great sovereigns, the Russian tsars, from the beginning are on their great lordships of the Russian tsardom, according to their czarish degree, majesties from their great ancestors, great sovereigns and not by the choice of people, and they rule and decree in all their lordships according to their czarish, most wise understanding.

The Russian tsars had to be crowned with the crown of Vladimir Monomakh and no other. Furthermore, Boris and his son Fyodor were healthy and their heirs (*nasledniki*) would be their children. They would speak no more of this issue: "our tongue does not open to speak such things of God's anointed."[74]

[73] Prose version: Elias Pilgrimovius [Eliasz Pielgrzymowski], *Didžioji Leono Sapiegos pasiuntinybė i Moskvą 1600–1601 m.*, ed. Jūratė Kiaupienė. Historiae Lituaniae Fontes Minores IV (Vilnius: Žara, 2002); Verse: Eliasz Pielgrzymowski, *Poselstwo i krótkie spisanie rozprawy z Moskwą. Poselstwo do Zygmunta Trzeciego*, ed. Roman Krzywy. Humanizm: Polonika IV (Warsaw: Neriton, 2010). See also Tyszkowski, *Polselstwo Lwa Sapiehy w Moskwie*; Czwołek, *Piórem i Buławą*, 147–157; and Floria, *Russko-pol'skie otnosheniia i baltiiskii vopros*, 140–161.

[74] "Wielikije hospodary, cary rosiejskije i z naczała na swoich presławnych hospodarstwach Rosyjskoho Carstwa bywajuć po swojej carskoj stepieni wieliczestwa z praroditelej swoich, wielikich hospodarej, a nie po ludzkomu obiraniu, i władiejuć, i powieliwajuć

If we believe the Polish diplomat, the boyars in their desire to reject the Polish union plan asserted something they all knew not to be true, that Boris ruled by inheritance and not the choice of men (*liudskoe obiranie*). It was also not the case that Boris was healthy, for Pielgrzymowski reported earlier that Boris "now suddenly became ill in his toe", presumably suffering from an attack of gout.[75] If the assertion of heredity was specious, the repeated presence of Tsarevich Fyodor at the ceremonies for the Polish embassy, his occasional brief speeches, and the almost universal invocation of his name with that of his father was a real fact. The boy was only eleven years old, so his appearance was clearly a statement of his future role, not an attempt to find a replacement for the tsar during his illnesses.[76] A few months later, in February 1601, Fyodor Borisovich joined his father at the banquet for a Swedish embassy.[77] He had become a regular feature of the court ceremonial.

The third attempt by Boris to secure a foreign husband for Kseniia came in 1602, and this time it was much more substantive and came much closer to success.[78] Late in 1601, Christian IV sent a mission to

wo wsiech swoich hospodarstwach po swojemu carskomu premudromu razumu. . . . jazyk nasz nie otwierżetsa pro takich pomazannikow Bożych howorić takije dzieła," Pielgrzymowski, *Poselstwo*, 94–95.

[75] "z nagła teraz na palec zachorzał," Pielgrzymowski, *Poselstwo*, 51, 53.

[76] See, for example, Pielgrzymowski, *Poselstwo*, 54 (Fyodor at the first audience, November 15), 60–61 (greetings and banquet in the name of Boris and Fyodor), 163–166 (Polish envoys received in the palace by Fyodor, Boris is again ill, February 16, 1601), 189 (Fyodor, "kniaź młody," makes a speech to the Polish envoys, March 3, 1601), 204–207 (Fyodor, "kniaź młody," at the final banquet, March 11, 1601). Dates NS. Fyodor Borisovich had appeared with his father at court ceremonies earlier, during the reign of Tsar Fyodor, starting in 1595 (when he was six years old!): Zimin, *V kanun groznykh potriasenii*, 205.

[77] *RK 1550–1636*, vol. 2 pt. 1, 184.

[78] D. Tsvetaev, *Protestantstvo i protestanty v Rossii do epokhi preobrazovanii, ChOIDR*, no. 4 (1889): 1–328; no. 1 (1890): 329–782, esp. 440–457; G. V. Forsten, "Snosheniia Danii s Rossiei v tsarstvovanie Khristiana IV," *Zhurnal Ministerstva narodnogo prosveshcheniia* 280 (1892): 281–335, esp. 288–298. The main source for the Danish mission is the unpublished diary of Axel Gyldenstjerne, who oversaw the mission, in TKUA, Rusland 18. A paraphrase with a few quotations is L. Engelstoft, "Udtog af Rigsraad Axel Gyldenstiernes Dagbog holden paa hans reise til og under hans Ophold i Moskow 1602–1603," *Historisk Calender* I (1814): 73–212 (Tsarevich Fyodor 104–106, 120, 131–137, 145, 147–148, 177). A Russian translation of the unpublished diary is Iu. N. Shcherbachev, trans., "Puteshestvie ego kniazheskoi svetlosti Gertsoga Gansa Shlezvig-Golshtinskogo v Rossiiu 1602 goda," *ChOIDR* 238, 3 (1911): 1–64. See also the anonymous German diary of the embassy, *Wahrhaftige Relation der Reussischen und Muscowitischen Reyse . . . des Herren Herzog Johansen des Jüngern . . .*, Lübeck, 1603 and Hamburg, 1604 (both with pages unnumbered and found in the Herzog August Bibliothek, Wolfenbüttel; another copy, Magdeburg, 1604, reprinted in *Magazin für die neue Historie und Geographie* VII (1773), 269, 272. Russian translation of the latter: A. N. Shemiakin, trans., "Dva svatovstva inozemnykh printsev k russkim velikim kniazhnam v XVII stoletii: Izvestie o puteshestvii v Rossiiu i Moskvu gertsoga Gansa mladshego datskogo," *CHOIDR* 4, 4 (1867): 1–56.

Boris (and Fyodor) over border and other issues as well as with the suggestion that Hans, Duke of Schleswig-Holstein, his younger brother born in 1583, marry Boris's daughter Kseniia. The conditions for the marriage laid down by the king of Denmark stipulated that Hans would be free to practice his religion and to go back and forth to Denmark, and that he would receive as Kseniia's dowry the principality of Tver'. Should she die before him, he would retain the principality, and it would pass to their children. The agreement did not specify what rights Kseniia would have to the Russian throne, if any, in the case of the death without heirs of her brother Fyodor, or what the position of Hans would be in that case.[79] In the summer of 1602 a Danish embassy of more than 300 persons went to Russia under the leadership of Axel Gyldenstjerne, Councillor of State and a great aristocrat at the Danish court. When Russian officials greeted them at their arrival in Ivangorod, tsarevich Fyodor's emissary was among the greeters.[80] It took the Danes several weeks to reach Moscow. According to Isaac Massa, on September 19 Boris and his son secretly watched the entrance of the Danes from the wall of the Kremlin, and later both greeted the Danes at a great banquet. Fyodor sat at the right hand of Boris, and Duke Hans next to him.[81] The Danish accounts of the embassy confirm Massa's account of the reception and indeed show that the young Fyodor was present at most of the formal occasions at the Palace and elsewhere. At the first meeting of the new head of the Ambassadorial Office, Afanasii Vlas'ev, with the Danes on their arrival at Ivangorod, Vlas'ev greeted them on behalf of the tsar and his son. On their entrance to Moscow, two boyars greeted the Danes for Boris and two for his son. At the first audience on September 30, Fyodor sat near his father, sharing in the banquet, the courtesies, and the giving of gifts. The Danes also reported in some detail the pilgrimage of the tsar and his family on October 6, to the Trinity-St. Sergii Monastery, the first for which we have a description since the 1560s. By the time of Boris it was clearly a matter of tradition, and the Tsar and his son rode in magnificent carriages accompanied by hundreds of guards and the boyars. The tsaritsa followed in another carriage with their daughter, and many women with them. The pilgrimage was not just a matter of personal piety, but a display of the ruling family to the people. The discussions about conditions had not proceeded very far, however, when Duke Hans fell ill on October 15. During his illness, tsarevich Fyodor accompanied the tsar to visit him and

[79] Shcherbachev, ed., *Russkie akty*, 333–342. [80] *RK 1550–1636* vol. 2, pt. 1, 203.

[81] Isaac Massa, *Histoire des guerres de la Moscovie*, 2 vols. (Brussels: Fr. J. Olivier, 1866), vol. 1, 64–66: Isaac Massa, *A Short History of the Beginnings and Origins of These Present Wars in Moscow*, trans. G. Edward Orchard (Toronto: University of Toronto Press, 1982); *RK 1550–1636*, vol. 2, pt. 1, 204.

later went with his uncle, the *koniushii* (master of the horse) Dmitrii Godunov. The death of Hans on October 28, 1602, put an end to the story.[82] Boris wrote to Christian of his own grief and condolences, and asked if there were another Danish prince to replace Hans. Boris then sent a Russian embassy to Denmark, but by the time it arrived Russia was in full crisis and Kseniia's future was no longer relevant.[83] For no part of this story is there any evidence of discussion among the boyars or any reaction from the Orthodox Church. It is the case that V. Ia. Shchelkalov lost his position as head of the Ambassadorial Office in 1601, on the eve of Hans's arrival, to Afanasii Vlas'ev, but we do not know whether that had anything to with the Danish marriage project.[84] There is no evidence of either support for the policy or opposition to it from the boyars, other than the remark quoted by Isaac Massa to the effect that the boyar Semen Nikitich Godunov opposed marrying the tsarevna to a heretic who was not worthy to come to the holy land of Russia.[85] The church does not seem to have taken a position publicly.

The Danes stayed in Moscow until the summer of 1603, and while there they had the opportunity to witness tsarevich Fyodor in more public ceremonies. On January 6, was the blessing of the waters at Epiphany, and both Tsar Boris and his son came, in similar clothing and to the same place in the ceremony.[86] The Danes also saw the Palm Sunday procession on April 17, 1603. Tsar Boris led the patriarch's horse as usual, and the tsarevich followed behind them.[87] On May 21 there was another procession, led by the patriarch and tsarevich Fyodor. The German diarist of the Danish embassy reported that they proceeded to a local monastery, which must have been the Sretenie (Presentation of Christ in the Temple)

[82] In the Gyldenstjerne diary Fyodor Borisovich was usually called the "young emperor" (unge keyser): Gyldenstjerne Journal, TKUA Rusland 18, ll. 3, 24v, 31v, 51v, 59, 64v, 131; Shcherbachev, trans., "Puteshestvie ego kniazheskoi svetlosti Gertsoga Gansa Shlezvig-Golshtinskogo," 6, 15, 17–18, 25, 28, 30, 54; Forsten, "Snosheniia Danii s Rossiei" 290–295.

[83] Iu. N. Shcherbachev, "Datskii arkhiv: Materialy po istorii Drevnei Rossii, khraniashchiesia v Kopengagene 1326-1690 gg.," *ChOIDR*, 1 (1893): 150–175; Shcherbachev, ed., *Russkie akty*, 327–396; Tsevtaev, *Protestantstvo i protestanty v Rossii*, 440–457.

[84] Pavlov, Gosudarev *dvor i politicheskaia bor'ba pri Borise Godunove*, 76; D. M. Liseitsev, *Prikaznaia sistema Moskovskogo gosudarstva v epokhu Smuty* (Moscow: Institut rossiskoi istorii RAN, 2009), 593.

[85] Massa, *Histoire des guerres de la Moscovie*, vol. 1, 68. S. N. Godunov was certainly an important figure in the duma, the most important of the Godunov relatives: Pavlov, *Gosudarev dvor i politicheskaia bor'ba pri Borise Godunove*, 64–67. Massa thought that he was the tsar's "right ear" and a "great tyrant": Massa, *Histoire des guerres de la Moscovie*, vol. 1, 65.

[86] "Wahrhaftige Relation der Reussischen und Muscowitischen Reyse," *Magazin* VII, 278–281. The first weeks of January 1603 are missing in the Gyldenstjerne diary, and it ends on February 21.

[87] Ibid., *Magazin* VII, 282–286.

Monastery on the edge of the city, to which there was traditionally an annual procession. On the way tsarevich Fyodor stopped by the place of execution, the Lobnoe mesto (*Heuptpand*) on Red Square and vowed to rebuild it.[88]

The Danes were not the only ones to see these ceremonies. In 1603, one last embassy arrived that had nothing to do with succession but recorded in detail the participation of tsarevich Fyodor Borisovich in the court ceremonial. This was the embassy from the Hanseatic League, or more precisely from Lübeck and Stralsund. Both the Lübeckers and the Stralsunders recorded the events, with somewhat different details. At their arrival in the capital on March 25 (Annunciation Day) one of the boyars greeted them in the names of Boris and his son. Their first audience on April 3, 1603, was with Boris and his son Fyodor, sitting to his left. Boris wore the Monomakh crown: "a black velvet cap fitted with sable furs a hand wide and on it a gold crown with all sorts of magnificent diamonds and noble stones."[89] Fyodor sat on a lower level from his father and wore only a tall hat decorated with black fox fur.[90] On Palm Sunday (April 17) the Hanseatic envoys witnessed the procession, with Tsar Boris and the young tsarevich.[91] A month later (May 21) they were witnesses to another procession, this time led by tsarevich Fyodor alone. The Lübeckers reported that "the young tsar in a great solemn procession of innumerable priests, monks, boyars, and the common people went past our yard in order to bless the fruits of the fields."[92] The Stralsund account also noted the presence of both the patriarch and the tsarevich. The next day the Germans learned that if they wanted to give a petition, they should give it to the "young tsar" or to Afanasii Vlas'ev.[93]

Even as the divisions in Russian society were beginning to appear, Boris went on to the next stage in moving his son toward the throne and finding him a bride. In May 1604 a Russian embassy departed for Kakheti, the

[88] Ibid., *Magazin* VII, 287.
[89] Otto Blümcke, *Berichte und Akten der hansischen Gesandtschaft nach Moskau im Jahre 1603*. Hansische Geschichtsquellen VII (Halle: n.p., 1894), 46, 97, 100 ("Der Kayser ist bekleidett gewesen mitt einer schwartzenn sammittenn Mutzenn ufm heuptte, mit zobelnn ein handtt breitt aussgeschlagenn, unnd daruber her eine goldene Krone mitt allerlei herlichenn Demanten unnd edlenn Steinen gezirett").
[90] Ibid., 101.
[91] Ibid., 51, 109–110. Cf. Robert O. Crummey, "Court Spectacles in Seventeenth Century Russia: Illusion and Reality," in *Essays in Honor of A. A. Zimin*, ed. Daniel Clarke Waugh (Columbus, Ohio: Slavica, 1985), 130–158.
[92] Blümcke, *Berichte und Akten der hansischen Gesandtschaft*, 52 ("der junge Kayser in grosser solennischer procession mite in hauffen unzehliger Pfaffen, Munchen, Bayoren unnd gemeinen volcks unsern hoff vorbey gangen, umb die fruchte des feldes zu gesegnen").
[93] Ibid., 112–113.

eastern Georgian kingdom, and Kartli, the traditional Georgian center, both Orthodox countries. The embassy spoke in the name of both Boris and his son Fyodor. They knew from an earlier embassy from Alexander of Kakheti that both Alexander and his neighbor George of Kartli had marriageable daughters and granddaughters. The discussions were inconclusive, lasting into the early months of 1605, by which time Tsar Boris had already died.[94] As Boris assembled an army late in the year to confront the threat posed by the first pretender, he included his son's entourage, a little over 100 men, in its ranks. Most likely Fyodor Borisovich stayed in Moscow with his father, but from the list it is clear that he had his own group of noblemen and others in his service.[95]

For the whole brief reign of Boris Godunov, his son tsarevich Fyodor Borisovich was prominent in the court ceremonies for foreign ambassadors, taking on lesser roles with brief speeches and receiving petitions. He also participated in the Palm Sunday procession and the Epiphany ceremonies, for which the audience was primarily Russian and went beyond the court to include the people of Moscow.[96] The message was quite obvious that he was the future tsar. Both the Polish embassy and the Hanseatic embassy saw him as the "young tsar" (*kniaź młody* or *der junge Kayser*), not just as the son of the tsar. They understood him to be associated with his father in ruling the country. Boris did everything he could to ensure that his son would succeed him, and tried to provide for his daughter a husband who would be a credible consort if the son died or left no heirs himself. The crisis that began when Grigorii Otrep'ev, a former monk and pretender to the throne sponsored by Polish aristocrats, crossed the border into southern Russia in autumn 1604 rendered all these efforts fruitless.

The Time of Troubles

The Time of Troubles was a massive social and political upheaval, but it began and remained a battle about succession to the Russian throne.[97]

[94] S. A. Belokurov, *Snosheniia Rossii s Kavkazom* (Moscow: Universitetskaia tipografiia, 1889), 428, 430, 492–517; W. E. D. Allen, "The Georgian Marriage Projects of Boris Godunov," *Oxford Slavonic Papers* 12 (1965): 69–79.

[95] Mordovina and Stanislavskii, *Boiarskie spiski*, 31, 46, 64.

[96] At the Epiphany ceremony of January 6, 1603, both Tsar Boris and his son kissed the Gospel, and the patriarch sprinkled both of them with holy water before anyone else. The Danish envoys noted that Fyodor stayed for the whole ritual in spite of the intense cold: "Wahrhaftige Relation der Reussischen und Muscowitischen Reyse," *Magazin* VII, 280–281; Bushkovitch, "The Epiphany Ceremony of the Russian Court in the Sixteenth and Seventeenth Centuries," *Russian Review* 49, 1 (1990): 1–17.

[97] Platonov, *Ocherki po istorii Smuty*; Maureen Perrie, *Pretenders and Popular Monarchism in Early Modern Russia: The False Tsars of the Time of Troubles* (Cambridge: Cambridge

Furthermore, it was a struggle that pitted pretenders claiming the throne by hereditary succession against elected tsars, Boris and Vasilii Shuiskii.[98] The sudden death of Boris in April 1605, allowed Grigorii Otrep'ev, the First False Dmitrii, to come to the throne. Boris had tried to pass the throne to his son, then only sixteen years old, in the traditional manner: he had blessed him with the throne and lands of Russia. At the same time, however, he also left the state in the hands of his widow, Tsaritsa Mariia, for the time being.[99] Like his father, Fyodor Borisovich ordered the population to swear an oath to serve him, his mother, and his sister. According to the *razriad* account, they did.[100] Neither Boris nor his son, however, could maintain power against the rebellion spreading from the southwestern frontier toward Moscow. The commanders of the tsar's army began to go over to the False Dmitrii. Boyar intrigue in Moscow removed both Fyodor and his mother from power, and both soon perished.[101] Only Boris's daughter Kseniia was allowed to live out her life, as a nun. Neither the First False Dmitrii nor the later pretenders claimed that Tsar Ivan IV had designated (*blagoslovil*) them as heir. They merely asserted that they were the heirs because they were, each one, the son of Ivan IV, Dmitrii, who had not died at Uglich in 1591 but had gone into hiding to escape the persecution of Boris Godunov. They thus negated the election of 1598, but they also avoided the fact that neither Ivan nor Fyodor had ever designated Dmitrii as his heir. As the First False Dmitrii entered Russia he called on the people to join him, the "born sovereign" (*gosudar' prirozhdennyi*). Soon after he took the throne in summer 1605, he sent around orders that the whole population should swear an oath of loyal service to him, again the "born sovereign" and his "mother," the nun Marfa (Mariia Nagaia, Ivan IV's last wife).[102] "Born sovereign" was a new term that earlier rulers had never used, and the

University Press, 1995); A. L. Stanislavskii, *Grazhdanskaia voina v Rossii XVII v.: Kazachestvo na perelome istorii* (Moscow: Mysl', 1990); Dunning, *Russia's First Civil War*; B. N. Floria, *Pol'sko-litovskaia interventsiia v Rossii i russkoe obshchestvo* (Moscow: Indrik, 2005), 200–226, 371–372; I. O. Tiumentsev, *Smutnoe vremia v Rossii v nachale XVII veka: Dvizhenzie Lzhedmitriia II* (Moscow: Nauka, 2008); G. A. Zamiatin, *Rossiia i Shvetsiia v nachale XVII veka* (St. Petersburg: RGGU, 2008).

98 Perrie notes that "the pretenders appealed to the traditional principle of hereditary succession, in contrast to the various types of election that had brought their opponents to the throne," Perrie, *Pretenders and Popular Monarchism*, 239. As she herself described, however, the Cossacks in 1605 seem to have supported collateral, not lineal, succession: Ibid., 94–95.

99 *SGGD* II, 187–190 (announcement from Tsaritsa Mariia and Fyodor Borisovich and Patriarch Iov).

100 *SGGD* II, 191–194; *RK 1550–1636*, vol. 2, pt. 1, 224.

101 *RK 1550–1636*, vol. 2, pt. 1, 228.

102 *AAE* II, 76, 92–95; *SGGD* II, 200–003: Perrie, *Pretenders and Popular Monarchism*, 64–65.

inclusion of his "mother," brought from her convent, added to the show of heredity. They also used foreign models to make that claim. In his title the First False Dmitrii described himself in official documents as "*gosudar' i dedich*" (in Polish "pan i dziedzicz," in Latin "dominus et haeres"), a combination that the Russian rulers had also never used.[103] The Second False Dmitrii used the same terminology to describe himself, starting from his appearance on the scene in 1608.[104] Neither of the two was relying on Russian tradition, but instead drew on new terms, including Polish legal terminology, to assert a hereditary claim. The followers of the two False Dmitriis may well have reasoned according to some sort of Russian popular tradition based on reverence for simple hereditary succession as an argument. The first two pretenders' claims were formulated in a new language, some of it borrowed from Poland's titulature of kings that was the norm before the 1573 election of Henry of Valois.[105]

Grigorii Otrep'ev did not last. He managed to stay in power long enough to marry Marina Mniszech, the daughter of his principal patron in Poland, Jerzy Mniszech. This First False Dmitrii and his Polish entourage had managed to offend the boyars and people of Moscow, who overthrew him in May, 1606. Fast on the heels of that event, a relatively narrow group of boyars and some townspeople chose Prince Vasilii Shuiskii as tsar. The choice did not involve the larger social groups who played a role in 1598 and later in 1613. These boyar circles chose Shuiskii among other possible candidates: they had sent secret messages to King Sigismund eploring the king's support for Dmitrii, whom they saw as low-born and tyrannical, and had suggested that they might choose his son Władysław instead.[106] Before this plan could come to fruition, Dmitrii perished and Shuiskii came to power. On May 19, 1606, Shuiskii issued a series of promises to the boyars, stating on his oath that he would pass no sentence of death or confiscation of property without the participation of the boyars, nor would he confiscate the property of the wives and children of townsmen convicted

[103] A. V. Lavrent'ev, *Tsarevich – tsar' – tsesar': Lzhedmitrii I, ego gosudarstvennaia pechat', nagradnye znaki i medali 1604–1606 gg.* (St. Petersburg: Dmitrii Bulanin, 2001), 12; SGGD II, 159–162, 165–166.

[104] *SGGD* II, 327–328, 336–341, 348, 352–353, 361–363.

[105] For the Polish terminology, see *Volumina Legum* (St. Petersburg: J. Ohryzk, 1859), vol. I, 277 (1542), 287 (1547); vol. II, 107 (1570). After 1573, the title was merely "Deo gratia rex," in Polish "król z Bożej łaski": *Volumina Legum* II, 134–135. The most thorough account of the pretender phenomenon, that of Maureen Perrie, makes clear that the extent of popular enthusiasm for the various pretenders may have been occasionally exaggerated by historians but was certainly real. Perrie, *Pretenders and Popular Monarchism*, 245.

[106] Floria, *Pol'sko-litovskaia interventsiia*, 62–63.

of crime or listen to false accusations.[107] The "constitutional" ring of the text has excited much discussion over the years, but the first part of the text, describing Shuiskii's right to the throne, has not. Before he got to the promises, Shuiskii asserted that he came to throne by heredity:

> "we," he said, "have come by the philanthropy of God and the prayers of the clergy and all Orthodox Christians to the patrimony (*otchina*) of our ancestors, the Russian sovereignty (*gosudarstvo*) as tsar and grand prince, and God had given it [the sovereignty] to our ancestor Riurik, who was from the Roman Caesar, and after many years to our ancestor Great Prince Aleksander Iaroslavich Nevskii; on this Russian sovereignty were my ancestors, and after that, having divided up to the Suzdal' district, not by seizure or compulsion, but by kinship, as great brothers [*bol'shie brat'ia*] were accustomed to sit on great places [thrones]."[108]

Tsar Vasilii declared that he had been elected but also made a direct hereditary claim as a Riurikovich and Suzdal' prince, whose lands came to him by heredity as was proper for "great brothers." Shuiskii's main potential rival for the throne was Prince F. I. Mstislavskii, a Gediminovich, so the genealogy may have also been intended to present a superior claim as a Riurikovich.[109] In any case, heredity went along with aristocracy.

The 1606 Order of Coronation (*chin venchaniia*) for Tsar Vasilii Shuiskii is another story. The 1598 document served as a template for this official 1607 document and described the process of election as well as the coronation. Patriarch Iov's speech from the 1598 Affirmation Charter appeared in the Order, this time putting the words in the mouth of the metropolitan of Novgorod Isidor (died 1619). The Order also included a story of the death of Fyodor and the election of Boris. Until the reign of Fyodor, the metropolitan said, the fathers had given the scepter and throne to their sons. After the death of Fyodor "*tsarskogo ego koreni chad ne ostasia*" ("no children of the tsar's descent remained"), and he said that Boris "*ne ot tsarskogo koreni izbran byst'*" ("was not chosen from the descent of a tsar") and that he was elected by the Boyar Duma (*tsarskii sinklit*). The rest of the speech stressed Tsar Vasilii's kinship with the previous rulers, asserting that he was taking the throne of his ancestors without mentioning the election.[110] Following the example of his predecessors, Tsar Vasilii required the population to kiss the cross to swear

[107] *SGGD* II, 299–300; Platonov, *Ocherki po istorii Smuty*, 282–287; G. V. Abramovich, *Kniazia Shuiskie i Rossiiskii tron* (Leningrad: Izdatel'stvo Leningradskogo universiteta, 1991), 134–138; Dunning, *Russia's First Civil War*, 237–243.
[108] *SGGD* II, 299.
[109] In late May 1606, there was some sort of plot in favor of Mstislavskii: Platonov, *Ocherki po istorii Smuty*, 292–293.
[110] *AAE* II, 104–106.

loyal service to him, and also to his tsaritsa and the children God would give him in the future.[111] The oaths clearly did not work very well, for almost immediately in the summer of 1606 Vasilii faced a rebellion in the south under one Ivan Bolotnikov, involving a motley collection of Cossacks, rebellious bondsmen, and gentry, who managed to hold a number of towns for nearly a year before falling apart.

Starting in early 1607, a new threat appeared, and for most of his short reign Vasilii struggled in vain against the other "hereditary" option, the "Thief of Tushino," the Second False Dmitrii.[112] The pretender took up camp with his army near the village of Tushino on the western outskirts of Moscow (hence the nickname) and asserted himself as the true Dmitrii, who not only had not perished in 1591 but also had survived in 1606. He soon attracted not only Russian support but also that of the numerous bands of Polish soldiers and nobles who had come to Russia with Otrep'ev, as well as new recruits from the Commonwealth. The documents that the Second False Dmitrii sent out to his followers thus reminded them of their 1605 oath of loyal service and called him their "born sovereign."[113] He asserted hereditary right against election and against Shuiskii's kinship with the old dynasty.

To cope with the growing civil war in Russia, Tsar Vasilii turned to Sweden, and in the spring of 1609 Jakob Delagardie led a Swedish army into Russia to help fight the pretender and his Russo-Polish forces. The Russian situation, however, had also attracted the attention of the king of Poland, who laid siege to Smolensk in late 1609. Vasilii's Swedish allies proved useless at the battle of Klushino, a Polish victory: many of the mercenary units left Swedish service for Polish. Soon after, the boyars and the people of Moscow on July 17, 1610, overthrew Tsar Vasilii. The throne was now vacant, and the Thief of Tushino himself perished in December 1610. For the next few months the "Seven boyars" ruled Russia, searching also for a more permanent solution to the crisis. In the days after the expulsion of Tsar Vasilii, the Moscow "ranks" (*chiny*) had informed the provinces that Tsar Vasilii had abandoned the throne at the petition of all the people, a formula that recalled the Affirmation Charters of 1598 and 1606. They sent out calls for an Assembly of the Land to choose a new tsar, and something like that did manage to come together in Moscow, though not with the participation of the Tushino camp. The Polish army under Stanisław Żółkiewski began its advance to

[111] *SGGD* II, 301–302. Tsar Vasilii had no children in 1610. Two daughters were born to him during his reign, but both died in infancy.

[112] Perrie, *Pretenders and Popular Monarchism*, 157–207; Tiumentsev, *Smutnoe vremia*.

[113] *Akty istoricheskie*, 5 vols. (St. Petersburg: Tipografiia Ekspeditsii zagotovleniia gosudarstvennykh bumag, 1841–2), vol. II, 132–133 (October 23, 1608).

Moscow, which created a new situation. As a result, the boyars and the assembled sobor decided to accept King Sigismund's son Władysław as the new tsar, with a series of conditions to secure the place of Orthodoxy and the rights of the boyars and gentry.[114] When the Poles agreed, the Moscow authorities sent orders to the provinces informing them of the resultant treaty and its provisions and ordering them to swear an oath of loyalty to Władysław. It naturally said nothing about succession, as Władysław was only fifteen years old and unmarried.[115] As the Polish option grew more and more unpopular, the Russian First Militia under Prince D. T. Trubetskoi and Prokopii Liapunov moved toward Moscow in 1611. As they assembled, they began to form an embryonic government, which they described as elected by the "whole land." In their messages to the town they did not announce any intention to elect a tsar, however, only the need to fight the Poles and free Moscow. In their oath, they swore only to expel the Poles and then serve the sovereign of Russia whom God would give them.[116] The First Militia stalled from internal discord, but they were clearly thinking about the possibilities. For a new tsar, they first turned to Sweden, looking to one of the sons of Karl IX, either Gustav Adolf or Karl Philip. The Swedes captured Novgorod in July 1611, which gave them an apparently firm position in Russia, and the Novgorodians expressed a desire for one of Karl's sons to be the new tsar.[117] The assassination of Liapunov in the summer put an end to the first Swedish project as well as to the First Militia.

The Second Militia came into being in Nizhnii Novgorod at the end of 1611 under the leadership of Prince D. M. Pozharskii and with the intention of electing a tsar. For that reason, it was even more a major turning point than it has seemed to many historians. Behind the Second Militia were the assembled townsmen, soldiers, and gentry of the Nizhnii Novgorod and other Volga districts. Around August 1611, the people of Kazan' called on Perm' to join them, stating explicitly that their aim was

114 The agreement also specified that changes to the law code could be made only with the consent of the boyars and the "whole land." *SGGD* II, 388–389, 391–398; *AAE* II, 277–279; Platonov, *Ocherki po istorii Smuty*, 425–438; Władysław Czapliński, *Władysław IV i jego czasy* (Warsaw: Wiedza Powszechna, 1976), 24–54; Floria, *Pol'sko-litovskaia interventsiia*, 200–226.

115 *AAE* II, 279–284; *SGGD* II, 439–444.

116 *AAE* II, 315–316 (April 11, 1611, First Militia to Sol'vychegodsk); *SGGD* II, 537–538 (oath); Platonov, *Ocherki po istorii Smuty*, 460–489. The letter from the Hegumen Dionisii and Avraamii Palitsyn of the Trinity-St. Sergii Monastery of October 6, 1611, also calls for help in expelling the Poles but says nothing about electing a tsar: *SGGD* II, 577–579.

117 Zamiatin, *Rossiia i Shvetsiia*, 33–59; Almquist, *Sverge och Ryssland*, 195–268; Michael Roberts, *Gustavus Adolphus*, 2 vols. (London and New York, New York: Longmans, Green and Co., 1953–8), vol. 1, 72–75.

to "elect a sovereign to the Moscow sovereignty by the whole land of the Russian state." A bit later, Prince Pozharskii and the people of Nizhnii Novgorod sent the same message to Vologda.[118] Pozharskii repeated the call for an election in June 1612, as he was preparing to move toward Moscow.[119] This intention was hardly surprising, since the Second Militia, like the first, arose from the assemblies of the people, townsmen and gentry, of the inner Russian areas, not from among the administrative officers, *voevodas* and others, left over from the reign of Vasilii Shuiskii. It came from below, and elected its own commanders, starting with Pozharskii. Historians have stressed the "national" composition and aims of the Second Militia, but in the early months of 1612 the Militia and Prince D. M. Pozharskii were interested in a Swedish candidate, Karl Philip, the second son of King Karl IX, for the throne of the tsars. Karl Philip in this plan would have had to become Orthodox.[120]

The victory of the Second Militia over the Polish forces before Moscow in August–October 1612, was the culmination of one of the great epics of Russian history. The Russians soon recaptured the Kremlin and formed an interim government, which immediately called an Assembly of the Land from all the provinces of Russia not under occupation by rebels or foreign armies. The interim authorities fulfilled the promises made in their first calls for unity and assistance. The deliberations occupied several weeks over the winter of 1612–13, and have been the matter of much discussion by historians. The Swedish candidacy was still quite serious in January 1613, but soon lost support.[121] The successful candidate was Michael Romanov (born 1596), the son of Fyodor Nikitich Romanov, who was proclaimed tsar

[118] "vybirati by nam na Moskovskoe gosudarstvo gosudaria vseiu zemleiu Rossiiskoi derzhavy." *AAE* II, 346, 350. P. G. Liubomirov, *Ocherk istorii nizhegorodskogo opolcheniia 1611–1613 gg.* (Moscow: Izdatel'stvo sotsial'no-ekonomicheskoi literatury, 1939), 45–46, 75–76; Iu. M. Eskin, *Dmitrii Mikhailovich Pozharskii* (Moscow: Kvadriga, 2013).

[119] *SGGD* II, 593–597. Similar messages from Pozharskii: *SGGD* II, 598–599.

[120] Pozharskii also wanted a united choice and that the tsar be the son of a sovereign: "gosudarskii syn," *AAE* II, 26–70; Zamiatin, *Rossiia i Shvetsiia*, 59–92; Roberts, *Gustavus Adolphus*, vol. 1, 75–79; B. N. Floria, "Izbranie tsaria Mikhaila," *Istoricheskii vestnik* 3, 150 (2013): 6–23. A bit later Pozharskii also discussed a Habsburg candidacy with an Imperial envoy to Persia who was passing through Iaroslavl': Walter Leitsch, *Moskau und die Politik des Kaiserhofes im XVII. Jahrhundert.* Wiener Archiv für die Geschichte des Slaventums und Osteuropas IV (Graz and Cologne: Böhlau, 1960), 64–87.

[121] Zamiatin, *Rossiia i Shvetsiia*, 140–162. According to Swedish informants, there were briefly other candidates, namely the Princes D. T. Trubetskoi and D. M. Cherkasskii, and the boyars generally opposed Michael: G. A. Zamiatin, "K istorii zemskogo sobora 1613 g.," *Trudy Voronezhskogo gosudarstvennogo universiteta* III (1926): 71–74. Gustav Adolf (king since the end of 1611) and his family were not fully united on the Karl Philip project, nor was the Swedish government: Roberts, *Gustavus Adolphus*, vol. I, 79–91.

by the Sobor in February.[122] Fyodor had been born around 1554 and was the eldest and most important of the Romanov clan that Boris Godunov had exiled in 1600. He and his wife then both entered monasteries, leaving their young son Michael in the care of relatives. In the time of the First False Dmitrii, Fyodor/Filaret Romanov became metropolitan of Rostov, and then in 1608 the forces of the Thief of Tushino brought him to their camp and made him patriarch in opposition to Germogen, Tsar Vasilii's patriarch. Filaret got to Moscow after the fall of Vasilii Shuiskii and headed the Russian embassy to Sigismund III in Smolensk. Filaret did not accept Sigismund's conditions, and as a result went as a prisoner to Marienburg in Royal (Polish) Prussia, where he remained until the Truce of Deulino of 1619. Consequently, he was not on the scene in 1613, and his seventeen-year-old son Michael Romanov was living with his mother near Kostroma on the upper Volga River.

For Michael Romanov's election, there are somewhat fuller sources beyond the Affirmation Charter (*Utverzhdennaia gramota*) of 1613 and narratives, so that historians can make more solid judgments about the actual events. They have generally concurred that his support was quite broad, though they continue to argue about specific issues such as the extent and importance of Cossack backing for the Romanov candidate. The versions of the Affirmation Charter bear the signatures of 256 to 283 (varying in the manuscripts) people from boyars on down through the ranks, and some of the signatures may have been added later. There may have been twice as many or more people present during the proceedings, including many elected deputies from the provinces and even (non-serf) peasants.[123] The Affirmation Charter of the 1613 election used for its text that of Boris and the *chin venchaniia* of Vasilii Shuiskii, but added new material.[124] The

[122] Platonov, Ocherki *po istorii Smuty*, 528–534; Dunning, Russia's First Civil War, 424–442; Stanislavskii, Grazhdanskaia voina v Rossii, 80–92. Zamiatin, Rossiia i Shvetsiia, 140–182; E. I. Kobzareva, *Shvedskaia okkupatsiia Novgoroda v period Smuty XVII veka* (Moscow: Institut rossiskoi istorii RAN, 2005), 199–244; G. Edward Orchard, "The Election of Michael Romanov," *Slavonic and East European Review* 67 (July 1989): 378–402; Viacheslav Kozliakov, *Mikhail Fedorovich* (Moscow: Molodaia gvardiia, 2004), 30–52. L. E. Morozova, *Rossiia na puti iz Smuty: Izbranie na tsarstvo Mikhaila Romanova* (Moscow: Nauka, 2005), denies the importance of the Cossacks. See also Isolde Thyrêt, "Marfa Ivanovna and the Expansion of the Role of the Tsar's Mother in the 17th Century," in *Rude and Barbarous Kingdom Revisited: Essays in Russian History in Honor of Robert O. Crummey*, ed. Chester Dunning, Russell Martin, and Daniel Rowland (Bloomington, Indiana: Slavica, 2008), 109–130.

[123] Cherepnin, *Zemskie sobory Russkogo gosudarstva*, 192; Dmitrii Liseitsev, "Legitimnost' verkhonvnoi vlasti v Rossii v epokhu Smuty: K voprosu o statuse 'vybornykh liudei'," *Rossiiskaia istoriia* 4 (2014): 146–154.

[124] S. A. Belokurov, ed., *Utverzhennaia gramota ob izbranii na Moskovskoe gosudarstvo Mikhaila Fedorovicha Romanova* (Moscow: Tipografiia Obshchestva rasprostraneniia poleznykh knig, 1906) (*ChOIDR*, 3, 1904).

1613 Charter pointed to the family connections with the Riurikovich dynasty (through Anastasia Romanova, the wife of Ivan IV) but devoted most of the space to a description of the Sobor. The Charter stressed that Michael's mother Marfa had to be convinced to allow her son to be the tsar before the boy himself. As there was no patriarch, Archbishop Feodorit of Riazan' and Murom took the role of the leader of the church, trying to convince Michael to take the throne. Again the document included the speech from 1598 in defense of the election of monarchs of non-royal families. It opened with the same statement, substituting Michael's name for that of Boris, that the old *koren'* of the tsars had ended with Fyodor and that Michael was the flower chosen by God for the kinship of his nature to that of rulers.[125] The official documents also stressed the dynastic tie, the role of the women members of the relevant clan, the leadership of the church, and unanimity of the people in the Sobor.[126] At the Sobor on April 14, 1613, the final act of election, Marfa blessed her son with the throne and Michael obeyed his mother, accepting the sovereignties of Moscow and Vladimir and becoming the ruler (*gosudar'*) of all Russia.[127] Not surprisingly, the coronation ritual on July 11 told the same story.[128] Metropolitan Efrem of Kazan', who officiated in the ceremony, gave a long oration, which followed the example of the text of the 1613 Charter. He did not try to concoct any story of blessing by previous tsars, and instead recounted the death of Fyodor without children, the election of Boris Godunov, and the evil deeds of the First False Dmitrii and King Sigismund of Poland, concluding that the people had chosen Michael (*po izbraniiu vsekh chinov liudei vsego vashego velikogo Rossiiskogo tsarstviia*) in accord with God's will. The document also recounted the story of the crown of Monomakh, as in 1547 and 1584, showing that the crown and dignity of tsar was inherited.[129] The only element of family inheritance from the previous tsars was the connection of the Romanov clan to Ivan IV's first wife, Anastasiia Romanova. As she was the sister of Michael's great-grandfather, it was hardly a matter of direct descent.[130] In his final prayer, Metropolitan

[125] Belokurov, *Utverzhennaia gramota*, 56–58. In recounting the events of 1613 S. M. Solov'ev ignored the speech, paraphrasing instead the more "realistic" arguments of Feodorit: S. M. Solov'ev, *Istoriia Rossii s drevneishikh vremen* (Moscow: Izdatel'stvo sotsial'no-ekonomicheskoi literatury, 1960–6) (originally Moscow: Universitetskaia tipografiia 1851–79), vol. V [= 9], 1961, 7–14). Similarly Morozova, *Rossiia na puti iz Smuty*, 143–152; and Marie-Karine Schaub, "Les élections des tsars russes," 325–338.

[126] Belokurov, *Utverzhennaia gramota*, 51–55. [127] Ibid., 70. [128] *SGGD* III, 70–87.

[129] *SGGD* III, 75–77.

[130] The story of the events in the Affirmation Charter of 1613 formed the basis of the abbreviated account of his accession that the young Tsar Michael communicated to the European states in the months immediately following his election. The letters to foreign

Efrem prayed for long life to the tsar and that he would see his grandsons, and that God would strengthen the Russian tsardom, but he did not connect the two. As Iov had prayed in the coronation of Boris Godunov, Efrem prayed that Michael would see his grandsons, but not *v svoem tsarstvii.*[131] The succession was left unmentioned, not surprisingly as Michael had been elected at age sixteen without a wife or children.

The First Romanov, His Wives, and His Heir

Tsar Michael's reign from 1613 until his death in 1645 at the age of forty-nine was a period of retrenchment and recovery.[132] The new government headed by Michael's mother Marfa (born Kseniia Ivanovna Shestova) in her nun's habit and her Saltykov relatives and favorites managed to put an end to the conflicts. It defeated and executed the Cossack leader Ivan Zarutskii in 1614 and made peace with Sweden at Stolbovo in 1617, at the price of losing the coast of the Gulf of Finland, which had been Russian since the ninth century. Actual warfare with Poland continued until the Truce of Deulino in 1618, in which Russia accepted the loss of Smolensk. Russia was now at peace. After the truce, Poland continued to assert Władysław's claim to the Russian throne. At that point Michael's father Filaret returned to Russia. The new government had needed revenue and soldiers to keep fighting until it could make a bearable peace, for the existing financial system was a wreck. The answer was a series of meetings of the Zemskii sobor, a practice that continued until 1642. The tsar called the sobor no less than fourteen times in a reign of thirty-two years, a frequency not equaled before or after. The subjects of discussion were always the same, either special taxes to meet military expenses, or matters of war and peace, all of them necessarily entwined

rulers and the instructions to the ambassadors stressed both the family tie to Tsar Fyudor and the unanimous election by all the people of Russia. England: N. M. Rogozhin, ed., *Posol'skaia kniga po sviaizam Rossii s Angliei 1613–1614 gg.* (Moscow: Institut istorii SSSR, 1979), 118–122; translation: Maija Jansson, Paul Bushkovitch, and Nikolai Rogozhin, *England and the North: The Russian Embassy of 1613-1614.* Memoirs of the American Philosophical Society 210 (Philadelphia, Pennsylvania: American Philosophical Society, 1994), 115–117; Holy Roman Empire: *PDS* II, 927–930, 956–957 (Michael's mother Marfa blesses him with the throne), 966–969, 1029–1031; Denmark: Shcherbachev, ed., *Russkie akty*, 452–454.

[131] *SGGD* III, 83.

[132] The literature on the reign of Tsar Michael has been sparse. See Kozliakov, *Mikhail Fedorovich*; E. Stashevskii, *Ocherki po istorii tsarstvovaniia Mikhaila Fyodorovicha* (Kiev: Tipografiia vtoroi Arteli, 1913), pt. 1; and E. I. Filina, *"V poiskakh al'ternativy": "Pridvornye partii" v politicheskoi bor'be v Rossii 30–50-gg. XVII v.* (Moscow: Izdatel'stvo Prometei, 2011). Fundamental is now A. P. Pavlov, *Dumnye i komnatnye liudi tsaria Mikhaila Romanova: Prosopograficheskoe issledovanie*, 2 vols. (St. Petersburg: Dmitrii Bulanin, 2019).

with one another.[133] The most important of these conflicts was the Smolensk War of 1632–4, the attempt engineered by Michael's father, Patriarch Filaret, to take back Smolensk, a dismal failure in all respects except that Poland abandoned the claim to the Russian throne.[134] After that moment and Filaret's death, there were no more grand schemes. Michael's government concentrated on reinforcing the southern border against the Crimean Tatars. In 1637 the Don Cossacks captured the Ottoman fort of Azov at the mouth of the Don, creating a crisis in the south. The government responded by calling a Zemskii sobor, the last of the reign, in January 1642. The government had no intention of supporting the Cossacks at the risk of war with the Ottoman Empire, and the sobor agreed that it was prudent to withdraw. Tsar Michael spent his last years trying to make an agreement with King Władysław IV of Poland against the Crimeans and on the Danish marriage project for his daughter. A cautious foreign policy was the background to the rapid recovery of the Russian villages, colonization of new lands in the Volga river basin, and the expansion of Russian settlement in Siberia to the Pacific Ocean. Russian trade boomed as the Dutch consolidated their primacy in Russian trade with the West through Archangel. The recovery of the population was the continuation of a population boom without parallel in the Europe of the seventeenth century, the reward of peace and the guarantee of Russia's prosperity and increasing importance in the world. A revived Russia and its monarch had to deal with the problem of succession once again.

Tsar Michael and his son Tsar Aleksei both managed to produce at least one viable heir throughout the century, but they did not seem to think that the succession was automatic. The 1613 Charter did not unambiguously elect a new dynasty as well as a new tsar, for at the end the Sobor pledged only to serve the tsar, the future tsaritsa, and the "*tsarskie deti*" whom God would give. In other words, they swore to serve the tsaritsa when one appeared and the tsar's children, plural, and not restricted to boys.[135] The same formula occurred in the oath sent around the country by the Sobor immediately after its decision for the population to swear.[136] This was an oath of loyalty to a new ruling family,

[133] Paul Bushkovitch, "The Tsar and the Sobor: 1613–53," in *The State in Early Modern Russia*, ed. Paul Bushkovitch (Bloomington, Indiana: Slavica, 2019), 133–162.

[134] Paul Bushkovitch, "The Court of Tsar Michael in Swedish Sources," *Forschungen zur osteuropäischen Geschichte* 58 (2001): 235–242; E. Stashevskii, *Smolenskaia voina 1632–1634 gg.: Organizatsiia i sostoianie Moskovskoi armii* (Kiev: Universitetskaia tipografiia N. T. Korchak-Novitskogo, 1919); Czapliński, *Władysław IV i jego czasy*, 158–170.

[135] Belokurov, *Utverzhennaia gramota*, 70.

[136] *SGGD* III, 11–15; DAI II, 1–2; Morozova, *Rossiia na puti iz Smuty*, 321–322, 325–328, 341–344, 405–407.

not a dynasty, and replicated the oath to Boris Godunov of 1598. The succession question was left open. Immediately after the election, the population also swore loyal service to the new tsar.[137] The 1613 oath included future children, though Michael was not yet married.

The birth of a potential heir required a wife for Michael, and the story of how that came about is a tangled web that raises a variety of questions about the succession and the plans of Tsar Michael's mother and, after 1619, of his father, Patriarch Filaret. Marfa ruled the country until 1619 in company with her favorites from the Saltykov clan, Boris and Mikhail Mikhailovich.[138] During that period, in 1615–16, Marfa made one attempt to marry her son the tsar to Mariia Ivanovna Khlopova, the daughter of a family of upper-middle-level nobles. The process may have advanced as far as a betrothal, and Mariia certainly began to reside in the women's part of the palace, the Terem, when she fell ill in the summer of 1616. The tsar's doctors investigated the illness, and Mikhail Saltykov, the cupbearer (*kravchii*) of the court, reported that they pronounced the disease incurable. The marriage was canceled, and Mariia and her family went into exile.[139] The circumstance and true story of these events are a matter of question. In September 1623, the issue came up again, and a new investigation produced a story that Khlopova's uncle had been disrespectful to Boris Saltykov in front of Tsar Michael, who was visiting the Armory, the head of which was Saltykov. Allegedly after that encounter they changed their minds about the girl and falsified the doctors' reports to disqualify her.[140]

This story was not unlikely. Given the lineup in the Duma in 1616, it is difficult to believe that Khlopova could have made it so far if Tsaritsa Marfa and her favorites, who were precisely the Saltykov brothers and Prince A. V. Lobanov-Rostovskii, had opposed her from the start. The sources of the 1620s (discussed later in this chapter) asserted that Khlopova had the support of Princes I. B. Cherkasskii and Dmitrii

[137] On earlier oaths, see Chapter 1. In 1598 the oath had been to Boris, the tsaritsa, their two children, and any children whom God would give. The people also swore not to support Semen Bekbulatovich to replace Boris on the throne: *AAE* II, 57–61. The oath to Boris Godunov's son Fyodor was actually to serve Tsaritsa Mariia and her children Fyodor and Irina: *SGGD* II, 191–194. The one surviving oath to the First False Dmitrii mentions only him and his mother (Mariia Nagaia), but he was not married yet. Similarly, the oath to Tsar Vasilii Shuiskii in 1607 was to his wife and future children: *AAE* II, 94–95, 102–103.

[138] Stashevskii, *Ocherki po istorii tsarstvovaniia Mikhaila Fyodorovicha*, 93–189; Thyrêt, "Marfa Ivanovna," 124–129; Pavlov, *Dumnye i komnatnye liudi tsaria Mikhaila Romanova*, vol. I, 147–260.

[139] Russell E. Martin, *A Bride for the Tsar: Bride Shows and Marriage Politics in Early Modern Russia* (DeKalb, Illinois: Northern Illinois University Press, 2012), 167–176.

[140] *SGGD* III, 257–268; Martin, *A Bride for the Tsar*, 176–185.

Mikhailovich Pozharskii, the hero of the Time of Troubles. The later sources identified F. I. Sheremetev, M. B. Shein, and Ivan Nikitich Romanov as the only supporters of Filaret, thus presumably they were not the friends of the ruling coalition in 1616. None of them had important offices in that year. These factional groupings were reflected in the reshuffling of offices after Filaret returned.[141] As a result of the change of mind on the part of the Saltykovs, there was no progress toward a succession to Tsar Michael until his father arrived in Moscow in 1619.[142]

The provisions of the Truce of Deulino had released Filaret from imprisonment, after which he returned to Russia and immediately ascended the patriarchal throne on June 21–23.[143] In Russian historiographical tradition, he ruled as a strong father commanding his weak-willed son and carrying the title "great sovereign" (*velikii gosudar'*) until his death in 1633.[144] That he had the title of great sovereign and was the most powerful figure at court is undoubted, but Filaret was not unchallenged. The boyars were not united, and he had powerful opponents, not least his former wife, the nun Marfa. The boyars who had ruled with Marfa gradually lost their offices as heads of chancelleries to supporters of the patriarch.[145] Marfa, however, still had strong supporters. For the 1620s, the Dutch and Swedish diplomats recorded their impressions of the politics of the court.[146] The 1624 report, probably the work of Isaac Massa, stated that Marfa and Filaret each headed their own faction, and that Tsar Michael inclined much more toward his mother than toward his father. The principal issue at stake was his marriage. Filaret wanted a foreign bride, while Marfa wanted a Russian. The description is at odds with the usual portrait of Filaret as a sort of xenophobe, hostile to Poland and suspicious of the Orthodox of the Commonwealth, but that

141 There were twenty-six boyars in that year, of whom four died before the Khlopova incident, and five more were administering distant provinces. Poe, *The Russian Elite*, 88; Aleskandr Barsukov, *Spiski gorodovykh voevod i drugikh lits voevodskogo upravleniia Moskovskogo gosudarstva XVII stoletiia* (St. Petersburg: Tipografiia M. M. Stasiulevicha, 1902). Pavlov sees Khlopova as having some support at the court but opposed by the Saltykovy and perhaps Tsaritsa Marfa: Pavlov, *Dumnye i komnatnye liudi tsaria Mikhaila Romanova*, vol. I, 249–255, 276–282.

142 The Russian envoys sent to Stockholm in 1617 for the ratification of the Stolbovo treaty were instructed to inquire if Gustav Adolf had any marriageable sisters and if they had any proposals of marriage. B. N. Floria believes that they were to inquire on behalf of Tsar Michael: B. N. Floria, *Rossiia i cheshskoe vosstanie protiv Gabsburgov* (Moscow: Nauka, 1986), 40.

143 *DAI* II, 185–221 (*Izvestie* on the election and installation of Filaret).

144 Ia. G. Solodkin and D. M. Bulanin, "Filaret," *SKKDR* 3 (XVII v.), pt. 4, 161–168.

145 Filina, "*V poiskakh al'ternativy*," 49–51; Pavlov, *Dumnye i komnatnye liudi tsaria Mikhaila Romanova*, vol. I, 260–401.

146 Paul Bushkovitch, "Shvedskie istochniki o Rossii 1624–26 gg.," *Arkhiv russkoi istorii* 8 (2007): 359–381.

image is incomplete, to say the least.[147] The patriarch pursued his marriage plans quite actively, almost immediately after his return, a situation that implied that he had the upper hand in spite of the "inclination" of the tsar toward his mother. The head of the Ambassadorial office, the duma secretary Ivan Gramotin, does not seem to have taken sides, though he faithfully supervised the embassies. Filaret's allies in the duma were his brother Ivan Nikitich Romanov, Fyodor Ivanovich Sheremetev, and M. B. Shein, while Prince A. V. Sitskii and Prince D. M. Pozharskii supported Marfa. The most important of the boyars, Prince Ivan Boriskovich Cherkaskii, head of the Musketeers', Apothecary, and Great Treasury chancelleries, and Prince B. M. Lykov, the head of the Investigations Chancellery, were close to both Filaret and Marfa.[148] The first Russian emissary with the mission to find a bride for the tsar left for Europe in the spring of 1621. Before he could report, in Moscow the information had arrived that Christian IV of Denmark had nieces who would make suitable brides, and by March 1, 1622 a Russian embassy had arrived in Copenhagen. Christian was not interested, whether dubious about the match or about Russia's condition after the Time of Troubles, or just preoccupied with Danish affairs.[149] The same summer the Russians turned to Gustav Adolf in Sweden, asking him to help them to make contact with Brandenburg, as the elector Georg Wilhelm also had a suitable daughter. Objections from the king of Poland made the Brandenburg match impossible.[150] These Danish and Brandenburg stories leave many uncertainties. The instructions to the Russian ambassadors

[147] In 1620, Filaret presided over a council of the church which decreed rebaptism for Orthodox believers from the Polish Commonwealth, and in 1626 attempted (unsuccessfully) to ban Orthodox books from Poland. The 1627 dispute with the Ukrainian monk Lavrentii Zizanii also resulted in criticism of Ruthenian Orthodoxy. Makarii, *Istoriia Russkoi tserkvi* (Moscow: Izdatel'stvo Spaso-Priobrazhenskogo Valaamskogo monastyria, 1996), vol. 6, 285–290; Paul Bushkovitch, *Religion and Society in Russia: The Sixteenth and Seventeenth Centuries* (New York, New York: Oxford University Press, 1992), 52–53; A. A. Bulychev, *Istoriia odnoi politicheskoi kampanii XVII veka* (Moscow: Iazyki slavianskoi kul'tury, 2004); Margarita Korzo, *Ukrainskaia i belorusskaia katekheticheskaia traditsiia kontsa XVI–XVIII vv.: Stanovlenie, evoliutsiia i problema zaimstvovanii* (Moscow: KANON+, 2007), 292–354. Both Bulychev and Korzo see these incidents as examples of political and other issues rather than xenophobia and intolerance.

[148] Bushkovitch, "Shvedskie istochniki o Rossii," 364–365, 367, 371–373, 376–377; S. K. Bogoiavlenskii, *Moskovskii prikaznyi apparat i deloproizvodstvo XVI–XVII vekov* (Moscow: Izdatel'stvo Moskovskogo universiteta, 2006), 259, 301. I. N. Romanov held no offices in the chancelleries though the Dutchman reported that he was master of the horse (*stallmeester*, presumably *koniushii*).

[149] Tsvetaev, *Protestantstvo i protestanty v Rossii*, 458–469; Forsten, "Snosheniia Danii s Rossiei," 303–304. Christian also had complaints about Russian trade policy. The Russians asked for the hand of Dorothea Augusta, the daughter of Hans Adolf of Holstein-Gottorp (1575–1616). Christian IV referred them to her family.

[150] Tsvetaev, *Protestantstvo i protestanty v Rossii*, 469–474; Kurt Forstreuter, *Preußen und Rußland von den Anfängen des Deutschen Ordens bis zu Peter dem Großen*. Göttinger Bausteine zur Geschichtswissenschaft 23 (Göttingen: Musterschmidt, 1955), 154–155.

specified that the bride would have to convert to Orthodoxy and that she would be supported in accord with her rank, but said nothing about succession. We do not know whether the Russian ambassadors had any oral communications with the foreign courts beyond the written instructions. What would happen if Michael were to die childless, or with daughters only? What would be the position of the tsaritsa in that case? Would her Danish or Brandenburg relatives have any rights? It is difficult to believe that these thoughts were absent from the minds of Russians, Danes, Swedes, or Brandenburgers. By early 1623, in any case, it was clear that these attempts at arranging a foreign marriage for Michael would go nowhere.

It was only then that Filaret admitted defeat, and it was Marfa who chose Princess Mariia Vladimirovna Dolgorukaia to be Michael's wife.[151] The bride was the daughter of Prince Vladimir Timofeevich Dolgorukii. The Dolgorukii clan had not yet attained its later importance. It sprang from the Princes Obolenskii, who had served the grand princes of Moscow since the later fourteenth century, but the Dolgorukiis had not been prominent.[152] Prince Vladimir Timofeevich was the first to make something of a career. He had held the rank of Moscow gentleman (*moskovskii dvorianin*) in the 1590s, one of 246 men to have that rank, and he was not wealthy.[153] During those years he commanded regiments in the army and on the southern border.[154] He obtained boyar rank in 1606 from Tsar Vasilii Shuiskii, serving in the army and occasionally in chanceries during the fighting. In 1612, he was one of only two boyars to join Prince Pozharskii and the militia in Iaroslavl'.[155] He was not present, however, for Michael's election, perhaps because he had been sent as *voevoda* to Nizhnii Novgorod, where he later administered the oath of allegiance to the tsar to the people of the town.[156] After the election, Dolgorukii dined with the tsar on Palm Sunday and was one of the boyars in charge of Moscow while the tsar made a pilgrimage to the Trinity-St.

[151] Bushkovitch, "Shvedskie istochniki o Rossii," 364, 370.

[152] A. A. Zimin, *Formirovanie boiarskoi aristokratii v Rossii vo vtoroi polovine XV–pervoi terti XVI v.* (Moscow: Nauka, 1988), 43–47; Petr Dolgorukov, *Rossiiskaia Rodoslovnaia kniga* (St. Petersburg: Tipografiia Karla Vingebera, 1854), vol. 1, 86–109.

[153] Pavlov, *Gosudarev dvor i politicheskaia bor'ba pri Borise Godunove*, 114, 116, 176.

[154] *RK 1475–1598*, 397, 416, 422, 430–432, 460, 525.

[155] Platonov, *Ocherki po istorii Smuty*, 518, 520; Liubomirov, *Ocherk istorii nizhegorodskogo opolcheniia*, 129, 137, 279; Belokurov, *Razriadnye zapisi za Smutnoe vremia*, 12, 14, 18, 45, 48, 87, 91, 92, 96, 98, 103, 105, 106, 109, 118–127. In 1608 he also was briefly the head of the Monastery Office: Liseitsev, *Prikaznaia sistema Moskovskogo gosudarstva*, 376–377, 683.

[156] Dolgorukii served in Nizhnii Novgorod in 7121 (1612–13): Belokurov, *Razriadnye zapisi za Smutnoe vremia*, 109, 264; Liubomirov, *Ocherk istorii nizhegorodskogo opolcheniia*, 172, 200–201; *DR* I, 1085–1086. After the election of Michael he served in the Moscow Judicial Office during 1614–15: Bogoiavlenskii, *Moskovskii prikaznyi apparat i deloproizvodstvo*, 176; Liseitsev, *Prikaznaia sistema Moskovskogo gosudarstva*, 343.

Sergii Monastery, and spent time as *voevoda* in Kazan'.[157] Tsar Michael appointed him to the patriarchal *Razriad* on the same day as the return of Filaret to Moscow on June 14, 1619.[158] In ensuing years, he again occasionally appeared at the tsar's table. A brief note from the summer of the same year listed Dolgorukii as the head of the "patriarchal court, with spiritual affairs."[159] Then the sources are silent until July 12, 1623, the tsar's name day, when the prince again participated in the banquet.[160] For the last months (September–December) of 1623 there are also the records of Filaret's meals kept by his servants, which list Dolgorukii as eating with the patriarch on December 21 and record the enormous amount of fish consumed that day, at least a dozen varieties of fish cooked in various ways and several types of caviar.[161] During the first part of 1624, Dolgorukii continued to appear at the small banquets of the tsar on feast days.[162]

157 *DR* I, 170, 176, 178. He was *voevoda* in Kazan' 1614–17: *RK 1550–1636*, II/2, 281 (Kazan', 7123 = 1614–15); *DR* I, 193 (Kazan', 1615), 246 (Kazan', 1616), 295 (Kazan', 1617).

158 *RK 1550–1636*, vol. II, pt. 2, 322. "na Moskve velel gosudar' byt' u ottsa svoego boiarinu kniaz'iu Volodimeru Timofeevichiu Dolgorukomu da Ivanu Momotu Aleksandrovu synu Koltovskomu." Koltovskii had served with Dolgorukii during the Smuta: Belokurov, *Razriadnye zapisi za Smutnoe vremia*, 14, 48, 96. He became a patriarchal boyar rather than the tsar's boyar and served until Dolgorukii left the position in 7132 (1623–4): Bogoiavlenskii, *Moskovskii prikaznyi apparat i deloproizvodstvo*, 111. The Stoglav council of 1552 mandated that the tsar appoint the officials of the patriarchal chanceries: I. A. Ustinova, *Knigi patriarshikh prikazov 1620–1649 gg. kak istoricheskii istochnik* (Moscow: Institut rossiskoi istorii RAN, 2011), 90.

159 He dined with Tsar Michael in 1620 on Transfiguration Day (August 6) and to celebrate the Birth of the Mother of God (September 8); in 1621 on Annunciation Day (March 25), Tsar Michael's name day (July 12, St. Michael Maleinos), Dormition, at the table of Patriarch Filaret with the tsar and other boyars (August 15), the feast of St. Peter the Metropolitan, again with Filaret and other boyars (December 21), and at Christmas at the table of the tsar; in 1622 on Palm Sunday (April 14) Dolgorukii dined with the patriarch, not the tsar, the only other boyar present being Ivan Nikitich Romanov: *DR* I, 454, 465, 471, 476 note, 482, 493–494, 506, 512.

160 The Dormition feast in 1623 was the occasion for another banquet at the patriarch's table, with the tsar and three boyars, including Dolgorukii, as guests. Dinner was held again with the patriarch on St. Peter's day in December of that year, with Dolgorukii and only one other boyar: *DR* I, 563, 566, 578.

161 "Stolovaia kniga patriarkha Filareta Nikiticha," *Starina i novizna* 6 (1911): 152–154. Filaret ate every day with various monks and clerics, usually unnamed unless they were bishops or hegumens, rarely with laymen. Only once did he host the tsar alone, on October 5, the feast of the three Moscow miracle-workers, Metropolitans Sts. Petr, Aleksei, and Iona. The largest banquet was on December 14, the day of the "Peshchnoe deistvo," the commemoration of the three Hebrew boys in the fiery furnace (Daniel 3), with the metropolitan of Krutitsa Iona, the archbishop of Pskov Pavel, six archimandrites, two hegumens, and assorted other clergy. On the day before the St. Peter feast of December 21, Filaret hosted the lay staff of the patriarchal offices. Ibid., 91, 144, 151.

162 Presentation (Sretenie, February 2), possibly at a dinner at the Novospasskii Monastery (April 25), and on the Dormition at the table of Filaret with the tsar and two other boyars (August 15): *DR* I, 581, 614, 624.

There is at least some indication of Marfa's reasons in arranging the Dolgorukii marriage. Prince Vladimir Dolgorukii, aside from his record of service, was connected to the Saltykov family who had been influential in the early years of Michael's reign, before the return of Filaret. The Saltykovs in turn were also related to the clan of Michael's mother, the Shestovs. It seems that Marfa was trying to hold on to the power that she had possessed in 1613–19.[163] At the same time, Dolgorukii's role in the patriarchal administration and household suggests that Marfa had found a bride whose father was not unwelcome to Filaret. Perhaps she is best seen as a compromise candidate between the two factions. The wedding was a grand affair, and a detailed record remains. Tsar Michael took the decision to marry Princess Dolgorukaia on September 14, 1624, on the advice of his father Patriarch Filaret. Feasting continued for several days, until the actual wedding on the nineteenth. Afterward they feasted again until September 22, and on the next day the tsar went with many boyars and courtiers on the annual pilgrimage to the Trinity-Saint Sergii Monastery.[164] Unfortunately, Tsaritsa Mariia lived only a few months and died in January 1625, taking with her the fortunes of her father's family.[165] The more famous boyar princes Dolgorukii of the later seventeenth and eighteenth centuries sprang from different branches of the clan.[166]

Tsar Michael again needed a wife. On February 6, 1626, he married Evdokiia Streshneva, who survived to bear him a son, the future Tsar Aleksei, and several daughters.[167] There is no direct evidence that explains who was behind the choice of Streshneva, but Massa reported in 1624 that the most influential of the young men

[163] Martin, *A Bride for the Tsar*, 182–187; Pavlov, *Dumnye i komnatnye liudi tsaria Mikhaila Romanova*, vol. I, 403–412.

[164] *DR* I, 629–644, 1217–1222; *DRV* XIII, 137–144. At the wedding Prince Vladimir Dolgorukii petitioned the tsar against the boyar F. I. Sheremetev for "unfriendliness" (*nedruzhba*), a form of precedence suit: *DR* I, 1222.

[165] *DR* I, 658. Dolgorukii lost any chance of greater influence with his daughter's death. Prince Vladimir was no longer in the patriarchal *Razriad*, for in 1623–4 the boyar Prince A. I. Khilkov had already replaced him, and he died in 1632 or 1633: Bogoiavlenskii, *Moskovskii prikaznyi apparat i deloproizvodstvo*, 111.

[166] Prince V. T. Dolgorukii could not expect relatives to attain high position as in-laws of the tsar, since he had very few relations. He had only one other child than Mariia, a daughter Elena of whom we know nothing. Two brothers, Petr and Fyodor, also do not appear in any records. All of them may have died in infancy, for the two brothers had no recorded children. The third brother, Prince Fyodor Timofeevich, had attained boyar rank, but died in 1612. Neither his son nor his grandson attained boyar rank: Dolgorukov, *Rossiiskaia Rodoslovnaia kniga*, vol. I, 87–89.

[167] Martin, *A Bride for the Tsar*, 185–189. Martin asserts that Marfa had no impact on the choice, but in fact it is not known who did.

around the tsar was the *stol'nik* Vasilii Ivanovich Streshnev.[168] The Streshnevy were a provincial landholding family on the rise in the early seventeenth century, but V. I. Streshnev seems to have been the only one with court connections before the marriage. He was only Evdokiia's cousin, from another branch of the clan, but that seems to have been enough. After the marriage they all received various promotions, though they do not seem to have had the support of Patrarch Filaret. At the end of the 1630s, their star waned with the rising influence of the boyar Prince B. A. Repnin. Later the Streshnev relatives of Tsaritsa Evdokiia seem to have supported the idea of the marriage of Tsarevna Irina to the Danish Prince Valdemar.[169] Whatever the long-run fate of the Streshnev clan, the marriage was successful, and Tsar Michael produced ten children, seven girls and three boys. Three of the girls, Irina, Anna, and Tatiana, lived to a long adult life. Most importantly for the throne, Aleksei was born in 1629 and lived to rule for many years.

As soon as Tsar Michael had married, the service oaths included the tsaritsa and their children. The 1626 service oath, apparently administered to the army, boyars, and officials soon after Michael's second marriage, had the same formula as the earlier ones, namely that they would serve Michael, Tsaritsa Evdokiia, and the children whom God would give.[170] As the children appeared, the service oaths administered yearly added them in. The 1626–7 oath preserved in the *Razriad* archive was only to Michael himself, but in the next year, 1627–8, his daughters Irina and Pelageia, born in 1627 and 1628, respectively, were added. The text of the oath dated March 1, 1629 had Pelageia crossed out (she died in January of that year in infancy), but added Aleksei, born on March 10, 1629. From then on the children were all added, with Aleksei, the only boy, placed first, then the girls in birth order. The oath for 7151 (1642–3) listed the living children, but added the phrase about children "whom God will give."[171] In

[168] Bushkovitch, "Shvedskie istochniki o Rossii," 367, 377. V. I. Streshnev held important offices only after the marriage to Evdokiia: Bogoiavlenskii, *Moskovskii prikaznyi apparat i deloproizvodstvo*, 290; Filina, "*V poiskakh al'ternativy*," 232–233.

[169] Andrei P. Pavlov, "Les Strešnev et les Miloslavskij dans la première moitié du XVIIe siècle: Liens de famille et liens sociaux, carrière à la cour, voies d'accès à l'élite dirigeante," *Cahiers du monde russe* 57, 2–3 (2016): 276–292; Pavlov, *Dumnye i komnatnye liudi tsaria Mikhaila Romanova*, vol. I, 412–418.

[170] For the oaths to serve Tsar Michael from or shortly after 1613: *DAI* I, 1–3; for 1626: *DRV* VIII, 60–67 = RGADA, f. 210 (Razriad) d. 177, ll. 1–23. The *DRV* version omits the oath of the *postel'nichii* on ll. 9–10.

[171] RGADA, f. 210 (Razriad), d. 177 (Formy krestoprivodnykh zapisei), ll. 1–349, esp. ll. 1–75, 309–349. The oath published in *DRV* 8, 67–83 is not dated but is the same as in d. 177, ll. 214–252 from 7146 (1637–1638), where the same children are listed but Ivan's name is crossed out. Ivan died on January 10, 1639 at the age of five and a half, so the *DRV* text is either the 7146 oath or that for one of the years from the birth of Tatiana in 1636 to 1638.

none of these oaths, as in the earlier ones, is the eldest son described as the heir. He is merely listed first after his mother as the oldest boy.[172] Other public statements and rituals were for the family, not just the tsar and his heir. Tsar Michael's announcement of the birth of Aleksei Mikhailovich to provincial officials and the orders from the clergy to include him in prayers also used no word to imply succession. He was called not the heir (*naslednik*) but merely the tsarevich, the son of the tsar, as his older sister Irina was a tsarevna, a daughter of the tsar.[173] The tsar's family came up twice in the meetings of the Zemskii sobor. In January 1634, Tsar Michael's opening speech summarized the course of the Smolensk war to that point, reminding his audience that the army had taken many lesser towns by the grace of God and the aid of His Mother and of all the Moscow saints and by the fortune (*schastiem*) of himself and his sons the tsarevichi Aleksei and Ivan.[174] Fortune was not confined to the tsar and his eldest son. In the 1639 sobor, the clergy in its opinion (supporting Michael in his conflict with Crimea) justified their advice by noting that their duty was to pray for the land and for the health of Tsar Michael, his Tsaritsa Evkokiia, and their children (*chadekh*), the same formula as in the oaths.[175] The ritual of drinking the health of the tsar, practiced at meals among laymen and monks and included in liturgical manuals, mandated that the celebrants drink to the tsar, his wife, and all their children.[176] Finally, the prayers for the ruling family in churches were not just for the tsar, but also for the tsaritsa and all children, male and female.[177]

During the reign of Tsar Michael the principal ceremony exclusively featuring the tsar's children was baptism, as had been the case in the sixteenth century. The baptisms did not vary by the birth order or sex of the child. The officiating priests and the godparents were often the same people, or people with the same sort of relationship to the tsar. The first

[172] During the same period the *Novyi letopisets* described the election of the new tsar as an election of the clan as well (*rod, srodstvo*). As a work of the 1620s, the *Novyi letopisets* reflected the then-powerful position of Patriarch Filaret, Michael's father. *PSRL* 14, 129; Vovina-Lebedeva, *Novyi letopisets*.

[173] *AAE* III, 266–268. [174] *KR* II, 615.

[175] "Mnenie Iosafa patriarkha i vsego osviashchennogo sobora," in *Zapiski otdeleniia russkoi i slavianskoi arkheologii imperatorskogo Russkogo arkheologicheskogo obshchestva*, ed. Vladimir Lamanskii (St. Petersburg: Russkoe arkheologicheskoe obshchestvo Otdeleniia russkoi i slavianskoi arkheologii, 1861), vol. II, 372–373; Cherepnin, *Zemskie sobory Russkogo gosudarstva*, 258.

[176] Nikolaos Chrissidis, "Whoever Does Not Drink to the End, He Wishes Evil: Ritual Drinking and Politics in Early Modern Russia," in *The New Muscovite Cultural History: A Collection in Honor of Daniel B. Rowland* ed. Valerie Kivelson, Karen Petrone, Nancy Shields Kollmann, and Michael S. Flier (Bloomington, Indiana: Slavica, 2009), 107–124.

[177] *Sluzhebnik* (Moscow: Pechatnyi dvor, 1627), l. 54 (chapter 4); *Sluzhebnik* (Moscow: Pechatnyi dvor, 1633), l. 54; *Sluzhebnik* (Moscow: Pechatnyi dvor, 1640), l. 53.

child was Irina, born on April 22, 1627, baptized on May 6. The *Novyi letopisets* chronicle asserted that Patriarch Filaret conducted the service, but the official *razriad* record was quite different. According to that source, the tsar's spiritual father Maksim Maksimov, priest of the Annunciation Cathedral, performed the service. Her godfather was the cellarer of the Trinity-St. Sergii Monastery, Aleksandr Bulatnikov, and her godmother was Anna Konstantinovna Streshneva, the wife of Luk'ian Stepanovich Streshnev.[178] Thus Irina's godmother was also her grandmother, Tsaritsa Evdokiia's mother. Irina would live until 1679 and play an important role in the family of the tsar. The second child was Pelageia, born around April 20, 1628 and baptized on May 1 in the Chudov Monastery, who lived a bit more than a year.[179] After two girls, the birth of a boy was undoubtedly a relief. The court records noted the birth of Aleksei Mikhailovich in 1629, his baptism, and his name day celebrations in 1630, 1631, and 1632.[180] He was born on March 10, a Tuesday, and he was given the name of St. Alexius, the Man of God, who is remembered on March 17. The actual baptism took place on March 22 in the Chudov Monastery in the Kremlin. The officiating priest was again Tsar Michael's spiritual father, Maksim Maksimov of the Annunciation Cathedral, the main palace church. The godfather was the cellarer of the Trinity-St. Sergii Monastery, Aleksandr Bulatnikov, and the godmother was the nun Irina Nikitichna Romanova, the patriarch's sister.[181] The officiating priest was an important part of the tsar's household as well as being important to the personal spiritual life of the tsar. Father Maksim had held his position at the Annunciation Cathedral since 1618 and kept it until 1635, when he became a monk in the Trinity-St. Sergii Monastery. He maintained good relations with the ruling family. In 1634 he was in Novgorod, where he received a letter from Tsaritsa Evdokiia. She asked him to send her a description of the miraculous places in Novgorod and the Novgorod area, places where miracles had occurred. She also assured him that he had no reason to fear the "angry word" of the tsar, and she sent him a present of some cloth. He replied that he would copy the places in the saints' lives that described the miracles, and that he hoped also to return to see the icon of the Vladimir Mother of God, to pray to the saintly Moscow metropolitans, and receive forgiveness at the grave of Patriarch Filaret (all places in the Dormition Cathedral). He also carried out the request, and compiled

178 *PSRL* XIV, 153: *DR* I, 913–914, 921–922.
179 *DR* I, 1004, 1009. The *razriad* gave no information about the persons involved in the baptism.
180 *DR* II, 40, 46, 51–52, 127, 193 (mistakenly for Tsar Michael), 265.
181 *DR* II, 40, 51.

a list and brief description of the miracle-working relics of Novgorod.[182] The godfather of Irina and Aleksei, Aleksandr Bulatnikov, had played an important role at the Trinity-St. Sergii Monastery as cellarer since 1622, managing the extensive monastery estates until 1641. He had been first a monk in the northern Solovetskii Monastery and kept up his contacts there, sending many gifts, including books. The books were a standard collection of Biblical texts, monastic lives, and the *Khronograf*.[183] The godmothers were female relatives of the tsar, starting with Irina's grandmother Anna Streshneva. About Irina Romanova very little is known, but the crucial point was that she was Filaret's sister and thus Aleksei's great aunt, a traditional role at a baptism. Thus the godparents established a spiritual relationship on the male side with the Trinity-St. Sergii Monastery, and on the female side with the relatives of the tsar.[184]

[182] Father Maksim stayed at the Trinity-St. Sergii Monastery until 1638, when he became bishop of Riazan', remaining there until his death in 1651. Ivan Zabelin, ed., "Opisanie novgorodskoi sviatyni v 1634 godu," *ChOIDR* 4 (1862): smes', 50–56; M. D. Kagan, "Maksim," *SKKDR* III, pt. 2, 323–326. On the Kremlin churches and their clergy, see N. D. Izvekov, *Moskovskie kremlevskie dvortsovye tserkvi i sluzhivshie pri nikh litsa v XVII veke* (Moscow: Pechat' A. I. Snegirevoi, 1906).

[183] O. V. Panchenko, "Iz istorii kul'turnykh sviazei Solovetskogo i Troitse-Sergieva Monastyrei v pervoi polovine XVII v.: Troitskii kelar' Aleksandr Bulatnikov," *TODRL* 55 (2004): 488–507.

[184] The choice of St. Aleksei for the name of Tsar Michael's first son was not an obvious one. Aleksei the man of God was a late-fourth-century saint whose relics rest today in Rome, and has been a well-recognized saint for centuries. He appeared in most medieval Russian lists of saints under the day of his commemoration in the East, March 17: O. V. Loseva, *Russkie mesiatseslovy XI–XIV vekov* (Moscow: Pamiatniki istoricheskoi mysli, 2001), 293. Metropolitan Makarii included him in his great *Chet'i Minei*: Arkhimandrit Iosif, *Podrobnoe Oglavlenie Velikikh chetiikh minei vserossiiskogo mitropolita Makariia* (Moscow: Sinodal'naia tipografiia, 1892), vol. II, 28. At the same time there were virtually no churches or monasteries dedicated to the saint, and none of the Romanovs before 1629 had the name. The life of St. Aleksei in its Slavic variants is the life of a radical ascetic. Born to a rich family in Rome, he left his family and wife and went to Syria, giving away all his money to the poor. There he became too well known, so he escaped. A storm at sea brought him back to Rome, where he lived seventeen years unrecognized in the house of his father, still as an ascetic. Eventually, through a voice heard in the church of St. Peter, everyone – the clergy, the Caesars, the family – realized that a holy man had been living among them. By the time that they recognized him, he had died, and his remains worked many miracles: N. F. Droblenkova and L. S. Shepeleva, eds., "Zhitie Aleksiia cheloveka Bozhiia," *BLDR* 2 (St. Petersburg: Nauka, 1999), 244–253, 534–535. This was the saint whom Tsar Michael (or perhaps Filaret?) chose to take as the patron saint of the next tsar. Earlier tsars and their sons had had various patron saints: for Ivan the Terrible, it was St. John the Baptist; for his son Ivan, St. John Climacus; and for the various Vasiliis and Dmitriis, there were St. Basil, the church father, and St. Demetrios of Salonika, the soldier-martyr. All of those, however, were common patrons for common names. Aleksei was something new, and it was precisely in the seventeenth century that the saint became popular to the point of entering Russian folklore: V. P. Adrianova-Peretts, *Zhitie Alekseia cheloveka Bozhiia v drevnei russkoi literature i narodnoi slovestnosti* (Petrograd, n.p., 1917). The most likely explanation is the association of St. Aleksei the Man of God with St. Aleksii,

Tsaritsa Evdokiia had ten children altogether. The baptisms of the last seven also give some sense of the function of the ritual beyond the basic one of admitting the newborn child into the community of Christians. Anna, born on July 14, 1630, was baptized on July 25 in the Chudov Monastery by Filaret. She lived until 1692. Her sister Marfa (born August 19, 1631) lived only a bit more than a year, and the only record of her baptism is that it took place in the Chudov Monastery on August 28. After Marfa another boy, Ivan, was born on June 1, 1633. For his baptism in the Chudov Monastery on June 16, the court record notes only which boyars and gentry accompanied him: Filaret may have been too ill to participate, as he died on October 1 of that year. Ivan Mikhailovich lived only five years, leaving his brother Aleksei as the only son. The next birth was that of Sofiia, who was born on September 30, 1634, but survived only a little less than two years. She was baptized on October 5 in the Chudov Monastery. The court records say nothing else about the ceremony, but Adam Olearius, who was in Moscow at the time with the Holstein embassy, wrote that there was not much festivity, as that was not the Russian custom. Patriarch Ioasaf, he said, was her godfather (*Gefatter*), "as with all the children of the grand prince." In this statement Olearius was wrong: of the children of Tsar Michael up to this point, Sofiia was the first to have the patriarch as her godfather. The next daughter, Tat'iana, was more long-lived, as she died only in 1706, having been born on January 5, 1636 and baptized on January 24 in the Chudov Monastery.[185] After 1639 there were no more children.[186] Though Olearius was right in that the ceremony was not a major show as in the West, the court elite was present to some extent, and there was usually a banquet after the birth or the baptism.

What the baptisms do show is that the patriarch was not the main actor in the service, as had often been the case in the century before. Where the records seem to be complete, the tsar's spiritual father conducted the service for Irina and Aleksei, and Filaret only for Anna. What was new was the presence of two godparents, another change from previous practice. For those children for whom the records are complete, Irina and Aleksei's godfather was a monk of the Trinity-St. Sergii Monastery, a violation of

Metropolitan of Moscow, whose relics rested in the Chudov Monastery where the baptism took place.

[185] *DR* II, 156–157, 231–234, 330, 332, 402, 490; "die Russen . . . bey der Taufe nicht wie in Deutschland grosse Gepränge und Gastereyen halten": Adam Olearius, *Vermehrte Newe Beschreibung Der Muscowitischen und Persischen Reyse* (Holwein: Dieter Lohmeier, 1656; Tübingen: Niemeyer, 1971), 41.

[186] The next child, Evdokiia, lived less than a day when she was born in 1637, and the last, Vasilii, only a few days in 1639. Both are known only from their graves in the Archangel cathedral and a brief notice of Vasilii's death: *DR* II, 963.

the canonical rules for baptism in the seventeenth century. Earlier regulations had not touched on this issue, but starting in the 1620s a translation of a late Greek canonical compilation called the *Nomokanon* was published in the Ukraine and in 1639 and 1658 in the Moscow *Trebnik*. It explicitly prohibited monks from serving as godfathers.[187] Tsar Michael had already ignored this prohibition, and Tsar Aleksei would do the same. Apparently the desire for a monk of good reputation as the godfather outweighed the published rules of the church. On the female side, the godmothers were relatives of the tsar and his wife, Streshneva and the nun Irina Romanova. Probably the latter's relationship to the family was more important than her role as a nun, judging by later practice.

If his baptismal name emphasized asceticism, Aleksei was brought up by his nurses in the usual manner. He had the same assortment of toys, pictures, games, and religious observances as his sisters and brothers.[188] He and his father, the tsar, attended the shows with rope-dancers and other German (or at least foreign) entertainers.[189] On February 13, 1633 Boris Ivanovich Morozov, a *stol'nik*, appeared in the court records as the *diad'k*a of tsarevich Aleksei, who was now nearly four years old. A year later, on January 6, 1634, the tsar raised Boris Morozov to the rank of boyar, bypassing all intermediate ranks.[190] In appointing a *diad'ka* Michael was following the precedent set by Boris Godunov for his son in 1598. Boris Morozov would become a major figure in the politics of the Russian court after 1645, but he and his family were not minor at the time of his appointment. His grandfather, the boyar Vasilii Petrovich, had served Boris Godunov and then Vasilii Shuiskii, the latter as *voevoda* of Kazan'. He joined Pozharskii at Iaroslavl', and served as *voevoda* of that city. It was he who proclaimed the election of Tsar Michael to the crowd. V. P. Morozov went on to hold office in Moscow and as *voevoda* of Kazan' in the late 1620s.[191] The Dutch and

[187] A. Pavlov, *Nomokanon pri Bol'shom Trebnike* (Odessa: Tipografiia Ul'rikha i Shul'tse, 1872), 9–15. The prohibition is in Pavlov, *Nomokanon*, 100–101(article 84); *Trebnik inocheskii* (Moscow: Pechatnii dvor', 1639), l. 453 ff. (Nomokanon); and *Trebnik* (Moscow: Pechatnyi dvor, 1658), l. 488v. See also E. V. Beliakova, L. V. Moshkova, and T. A. Oparina, *Kormchaia kniga: Ot rukopisnoi traditsii k pervomu pechatnomu izdaniiu* (Moscow and St. Petersburg: Tsentr gumanitarnikh initsiativ, 2017), 150–157.

[188] Ivan Zabelin, *Domashnii byt russkikh tsarei v XVI–XVII stoletiiakh* (Moscow: Kniga, 2000) (originally 4th ed., Moscow: Sinodal'naia tipografiia, 1915), vol. II, 62–65, 73–76, 81–82, 101–108.

[189] S. M. Shamin, "Tsirk tsarevicha Alekseia Mikhailovicha," *Peterburgskie slavianskie i balkanskie issledovaniia*, 2, 20 (2016): 136–151.

[190] *DR* II, 317, 354. On the rise of Boris Morozov: Pavlov, *Dumnye i komnatnye liudi tsaria Mikhaila Romanova*, vol. I, 636–652.

[191] Bogoiavlenskii, *Moskovskii prikaznyi apparat i deloproizvodstvo*, 135, 168; Barsukov, *Spiski gorodovykh voevod i drugikh lits voevodskogo upravleniia Moskovskogo gosudarstva*, 87.

Swedish diplomats in Moscow in the 1620s listed him among the boyars, though not among the most powerful. He died in 1630.[192] His son Ivan Vasil'evich, whom Boris Godunov had put in charge of his son Fyodor Borisovich in 1598 (though not as *diad'ka*) had joined his father in Iaroslavl' in the ranks of the Second Militia.[193] They both signed the Affirmation Charter for Tsar Michael, as did Ivan's sons Boris and Gleb. Ivan Vasil'evich and his two sons all held the rank of *stol'nik* at that moment.[194] I. V. Morozov's service to Tsar Michael was mainly at court. He commanded the garrison at Belaia near Smolensk in 1614–15 and was one of the officers in charge of the defense of Moscow in 1616–18. He then had no terms as provincial governor for twenty years, nor did he head any important office until after his son's rise to prominence. He did serve as a *rynda* in March 1619, a fact that suggested that he was still comparatively young. He had various duties at the tsar's banquets, but attained boyar rank only later in 1634, clearly as a result of his son's position. Like his son, he went directly from *stol'nik* to boyar, skipping the intermediate ranks. He became a monk in 1654 or 1655 and disappeared from the records.[195]

The Morozov family had a distinguished ancestry, but it had lapsed since the middle of the sixteenth century, and it was clearly V. P. Morozov and his grandsons who brought it back to prominence. Boris Morozov became a very wealthy landowner, and by the accident of conservation his estates records are among the few to survive from the seventeenth century.[196] Morozov was not uncultured, and his library included books in Latin, a surprising collection of medical and religious works, together with Cicero and Sallust, mostly from the sixteenth century. His library included some of the first works of Renaissance authors found in Russia (Jacques Lefèvre d'Étaples).[197] The author of a Russian translation of the work of the first-century BC Roman historian Pompeius Trogus, one of the few classical authors translated in seventeenth-century Russia,

192 Bushkovich, "Shvedskie istochniki o Rossii," 365, 368, 371, 378; Poe, *The Russian Elite*, 424.

193 Liubomirov, *Ocherk istorii nizhegorodskogo opolcheniia*, 286–287; Derzhavina and Kolosova, *Skazanie Avraamiia Palitsyna*, 232.

194 Belokurov, ed., *Utverzhennaia gramota*, 77–80.

195 *DR* I, 148, 190, 386; *DR* II, 354; Poe, *The Russian Elite*, 424.

196 D. I. Petrikeev, *Krupnoe krepostnoe khoziaistvo XVII v.: Po materialam votchiny B. I. Morozova* (Leningrad: Nauka, 1967).

197 E. V. Chistiakova, "Boiarskaia biblioteka," in *Problemy istorii, russkoi knizhnosti, kul'tury i obshchestvennogo soznaniia*, ed. E. V. Romodanovskaia (Novosibirsk: Sibirskii khronograf, 2000), 252–258; E. A. Savel'eva, *Katalog knig iz sobraniia Aptekarskogo prikaza* (St. Petersburg, Alfaret, 2006); Paul Bushkovitch, "Latinskie politicheskie knigi v Rossii 17-go veka," *Sbornik statei i publikatsii posviachchennyi Andreiu Alekseevichu Bulychevu* (Moscow: Drevlekhranilishche, 2019), 38–55.

dedicated his work to Morozov.[198] This culture had not previously been part of the education of the sons of the Russian tsars.[199]

Boris Morozov was not in charge of the tsar's eldest son alone. In January 1635, the tsar appointed the *stol'nik* Fyodor Borisovich Dalmatov-Karpov as his assistant ("*v tovarishchakh*").[200] He remained in that position for the next three years.[201] Boris Morozov's brother, Gleb Ivanovich, also participated in the upbringing of the tsar's sons. By June 1638, Gleb Morozov, who had recently been made a boyar, was the *diad'ka* of Ivan Mikhailovich, while Fyodor Borisovich Dalmatov-Karpov seems to have served both boys along with the Morozov brothers.[202] When tsarevich Ivan died on January 10, 1639, Gleb Morozov stood watch by the boy's coffin.[203] During the remainder of Tsar Michael's reign, Boris Morozov had no administrative position among the Moscow offices or in the provinces. After tsarevich Ivan's death, Gleb Morozov served as governor of Novgorod for 1642–5. At least for the Morozov brothers, the care of the tsar's children was a full-time occupation that admitted of no distraction.[204] Dalmatov-Karpov also was not present in the records of administration until after the death of Tsar Michael. Then his former charge, now Tsar Aleksei, promoted him to the Duma, from *stol'nik* to *okol'nichii*.[205] Dalmatov-Karpov was also involved with the Romanov dynasty's spiritual patronage, for his family appeared among the miracles of St. Savva and the Savva-Storozhevskii Monastery near Moscow, one of Tsar Aleksei's favored sites.[206]

Tsarevich Aleksei played no role in the court ceremonies other than as the object of occasional toasts and name-day banquets until 1642.[207] In

[198] O. A. Belobrova, "Morozov, Boris (Il'ia) Ivanovich," *SKKDR* III, pt. 2, 362–363.
[199] For the usual education, see Zabelin, *Domashnii byt russkikh tsarei*, vol. II, 138–189.
[200] *DR* II, 409. F. B. Dalmatov-Karpov was largely unknown. He appeared in the records only twice before, as *stol'nik* among an extremely long list of those present at the audience of the Persian ambassador in 1625, the ambassador who brought the relic of the Lord's robe to Tsar Michael, and again in 1637 for another diplomatic audience: *DR* I, 691, 870. His uncle Lev Ivanovich Dolmatov-Karpov had been a chamber *stol'nik* in 1618, was an *okol'nichii* in 1633, and died in 1642. Pavlov, *Dumnye i komnatnye liudi tsaria Mikhaila Romanova*, vol. I, 227, 490, 508–509.
[201] *DR* II, 465, 483, 525 (November 1636).
[202] *DR* II, 559, 579–580.
[203] *DR* II, 598, 931, 933.
[204] In 1633, the Morozov brothers provided grain for the Russian army besieging Smolensk and soldiers to defend Moscow in case of a feared Crimean Tatar raid. It seems that they stayed in Moscow with Tsar Michael rather than serving in the army; *KR* II, 448, 519.
[205] *DR* I, 19 (September 30, 1645). He received boyar rank in 1649 and died in 1659 or 1660: Poe, *The Russian Elite*, 154, 185. He was one of the boyars in charge of artillery in the campaigns of 1654 and 1655 against Poland: *DR* III, 420, 468, 478.
[206] Bushkovitch, *Religion and Society in Russia*, 113–114, 215–216.
[207] *DR* II, 359, 409, 428, 502, 525, 563, 580, 650, 674.

that year he took part with his father in the traditional ceremony, on September 1, New Year's Day in the Russian calendar. The New Year had been an important ceremony at the court, but the tsar's son had not always been present. In 1581, fathers Possevino and Campana had reported that the "people" greeted both Tsar Ivan and his son Ivan Ivanovich on New Year's Day and wished them long life. As the tsar and his court were in Staritsa at that moment, the ceremony must have taken place there. In 1598, the Imperial envoy Michael Schiel had witnessed the same ceremony in Moscow during the reign of Boris Godunov, but did not specify whether Boris's son was present or not. Both accounts convey the impression that the ceremony took place annually, and on a platform erected for the tsar.[208] In the seventeenth century the ceremony was similar. On September 1, the tsar and patriarch appeared on a platform erected between the Kremlin palace and the cathedrals. Patriarch Filaret spelled out the ritual in his 1622 ceremonial order for the Dormition Cathedral. The core was the meeting of the tsar and patriarch in the middle of the square before the palace, between the churches. After much chanting, the patriarch blessed the tsar with a cross and sprinkled holy water on him as well as on the boyars and the "whole people."[209] In 1634, Adam Olearius witnessed the ceremony and described it in some detail. In his account, some 20,000 people filled the main square in the Kremlin before the palace, clearly an exaggeration but conveying the scale of the event. Patriarch Ioasaf I came out of the Uspenskii cathedral accompanied by 400 clergymen carrying icons and open books. The tsar and the boyars came from the other side bareheaded, and the tsar and patriarch exchanged kisses. The patriarch gave to the tsar a jewel-encrusted cross to kiss and then, "in a long speech," blessed the tsar and the whole people, wishing them happiness in the New Year. The people answered with a loud "Amen," and many came forward

208 Latin original: A. M. Ammann, ed., "I. P. Campani Relatio de itinere Moscovitico," in *Antemurale* VI (1960–1): 1–85, esp. 32; German translation, A. M. Ammann, ed., "Ein russischer Reisebericht aus dem Jahre 1581," *Ostkirchliche Studien* X, 2–3 (September 1961): 156–193, esp. 184; X, 4 (December 1961): 283–300; Paul Pierling, ed., *Antonii Possevinii Missio Moscovitica* (Paris: Apud Ernestum Leroux, 1882), 70; "Relation wegen der jungsten Anno 98," 461; Russian translation: A. Shemiakin, ed., "Donesenie o poezdke v Moskvu pridvornogo rimskogo imperatora Mikhaila Shilia v 1598 godu," *ChOIDR* 2 (1875): 16–17; Michael S. Flier, "Political Ideas and Rituals," in *The Cambridge History of Russia*, ed. Maureen Perrie (Cambridge: Cambridge University Press), vol. I, 401–402. The 1642 appearance of Tsarevich Aleksei on September 1: Pavel Stroev, ed., *Vykhody gosudarei tsarei i velikikh kniazei Mikhaila Fedorovicha, Aleksiia Mikhailovicha, Fedora Aleksievicha vseia Rusi samoderzhtsev s 1632 po 1682 god* (Moscow: Tipografiia A. Semena, 1844), 106.

209 "Skazanie deistvennykh chinov sviatyia sobornyia tserkvi Uspeniia Presviatoi Bogoroditsy," *DRV* VI, 163–168; Makarii, *Istoriia Russkoi tserkvi*, vol. VI, 307–308.

to present petitions to the tsar. The five-year-old Aleksei was not present.[210] Over the next few years the New Year ceremony was repeated, normally under the name of the ritual (*deistvo*) of "*Mnogoletnoe zdravie*."[211] The New Year of September 1, 1642, however, was the first major ceremony to include tsarevich Aleksei. The tsarevich merely appeared, as he did at diplomatic ceremonies later. There was no formal presentation.[212] The sparse records do not explain why Tsar Michael decided to include his eldest son, but he chose the moment when the boy was thirteen years old, the age around which the rulers of the fifteenth and sixteenth centuries had usually chosen to ensure the succession of their sons or to begin to include them in court ceremonies or even government and military affairs. As far as can be established, Aleksei did not appear at later New Year's ceremonies during his father's lifetime, but he did play an increasing role in other major ceremonies. In January 1643, he joined his father for the Epiphany ceremony on the Moscow River, and the next year he went without his father. Tsar Michael seems to have been increasingly absent for major ceremonies in the last year and a half of his life. For Palm Sunday, 1644, the tsarevich conducted the procession without his father, the tsar, and again at Epiphany, 1645, he appeared alone.[213] As we shall see, he also participated in many, but not all, diplomatic ceremonies. These appearances all associated him with his father, and even showed him taking his father's place in 1644–5. He was obviously the heir, though there had been no formal designation.

The Danish Marriage

The last years of Tsar Michael's reign saw another complex tangle involving his family and potentially the succession. Patriarch Filaret had died in 1633, in the middle of the Smolensk War. The war had not been popular among the boyars, and his death led to changes at court.[214] Of Marfa's erstwhile favorites, Lobanov-Rostovskii had also died, but B. M. Saltykov returned to favor, heading the Petitions and Cossack Chancelleries, with

[210] Olearius, *Vermehrte Newe Beschreibung Der Muscowitischen und Persischen Reyse*, 37–38.

[211] Stroev, ed., *Vykhody gosudarei tsarei i velikikh kniazei*, 21, 41, 68, 78, 87, 97. This is the records of the clothing the tsar wore at various ceremonies, and is more complete for September 1 than the *Razriad* books. On the rite, see Konstantin Nikol'skii, *O sluzhbakh russkoi tserkvi byvshkikh v prezhnikh pechatnykh bogosluzhebnykh knigakh* (St. Petersburg: Tipografiia tovarishchestva Obshchestvennaia Pol'za, 1885), 98–168.

[212] *DR* II, 691; Stroev, ed., *Vykhody gosudarei tsarei i velikikh kniazei*, 106, 115; Philip Longworth, *Alexis, Tsar of All the Russias* (New York, New York: F. Watts, 1984), 15–16.

[213] Stroev, ed., *Vykhody gosudarei tsarei i velikikh kniazei*, 109, 115, 117, 123, 125–126.

[214] Bushkovitch, "The Court of Tsar Michael", 235–242.

his brother M. M. Saltykov heading the Banditry Chancellery. The brothers' offices in the 1613–20 period had been palace offices, but these new positions were concerned with military and security issues.[215] However, the Saltykovs were no longer the only important figures in the government. Cherkasskii (until his death in 1642) and Sheremetev, among others, remained powerful.[216] At the Ambassadorial Office, Gramotin gave way to Fyodor Likhachev, after 1640 accompanied by Grigorii L'vov, who was the sole head from 1643.[217] Another newly influential boyar from 1638 was Prince Boris Aleksandrovich Repnin.[218] All these men would have had to take a position on the marriage of the heir, as would Tsaritsa Evdokiia. Unfortunately, information on their views is scarce.

The new configuration of power at court had to deal with the tsar's attempt to marry his daughter Irina to the Danish Prince Valdemar, an illegitimate son of Christian IV. The relation to succession was indirect, since in no case could Irina succeed if her brother was alive and in good health. At the same time, Tsar Michael and Evdokiia by 1642 had already lost six children, two of them boys. The tsarevny Irina, Anna, and Tat'iana survived, but the only boy to survive was Aleksei. No ruler, or indeed any parent, in early modern Europe could look at this group of children and be sure that his son would live to adulthood and himself produce an heir. Thus any marriage for the daughters raised the issue of succession. The idea of a Danish connection arose in Moscow in 1640, when Irina was only thirteen. Until then Michael's relations with Denmark had not been particularly active, revolving mainly around commercial issues. The intended bridegroom, Valdemar, count of Schleswig-Holstein and the son of Christian IV by his second wife Kirsten Munk, was born in 1622 and thus eighteen at the beginning of the story. The Russian court had learned about Valdemar from Peter Marselis (1595–1672), the Dutch–Danish merchant who played so large a role in Russian iron production and Danish–Russian relations as well as other affairs in those years.[219] The

[215] Bogoiavlenskii, *Moskovskii prikaznyi apparat i deloproizvodstvo*, 284–285.

[216] Kozliakov, *Mikhail Fedorovich*, 229–237; Filina, "*V poiskakh al'ternativy*," 148–149, 324–330; and especially Pavlov, *Dumnye i komnatnye liudi tsaria Mikhaila Romanova*, vol. I, 471–652.

[217] Bogoiavlenskii, *Moskovskii prikaznyi apparat i deloproizvodstvo*, 131–132. The Swedes reported that Likhachev was the second most important man in the Ambassadorial Office already in 1626, though Russian sources do not show an appointment in that office. Bushkovitch, "Shvedskie istochniki o Rossii," 369, 379.

[218] A. P. Pavlov, "Ob odnom episode pridvornoi bor'by vremeni tsarstvovaniia Mikhaila Romanova v rasskaze V. N. Tatishcheva," *Canadian–American Slavic Studies* 48 (2014): 146–156.

[219] Erik Amburger, *Die Familie Marselis: Studien zur russischen Wirtschaftsgeschichte.* Osteuropastudien der Hochschulen des Landes Hessen; Reihe 1: Gießener

result was a Russian mission to Denmark, ostensibly for commercial issues, but in fact to find out about the Danish prince. Word of the Russian interest in Valdemar got out, and this time King Christian was interested. In 1641, he in turn sent Valdemar as part of a mission to Moscow supposedly to discuss the commercial issues, and that September Michael sent Christian a tepid response to the Danish mission. By the next summer Michael had made a decision to try to marry Irina to Valdemar, and this time a mission with a more formal proposal left for Copenhagen.[220] The negotiations were not easy, as the Danes were concerned about whether or not Valdemar would get his own lands and did not want him to abandon Lutheranism for Orthodoxy.[221] Only in 1643 was another mission with Marselis able to convince Christian to send his son to try to complete the agreement, and a very large Danish suite arrived in Moscow with the king's son in January 1644. The next year and a half were filled with incident and long disputes over faith between the Danes, especially the pastors in the suite, and the Russian clergy. This series of disputes incidentally left a large body of polemical literature on the Russian side that was a major contribution to Orthodox theology in seventeenth-century Russia.[222] Ultimately it seems that the proponents of the marriage were not numerous enough among the Russian elite. Valdemar would not budge on the issue of conversion, nor would Tsar Michael let him leave, and the issue was unresolved when Michael died suddenly on July 12, 1645. The young Tsar Aleksei released Valdemar and the Danes to return home.[223] Tsarevna Irina never married, though she remained an important figure at court. Valdemar did not get along with his half-brother, Frederick III, who succeeded Christian in 1648. He later served in the Swedish army against Poland, and died there in 1656.

The whole story of the courtship of Valdemar is filled with complexities, increased by the absence of any investigation of Danish or most Russian archives since the 1890s. Tsar Michael's motives in pursuing the marriage are not clear from the sparse literature, and Russian historians

Abhandlungen zur Agrar- und Wirtschaftsforschung des europäischen Ostens, vol. 4 (Gießen: W. Schmitz, 1957); T. A. Oparina, *Inozemtsy v Rossii XVI–XVII vv.* (Moscow: Progress–Traditsiia, 2007), 42–78, 106–109.

[220] Shcherbachev, ed., *Russkie akty*, 717–728.

[221] Forsten, "Snosheniia Danii s Rossiei", 331; also RGADA, f. 53, d. 7 and 8.

[222] Aleksandr Golubtsov, ed., "Pamiatniki prenii o vere," *ChOIDR* 2, pt. 2 (1892): 1–350; Bushkovitch, *Religion and Society in Russia*, 134–136; T. A. Oparina, *Ivan Nasedka i polemicheskoe bogoslovie kievskoi mitropolii* (Novosibirsk: Nauka, 1998).

[223] Tsvetaev, *Protestantstvo i protestanty v Rossii*, 476–510. Pavlov believes that only F. I. Sheremetev, the Streshnevs, and Tsaritsa Evdokiia were strongly for the marriage: Pavlov, *Dumnye i komnatnye liudi tsaria Mikhaila Romanova*, vol. I, 652–672. Filina's account of court politics at that moment is unfortunately largely speculative: Filina, "*V poiskakh al'ternativy*," 147–149.

have been interested only in the disputes over baptism and religion. An important issue was the relationship of the marriage to Russian foreign policy, which may have been as important as, or more important than, the religious issues.[224] Danish sources have so far not revealed much. The only substantial record of the Danish embassy in 1644–5 to be published is an anonymous German account printed in 1776 by Anton Friedrich Büsching, a German pastor, antiquarian, and geographer, in his *Magazin für die neue Historiographie und Geographie.*[225] The account was lacking the title and first page, so it was anonymous, but it clearly came from the Danish embassy and corresponds in most details of events to the unpublished Danish account of Oluf Parsberg and Steen Billde in the Danish archive. In Büsching's copy there was a note at the end by Wendelin Sybelist (1597–1677/9), who was Tsar Michael's doctor in those years and often a Russian informant on European affairs and agent for purchases for the Russian court.[226] The note asserted that there were many mistakes and omissions in the German report and went on to assert that "Religion was not the cause for the failure of the marriage, but only a pretext, and if the Swedes had not intervened as victorious invaders of Denmark, and if Tsar Michael had not ended his days from the greatest sadness of soul, the marriage would have been long ago consummated. For the tsar loved Prince Waldemar deeply."[227] Sybelist described himself as an eye- and ear-witness, admitted to and involved in many things (*testis ocularis et auritus, imo in multis admissus et commissus*). From what we

[224] S. M. Solov'ev, *Istoriia Rossii*, vol. V (= 9), 229–236; G. V. Forsten, *Baltiiskii vopros v XVI i XVII vekakh (1544–1648)*, 2 vols. Zapiski istoriko-filologicheskogo fakul'teta Sankt-Peterburgskogo universiteta 33, 34 (Saint-Petersburg: Tipografiia V. S. Balasheva, 1893–4), vol. 2, 494–502; Forsten, "Snosheniia Shvetsii s Rossiei v tsarstvovaniia Khristiny," *Zhurnal Ministerstva narodnogo prosveshcheniia* 275 (1891): 347–375; Forsten, "Snosheniia Danii s Rossiei"; C. Nyrop, "Nogle oplysninger om Grev Valdemar Christians Ruslandsfærd 1643–45," *Historisk Tidsskrift* series 6, 3 (1891–2): 237–338; Oparina, *Ivan Nasedka*, 219–243.

[225] "Nachricht von Woldemar Christian Guldenlöwe, Grafen von Schleswig-Holstein . . . Reise nach Russland," *Magazin für die neue Historie und Geographie* X (1776): 211–276. Russian translation: A. Shemiakin, ed. and trans., "Poezdka v Rossiu Vol'demara Khristiana Gil'denleve," *ChOIDR* 4 (1867): i–ii, 1–72. The Danish version: Danske Rigsarkiv, Tyske Kancelli, Udenrigske Avdelning [hereafter TKUA], Rusland A II, no. 25. The German-language account stems from the Danish embassy and may be the work of the embassy's pastor, Mathias Velhaver: Nyrop, "Nogle oplysninger," 238, note 2.

[226] On Sybelist, see Sabine Dumschat, *Ausländische Mediziner im Moskauer Russland.* Quellen und Studien zur Geschichte des östlichen Europas 67 (Stuttgart: Franz Steiner, 2006), 681–683.

[227] "Non religio fuit causa non confirmati matrimonii, sed tantum praetextus et nisi Sueci praeveniendo invasissent Daniam victores, et Zaar Mich. Fedorowitz diem suum ex summo moerore animi obiiset, consummatum omnino fuisset iam dudum connubium. Amabat enim Zaar principem Woldemarum intime." "Nachricht von Woldemar Christian Guldenlöwe," 213.

know, that last statement was correct. Since Sybelist also described himself in the text as *comes palatinus caesareus* (Imperial count palatine), he must have composed the note after he received that rank in 1652–5.[228]

The more detailed history of the negotiations throws some light on the significance of the issue for Tsar Michael's ideas about the role of his heir, tsarevich Aleksei, and succession generally. When Peter Marselis arrived in Copenhagen in March 1643 and delivered his credentials, Christian IV's agreement to the proposal followed. On April 8, Marselis returned to Moscow with the answer, and the Tsar sent him back in the late summer so that he could accompany Valdemar to Russia. Christian's instructions to the Danish embassy with Valdemar came on September 29, and the count reached Moscow in the first days of January (Old Style) 1644.[229] While all this was going on, Sweden suddenly attacked Denmark; this was the beginning of the so-called Torstenson War of 1643–5. Count Axel Oxenstierna and the regency for Queen Christina had decided in secret in May 1643 to attack Denmark, and while Valdemar was traveling through Poland to Russia in the autumn, the Swedish Field Marshal Lennart Torstenson marched rapidly north from Moravia to occupy Jutland. The next year Christian tried to fend off the invasion by land and sea, but ultimately had to sign away Danish territory to (the now regnant) Queen Christina of Sweden in exchange for peace in the Second Treaty of Brömsebro on August 13, 1645. The war placed the Russians in a dilemma. Since the inglorious end of the Smolensk War in 1634, Tsar Michael had striven for good relations with Poland and had hoped for an alliance against Crimea. As Sweden was hostile to Poland, both Poland and Russia were favorable to Denmark, but Tsar Michael had no reason to provoke the Swedes. Thus, soon after his arrival in Moscow, Count Valdemar brought up the Swedish invasion (February 4, 1644 OS), and Tsar Michael reminded him that Russia and Sweden had signed a treaty of eternal peace.[230] In other words, Russia was not going to do anything against Sweden. The Danes do not seem to have had much sense of the political discussions behind the scenes, but the Swedish envoy Peter Krusebiörn, when he arrived in Moscow a year later, early in 1645, got better information. He reported that the two boyars most hostile to Sweden were Fyodor Ivanovich Sheremetev and Prince Aleksandr Petrovich Repnin (obviously a mistake for Boris Aleksandrovich). Presumably they were also the most enthusiastic about the Danish marriage, but Krusebiörn did not say that. He did report that the marriage

[228] Dumschat, *Ausländische Mediziner im Moskauer Russland*, 681–682.
[229] Shcherbachev, "Datskii arkhiv," 222–224.
[230] Solov'ev, *Istoriia Rossii*, vol. V (= 9), 238. Solov'ev's account was a summary of the conversations from the Danish affairs in the Russian archive.

problem, at least by early 1645, absorbed all the attention of the Russian court, and prevented them from dealing with other matters such as the Polish embassy that had arrived also in January 1645, or his own mission.[231] By June, matters had reached a state of considerable confusion: "Public affairs right now are in such a confused state that neither His Majesty the Tsar nor his councilors know how to extricate themselves or to move on." The Chancellor, that is, the head of the Ambassadorial Office Grigorii L'vov, would have gladly left his post if he could.[232]

Whatever were the hopes and whoever were the main actors behind the confusion at the Russian court, tsarevich Aleksei played a major role in at least the ceremonial part of the whole episode, as is clear from the report of the Danish ambassadors Oluf Parsberg and Steen Bilde, the published Danish account of the affair, and the Russian records of court occasions.[233] When Valdemar came to Russia in 1641 only as an ambassador, tsarevich Aleksei did not appear. This was not unusual, however, since he did not appear for any other diplomatic reception. Before 1642, the only ceremonies for which his presence is mentioned are his own name-day banquets on March 17.[234] The first recorded acts of participation of the young Aleksei in any court ceremonies after his appearance at the 1642 New Year were precisely the audiences and meetings with Count Valdemar beginning on January 28, 1644. That was the day of the first formal audience with Valdemar.[235] The Danes reported that the tsarevich entered the reception hall in the House of Facets just as they were themselves arriving, immediately greeted the count in a friendly manner, and then went to stand by his father. After the welcome, the count kissed the hand of Tsar Michael and that of his son, who also sat with Valdemar and his father at the banquet.[236] The next few weeks were taken up with the dispute over Valdemar's conversion to Orthodoxy. The next time that the Tsar met Valdemar with the tsarevich was not until September 17. Michael and his son went to the count's residence in Moscow, the old house of Boris Godunov. As this had more

[231] Forsten, "Snosheniia Shvetsii s Rossiei," 362–366.

[232] "Die Respublicae stehen ietzo allhier in solchem verwirrten statu, daß weder Ihr. Zaar. Maytt. noch seine Räthe sich wißen zu extriciren oder zu entwickeln." Svenska Riksarchiv, Muscovitica, 33 (23 June, 1645, Krusebiorn to Christina).

[233] TKUA, Rusland A II, no. 25; "Nachricht von Woldemar Christian Guldenlöwe."

[234] *DR* II, 563 (1638), 650 (1641), 674 (1642).

[235] TKUA, Rusland A II, no. 25, January 28, 1644 (folios unnumbered); *DR* II, 723–724 (1643). Tsarevich Aleksei also participated in the audiences for Hasan aga, the envoy of Shah Abbas of Iran, in December 1645 and May 1645: *DR* II, 746–747, 755–756. He did not participate in the audiences for the ambassador of King Władysław of Poland, Gabriel Stempkowski, in January and February 1645: *DR* II, 748, 750–751.

[236] "Nachricht von Woldemar Christian Guldenlöwe," 221–223; Nyrop, "Nogle oplysninger," 251.

the character of a private meeting, the ceremonial records had no entries for that day. There was much eating and drinking, and Aleksei also handed out vodka (Branntwein) from a small golden box. Aleksei's tutor Boris Ivnovich Morozov tried another time to convince Valdemar to show his love for his future relatives by conversion. Valdemar graciously refused. The party then moved to the garden, where more was drunk and furs were brought against the evening chill. Morozov made yet another attempt to convince Valdemar to convert, but the tsar, who realized that his speeches were just irritating, told Morozov to leave. Morozov, however, was by this time drunk and refused. Tsarevich Aleksei "then finally stood up, took him by the breast of his coat and ordered him to go away, and he was immediately dragged away by two noblemen." Shortly before midnight, the party broke up. The next day the tsarevich paid a visit to Count Valdemar on his own, staying two hours.[237] Nothing much happened with the Danish embassy again other than correspondence back and forth until October 19, when tsarevich Aleksei again paid a visit.[238] Difficult discussions followed, and on December 15, the tsarevich came again and this time was very friendly. Two weeks later he invited Valdemar to see the entrance of the Persian ambassador.[239] The marriage project, however, was now at an impasse, and neither the offices of the Polish ambassador nor further disputation on matters of faith helped. Tsarevich Aleksei played no further role, perhaps because friendly visits gradually ceased. The Russians kept the Danish mission in Moscow while they argued among themselves. Then Tsar Michael died on July 12, 1645.

The Succession of Tsar Aleksei

The events of 1645 suggest that Michael's concern to present the heir was not irrational. These were dramatic events at the Russian court. Michael's death came when the negotiations over the Danish marriage were at an impasse and the government was in a state of confusion over the matter. It was also sudden.[240] July 12 was Tsar Michael's name-day (St. Michael Maleinos) and the occasion of yearly celebration. The festivities started at noon that year, and Michael felt well at first, but soon fell ill and died in

[237] "Nachricht von Woldemar Christian Guldenlöwe," 233–237; "daher endlich der Zarewitz aufgestanden, ihn bey dem Rocke and der Brust gefasset, und ihm befohlen wegzugehen, und er ward alsobald von zweyen von Adel weggetrecket" (236). There is no entry for this day in the unpublished Parsberg and Bilde report.

[238] "Nachricht von Woldemar Christian Guldenlöwe," 237. The text has February, but from the context it must have been October 19.

[239] "Nachricht von Woldemar Christian Guldenlöwe," 238–239.

[240] Pavlov, *Dumnye i komnatnye liudi tsaria Mikhaila Romanova*, vol. I, 675–683.

the night.[241] Twenty years later Grigorii Kotoshikhin, a former official who had fled to Sweden, claimed that very soon after Michael's death a sobor chose Aleksei, but historians have never found evidence of such a sobor.[242] Regardless, the succession was not simple. The *Razriad* documents of the service oath to the new ruler had two versions, the earlier stating that people were to swear to obey Tsaritsa Evdokiia and Tsar Aleksei in that order, and the second putting Aleksei's name first ahead of his mother, the tsaritsa. The change came on the first or second day after Michael's death.[243] There was more. The Swedish resident Krusebiörn reported on July 17 (when the first provincials were already swearing the oath) that the whole succession had been handled with unseemly speed. Michael had been laid to rest almost immediately in a simple coffin. The Danish embassy told the same story, namely that Michael was laid to rest in the Archangel Cathedral the next morning, with great ceremony, involving hundreds of monks with burning candles and the court, led by Tsar Aleksei and the boyars.[244] Krusebiörn reported further: "Soon after his Majesty the Tsar's death, during the very same night, the young tsarevich Aleksei Mikhailovich immediately was declared and inaugurated in place of his late father as tsar and grand prince of all Russians by all the lords present. His lord cousin Prince [sic] Nikita Ivanovich Romanov was the first so sworn and immediately the other lords by unanimous agreement obliged themselves and swore with him." Only then did the other ranks swear the oath, presumably on July 13.[245] The oath that the other ranks swore, at least in Tula on July 17–20, was to serve Tsar Aleksei and his mother Evdokiia (in that

241 "Nachricht von Woldemar Christian Guldenlöwe," 266–267; TKUA Rusland A II, no. 25 [0070]. St. Michael was a tenth-century Byzantine monk, the uncle of Emperor Nikephoros II Phokas (ruled 963–969). The day was Tsar Michael's birthday as well as his name day.

242 G. K. Kotoshikhin, *O Rossii v tsarstvovanie Alekseia Mikhailovicha* (Moscow: Rosspen, 2000), 25.

243 Ol'ga E. Kosheleva, "Leto 1645 goda: Smena lits na Rossiiskom prestole," in *Kazus: Individual'nie i unikal'nie v istorii*, ed. Iu. L. Bessmertny and M. A. Boitsov (Moscow: Izdatel'skii tsentr Rossiiskogo gosudarstvennogo gumanitarnogo universiteta, 1999), 148–170. Aleksei was only sixteen (birthday March 19, 1629) and unmarried. The oath does not seem to have included any future children. Kosheleva believes that the first version, with Evdokiia first, reflected Tsar Michael's wishes, perhaps of long standing, given his son's age.

244 "Nachricht von Woldemar Christian Guldenlöwe," 267.

245 "Kurtz nach Ihr. Zaar. Maytt. seel. hintritt, noch in der Nacht, ist der iunge Zaarowitz Alexé Michalowitz auch alsofortt an seines seel. Herres Vaters statt von sämptlichen anwesenden herren ein Zaar undt Großfürst aller Reußen declariret undt inauguriret worden. Sein herr Vätter Knäs Mykita Ivanowitz Romanoff ist der erste gewesen, so geschworen, dem alsobaldt die andere herren unanimi consensu beygepflichtet undt mitgeschworen." Svenska RA, Muscovitica 33, July 17, 1645. Cf. Forsten, "Snosheniia Shvetsii s Rossiei," 348–375; Forsten, *Baltiiskii vopros*, vol. II, 503. N. I. Romanov was

order), and stated that as he was dying Tsar Michael had blessed Aleksei with the throne of the tsars over the sovereignty of Vladimir and Moscow and all other great sovereignties of the Russian tsardom.[246] Putting this report together with the *Razriad* documents, it seems that there was some uncertainty over the succession, not about Aleksei, however, whom his father had "declared" to the court and people in 1642, but about the status of his mother. After the decision for Aleksei alone, the boyars rushed the oath ceremony and put out a story that claimed unanimity, all in a few days. In the version that reached Krusebiörn, the crucial figure was Nikita Romanov, not Boris Morozov as in later accounts.[247] The "declaration" and "inauguration" of Aleksei on the part of the court and church elite seems to be the event that Kotoshikhin remembered as a sobor.

The *Razriad*'s daily records stated simply that Michael's son Aleksei "came to be" (*uchinilsia*) on the tsar's throne "according to the blessing" (*po blagosloveniiu*) of his father.[248] The coronation ceremony also mentioned nothing resembling an election, and it followed the older precedents. As in 1547 and 1584, Aleksei's speech to Patriarch Iosif retold the story of the Monomakh crown and described the election of Tsar Michael, this time without the word selection/election (*izbranie*) and instead asserting that he ascended the throne at the "petition" (*chelobit'e*) of all the people. The speech included the formula that Tsar Michael had blessed his son Aleksei with the tsardom. Once again, the blessing appeared to be crucial to the succession.[249]

a chamber *stol'nik* and had been since 1639, receiving boyar rank only in September. He was very young for the rank: Pavlov, *Dumnye i komnatnye liudi tsaria Mikhaila Romanova*, vol. I, 613–614, 679. His position as chamber *stol'nik* presumably accounts for his presence among the boyars. He does not seem to have taken sides among the court factions.

[246] RGADA, f. 210, Razriad, moskovskii stol, d. 201, ll. 24–28. For the oath in Kaluga (July 20) see ll. 112–116. Kosheleva, "Leto 1645 goda," 159–160.

[247] The later work "Kniga o prestavlenii . . . Mikhaila . . ." attributed the major role in events to Morozov; Vremennik *OIDR* 17 (1853), 203–212; Kosheleva, "Leto 1645 goda," 150, 157. See also "Povest' izvestno o ezhe sluchisia byti v nashei rustei zemle . . .," in *Pamiatniki prenii o vere, voznikshikrefh po delu korolevicha Val'demara i tsarevny Iriny*, ed. A. Golubtsov, *ChOIDR* 2, 2 (1892): 1–22. The Danish reports "Nachricht von Woldemar Christian Guldenlöwe," 266–267, as well as the Parsberg/Billede report, TKUA Rusland A II, no. 25 [0070], describe the death of Michael and the accession of his son on July 12, 1645, without mention of Romanov or Morozov.

[248] *DR* II, 756; *DR* III, 1; *Povsiadnevnykh dvortsovykh vremen gosudarei tsarei Mikhaila Fedorovicha i Alekseia Mikhailovicha zapisok, chast' 1 i 2* (Moscow: Pechatana pri Imperatorskom Moskovskom universiteta, 1769), vol. I, 269–270. On the *Razriad* records, see O. A. Novokhatko, *Zapisnye knigi Moskovskogo stola Razriadnogo prikaza XVII veka* (Moscow: Pamiatniki istoricheskoi mysli, 2000), esp, 167–226.

[249] Leonid, ed., *Chin postavleniia na tsarstvo tsaria Alekseia Mikhailovicha*, (Pamiatniki drevnei pis'mennosti 16) (St. Petersburg: I. Voshchinskii, 1882), 12–14. Cf. Longworth, *Alexis*, 21–22.

Thus succession to the Russian throne had come almost full circle. There was no more talk of choosing the tsar, either by God or by the people assembled in a sobor. The only issue that mattered, so it seemed, was the blessing by the previous tsar. It looks very much as if that blessing did not actually take place in the traditional form in 1645, if only because Tsar Michael died too quickly, though the oath sworn by the army and gentry asserted that it did. In any case, Tsar Michael had only one living son in Aleksei, and he had made it perfectly clear to everyone that he intended Aleksei to be his successor. He had done that by including Aleksei in the important ceremonies of the court from the New Year ritual of 1642 onward. Here the Russian elite, clerical and lay, and the representatives of foreign potentates saw him with his father and sometimes acting as his deputy. The latter role was not new, for Ivan III and Ivan the Terrible had done the same with their sons. The public role of the tsarevich reinforced his character as heir to throne. The only other living Romanov relative was Aleksei's first cousin Nikita Ivanovich Romanov, a young man whose first court rank as *stol'nik* had come only in 1639.[250] Nikita Romanov not only did not claim the throne but (according to Krusebiörn) was the first to swear allegiance to Aleksei. The only alternative to Aleksei would have been either Nikita Romanov or someone from outside the tsar's family, and that could happen only at a sobor or, as in the Time of Troubles, by civil war. Tsar Michael had avoided both those eventualities by the traditional means of associating his son with himself in the public acts of the ruler. Count Waldemar soon returned to Denmark, and the new reign began with a clean slate.

[250] V. Korsakova, "Romanov, Ivan Nikitich," in *Russkii Biograficheskii Slovar'*. Romanova–Riasovskii (Petrograd: Izdanie Imperatorskogo Russkogo istoricheskogo obshchestva, 1918), vol. 17, 39–42. I. N. Romanov never married and died in 1654.

5 Succession and the New Culture of the Court 1645–1689

Succession to the throne from Tsar Michael's death to the accession of Peter the Great was relatively simple in the sense that Tsar Aleksei succeeded without challenge and over the years had several sons to whom he could leave the throne. The only contentious succession was in 1682, when revolt from the musketeers forced the boyars to proclaim two co-tsars, Ivan and Peter. Tsar Aleksei followed the precedent of earlier rulers in making clear whom he considered his heir and gradually introducing him to the formalities of presentation and even (as appropriate to the heir's age) government. Two differences, however, marked the period. One was the presentation of the heir on the traditional day of the New Year, September 1, beginning in 1667. The other, and more far-reaching, was the recasting of the ceremonies of the court year in a new form, with speeches and poetry in Baroque fashion, in which the heir played an important role. These speeches and poems were the work of Simeon Polotskii and his successors and constituted the first significant introduction to the Russian court of West European forms of court ceremony and even, to a limited extent, of ideas about monarchy. The court ceremonial ceased to be exclusively religious, and the repeated presentation of the heir at various moments played a central role in that change.[1] Simeon and the others did not confine themselves to form: they also began to introduce much more distinct ideas of hereditary monarchy, especially in compositions intended primarily for the ruling family.

Succession and Politics to 1667

During the first years of Aleksei's reign, the new tsar married as well as dealt with political storms. His former "tutor" (*diad'ka*) Boris Morozov was the most powerful of the boyars in the first years of the new reign and

[1] On the more traditional ceremonies and their documentation see O. V. Novokhatko, *Zapisnye knigi Moskovskogo stola Razriadnogo prikaza XVII veka* (Moscow: Pamiatniki istoricheskoi mysli, 2000), 167–226.

was most likely behind the failure of Tsar Aleksei's first attempt at finding a wife in February 1647, and certainly behind the marriage of the tsar to Mariia Il'inchna Miloslavskaia on January 16, 1648. She was the daughter of Morozov's client Il'ya Miloslavskii, whose other daughter Morozov himself almost immediately married. Morozov was now the tsar's brother-in-law. Tsaritsa Mariia gave birth in quick succession.[2] A son Dmitrii was born on October 22, 1648, the day of the festival of the Kazan' Icon of the Mother of God. The baptism was on October 29, and the officiating priest was Patriarch Iosif, the godmother Tsarevna Irina Mikhailovna, and the godfather the archimandrite Adrian of the Trinity-St. Sergii Monastery. Dmitrii died a year later.[3] Two daughters, Evdokiia and Marfa, arrived in 1650 and 1652, and both lived long lives, but were not normally considered possible heirs.[4] Finally, on February 5, 1654, during Butter Week, Tsaritsa Mariia provided Tsar Aleksei with a son, also named Aleksei. The baptism took place on the second Sunday of Lent, February 19, in the Dormition Cathedral of the Kremlin, with Patriarch Nikon himself conducting the service. The godmother was again Tsarevna Irina and the godfather Archimandrite Adrian. His patron saint was not the same as that of his father; rather it was St. Aleksei, the fourteenth-century metropolitan of Moscow.[5] This time the tsar's son was baptized not in the Chudov Monastery, but in the Dormition Cathedral. As that was the patriarch's church, the message was hard to miss: Nikon was in charge. The church ordered prayer services to be celebrated, ordering the people to pray for long life for the whole ruling family, not just the tsar, the tsaritsa, and their new son but all the aunts and daughters as well.[6] From then on until the boy's death on January 17, 1670, he was the eldest son of the tsar, and his

[2] Russell E. Martin, *A Bride for the Tsar: Bride Shows and Marriage Politics in Early Modern Russia* (DeKalb, Illinois: Northern Illinois University Press, 2012), 190–196.

[3] *DR* III, 106–107; *AAE* IV, 43–44, 61. Adrian Novgorodets was archimadrite during the years 1640–56, and was involved with spreading the cults of icons of the Mother of God at monasteries near Iaroslavl'. See Pavel Stroev, *Spiski ierarkhov i nastoiatelei monastyrei rossiiskiia tserkvi* (St. Petersburg: Tipografiia V. S. Balasheva, 1877), 139; M. D. Kagan and A. A. Turilov, "Skazanie o ikone Bogomateri Tolgskoi," *SKKDR* III, pt. 3, 400–407; D. M. Bulanin, "Skazanie o ikone Bogomateri Smolenskoi v Smolenskom monastyre pod Iaroslavlem," *SKKDR* III, pt. 4, 581–585; and Andreas Ebbinghaus, *Die altrussischen Marienikonen-Legenden*. Slavistische Veröffentlichungen 770 (Berlin: Harrassowitz, 1990), 93, 193–199.

[4] Evdokiia was baptized in the Chudov Monastery, but the court records provide no other details, nor do they even describe the baptism of Marfa: *DR* III, 149, 325.

[5] *DR* III, 399–401.

[6] *AAE* IV, 106–107 (circular letter of Makarii, Metropolitan of Novgorod, to northern towns and villages, February 9, 1654, ordering prayers for the tsar, his new born son, and the rest of his family.)

father made sure that it was clear to all that Aleksei Alekseevich was to be the heir.[7]

At the same time, Tsar Aleksei in his title proclaimed himself the hereditary heir to the throne, unlike his elected father Tsar Michael. In the letters to other sovereigns from the first years of his reign he had used the same title as his father, "Tsar and Grand Prince of All Russia, autocrat," followed by a list of territories he ruled or claimed to rule, ending with the phrase "sovereign and possessor" (*gosudar' i obladatel'*).[8] A letter from Russian officials to Adam Kisiel in Kiev complaining of omissions in the tsar's titles in Polish correspondence concerned the last few words, but they were not about heredity.[9] In 1649, letters from the tsar to the king of Poland had the traditional title from Tsar Michael's time, as did the tsar's letter to Hetman Bohdan Khmel'nys'skyi, and the treaty with Poland of July 1650, had the same, with no mention of heredity.[10] In September 1653, the tsar's letter to the hetman still had the traditional form of the title.[11] On the birth of Tsarevich Aleksei in 1654, however, he sent an announcement of the event to Khmel'nyts'kyi, who had only weeks before accepted the overlordship of the tsar. Here Tsar Aleksei styled himself with all the traditional territorial titles, Moscow, Vladimir, Kazan', and so on, but also used the phrase from Tsar Fyodor's 1584 coronation, *otchich i dedich i naslednik*, that proclaimed the hereditary

[7] At the death of Aleksei Alekseevich, the eldest son was Fyodor, born May 30, 1661, ultimately Tsar Aleksei's successor. There is no information on his baptism, but as his name day was celebrated on June 8 (St. Theodore), that must have been the day of the baptism: *DR* III, Dopolneniia, 271–272, 337–338. As his later life would demonstrate, Fyodor was not healthy and died a few days short of his twenty-first birthday in 1682, after a reign only six years. A second son, Simeon, was born on April 3, 1665 and was baptized on April 22: Pavel Stroev, ed., *Vykhody gosudarei tsarei i velikikh kniazei Mikhaila Fedorovicha, Aleksiia Mikhailovicha, Fedora Aleksievicha vseia Rusi samoderzhtsev s 1632 po 1682 god* (Moscow: Tipografiia A. Semena, 1844), 439. His godfather was to be "a monk from a local monastery" according to the Dutch diplomat Nicolaas Witsen: Nicolaas Witsen, *Moscovische Reyse 1664–1665*. Werken uitgeven door de Linschoten-Vereeniging 67 (The Hague: Martinus Nijhoff, 1966), vol. II, 202; Nikolaas Vitsen, *Puteshestvie v Moskoviiu 1664–1665*, trans. V. G. Trisman (St. Petersburg: Simpozium, 1996), 156–157. The third son was Ivan, who came into the world in 1666, another unhealthy boy who would "reign" as co-tsar to Peter 1682–96. To make matters worse, Tsaritsa Mariia died at the beginning of 1669, shortly after the birth of her thirteenth child (a girl, who survived only briefly), and their second son, Simeon, died only a few months later. Tsar Aleksei was in a dilemma, and he solved it by his marriage to Natal'ia Naryshkina in 1671. A year later a healthy son was born, the future Peter the Great.

[8] For example, *PDS* II, 1234–1235 (June 14, 1616, Tsar Michael to Emperor Matthias).

[9] *AIuZR* III, 160–163 (March 15, 1648); 176–179 (April 1648, Kisiel's explanation).

[10] *AIuZR* III, 310 (May 8, 1649, Aleksei to Jan Kazimierz); 320 (June 13, 1649, Aleksei to Khmel'nyts'kyi); 362 (October 1649, Aleksei to Jan Kazimierz); *PSZ* I, 238.

[11] *SGGD* III, 480 (September 6, 1653).

nature of his rule.[12] He used the same phrase in his letters to Emperor Ferdinand III in 1654–6 and to Emperor Leopold in 1665.[13] The Ambassadorial Office's reply to the 1667 memorandum of Sir John Hebdon, the envoy of Charles II of England, contained the phrase as well in the title, and the English have left us a contemporary translation: "of many dominions and countryes east, west, and north heire thereof from Father and Grandfather."[14] The 1673 letters to Pope Clement X, Emperor Leopold, and the Doge of Venice had it as well.[15] The title remained in this form until the end of the reign of Tsar Aleksei.[16]

Why the title changed between the beginning of September 1653 and February 1654 is not explicit in the sources. The most important intervening event was the Assembly of the Land in October 1653, which took the decision to go to war with Poland and accept the Ukrainian offer to be incorporated into Russia.[17] This was a major event, ratifying the decision of the tsar and his advisers to support the hetman against Poland. It meant a major war with the (apparently) still much stronger Poland and, if successful, an important addition to Russia's population and territory. The tsar's title figured in these decisions, if only as an extra reason to go to war. In the 1634 Polianovka treaty, Poland had agreed that its king would not claim the title of tsar of all Russia, as he had since the Time of Troubles.[18] In the Assembly, the final decision claimed that many of the officials of the Polish-Lithuanian state had not honored that treaty and in this and other ways dishonored the tsar.[19] This claim had nothing do with heredity.

The only likely explanation for the new title is the birth of the tsar's first heir, Tsarevich Aleksei, on February 5, 1654.[20] He now had a son, and

[12] E. E. Rychalovskii, ed., *Perepiska getmanov levoberezhnoi Ukrainy s Moskvoi i Sankt-Peterburgom 1654–1764 gg.*, vol. 1, *Getmanstvo Bogdana Khmel'nitskogo 1654–1657 gg.* (Moscow: Drevlekhranilishche, 2017), 56–57 (February 9, 1654); *AIuZR* 10, 307–308. In his letter to the hetman, he described his infant son as tsarevich and grand prince.

[13] *PDS* III, 88–89, 98, 264–265, 535–536; *PDS* IV, 542.

[14] S. Konovalov, "England and Russia: Two Missions, 1666–1668," *Oxford Slavonic Papers* XIII (1967), 66.

[15] *PDS* IV, 755, 763, 766.

[16] It also appeared in certain documents besides diplomatic correspondence, such as the charter confirming the privileges of the city of Kiev (July 16, 1654): *SGGD* III, 524.

[17] L. V. Cherepnin, *Zemskie sobory Russkogo gosudarstva v XVI–XVII vv.* (Moscow: Iazyki slavianskoi kul'tury, 1978), 327–337.

[18] *Traktaty pokojowe pomiędzy Rzeczpospolitą a Rosją w XVII wieku/Mirnye dogovory mezhdu Rech'iu Pospolitoi i Rossiei v XVII veke.* Świadectwa minionych wieków (Kraków: Platan, 2002), 22–47, 67–100.

[19] *AIuZR* 10, 6–8 (October 1, 1653, decision of the Assembly).

[20] *DR* III, 399. The boy was not baptized until February 12 (*DR* III, 400), after the letter to the hetman announcing his birth.

that son would obviously benefit from his father's claim to have inherited the territories that he himself ruled. As we shall see, it was a signal that succession, and particularly the presentation of succession and the successor, was to be an important theme in the reign of Aleksei Mikhailovich.

The issue of succession unfolded against a backdrop of dramatic events in Russia and among her neighbors. Morozov was responsible for introducing a salt tax to replace some older levies in the hope that it would bring more revenue. In the summer of 1648, however, Moscow erupted in a revolt of the townspeople against Morozov's salt tax, and the favorite barely escaped with his life. His associates were not so lucky, and the revolts spread to a number of smaller towns and border fortresses in the south and even Siberia. Lesser nobles and soldiers joined, and in some places led, the revolts. Ultimately the tsar rescinded the salt tax, and in the autumn called an Assembly of the Land to deal with the grievances. The result was Russia's first law code, the 1649 Conciliar Code (*Sobornoe Ulozhenie*), but the revolts did not end there, for in 1650, Novgorod and Pskov rose in rebellion.[21] While the towns were the scene of social unrest, the church was gradually moving into internal debates fraught with consequences. Since the 1630s, at least some of the parish clergy had been discontented with the existing forms of liturgical celebration and the lack of propagation of Christian teaching. In 1645, Stefan Vonifat'ev received the position of archpriest (*protopop*) of the Kremlin Annunciation Cathedral attached to the tsar's palace and simultaneously took over as the spiritual father of the tsar. A supporter of reform of the liturgy, he was largely unsuccessful until the death of Patriarch Iosif in 1652.[22] The new patriarch was Nikon, formerly archbishop of Novgorod and known for his homilies and as a supporter of reform. His first measures in the early months of 1653 would split the church, but for the time being Nikon exiled and imprisoned his opponents (the most famous being archpriest

[21] P. P. Smirnov, *Posadskie liudi i ikh klassovaia bor'ba do serediny XVII veka*, 2 vols. (Moscow: Izdatel'stvo Akademii nauk SSSR, 1947–8); E. V. Chistiakova, *Gorodskie vosstaniia v Rossii v pervoi polovine XVII veka: 30–40-e gody* (Voronezh: Izdatel'stvo Voronezhskogo universiteta, 1975); Richard Hellie, "Early Modern Russian Law: The Ulozhenie of 1649," *Russian History* 15, 2–4 (1988): 181–224; Richard Hellie, "Ulozhenie-Preamble," *Russian History* 15, 2–4 (1988): 155–179; Valerie Kivelson, "The Devil Stole His Mind: The Tsar and the 1648 Moscow Uprising," *American Historical Review* 98, 3 (1993): 733–756.

[22] Paul Bushkovitch, *Religion and Society in Russia: The Sixteenth and Seventeenth Centuries* (New York, New York: Oxford University Press, 1992), 51–73. On religion in the 1640s, see T. A. Oparina, *Ivan Nasedka i polemicheskoe bogoslovie kievskoi mitropolii* (Novosibirsk: Nauka, 1998); and O. S. Sapozhnikova, *Russkii knizhnik XVII veka Sergei Shelonin* (Moscow and St. Petersburg: Al'ians-Arkheo, 2010).

Avvakum Petrov) and also replaced Morozov as the most important of the tsar's advisors.[23]

The storm that broke in the Ukraine early in 1648 presented Aleksei with a whole series of new issues. There the Cossacks rose in revolt against Polish rule, destroying the Polish army and unleashing a peasant revolt among the Orthodox Ruthenian people of the Commonwealth. The Cossacks set up a whole political structure in the Ukrainian lands, challenging the king of Poland for control of the area. For Russia, it was a foreign policy dilemma of major proportions, rendering irrelevant Aleksei's father's attempts at a Polish alliance against Crimea. From the first weeks of the revolt, its leader Hetman Bohdan Khmel'nyts'kyi sent emissaries to Moscow begging the tsar to take the Ukrainian Cossacks under his "high hand." The tsar now had to decide whether he wanted to go to war with Poland, the hitherto hegemonic power of Eastern Europe, the victor over Russia in its two latest wars. He called a sobor in 1651 to discuss the topic, but the conclusion was to ask the king of Poland yet another time to cease his mistreatment of Orthodoxy. Only in the spring of 1653, probably at the urging of the new patriarch, Nikon, did Aleksei decide to go to war. Even then he secured the agreement of the Assembly of the Land (October 1653) before making the treaty with the Cossacks at Pereiaslav in January 1654.

The Pereiaslav agreement, establishing the Ukrainian hetmanate as an autonomous unit under the tsar, preceded by only a few weeks the birth of Tsarevich Aleksei.[24]

Only a few months after the birth of his son, the tsar went off to war. Back in Moscow, Patriarch Nikon remained in charge of the state. The first summer campaign of 1654 was spectacularly successful, for several towns surrendered to the Russians without a shot, and others were quickly taken. The Russian army penetrated far into the lands of the king of Poland, taking Polotsk and Mstislavl' and then in September, the great city and fortress of Smolensk. Tsar Aleksei had recaptured all the land lost to Poland in the Time of Troubles and now also controlled the eastern parts of the Grand Duchy of Lithuania. The court registers of the *Razriad* recorded the events. The tsar sent messages with news of the greater victories to the tsaritsa, Tsarevich Aleksei, and Patriarch Nikon (listed in that order). The commanders

[23] N. F. Kapterev, *Patriarkh Nikon i tsar' Aleksei Mikhailovich*, 2 vols. (Sergiev Posad: Izdatel'stvo Spaso-Priobrazhenskogo Valaamskogo monastyria, 1909–12); S. V. Lobachev, *Patriarkh Nikon* (St. Petersburg: Iskusstvo-SPB, 2003).

[24] There is no comprehensive history of Russia's decision to go to war over the Ukrainian revolt. See Paul Bushkovitch, "Russian Boyars and the Ukrainian Hetmanate," *Journal of Ukrainian Studies* 29, 1–2 (Summer–Winter 2004): 47–63 for some suggestions.

sent in reports of their successes to the tsar, which they attributed in each case to the prayers of the Mother of God and the Russian and other saints to God himself, and the good fortune (*schastie*) of Tsar Aleksei and his infant son.[25] This was the same formula that Tsar Michael had used at the Assembly of the Land in 1634. These messages continued with the capture of Wilno in 1655 and, during the new war with Sweden in Livonia, with the capture of Dorpat and the fortress of Kokenhausen in 1656.[26] At the same time as the victories, there was disaster, for in 1654–5 plague struck Moscow, with thousands of casualties. Patriarch Nikon and the whole family of the tsar left the city. Nikon was clearly in charge, giving orders to the boyars in Moscow.[27] During the absence of the tsar, orders also came from the infant tsarevich (presumably in fact from Nikon) in October to take measures against the plague in various places. In the spring, orders came in his name to grant tax relief to the villages belonging to Nikon's favorite Iverskii Monastery, and again in 1656 orders were given about collecting tolls in Bezhetskii verkh.[28] Thus, even as a baby, Aleksei Alekseevich had a role in the state, even if only a nominal one. It was not unusual for orders and decrees to come from an infant monarch (this had been the case with Ivan the Terrible), but the issuing of orders from an infant tsarevich whose father was alive was an innovation.

The next years of the war were less eventful, Tsar Aleksei stayed back in Moscow, and peace came with Sweden. The great event of those years was his clash with Patriarch Nikon, who abandoned the exercise of his office in 1658 and retreated to the Monastery of the New Jerusalem that he had recently built. At first it seemed merely a matter of precedence, but it grew into a struggle for power: tsar or patriarch. For nearly a decade Tsar Aleksei tried to make peace, but neither he nor Nikon would give in. While the dispute continued, resistance to the patriarch's liturgical reforms gradually split the church. A substantial minority of clergy and laymen refused to obey, laying the foundations of the Old Belief, Russia's largest movement of religious dissent.[29] In the midst of this contention, on May 30, 1661, Tsaritsa Mariia gave birth to a second son, Fyodor Alekseevich.[30] A month later, the

[25] *DR* III, 425–426, 429–432, 435–436, 449–450.

[26] *DR* III, 485; *DR* III, Dopolnenie, 6, 64, 68–69, 80–83.

[27] *DAI* III, 442–521. Nikon also received ambassadors and made decisions jointly with the boyars before the plague hit: Lobachev, *Patriarkh Nikon*, 147–157.

[28] *AAE* IV, 111–112, 133; *AI* IV, 233, 240; *SGGD* III, 533–534. On the monasteries, see Kevin M. Kain, "Before New Jerusalem: Patriarch Nikon's Iverskii and Krestnyi Monasteries," *Russian History* 39 (2012): 173–231.

[29] Kapterev, *Patriarkh Nikon*, vol. I, 394–431; Lobachev, *Patriarkh Nikon*, 189–202.

[30] *DR* III, Dopolnenie, 271, 276; Stroev, ed., *Vykhody gosudarei tsarei i velikikh kniazei*, 358. The palace records note that the tsar sent the news to Patriarch Nikon in his self-imposed exile in the Monastery of the New Jerusalem, but for the baptism only that it took place on June 30 and on that day Tsar Aleksei heard mass in one of the interior palace churches.

Razriad records stated that the tsar's envoys attributed the conclusion of the peace treaty with Sweden (Kardis, June 1661) to the intercession of the Mother of God and the saints, and to the good fortune of Aleksei and both his sons, Tsarevichi Aleksei and Fyodor.[31] Good fortune belonged to the tsar and all his sons, not just the eldest. The happy events notwithstanding, the continuing war began to wear on the fabric of society. In the summer of 1662, the Moscow populace rioted, attributing the debasement of the currency and their other sufferings to the tsar's favorites, Il'ya Miloslavskii and F. M. Rtishchev.[32] (Boris Morozov escaped their wrath, for he had died in 1661.) Finally, the war began to wind down. Russian negotiations with Poland resumed at the end of 1662, and after much maneuvering and further fighting the two sides came together at Andrusovo near Smolensk on April 30, 1666. The final treaty concluded on January 30/February 9, 1667. It was a truce, not a peace treaty, but most importantly it put an end to the war and gave Russia Smolensk and its surrounding territory, the Ukrainian hetmanate, and the city of Kiev (in theory for a period of years). Russia was now at peace and had replaced Poland as the dominant power in Eastern Europe. Russia's chief negotiator, A. L. Ordin-Nashchokin, returned home in triumph, bringing back the icon from the Savior Church in the Kremlin Palace that had accompanied him to the negotiations.[33]

During these years the tsar's family, not just the tsar himself, was present in official documents. The prayers for the tsar in the mass continued as in the reign of Tsar Michael, with prayers for the tsar, the tsaritsa, and all the children, each named. This form of prayers survived unchanged during all the liturgical reforms of the early years of Aleksei's reign, including Nikon's revisions. The Byantine and Greek versions of those prayers had included only the emperors, not the family, so Nikon's predilection for Greek liturgy did not extend this far.[34] We know relatively little about the service oaths of Aleksei's reign, but the surviving examples suggest that the earlier formula, swearing to serve the tsar, the tsaritsa, and the children whom God would give, remained in force.[35] In other

[31] *DR* III, Dopolnenie, 275.

[32] V. I. Buganov, *Moskovskoe vosstanie 1662 goda* (Moscow: Nauka, 1964).

[33] Zbigniew Wójcik, *Traktat andruszowski 1667 roku i jego geneza* (Warsaw: Państwowe Wydawnictwo Naukowe, 1959); B. N. Floria, *Vneshnepoliticheskaia program A. L. Ordina-Nashchokina i popytki ee osushchestvleniia* (Moscow: Indrik, 2013), 12–195; *DAI* V, 102.

[34] Paul Meyendorff, *Russia, Ritual and Reform: The Liturgical Reforms of Nikon in the Seventeenth Century* (Crestwood, New York: St. Vladimir's Press, 1991), 144, 172–173. Cf. Jacobus Goar, ed., *Euchologion* (Venice: Typographia Bartholomei Javarina, 1730), 56.

[35] *PSZ* I, 255–256 (no. 69, August 31, 1651); 308–315 (no. 114, 1653); *DRV* 8, 84; Ia. G. Solodkin, "Prisiagi moskovskim gosudariam po dannym sibirskogo letopisnogo svoda," *Vestnik All'ians-Arkheo* 17 (2016): 90–102.

respects, the surviving record shows that Aleksei included his eldest son in official documentation and, as the boy grew older, in appropriate occasions at court. The court registers of the years from 1657 through 1665 are not complete, but it is clear that as Tsarevich Aleksei grew up, he took a larger role in the life of the court. In his infancy, the registers recorded only his formal inclusion in the messages from the army or diplomatic exchanges and the yearly celebration of his own name day (February 12) and those of his siblings.[36] The first court ceremony in which Tsarevich Aleksei played some minor part, the reception of the English ambassador Charles Howard, the earl of Carlisle, came in 1664.[37] Later on, in December 1664, he and his younger brother Fyodor "interceded" (successfully) for Nikolai Ziuzin, who had been condemned to death for his intrigues on the part of Patriarch Nikon.[38]

The only more notable events were the appointment of the boyar Prince Ivan Petrovich Pronskii as the *diad'ka* of Tsarevich Aleksei on May 16, 1658, and the installation of Aleksei Alekseevich in new rooms in the Kremlin Palace in June 1662.[39] By 1664 the tsarevich had acquired another tutor in the person of the *okol'nichii* F. M. Rtishchev (1625–73). Rtishchev, aside from his being in favor with the tsar, was an important figure in the new currents in religion and culture at the court. He was the patron of the Ukrainian scholar and preacher Epifanii Slavinetskii, who had come to Moscow in 1649 to teach the new skills to young Russians. Rtishchev was also the subject of a hagiographic biography, one of the first of a layman, that stressed his piety, humility, and generosity to the poor.[40] His other official post was that of the head of the Great Palace, the principal office serving the tsar's household, and informally he served as the head of the Printing Office from 1658 to

[36] *DR* III, 457; *DR* III, Dopolnenie, 24–25, 89, 173, 214, 253, 309, 337–338, 368, 378; S. A. Belokurov, *Dneval'nye zapiski Prikaza tainykh del 7165–7183 gg., ChOIDR* 1–2 (1908): 45, 59, 134 (hereafter *DZ*).

[37] *DR* III, 556–579. The tsarevich received some of the food from the banquet of February 19, 1664, but was not actually present (*DR* III, 576).

[38] *SGGD* IV, 142–143; N. Gibbenet, *Istoricheskoe issledovanie dela Patriarkha Nikona* (St. Petersburg, Tipografiia Ministerstva vnutrennikh del, 1884), vol. II, 137. It is not clear who was behind the intercession, the tsar himself or someone else.

[39] *DR* III, Dopolnenie, 133, 339. Pronskii first served at court in 1627, received boyar rank in 1652, and died in 1683. His wife was Anastasiia, the daughter of Prince D. M. Pozharskii, the great commander of the Time of Troubles: Marshall Poe, *The Russian Elite in the Seventeenth Century* (Helsinki: Academia Scientarium Fennica, 2004), vol. I, 436; Iu. M. Eskin, *Dmitrii Mikhailovich Pozharskii* (Moscow: Kvadriga, 2013), 182.

[40] I. Kozlovskii, *F. M. Rtishchev: Istoriko-biograficheskoe issledovanie* (Kiev: n.p., 1906), 101–113, originally in *Kievskie universitetskie izvestiia* 46 (January 1906): 1–52; (February 1906): 53–100; (June 1906): 101–132; (November 1906): 133–152; (December 1906): 153–201; Bushkovitch, *Religion and Society in Russia*, 160–163.

1666–7.[41] As such he must have inspired or at least approved the publication of the one printed text then available to address the education of the son of a ruler. That was the *Testament* of the Byzantine tsar Basil I the Macedonian (867–86), written for his son and successor Leo the Wise (886–912). In fact, Basil did not write the text, but no one realized that until modern times.[42] It was circulated well in Byzantium and was early on translated into Slavic. In 1638, the Belorussian printer Spiridon Sobol' published the Slavic version in Mogilev, supplying it with an afterword that praised Basil and especially Leo for spreading Christianity among the Slavs through Sts. Cyrill and Methodius. The Moscow text of 1661–3 reproduced the afterword.[43] The *Testament* was mostly a traditional Byzantine text of advice to the ruler, perhaps with occasional emphasis not found elsewhere, stressing respect for the church and the importance of friendship over family ties for rulers.[44] Byzantine as it may seem, the text was published and translated into Latin and vernacular languages several times in early modern Europe, in France by David Rivault de Fleurance, one of the teachers of Louis XIII.[45]

[41] S. K. Bogoiavlenskii, *Moskovskii prikaznyi apparat i deloproizvodstvo XVI–XVII vekov* (Moscow: Izdatel'stvo Moskovskogo universiteta, 2006), 283; I. V. Pozdeeva, A. V. Dadykin, and V. P. Pushkov, *Moskovskii pechatnyi dvor – fakt i faktor russkoi kul'tury 1652–1700 gody*, 2 vols. (Moscow: Nauka, 2007–11), vol. I, 132; vol. 2, 94, 109, 133, 135, 137–138, 141, 370, 395, 516, 545.

[42] Kurt Emminger, *Studien zu den griechischen Fürstenspiegeln* (Munich: Lindl, 1913), 23–73; Konstantinos D. S. Paidas, *Vasileios A' Makedōn: Dyo parainetika keimena pros ton autokratora Leonta 6. ton Sopho* (Athens: Ekdoseis Kanake, 2009). The other available Byzantine political text, printed in 1661, was that of the deacon Agapetus (sixth century), which was already known and used in Russia but not directed specifically at the heir: [Arsenii Grek], *Anfologion* (Moscow: Pechatnyi dvor, 1660), 82–114. On Agapetus, see Chapter 1. Tsar Aleksei brought St. Filipp's relics from the Solovetskii Monastery to Moscow in 1652 with great ceremony.

[43] A. S. Zernova, "Belorusskii pechatnik S. Sobol'," *Kniga: Issledovaniia i materialy* 10 (1965), 126–145; Angel Nikolov, "Srednevekovyi slavianskii perevod 'Uchitel'nykh glav' imperatora Vasiliia I: Problemy izucheniia rukopisnoi traditsii i rannikh pechatnykh izdanii," in *XIX Ezhegodnaia bogoslovskaia konferentsiia* (Moscow: Sviato-Tikhvinskii bogoslovskii institut, 2009), vol. I, 41–47.

[44] I. S. Chichurov, *Politicheskaia ideologiia Srednevekov'ia: Vizantiia i Rus'* (Moscow: Nauka, 1990), 67–106; Shaun Tougher, "Macedonian Mirrors: The Advice of Basil I for His Son Leo VI," in *Concepts of Ideal Rulership from Antiquity to the Renaissance*, ed. G. Roskam and S. Schorn (Turnhout: Brepols, 2018), 355–382; Dimiter Angelov, *Imperial Ideology and Political Thought in Byzantium 1204–1330* (Cambridge: Cambridge University Press, 2006), 185–187, 194–195.

[45] Editions: *Basilii Romanorum Imp. exhortationum capita LXVI. ad Leonem filium* (Paris: Apud F. Morellum, 1584); Johann von Fuchte, ed., *Basilii imperatoris constantinopolitani capita sexaginta sex* (Helmstedt: Lucius, 1616); translations: James Scudamore, trans., *The Sixty-Six Admonitory Chapters of Basilius, King of the Romans, to His Sonne Leo* (Paris: n.p., 1638); David Rivault de Fleurance, *Remonstrances de Basile, empereur des Romains, à Leon son fils* (Paris: A. Estiene, 1612, 1646); Pascale Mormiche, *Devenir prince: L'école du*

The tsarevich soon had not just tutors to supervise his upbringing, but an actual teacher. The teacher was the Kiev-trained Belorussian monk Simeon Polotskii, soon to become a major figure at the Russian court. What Simeon taught the tsarevich cannot be exactly known, but it seems to have included Latin, and someone may have taught him Greek: in the library of Aleksei Alekseevich were two manuscript dictionaries: *Leksikon pismenoi slovenskoi s grecheskim* and *Leksikon latinskoi pismannoi s slovenskim.*[46] Someone took the trouble to make Slavic dictionaries for the two languages, as printed books did not exist.[47] Latin had been part of the education of European princes since the Middle Ages, but in Russia it was an innovation. Later on Paisios Ligarides, the Greek metropolitan of Gaza, spoke to the tsar's family in Latin and claimed that Tsarevich Aleksei could speak Greek. On August 26, 1666, Tsarevich Aleksei acquired another brother with the birth of Ivan.[48] By the summer of 1667, Aleksei Alekseevich was taking part in the court's religious observances with his father.[49] On September 1 of that year, Tsar Aleksei introduced a new element into the usual New Year's ceremony in the Kremlin: the presentation (*ob"iavlenie*) of the tsarevich. This new ceremony was not only an innovation in substance, but also a major example of the new culture of the court that appeared in the 1660s.

The New Culture of the Court

The new elements in court culture represented a departure from the religious culture that had developed at the court of the sixteenth rulers of Russia. Some of these were a matter of the importation of Western artistic genres and devices: a move toward three-dimensionality in icon painting and fresco (in the work of Simon Ushakov and others), the development of verse and declamation on mostly Polish baroque models

pouvoir en France XVIIe–XVIIIe siècles (Paris: Éditions CNRS, 2009), 24–26, 227. The young Louis XIII also read and translated Agapetus.

46 Ivan Zabelin, *Domashnii byt Russkikh tsarei v XVI i XVII stoletiiakh* (Moscow: Kniga, 2000, 2003), vol. I, pt. 2, 185–186; vol. III, 599.

47 Slavinetskii produced manuscript dictionaries of Latin to Slavic and Slavic to Latin which remain in the Moscow archives: V. V. Nimchuk, *Leksykon latyns'kyi E. Slavynets'koho, Leksykon sloveno-latyns'kyi E. Slavynets'koho ta A. Korets'koho-Satanovs'koho* (Kiev: Naukova dumka, 1973). These may or may not be the ones in the library of Aleskei Alkekseevich, but they demonstrate that such manuscripts did circulate in the court.

48 Tsarevich Ivan was baptized on 20 September in the church of the Uncreated Image of the Savior. This was the church built in 1661 for the apartments of Tsar Aleksei's sisters, Irina, Anna, and Tat'iana. *DR* III, 641; Stroev, ed., *Vykhody gosudarei tsarei i velikikh kniazei*, 466, 468; Belokurov, *Dneval'nye zapisi*, 227: Izvekov, *Moskovskie kremlevskie dvortsovye tserkvi*, 75.

49 *DZ*, 248.

mediated through Kiev, and even the study of Polish and Latin by some of the sons of the court elite. It also involved a changing religious culture, and the beginnings of secular reading and education. These were not merely the exercises of scholars and their students behind closed doors, for they formed part of the action and texts of the important rituals of the court. The new poetry and panegyric oratory celebrated the stages of succession to the throne in Tsar Aleksei's reign and after, for the poets and orators marked the marriages, births, and presentations of the heirs and their coronation with elaborate creations, both for the public and for the private pleasure of the ruling family. The most important, but not the only, voice of these changes was that of the Belorussian monk, Simeon Polotskii. Simeon and others adapted to Russia the whole panoply of panegyric of monarchs current in the West, a genre with roots going back to the Roman Empire.

These changes began to appear on a limited scale from at least the 1630s, but only a generation later did they gather speed and scope. New impulses came from several directions. Tsar Aleksei brought learned monks from Kiev starting in 1649, the most important of them being Epifanii Slavinetskii (died 1675). His main contribution was to introduce the Baroque sermon into the Russian court, certainly an innovation but one that remained within a religious culture.[50] The process of change quickened with the appearance of Simeon Polotskii (1629–80) at the Russian court early in 1664.[51] Simeon, born in 1629 in Polotsk in the Lithuanian part of the Polish commonwealth, was a product of the Jesuit academy in Wilno and the Orthodox academy in Kiev. He returned to Polotsk where he started a school and first met Tsar Aleksei in 1656, when the tsar passed through the town and heard two of Simeon's panegyric verses in his honor. Later, in 1660, Simeon went to Moscow with the pupils from his school, who performed a poetic declamation on January 19 in the tsar's honor. These were typical products of Baroque culture, praising the glory and virtue of the tsar and comparing him to the sun. The 1660 verses also compared Tsaritsa Mariia to the moon, and

[50] Bushkovitch, *Religion and Society in Russia*, 150–178.

[51] I. Tatarskii, *Simeon Polotskii (ego zhizn' i deiatel'nost')* (Moscow: M. G. Volchaninov, 1886); A. N. Robinson, *Bor'ba idei v russkoi literature XVII veka* (Moscow: Nauka, 1974); A. N. Robinson, ed., *Simeon Polotskii i ego knigoizdatel'skaia deiatel'nost': Russkaia staropechatnaia literature: XVI–pervaia chetvert' XVIII v.* (Moscow: Nauka, 1982); Bushkovitch, *Religion and Society in Russia*, 163–172; A. M. Panchenko, D. M. Bulanin, and A. A. Romanova, "Simeon Polotskii," *SKKDR* III, pt. 3, 362–379; Irina A. Podtergera, "Reconstructing the Life of Simeon Polotskii on the Basis of Manuscripts," *Canadian Slavonic Papers* 49, 3–4 (2007): 293–306; Margarita A. Korzo, *Nravstvennoe bogoslovie Simeona Polotskogo: Osvoenie katolicheskoi traditsii Moskovskimi knizhnikami vtoroi poloviny XVII veka* (Moscow: IFRAN, 2011).

Tsarevich Aleksei to the morning star (*dennitsa*). Thus praise of the tsar already included Tsarevich Aleksei, singled out in the text from the tsar's aunts and daughters.[52] Simeon also produced other compositions in praise of Tsar Aleksei's victories and of his sons the tsarevichi Aleksei and Simeon.[53] The monk moved permanently to Moscow in 1664 and soon found a home in the Zaikonospasskii Monastery, in the Kitaigorod next to Red Square, that is to say, across the square from the Kremlin. He soon found a task in the wake of the Church Council of 1666–7, which deposed Nikon and condemned the Old Ritualists. Simeon composed the *Zhezl pravleniia* (*Staff of Governance*), a defense of the Council's position against the Old Ritualists. Simeon's knowledge and writings included fat volumes of sermons but also ranged far beyond, to theater and poetry on the model of neo-Latin and Polish verse and declamations for court ceremonies. Among these ceremonies was that for the presentation of the tsarevich in 1667 and 1674, contributions which form a modest part of his extensive work redirecting Russian court culture from an exclusively religious culture toward the combination of religious and secular themes that made up the European Baroque.[54]

In writing about the tsar and his sons, Simeon's prose orations and poetry were products of the rhetorical culture of the Baroque era. These were founded on the classical models of panegyric verse to honor Roman emperors (Ovid, Virgil, and especially Horace) and the prose panegyric such as that of Pliny the Younger for the Emperor Trajan.[55] Panegyric poetry and prose in praise of monarchs returned with the Renaissance, continuing on into the seventeenth century. In France, Joachim Du Bellay compared Francis I and Henry II to the sun long before Louis XIV and even wrote a poem to explain to the king the value of poetry to kings. Pierre de Ronsard produced a great many poems for the king, including a series of odes and sonnets to the kings of France and other

[52] Tatarskii, *Simeon Polotskii*, 47–51; Simeon Polotskii, *Izbrannye sochinennia* (Moscow: Izdatel'stvo Akademii nauk SSSR, 1953), 97–102.

[53] Simeon Polotskii, *Virshi*, ed. V. K. Bylinin and L. U. Zvonareva (Minsk: Mastatskaia literatura, 1990), 22–86.

[54] On the culture of the court see Bushkovitch, Religion *and Society in Russia*, 150–175; A. S. Eleonskaia, *Russkaia oratorskaia proza v literaturnom protsesse XVII veka* (Moscow: Nauka, 1990); L. I. Sazonova, *Literaturnaia kul'tura Rossii: Rannee Novoe vremia* (Moscow: Iazyki slavianskikh kul'tur, 2006); I. A. Buseva-Davydova, *Kul'tura i iskusstvo v epokhu peremen: Rossiia semnadtsatogo stoletiia* (Moscow: Indrik, 2008); P. V. Sedov, Zakat *moskovskogo tsarstva: Tsarskii dvor kontsa XVII veka* (St. Petersburg: Dmitrii Bulanin, 2007). It should be noted that none of these authors other than Sedov and Sazonova focused specifically on the court, though in fact that was the location of almost all the religious and cultural phenomena these historians discussed.

[55] Paul Roche, ed., *Pliny's Praise: The Panegyricus in the Roman World* (Cambridge: Cambridge University Press, 2011); Roger Rees, ed., *Latin Panegyric* (Oxford: Oxford University Press, 2011).

members of the royal family. After the Wars of Religion, François de Malherbe produced verse in honor of Henri IV and Louis XIII. The Jesuits Nicolas Caussin and Denis Pétau published a collection of prose panegyrics on the majority of Louis XIII.[56] One of Jean Racine's first works was an ode on the recovery of Louis XIV from illness written in 1663 that compared Henri IV to the sun, and of course it became the standard metaphor for Louis himself later on.[57] The Académie française sponsored a panegyric of the king on his name day (the day of St. Louis of France, August 25).[58] These panegyrics did not ignore the king's presumed piety, but that was only one virtue among others – justice, modesty, courage, prudence, graciousness, and restraint of passion – the normal panoply of human virtues since ancient times and the Renaissance.

Panegyric of the monarch was not confined to France or the Catholic monarchies. England was especially rich in such compositions, though they have not attracted as much scholarly attention as the visual images of kingship.[59] Edmund Spenser's *Faerie Queene* was dedicated to Queen Elizabeth and featured her in allegorical form both as royal queen (Gloriana) and as a "most virtuous and beautiful lady" (Belphoebe). The much lesser known Samuel Daniel provided the same for James I. His text was largely about English history and the political virtues of James, but included the traditional account of the ideal king: "Religion comes with thee, peace, righteousnesse//Judgement and justice, which more glorious are//Then all thy Kingdomes . . ."[60] Ben Jonson displayed similar sentiments. In his verse King James came to England with Themis (right custom and order), Dice (justice), Eunomia (good laws), and Irene (peace), and James, unlike a tyrant, could control his

[56] Joachim Du Bellay, "Prosphonématique," "Louange de la France et du roy treschrestien Henry II," in *L'Olive* (Paris: Arnoul L'Angelier, 1549–50); and in Joachim Du Bellay, *Œuvres complètes*, ed. Olivier Millet (Paris: Honoré Champion, 2003), vol. 2, 90–96, 136–137; Pierre de Ronsard, "Avant-Entrée du roy tres-chrestien à Paris" (1549), in *Œuvres* (Paris: Alphonse Lemerre, 1893), vol. 6, 201–205, and other works; François de Malherbe, "Prière pour le roi Henri le Grand allant en Limousin" (1605–7), in *Recueil des plus beaux vers de messieurs de Malherbe, Racan* . . . (Paris: Pierre Mettayer, 1638), 8–13; and in *Les Poésies* (Paris: Société des textes français modernes, 1999), 27–32. Nicolas Caussin and Denis Pétau, *Pompa regia* (La Fleche: Flexiae, 1615).

[57] Louis Hautecœur, *Louis XIV: Roi soleil* (Paris: Plon, 1953); Peter Burke, *The Fabrication of Louis XIV* (New Haven, Connecticut: Yale University Press, 1992), 26, 45, 66, 130, 180.

[58] Pierre Zoberman, *Les panégyriques du roi prononcés dans l'Académie française* (Paris: Presses de l'Université de Paris-Sorbonne, 1991).

[59] Kevin Sharpe, *Selling the Tudor Monarchy: Authority and Image in Sixteenth-Century England* (New Haven, Connecticut: Yale University Press, 2009), 109–113, 348–355, 464–466.

[60] Samuel Daniel, "A Panegyric Congratulatorie to the King's Most Excellent Majestie," in *The Complete Works in Verse and Prose* (London: Hazell, Watson and Viney, 1885), vol. 1, 144 (stanza 4), originally 1603.

passions.[61] Religion was not absent in this poetry but justice was more important. At the equally Protestant court of Denmark, the royal chaplain, Anders Sørenson Vedel, praised King Frederick II at the occasion of the investiture of the dukes of Holstein (1580) and the king's death (1588). Neither text had much to say about the king's piety. The investiture oration was mainly devoted to praise of the Danish monarchy. The funeral sermon devoted some ten pages (out of ninety) to Frederik's virtues. Fear of God came first, followed by mercy, justice, and mildness. The rest of the text was a chronicle of the king's accomplishments.[62] Perhaps the most striking work to come out of Protestant Europe on the ideal king was the work of a king himself: the *Basilikon Doron* of James I of England. The small book was advice to his son and heir, and actually devoted the first 20 pages of 150 to piety. The good king should fear God and be firm in his faith, he wrote. To accomplish that, he needed to read and know the Bible and pray frequently to the Lord. After this introduction, James advised his son to cultivate the usual virtues of a good king, such as justice and clemency.[63] None of these modern works, of course, was known to Simeon Polotskii, as his only foreign languages were Latin and Polish, but they formed the background to the Polish writers whom he did read.

The fashion for praise of the king, especially in verse, had reached Poland in Latin and Polish poetry already by the beginning of the sixteenth century. Ioannes Dantiscus and Andrzej Krzycki, both clerics, praised Sigismund August, his marriage, and his victories.[64] Poland's greatest Renaissance poet, Jan Kochanowski, composed a Latin "Epinicion" in honor of King Stefan Batory's victory over Russia in 1582.[65] In the seventeenth century the Jesuits Jan Rywocki and Jakub Olszewski praised King Władysław IV, the latter in Polish prose from his

[61] Ben Jonson, "A Panegyre on the Happy Entrance of James, Our Sovereign" (1603), in *Workes* (London: Richard Bishop, 1640), 87–90 (second count).

[62] Anders Sørenson Vedel, *Oratio panegyrica oblata ... Frederico II* (Copenhagen: Andreas Gutterwitz, 1580); Anders Sørenson Vedel, *En sørgelig Ligpredicken ... Frederich den anden* (Copenhagen: Aff Laurentz Benedicht, 1588).

[63] James I, *Basilikon Doron* (London: Felix Kyngston, 1603). For panegyrics and other forms of praise of the Stuart kings, see Kevin Sharpe, *Image Wars: Kings and Commonwealths in England 1603–1660* (New Haven, Connecticut: Yale University Press, 2010), 46–57, 173–189.

[64] Ioannes Dantiscus [Jan Dantyszek], *Sylvula de victoria inclyti Sigismundi regis Polonie contra Moschos* (Kraków: Grachovie per Florianum Unglerium XXIII, 1514); [Andrzej Krzycki], *Andreae Cricii Carmina*, ed. Kazimierz Moraswski. Corpus antiquissimorum poetarum Poloniae latinorum III (Kraków: Typis Universitatis Jagellonicae, 1888), 20–88.

[65] Jan Kochanowski, *Carmina latina*, ed. Józef Przyborowski (Warsaw: Officina Fratrum Jezynsciorum 1884), 285–336.

chair at the Wilno Academy.[66] The Jesuit Maciej Kazimierz Sarbiewski (1595–1640), Poland's most important Latin poet, praised Pope Urban VIII, Holy Roman Emperor Ferdinand II, and Poland's Sigismund III.[67] Samuel Twardowski (died 1660) published in 1649 a verse account of King Władysław IV that Simeon Polotskii had in his library.[68]

The Polish examples demonstrate that these panegyrics had nothing to do with the power of the monarch, much less with "absolutism." These panegyrics did not distinguish among monarchs in different "constitutional" structures. Twardowski praised an elected king who regularly dealt with a recalcitrant diet. He described the distinguished ancestry of the Wasas and his hero's royal birth, but he also described the election of the king in some detail, stressing his popularity even before the election. Władysław's wisdom, self-restraint, humanity, grace, and simplicity of life called forth universal approval.[69] Following this Western tradition, Simeon Polotskii and his successors began to feature extravagant praise of the tsar not just for his piety but also for his secular glory and achievements. Implicit in the panegyrics was also a conception of the ideal monarch, one that included secular as well as religious virtues. This sort of praise of the tsar was a radical innovation in Russian culture, and it affected the image and presentation of the heir as well.[70]

[66] Jan Rywocki SJ, *Monumentum gratae testificationis invictissimo et potentissimo Poloniae et Sueciae regi Vladislao IV* (Wilno: Vilnae Typis Akademicis, 1639); Jakub Olszewski, *Kazania* (Wilno: Drukarnia Akademicka, 1645).

[67] Matthias Casimirus Sarbievius [Maciej Kazimierz Sarbiewski], *Lyricorum libri IV* (Antwerp: Ex officina Plantinia Balthasaris Moreti, 1634), 59–61 (Sigismund, Book II, ode 23); Sarbiewski influenced all the Eastern Slavic poets of the time, including Simeon Polotskii: Sazonova, *Literaturnaia kul'tura Rossii*, 118–24.

[68] Samuel Twardowski, *Władysław IV, król polski i szwedzki*, ed. Roman Krzywy (Warsaw: PAN, 2012) (originally Leszno, 1649); Anthony Hippisley and Evgenija Luk'janova, *Simeon Polockij's Library: A Catalogue*. Bausteine zur slavischen Philologie und Kulturgeschichte. Series B, Editions, new sequence, vol. 22 (Cologne, Weimar, and Vienna: Böhlau, 2004), 145.

[69] Twardowski, *Władysław IV*, 209–211. Twardowski did not stress the king's piety, though he did not omit it. Describing Władysław's trip to Italy in 1625, he notes the king's visit to the Marian shrine at Loreto, but gives it no more space than the visit to the Papal arsenal, and devotes only some 100 lines to the shrines in Rome: Twardowski, *Władysław IV*, 186–188.

[70] Simeon and other clergy trained in Kiev do not seem to have had Ruthenian prototypes for their panegyrics. The closest analogy is Peter Mohyla's hymn in praise of King Władysław on his election in 1632. Its content is a traditional prayer for a pious ruler with Christian virtues: *Arkhiv Iugo-Zapadnoi Rossii* (Kiev: Kommisiia dlia razbora drevnikh aktov, 1887), vol. I, pt. 7, 168–170. Books from the Kiev presses included poems and prose in praise of patrons and Orthodox magnates, but not the king of Poland.

The First Presentation and After

The first public presentation of the heir took place on September 1, 1667 in the Dormition Cathedral of the Kremlin and the square between the cathedral, the tsar's palace and the bell tower known as Ivan the Great. It had, however, a series of preludes through the earlier part of the year. The reason for those preludes may well have been the tsar's preoccupation with the end of the church council that condemned Avvakum and Old Belief and deposed Nikon, for it lasted into the early part of 1667. The council included also the Greek Patriarch Paisios of Alexandria and Makarios of Antioch. They had come to Russia at the request of Tsar Aleksei to help solve the conflict with Patriarch Nikon. At the end of the council, the Russian church and Tsar Aleksei selected as patriarch the archimandrite of the Trinity-St. Sergii Monastery, Ioasaf, whom Paisios and Makarios then placed on the patriarchal throne.[71] Both patriarchs would also be part of the presentation of the heir, and in the background was also the Greek metropolitan of Gaza, Paisios Ligarides (1610–78), who later produced a polemical account of the author's time in Russia and the case of Patriarch Nikon.[72]

According to the account of Ligarides, the tsar assembled his family in the palace on January 1, 1667, "privately" (*kat'idian*), before the church ceremonies in the palace and invited the Greek patriarchs. Ligarides believed that Tsar Aleksei was thinking of introducing the Roman New Year.[73] At this meeting, Patiarch Paisios of Alexandria made three brief speeches, to the children of the tsar, to the Tsaritsa Mariia, and to the tsarevny, the tsar's sisters. Ligarides summarized the speeches, which are also extant in a manuscript of the patriarchal library of Alexandria.[74] Patriarch Paisios addressed all of the ruling family, not just the tsar and

[71] Kapterev, *Patriarkh Nikon*, vol. II, 256–420, 465–519; Kapterev, *Kharakter otnoshenii Rossii k pravoslavnomu vostoku v XVI i XVII stoletiiakh*, 2nd ed. (Sergiev Posad: Izdanie knizhnogo magazina M. S. Elova, 1914), 426–454; Paul Meyendorff, *Russia, Ritual and Reform*; Bushkovitch, *Religion and Society in Russia*, 66–68, 165–168, 202–203; Wolfram von Scheliha, *Russland und die orthdoxe Universalkirche in der Patriarchsperiode (1589–1721)*. Forschungen zur Geschichte Osteuropas 62 (Wiesbaden: Harrassowitz, 2004); Lobachev, *Patriarkh Nikon*, 174–226.

[72] On Ligarides, see Harry T. Hionides, *Paisius Ligarides* (New York, New York: Twayne Publishers, 1972). For his account of Nikon, see Gennadius Library Athens, MS 260; and William Palmer, *The Patriarch and the Tsar* (London: Trubner and Co., 1873), vol. III. Ligarides came from the Greek island of Chios, received his education in Rome and became Orthodox metropolitan of Gaza in 1652. There was considerable suspicion of his religious loyalties from the Greek clergy.

[73] *DZ*, 234; *DAI* V, 100; Gennadius Library Athens, MS 260, ff. 96–97; Palmer, *The Patriarch and the Tsar*, vol. III, 202–204.

[74] Panagiotis Tzoumerkas, *Ho Kodiks arithm. 393 tes Alexandrines Patriarkhikes Vivliothekes ho legomenos tou Patriarkhou Paisiou* (Alexandria: Ekdose Patriarkhikes Bibliothekes tou Patrikarkheiou Alexandreias, 2010), 143–148.

his heir. According to Ligarides, the patriarch delivered these speeches. Ligarides claimed that at this private meeting the tsarevich wanted to reply in Greek to Paisios, but his father interrupted him and answered himself, also in Greek.[75] The speeches from January 1 were not the only event of that year that brought new cultural impulses into the celebration of the ruling family and the heir. Tsarevich Aleksei's name day fell on February 12, two days after the consecration of the new patriarch, Ioasaf.[76] The palace records are not extant for those weeks, but Simeon Polotskii's brief greeting to the tsarevich does survive. It reminds the listeners of St. Aleksei, "the helmsman of the ship of the Russian church." He is an intercessor for all Orthodox people, but has especial "protection of your inheritance the state" (*nasledіia ti derzhavy pokrovitel'stvom*).[77] Name days were usually a small ceremony in the palace, and the circumstances meant that it was unlikely to be more than that, but Simeon's terminology was revealing: Tsarevich Aleksei was to be the ruler by heredity.

Finally, on September 1, 1667, Tsar Aleksei presented his son Tsarevich Aleksei (aged thirteen) to the people in an elaborate public ceremony in the Kremlin.[78] The people included the boyars and court ranks, but also a variety of others, including foreign merchants and diplomats.[79] The clergy carrying out the ceremony included not only the Russian patriarch, Ioasaf, but also the Orthodox patriarchs Paisios

[75] Gennadius Library Athens, MS 260, ff. 96–97; Palmer, *The Patriarch and the Tsar*, vol. III, 202–204.

[76] Gennadius Library Athens, MS 260, f. 149v; Palmer, *The Patriarch and the Tsar*, vol. III, 284.

[77] Gosudarstvennyi istoricheskii Muzei (GIM), Sinodal'noe sobranie 229 (Simeon Polotskii, speeches and greetings), ll. 183ob.–184; Russian National Library. Osnovnoe sobranie F XVII 83 (Simeon Polotskii, works), ll. 280–280ob. (dated 1667). Sinodal'noe sobranie 229 also contains another greeting for the name day of Tsarevich Aleksei, unfortunately undated, ll. 183–183ob.

[78] On the ceremony, see Konstantin Nikol'skii, *O sluzhbakh russkoi tservki byvshikh v prezhnikh pechatnykh bogosluzhebnykh knigakh* (St. Petersburg: Tipografiia tovarishchestva Obshchestvennaia pol'za, 1885), 98–168; N. Krasnosel'tsev, *K istorii pravoslavnogo bogosluzheniia* (Kazan': Tipografiia Imperatorskogo universiteta, 1889), 27–56; M. Lisitsyn, *Pervonachal'nyi slaviano-russkii tipikon* (St. Petersburg: Tipografiia V. D. Smirnova, 1911), 110–114; Ivan Zabelin, *Domashnii byt Russkikh tsarei*, 397–401. Iu. E. Shustova, "Prazdnik Novogo Goda v Rossii XVII vv.," in *Kalendar': Khronologicheskaia kul'tura i problemy ee izucheniia* (Moscow: Rossiiskii gosudarstvennyi gumanitarnyi universitet, 2006), 192–201; and Iu. E. Shustova, "Prazdnik Novoletiia v epokhu tsaria Alekseia Mikhailovicha: Zarozhdenie novoi prazdnichnoi kul'tury," *Kolomenskoe: Materialy i issledovaniia* 13 (2011): 31–48. The usual court records (*DR*, *DZ*) have missing pages for these events.

[79] The files in RGADA, f. 210, d. 445, ch. 2, l. 2 ff. represent over sixty petitions from various ranks asking to receive the gifts promised at the time of the presentation of the tsarevich (see l.3, for example). The presentation was thus a widely known event, though all the petitioners may not have been present in the Kremlin on that day.

of Alexandria and Makarios of Antioch. The conflict in the church was resolved at the moment that the tsar's eldest son became thirteen years old.

The presentation ceremony for the heir was the most visible form of paternal designation that the Russian tsars ever devised. The sources do not explicitly explain why the tsar chose the Orthodox New Year to present his son, but some of the associations with that holiday make the choice more comprehensible. The ceremony began with the tsar, his heir, and the court leaving the palace to walk a few meters to the Dormition Cathedral. The center of the palace as it then was, before much of it was torn down in the eighteenth century, was the Golden Chamber (*Zolotaia palata*), built in the 1550s by Ivan the Terrible as the principal room for the throne and audiences. The room was covered with frescoes that expressed the Russian court's conception of the order of the natural and human world at that time. Though no longer extant, the subjects are known from the detailed description made in March 1672, by the court icon painter Simon Ushakov (1626–86) at the time of restoration. On the walls were depictions of Joshua's conquest of Canaan and the story of the tsar's regalia, the cap of Monomakh from the *Tale of the Vladimir Princes*. At the very top was an image of Christ Emmanuel, and below his feet descending over the curve of the vault were the four virtues from Wisdom 8:7, "if a man love righteousness, her [wisdom's] labors are virtues: for she teacheth temperance and prudence [*sophrosyne* ... *kai phronesis*], justice, and fortitude [*dikaiosyne kai andreia*]." The Slavic inscriptions gave the virtues as "tselomudrie, razum, chistota, pravda," replacing *andreia* (fortitude or courage) with *chistota* (purity).[80] These are images that the viewer saw in the center, looking straight on at Christ. Next to the images of the virtues (and the corresponding vices) on the left were pictures of the circle of time, the four seasons, and on the right the circles of the sun, moon, and fire. Air was depicted between the two groups. The rest of the ceiling was taken up with the images of Wisdom ("Wisdom hath builded her house": Proverbs 9:1).[81] The ceiling paintings contained one more reference: next to the image of Christ Emmanuel were three inscriptions, two of them from the service for the New Year on September

[80] Robert Hanhart and Alfred Rahlfs, eds., *Septuaginta*, 2 vols., 2nd ed. (Stuttgart: Deutsche Bibelgesellschaft, 2006), vol. II, 356.

[81] Ivan Zabelin, ed., *Materialy dlia istorii, arkheologii i statistiki goroda Moskvy* (Moscow: Moskovskaia gosudarstvennaia duma, 1884), vol. I, 1238–1240; O. I. Podobedova, *Moskovskaia shkola zhivopisi pri Ivane IV: Rabota v moskovskoi Kremle 40kh–70kh godov XVI veka* (Moscow: Nauka, 1972), 62–63; Frank Kämpfer, "'Rußland an der Schwelle zur Neuzeit': Kunst, Ideologie und historisches Bewußtsein unter Ivan Groznyj," *Jahrbücher für Geschichte Osteuropas* Neue Folge 23, 4 (1975): 509; Justin Willson, "Virtue Idealized in the Palace Murals of Ivan the Terrible," (Slavic Review).

1: "*Blagoslovi venets leta blagosti Tvoeia Gospodi*" (Bless, o Lord the crown of the year of your goodness) and "*Prevechnoe Slovo otchee, izhe vo obraze Bozhii syi, i sostavliaiai tvar' ot nebytiia v bytie, izhe vremena i leta svoeiu oblastiiu polozhei, blagoslovi venets letu blagostiiu svoeiu, darui mir tserkvam tvoim, pobedy vernomu tsariu, blagoplodie zhe zemli i nam veliu milost'*" (Most eternal Word of the Father, who is in the image of God and has made creation from unbeing to being, who put the times and the years by his power, bless the crown of the year with your goodness, give peace to your churches, victory to the faithful tsar, fertility to the land and great love to us).[82] The sixteenth-century frescoes contained no reference to succession to the throne, but they did explain the larger context of the New Year ceremony as it was before Tsar Aleksei attached the presentation of the heir to it. The ceremony's purpose was to remind the believer of God's creation of the world, including time (hence the New Year) and of the importance of wisdom and virtue. Wisdom and virtue were necessary for all Christians, but placing the images on the ceiling (the closest part to heaven) of the throne room in the tsar's palace underlined their relevance for the ruler. The prayers, pronounced by the clergy and the metropolitan/patriarch, called on God to bless the cycle of the year, the tsar, and the people. This message was still clearly understood in 1667, as Ushakov's description, made only five years later, demonstrates.

The 1667 presentation (*ob"iavlenie*) was not only a court ceremony, for it took place in the courtyard of the Kremlin between the palace and the churches under the open sky. The new ceremony encapsulated the more traditional celebration of the New Year.[83] There are two accounts of the ceremony extant, an official account from the state archives and an account from the church.[84] The official Russian church record described the events with flowery language: "by God's mercy there was a new work of grace: the sovereign tsarevich and grand prince Aleksei Alekseevich was with his father . . . at the New Year (*letoproshenie*), [and] was presented to the whole world."[85] The state account recorded that at three o'clock the men of duma rank, with the "foreign" tsarevichi of Georgia, Kasimov, and Siberia, assembled in the entrance chamber (*perednaia verkhnaia*

[82] Zabelin, *Materialy dlia istorii, arkheologii i statistiki goroda Moskvy*, vol. I. 1238–1239. For the text of the New Year service, see *Trefologion, I (sentiabr'–noiabr')* (Moscow: Pechatnyi dvor, 1637), ll. 1–22 (the quotations in the fresco are on l. 20v). A later description of the service is in the Ustav of 1668: *DRV* 2nd ed. (Moscow: Kompaniia tipograficheskaia, 1789), vol X, 1–9.

[83] Stroev, ed., *Vykhody gosudarei tsarei i velikikh kniazei*, 480. One new element in 1665 and 1666 was a speech (*rech'*) from the boyar Prince Nikita Ivanovich Odoevskii: *DZ*, 190, 224–225. There is no information on its content.

[84] *PSZ* I, no. 415, 719–724; *DAI* V, 112–113 (vykhody patriarshie = Sin. 423, ll. 11–12ob.).

[85] *DAI* V, 112 (= Sin. 423, ll. 11).

palata) of the Kremlin palace. The audience there was only the boyars and duma ranks, and Tsar Aleksei declared that this was the proper time for him to present his son for all of them to hear, to the Patriarchs Paisios of Alexandria, Makarios of Antioch, and Ioasaf of Moscow, as well as the whole clergy, the Duma, and the whole people. The boyars assembled in the Entrance Chamber, then petitioned the tsar to present his son, and wished both tsar and son long life and victory over their enemies. The tsar then went to the rooms of the tsarevich, while the "near boyars" waited in the palace church of the Savior and the rest remained in the Entrance Chamber. As the procession moved from the rooms of the tsarevich to the rooms of the tsar, Archimandrite Ioakim of the Kremlin Chudov Monastery carried the icon of the Savior from the Kremlin church before the tsar and Tsarevich Aleksei. According to the church records, this was the icon that had accompanied A. L. Ordin-Nashchokin on his latest embassy.[86] They moved down the stairway by the Granovitaia palata outside to the Dormition Cathedral. They walked on carpets spread on the ground, and during the procession Prince I. P. Pronskii (the *diad'ka* of the tsarevich) asked the lesser ranks in his name about their health. In the cathedral, father and son kissed the icons and relics. After the cathedral service, everyone went on the platforms that had been erected in the Kremlin square for the New Year's ritual, "where it is the custom every year to pronounce prayers of thanks and for the New Year to the Triune Light."[87] The clergy assembled on one platform, the tsar and court on the other. After the usual prayers, Patriarch Paisios pronounced a greeting in Greek (*grecheskim dialektom*) to the tsar and his son, and Pavel, the Sarskii metropolitan, read a Russian translation. The deacons then sang the prayer for long life, and the tsar greeted the patriarchs. According to the church account, Tsarevich Aleksei made his own speech, greeting and praising his father: "the sovereign tsarevich greeted the sovereign tsar his father, standing in front of him."[88] The state account merely recorded the fact of the speech and praised the tsarevich. The tsar then thanked his son, then kissed him on the head; and everyone thanked and greeted one another. Prince N. I. Odoevskii made a speech, as he had done for previous New Year's ceremonies, concluding the proceedings.[89] The

[86] *PSZ* I, 719; *DAI* V, 112 (= Sin. 423, l. 11v). [87] *PSZ* I, 721–722.

[88] "gosudar' tsarevich szdravstvoval gosudariu tsariu, ottsu svoemu, stav priamo litsu ego," *DAI* V, 113 (= Sin. 423, l. 11v).

[89] *PSZ* I, 722–723; Pawel Potocki thought Odoevskii learned in Slavic letters: Bushkovitch, *Peter the Great: The Struggle for Power 1671–1725* (Cambridge: Cambridge University Press, 2001), 31–32. An anonymous English newsletter from September 1667 gave an eyewitness account of the ceremony and reported that both the tsar and the tsarevich made speeches. It also noted that the nobility, strangers (foreigners), and "commonalty" congratulated the tsar at the ceremony. National Archives of the United Kingdom, Public

tsar then bestowed gifts on his subjects, from the greatest boyars down to the commanders of the musketeers.[90] A banquet followed, the first of several, this one with all the duma ranks, the clergy, and the soldiers, but without the tsarevich.[91]

Tsarevich Aleksei appeared for the name day of Tsarevna Marfa on September 5.[92] Two days later, on Saturday September 7, the tsar held a banquet in honor of the presentation of his son (*stol dlia obiavleniia*). As was the case with the September 1 banquet, Aleksei Alekseevich himself was not present. The banquet did not include all the boyars, only Prince Ivan Alekseevich Vorotynskii, Prince Ivan Andreevich Khovanskii, the *okol'nichii* Prince Ivan Dmitrievich Pozharskii, and the duma secretary Dementii Bashmakov. Bashmakov had been head of the tsar's Privy Chancery since 1664, and one of the few other guests to be named was Fyodor Mikhailov, also a secretary of that chancery. The other unnamed guests included the commanders of the musketeer regiments, the foreign colonels of the new regiments, the staff of the Chancery of the Horse, the priests of the Annunciation Cathedral, the falconers, some Greek merchants, the staff of the Goldsmiths Chancery, the doctors, and the apothecaries, and then by name Lieutenant General Nicholas Baumann. In the Hall of Facets on the left side of the tsar at a separate table sat "the teacher, the monk Simeon (*uchitel' starets Simeon*)," that is to say, Simeon Polotskii.[93] The guests were the military officers and the staffs of the household and offices that served the ruling family in various capacities, from the stables to the doctors and some Greek merchants. Also present were some who made up the inner circle of the tsar in political matters as well: Bashmakov, Khovanskii (already a favorite for some years), head of the Post (*Iam*) Chancery, and Pozharskii, head of the Petitions Chancery. The only other boyar was Prince I. A. Vorotynskii, a boyar since 1664, who never headed any chancery or served as provincial governor, but was prominent in many ceremonies at court. It seems as if this banquet was largely for the household, but including a few officials

Record Office, State Papers 91/3, ff. 132–132v., printed in S. Konovalov, "Patrick Gordon's Dispatches from Russia 1667," *Oxford Slavonic Papers* XI (1964): 11–12.

90 *PSZ* I, 723. In the next few days the tsar also gave gifts to the most important *d'iaki*, Dementii Bashmakov (Privy Chancery), Luk'ian Golosov (Ambassadorial Chancery), and others, as well as to the ordinary soldiers and musketeers with their families. The process of gift-giving continued into 1669: Russkaia istoricheskaia biblioteka (RIB) 23, 1488–1492, 1522–1526, 1528, RIB 21, 125 (to the wives and mothers of musketeers, 7178, misdated in RIB to 7168).

91 *PSZ* I, 723–724; *DR* III, 659–660; *DAI* V, 113 (= Sin. 423, l. 12).

92 *DAI* V, 113–114 (= Sin. 423, l. 12v).

93 *DZ* 253. Baumann served in the Russian army as early as in 1663–4: Dmitry Fedosov, ed., *The Diary of General Patrick Gordon of Auchleuchries 1635–1699* (Aberdeen: AHRC Centre for Irish and Scottish Studies, University of Aberdeen, 2010), vol. II, 181,199.

and four men of duma rank.[94] This second banquet ended the ceremony of presentation.

Just as new as the ceremony itself were the speeches. The presentation of Tsarevich Aleksei was the occasion for speeches that Simeon Polotskii wrote for the heir and even the tsar himself as well as declamations that he and others delivered. Several days after the event, Simeon received a reward for a speech on the presentation of the tsarevich, presumably the speech that is preserved in the manuscript of his declamations, the "Book of Greetings."[95] In it the speaker addressed the tsar directly, congratulating him that a new sun (the tsarevich) had appeared. The whole people, he said, had rejoiced, like the birds in the spring seeing the rising sun. He told the story of "a certain Ammon, [perhaps a mistake for Memnon] an Egyptian who built an organ to sing at the sight of the sun: we also will play with our organs of the soul, singing as in Psalm 118:24," that is, "This is the day which the Lord hath made; we will rejoice and be glad in it," "God has made two great lights, you [the tsar] and your son, to hold the Orthodox Russian tsardom. Let him give you victory over the night, the pagans. The natural sun has no offspring, but you our animated sun have produced another sun, with your name and your virtues. As you live for God, the church, and your tsardom, so will your son, for the apple does not fall far from the tree. The eagle produces an eagle, not a weak dove. Like father, like son. Likeness has a certain natural power," the text continued. "Like enjoys like, and even God made man in his own image." [Gen. 1: 27] "The Virgin Mary, when she saw an icon of herself, said that with the icon would be her grace and power. When we honor icons, the honor goes to the prototype: so when we honor the son, we honor the father. Alexander the Great took honor for one of his councilors as honor to himself. So you should take honor to your son as honor to you. You, the boyars (*sigklit*), should also rejoice, as you see the establishment of our strength (*utverzhdenie kreposti nasheia*). The whole Orthodox Russian world rejoices, and with me says, let there be long life to father and son."[96]

Who actually delivered the speech? It occupies little more than two pages in the manuscript and was written in a language full of metaphors,

94 *DR* III, 661–662; Bogoiavlenskii, *Moskovskii prikaznyi apparat*, 188–189, 208, 211–112; Poe, *The Russian Elite*, vol. I, 395.

95 Zabelin, *Domashnii byt Russkikh tsarei*, vol. II, 187; [Simeon Polotskii], "Kniga privetsv na gospodskiia i inyia prazdniki i inyia rechi raznyia", GIM, Sin. 229. The collection was edited by Simeon himself, with folios 1–3, 11–12, and some notes in the hand of Simeon's pupil Sil'vestr Medvedev: Sazonova, *Literaturnaia kul'tura Rossii*, 161–163.

96 [Simeon Polotskii], "Rech' o iavlenii gosudaria tsarevicha Aleksiia Aleksiievicha," GIM, Sin. 229, ll. 175–176. Another copy is Russian National Library, Manuscript Division, F XVII 83, ll. 46–48ob., not in Simeon's hand but rather in that of a contemporary Belorussian scribe (identification by Dr. Irina Podtergera).

with classical allusions and Biblical quotations. It was not in the name of the tsarevich, and Simeon Polotskii himself did not speak, according to the records of the events.[97] It is possible that Pavel, the Krutitsy Metropolitan, or Patriarch Ioasaf, pronounced the words, for both of them spoke at the ceremony. Metropolitan Pavel was Simeon's principal patron in the church from the time of his arrival in Moscow until Pavel's death in 1675, and Simeon wrote other texts for him to deliver.[98] Similarly, Simeon wrote epistles and other writings for Ioasaf.[99] In any case, Simeon adapted the text for his audience and for the occasion, but it was no less an innovation. Russia had no tradition of secular oratory, and only the Ukrainian preachers in Moscow such as Epifanii Slavinetskii occasionally alluded to texts or events outside the traditional Russian religious culture. The declamation, with its central metaphor of the sun and the reference to the eagle also served as a foretaste of a much more ambitious and innovative work, Simeon's *Orel Rossiiskii*.

The other surviving speech, or speeches, from the ceremony belonged to Patriarch Paisios. According to the Russian patriarchal record, Paisios made a speech of greeting to the tsar and then Pavel made the same speech "according to writing in a small notebook" in Russian.[100] In the Russian state record, Paisios greeted both the tsar and Tsarevich Aleksei.[101] According to the Greek texts, the patriarch greeted the tsar as the protector of the church and the descendant of the Palaiologos emperors of Byzantium by way of Sophia Palaiologina (a genealogical phantasy). He praised the tsar's gentleness, wisdom, and love of humanity, and called blessed the womb of his mother Evdokiia. Tsar Aleksei was a new Constantine.[102] The greeting (*khairetismos*) to the tsarevich was a bit more elaborate. Alexander the Great had completed the work of his father Philip II, and Solomon completed the Temple of Jerusalem that King David had left unfinished. Constantius Chlorus, the father of Constantine the Great, ruled the western provinces of the Roman empire before his son defeated his enemies, Maximinus, Maxentius,

97 Sazonova believes that Simeon delivered the speech, but not at the public ceremonies: Sazonova, *Literaturnaia kul'tura Rossii*, 52.

98 V. K. Ziborov and V. V. Iakovlev, "Pavel," *SKKDR* III, pt. 3, 4–8. For Pavel's library, see V. Undol'skii, ed., "Biblioteka Pavla, mitropolita sarskogo i podonskogo," *Vremennik OIDR* 5 (1850): 65–73. It is theoretically possible that the speech was delivered by Patriarch Ioasaf, but Simeon does not seem to have had close relations with him.

99 Robinson, *Bor'ba idei v russkoi literature*, 234; O. B. Belobrova, "Ioasaf II," *SKKDR* III, pt. 2, 80–82.

100 *DAI* V, 113 (= Sin. 423, l. 11v): "govoril prezhe Paisii patriarch, potom govoril po pismu, po tetradi poludestovoi Pavel mitropolit sarskii." The punctuation in Sin. 423 makes clear that it was Pavel who spoke from a notebook, not Paisios.

101 *PSZ* I, 721–722.

102 *DAI* V, 113; Tzoumerkas, *Ho Kodiks*, 143.

and Licinius, and took the whole state. Your father Aleksei, he said, has enlarged the boundaries of Russia, thus strengthening Orthdoxy like a new Constantine. It is your task to complete your father's work. The Byzantine emperor Leo VI the Wise (886–912), the son of Basil the Macedonian, fulfilled his father's accomplishments with science and prophecy, including that of the yellow-haired race [*ksanthon genos*] that would free us [Greeks] from slavery. Constantine had come from the west, but learned to love Greek language and wisdom, and founded Constantinople, the queen of cities. Now we see and hear with our own ears that the God-blessed tsarevich, the grand prince [*ho megas knezes*] Aleksei Alekseevich speaks Greek [*hellenize*] and even loves our tribe [*phyle*] and the whole Rhomaic people. Let him and his father, like two Alexanders, restore and liberate us. We rejoice like the old Persians who saw Alexander the Great speak Persian and wear Persian clothes. Paisios ended with a prayer for God to fulfill his request for long life for father and son Aleksei as well as for the other sons, Fyodor, Simeon, and Ivan.[103] Finally, there may have been another short text at the ceremony from Paisios, a *polychronion*, a form of the traditional wish for many years of life to the ruler. The text is found in the Paisios manuscript with the orations and greetings to the tsar's family, and, as Tzoumerkas noted, it could have been delivered at any or all of several occasions when Patriarch Paisios conducted a service with the presence of the tsar and other members of his family. Most of the text is the traditional wishes for long life, not just for the tsar but also the tsaritsa, all the tsar's children and his sisters. The patriarch also explicitly named Tsar Aleksei the "heir and successor" (*kleronomos kai diadochos*) of Russia and other

[103] Tzoumerkas, *Ho Kodiks*, 144–145. The idea of Leo VI as a prophet comes from the *Oracula Leonis*. See Wolfram Brandes, "Oracula Leonis," in *Christian–Muslim Relations: A Bibliographical History*, ed. David Thomas and Alex Mallett (Leiden: Brill, 2012), vol. 4, 124–127. The prophecies of the *ksanthon genos* go back at least to the tenth-century Byzantine life of St. Andreas Salos, and appeared in the work of both Paisios Ligarides and Nicolae Spatharii Milescu: Lennart Ryden, "The Andreas Salos Apocalypse: Greek Text, Translation and Commentary," *Dumbarton Oaks Papers* 28 (1974): 197–261; Petre Guran, "Historical Prophecies from Late Antique Apocalypticism to Secular Eschatology," *Revue des études sud-est européennes* 52 (2014): 47–62; Michael Pesenson, "Nicolae Milescu Spafarii's 'Khrismologion' and 'Kniga o Sivillakh': Prophecies of Power in Late Seventeenth Century Russia," in *Religion and Identity in Russia and the Soviet Union*, ed. Nikolaos A. Chrissidis, Cathy J. Potter, David Schimmelpenninck van der Oye, and Jennifer Spock (Bloomington, Indiana: Slavica, 2011), 63–80; V. G. Chentsova, "Paisii Ligarid, Nikolai Spafarii i Franchesko Barotstsi: Eskhatoligicheskie idei pri dvore tsaria Alekseia Mikhailovicha," *Drevniaia Rus': Voprosy medievistiki* 55, 1 (2014): 69–82; Asterios Argyriou, *Les exégèses grecques de l'Apocalypse à l'époque turque (1453–1821): Esquisse d'une histoire des courants idéologiques au sein du people grec asservi* (Thessaloniki: Hetaireia makedonikon spoudon, 1982).

dominions.[104] The patriarch was not the only one from the Greek clergy to use this terminology: in the dedication to his history of the Nikon affair, Paisios Ligarides addressed Tsar Aleksei as the "natural heir and successor" (*physikos kleronomos kai diadochos*) to the Russian throne.[105]

Insofar as the Greeks were concerned, the patriarch of Alexandria presented the tsar and his son in this short oration with an entire political platform, one that had little to do with actual Russian foreign policy. The tsars had strenuously avoided conflict with the Turks for more than a century, and that was not to change until 1677. The Russians did think about the Orthodox peoples of the Balkans, and they did know about the prophecies of the fall of the Turks, not least from Ligarides himself, but the context of the patriarch's speech seems more cultural than political. It was part of the new culture of the Russian court, with impulses from the Greeks alongside the more powerful stream from Kiev and the West.[106] At the same time, the claim of descent from the Palaiologan emperors of Byzantium, however fanciful, presented the tsarevich with an assertion that he was a hereditary monarch. The claim of rule by heredity came this time in a speech before the assembled elite of church and state, even if it was not the clearest statement. The *polychronion* was much clearer, but may not have been pronounced before a large audience and Ligarides's history was scarcely, if at all, known in Russia. The Greek description of Russia as a hereditary monarchy remained in the small circles of the ruling family and inner court.

Simeon Polotskii was for the time being the main conduit of the stream of western culture through Kiev. His contribution to the presentation of the tsarevich, *Orel Rossiiskii*, was a long poetic panegyric, which he later included in his voluminous collection of occasional verse, the *Rifmologion*, completed shortly before his death in 1680. The poem was a product of Baroque poetics, with word games, words arranged to make pictures, a *carmen echicum*, anagrams, classical analogies, and the whole revolving around the image of the tsar and his son as the sun, the source of light, and

[104] Tzoumerkas, *Ho Kodiks*, 47, 147–148. In the relevant passage Paisios seems to have been summarizing and translating the tsar's title. The words *kleronomos kai diadochos* may have been an attempt to render *otchich i dedich*.

[105] Gennadius Library Athens, MS 260, f. 3; Palmer, *The Patriarch and the Tsar*, vol. III, 15.

[106] V. G. Chentsova, "Eschatologie byzantine et pensée historique à la cour d'Alexis Romanov: Paisios Ligaridès, Nicolas le Spathaire et Francesco Barozzi aux origines du messianisme russe (1656–1673)," in *Écrire et réécrire l'histoire russe d'Ivan le Terrible à Vasilij Ključevskij (1547–1917)*, ed. Pierre Gonneau and Ecatherina Rai. Collection historique de l'Insitut des études slaves 51 (Paris: Institut d'études slaves, 2013), 41–51; V. G. Chentsova, "Paisii Ligarid, Nikolai Spafarii i Franchesko Barotstsi"; D. N. Ramazanova, "Bukharestskii spisok 'Khrismologiona' Paisiia Ligarida: Paleograficheskoe i kodikologicheskoe issledovanie," *Vestnik RGGU* (50), 10, 7 (2010): 178–191.

of the Russian eagle.[107] Simeon accompanied the text with a "speech" (*rech'*), on the actual delivery of which we have no information. It followed the model of the speech for the public ceremony on September 1, repeating the metaphor of the sun and rejoicing at the presentation of the tsarevich, "the true heir and inheritor of the Orthodox Russian tsardom" (*istinnogo naslednika i dedicha pravoslavnogo rossiiskogo tsarstva*). He called on the tsar, the patriarchs Paisios and Makarios, the boyars, and the Russian people to rejoice with him.[108]

The poem carried three quotations from the Bible as its epigraph: "In them [the heavens] he set a tabernacle for the sun, which is as a bridegroom coming out of his chamber, and rejoiceth as a strong man to run a race" (Psalm 19: 4–5); "this is my beloved son, in whom I am well pleased" (Mat. 3: 17); and "The father of the righteous shall greatly rejoice: and he that begetteth a wise child shall have joy of him. Thy father and mother shall be glad, and she that bare thee shall rejoice" (Prov. 23: 24–25). Immediately following were two dedications (*afierosis*) of the work to Tsar Aleksei in the form of complicated poetic puzzles.[109] A prose "encomium" of Tsar Aleksei served as preface to the poem. Again repeating the sun image, Simeon praised the virtue, wisdom, and piety of the tsar at some length. Tsar Aleksei was not a slave to his passions like Nebuchadnezzar and Solomon. The tsarevich gives us all hope, he said, of light instead of darkness and the turning and inconstantly running wheel of Fate (*Imarmena*, from Greek *heimarmene*). The news of the heir, the second sun (*izvestie nasledstva vtorogo solntsa*), gives hope. Tsar Aleksei's victories over the Poles and Lithuanians have freed White and Little Russia from the hands of the faithless as from a second Babylonian

[107] N. A. Smirnov, ed., *Orel Rossiiskii: Tvorenie Simeona Polotskogo*. Obshchestvo liubitelei drevnei pis'mennosti 133 (St. Petersburg: Obshchestvo liubitelei drevnei pis'mennosti, 1915); Simeon Polotskii, *Orel Rossiiskii*, ed. L. I. Sazonova (Moscow: Indrik, 2015). For the text in the context of Simeon's larger collection of panegyric poetry, the *Rifmologion*, see Simeon Polockij, *Rifmologion: Eine Sammlung höfisch-zeremonieller Gedichte*, (Vienna, Cologne, and Weimar: Böhlau, 2017), vol. 2, 209–260. There were at least two copies from Simeon himself, one a presentation copy in the tsar's library and the other included in the *Rifmologion*. On *Orel Rossiiskii* and other undated "*privetstva*" to the tsarevich and other members of the ruling family, see V. P. Grebeniuk, "'Rifmologion' Simeona Polotskogo (Istoriia sozdaniia, struktura, idei)," in *Simeon Polotskii i ego knigoizdatel's-kaia deiatel'nost': Russkaia staropechatnaia literatura: XVI–pervaia chetvert' XVIII v.*, ed. A. N. Robinson (Moscow: Nauka, 1982), 269, 274–276, 283–284, 288–292. On the imagery (new to Russia) see Sazonova, *Literaturnaia kul'tnura Rossii*, 385–413. The image of the "sun-king" was not confined to Louis XIV in seventeenth-century Europe: Burke, *The Fabrication of Louis XIV*; Harsha Ram, *Imperial Sublime: A Russian Poetics of Empire* (Madison, Wisconsin: University of Wisconsin Press, 2003), 34–38.

[108] Smirnov, ed., *Orel Rossiiskii*, xxv–xxvii; Simeon, *Orel Rossiiskii*, 295–297.

[109] Smirnov, ed., *Orel Rossiiskii*, 4–6; Simeon, *Orel Rossiiskii*, ll. 3–3v; Sazonova, *Literaturnaia kul'tura Rossii*, 254–257.

captivity. The glory of the tsar's right hand has risen to the heavens. Now God will allow the moon of Islam to wane. At the end Simeon wished long life to the tsar, Tsaritsa Mariia, Tsarevich Aleksei, the younger sons, and the tsar's aunts and daughters.[110] The verse began in the next section, the "elogion," which also introduced the image of the Russian eagle soaring in the heavens before the sun. Again it gave praise to Tsar Aleksei, whose justice and avoidance of flattery made his fame spread to all over the world, even to America(!) and the Ganges. Tsarevich Aleksei is now the second sun, and sadness will move to the land of the Hagarites (Muslims). After this section, the presentation copy in the tsar's library had a picture of the Russian eagle as a coat of arms, with three crowns, sword and scepter, and St. George on his chest, all against the disk of the sun. On the sun's rays were the forty-seven virtues of the tsar, and over all the quotation from Psalm 19.[111] The author then called on Apollo and the Muses to prophesy. They fulfilled the request over the next ten folios, though their responses are not exactly prophecies but more variations of the images of the sun and the eagle, all pointing to true faith and to the tsar's glory. Finally, Apollo himself claimed that Homer, Virgil, Demosthenes, Cicero, and Aristotle would not be able to describe Russia's glory, and Tsarevich Aleksei is Russia's joy.[112] Then the reader found a drawing of the twelve signs of the Zodiac encircling the second line of the quotation from Psalm 19 ("rejoiceth as a strong man to run a race"). The description of each of the twelve signs, beginning with Aries, illustrated one of the virtues of the tsarevich, and constituted the longest section of the poem. The ram was humility, Taurus labor, and Gemini love, including that of one's people, as in the story of Marcus Curtius jumping into the lake for the Romans. Next was Cancer, whose realm the tsarevich would enter when he expanded Russia, especially to the sea against the Tatars. He would enter the realm of Leo when he defeated the lion of (Swedish) Livonia. Virgo would show him how to defeat his spiritual and fleshly enemies, and free the Greeks as well. Libra was the sign of justice (*pravda*). Aleksei will be a just tsar, for now he prays to be just. In contrast, Scorpio is the flatterer, whom the tsarevich must avoid. Sagittarius, the archer, will help the future Tsar Aleksei against the Turks, for the city of Constantine awaits him. Capricorn will be the place of the tsarevich when the pagans in the dark forests turn away from idols to accept the true faith. Similarly, the water that Aquarius dispenses is the

[110] Smirnov, ed., *Orel Rossiiskii*, 7–13; Simeon, *Orel Rossiiskii*, ll. 4–9v.

[111] Smirnov, ed., *Orel Rossiiskii*, 14–24; Simeon, *Orel Rossiiskii*, ll. 10–17. The *Rifmologion* copy of the text had a simplified drawing: Grebeniuk, "'Rifmologion' Simeona Polotskogo," 289–290.

[112] Smirnov, ed., *Orel Rossiiskii*, 25–40; Simeon, *Orel Rossiiskii*, 17v–29.

water of faith, of baptism: "As you are the inheritor of this tsardom, which is the gates to the bright heaven. From your power water flows, which deifies the human race" (*Iak naslednik sego tsarstva esi, ezhe est' vratmi k svtlomu nebesi. S tvoei derzhavy voda istekaet. Rod chelovechesk iazhe obozhaet*). The last sign, Pisces, signified the human race born in the water of baptism.[113] The praise and advice to the tsarevich by means of the Zodiac was the climax of the poem. The remaining parts were a series of Baroque devices. First came a greeting and wish of long life to the tsarevich and the whole ruling family in verse shaped like a heart, then a more conventionally arranged request to accept the poem. After the heart was a *carmen echicum*, a dialogue of Phaeton and Echo on the tsar's virtues in which the answer rhymed with the question, an acrostic, several anagrams, and a final wish of long life to the tsar.[114] Simeon's *Orel Rossiiskii* was not only the beginning of a new era in Russian poetry. It also marked a sharp innovation in the court culture, both esthetically and in content. It was the first praise in Russian history of the tsar for his glory and earthly virtues in addition to his piety.

Simeon's may not have been the only verse for the occasion, for a similar impulse toward a new court culture came from the Greeks. Paisios Ligarides, the Metropolitan of Gaza, had come to Russia even before Simeon Polotskii, in 1662. As early as Palm Sunday 1665, he gave a speech in Latin before Tsarevich Aleksei and his mother (with the tsar looking on) comparing certain Byzantine empresses to the tsaritsa, according to Nicolaas Witsen, who was then a younger member of a Dutch diplomatic mission. A few weeks later he wrote an epigram for the birth of Tsarevich Simeon, which he read to Witsen.[115] He also provided epigrams for Aleksei Alekseevich, his brother Fyodor, and Simeon, wishing long life to the tsarevichi. The last line of the epigram to Aleksei Alekseevich refers to the tsarevich and his father as "both emperors" (*amphoteroi basileis*), implying that the occasion for the verses was associated with, or came after, the 1667 presentation.[116] It is not certain that these poems were written for the presentation, rather they

[113] Smirnov, ed., *Orel Rossiiskii*, 41–64, Simeon, *Orel Rossiiskii*, 29v–46.

[114] Smirnov, ed., *Orel Rossiiskii*, 64–77, Simeon, *Orel Rossiiskii*, 46v–54v.

[115] Witsen, *Moscovische Reyse*, vol. II, 198–199, 201–203; Vitsen, *Puteshestvie*, 154–158. On Witsen and his mission to Russia, see Marion Peters, *De wijze koopman: Het wereldwijde onderzoek van Nicolaes Witsen (1641–1717), burgemeester en VOC-bewindhebber van Amserdam* (Amsterdam: Bakker, 2010), 37–45.

[116] RGADA, f. 27 (Tainyi prikaz), no. 352, ll. 1–1ob. The epigram on Aleksei is published in Ihor Ševčenko, "A New Greek Source Concerning the Nikon Affair," *Palaeoslavica* 7 (1999): 80–83. The poem to Fyodor expresses the wish that the latter reveal himself the "gift of God" as befits his name. See also Fedor B. Poljakov, "Paisios Ligarides und die ostslavische Barockliteratur in Moskau," *Wiener Slavistisches Jahrbuch* 49 (2003): 143–156.

seem to have been for the birth of the heir but also for his brothers. Ligarides was celebrating the ruling family, if not the heir alone.

Paisios and Simeon were not the only learned clergy celebrating the presentation. Lazar' Baranovych (1616–93), bishop of Chernigov and a former teacher of Simeon, also wrote a sermon, which he published in 1674 in Kiev in his sermon collection *Truby sloves propovednykh*. Baranovych took as his text the prayer of Jesus in John 17:1, "Father, the hour is come; glorify thy Son, that thy Son may also glorify thee." The first part of the sermon was a variation on the words of God at the baptism of Christ, repeated at the transfiguration (Mat. 3:17, 17:5) "This is my beloved Son, in whom I am well pleased" (*Se est' syn moi vozliublennyi, o Nemzhe blagovolikh*). The idea is a parallel of God's love for his son with the love of Tsar Aleksei for Tsarevich Aleksei. The second part took the New Year as the example of Christ's words in Matthew 18:20, "Where two or three are gathered together in my name, there am I in the midst of thee," though Baranovych omitted the words "or three," presumably to focus the text on the tsar and his son. Finally, he prayed for the happiness of the tsar and the tsarevich. As Christ had three apostles at his transfiguration, so the three patriarchs, Paisios, Makarios, and Ioasaf, have blessed the tsarevich. At that moment, St. Peter said that it was good under three tabernacles (Mat. 17: 4, a bit freely), so we are under the three crowns (*ventsy*) of your eagle and we rejoice under the protection of the eagle's wings.[117] The three crowns presumably referred to Great, Little, and White Russia.

Baranovych thus shared Simeon Polotskii's extravagant praise of the tsar. In his text he used the eagle metaphor, but the basic structure was the parallel of God and Christ to the tsar and his son. It would be difficult to find a more powerful analogy. He carried it forth in the analogy of the patriarchal blessings to the transfiguration of Christ.[118] What we do not know is whether he actually delivered the sermon in Moscow on the day of the presentation of the tsarevich or not. He had been present at the 1666–7 church council, and seems to have left Moscow sometime at the end of the summer of 1667. It seems odd that he would compose the sermon later, but it is certainly possible.[119] In any case, by printing the text in his book, Baranovych insured that the news of the presentation of the

[117] Lazar' Baranovich, *Truby sloves propovednykh* (Kiev: Tipografiia lavry, 1674), 398v–400v.

[118] Cf. Serhii Plokhy, *The Cossacks and Religion in Early Modern Ukraine* (Oxford: Oxford University Press, 2001), 224, n. 57.

[119] *DAI* V, 108. On Baranovych in Moscow in 1666–7 see V. O. Eingorn, "O snosheniiakh Malorossiiskogo dukhovenstva s Moskovskim pravitel'stvom v tsarstvovanie Alekseia Mikhailovicha," *ChOIDR* 3 (1894): 378–398, 401–406, 425.

tsarevich and the new forms of praise of the monarch acquired an audience well beyond Moscow. Though it was never printed in Moscow itself, the book was printed on paper provided by the tsar and it circulated in Russia, not just the hetmanate.[120] Metropolitan Pavel of Krutitsy had it, and the library of Tsar Fyodor later had five copies of the work.[121]

The Final Years of Tsar Aleksei

After the presentation, Tsarevich Aleksei was a regular participant in court ceremonies until his health began to fail. In October and November of 1667 he was present at the audiences for the Polish ambassador. On January 6, 1668, he accompanied his father at the blessing of the waters at Epiphany, and on Palm Sunday the same year he walked with his father, leading Patriarch Ioasaf's horse.[122] The tsarevich appeared for the New Year with his father again on September 1, 1668, and in the ensuing months Aleksei Alekseevich regularly appeared to the court and people at the most important ceremonies of the following Orthodox year. The tsarevich did not join his father for the Palm Sunday procession, but he was present at all the other liturgies for the Easter cycle. The last such appearance, if it can be called that, was for Dormition, August 15, 1669, in the tsar's suburban residence at Preobrazhenskoe. The tsarevich went to mass in the church, but heard the rest of the liturgies in his rooms.[123] Tsar Aleksei attended the New Year ritual without his son that autumn, and the tsarevich disappeared from the records until his death in January 1670.[124]

The death of the tsarevich Aleksei left Tsar Aleksei with two sons, Fyodor and Ivan, born in 1661 and 1666. As their later lives revealed, neither was healthy. Fyodor, tsar in 1676–82, was never strong, and died shortly before his twenty-first birthday. Ivan, the future co-tsar Ivan V (1682–96), was also unhealthy, and seems to have had impaired sight and hearing. In addition, Tsaritsa Mariia had died in March 1669, after having given birth to thirteen children, and in the summer the four-year-old Tsarevich Simeon followed her to the grave. Five of her

[120] Simeon Polotskii believed that Baranovych's espousal of the Catholic notion of the Immaculate Conception and original sin in his sermons on the Annunciation made it unacceptable in Moscow: Peter Rolland, "'Nie skoro prawi monsztuk do tych trąb otrzymacie': On Lazar' Baranovyč's 'Truby sloves propovidnyx' and Their Non-publication in Moscow," *Journal of Ukrainian Studies* 17, 1–2 (1992): 205–216.

[121] Undol'skii, ed., "Biblioteka Pavla," 65; Zabelin, *Domashnii byt Russkikh tsarei*, vol. III, 600.

[122] *DR* III, 675, 696–699, 712–713, 727–728; *DZ*, 271, 274.

[123] Stroev, ed., *Vykhody gosudarei tsarei i velikikh kniazei*, 502, 511–512, 516.

[124] Tsar Aleksei attended his funeral on January 16: Ibid., 518, 521.

daughters lived long and apparently healthy lives, but the tradition was to pass the throne to males in normal circumstances. Tsar Aleksei was naturally concerned about the succession. As early as in November 1669, he realized that he needed a new wife and thus a new bride-show. In late December the Dutch envoy Nicholas Heinsius reported back to the States General:

> The tsar has entirely put away his mourning for his wife, deciding to eventually make a second marriage; God forbid there would be some delay about that for one or other inconvenience, the long indisposition of the tsar's oldest prince, now entering the seventeenth year of age, taking continuously the upper hand. As far as can be learned of the position of the tsar's wife, it is not yet certain, there being three or four Russian ladies with greater claim than others to be considered for it.[125]

Three days later the tsarevich had gotten worse, and the tsar took his illness very much to heart. The marriage plans were apparently postponed, and nothing could be learned of any prospective bride.[126] Heinsius soon had the death of Tsarevich Aleksei to report. The burial was accompanied by a "small ceremony, following the custom," a comment that reflected how much Russian practices at court still differed from the West: there were no great state funerals.[127] There was great grief among the common people, especially since the sickness of the heir had been concealed. In spite of the secrecy, the Dutch envoy had it for eleven weeks from a "good hand" that the illness of the tsarevich was incurable. The good character and virtues of the tsarevich doubled the grief, and all the houses in Moscow were closed. The Dutchman went on to report that it was said that the tsar's oldest daughter (Evdokiia), now of marriageable age, had a similar disease, and that the deaths in the last year of the tsaritsa, her sister, her father I. D. Miloslavskii (once ambassador to The Hague), and the youngest tsarevich had brought sorrow to the court.[128]

[125] Martin, *A Bride for the Tsar*, 196–197; Allgemeene Rijksarchiev, The Hague, Staaten General Deel II (henceforth ARSG), 7364, January 8, 1670 NS/December 29, 1669 OS; Bushkovitch, *Peter the Great* (2001), 61, note 30; Martin.

[126] ARSG 7364, January 11, 1670.

[127] Cf. the funeral of Henry, Prince of Wales in 1612: Roy Strong, *Henry, Prince of Wales and England's Lost Renaissance* (London: Thames and Hudson, 1986), 7.

[128] "Op gisteren is den oudsten Czaarsen Prince alhier dessen weerld ooverleeden, ende op hoyden ter aarden geset, tgeen met kleyne ceremonien, volgens t gebruyck hier te lande, is toegegaan. Dit verlies maeckt allesints onder de gemeente seer droefenisse ende verslagenheyd, also de langwylige onpasselickgheyd van hoochgemelten Prince int public wierde gesecreteert. Doch des niet tegenstaende ben ick al voor thien ofte elf weecken van geode handt wel geinformeert, dat deese quynende sieckte voor ongeneeselick was te houden. De goeden inborst en uytsteeckende deugden van deesen Heer verdubblden de droefheydt allenomstaende alle huysen binnen deese stadt toegesloeten.

Thus the death of Tsarevich Aleksei in 1670 actually postponed the tsar's second marriage, but only until the next year. The maneuvers that led up to that marriage were complex, involving the rise of Artamon Matveev and other intrigues at court.[129] Eventually, Aleksei married Natal'ia Naryshkina in January 1671. Sixteenth months later the tsaritsa gave birth to Peter, the future Peter the Great, on May 30. At his baptism Tsarevich Fyodor and his aunt Irina Mikhailovna (the eldest of Tsar Michael's daughters) were the godparents. The baptism service took place in the Chudov Monastery, with Archimandrite Ioakim (the future patriarch) and father Andrei Savinovich, the archpriest of the Annunciation Cathedral and Tsar Aleksei's spiritual father, giving the service.[130] Tsar Aleksei had no more sons, but two daughters soon followed Peter. The first was Natal'ia, born on August 22, 1673 and baptized on September 14 in the church of St. Aleksii in the Chudov Monastery. The godparents were the same as Peter's, but the officiating priest was not recorded.[131] Finally, Tsarevna Feodora was born on September 4, 1674 and baptized on October 4 in the Dormition Cathedral with the same godparents as Peter. Patriarch Ioakim and a whole group of hierarchs, as well as father Andrei Savinovich, took the service.[132] The two girls had very different fates: Feodora lived only three years, but Natal'ia survived until 1716 and played a major role in the court of her brother Peter. Eventually the women of the tsar's family would come to exercise power and even mount the throne, but that was not yet on the horizon. For the time being, Russia had three possible heirs to the throne, and the last born, Peter, was actually healthy. The tsar's marriage had also signaled a new constellation of power at court, for it was with the marriage that Artamon Matveev came into the tsar's favor, a position that lasted until the end of the reign.

Men will seggen, dat de oudste Princesse, synde van hubaere jaeren, door diergelyke indispositie sich medgeincommodeert bevindt. Binnen den tydt van een jaer heft dit Hoff betreuet het afsterven van de Czaarinne, haer suster, haer vaeder Ilia Danilovitz [Miloslavskii] de welcke voor deesen in estraordinaire Ambassade by Haere Ho. Mo. weegens syne Czaarse Majts Heer Vaeder is geweest; ende twee jonge Czaarse Princen." ARSG 7364, January 10/20, 1670. Tsarevna Endokiia, born 1658, whatever her health at that point, lived until 1723.

129 Tsar Aleksei's oldest sister Irina had an alternative candidate to Naryshkina, one Avdot'ia Beliaeva, who was introduced by her uncle, Ivan Shikhirev, a Moscow *dvorianin* by rank. Bushkovitch, *Peter the Great*, 61–64; Martin, *A Bride for the Tsar*, 197–202; [P. I. Ivanov], *Alfavitnyi ukazatel' familii i lits upominaemykh v boiarskikh knigakh* (Moscow: S. Selivanovskii, 1853), 477.

130 *DR* III, 889–892, Dopolnenie, 463–479; O. A. Belobrova, "Andrei Savinov Postnikov," *SKKDR* III, pt. 1, 86; Sedov, *Zakat moskovskogo tsarstva*, 113–119, 122–149.

131 *DRV* III, 899, 901.

132 *DRV* III, 985, 1060.

Tsarevich Fyodor

Fyodor, the next-eldest son of the tsar, was only nine years old at his brother's death. The years between 1670 and the death of Tsar Aleksei were rich in events, political and cultural, and the latter marked the increasing and widening transformation of the culture of the court. The culture of the court evolved against a background of major political shifts. After the Truce of Andrusovo with Poland, the main political figure at court and in government was Afanasii Ordin-Nashchokin, the head of the Ambassadorial Office. As the main Russian negotiator for the truce, he returned in triumph with the full favor of the tsar. He had few rivals. Boris Morozov had died in 1661, and Il'ya Miloslavskii, his brother-in-law and father-in-law of the tsar, followed him early in 1668. Nikon was formally deposed in 1666, and his successor, Ioasaf II (1667–72), was not a powerful figure. Ordin-Nashchokin's own culture was not traditional: he clearly was open to the new cultural impulses from Kiev, but his relations with the Ukrainian hetmans were not good. He was unable to manage the intrigues and internal violence of the hetmanate, and the tsar removed him from office in 1671. His replacement, Matveev, was not only in charge of foreign policy but also the tsar's favorite, and his influence was strong throughout the government.[133]

After the rise to predominance of Matveev, the new style in court culture only increased in breadth and depth. Verse and declamation played an ever increasing role in court ceremony. The production of luxurious illustrated manuscripts for the court provided books on the history of the Romanov dynasty, the monarchs of the rest of the world, and many other topics for the reading of the tsar and his heirs. The appearance of theater in 1672 added a radically new element to the culture of the court. Not only had Russia never had a theater before, but the theater used German, not Polish or Ukrainian, models.[134] Theater had been a central part of European court culture since the Renaissance, and now it had come to Russia. The new culture also had

[133] Bushkovitch, *Peter the Great*, 42–79. Sedov, *Zakat moskovskogo tsarstva*, 111–113, 119–122.

[134] The high point of Polish court theater was in the reign of Władysław IV, a great lover of Italian opera and culture. It was in abeyance during the wars of the 1650s and 1600s, but had a certain revival under Jan Sobieski (1674–96). The inspiration was again Italian and French. George Gömöri, "Drama in Poland," "Opera in Poland," and "Ballet in Poland," in *Spectaculum Europaeum*, ed. Pierre Béhar, Helen Watanabe-O'Kelly (Wiesbaden: Harrassowitz, 1999), 309–320; 477–481, 585–590; Karolina Targosz-Kretowa, *Teatr dworski Władysława IV, 1635–1648* (Kraków: Wydawnictwo Literackie, 1965). For German court theater, see, for example: Helen Watanabe-O'Kelly, *Court Culture in Dresden: From Renaissance to Baroque* (Basingstoke and New York, New York: Palgrave, 2002).

a powerful patron in Artamon Matveev, the head of the Ambassadorial Office after 1671. Earlier Tsar Aleksei had shown an interest in the theater, for in 1660 he had asked John Hebdon, an English merchant in the tsar's service, to hire comedians for him in England.[135] Nothing came of that request, however, and it was Matveev who sponsored the first court theater in 1672. Several texts of the plays survive, and recent discoveries demonstrate that the first performance of the theater was in February, not October, 1672. It was a "ballet" in the meaning of that time in Western Europe, that is, a series of short performances of comedy, music, and some dancing. It included a brief speech in praise of the tsar, but otherwise had no dialogue. The performers were all the sons of merchants, doctors, and teachers from the German Quarter (*Nemetskaia sloboda*). Matveev was one of the few boyars in attendance, but the tsar and his family (including the women) were all present. A similar performance followed in May, with Tsaritsa Natal'ia present and visible, only a few weeks before she gave birth to Peter the Great. The first play with dialogue came in October under Matveev's sponsorship and was the Old Testament story of Esther, a common theme in German Protestant theater of the sixteenth and seventeenth centuries. The author was one of the Lutheran Pastors, Johann Gottfried Gregorii, and again the performers were boys from the school in the German Quarter. The Esther play, like later ones with the stories of Judith, Tamerlane, and Bayazet, and others, all presented the stories of kings. None of the plays had succession as the theme, but they were political plays in that their stories were of the virtue and piety of rulers, or the opposite, such as the pride of kings in the case of Bayazet, who was punished by God. At other times, there were performances of comedy and "ballet" based on the stock characters of the early modern German stage such as Pickelherring.[136] Performances

[135] In a long list of items to be obtained in England, the tsar included "masterov komediiu delat'" in his own hand: I. Ia. Gurliand, *Ivan Gebdon: Kommissarius i resident* (Iaroslavl': Tipografiia Gubernskogo pravleniia, 1903), 49; Paul Dukes, Graeme P. Herd, and Jarmo Kotilaine, *Stuarts and Romanovs: The Rise and Fall of a Special Relationship* (Dundee: Dundee University Press, 2009), 99–101. Tsar Aleksei must have heard of the "English comedians" popular in Central Europe in the first half of the seventeenth century: Jerzy Limon, *Gentlemen of a Company: English Players in Central and Eastern Europe 1590–1660* (Cambridge: Cambridge University Press, 1985).

[136] Bushkovitch, *Peter the Great*, 44–47; Claudia Jensen and Ingrid Maier, "Orpheus and Pickelherring in the Kremlin: The 'Ballet' for the Tsar of February, 1672," *Scando-Slavica* 59, 2 (2013): 145–184; Claudia Jensen and Ingrid Maier, "Pickelherring Returns: More New Sources on the Prehistory of the Russian Court Theater," *Scando-Slavica* 61, 1 (2015): 7–56; Claudia Jensen and Ingrid Maier, *Pridvornyi teater v Rossii XVII veka* (Moscow: Indrik, 2016); A. N. Robinson, O. M. Derzhavina, A. S. Demin, and E. K. Romodanovskaia, eds., *Ranniaia russkaia dramaturgiia*, vols. 1–2 (Moscow: Nauka, 1972–7); V. N. Vsevolodskii-Gerngross, *Russkii teatr ot istokov do serediny XVIII veka* (Moscow: Izdatel'stvo Akademii nauk SSSR, 1957); M. P. Odesskii,

like these continued, under Matveev's patronage, to the end of Tsar Aleksei's reign.

The series of illustrated manuscripts, mostly for presentation to the tsar and ruling family, were also prepared in the Ambassadorial Office under Matveev's supervision. The *Kniga ob izbranii tsaria Mikhail Fyodorovicha* (*Book of the Election of Tsar Michael Fyodorovich*) came into being starting in the summer of 1672, a few months after the birth of Peter. The book was primarily an account of the coronation of Michael and the installation of Patriarch Filaret, but the preface gave an account of the death of Tsar Fyodor in 1598 that stressed the legend that he had blessed Fyodor Nikitich Romanov with the throne. In this version Boris simply took power with no mention of the Assembly of the Land. The account of Michael's election was quite elaborate, eliding the controversy over the proper candidate and the role of the Cossacks. In this account the choice of Michael was unanimous. The book faithfully reproduced the 1613 *Chin venchaniia*, with the speech of the officiating metropolitan that contradicted the preface in noting the election of Boris in its historical narrative. Repeatedly the book stressed the designation of Fyodor Romanov by Tsar Fyodor, a result that combined designation with inheritance and popular choice.[137] The other manuscript books in this series included the *Tituliarnik*, a series of pictures of current monarchs and lists of their full titles, but also a long account of the genealogy and history of Russia's rulers through Tsar Aleksei. Its version of the election of Tsar Michael was similar to that of the book on his election.[138] Matveev's major collaborator in these projects was Nicolae Milescu-Spafarii, a Rumanian nobleman who had come to Russia in 1671 after years of exile in Western Europe. He served also as a translator to the Danish resident (see below), leaving Moscow on an expedition to China in 1675. In his Moscow years he produced several books, some with obvious political content, such as the *Vasiliologion* of 1674. This book was a series of sketches of great kings from Biblical and Roman times through recent Russian rulers, one of the first in Russia to present states in the Aristotelian terminology (monarchy, aristocracy, democracy) normal in the West since the Renaissance. It also simply ignored the election of

Poetika russkoi dramy: Posledniaia tret' XVII–pervaia tret' XVIII v. (Moscow: Rossiiskii gosudarstvennyi gumanitarnyi universitet, 2004). Biblical drama and ballet in Dresden: Watanabe-O'Kelly, *Court Culture in Dresden*, 5–36, 132–140, 174–189.

137 *DAI* VI, 191–192, 199; A. L. Batalov and I. A. Vorotnikova, eds., *Kniga ob izbranii na prevysochaishii prestol Velikogo Rossiiskogo Tsarstviia velikogo gosudaria tsaria i velikogo kniazia Mikhaila Fyodorovicha vseia Velikiia Rossii samoderzhtsa: Rukopis', kommentarii, tekst* (Moscow: Federal'noe gosudarstvennoe biudzhetnoe uchrezhdenie kul'tury – Gosudarstvennyi istoricheskii kul'turnyi muzei-zapovednik Moskovskii kreml', 2014).

138 Iu. M. Eskin, ed., *Tsarskii tituliarnik*, 2 vols. (Moscow: Fond Stoliarova, 2007).

Michael Romanov and presented a series of rulers back to Kievan times, each taking up the throne of his father, with the exception of Boris Godunov.[139]

During these years Simeon Polotskii continued his activity, both preaching and the production of poetry and declamations for the court and clergy. The tsar's new palace at Kolomenskoe was the occasion in 1672 for another poetic "greeting" celebrating the new structure and wishing health to the whole ruling family.[140] He was also involved in some way in the upbringing of Tsarevich Fyodor. Since the eighteenth century, the legend has persisted that Simeon was actually Fyodor's teacher and taught him Latin, but there is no evidence for that. The palace records have only the names of his teachers as a boy, the ones who taught him to read and write Russian and Slavonic. He does not seem to have been taught Latin, or not very much, perhaps because of his poor health.[141] What is clear is that Simeon wrote a number of declamations for Fyodor, and that his library contained many books in Latin. He may not have been able to read them very well, but the library also contained books from the Ukrainian presses as well as those of Simeon Polotskii himself. The culture that they represented was not that of Western Europe, but it was part of the new culture that appeared in the Moscow court after the 1660s.[142]

Historical texts, theater, poetry, and declamations provided images of succession to the throne, and Tsar Aleksei gave a role to his sons even before their maturity. In 1672, Dem'ian Mnohohrishnyi, the hetman of the Ukrainian Cossacks was deposed by his enemies among the Cossack elite, the *starshyna*, and sent to Moscow for trial. There he was convicted of treasonous dealings with the Poles and sentenced to death. Tsar Aleksei commuted the sentence to exile to Siberia and confiscation of property on the petition of his children, the tsarevichi Fyodor and Ivan "of all great, little, and white Russia," then still young children (*po uprosheniiu nashego tsarskogo velichestva detei blagovernogo gosudaria tsarevicha i velikogo kniazia Fyodora Alekseevicha vseia velikiia i malyia i belyia Rossii i ...*

139 "Vasiliologion," Biblioteka Akademii nauk, Arkhangel'skoe sobranie S 129, ll. 286ob.–288ob.; Paul Bushkovitch, *Peter the Great*, 43–44; Paul Bushkovitch, "The *Vasiliologion* of Nikolai Spafarii Milescu," *Russian History* 36 (2009): 1–15.

140 Polotskii, *Izbrannye sochineniia*, 103–107; Simeon Polockij, *Rifmologion* 2, 130–134.

141 Sedov, *Zakat moskovskogo tsarstva*, 178–183.

142 See Robinson, *Bor'ba idei v russkoi literature*; Sazonova, *Literaturnaia kul'tura Rossii*, 34–112; Paul Bushkovitch, "Cultural Change among the Russian Boyars 1650–1680: New Sources and Old Problems," *Forschungen zur osteuropäischen Geschichte* 56 (2000): 91–111. For Tsar Fyodor's library, see Zabelin, *Domashnii byt Russkikh tsarei*, vol. III, 599–607; I. N. Lebedeva, "Lichnaia biblioteka tsaria Fedora Alekseevicha," in *Kniga v Rossii XVIII–pervoi polovine XIX v.* (Leningrad: Biblioteka Akademii nauk SSSR, 1989), 84–90.

[same title] *Ioanna Aleskeevicha*).[143] This was a matter of protocol rather than substance, but the tsar's act of mercy placed his heirs at the center of the event.

A more important role came for the young Fyodor on the death of the king of Poland, Michał Korybut Wiśniowiecki, at the end of 1673. Several of the Lithuanian magnates had the idea of proposing the tsarevich as their future king. The main figure was the Grand Hetman of Lithuania, Michał Kazimierz Pac (1624–82), who sent an embassy to Moscow to discuss the subject. He asked for Fyodor on the condition that the tsarevich convert to Catholicism and marry the twenty-year-old widow of the late Polish king, Eleonore Maria of Austria, and that Russia return the lands acquired from Poland in the Truce of Andrusovo as well as grant a subsidy to the Polish army. Not surprisingly, the boyar Prince Iu. A. Dolgorukii, speaking for the tsar, refused, though he proposed Tsar Aleksei for the Polish throne in his son's place. In Warsaw, the Russian resident Vasilii Tiapkin heard the same proposal from Pac.[144] It is not clear that the Russians took the proposal very seriously, but they did try to keep Pac and the Lithuanians friendly.[145] In the event, the Polish throne went in May 1674 to Jan Sobieski, who would rule the country until his death in 1696 and earn eternal glory for his role in the defense of Vienna against the Ottomans in 1683.

In Russia, the heir remained Tsarevich Fyodor, and Tsar Aleksei made sure that everyone knew who the heir was. He repeated the presentation ceremony on September 1, 1674 for Fyodor, aged thirteen. The tsar planned for the event in advance. At the end of July, he ordered the *Razriad* to provide him with the description of the presentation of Aleksei Alekseevich from their archives and took the two volumes to his rooms.[146] The sources are fuller for this event, explicitly called "*ob"iavlenie*. They fall into two versions, a detailed description of the event with

143 RGADA, f. 229, op. 3, delo 26 (letter from Malorossiiskii prikaz in the name of Tsar Aleksei to the heads of the *starshyna* of the Ukrainain hetmanate Petr Zabila, Ivan Samoilovich, and others); P. A. Matveev, "Baturinskii perevorot 13-go marta 1672 goda (Delo Dem'iana Mnogogreshnogo)," *Russkaia starina* 11 (1903): 467; A. S. Almazov, *Politicheskii portret ukrainskogo getmana Ivana Samoilovicha v kontekste russko-ukrainskikh otnoshenii* (Moscow: MGU, 2012), 47. (Thanks for the archival reference to Ievgeniia Sakal.)

144 S. M. Solov'ev, *Istoriia Rossii s drevneishikh vremen* (Moscow: Izdatel'stvo sotsial'no-ekonomicheskoi literatury, 1960–6), vol. 6, 505–512 (originally Moscow: Universitetskaia tipografiia 1851–79); Zbigniew Wójcik, *Rzeczpospolita wobec Turcji i Rosji: 1674–1679: Studium z dziejów polskiej polityki zagranicznej* (Wrocław: Zakład Narodowy im. Ossolińskich, 1976).

145 On the relations of the Lithuanian magnates with Russia in the 1670s and 1680s, see K. A. Kochegarov, *Rech' Pospolitaia i Rossiia v 1680–1686 godakh: Zakliuchenie dogovora o vechnom mire* (Moscow: Indrik, 2008), 50–57.

146 *Dela tainogo prikaza* I (RIB 21), 1745.

brief speeches (in two versions) and a *Razriad* account that recounted the action of the ceremony with a fuller list of the participants.[147] The more detailed account, called *zapiska* in the text, began with the statement that Tsar Aleksei, with his full title, including *otchich i dedich i naslednik i gosudar' i obladatel'*, had decided to present (*ob"iaviti*) his son Tsarevich Aleksei to the whole clergy and people of the Moscow state. The *zapiska* went on to relate that Tsar Aleksei, before the actual ceremony, sat upon his throne in the Anteroom (*Perednaia palata*) of the palace and called the duma to sit before him. He then stood up, prayed, and called the duma to approach him. He announced that the day and time had come to give his second son Fyodor Alekseevich to serve God, and to bring him to the cathedral to present (*ob"iaviti*) him to Patriarch Ioakim and the whole clergy as well as to the duma ranks, the lesser gentry ranks, the chancery secretaries, and the people of all ranks.[148] After his speech, the tsar went to the Kremlin Church of the Savior to pray, and then returned to the anteroom, this time with the tsarevich. His two *diad'ki*, the boyar Prince F. F. Kurakin and the duma gentleman I. B. Khitrovo, led him.[149] The assembled duma ranks greeted them, and they all went back to the Church of the Savior. There they crossed themselves before the icons, and the tsar asked Archimandrite Vikentii of the Trinity-St. Sergii Monastery to carry the icon of the Savior before the procession. Vikentii took the icon and led them all down the Red Staircase and out of the palace over Persian carpets toward the cathedral of the Dormition of the Mother of God with the deacons singing. The path was lined with lesser courtiers (*stol'niki*) and the musketeers of Iurii Lutokhin's regiment, who carried banners and their long muskets, and those of Vasilii Bukhvostov's regiment, with sabers but no muskets. On a platform near the Archangel Cathedral were the foreign officers and merchants. Nearby was the Polish ambassador, Paweł Świderski, and the Danish resident, Magnus Gjøe, with his translator, Nicholas Milescu-Spafarii, and the sons, Semen and Grigorii, of the Ukrainian Hetman Samoilovych. In the cathedral the patriarch's deacons sang the wishes for long life, and the tsar and his son crossed themselves before the icons and relics. Patriarch Ioakim blessed them. At this point, the tsar's secretaries made the usual inquiries

147 The more detailed accounts are in *PSZ* I, no. 586, 987–991and *SGGD* IV, 316–321 [= RGADA, f. 135, d. 329] and the *Razriad* records are *DR* III, 973–981. Briefer accounts are given in Stroev, ed., *Vykhody gosudarei tsarei i velikikh kniazei*, 581; *DAI* V, 152–153; Sin. 423, 43–44ob. (*ob"iavlenie*); Cherepnin, *Zemskie sobory*, 343–346; Philip Longworth, *Alexis, Tsar of All the Russias* (New York, New York: F. Watts, 1984), 185–187.

148 *PSZ* I, 987; *SGGD* IV, 316–317.

149 *PSZ* I, 988, *SGGD* IV, 317. This appears to be the first mention of Tsarevich Fyodor's *diad'ki* in the known records.

of the two ambassadors about their health, and the emissaries petitioned for their rewards.[150]

Next came the actual ceremony, the New Year ritual augmented by the presentation of the tsarevich. As usual, there was a platform near the Annunciation Cathedral, covered also with Persian carpets and with three places for the patriarch, tsar, and tsarevich, the patriarch's with two steps and those for Aleksei and his son with three. The procession came from the cathedral and the tsar, tsarevich, and patriarch stood at their places. The clergy bowed before all three. The patriarch censed the icons, the tsar and tsarevich, and the regalia. The clergy then censed the tsar, tsarevich, and patriarch, and then the deacons sang psalms and the reading for the day from the Prophet Isaiah, while the patriarch, tsar, and tsarevich sat, the two last on folding chairs. Two priests sanctified holy water, and deacons read from the Gospels and Acts. The patriarch plunged the cross into the holy water. After more censing and prayers, the patriarch was brought the icon of the Savior, and he made a blessing with it in all four directions. The patriarch and the clergy then came up to the tsar and his son, and Ioakim made a speech. The deacons sang "many years" to the tsar, to Tsaritsa Natal'ia, and to all three tsarevichi. The tsar replied with another speech to the patriarch. Tsarevich Fyodor greeted his father, made his own speech, and bowed to him, after which the tsar kissed him on the head. Then the duma and the merchants greeted the tsar and his son. The boyar Prince Iu. A. Dolgorukii made another speech, and the clergy again greeted the patriarch. The tsar, Tsarevich Fyodor, and Patriarch Ioakim returned all the greetings to the Duma and all Orthodox Christians while the deacons again sang "many years."[151]

Thus the public ceremony ended, and the patriarch and clergy returned to the cathedral. The tsar and court returned to the palace by way of the porch of the Annunciation Cathedral. The process of the tsar's bestowal of rewards began with the promotion of I. B. Khitrovo to *okol'nichii*, and the court and clergy went to the banquet in the room of facets.[152] Khitrovo was one of several, for the tsar distributed all sorts of rewards to the court and the country at large to mark the occasion. All boyars received 100 rubles, as did lesser ranks down to secretaries, musketeers, and provincial gentry. They received additional *pomest'e* lands as well, all according to their rank. Prince F. F. Kurakin had a special award of 150 rubles.[153] During the banquet there were more gifts, and present were not only the clergy and court, but also Grigorii Dmitrievich Stroganov,

[150] *PSZ* I, 988–989, *SGGD* IV, 317–319; *DR* III, 976, 980.
[151] *PSZ* I, 989–990, *SGGD* IV, 319–320.
[152] *PSZ* I, 990–991, *SGGD* IV, 320–321; *DR* III, 978. [153] *DR* III, 977–978.

Russia's richest merchant and manufacturer, and the senior merchants (*gosti*).[154] The next day the tsar ordered the news of the presentation to be sent to all provincial governors, and three days later special rewards given to the governor and gentry of Smolensk.[155]

All the surviving sources record speeches by Tsarevich Fyodor himself to his father and by Prince Iurii Alekseevich Dolgorukii. While the official records only indicate the fact of Fyodor's speech, Simeon Polotskii's manuscripts include a "greeting" for the presentation of Tsarevich Fyodor. Who pronounced the speech is not indicated, but from the text it was not the tsarevich himself. The speech was short, beginning with a declaration of the joy of the event. Fyodor was the apple of his father's eye and would be his support in old age. Like the eagle, he was used to soaring under the rays of the sun of Orthodoxy. The author wished that God would give him the wisdom of Solomon, the glory and bravery of Alexander the Great, the bodily strength of Samson, and the victory over his enemies of Joshua. It concluded with wishes for long life for the whole ruling family on behalf of the speaker, Patriarch Ioakim, and all the clergy, the princes, boyars, and all the "Christ-loving soldiers," that is, the gentry.[156] This final passage seems to exclude anyone from the clergy, leaving only Dolgorukii as the most likely speaker.[157]

If the only extant text of a speech from the event was not the one pronounced by Tsarevich Fyodor, he nevertheless made an impression. The Danish resident Gjøe reported back to Copenhagen the day after the ceremony:

> Yesterday the elder prince was shown to the people for the first time, having at this time attained the age of fourteen years. This was done with great pomp and ceremony, at which I had the honor also to assist. The prince harangued his Tsarish Majesty in the lower court before the whole people and wished him a happy year, since they begin theirs the first day of September, and after the father had responded to this compliment all the boyars and the patriarch with the metropolitans and all their suite saluted their new prince by striking their foreheads.

[154] *DR* III, 978–979.

[155] *DR* III, 981; *SGGD* IV, 320–322; *PSZ* I no. 588, 992–994; RGADA, f. 135, d. 332, ll. 4–5 (letter to F. P. Naryshkin, governor of Archangel, September 14, 1674).

[156] "Privetstsvo o iavlenii gosudaria tsarevicha i velikago kniazia Feodora Aleksievicha," GIM, Sinodal'noe sobranie 229, ll. 177–178. Simeon was not, however, Fyodor's tutor, contrary to the legend stemming from Tatishchev: Sedov, *Zakat moskovskogo tsarstva*, 178–184.

[157] The speech also has only one Biblical quotation ("This is my beloved son," Mat. 3:17), and Simeon wrote a poem in 1673 to console Dolgorukii on the death of his brother Dmitrii: Polotskii, *Virshi*, 281–283.

It was also the first time for the Danish resident to be ordered to see the ceremony and be asked about his health.[158] In his account, the fact that the tsarevich made a speech was the most striking aspect of the event. Gjøe understood it as a compliment for the New Year, which suggests that it was very likely the speech that Simeon wrote was a greeting on that occasion from tsarevich to tsar, or something very like it. The speech began with general reflections on beginning and ending. Orthodox people had the custom of greeting one another on the occasion, so the tsarevich-speaker greeted his father. As the eagle molted, so he wished new external and internal clothing for the tsar. The external clothing would be victory over the enemies of the faith. The inner clothing would be God's grace, which would give him all the virtues. May you live as long as Methuselah, he concluded, healthy and joyful along with our mother, his tsaritsa, my brothers Ivan and Petr, and my sisters and aunts.[159]

After his presentation, Tsarevich Fyodor, however, did not play a major role in court ceremonies right away. He did not seem to have been present at audiences for ambassadors and certainly stayed behind in the palace (*v verkhu*) with Tsaritsa Natal'ia, his two *diad'ki*, his younger brother Ivan, and his sisters, both for the Epiphany ceremony and for the Palm Sunday procession in 1675.[160] Perhaps this was a matter of health, since he also did not accompany his father to the many liturgies and other visits to churches and monasteries over the winter of 1674–5. By the autumn his health may have recovered. At the New Year of 1675, Tsar Aleksei attended the ceremony without his son, this time observed by the Imperial Embassy of Annibale Bottoni, representing Leopold I. His secretary, Adolf Lyseck, described the proceedings and recorded that once again Prince Odoevskii made a speech. The next day, however, at the reception for Bottoni at Kolomenskoe, the tsarevich was present, "who on this day had been first presented in the public audience as the legitimate heir and successor of his father." The young Fyodor followed his father in asking about the health of Emperor Leopold. Indeed, Lyseck noted that Tsaritsa

[158] "Hier le Prince aisné fust montré au peuple pour la première fois, ayant à cet heur attaint l'age de quatorze ans, cela se fist avec grande pompe et ceremonie, à la quelle j'eu l'honneur aussi d'assister, ce Prince harangua sa Majesté Zarique dans la basse cour devant tout le peuple et luy souhaittait l'heureuse année car ils commencent la leur le 1 jour de septembre et apres que le Pere avoit respond à ce compliment tous les Bayares et le Patriarche avec les Metropolites et toute leur suite saluerent leur novau Prince en se buttant le front." Danske Rigsarkivet, TKUA Rusland B 38 (September 2, 1674).

[159] "Privetstvo k velikomu gosudariu tsariu ot gosudaria tsarevicha," Sin. 229, ll. 15–16. The references to Ivan and Petr mean that the speech could not have been written for Tsarevich Aleksei, and the only other New Year celebrations where Peter and Ivan could have been mentioned were in 1672 and 1673. Unfortunately, the palace records for those occasions seem not to have survived, or at least have not been published.

[160] *DR* III, 1167–1170, 1304–1306.

Natal'ia and the younger tsarevich looked on from a nearby room, and that the younger prince (Ivan?) opened the door a crack to see the foreigners better. A few days later, the Imperial diplomats watched the departure of the tsar and his court for the pilgrimage to the Trinity-St. Sergii Monastery, and the tsarevich noticed and greeted them from his carriage.[161] The pilgrimage of that year was a particular show of the wealth and magnificence of the tsar's court, and Fyodor was taking the accustomed place of the heir.[162]

If Tsarevich Fyodor was not very visible at the court until late in 1675, his younger brothers were necessarily less so. The first mention of Tsarevich Ivan's *diad'ka*, Prince Petr Ivanovich Prozorovskii, came shortly after the presentation of Tsarevich Fyodor. Tsar Aleksei went out to one of the nearby villages, and Tsaritsa Natal'ia and the whole family remained behind in Moscow. Peter was too young for a *diad'ka*, but the eight-year-old Ivan now had his. Prince Prozorovskii was only a chamber *stol'nik* in rank, but a chamber *stol'nik* was part of the court inner circle, even if junior in rank. His father was the governor of Astrakhan', whom Stenka Razin's Cossack rebels had killed in 1670.[163] Staying with Ivan while his father was away was a serious task for Prince Prozorovskii, as *diad'ka* and *blizhnii chelovek*, for Ivan was too young (aside from his health) to participate in court ceremonies.[164] Tsarevich Peter, who was still a small child, appeared in the records of court activities with his nurse and the boyar women in charge of him (the *mamki*).[165] Tsarevich Fyodor's younger brothers had the entourage and household appropriate for sons of the tsar.

Succession 1676–1689

The succession to Tsar Aleksei was similar in many respects to the event thirty-one years before at his own father's death. Tsar Aleksei fell ill on January 22, 1676, and died eight days later, on January 30 in the fourth hour of the night, according to the official description of the *Razriad*

[161] Adolph Lyseck, *Relatio, eorum quae . . . ad Magnum Moscorum Czarum, . . . 1675 gesta sunt* (Salzburg: Aulico-Academici, 1676), 37–56: "qui hac primum die in publica audientia legitimus haeres et patris successor proponebatur" (50); translation by I. Tarnava-Borichevskii, "Skazanie Adol'fa Lizeka," *Zhurnal Ministerstva narodnogo prosveshcheniia* 16 (November, 1837), 345–350, 355–355, 366. See also the report of the Brandenburg emissary: Joachim Scultetus, "Beschreibung der zwoten Gesandschaft," *Magazin für die neue Historie und Geographie* IX (1775): 48–49.

[162] Sedov, *Zakat moskovskogo tsarstva*, 184–189.

[163] *DR* III, 1013; Dolgorukov, *Rossiiskaia rodoslovnaia kniga*, vol. I, 191.

[164] *DR* III, 1034, 1040, 1066, 1183, 1306 (Easter 1675), 1584, 1594.

[165] *DR* III, 1320 (April 1675).

office. Unlike his father, he seems to have been conscious long enough to bless his son with the staff of rule and the throne: "he passed the staff of governance and blessed his son . . . the tsarevich and grand prince Fyodor Alekseevich on his throne of his tsarish majesty" (*zhezl pravlenia vruchil, i na svoi tsarskogo velichestva prestol blagoslovil syna svoego . . . tsarevicha i velikogo kniazia Fyodora Alekseevicha*).[166] The Danish resident Gjøe had already heard of the tsar's illness on January 26 from "one of his friends who had business at the court," though it was kept very secret.[167] A few days after Aleksei's death he was able to describe the event in some detail. He reported the blessing and that the tsar had, it was said, exhorted his son to rule mildly and in fear of God and put the scepter into his hands. He urged him to follow the advice of the good servants whom he was leaving to him, especially that of B. M. Khitrovo.[168] Immediately after the tsar had died, the official record continued, Fyodor "came to be on the Moscow, Kiev, and Vladimir sovereignties" (*uchinilsia na Moskovskom, i na Kievskom, i na Vladimirskom gosudarstve*) and on all his other "sovereignties"; literally he "became" on them. The new tsar's subjects, led by the Kasimov and Siberian tsarevichi and the boyars assembled to swear the oath of fidelity to the tsar, his heirs (*naslednikom ikh gosudarskim*), his stepmother Tsaritsa Natal'ia, his brothers Ivan and Peter, and all his aunts and sisters. Besides the boyars, the lesser duma and court ranks, the secretaries, the Moscow gentry, the various sorts of soldiers, and the townspeople of various ranks all swore the oath in the presence of Patriarch Ioakim and the clergy. Those not present were brought to the oath later.[169] Gjøe was able to provide more details. At his death, Tsar Aleksei

> left the the succession to the crown to his eldest son Tsarevich Fyodor Alekseevich, who is not yet sixteen. The boyars, immediately after his death, sat their new tsar on the throne of his father that evening and according to the received usage had him kiss the cross, which the boyars then received from him

[166] RGADA, f. 210 (*Razriad*) d. 500, stolpik 6, ll. 8–9: *DR* III, 1635–1636.

[167] TKUA Rusland, B 38, January 26, 1676; "un de mes amis qui pratiquet à la cour, me vient dire que le Zar doit ester dangeureusement malade, mais on le tient fort secret." Gjøe had been close to the Marselis family, long settled in Russia and well connected, but after the death of Peter Marselis he had acquired the services of Paul Menzies, a Scottish mercenary officer who had married the widow of Marselis: Bushkovitch, *Peter the Great*, 75 and TKUA Rusland B 38, January 19, 1676.

[168] "Le dernier jour il communia et sentant le mort approcher il fist appeler le Prince aisné à present Zar, à qui il donna sa benediction, et à ce qu'on dit, de tres belles et Chretiennes moralitez, lui donna mesme le Sceptre entre les mains l'exhortant surtout de gouverner avec douceur et dans la crainte de Dieu et de suivre les Conseils des Bons Serrviteurs que lui laissait, et nommément luy recommanda un Boyar appellee Bogdan Matveivitz [Khitrovo]." TKUA Rusland, B 38, February 3, 1676.

[169] *DR* III, 1636–1640.

to kiss it as well, and at the same time they gave the oath of fidelity; this done, the garrison also gave its oath before the boyars in front of the palace and the foreign officers before the secretaries of the Foreign Chancery, so that everything was done before dawn and almost before the news of the death of the tsar.

The next day was the funeral, "without pomp" (at least by Western standards). Both the young tsar and Tsaritsa Natal'ia were carried, Fyodor in a chair and Natal'ia in a sledge, to the church, surrounded by a great crowd of weeping mourners.[170] The Dutch ambassador told the same story.[171]

The accession of Fyodor Alekseevich to the throne did not solve the succession problem. As the Danish resident reported again:

There is also great appearance that the present tsar [Fyodor], having been very unhealthy and melancholic since childhood, cannot live long and his brother [Ivan] being nearly blind and humpbacked, the succession will infallibly fall on the prince and son [Peter] of the present tsaritsa [Natal'ia].[172]

The succession issue, however, immediately became part of the factional struggles at the court. Tsar Fyodor recalled to the court his Miloslavskii relatives, and by the summer Artamon Matveev fell from favor, soon going into exile. Tsaritsa Natal'ia, though she was the tsar's stepmother and appeared in the oaths of loyalty, had no part in the politics of the court until the death of Fyodor, as the boyars took control and the most powerful of the Romanov women was Tsarevna Irina, Fyodor's aunt, until her death in 1680.[173]

Russia's Ambassadorial Office immediately sent the news of the tsar's death and the accession of Fyodor to the European courts with which the tsars were in regular relations. To the kings of Denmark, Sweden, and England, the elector of Brandenburg and the prince of Orange the

[170] TKUA Rusland B 38, February 3, 1676. Aleksei "laisse la succession à la couronne à son Filz aisné Prince Foeder Alexeivitz, qui n'a pas encore seize ans accomplish. Les Boyars, incontinent apres sa mort, fisrent encore le mesme soir assoir leur novau Zar sur le throne de son Pere, et selon l'usage reçeu luy fisrent baisser la croix laquelle les Boyars reçeurent de luy pour la baisser aussi, et en mesme temps presterent le serment de fidelité, cela fait, la guarnison presta le serment aux Boyars devant le chastau et les officiers Estrangers aux Chancelliers du Pricas Estranger, si bien que tout fust fait devant le jour, et qu'on eust presque connoissance de la mort du Zar." See also Iu. N. Shcherbachev, "Iz donesenii pervogo datskogo rezidenta v Moskve (1672–1676 gg.)," *ChOIDR* 2 (1917): smes', 32–42, esp. 38–39.

[171] B. Coyet, *Posol'stvo Kunraada fan-Klenka*, ed. A. M. Loviagin (St. Petersburg: Izdatel'stvo Arkheograficheskoi Komisii, 1900), 136–139.

[172] TKUA Rusland B 38, February 3, 1676: "Il y a une aussi grande apparence, que le Zar à present ayant esté de son enfance tout à fait malsain et melancolique, ne pourra vivre long temps et son frere estant presque aveugle et bossu, la succession tombera infailliblement sur le Prince et Filz de Zaritsa à present . . ."

[173] Bushkovitch, *Peter the Great*, 80–82; Sedov, *Zakat moskovskogo tsarstva*, 193–200.

announcement, giving the tsar's title with the list of territories and then "*otchich i dedich i naslednik*," stated that Tsar Aleksei had blessed Fyodor and given him the regalia. Jan Sobieski, king of Poland, and Leopold, the Holy Roman Emperor, were to receive the same message, that Aleksei had blessed his son with the tsardom. Fyodor was the heir to the throne, but his father had also explicitly passed on the throne.[174]

The young and sickly tsarevich formally ascended the throne on June 18, 1676, with the same coronation ceremonial as his father. There were a few modifications: in the two speeches the tsar and Patriarch Ioakim omitted the account of the Time of Troubles that still figured in 1645, and went from the story of the Monomakh crown to the lives and deaths of Michael and Aleksei. Once again, they stressed that Tsar Aleksei had blessed his son with the tsardom.[175] In his final speech, Ioakim prayed to the Lord to give an heir to the throne.[176] The real innovation in the coronation, however, was not in the speeches. After the anointment, Fyodor went through the Royal Doors (*tsarskie vrata*) in the iconostasis to the altar behind. There he took communion, an act normally reserved for the clergy. This act set off the tsar from the rest of the faithful, by means of a practice that had existed in late Byzantium but appeared for the first time in a Russian coronation. The first scholar to note the fact, B. A. Uspenskii, saw it as a case of the alleged "Byzantinization" of the court in the seventeenth century, a dubious concept.[177] Whatever the Russians knew about Byzantium at that point came from the West.[178]

[174] *PDS* V, 422–426, 437–438, 475–476, 484–486.

[175] *PSZ* II, no. 648, 42–68 (quotations 52–54); Barsov, *Drevnerusskie pamiatniki*, 98–106; Sedov, *Zakat moskovskogo tsarstva*, 237–240.

[176] *PSZ* II, 65.

[177] B. A. Uspenskii, *Tsar' i Patriarkh: Kharizma vlasti v Rossii* (Moscow: Shkola iazyki russkoi kul'tury, 1998), 154–155.

[178] Indeed, Uspenskii, in his search for the path by which the Russians could have heard of the practice, could only find as his likely candidate Paisios Ligarides, himself a product of Catholic schools in Rome. The Russians in the later seventeenth century had no memory of the Byzantine practices, and certainly their Greek contemporaries had no better idea: their "Emperor" was the Ottoman Sultan. The only written sources for the practice were and still are a variety of late Byzantine writers, Pseudo-Codinos, Symeon of Thessalonika, and others, who were not known in Russia. They could have been known to Ligarides from the editions of their works published in Italy and elsewhere from the Renaissance onward. If the Russians had a "Byzantine" source, it came via Western humanist scholars. Symeon of Thessalonika's works on the liturgy were translated only in the 1680s, by Evfimii Chudovskii, from a printed text of 1683: Olga B. Strakhov, *The Byzantine Culture in Muscovite Rus': The Case of Evfimii Chudovskii (1620–1705)*. Bausteine zur slavischen Philologie und Kulturgeschichte. Series A, Slavistische Forschungen; New sequence, vol. 26 (Cologne: Böhlau, 1998), 148–154; T. A. Isachenko, *Perevodnaia moskovskaia knizhnost': Metropolichii i patriarshii skriptorii XV–XVII vv.* (Moscow: Pashkov dom, 2009), 236.

The tsar's communion by the altar was not the only innovation on the day of the coronation.[179] The death of the tsar and the succession of his son had already provided Simeon Polotskii with an occasion for another long poem, *Glas poslednii*. Constructed as the voices of the tsar and his courtiers and people, it began with a prayer from the tsar asking God's forgiveness for his sins, and then going on to bless his son with the tsardom and commend his family to his son's care. Most of the text was Aleksei's advice to his son about how to be a good Orthodox ruler. It combined the traditional commands to piety, justice, and mercy with bits of advice gleaned from the clichés of early modern (and earlier) political literature. These were exhortations to prudence: to conquer one's enemies, conquer one's own passions; reward good people and avoid the bad, for they will repay with good and evil accordingly; read history books, for they provide examples for life; virtue leads to power and success. Toward the end the tsar's voice repeats to all Orthodox Christians "In my place I leave my son, I name Fyodor the tsar for you." The poem, which was composed quickly after Aleksei's death, concluded with a series of laments for the dead tsar. Simeon presented it to the new Tsar Fyodor, and it became one of the most widely copied of the poet's works.[180] For the coronation itself Simeon Polotskii contributed yet another poem, called *Gusl' dobroglasnaia* (*The Well-Tempered Lyre*), a series of greetings as if sent from the members of the ruling family, the boyars, the clergy, and the population at large. He presented this work

[179] Sometime during the ceremony or elsewhere during the day Patriarch Ioakim pronounced another speech written for him by Simeon Polotskii. There are a number of places in the ceremony where the order of coronation simply says the patriarch made a speech without giving the text. Medvedev's index to the manuscript, however, gave the title of the speech as "From the most holy patriarch on the day of the coronation of the sovereign Fyodor Aleksievicha" ("Ot sviateishego patriarkha v den' gosudaria tsaria Feodora Aleksievicha." GIM, Sin. 229, l. 2) which would seem to mean not necessarily at the actual coronation. Unfortunately, the *Razriad* documents for that day are lost or unpublished, so the full course of events is not known, but most likely the speech was given outside the immediate ceremony, perhaps in the palace. The speech itself was brief, beginning by reminding the audience of the anointment of Saul by the prophet Samuel, the Biblical precedent for the anointment of all Christian kings and emperors (1 Kings 10:1). "I speak with Samuel: the Lord has anointed you for the kingdom over his people in the Russian Israel" (*Glagoliu zhe s Samuilom: Pomaza tebe Gospod' na tsarstvo liudem svoim izhe vo Israili Rossiistem*), echoing the notion current in Russia since the sixteenth century that Russia was the New Israel. The anointment is God's grace, which instructs you in government, and brings wisdom in judgments and councils, and strength in warfare. He exhorted the tsar to fight the schismatics, look after the faithful, and keep the enemies of the church away from the borders. He continued in this vein briefly and then concluded with wishes for success, health, and long life to Fyodor and the entire ruling family. GIM, Sin. 229, ll. 187–188ob.

[180] Polockij, *Rifmologion* 2, 332–394, esp. 341, 344, 353, 355, 372 (Vmesto zhe sebe syna ostavliaiu, vam Feodora Tsaria naritsaiu); Grebeniuk, "'Rifmologion' Simeona Polotskogo," 260, 294–295, 303–308.

too to the new tsar.[181] Simeon began with a prose introduction adducing the anointment of Solomon by the priest Zadok (3 Kings 1:39). He paraphrased Psalm 88/89 ("I have found David my servant; with my holy oil I have anointed him.") as "I have found Fyodor my servant; with my holy oil I have anointed him."[182] Precedents for Tsar Fyodor were Trajan for his justice as described in Pliny, Constantine and Vladimir of Kiev for their support of the church, Alexander the Great for his strength, Titus for his goodness, David for his meekness, Solomon for his wisdom, Hezekiah for his piety, and Joseph for his foresight (*promysel*). Let the new Israel, the Russian tsardom, rejoice.[183] Repeatedly the poem referred to Fyodor as the inheritor (*dedich*) or even "rightful" or "true" inheritor (*prava* or *istinna dedicha*) of the throne. Once again Simeon stressed the hereditary claim to rule, and, finally, he concluded with a poetic appeal for the work to be printed, not included in the presentation copy. He wanted it printed because it would proclaim the tsar's glory to all Russia and wherever there were Orthodox Slavs. Books carried glory around the world, and would spread Russia's, as poets usually did. There were few Slavic verses, he said, and their time had come.[184] This request was a new direction that Russia had not seen before.

Tsar Fyodor was the recipient and presumed patron of the new court poetry, but he also was a reigning monarch. He made two attempts to provide himself with an heir to the throne. His first marriage was to Agaf'ia Grushetskaia on July 18, 1680, a very modest affair in contrast to earlier weddings. Unfortunately, Tsaritsa Agaf'ia died exactly a year later, having given birth to a son, Il'ia, who himself died three days later.[185] The baptism took place in the Kremlin palace and Patriarch Ioakim officiated. The godmother was Tsarevna Tat'iana and the godfather was the hegumen Ilarion of the Florishchev hermitage near Vladimir. Ilarion combined his monastic calling with deep involvement in the new culture, as the monatery library attests.[186] The last years of

[181] Polockij, *Rifmologion* 2, 394–442; Polotskii, *Izbrannye sochineniia*, 108–159.

[182] "Obretokh Feodora, raba moego, eleem sviatym moim pomazakh ego," Polockij, *Rifmologion* 2, 395–396; Polotskii, *Izbrannye sochineniia*, 109–111.

[183] The poem also described Fyodor as "Rossiiska tsarstva istinnyi dedichu" and quoted the full post-1654 title: Polockij, *Rifmologion* 2, 407 (quotation), 425 (title), 433–434, 438; Polotskii, *Izbrannye sochineniia*, 123, 141, 150, 154.

[184] Polockij, *Rifmologion* 2, 442–445. The text was not printed.

[185] Bushkovitch, *Peter the Great*, 112–118; Martin, *A Bride for the Tsar*, 206–216; Sedov, *Zakat moskovskogo tsarstva*, 350–360.

[186] Sedov, *Zakat moskovskogo tsarstva*, 368. The monastery dates from the 1650s, and Ilarion was the main figure early on. Among more traditional texts, the library contained the writings of the Ukrainian Innokentii Gizel' as well as those of Simeon Polotskii, Karion Istomin, and the Leichoudes brothers. One curiosity was a translation of the

Tsar Fyodor's reign were filled with many important political events and important reforms, but he still did not have an heir.[187] Fyodor also made other provisions for the future: he took care of his younger brothers. Late in 1679, he appointed Rodion Matveevich Streshnev to be Peter's *dia-d'ka*. Streshnev came from the family of Tsar Michael's wife, Peter's grandmother, and had a reputation for probity.[188] Both Streshnev and Ivan's governor Prozorovskii had received boyar rank on June 18, 1676, the day of Fyodor's coronation.[189]

Fyodor's court did not continue his father's theater, but Simeon Polotskii continued to write poetry and sermons for the relevant occasions. When he added the last parts of the *Rifmologion* in 1680, it included a poetic greeting to the tsar on his first marriage in that year.[190] Equally importantly, Simeon was able to get permission to organize his own printing press in February 1679. It lasted three years after his death on August 25, 1680, and produced several of his major works. Besides his two collections of sermons, the "Upper Typography" ("upper" – *verkh* – normally indicated the Kremlin palace), he and his pupils printed a primer (*Bukvar'*), the Slavic translations of Pseudo-Basil and the story of Varlaam and Ioasaph, as well as Simeon's verse translation of the Psalms.[191] Pseudo-Basil was a reedition of the earlier Moscow edition that was based on the Ruthenian translations of the early seventeenth century. To be sure, the text was frequently printed in the West during the early modern era, but that was in another context.[192] Panegyric poetry and prose, on the moments relevant to succession to the throne as well as other events at court, did not cease with Simeon's death. Simeon's pupil Sil'vestr Medvedev continued his work, inheriting his books and

work of the German doctor Johann Ludwig Remmilin, *Catoptrum microcosmicum* (1619), apparently from the 1632 German version, *Kleiner Welt-Spiegel*: V. Georgievskii, *Florishcheva Pustyn'* (Viazniki: Izdatel'stvo Arkhimandrita Antoniia, nastoiatelia Florishchevoi pustyni, 1896), 161–288, esp. 179, 181, 190–192, 194–197, 199–200, 248–251, 257–258, 262, 267–268. See D. M. Bulanin, "Ilarion," *SKKDR* III, pt. 4, 425–429.

187 Bushkovitch, *Peter the Great*, 114–124; Sedov, *Zakat moskovskogo tsarstva*, 397–490.

188 Bushkovitch, *Peter the Great*, 111; E. F. Shmurlo, "Kriticheskie zametki po istorii Petra Velikogo," *Zhurnal Ministerstva narodnogo prosveshcheniia* 330 (August, 1900), 218–219.

189 Poe, *The Russian Elite*, vol. I, 234–235.

190 Polockij, *Rifmologion*, 17–21; Grebeniuk, "'Rifmologion' Simeona Polotskogo," 280, 282.

191 A. S. Zernova, *Knigi kirillovskoi pechati izdannye v Moskve v XVI–XVII vekakh* (Moscow: Tipografiia Biblioteki SSSR imeni V. I. Lenina, 1958), 105–107; L. A. Chernaia, "Verkhniaia tipografiia Simeona Polotskogo," in *Simeon Polotskii i ego knigoizdatel'skaia deiatel'nost': Russkaia staropechatnaia literatura: XVI–pervaia chetvert' XVIII v.*, ed. A. N. Robinson (Moscow: Nauka, 1982), 46–59.

192 F. I. Setin, "'Testament' v izdanii Simeon Polotskogo," in *Simeon Polotskii i ego knigoizdatel'skaia deiatel'nost': Russkaia staropechatnaia literatura: XVI–pervaia chetvert' XVIII v.*, ed. A. N. Robinson (Moscow: Nauka, 1982), 105–116.

manuscripts. Medvedev seems to have been close to Tsar Fyodor and also produced a poem for the birth of Tsar Fyodor's short-lived son Il'ia in 1681, another for his second marriage in 1682, this time on Tsar Fyodor's orders, and a longer effort on the death of the tsar.[193] As we shall see, he was not the only court poet.

The Regency of Sophia

Fyodor died on April 27, 1682, only three months after his second marriage. He died after a long period of illness and without issue. His second marriage in February had been unpopular with most of the great men of the court, according to the Dutch resident Johan Keller, and there were already rumors that Peter would be the successor.[194] In no source is there any indication that Fyodor designated an heir. Shortly after his death, the boyars decided that the new tsar should be the ten-year-old Peter. The Danish resident Heinrich Butenant reported that in place of Fyodor,

> immediately the youngest brother named Peter Alekseevich . . . was chosen tsar; to be sure at the beginning there was some disunity among the great lords, for some wanted the eldest prince from the first bed, namely Ivan Alekseevich (who is now sixteen) for the succession, but since the latter is a very god-fearing prince and has a great defect in his face he did not want to take over the government.

Peter's mother Natal'ia took over the government with her son and was always with him.[195] The rising star of Russian court poetry, Karion

[193] Aleksandr Prozorovskii, *Sil'vestr Medvedev, ego zhizni i deiatel'nost', ChOIDR* 2, 4 (1896): 1–148; 3, 6 (1896): 149–378; 4, 3 (1896): 379–606. On his relations with Fyodor, see Prozorovskii, *Sil'vestr Medvedev*, 187–205 and Sedov, *Zakat moskovskogo tsarstva*, 448–449. N. N. Durnovo, "'Privetstvo brachnoe' Sil'vestra Medvedeva," *Izvestiia Otdeleniia russkogo iazyka i slovesnosti Akademii nauk*, new series, 9, 2 (1904): 303–350: for the poem "pisasia ... za bogougodnym ego tsarskogo presvetlogo velichestva ukazom," 304; for the poem on tsarevich Il'ia, 305–306; I. P. Kozlovskii, *Sil'vestr Medvedev: Ocherk iz istorii russkogo prosveshcheniia i obshchestvennoi zhizni v kontse XVII veka* (Kiev: Tipografiia universiteta Sv. Vladimira, 1895), 74–76 (originally in *Kievskie universitetskie izvestiia* 35, 1895).

[194] Sedov, *Zakat moskovskogo tsarstva*, 391–394; Bushkovitch, *Peter the Great*, 124; Martin, *A Bride for the Tsar*, 216–219; ARSG 7365, February 23, 1682.

[195] TKUA Rusland B 40, May 2, 1682: "ist strax der jungste Bruder nahmens Peter Alexejevitz (nähmlich von der verwitben Zarinnen dess nunmehr in Gott Ruhenden Zaaren Alexej Michaylowitz) zum Zaaren erwehlet worden, es war zwar im Anfang einege Uneinigkeit zwischen den grossen Herren, weiln ezliche, den ältesten Prinz vom erster Bette, nahmens Ivan Alexejewitz (welche nun in Sechszehnten Jahre begriffen) zum Nachfolgte begehreten weiln aber dieser ein sehr Gottesfurchtige Prinz, undt grossen Mangel am Gesichte hatt, hat er die Regierung nicht wollen annähmen. Der neuer erwehlte Zaar ist nur gestern den Primo Maii zehen Jahr alt geworden, seine frauw Mutter die verwitbe Kayserinne Natalja Kirilowna Narüskin nimt dass Regiment mit Ihren shone an, undt last sich allezeit present bey dem Zaaren finden."

Istomin (*c.* 1640–*c.* 1720), was not far behind the changes with his poetry. In the weeks after the decision for Peter, he produced a poem celebrating the event, calling the young tsar "called, chosen" (*zvannyi izbrannyi*), though in Istomin's version it was God who chose Peter.[196]

The result of the elevation of Peter to the throne was the revolt of the musketeers on May 15–17. The musketeers were discontented with the "election" of Peter and came out against their commanders and for Ivan.[197] The result was a revolt that ended in the murder of the recently returned Artamon Matveev and the leading boyar Prince Iu. A. Dolgorukii. All these events were complicated by the factional struggles at court, the Naryshkin faction of Peter's mother's family against his Miloslavskii half-sister Sofiia and her favorite, Prince V. V. Golitsyn. A further complication was Prince I. I. Khovanskii's bid for power. The outcome was the election of Ivan as Peter's co-tsar on May 2.[198] The Danish resident Heinrich Butenant von Rosenbusch told the story:

> Only on the past Friday the 26 of this month [May] the Tsarevich Ivan Alekseevich was elected tsar as well, and all the lords, the commons and also the musketeers have sworn the oath of obedience, so that they now have two tsars, and all petitions and writings are to be presented to both names.

Prince Vasilii Golitsyn had already been appointed to head the Ambassadorial Office, "a very intelligent man and friendly to foreigners."[199]

Was there an election or merely a coup d'état? Is the distinction meaningful? The Russian documentary record of the events is complicated. The brief

196 A. P. Bogdanov, *Pamiatniki obshchestvenno-politicheskoi mysli v Rossii kontsa XVII veka: Literaturnye panegiriki* (Moscow: Institut istorii SSSR, 1983), 49–85; S. N. Brailovskii, *Odin iz 'pestrykh' XVII stoletiia: Istoriko-literaturnoe issledovanie*. Zapiski Imperatorskoi Akademii nauk, series 8, Istoriko-filologicheskoe otdelenie 5 (St. Petersburg: Tipografiia Akademii nauk, 1902). Istomin was another learned monk who worked in the Moscow Printing House and had connections with both Patriarch Ioakim and Sil'vestr Medvedev: L. I. Sazonova, "Karion Istomin," SKKDR III, pt. 2, 140–152.

197 Keller wrote that the musketeers were against the election of Peter: ARSG 7365, May 2, 1682. "Tegens geseide Electie schynen de Strelitsen … haer te willen opposeren"; Bushkovitch, *Peter the Great*, 127.

198 V. I. Buganov, *Moskovskie vosstaniia kontsa XVII veka* (Moscow: Nauka, 1969), 87–362; Lindsey Hughes, *Sophia, Regent of Russia 1657–1704* (New Haven, Connecticut: Yale University Press, 1990), 52–88; A. S. Lavrov, *Regenstvo tsarevny Sofii Alekseevna* (Moscow: Arkheologicheskii tsentr, 1999), 15–78; Bushkovitch, *Peter the Great*, 125–136.

199 TKUA Rusland B 40, May 30, 1682: "Allein auf vergangene Freytag den 26ten dieses ist der Zarewitz Ivan Alexejewitz auch zum Zaaren erwehlet worden, und haben Ihme alle Herren, die gemeine, wie auch die Strelizen den Eyde der gehorsamkeit geschworen, so dass sie hier nun zwo Zaaren haben, und warden alle Suppliquen undt Schriften auf beider Nahmen eingerichtet … zu einem Herrn über die Posolsche Pricas, ist der Bojar, Knaes Wasieley Wasiljewitz Galitzin ernennet worden, ein sehr verständige Herr, und freundlich gegen die Ausländer."

Razriad documents simply say "*narekli na tsarstvo*" Peter and later Ivan; in other words, the impersonal verb meant that someone unspecified appointed them.[200] There is also another *Razriad* document that described the process of the election of Peter on April 27: Patriarch Ioakim asked the lesser ranks of courtiers and the people of Moscow whom they wanted as tsar, and they answered Peter. He turned to the boyars and they gave him the same answer.[201] Official notices sent out with the order to swear the oath of loyalty did not go into any detail, and just stated that Peter had ascended the throne.[202] A few weeks later, on May 15–17 the musketeers revolted and succeeded in getting Ivan on the throne as co-tsar with Peter. These events required new official documentation. The official notice of the addition of Ivan (May 27) and Sophia as regent (May 29) was published as a contemporary document.[203] As A. S. Lavrov established, this document was compiled only after Sophia's defeat of Khovanskii at the end of the year and backdated her official position as regent.[204] Lavrov and other historians focused on the issue of Sophia's regency. The document, however, also throws light on the election. It asserted that Ioakim and the people asked Ivan and Peter to rule on the throne of their ancestors. Ivan supposedly answered that Peter had a living mother, and gave the throne to his younger brother. A month later, on May 26, Ioakim, the clergy, the duma ranks, and the people went to Ivan. They told him that he was the elder brother and that a dispute (*raspria*) had arisen among the people, and they asked him to rule as well, and he agreed "for the quieting of the whole people" (*dlia vsenarodnogo usmireniia*). Then the two tsars consulted Natal'ia and the rest of the family and Ioakim and all ranks, and decided to give the ruling power to Tsarevna Sophia. The tsars decreed the regency of Sophia and the boyars agreed on May 29. The insertion of Sophia's appointment was probably fictitious, for she most likely came to power some weeks later and the rest reflected the official conception of the succession that Sophia wanted to present. This version muffled the story of the election, but did not eliminate it. In this version the appointment of Sophia was the outcome of consultation among the elite and the people.

[200] Solov'ev, *Istoriia Rossii s drevneishikh vremen*, vol. VII [= 13], 320, 338. Solov'ev published the documents as an appendix to his narrative.

[201] *SGGD* IV, 412–413 (April 27).

[202] *SGGD* IV, 415–416 (May 3, to the Don Atamans).

[203] *SGGD* IV, 441–445.

[204] Lavrov, *Regentstvo tsarevny Sofii Alekseevna*, 72–78. Lavrov argued that Hughes was wrong that the *SGGD* document was taken from Sil'vestr Medvedev's history of the events: Hughes, *Sophia, Regent of Russia*, 70, 286, note 110. For Medvedev's history see A. Prozorovskii, ed., *Sil'vestra Medvedeva sozertsanie kratkoe let 7190, 91, i 92, v nikh chto sodeiasia v grazhdanstve*, *ChOIDR* 4, 2 (1894), i–lii, 1–198. Medvedev's text covers the period from the treaty of Bakhchisarai (January 1681) to January 1684.

There are also two narratives of the events, one by Sil'vestr Medvedev (1641–91) and the other from the pen of Andrei Artamonovich Matveev, which provide additional details, if they are accurate. They come from different sides of the court politics of the 1680s, for Medvedev was favorable to Sophia and Matveev was a fervent supporter of Peter and his Naryshkin clan. Medvedev's history, the *Sozertsanie kratkoe* (*Brief View*), described the events without equivocation as an election. The relevant section began with the notice that Peter "was elected" (*izbran byst'*) and then went on to give a detailed account of the election (*izbranie*). In his version Ioakim assembled the clergy in the Kremlin Palace after the death of Fyodor, and the boyars and other duma ranks joined them. They all then went out onto the porch to stand before the lesser court ranks, the soldiers, and the people of Moscow assembled in the courtyard, and asked whom they wished to have as the tsar. The answer was Peter. Only then, in Medvedev's version, did Ioakim turn to the duma and ask their opinion, which was the same. Thus Peter became the tsar, and everyone from the duma down to the townsmen swore faithful service to him, his mother and brother, and all the family. His mother Natal'ia was with him the whole time.[205] Medvedev's text had no mention of Ivan's refusal to take the throne, as in Sophia's official announcement, and supported the official record of April 17, as well as the contemporary account of Butenant. After describing the revolt, Medvedev went on to the choice of Ivan as co-ruler. In his account, the soldiers (*vybornye, sluzhilye liudi*) assembled in the Kremlin only on May 23, and sent Prince Khovanskii into the palace to declare that they wanted Ivan in addition to Peter. Ioakim assembled the clergy, the duma, and the people. "There was much talk about election."[206] Some were not happy with the idea of two tsars, but eventually they agreed. The actual proclamation of both Ivan and Peter came on May 26, with Ivan as first tsar and Peter second. The musketeers and the whole people swore the oath of loyalty. On May 29, Sophia took charge of the government in view of the youth of the tsars.[207] Matveev's account, though written much later, was also unambiguously a story of election. In his version Ioakim assembled the duma and the courtiers immediately after the death of Tsar Fyodor, as many already inclined to the election (*izbranie*) of Peter. They then swore the oath of loyalty. What is missing from his version is any mention of the larger group of soldiers, nobles, and townsmen in Peter's election. Matveev went on to recount the revolt in vivid detail and then the election of Tsar Ivan by the musketeers. In his account, only the musketeers

[205] Prozorovskii, ed., *Sil'vestra Medvedeva sozertsanie kratkoe*, 42–46.
[206] Ibid., 60–61: "mnogoe glagolanie v polate o izbranii byst'." [207] Ibid., 65–67.

elected Ivan.[208] The details varied, but all the sources, namely official documents, Medvedev, and Matveev, presented the events of 1682 as the election of the tsars.

The Ambassadorial Office now had the task of informing Russia's neighbors of the new reign. The first letters were ready to go on June 9, when the new arrangements seemed stable. To Emperor Leopold, King Jan Sobieski, Shah Suleiman of Iran, and the Ottoman Sultan Mehmet IV the message was laconic: Tsar Fyodor had died and Ivan and Peter had become the tsars on the ancestral throne of the great and most glorious Russian tsardom: "*na praroditel'skom velikogo i preslavnogo Rossiiskogo tsarstva prestole uchinilis'*."[209] There was nothing here of the real events and the election of the new tsars, even though, in Europe at least, the news had already spread through reports of diplomats and the many newsletters and gazettes that were already a major part of European culture.

In the midst of all these maneuvers, on June 25, 1682, both boys were crowned by the patriarch. Both were led through the ceremony by their *diad'ki*, Prince Prozorovskii and Streshnev.[210] The coronation document began with a speech in the mouths of Ioakim and the assembled clergy and boyars, gentry, and townspeople that explained the double coronation, in which the audience heard that Tsar Fyodor had simply "left" (*ostavil*) the throne to Ivan and Peter. The speeches of the tsars and the patriarch in the actual ceremony followed the tradition in repeating the story of the Monomakh crown, but did not say that Fyodor had blessed one or both of the boys. Rather, it asserted both in the tsars' version and in the patriarch's version that they had ascended the throne by the will of God. They came to sit on their "ancestral throne" (*na praroditel'skom prestole*) and took up the throne and regalia together. It repeated the most recent version of their title, with the expression *otchichi i dedichi i nasledniki*.[211] In other words, in a case where everyone knew that the church, the boyar elite, and the musketeers had decided on Ivan and Peter, the coronation document presented them as the result of heredity and divine will. Ioakim anointed both

208 A. A. Matveev, "Zapiski Andreia Artamonovicha Matveeva," in *Zapiski russkikh liudei*, ed. I. Sakharov (St. Petersburg: Tipografiia I. Sakharova, 1841), 4, 34. Matveev's text follows the events from 1682 to 1697 and was most likely composed after the latter date. The title "zapiski" was imposed by Sakharov in the nineteenth century. The manuscripts have "Gistoriia" as Matveev's title.

209 *PDS* VI, 25–28, 53–54, 101.

210 Solov'ev, *Istoriia Rossii s drevneishikh vremen*, vol. 7, 345 (the *Razriad* account).

211 *PSZ* II, 413, 422–425. The ceremony differed in several other respects from the traditional, not least being the prominent role of Golitsyn: Ibid., 420.

young tsars and both took communion by the altar, inside the royal doors.[212] It was these last two parts of the ceremony that Medvedev described in his brief account of the coronation.[213] Here he did not touch on election or heredity, for his earlier narrative had made it clear that what had occurred was two elections. In his verses for the coronation Karion Istomin celebrated God's will as the basis of the accession of the two boys. Ivan and Peter were "two autocrats, tsars known to God, grand dukes chosen in justice." They were also the inheritors (*otchichi i dedichi*) of the tsardom of Moscow. Istomin noted the anointment with oil and the communion, though he did not specify where it took place. He wished both of them glory, long life, and children.[214]

In the case of the succession of Ivan and Peter in 1682 the attention of historians has been focused, as for 1598 and 1613, on the maneuvers of the various factions and the political realities. It was the boyars and Patriarch Ioakim who made the decision. They felt that it was perfectly normal to name Peter as the tsar, given the situation of his older brother's incapacity. This was a conscious choice for a younger son. As the diplomats, Medvedev, and the first Russian records of the events all agree, Ioakim, the boyars, and the people did at first elect Peter. The addition of Ivan to the throne was not a trivial issue. He may have been unable to rule by himself, but no one knew at that moment whether or not Ivan would produce an heir. As he was the older brother, his future son would be the more obvious heir than Peter. If Russia had really been a hereditary monarchy with primogeniture, Ivan, not Peter, was obviously the correct choice. As we know, he did have an infant daughter born in March 1689 (who died in 1692), and later produced several healthy girls, including the future empress Anna. Before he could do that, however, Tsar Ivan had to marry.

The marriage of Tsar Ivan V Alekseevich to Praskov'ia Saltykova on January 9, 1684, has not attracted much attention from historians.[215] It was a very modest affair, like the marriages of Tsar Fyodor. Yet contemporaries took it seriously, for they did not know how events would play out

212 *PSZ* II, 434–435. The *Razriad* record, which omitted the speeches, included the anointment and communion by the altar, Solov'ev, *Istoriia Rossii s drevneishikh vremen*, vol. 6, 346.

213 Prozorovskii, ed. *Sil'vestra Medvedeva sozertsanie kratkoe*, 96–97. Matveev mentioned the coronation only briefly: Matveev, "Zapiski Andreia Artamonovicha Matveeva," 36.

214 "Dva samoderzhtsa/tsari bogoznani/Velikie kniazi/vo pravde izbrani./Ioann i Petr/Aleksievichi/Moskovskogo tsarstva/otchichi i dedichi." A. P. Bogdanov, *Stikh torzhestva: Rozhdenie russkoi ody posledniaia chetvert' XVII–nachalo XVIII veka* (Moscow: Rossiiskaia akademiia nauk, Institut rossiskoi istorii, 2012), 383–385.

215 *DRV* XI, 196–197; M. I. Semevskii, *Tsaritsa Praskov'ia 1664–1723*, 2nd ed. (St. Petersburg: Russkaia starina, 1883), 8–12; Martin, *A Bride for the Tsar*, 219–222.

in the next few years. The Scottish mercenary officer Patrick Gordon recorded it in his diary, noting that it was a private affair, "as usual" he thought, for the only weddings he knew about were those of Tsar Fyodor.[216] The new Danish resident, Hildebrand von Horn, commented on the bride's beauty, but he expected trouble. The wedding, he thought, was Sophia's work and it was part of her designs for sole power. In this she was prompted by I. M. Miloslavskii, but even Prince V. V. Golitsyn was opposed to the idea. Horn said nothing about potential heirs: perhaps he assumed that Ivan was not capable of fatherhood.[217] Needless to say, Horn was also close to Sophia's opponents, the Naryshkins. Neither Medvedev nor Istomin seem to have marked it with verse or oratory.

The marriage of Peter on January 27, 1689, to Evdokiia Lopukhina surpassed the precedent of Ivan's wedding in its modesty. Its political importance was not small, but that was not reflected in the ceremony.[218] The wedding took place not in the Dormition Cathedral but in one of the palace chapels, and the patriarch did not perform the service. That was the role of Peter's spiritual father, Archpriest Merkurii Gavrilovich. Again according to Gordon, the banquet did not take place until February 7.[219] The Swedish resident, Christopher von Kochen, could report very little other than the fact of the wedding itself, the name of the bride's father, and the fact that his clan had a good following. The bride, he wrote, had only moderate beauty but a good understanding.[220] The wedding was, however, the object of a book of poetry from Karion Istomin. An emblem book with more panegyric verse, it naturally wished the bride and groom children and the inheritance of the all-Russian tsardom by the God-given children.[221]

This was the only poetic present, for Peter's teacher since 1683, the duma secretary Nikita Zotov, was not a poet.[222] Peter's education was a more complicated affair than that of his father. He reached the normal age

[216] Fedosov, ed., *The Diary of General Patrick Gordon*, vol. IV, 1–2.

[217] "Relationer til K. Christian den Femte fra den danske envoyé i Moskov Hildebrand von Horrn November 1682–Juni 1684," *Aarsberetninger fra det Kongelige Geheimearchiv* 6 (1876–82) [= TKUA Rusland B 41], 172–173.

[218] Bushkovitch, *Peter the Great*, 156–157; K. A. Kochegarov, "Bor'ba boiarskikh gruppirovok vokrug planov zhenit'by tsaria Petra i russko-pol'skie otnosheniia v 1684–89 gg.," in *Rossiia, Pol'sha, Germaniia v evropeiskoi politike: Istoricheskii opyt vzaimodeistviia i imperativy sotrudnichestva*, ed. B. V. Nosov (Moscow: Indrik, 2012), 45–88.

[219] Martin, *A Bride for the Tsar*, 226–227; Fedosov, ed., *The Diary of General Patrick Gordon*, vol. IV, 234–235.

[220] Svenska Riksarkiv (SR), Muscovitica 115, January 18 and February 1, 1689.

[221] Karion Istomin, *Kniga liubvi znak v chestne brake*, ed. L. I. Sazonova (Moscow: Izdatel'stvo Kniga, 1989), 2ob., 94.

[222] M. M. Bogoslovskii, *Petr I: Materialy dlia bibliografii* (Moscow: OGIZ, 1940), vol. I, 33–37; Ernest A. Zitser, *The Transfigured Kingdom: Sacred Parody and Charismatic Authority at the Court of Peter the Great* (Ithaca, New York and London: Cornell University Press,

to advance from reading and writing to more sophisticated matter only toward the end of Fyodor's reign, and the appointment of Streshnev as his *diad'ka* in 1679 signaled that change. Streshnev does not seem to have had much impact on Peter's actual learning, and neither did his mother. Other than Zotov, Peter, at least according to legend, was left very much on his own in a time when the court was the site of various cross-currents in culture and education. While Peter was mostly in the suburban residences, in central Moscow the Greek Leichoudes brothers, Sophronios and Ioannikios, opened a school that followed Jesuit models, like most Greek schools of the time. They had opponents, allegedly even more Western in tastes than they, such as Sil'vestr Medvedev. Patriarch Ioakim seemed to be on the side of the Leichoudes.[223] None of this reached Peter, as far as we know; nor did it involve Zotov. Zotov became Peter's teacher when he was already tsar at the age of eleven. Normally this was the age at which more serious education began, but what Peter actually studied is hard to trace. As he was already the tsar, he participated in a great many of the court ceremonies and the September pilgrimage to the Trinity-St. Sergii Monastery. At the same time, he spent more and more time out of the Kremlin in the suburban residences of the tsars, especially Preobrazhenskoe to the northeast. He (or Zotov) took books from the library of the tsars, such as Maciej Stryjkowski's sixteenth-century history of Poland and Lithuania and the Bible in pictures. Neither religious nor historical reading matter was new, but these books were. The Bible as a unit of reading was unusual in Russia, where it had been read in parts or as part of liturgy: the first printed version came only in 1663, and Peter's version had pictures. Stryjkowski had been translated only in the 1670s as a classic work of Polish Renaissance historiography.[224] Peter also spent a great deal of time in military exercises with his *poteshnye* ("amusement") soldiers, the

2004), 28–29. Zotov, who had an administrative and diplomatic career before receiving the post of Peter's teacher, was a duma secretary from November 1, 1682, according to the sources used by Poe: *The Russian Elite*, vol. I, 270, 406. Other sources list him with that rank in May 1681, suggesting that the rank was the reward for his diplomatic service at the conclusion of the Treaty of Bakhchisarai earlier that year: *DR* IV, 188.

[223] Nikolaos A. Chrissidis, *An Academy at the Court of the Tsars: Greek Scholars and Jesuit Education in Early Modern Russia* (DeKalb, Illinois: Northern Illinois University Press, 2016); Strakhov, *The Byzantine Culture in Muscovite Rus'; Sazonova, Literaturnaia kul'tura Rossii.*

[224] Shmurlo, "Kriticheskie zametki po istorii Petra Velikogo," 429–439; Maciej Stryjkowski, *Kronika Polska, Litewska, Żmódzka, i wszystkiej Rusi*, 2 vols. (Warsaw: Gustaw Leon Glücksberg, 1846) (originally Königsberg, 1582); A. I. Rogov, *Russko-pol'skie kul'turnye sviazi v epokhu Vozrozhdeniia; Stryikovskii i ego Khronika* (Moscow: Nauka, 1966); Christine Watson, *Tradition and Translation: Maciej Stryjkowski's Polish Chronicle in Seventeenth-Century Russian Manuscripts*. Studia Slavica Upsaliensia 46 (Uppsala: Uppsala University, 2012). The interest in Stryjkowski may have been in his account of the early history of Russia, the most commonly translated section.

beginnings of the later regiments of guards, and with boats. He also had some mathematical training, perhaps for navigation. He learned how to use an astrolabe from the Dutch mariner Frans Timmerman, who also taught him to sail. As Peter later related in the introduction to his 1720 Naval Statute, he found a foreign boat in an old barn, and Timmerman told him that it could sail against the wind.[225] Peter was fascinated, and from then on remained obsessed with boats to the end of his life. The interest in mathematics, as well as his training in handicrafts with a lathe, was not unusual for a European monarch in the 1680s, but was all entirely new in the Russian court. The interest in military affairs was not new: the tsars in the sixteenth century had brought their sons to the army before they were adults.[226] Perhaps it was fortunate that Peter had no father to direct his education, and as the tsar he had to listen to no one but his mother.

Peter's education and life at court was the object of poetry and panegyric from Karion Istomin and the Leichoudes. They all also had verses and orations for his brother Tsar Ivan, Sophia, and even Prince Golitsyn. Ignatii Rimskii-Korsakov, archimandrite of the New Savior Monastery in Moscow (the Romanov "house monastery") and later Metropolitan of Tobol'sk, contributed sermons on the wars and campaigns against the Crimean Tatars, as did Patriarch Ioakim.[227] These compositions were now an established part of the culture of the court. They only occasionally touched on succession as they celebrated name days and birthdays. Sophronios Leichoudes lauded Tsar Ivan on his name day (August 29) in 1688, and Peter on his birthday (May 30) in 1689.[228] In the birthday panegyric Leichoudes noted the supposed descent of Peter from Prince Vladimir and, through him, the Byzantine emperors. This fanciful genealogy not only connected Russia to the Byzantine world, but also presented the Romanovs as a hereditary dynasty.[229] In this phantasy Leichoudes followed the precedent of the earlier Greeks in Moscow, Ligarides and Patriarch Paisios. Karion Istomin was prolific, greeting both Peter's mother Natal'ia and Prince Boris Golitsyn (the leader of the Naryshkin

[225] A. A. Preobrazhenskii and T. E. Novitskaia, eds., *Zakonodatel'stvo Petra I* (Moscow: Iuridicheskaia literatura, 1997), 236–237.

[226] Bogoslovskii, *Petr I*, vol. I, 30–37, 48–67; *PiB* I, 1–10; Mormiche, *Devenir prince*, 55, 57, 297, 336–341; Watanabe-O'Kelly, *Court Culture in Dresden*, 80–84, 96.

[227] Bogdanov, *Pamiatniki obshchestvenno-politicheskoi mysli v Rossii*, 135–182, 233–241; O. A. Belobrova, A. P. Bogdanov, "Ignatii," *SKKDR* III, pt. 2, 26–31. Ioakim's sermons were actually written by Istomin: Bogdanov, *Pamiatniki obshchestvenno-politicheskoi mysli v Rossii*, 118–181.

[228] Bogdanov, *Pamiatniki obshchestvenno-politicheskoi mysli v Rossii*, 185–186; Chrissidis, *An Academy at the Court of the Tsars*, 169–170.

[229] Vladimiro-suzdal'skii muzei-zapovednik MS Kr-388/V-5636/112, ff. 55–58v (transcript by Nikolaos Chrissidis).

faction) on Peter's name day in 1689.[230] Later in August, on the eve of the overthrow of Sophia, he wrote verse for the name days of both Tsaritsa Evdokiia and Tsaritsa Natal'ia. In the latter, he explicitly praised the *tsarskii rod* and hoped that they would rule eternally.[231] With the two young tsars only recently married, the succession to their thrones did not seem an immediate concern to the court poets and orators.

The issue of succession, however, was settled dramatically in August 1689, for Peter overthrew the regency of his sister with the support of Ivan and his court as well as the boyar elite and the army. In the middle of September, after Sophia had surrendered and when her supporters were under arrest, Peter wrote to his brother Ivan, telling him that it was now time for them to rule without her. It was they, the two brothers, who had the right to the title, as they had taken up the scepter of rule of their ancestral tsardom (*praroditel'skoe tsarstvo*), as shown in the messages sent to foreign rulers on the death of Tsar Fyodor and in the church council of 7190 (1681–2). What Peter meant by the church council is not clear, since that council met in the last months of Fyodor's reign, but the claim of the ancestral tsardom was perfectly clear.[232] Peter chose to ignore the "election" of 1682, though he in many ways repeated the process seven years later. It was the support of the elite and the army that made possible his assumption of power at the age of seventeen. He then ruled, formally with his brother Ivan, until the latter's death in 1696.

*

The seventeenth century did not leave Russia an unambiguous heritage of hereditary monarchy in the male line, either in fact or in conception. It was the foreigners, Simeon Polotskii, the Greeks, and their Russian pupils who emphasized heredity. The election of Boris, Vasilii Shuiskii, and Michael Romanov was in every chronicle and historical tale that circulated in Russia. The events of 1682 were also recounted by Medvedev, Andrei Matveev, and others, and were within living memory in Peter's time. To the Swedish scholar and traveler Sparwenfeld, it seemed that the Russians looked to the utility of the realm, not

[230] Bogdanov, *Pamiatniki obshchestvenno-politicheskoi mysli v Rossii*, 211–212; Bogdanov, *Stikh torzhestva*, 428–429.

[231] Bogdanov, *Pamiatniki obshchestvenno-politicheskoi mysli v Rossii*, 231–232, 242–243; Bogdanov, *Stikh torzhestva*, 447–452.

[232] *PiB* I, 13–14. For the church council see Sedov, *Zakat moskovskogo tsarstva*, 422–452. Sophia had used the title "autocrat" (*samoderzhitsa*) in internal documents after 1686: Hughes, *Sophia, Regent of Russia*, 194.

heredity. In fact, succession included a role for the ruling family's women: Tsaritsa Anastasia and Tsaritsa Irina Godunova were crucial to the presentation of the elections, as they provided a dynastic link alongside the will of God expressed by the people at the Sobor. Both in fact and in the realm of ideas, dynastic, testamentary, and electoral succession coexisted.

6 Peter the Great and Succession 1690–1719

The reign of Peter the Great brought to the surface all the ambiguities about succession to the throne in Russia since the fifteenth century.[1] Peter was not the oldest son of his father when the elite and the people of Moscow elected him tsar in 1682, but he was a member of the ruling Romanov family. He came to the throne by election as well as heredity, and the inclusion of his older brother Ivan a month later did not cancel his own election. When he overthrew the rule of his sister Sophia in 1689, he continued to rule with Ivan until the latter's death. Fortunately he never had to face the situation that would have existed if Ivan had produced a son, so he could treat his own son Aleksei as the heir from birth.

Peter the Great's first son Aleksei was born on February 19, 1690, six months after he overthrew Sophia. For the next twenty-eight years, succession to the throne revolved around Aleksei Petrovich. Peter had no more surviving male children until 1715 (Petr Petrovich), but he did have a number of daughters, two of whom, Anna and Elizabeth, survived to adulthood, the latter eventually to become Empress in 1741. His half-brother Ivan had only daughters, three of them living to adulthood and the second, also named Anna, reigning as empress during the years 1730–40. If the women were taken into account, there were many possible heirs, but the daughters do not seem to have been an option until late in Peter's reign, after the deaths of Aleksei Petrovich and Petr Petrovich. When the latter boy died in 1719, there was another possible male heir,

[1] The literature on Peter is immense. See Reinhard Wittram, *Peter I Czar und Kaiser*, 2 vols. (Göttingen, Vandenhoeck & Ruprecht, 1964); N. I. Pavlenko, *Petr Velikii* (Moscow: Mysl', 1994); E. V. Anisimov, *Gosudarstvennye preobrazovaniia i samoderzhavie Petra Velikogo* (St. Petersburg: Dmitrii Bulanin, 1997); Lindsey Hughes, *Russia in the Age of Peter the Great* (New Haven, Connecticut: Yale University Press, 1998); Paul Bushkovitch, *Peter the Great: The Struggle for Power 1671–1725* (Cambridge: Cambridge University Press, 2001), Russian translation by N. L. Luzhitskaia, *Petr Velikii: bor'ba za vlast' (1671–1725)* (St. Petersburg: Dmitrii Bulanin, 2008); James Cracraft, *The Petrine Revolution in Russian Culture* (Cambridge, Massachusetts: The Belknap Press of Harvard University Press, 2004).

Peter's grandson Petr Alekseevich, also born in 1715. Just four years old, he was a healthy boy and he was a direct descendant of the tsar.

Tsar Ivan V's daughters were only a year or two younger than Tsarevich Aleksei. After their father's death, they grew up mostly in and around Moscow, and served as brides in Peter's dynastic alliances. The first attempt to marry off the tsar's nieces came in September 1709, apparently in a response to an offer from the Landgrave of Hesse-Cassel, to marry one of the Russian "princesses" to the heir to Hesse-Cassel. These princesses could only have been Ekaterina and Anna Ivanovna, both of marriageable age. Peter showed some interest in the proposal, but for whatever reason nothing came of it.[2] The second daughter Anna was the first to be married, in 1710 to Friedrich Wilhelm, the duke of Kurland (born 1698), who died a few weeks after the wedding. The idea for the marriage came from Kurland, not from Peter. The Duchy's rulers not only wanted a bride for the young duke but also wanted a powerful ally to support the small territory. As Peter had just taken control of Livonia to the north, the tsar's family was an obvious choice. For Peter it gave him a chance to exert Russian influence in Kurland: he promised to help the duke against foreign and domestic enemies.[3] For the next twenty years Anna lived in Mitau as the Duchess of Kurland, a vassal state of the Kingdom of Poland, ruling with the help of her favorite, Ernst Johann von Biron. The next marriage alliance of Russia with a German ruler also came on the latter's initiative. Karl-Leopold, the duke of Mecklenburg-Schwerin (1678–1747), contentious in politics and temperamental in marriage, was looking for a new wife (he had divorced the first) from his accession to the throne in 1713 onward. He turned to Russia and the possibility of one of Peter's nieces.[4] The idea came to fruition only in

[2] The proposal was mediated by Johan Christoph Urbich, and the only documents are among his papers: Landesarchiv Sachsen-Anhalt, Standort Wernigerode H82, no. 1029, ff. 468–468v (September 1709), no. 1028, ff. 39–40 (February 24, 1710, Instructions to Urbich). The Landgrave of Hesse-Cassel at that moment was Karl (1654–1730, ruled from 1670), and his heir was Friedrich I (1676–1751), from 1720 king of Sweden as the husband of Queen Ulrike Eleonore.

[3] Wittram, *Peter I Czar und Kaiser*, vol. I, 354–361; *PiB* 1710, 161–168, 311–316; "Urkunden von der Vermälung des Herzogs zu Curland Friedrich Wilhelm mit der rußischen Prinzessin Anna," *Magazin für die neue Historie und Geographie* 15 (1781): 199–220. The only discussion of heirs was the provision that any sons should be raised Lutheran and daughters Orthodox, as well as details about the dowry's fate in case of the death of either spouse.

[4] Wittram, *Peter I Czar und Kaiser*, vol. II, 271–278; Walther Mediger, *Mecklenburg, Rußland und England-Hannover 1707–1721: Ein Betrag zur Geschichte des Nordischen Krieges*. Quellen und Darstellungen zur Geschichte Niedersachsens 70 (Hildesheim: Lax, 1967), vol. I, 87–105. He also explored marriages to the Swedish royal house and that of the emperor at the same time: Mediger, *Mecklenburg, Rußland und England-Hannover*, vol. I, 105–115.

1715, and Peter was at first not enthusiastic. He wanted assurance that Karl-Leopold's divorce was legitimate, and in general he did not trust Karl-Leopold.[5] Peter finally agreed to the marriage of the duke with Ekaterina Ivanovna early in 1716, and the marriage took place that summer. For Peter the main advantage was to provide a logistic base for an invasion of Sweden, with some commercial considerations (mostly chimerical) in the background. In return, Peter was to support Karl-Leopold in his aims, including his disputes with the Mecklenburg estates.[6] The third sister, Praskov'ia Ivanovna, remained in Russia, marrying late in life to a Russian nobleman. As the tsar's half-nieces, Ivan V's daughters were part of the ruling family but not likely heirs until well after Peter's death.[7] Succession seemed to be a simple matter, with Aleksei Petrovich the heir, until relations between father and son deteriorated, starting in 1715.

*

In the first years after 1689, the court ceremonies continued as before, including that for the baptism of the tsars' children. The first born was Ivan's daughter Mariia on March 21, 1689, before the overthrow of Sophia. As the tradition now demanded, she was baptized in the Chudov Monastery by Patriarch Ioakim, the godparents being Peter himself and his aunt Tat'iana Mikhailovna.[8] Both tsars came out for the blessing of the waters at Epiphany in 1690.[9] A few weeks later the birth of Tsarevich Aleksei on February 19, 1690, was the object of great thanksgiving, much of it in the traditional manner. On the day of his birth, Tsars Ivan and Peter went with Patriarch Ioakim and all the clergy to the Dormition Cathedral to pray for the health of the tsars and the new tsarevich. The boyars, courtiers, secretaries, and even the elite merchants and townspeople were present as well. Afterward the two tsars heard more services in the palace churches and gave gifts to all. There were many promotions that day, beginning with M. K. Naryshkin and

[5] Mediger, *Mecklenburg, Rußland und England-Hannover*, vol. I, 176–178.

[6] S. M. Solov'ev, *Istoriia Rossii s drevneishikh vremen* (Moscow: Izdatel'stvo sotsial'no-ekonomicheskoi literatury, 1960–6), vol. IX, 46–51, originally Moscow: Universitetskaia tipografiia, 1851–79; Mediger, *Mecklenburg, Rußland und England-Hannover*, vol. I, 205–220. Treaties: F. Martens, *Sobranie Traktatov i Konventsii zakliuchennykh Rossiei s inostrannymi derzhavami* (St. Petersburg: Tipografiia ministerstva putei soobshcheniia, 1880), vol. V, 137–151. The contention that Peter had greater aims for a position in northern Germany is unconvincing. The known documents say nothing beyond the military issues and various commercial projects and are very sparse on Peter's intentions.

[7] M. I. Semevskii, *Tsaritsa Praskov'ia 1664–1723*, 2nd ed. (St. Petersburg: Russkaia starina, 1883).

[8] *DR* IV, 438. She died in 1692.

[9] *DR* IV, 515–521.

P. A. Lopukhin the younger, both relatives of Peter's wife and mother, to boyar rank.[10] Patrick Gordon recorded that he was among those receiving a cup of vodka from Peter's hands, a traditional ritual, but he also related that "In the evening I was sent for by his Ma-tie, entertained & detained all night." The next day he went out with Peter to Fili, the Naryshkin estate near Moscow, for dinner and supper with L. K. Naryshkin, Peter's uncle and the most power of the boyars in those years. Gordon returned home only at three o'clock in the morning the next day.[11] Peter was supplementing the traditional ceremonies and banquets with drinking bouts with his relatives and foreign officers.

Three days later, six regiments of soldiers and musketeers came in uniform and formation to express their congratulations, and the colonels of the first regiments made speeches, which were recorded in the Musketeers' Chancery. Peter watched from the balcony, and the boyar Prince I. B. Troekurov thanked them in his name. They fired a salute from the muskets.[12]

The next day, February 23, 1690, was full of events. Tsarevich Aleksei was baptized in the monastery church of St. Aleksii in the Chudov Monastery. Patriarch Ioakim conducted the service and also was the boy's godfather. Tsarevna Tatiana Mikhailovna, Peter's aunt, was his godmother. The tsar's own mother, Tsaritsa Natal'ia, stood by for the baptism of her first grandchild. Peter was there, but Ivan was not. Afterward Peter distributed vodka to the boyars, soldiers, and secretaries. That day was the Sunday of the Last Judgment, a solemn festival that formed part of the preparation for Lent.[13] The court records listed no more festivities, but at 4 o'clock in the afternoon the military regiments came to the Kremlin again for another salute. Gordon described the ceremony:

> I marched in the Crimlina & into the court at the west gate & and the other Selected regiment at the east gate. Being come within the court wee did draw up the regiments fronting towards the palace. How soone the regiments were drawne up, the Tzaars with the boyars being descended to a staire-head, I caused them present their armes & then put their muskets under their armes with the musket

[10] *DR* IV, 527–529; SR Muscovitica, February 21, 1690 (Kochen).

[11] Dmitry Fedosov, ed., *The Diary of General Patrick Gordon of Auchleuchries 1635–1699*, 6 vols. (Aberdeen: AHRC Centre for Irish and Scottish Studies, University of Aberdeen, 2009–16), vol. V, 6.

[12] *DR* IV, 529–531; Fedosov, ed., *The Diary of General Patrick Gordon*, vol. V, 7: "Some regiments of the streltsees saluted & congratulated his Ma-tie, gave fire in the inner court. Myne was ready, but being late were dismissed."

[13] *DR* IV, 531–532. There was no further celebration as that day, February 23, was the Sunday of the Last Judgement, a solemn festival, the last day to eat meat in preparation for Lent.

backwards (a very unseemly posture). Then takeing of the their caps, by a sign of the drum wee all made a deep reverence to the Tzaars; then I standing directly befor their Ma-ties, & the colonels a little behind me, I according to my instructions spoke aloud the following speech, translated verbatim or ad verbum:

'The Lord grant that thou, Great Lord, Tzaar, and Great Duke Peter Alexeiowitz of all the Great, Litle, & White Russia self-upholder [*samoderzhets*], & of many Dominions & Countries East, West & Northerne from Father and Grandfather, Lord, successor & commander [*otchich i dedich, gosudar', naslednik i povelitel'*], be in health with your Ma-ties new borne successor and our Lord, the most illustrious Prince and Great Duke Alexey Petrovitz of the Great, Litle & White Russia, for many years.'

After which by a signe of the drumme wee all made a deep reverence.

At this point the boyar Prince F. S. Urusov, head of the Foreigners' Chancery (in charge of mercenary soldiers), wished them good health in turn. He then announced the gifts to the officers, consisting of expensive fine cloth, and gifts of cash to the men. All were then invited to the tsar's table for meat and drink, and they all in return made a "deep reverence."

Then I was commanded to cause the sojours give fyre, so being very throng, I drew forward the first three ranks to the very wall of the palace & made them face about, the collours being in the middle, and caused them make ready; & the first rank kneeling, the second stooping & the third standing upright, give fire altogether, the collours in the meane time flourishing, and the drums beating, which pleased his Ma-tie so well that he caused us fire againe & yet a third time; then leading them to their former station & clubbing their musquets & mounting their pikes, marched out of the court.[14]

The usual banquet came on February 28, where Peter presided but again Ivan did not join them. Patriarch Ioakim was at the table, as were the boyars, courtiers of lesser ranks, the generals and colonels of the army and musketeers, the senior chancery secretaries, and G. D. Stroganov and other privileged merchants.[15] Gordon was to have come to the banquet, but Patriarch Ioakim objected to the presence of foreigners.[16] In addition to all the ceremony, public and private, Karion Istomin contributed more poetry in honor of the events, something that was no longer an innovation. Istomin, among all the joyful exclamations and extravagant praise of the tsar, did not omit to say that Peter's son would be a sovereign

[14] Fedosov, ed., *The Diary of General Patrick Gordon*, vol. V, 7–8.

[15] *DR* IV, 534–536. Peter also made several promotions on this occasion, including advancing his long-time supporter Prince B. A. Golitsyn to full boyar from *kravchii* (a lesser duma rank) as well as P. A. Lopukhin the elder from *okol'nichii* to boyar.

[16] Fedosov, ed., *The Diary of General Patrick Gordon*, vol. V, 10. Gordon nevertheless received a reward for his congratulations: G. V. Esipov, *Sbornik vypisok iz arkhivnykh bumag o Petre Velikom* (Moscow: Universitetskaia tipografiia, 1872), vol. I, 110–111.

(*gosudar'*) and that Peter himself was the inheritor, *otchich i dedich*, of the tsardom of Russia.[17] Like the speech that Gordon was instructed to make before the salute, it stressed the hereditary nature of the monarchy.

The tsarevich was too young to participate in the traditional ceremonies in the ensuing years, but he was the object of numerous verses presented to him by the author, Karion Istomin. These were not really gifts to the infant Aleksei, they were part of the poetic additions to the court ceremonies, for the name day of the tsarevich or other family occasions.[18] Others of his works provided wise teachings, secular and religious, for the heir's future, especially the *Bukvar'* of 1696, and the *Edem* and *Ekklesia* in 1693.[19] The traditional public ceremonies continued, and Peter and Ivan took the customary role of the tsar together. The two tsars led Patriarch Adrian in the Palm Sunday procession (April 9) in 1693, and they went to the Moscow River with him for the blessing of the waters at Epiphany in 1694.[20] Peter's mother, Tsaritsa Natal'ia, died later in January 1694, and after that moment Peter began to ignore the traditional court calendar of ceremonies. There was no Palm Sunday procession in 1694.[21] In 1695, the Epiphany procession did take place, but it is not clear whether Ivan or Peter took part.[22] In January 1696, Peter was ill the whole month, and Tsar Ivan led the Epiphany ceremony alone.[23]

As long as Natal'ia was alive, the Naryshkins had ruled Russia in Peter's name, but with her death everything changed. Peter immediately went to Archangel and now went out to sea on ships. When he returned, he decided that Russia should once again take an active part in the war against the Turks, and this time not to move directly against Crimea but to capture the fortress of Azov that blocked the mouth of the Don River.[24] During these years the young Tsarevich Aleksei remained in the care of women. His governess (*mamka*) was Praskov'ia Alekseevna Naryshkina, the widow of Ivan Kirillovich Naryshkin, Tsaritsa Natal'ia's brother, who had been

[17] A. P. Bogdanov, *Stikh torzhestva: Rozhdenie russkoi ody posledniaia chetvert' XVII–nachalo XVIII veka*, 2 vols. (Moscow: Rossiiskaia akademiia nauk, Institut rossiskoi istorii, 2012), 489–500.

[18] Ibid., 506–511, 523–530.

[19] S. N. Brailovskii, *Odin iz 'pestrykh' XVII stoletiia: Istoriko-literaturnoe issledovanie*. Zapiski Imperatorskoi Akademii nauk, series 8, Istoriko-filologicheskoe otdelenie 5 (St. Petersburg: Tipografiia Akademii nauk, 1902), 273–277; Bogdanov, *Stikh torzhestva*, 568–573.

[20] *DR* IV, 775–780, 843–849. [21] *DR* IV, 853–862, 881.

[22] The court records are missing or unpublished for 1695. Gordon recorded that he saw the procession, but says nothing about it: Fedosov, ed., *The Diary of General Patrick Gordon*, vol. V, 341.

[23] *DR* IV, 911–916; Fedosov, ed., *The Diary of General Patrick Gordon*, vol. VI, 2; M. M. Bogoslovskii, *Petr I: Materialy dlia bibliografii*, 5 vols. (Moscow: OGIZ, 1940–8), vol. I, 285.

[24] Bushkovitch, *Peter the Great*, 170–183.

murdered by the musketeers in 1682.[25] Aleksei was seemingly a healthy boy, but Peter did not place all his hopes in him alone. On October 4, 1691, a second son, Aleksandr Petrovich, was born while Peter was in Preobrazhenskoe. He traveled immediately to Moscow, where he went with Tsar Ivan and Patriarch Adrian to give thanks in the Dormition Cathedral and then returned to Preobrazhenskoe. Two weeks later the soldiers again paid their respects, this time in Preobrazhenskoe, received their rewards, and fired a salute. Gordon made the same speech as he did before on the occasion of the birth of Tsarevich Aleksei, with Aleksandr Petrovich explicitly named as heir.[26] The baptism was on November 1, in the Chudov Monastery, the officiating priest being the tsar's spiritual father. The godparents were the cellarer of the Trinity-St. Sergii Monastery and Peter's sister, Tsarevna Natal'ia.[27] For a short time Peter had two potential heirs, but unfortunately Aleksandr died in May 1692.[28] The Swedish resident von Kochen reported at the time that Peter had managed only a little rest and did not want to see anyone. Tsar Ivan went to the funeral.[29]

Largely unnoticed by historians were another series of important events in the Romanov family, namely the birth of Tsar Ivan's daughters Feodosiia, Ekaterina, and Anna in 1690–3 and the death of Tsar Ivan. Feodosiia was born on June 4, 1690 and baptized on June 20 in the church of St. Aleksii of the Chudov Monastery by Tsar Ivan's spiritual father Merkurii. The godparents were Peter himself and Tsarevna Tat'iana.[30] Feodosiia lived only a year, but the next two girls would both play important roles in Russian history, Anna as no less than empress and tsaritsa in 1730–40. Ekaterina was born on October 29, 1691, and baptized on November 8 in the Chudov Monastery, with the tsar's spiritual father (presumably Merkurii) and the same godparents as Feodosiia.[31] For

[25] Ivan Zabelin, *Domashnii byt russkikh tsarei v XVI–XVII stoletiiakh* (Moscow: Kniga, 2000–3), vol. II, 392; A. B. Lobanov-Rostovskii, *Russkaia rodoslovnaia kniga* (St. Petersburg: Izdatel'stvo A. S. Suvorina, 1895), vol. II, 6; N. Iu. Bolotina, "Domashnii byt iunogo tsarevicha Alekseia Petrovicha (po materialam F. 396, Arkhiva Oruzheinoi palaty RGADA)," in *Petrovskoe vremia v litsakh 2013*. Trudy gosudarstvennogo Ermitazha 70 (St. Petersburg: Izdatel'stvo Gosudarstvennogo Ermitazha, 2013), 96–101. Naryshkina had already been part of Tsaritsa Natal'ia's household in 1674–5: Bogoslovskii, *Petr I*, vol. I, 23, 26, 28.

[26] *DR* IV, 610–616; Fedosov, ed., *The Diary of General Patrick Gordon*, vol. V, 97, 99. Gordon again received a reward: Esipov, *Sbornik vypisok*, vol. I, 129.

[27] *DRV* XI, 187–188. It is not clear whether the spiritual father was the official spiritual father of the tsar, Father Merkurii, Ivan's spiritual father, or Peter's personal spiritual father, Father Petr Vasil'evich, at that moment priest of the Savior Church inside the palace: N. D. Izvekov, *Kremlevskie dvortsovye tserkvi i sluzhivshie pri nikh litsa v XVII veke* (Moscow: Pechat' A. I. Snegirevoi, 1906), 111–112.

[28] *DR* IV, 685; Fedosov, ed., *The Diary of General Patrick Gordon*, vol. V, 149.

[29] SR Muscovitica 605, May 20, 1692.

[30] *DRV* XI, 185–187; *DR* IV, 565.

[31] *DRV* XI, 188–189; *DR* IV, 620–623.

Anna Ivanovna the account of events is a bit fuller. She was born on January 28, 1693, and baptized on February 3 in the church of St. Aleksii in the Chudov Monastery. The officiating priest was Patriarch Adrian himself. Her godparents were again Peter himself and Tsarevna Tat'iana Mikhailovna.[32] Congratulations and presents (icons and relics) came to the new father from the patriarch, clergy, and court a few weeks later. Both tsars had a banquet in honor of the occasion.[33] The father of all these baby girls, Tsar Ivan, died on January 29, 1696, in the winter between the two Azov campaigns. Peter, who had been ill the whole previous month, took his part in the funeral the next day, the last great ceremony of the old Russian court ritual. He came and followed his brother in mourning clothes to the cathedral of St. Michael the Archangel in the Kremlin, the burial place of the tsars. The boyars and the courtiers watched over the tomb, as was customary, for forty days, their service to the tsar carefully recorded for a system that was soon to come to an end.[34] Peter was now the sole tsar, and Tsarevich Aleksei was the sole heir, as Tsar Ivan had produced no sons. The future of Ivan's daughters was something no one could foresee in 1696, but the same was true of the tsarevich.

For the next decade or so succession was not an issue, and Peter was absorbed with other things: his victory at Azov in 1696, the trip to Western Europe in 1697–8, and the war with Sweden that broke out in 1700. Insofar as succession was concerned, the only issue was the proper upbringing of his son. In the past, the Russian tsars had appointed both a *diad'ka* from among the boyars, or at least the court elite, and a teacher for reading, writing, arithmetic, and eventually more sophisticated subjects. These appointments had come when the tsars' sons were about five years old. In the case of Tsarevich Aleksei Petrovich, his first teacher was Nikifor Viazemskii. His letters to Peter during the summer of 1696 in decorated Baroque style record the beginning of Aleksei's lessons in reading. The boy moved quickly on to mastering the *Chasoslov* (*Book of Hours*).[35] There is no record of any *diad'ka* for Aleksei Petrovich, and indeed the tsarevich is largely invisible until the summer of 1698. At a distance, he witnessed with his mother the arrival of an Imperial embassy at the end of April.[36] The rebellion of the musketeers of that year soon

32 *DR* IV, 754–759; SR Muscovitica, February 3, 1693 (birth of Anna Ivanovna).

33 *DR* IV, 765–766. 34 *DR* IV, 720–734.

35 N. G. Ustrialov, *Istoriia tsarstvovaniia Petra Velikogo*, 5 vols. (St. Petersburg: Tipografiia Vtorogo otdelenie sobstvennoi E.I.V. Kantseliarii, 1858–63), vol. VI, 297–298; *PiB* 1, 592–593 (July 29, 1696). Viazemskii came from a minor gentry (*deti boiarskie*) family according to the genealogist V. Rummel': "Viazemskie," in *Entsiklopediia Brokgauz-Efron* (St. Petersburg: Semenovskaia tipo litografiia, I. A. Efrona, 1892), vol. 7A, 718.

36 Johannes Georg Korb, *Diarium itineris in Moscoviam* (Vienna: Typis Leopoldi Voigt, 1700), 40. Russian translation: Iogann Georg Korb, *Dnevnik puteshestviia v Moskoviiu*

brought his name, if not his person, into view. In part, this was the result of the attitude of the rebels: they believed that Peter had died abroad (after having been enticed there by the foreigner Lefort) and that they wanted to put on the throne either Sophia or the tsarevich, or some combination of the two. Rumors also spread among the rebels that the boyars wanted to strangle Aleksei Petrovich.[37] The only direct impact of the rebellion on the boy's fate was the plan to send him to the Trinity-St. Sergii Monastery at the height of the rebellion, just before the defeat of the rebels by the army on June 18.[38]

More crucial at the time was Peter's decision to separate from his wife, an issue that had surfaced in June 1697, as well, though not apparently known to the rebels. Patriarch Adrian was strongly opposed to the idea, though he also had other objections to Peter's policies: he was against the tobacco contracts that Peter had made with Russian and English merchants.[39] Soon after the tsar's departure for Europe, Tikhon Streshnev, in Peter's name, had appointed I. I. Naryshkin head of the Workshop of Tsarevna Natal'ia Alekseevna, an office that continued the Tsaritsa's Workshop (*Tsaritsyna Masterskaia Palata*).[40] Its tasks were the supply of the female household, especially with cloth. The change in name implies that Peter was replacing his wife with his sister as the head of the female household in the Kremlin. The tsar had been writing to Streshnev, L. K. Naryshkin, and Evdokiia's spiritual father about the divorce, and his impending return brought the issue to a head.[41] The imperial ambassador Ignaz von Guarient reported that Peter was sending orders to Adrian to send Evdokiia to a convent and that the patriarch had not yet decided whether to obey or not. The Danish resident

(1698 i 1699 gg.), ed. and trans. A. I. Malein (St. Petersburg: A. S. Suvorin, 1906), 43; and see Friedrich Dukmeyer, *Korbs Diarium itineris in Moscoviam und die Quellen die es ergänzen: Beiträge zur moskowitisch-russischen, österreichisch-kaiserlichen und brandenburgisch-preußischen Geschichte aus der Zeit Peters des Großen*, 2 vols. Historische Studien 70, 80 (Berlin: Emil Ebering, 1909–10).

[37] Bogoslovskii, *Petr I*, vol. III, 36, 46, 52, 79, 88–92; V. I. Buganov, ed., *Vosstanie moskovskikh strel'tsov: 1698 god* (Moscow: Nauka, 1980), 126, 245; V. I. Buganov, *Moskovskie vosstanie kontsa XVII veka* (Moscow: Nauka, 1969), 371, 404, 411, 414, 421.

[38] Korb recorded under June 15–17/25–27: "Tzareiwizius ob proximiora in dies rebellionis pericula iter suum paravit ad Droizam" (The tsarevich has prepared his journey to the Trinity on account of the daily nearer dangers of the rebellion), Korb, *Diarium itineris in Moscoviam*, 59; Korb, *Dnevnik puteshestviia v Moskoviiu*, 64.

[39] Bushkovitch, *Peter the Great*, 199–200.

[40] *DR* IV, 1056. The decree on June 20, 1697, specified that Naryshkin was the new head of the office, but the *d'iaki* would remain the same. One of the *d'iaki*, D. Samsonov, had managed the office since 1685 for the tsaritsy: Bogoiavlenskii, *Moskovskii prikaznyi apparat*, 200–201; N. F. Demidova, *Sluzhilaia biurokratiia v Rossii XVII veka; biograficheskii spravochnik* (Moscow: Pamiatniki istoricheskoi mysli, 2011), 497. On the office, see Ivan Zabelin, *Domashnii byt russkogo naroda v XVI i XVII st.*, vol. 3. *Domashnii byt russkikh tsarits v XVI i XVII st.*, 401–403.

[41] *PiB* I, 700; T. N. Streshnev to Peter, April 1698 on Peter's letters of February about Evdokiia.

Butenant wrote the same summer that Evdokiia was popular among the Russians because of her hatred of foreigners, which also made her odious in the mind of the tsar. By the end of June Evdokiia had decided to enter a convent, but wanted to take her son Aleksei with her. At a recent procession, however, the tsarevich himself, only eight years old, had reproached Lev Naryshkin with causing the mistreatment that he and his mother had suffered and threatened him with execution.[42] Peter himself returned to Moscow on August 25, 1698. His main task was to deal with the defeated rebels, but he also had to solve the problem of his wife and son.

Even before ordering the boyars to shave their beards and beginning the interrogation of the rebels, Peter met with his son in the Kremlin two days after his return, but avoided the tsaritsa. There was a further meeting in Preobrazhenskoe of the tsarevich and Tsarevna Natal'ia, Peter's sister, and on September 23, Peter sent Evdokiia to a convent in Suzdal'. When he asked her why she had not obeyed the orders he had sent her from Western Europe, she said that she was only concerned for her son. Peter put the boy into the care of Tsarevna Natal'ia, and there were rumors that he might turn him over to Prince Boris Golitsyn.[43] These rumors proved to be false, but they are the only hint of a *diad'ka* of the traditional sort even being considered.

The tsarevich next appeared in public in the middle of February 1699, for the fireworks and audience of the ambassador of Brandenburg, in Western dress and both times with Tsarevna Natal'ia. A month later, on March 10/20, Peter established the first of Russia's orders, modeled on the European orders of chivalry like the Order of the Holy Spirit in France or the Knights of the Garter in England. This was the Order of St. Andrew the Apostle, and the first recipient was Fyodor Alekseevich Golovin, who was just at that time becoming Peter's right-hand man for diplomacy, warfare, and anything else the tsar could load on him. The insignia of the order, as Korb noted, bore Peter's image on one side and that of Tsarevich Aleksei on the other. In 1699, Palm Sunday fell on April 2, but there was no procession, apparently because Patriarch Adrian was ill. The plan, judging from the records of the court, had been for Tsarevich Aleksei to participate. Fyodor Golovin had ordered clothing and other equipment made for him. Whether Peter himself had planned to participate is not clear.[44] In June, again according to Korb, Aleksei organized prayers for his father on his name day, Sts. Peter and Paul. He was living

[42] Bushkovitch, *Peter the Great*, 200–202.

[43] Korb, *Diarium itineris in Moscoviam*, 74, 82, 83; Korb, *Dnevnik puteshestviia v Moskoviiu*, 80, 89; Bogoslovskii, *Petr I*, III, 48, 59; Bushkovitch, *Peter the Great*, 204–205, 208.

[44] *DR* IV, 1097; *PiB* I, 791; Bolotina, "Domashnii byt iunogo tsarevicha Alekseia Petrovicha," 97–98.

during the summer in the tsars' suburban house at Izmailovo, where Guarient and the imperial embassy encountered them. The Austrians were walking in the woods to avoid the summer heat and took musicians with them. There they met the tsaritsy (Marfa and Praskov'ia), Aleksei Petrovich, and the tsarevny, who heard and enjoyed the music. The same group witnessed the departure of the Habsburg embassy on July 3/13.[45]

Peter now had to decide about the further education and upbringing of his son. This issue arose during Peter's trip to Western Europe, and was partly the result of the good impression that Peter himself made in several of the courts that he visited. While Peter was still abroad, the idea that Peter would send the tsarevich to the West to be educated began to circulate. Electress Sophie of Hannover (1630–1714) recorded the story as early as August 1697, in a letter to her sister. Sophie did not say that Peter was the origin of the story: rather "one says" (*man sagt*) that the tsarevich would come to Berlin for his education.[46] The idea may have come from the agreement that Peter had made with the Elector of Brandenburg, which included a provision to accept Russian students coming to study.[47] Sophie was a princess of considerable sophistication. She had been impressed with Peter on meeting him in Germany: "the tsar is a tall handsome man, very well made in his face and has a great vivacity of spirit, a prompt and accurate repartee, but could have better manners than he does with such a great advantage from nature." Sophie, the granddaughter of James I of England, was an experienced princess and active in the marriage politics (if not in other politics) of the Hannoverian court.[48] The idea did not just circulate in the West. At the end of 1698 Prince Boris Golitsyn told Guarient that Aleksei would be sent to some European court for education. During the spring and summer of 1699 there were rumors in Moscow that he would send the boy abroad with Andrei Vinius or Andrei Matveev, Russia's newly appointed ambassador to the Netherlands, a man of considerable education (he conducted his

[45] Korb, *Diarium itineris in Moscoviam*, 117–118, 122, 141, 143; Korb, *Dnevnik puteshestviia v Moskoviiu*, 130–131, 135, 157–159; Bushkovitch, *Peter the Great*, 218

[46] Eduard Bodemann, ed., *Briefe der Kurfürstin Sophie von Hannover an die Raugräfinnen und Raugrafen zu Pfalz*. Publikationen aus den preußischen Archiven 37 (Leipzig: S. Hirzel, 1888, 163).

[47] Bogoslovskii, *Petr I*, vol. II, 90.

[48] Georg Schnath, *Geschichte Hannovers im Zeitalter der neunten Kur und der englischen Sukzession 1674–1714* (Hildesheim: August Lax Verlagsbuchhandlung, 1978), vol. III, 760–774: Bodemann, *Briefe der Kurfürstin Sophie*, 160–161: "Der Sar ist ein langer schöner Herr, von gesicht recht bien fait, undt hatt eine grosse vivasité d'esprit, la repartie pronte et juste, könte aber wol besser manihrt sein als er ist mit so grosse avantage von der Natur." Later Sophie and the Hannoverian family danced for several hours with Peter and the Russians "auf moscovitisch, welcher viel artiger ist als auf polnisch." Peter also told her that he did not like hunting and preferred navigation.

correspondence with the Dutch government in Latin). These rumors may have been false from the start, but in any case Matveev left with his wife and family but without the heir. Berlin may have been another possibility.[49] None of these schemes came to fruition, but they do demonstrate that Peter's trip to Europe had aroused interest in a Western education for the heir, both among the Russian elite and among the Europeans themselves. Peter's relative sophistication was, in the mind of the Europeans, a guarantee of the Western education of his son. The courts of Vienna and Berlin would continue to pursue the idea of a Western education for Aleksei in the ensuing years, and, as later events would show, the rumors and discussion of Aleksei's Western education would lead to schemes for his marriage in several of the European courts.

Peter, however, chose to keep his son in Russia and find for him teachers from the West. Peter's first choice for his son's mentor was the Saxon general Georg Carl von Carlowitz, but he was killed at the king of Poland's siege of Riga in early 1700. Carlowitz seems to have recommended Martin Neugebauer of Danzig (1670–1758), an unfortunate choice. Neugebauer did not last long and acquired notoriety for his political pamphlets against Peter after he lost the position in 1703. What he contributed to the heir's education is obscure. Most historians believe that Peter gave Menshikov overall charge of the boy around 1700. At the same time, Peter's sister Natal'ia seems to have often had daily care of the boy, as when both of them traveled to Voronezh to witness the launching of the boat *Predestinatsiia*, designed by the tsar himself, in April 1700.[50] The Habsburg resident Otto Pleyer called Menshikov the "obristhofmeister" (presumably, the German equivalent of *diad'ka*) of the tsarevich in April 1702, but how long he had held the position is not clear.[51]

Peter (or perhaps Menshikov) also looked after the boy's living spaces. In these years, his rooms in Preobrazhenskoe were decorated by the painter Mikhail Choglokov with a series of images that depicted the parables of Christ. In churches, this was a relatively new subject, uncommon before the latter part of the seventeenth century. In this case, the newer repertory of sacred images was appropriated for a secular dwelling, evidently for its pedagogical value in Christian faith and morals.[52] The new religious images in the rooms of the tsarevich were some of the

[49] Bushkovitch, *Peter the Great*, 219, 229–231. [50] *PiB* I, 801.

[51] Ustrialov, *Istoriia tsarstvovaniia Petra Velikogo*, vol. IV, pt. 2, 578.

[52] Bolotina, "Domashnii byt iunogo tsarevicha Alekseia Petrovicha," 99–100; T. L. Nikitina, *Russkie tserkovnye stennye rospisi 1670–1680-kh godov* (Moscow: Indrik, 2015), 74–75, 196. Choglokov (mentioned 1678–1723) worked in the Kremlin palace icon studio: I. A. Kochetkov, *Slovar' russkikh ikonopistev XI–XVII vekov* (Moscow: Indrik, 2003), 761–762.

manifestations of what eventually would become part of a European style of court culture. For the time being, however, Peter had let the old Russian court ceremonies fall by the wayside without producing a new series of ceremonies. He took up residence in Preobrazhenskoe, making it practically very difficult to continue the old rituals. One of the few to remain was the blessing of the waters at Epiphany, though Peter did not any longer play a role as his father and grandfather had.[53] Along with the older ceremonies such as the Palm Sunday ritual, new elements like the presentation of poetry for court events and the sermons and oratory for the weddings and anniversaries of the tsar's family and annual celebrations like Russian New Year faded away. Among the remaining ceremonies were the events that involved the participants in his "Most Comic and All-Drunken Council," his companions in drinking bouts and other social events who shared parodic titles and rituals with the tsar. One such was the wedding of F. P. Shanskii, one of his jesters and a participant in these parodic ceremonies, in January 1702. Shanskii married one of the Princesses Shakhovskaia in an elaborate event that included a great banquet with both sexes present and was immortalized by an engraving from the hand of the Dutch artist Adrian Schoonebeck. Tsarevich Aleksei was one of the celebrants, and was prominent in the procession leading up to the wedding itself.[54] The most detailed description of the wedding comes from the Dutch traveler and artist Cornelis de Bruijn, whom Peter shortly afterward asked to paint portraits of his nieces, the daughters of the late Tsar Ivan, and his wife Praskov'ia. There had been portraits of the tsars in the seventeenth century, but the commissioning of portraits of the daughters of the tsar was something new. De Bruijn did as he was asked, and also painted Tsaritsa Praskov'ia. The Dutch artist thought that she was an attractive and pleasant woman, as were her three daughters. Tsarevich Aleksei, he learned, took pleasure in the company of the girls. De Bruijn delivered the portraits before he went on to Persia.[55] Unfortunately the paintings do not seem to have survived.

[53] Cornelis de Bruijn, *Reizen over Moskovie door Persie en Indie* (Amsterdam: Willem en David Goeree, 1711), 23–24; P. P. Barsov and O. M. Bodianskii, eds. and trans., *Puteshestvie cherez Moskoviiu Korneliia de Bruina* (Moscow: Imperatorskoe obshchestvo istorii i drevnostei rossiskikh pri Moskovskom universitete, 1873) (originally *ChOIDR* 1872–3), 41–44.

[54] Ernest A. Zitser, *The Transfigured Kingdom: Sacred Parody and Charismatic Authority at the Court of Peter the Great* (Ithaca, New York and London: Cornell University Press, 2004), 113–115; de Bruijn, *Reizen over Moskovie*, 26–28 ("den Czaersen prins," "de jonge Prins," 28); Barsov and Bodianskii, eds. and trans., *Puteshestvie cherez Moskoviiu Korneliia de Bruina*, 47–53 (tsarevich, 52).

[55] De Bruijn, *Reizen over Moskovie*, 29, 31–33 (31: "de prins Alexey Petrowitz meenigmale by haer [Praskov'ia] komt om eenig vermaek te nemen met de jonge Princessen"); Barsov

Since Peter himself was often away on campaign with the army, Moscow did not really have a court for most of the decade after 1700. The foundation and building of St. Petersburg was another distraction, even if it was not yet formally a capital or the main residence of the tsar. Finally, the newer elements of court ritual from the end of the seventeenth century fell into abeyance with the old because there was simply no one to carry them on. This is a bit of a paradox, since precisely in 1700 Peter began the policy of appointing Ukrainians to the main episcopal offices in Russia, men with a more or less Western education. Peter's Ukrainians, however, were not poets and there was no court for them to edify and entertain. They were not involved with Peter's or the heir's household, as Simeon Polotskii had been. The first was Stefan Iavorskii (1658–1722), then a teacher at the Kiev Academy and head of a local monastery. Stefan so impressed Peter with his sermon on the funeral of the boyar Shein that the tsar appointed him "caretaker" (*mestobliustitel'*) of the patriarchal throne when Patriarch Adrian died late in 1700.[56] Stefan was no other-worldly monk: his orations celebrated all of Peter's victories, praised his achievements, and condemned Mazepa in 1708, but he did not regularly preach for court occasions such as birthdays. Very few of his sermons were published at the time (or later), even as print was becoming a more and more important part of the public display of Peter's monarchy.[57] Aleksei's education may have been "European," but in the absence of an organized court culture he was not at the center of any important events until he was much older.

While Aleksei was growing up and his father was looking for a tutor, the first marriage plans appeared, though not at Peter's initiative. The idea came from Vienna, from the Habsburg court that Peter had visited in the summer of 1698, his last major stop on his trip to Western and Central Europe. There he had met not only the Emperor Leopold I but also his eldest son and heir Joseph and his wife Eleonore-Magdalene and her daughters. The meeting with the empress took place on June 24. It was brief, but Peter met the daughters and was particularly gracious to them.

and Bodianskii, eds. and trans., *Puteshestvie cherez Moskoviiu Korneliia de Bruina*, 54–55, 58–59, 61–62.

[56] Bushkovitch, *Peter the Great*, 221.

[57] F. Ternovskii, "Stefan Iavorskii (Biograficheskii ocherk)," *Trudy Kievskoi dukhovnoi akademii* (1864): (1), 36–70; (3), 237–290; (6), 137–186; [Stefan Iavorskii], "Slovo pred prokliatiem Mazepy," *Trudy Kievskoi dukhovnoi akademii* (1865): (12), 499–512; I. Chistovich, "Neizdannye propovedi Stefana Iavorskogo," *Khristianskoe chtenie* 1 (1867): 259–279, 414–429, 814–837; V. P[evnitskii] "Slova mitropolita Stefana Iavorskogo," *Trudy Kievskoi dukhovnoi akademii* (1874): (7), 72–121; (10), 123–154; (12), 505–520; 1875 (1), 118–128; (3), 631–647; (5), 486–505; (9), 463–492; (10), 124–145; S. I. Nikolaev, "Iavorskii, Stefan," in *Slovar' russkikh pisatelei XVIII veka* (St. Petersburg: Nauka, 2010), vol. III, 456–458.

The meeting with Joseph on June 28 was also not long, it seems, since we know nothing about it other than the location, the Augarten. Peter met the second son, Karl, in July at one of the costumed banquets that formed part of the Viennese court tradition.[58] The available sources have nothing to say about marriage plans in 1698, but they are not very revealing about anything but formal audiences and entertainments.

The Habsburg court in Vienna began to explore the possibility of marrying Archduke Karl to one of the young women in Peter's family in 1701. For many months it was not clear whether the women in question were Peter's half-nieces, Tsar Ivan V's daughters Ekaterina, Anna, and Praskov'ia, whom the Habsburgs knew about from the Guarient mission two years before, or Peter's sister Natal'ia. Peter himself at that point had only the one child, Tsarevich Aleksei, and he too was a subject of discussion. These marriage plans were not, of course the main issues in Russia's relations with the Habsburgs. The subjects of discussion were the relations of both courts to the two unfolding wars, the War of Spanish Succession and the Northern War. For the Habsburgs, the war with France over Spain was a major issue. The last Habsburg king of Spain, Charles II, had left his throne to his nephew Philip of Bourbon, the grandson of Louis XIV. Emperor Leopold had his own candidate, his second son Karl, and both England and Holland, fearful of French hegemony in Europe and abroad, joined him in war with France. Russia explored possible alliances with both France and Austria, while the Austrians, suspicious of both Sweden and Russia and wary about the fate of Poland, tried to keep a balance.[59] Why anyone in the court at Vienna at this historic moment would want a Russian marriage of any sort is not clear. The war in the north was an unwelcome distraction for the Habsburgs. It is also not clear who in the Habsburg government was behind the schemes. At that moment the most important ministers were Count Ferdinand Bonaventura Harrach and Count Dominik Andreas Kaunitz, after 1696 the Imperial Vice Chancellor. Kaunitz eventually came into the discussions, while Harrach did not. The most important figure in the marriage plan seems to have been Empress Eleonore.[60] Whoever was behind the plan, the Austrian marriage proposal was the first to the Romanov dynasty in nearly a century.

[58] Bogoslovskii, *Petr I*, vol. II, 479–480, 491, 515.

[59] See Herman Brulin, "Österrike och det stora nordiske kriget före Karl XII:s infall i Sachsen (1700–1706)," *Historisk tidskrift* 29 (1909): 141–166, 197–242; and Jacek Burdowicz-Nowicki, *Piotr I, August II, i Rzeczpospolita 1697–1706* (Kraków: Arcana, 2010), esp. 222–234.

[60] Empress Eleonore played a major role in the marriage of her and Leopold's eldest son Joseph I to Wilhelmine Amalie of Braunschweig-Lüneburg: Schnath, *Geschichte Hannovers*, vol. III, 202–230.

The 1701 plans were for Peter's sister and daughters and not likely to involve succession, and Peter had only the one son, apparently healthy, but the future was unknown. Further, the idea appeared very quickly to bring Tsarevich Aleksei to Vienna for his education. Education could lead in many directions, and Emperor Leopold had several daughters only a bit older than the tsarevich.

It was the Russian emissary, Prince Petr Alekseevich Golitsyn (1660–1722), the younger brother of Prince Boris Golitsyn, who reported the Austrian feelers with evident surprise. Prince Petr Golitsyn had received his instructions in January 1701, and they contained nothing about any marriage plans for the heir or Peter's daughters. He was to go to Vienna not as an ambassador but as a "volunteer" to follow the Austrian army of Prince Eugene of Savoy fighting the French in Italy, the opening battles of the yet undeclared War of the Spanish Succession.[61] Golitsyn was not to announce himself as an ambassador. He was, however, to find out the "secret affairs" of the Habsburg court and to make contact with the relevant minister of state and tell him that he wished to meet the emperor with a message from the tsar. At this secret meeting he was to convey the tsar's greetings and inquire about the emperor's health. Then he was to reveal his business. In December 1700, the Habsburg envoy to the king of Poland had passed a request to the Russian resident in Warsaw for help to the emperor in the coming war against France over the Spanish succession. Peter's response to the Austrian request was to assure Leopold of his friendship and ask for his mediation in the war with Sweden.[62] Written shortly after the Russian defeat at Narva, Peter's request is understandable. Golitsyn arrived in Vienna in May and soon reported that he had acquired an informant at the court, Peter Linxweiler, a former servant of Boris Sheremetev, presumably from the latter's trip to Italy in 1698.[63]

Over the summer of 1701 it became clear that the discussions with Vienna about mediation in the war with Sweden would go nowhere, but Golitsyn did make contact with the Jesuit father Friedrich von Lüdingshausen Wolff, a very influential figure at the Viennese court.[64]

[61] The death of Carlos II of Spain in November 1700, led to the war. Though Emperor Leopold did not formally declare war until May 1702, the Austrian forces began to occupy the formally Spanish territory of Milan early in 1701: Jean Bérenger, *Léopold Ier (1640–1705): Fondateur de la puissance autrichienne* (Paris: Presses universitaires de France, 2004), 422; Linda Frey and Marsha Frey, *A Question of Empire: Leopold I and the War of the Spanish Succession 1701–1705* (Boulder, Colorado: East European Monographs, 1983).

[62] RGADA, f. 32, d. 3, 1701, ll. 1–5, January 1701, instructions to Golitsyn; *PiB* I, 432–433.

[63] RGADA, f. 32, d. 4, 1701, ll. 1–2, 7. Golitsyn to F. A. Golovin, May 9 and 16, 1701.

[64] RGADA, f. 32, d. 4, 1701, ll. 14–15ob., 24–24ob., 31–31ob., Golitsyn to F. A. Golovin, June 7, 21, and 28, 1701. Linxweiler is identified on l. 31 ob.

Father Wolff, who came from Dünaburg in the Polish part of Livonia, spent much of his youth at the Polish court and had met both Sheremetev and Peter himself on their ways through Vienna and preached to them in some sort of Slavic language.[65] In July, it was father Wolff who informed Golitsyn that Peter would have to make peace with Charles XII on his own, but the emperor was willing to help him in other things. In an encoded appendix to this report, Golitsyn added that father Wolff also had a message from Empress Eleonore: "that his tsarish majesty should give from his court a spouse for the archduke, the emperor's son, but which [woman] he did not say."[66] The archduke must have been Karl, since his elder brother Joseph was already married. Golitsyn did not know how to answer these suggestions, and asked for instructions. Empress Eleonore also proposed a few months later that the tsarevich be sent to Vienna for education (*nauchenie*).[67] The Russian emissary finally got an order from Golovin to discuss the marriage issue with the "relevant person" (*komu na[d]lezhit*), and that was the Empress. This time she proposed to him at an audience to send someone to Russia to discuss it, but she also wanted a portrait (*persona*) as was the custom in Europe.[68] A month later Golitsyn reported again, in the midst of his report on the discussion of international politics with Count von Kaunitz, that Eleonore again asked for the portraits.[69] These communications were all with Fyodor Golovin, the head of Peter's foreign policy, not with Peter directly. When the tsar himself sent further instructions to Prince Golitsyn at the end of the year, he merely ordered him to follow the army of Prince Eugene into Italy and to observe its movements and methods.[70] There was nothing about the marriage projects or sending the tsarevich to Vienna.

Moscow, presumably Golovin, did send a letter to father Wolff along with those to Emperor Leopold and Golitsyn, but it did not arrive. In February 1702, the prince reported that the empress was asking again for portraits of the Romanov women. He also conveyed another conversation

[65] Bogoslovskii, *Petr I*, vol. II, 493–495. On Wolff, see Joachim Köhler, "Lüdingshausen genannt Wolff, *Friedrich von*," *Neue Deutsche Biographie*, vol. 15, 457–459, www.deutsche-biographie.de/sfz54923.html#ndbcontent.

[66] "чтобы царское величество поволил из двора своего дать в супругу за сына цесарского Арцыдука, а о которой, того мне не сказал." RGADA, f. 32, d. 4, 1701, ll. 37–38, July 9, 1701, Golitsyn to Golovin.

[67] RGADA, f. 32, d. 4, 1701, ll. 82–85, September 5, 1701, Golitsyn to Golovin.

[68] RGADA, f. 32, d. 4, 1701, ll. 139–141, November 11, 1701, Golitsyn to Golovin.

[69] RGADA, f. 32, d. 4, 1701, ll. 165–166ob., December 13, 1701, Golitsyn to Golovin.

[70] RGADA, f. 32, d. 3, 1701, ll. 98–100ob., Peter to Golitsyn, Moscow, November 24, 1701; *PiB* I, 476, Peter to Leopold, November 27, 1701, asking permission for Golitsyn to accompany the army in Italy. Golitsyn was not happy about the assignment, preferring to stay in Vienna: *PiB* I, 882.

with Kaunitz, repeating the request to send the tsarevich to Vienna for education. Kaunitz conveyed the emperor's regret that he had heard that Peter might send his son to Prussia or other places and asked for Golitsyn's answer to all this. Golitsyn replied that he could not answer without instructions, and inquired what would the position of the tsarevich be in that case? He noted that the emperor wanted ambassadors to stand at table in the presence of the archduke: would that be the case with the tsarevich? (In other words, would there be equivalency in rank.) The answer from Kaunitz was that Leopold would treat him as a son.[71]

The emperor's confessor urged Golitsyn to get the portraits sent. It was, the prince thought, only the confessor and the Papal nuncio Gianantonio Davia who wanted the marriage.[72] Golitsyn submitted memoranda to the Austrian court showing willingness to consider the proposals.[73] After the Easter season had passed, the issue came up again, and this time Golitsyn had more information: the archduke was not small in stature, and the most appropriate bride for him would be the tsar's sister Natal'ia Alekseevna. It was she who was continuously discussed.[74] The nieces were not the object of interest in Vienna. As Natal'ia was twenty-nine in 1702 and the Archduke Karl only seventeen, Golitsyn's remark about Karl's height is understandable.

Over the summer all these plans languished, and in the autumn Peter's special envoy Johan Reinhold von Patkul was in Vienna to take over the whole range of business the tsar had with Emperor Leopold and his ministers.[75] Patkul had been one of the leaders of the Livonian opposition to the Swedish crown and an organizer of the coalition of Poland, Russia, and Denmark against it. He had just entered Russian service, serving

[71] RGADA, f. 32, d. 3, 1702, ll. 11–12ob., January 16, 1702, Golitsyn to Golovin; ll. 44–47ob., February 10, 1702, Golitsyn to Golovin; ll. 54–60, February 8, 1702, Golitsyn to Golovin; Solov'ev, *Istoriia Rossii s drevneishikh vremen*, vol. VIII, 38.

[72] RGADA, f. 32, d. 3, 1702, ll. 61–64ob., February 16, 1702, Golitsyn to Golovin. Golitsyn also heard that the king of Sweden was pressing his family's case and promising the empress to make her brother Elector Johann Wilhelm von der Pfalz the king of Poland in return, and that she was inclined to take up the offer. This must have been a rumor, as it has left no trace in Austrian records: see Brulin, "Österrike och det stora nordiske kriget."

[73] Brulin, "Österrike och det stora nordiske kriget," 225, quoting Golitsyn's memoranda from January 20 and March 26, 1702. The Papal nuncio in Warsaw, Francesco Pignatelli, archbishop of Taranto, reported that the Habsburg emissary to Russia, Count von Schirendorf, told him of the scheme to marry Aleksei to one of the archduchesses: Augustin Theiner, ed., *Monuments historiques relatifs aux règnes d'Alexis Michaélowitch, Féodor III, et Pierre le Grand, czars de Russie, extraits des Archives du Vatican et de Naples* (Rome: Imprimerie du Vatican, 1859), 389 (July 26, 1702). Pignatelli spoke to him in Poland, and it is not clear that Schirendorff reached Moscow.

[74] RGADA, f. 32, d. 3, 1702, ll. 240–242ob., June 1, 1702, Golitsyn to Golovin.

[75] Yella Erdmann, *Der livländische Staatsmann Johann Reinhold von Patkul* (Berlin: Haude & Spener, 1970), 132–148.

Peter faithfully until his imprisonment in Saxony by August II in December 1705, and his subsequent capture and execution by the Swedes in 1707. In the autumn of 1702, his task was to convince the Habsburg emperor to be helpful to Peter's cause and to the king of Poland, but only in the modest ways that the war with France permitted. The discussions with Kaunitz took up much of late September, and near the end Patkul asked Golitsyn about the marriage question, since Kaunitz had told him that the idea had not come from Vienna, that it was a Russian proposal. As Golitsyn told Patkul, this was a lie, and he clarified that Empress Eleonore, privy counselor "Skalvinii,"[76] and the emperor's confessor had proposed it to him. The marriage plan and the tsarevich came up in the discussions on November 16. Patkul reported that Kaunitz said a great deal about both, but provided no details.[77] After that moment, both the marriage project and the proposal to educate the tsarevich in Vienna disappeared from the record. Whatever the intentions of Empress Eleonore and her circle, the project to establish closer family ties between the Habsburgs and Romanovs had come to nothing, and does not seem to have held any priority with Leopold's ministers. Presumably it was incompatible with Habsburg policy, concerned as it was with the war with France and the complications caused by the Northern War on its own northern border. That the empress was the prime mover, however, does not mean that the plan was trivial. Married to Leopold in 1676, she was his third wife and the mother of his two sons. Born in 1655, Eleonore initially stayed away from public affairs but, after the 1690s, as a mature woman she was increasingly involved in political affairs.[78] There is no evidence that Peter took either of the Austrian plans seriously.[79] He did not mention them in his instructions to Golitsyn, and Patkul spent no time on them, nor were they discussed in his surviving letters to Leopold. The importance of the episode was that the Russians learned that one of the principal courts in Europe was interested in a Russian bride for the son of the emperor (as second son, not the heir apparent) and in pursuing close contact with Peter's heir.[80] This could

[76] Presumably Hieronymus Scalvinoni: Max Braubach, *Prinz Eugen von Savoyen* (Munich: R. Oldenbourg, 1963), vol. 1, 291.

[77] RGADA, f. 32, d. 13, 1702, ll. 44–70, esp. 65–65ob. and 69ob., Patkul's report on his discussions in Vienna, partially published in Ustrialov, *Istoriia tsarstvovaniia Petra Velikogo*, vol. VI, pt. 2, 258–266; Solov'ev, *Istoriia Rossii s drevneishikh vremen*, vol. VIII, 40–41.

[78] Braubach, *Prinz Eugen*, vol. I, 286–293; Bérenger, *Léopold Ier*, 248–249.

[79] The last letter of Golitsyn to mention the plans suggests that Golovin was annoyed that Golitsyn had pursued them to the extent that he did: RGADA, f. 32, d. 3, 1702, ll. 403–403ob., October 17, 1702, Golitsyn to Golovin.

[80] Vienna was not alone in trying to get Aleksei to be educated. In 1705, King Frederick of Prussia proposed to receive Peter's son for education in Berlin: Erich Hassinger,

not have been expected. The other important feature of the episode lay in preparing the network of contacts for the later negotiations about the marriage of Tsarevich Aleksei to Charlotte Christine of Braunschweig-Wolfenbüttel. The most important of these contacts was Johann Christoph von Urbich, then the ambassador of Denmark to Vienna, on whom Patkul relied for his contact with Kaunitz.[81]

Aleksei's Upbringing

While the Habsburg court in Vienna debated the future of the tsar's family, Peter began to take Aleksei on his journeys through Russia. Aleksei and Neugebauer went with the tsar to Archangel in 1702, where the tutor quarreled with some of the members of Peter's suite, an incident that ultimately led to his dismissal.[82] That autumn the tsar had his first important success over the Swedes, the capture of the fortress of Nöteborg on the Neva River. Judging from Menshikov's correspondence with the Arsen'ev sisters Dar'ia and Varvara, tsarevich Aleksei accompanied his father on the campaign, along with his teacher Viazemskii, though he got no closer to the action than Novgorod. Menshikov made sure to tell the ladies that both the tsar and the tsarevich were in good health, since the Arsen'evs were part of Tsarevna Natal'ia's household.[83] After renaming the fort Schlüsselburg and naming Menshikov as its governor, Peter returned to Moscow. When he stopped to celebrate at Chashnikovo, L. K. Naryshkin's estate, the tsarevich joined his father with the officers and the ambassadors of Prussia and Holland.[84] Tsarevich Aleksei continued to travel around the country with his father. In April 1703, he wrote a brief greeting to the Arsen'ev sisters from Schlüsselburg, announcing "I am alive" (*Ia zhiv*).[85] Again the heir was following his father, for that summer Peter took the last Swedish positions on the Neva and laid the foundations of St. Petersburg. Aleksei was still in St. Petersburg in August.[86] The next year he took the boy along to the capture of Narva in August, after which Aleksei returned to Moscow and participated in the

Brandenburg-Preußen, Rußland und Schweden 1700–1713 (Munich: Isar Verlag, 1953), 164.

[81] Erdmann, *Der livländische Staatsmann Johann Reinhold von Patkul*, 117, 133.

[82] Bushkovitch, *Peter the Great*, 231.

[83] G. V. Esipov, "Zhizneopisanie kniazia A. D. Menshikova po novootkrytym bumagam," *Russkii arkhiv* 13, 7 (1875): 238.

[84] Bushkovitch, *Peter the Great*, 233.

[85] *Pis'ma russkikh gosudarei i drugikh osob tsarskogo semeistva*, 4 vols. (Moscow: n.p., 1862), vol. III, 3.

[86] N. Murzakevich, ed., *Pis'ma tsarevicha Alekseia Petrovicha* (Odessa: n.p., 1849), 1; *PiB* 2, 610.

triumphal entrance to the capital celebrating the victory.[87] His earlier letter to the two Arsen'ev ladies suggests that Aleksei's permanent residence was still with Tsarevna Natal'ia, for they had been part of her household since 1686. Peter trusted them with other great responsibilities: from 1704 they were in charge of Marta Skavronskaia, the future wife of Peter as Ekaterina Alekseevna.[88] The Arsen'evs were close to Menshikov as well, and Dar'ia eventually married him in 1706 in Kiev.[89] In 1705–6, Tsarevich Aleksei's letters to his father, all of them formal inquiries about his health, came from Preobrazhenskoe, where Tsarevna Natal'ia spent her time.[90] Aleksei thus spent his formative years not only in the household of the tsarevna but with Menshikov, the Arsen'ev sisters, and his father's mistress and future wife. There is no evidence about the relationship between Aleksei and Ekaterina in these years, in spite of the legend that Aleksei had the role of godfather at the baptism of Marta/Ekaterina into the Orthodox faith.[91]

[87] Svetlana Korzun, *Heinrich von Huyssen (1666–1739): Prinzenerzieher, Diplomat und Publizist in den Diensten Zar Peters I., des Großen*. Jablonianа 3: Quellen und Forschungen zur europäischen Kulturgeschichte der Frühen Neuzeit (Wiesbaden: Harrassowitz, 2013), 37–38.

[88] Much of Ekaterina's early life is obscure, but she was brought up in the household of the Livonian pastor Johann Ernst Glück (1654–1705), the translator of the Bible into Latvian. Glück and his family were captured by the Russian army after the fall of the fortress of Marienburg near the Russian border in 1702. They were brought to Moscow, where he taught, including briefly Tsarevich Aleksei in 1703. Ekaterina came into Peter's life sometime around 1704 at the final separation from his previous mistress Anna Mons: Helmut Glück and Ineta Polanska, *Johann Ernst Glück (1654–1705): Pastor, Philologe, Volksaufklärer im Baltikum und in Russland* (Wiesbaden: Harrassowitz, 2005), 57–63, 72–83, 88–89; V. A. Kovrigina, *Nemetskaia sloboda Moskvy i ee zhiteli v kontse XVII–pervoi polovine XVIII veka* (Moscow: Arkheograficheskii tsentr, 1998), 313–332; S. A. Belokurov and A. N. Zertsalov, eds., "O nemetskikh shkolakh v Moskve v pervoi chetverti XVIII v. (1701–1715 gg.): Dokumenty moskovskikh arkhivov," *ChIODR* I (1907): i–xli, 1–244; Bushkovitch, *Peter the Great*, 238.

[89] On August 18: Esipov, "Zhizneopisanie kniazia A. D. Menshikova," 237, 241–247.

[90] Murzakevich, ed., *Pis'ma tsarevicha Alekseia Petrovicha*, 2–7.

[91] This legend has no foundation in fact. Both Ustrialov and Solov'ev reported it as a fact, but both historians had as their only source the memoirs of Alexander Gordon, a Scottish mercenary soldier and relative of Patrick Gordon, but Alexander Gordon was a prisoner of war in Sweden for the years in question, 1700–8. Later historians, B. A. Uspenskii, Hughes, Zitser, and even Kurukin, report the story as fact, claiming the baptism must have taken place around 1706. Alexander Gordon, *History of Peter the Great* (Aberdeen: F. Douglass and W. Murray, 1755), vol. I, x–xi; vol. II, 258; Ustrialov, *Istoriia tsarstvovaniia Petra Velikogo*, vol. IV, pt. 1, 141; Solov'ev, *Istoriia Rossii s drevneishikh vremen*, vol. VIII, 370–371: B. A. Uspenskii, "Historia sub specie semioticae," in *Izbrannye trudy*, 2nd ed. (Moscow: Gnozis, 1996), vol. II, 71–82 (originally 1976); Hughes, *Russia in the Age of Peter the Great*, 397, 450–451; Zitser, *The Transfigured Kingdom*, 118; I. V. Kurukin, *Ekaterina I*(Moscow: Molodaia gvardiia, 2016), 24–25. Yet the event must have taken place before September 1705, since Peter received a letter from her as Ekaterina in that month: *PiB* III, 954. At that point the tsarevich was only fifteen years old, young for a godfather. Only Gary Marker correctly calls the story "undocumented": Gary Marker,

Neugebauer's behavior and Menshikov's support of the teacher's opponents had brought his employment to an end. The replacement was at first the Livonian in Peter's service, Johann Reinhold von Patkul, but his diplomatic and political engagement meant that he had no time for pedagogy, and Peter turned to the Westphalian Heinrich von Huyssen (1666–1719), a man with a degree in law and some experience of travel and service to princes. He was also one of the correspondents of the philosopher and mathematician Gottfried Wilhelm Leibniz, who was the librarian to the Elector of Hannover. Leibniz wrote to him in Moscow looking for information about Russia and sent him political news. Huyssen produced an entire plan for the education of the heir when he took the position in November 1703. Huyssen wanted Aleksei to be brought up fearing the Lord, but, since his teacher was not Orthodox, he left religion to the Russian clergy and confined himself to inculcating virtue in general. He also wanted him to read the Bible and learn French, geography, and history. After two years of these basic subjects, he was to learn the details of statecraft and warfare.[92] This was a full European education plan.

Huyssen's evaluation of the tsarevich in his first letter to Leibniz was positive: "He is a prince who lacks neither wit nor liveliness. He has ambition moderated by reason, solid judgment, a great desire to strive, and to do everything that one tells him is proper for a great prince. He has a docile and tractable character, shows that he wishes to repair by serious application what was neglected in his education in the past. I note in him a great inclination for piety, justice, rectitude, and integrity of behavior. He loves mathematics, foreign languages and demonstrates a great desire to see foreign countries. He wants to learn French and High German well. He has begun dancing, the use of arms, and military exercises, which he likes very much." Peter had allowed him to dispense with some of the Orthodox fasts as possibly bad for his health, but the tsarevich insisted on observing them "par un movement de devotion."[93] At the age of thirteen, Tsarevich Aleksei made a good impression.

Imperial Saint: The Cult of St. Catherine and the Dawn of Female Rule in Russia (DeKalb, Illinois: Northern Illinois University Press, 2007), 4.

92 W. Guerrier, *Leibniz in seinen Beziehungen zu Rußland und Peter dem Großen* (St. Petersburg and Leipzig: Kaiserliche Akademie der Wissenschaften, 1873), 51–56; Gottfried Wilhem Leibniz, *Sämtliche Schriften und Briefe*. Series I. Allgemeiner, Politischer und Historischer Briefwechsel, 25 vols. (Berlin: Brandenburgische Akademie der Wissenschaften; Göttingen: Akademie der Wissenschaften zu Göttingen, 2011), vol. 22, 653–654; Huyssen's proposed curriculum is in J. H. von L[ohenstein], *Des grossen Herrens Czaars und Gross-Fürsten von Moscau Petri Alexiewitz ... Leben und Thaten* (Frankfurt and Leipzig: Johann Leonhard Buggeln, 1710), vol. 1, 56–62; Korzun, *Heinrich von Huyssen*, 34–36; and *PiB* 2, 527.

93 Leibniz, *Sämtliche Schriften und Briefe*, vol. 23, 7–9.

Exposure to the public, or at least the elite, did not enhance the heir's reputation. In 1699, Korb had been full of praise of the boy's appearance and demeanor, but by 1705 the Danish envoy Georg Grund said that "he was not so brought up that his subjects have any respect for him."[94] During the next year Aleksei remained in Moscow while Peter was with the army in Poland. Pleyer reported that the heir not only did not accompany his father to the army but also had no role in government, and nor was he learning any other sciences.[95] Huyssen was worried about the heir's education by 1704, and had more cause to worry when Peter sent him off to Vienna early in 1705. After his early optimism had passed, Huyssen was concerned that the boy did not seem yet to understand what he needed to know as heir to the throne, both in demeanor and in concrete knowledge.[96] Huyssen remained away for the next three years.

A decisive change took place in the role of Tsarevich Aleksei in 1707, as he reached the age of seventeen. He was now the object of intrigues by those in the elite and the country who were discontented with Peter's reforms. Pleyer wrote back to Vienna that a "secret party" had formed, which was in favor of the heir and opposed to the growing influence of Menshikov.[97] At the same time, Peter began to bring him into public view and put him to work. He called him to the Russian military headquarters at Żółkiew in Poland, where he participated at the audience for the Polish ambassadors in February 1707. This reception seems to have been the first time he took part in such occasions. From there he went back to Smolensk with orders to collect grain for the army, remaining there all summer.[98] Then his letters to his father suddenly took on real content, as he reported the collection of grain, hay, and recruits with details and numbers. He received orders not only from the tsar but also from various officials and commanders in the army, hastening to Minsk at the end of September to meet his father.[99] The tsar then put his son in charge of fortification works in Moscow. He was to oversee the preparations of the governor, Prince M. P. Gagarin, and attend meetings of the Privy Chancery. This was not an artificial assignment, since in the winter of 1707–8 the intentions of Charles XII were unknown, but they were threatening, since he was moving east through Poland.[100] Aleksei stayed

94 Bushkovitch, *Peter the Great*, 248.
95 Pleyer, July 5/15, 1706, in Ustrialov, *Istoriia tsarstvovaniia Petra Velikogo*, vol. IV, pt. 2, 656.
96 *PiB* 3, 364–365; Korzun, *Heinrich von Huyssen*, 38–39.
97 Bushkovitch, *Peter the Great*, 256, following Haus-, Hof- und Staatsarchiv, Russland I, January 27, 1707 in cipher.
98 *PiB* 5, 14, 383, 473–474, 655–656.
99 *PiB* 5, 726–727; Murzakevich, ed., *Pis'ma tsarevicha Alekseia Petrovicha*, 7–18; *Pis'ma russkikh gosudarei*, vol. III, 5.
100 Bushkovitch, *Peter the Great*, 256, 267–268.

on in Moscow, living mostly at Preobrazhenskoe, for the next few years, looking after the fortifications and rounding up recruits for the army and sending them on to his father and the other commanders. As Peter moved with the army (and made occasional quick trips to St. Petersburg), his son kept up the reports. He also sent on news of the progress and defeat of the rebellion among the Don Cossacks in 1708. He seems to have received regular dispatches from Prince V. V. Dolgorukii, the commander of the tsar's troops against the rebels, which he sent on to Peter. Huyssen returned to Moscow in October 1708, and took up his duties as teacher once more. In the interval Nikifor Viazemskii had taken over again, reporting to the tsar that Aleksei had made good progress in German, history, and geography. French and arithmetic remained for the future.[101] Aleksei remained in Preobrazhenskoe, constantly reporting on his tasks and receiving news of the war, until January 1709, when he went south to the Ukraine to join his father.[102] He brought with him 4,500 new soldiers for the army, and then returned to Moscow in June.[103] Clearly Peter did not want him near the army for the coming decisive battles with the Swedes. Aleksei received the news of the victory at Poltava right away, and participated in the victory parade in Moscow later that year. He was now old enough and, it seemed, mature enough for marriage. That issue had already been under discussion for several years.

Charlotte of Braunschweig-Wolfenbüttel

As Aleksei grew and learned to work in his father's new administration and army, Russia's diplomats were looking for a bride for him. The first approach came in 1706, from a rather unexpected quarter. Duke Friedrich Wilhelm of Mecklenburg-Schwerin (reigned 1692–1713) was restive under the hegemony of Sweden, whose Pomeranian possessions bordered on his own. Looking for potential allies, he turned to the king of Denmark, who was still smarting from his defeat at the hands of Charles XII in 1700. The king was friendly but unwilling to challenge the seemingly invincible king of Sweden. While Mecklenburg's envoy was in Denmark, he met the Russian ambassador Andrei Petrovich Izmailov in February 1706, who suggested to him that his master might think of an alliance with Russia. Peter, Izmailov claimed, wanted to imitate the king of France in the east, and reward any ruler who broke with Sweden. The Mecklenburg ambassador's report caused much discussion at Schwerin.

101 *PiB* 7, 250; 8, 133; Korzun, *Heinrich von Huyssen*, 39.
102 Murzakevich, ed., *Pis'ma tsarevicha Alekseia Petrovicha*, 19–55; *Pis'ma russkikh gosudarei*, vol. III, 8–20; Bushkovitch, *Peter the Great*, 280–284.
103 Murzakevich, ed., *Pis'ma tsarevicha Alekseia Petrovicha*, 55–59.

The idea of an alliance was much too dangerous (Mecklenburg had no army), but a commercial agreement might be useful. Duke Friedrich Wilhelm had a sister, however, and suggested a possible marriage between her and the tsarevich. Izmailov was interested. He said that the tsar was interested in finding a wife for his son among the German princesses, and that the Mecklenburgers should not worry that the young duchess would have to change her religion. The tsar had already decreed free exercise of religion for all Christians. Again the Mecklenburg ministers were afraid of the Swedish reaction, and the matter went no farther. Izmailov did not report the discussion to his superiors.[104]

Thus the Mecklenburg plan went nowhere, but greater things were afoot. At the same time Huyssen, now Russia's representative in Vienna, was looking for a bride as well. Vienna was a good place to start. It was the center of German politics as well as those of the rest of central Europe. In the last years before Emperor Leopold's death, the "young court" of his son and heir Joseph had already come to power, determined to prosecute the war against France with more vigor than the emperor's advisors had demonstrated. They counted heavily on Prince Eugene of Savoy, the Empire's most successful general.[105] Leopold's death on May 5, 1705 brought greater power to Prince Eugene, as well as to other imperial favorites such as Prince Karl Theodor Otto zu Salm and Count Johann Wenzel Wratislaw von Mitrowitz.[106] Most importantly, the victories of Prince Eugene and the Duke of Marlborough at Blenheim/Hochstädt (1704) and Marlborough's at Ramillies (1706) meant that the initially critical position of the Habsburgs, beset by France and the rebellion of Ferenc Rákóczi in Hungary, had stabilized for the better. Only in Spain were the Habsburg fortunes unfavorable. The Spanish elite and people favored the Bourbon king, Philip V, and inflicted a serious defeat on the partisans of Emperor Joseph's brother Karl at Almansa (1707). In the midst of these momentous events, the Northern War was a distraction for Vienna and its allies. Their main concern was to prevent Sweden from playing its hitherto traditional role as the ally of France. Thus the Habsburgs were mildly favorable to Peter, but most of all wanted to keep out of the northern conflict by all means necessary, as they showed

[104] Mediger, *Mecklenburg, Rußland und England-Hannover*, vol. I, 23–27. Izmailov had been a *komnatnyi stol'nik* of Tsar Ivan Alekseevich and was one of the men sent to Italy in 1697 to learn navigation. (His conversations with the Mecklenburg ambassador were in Italian.) He had been Peter's ambassador in Copenhagen since 1701: *PiB* 1, 133, 332, 467–468, 610. RGADA, F. 53, 1706, d. 2, l. 57ob. (March 12, 1706, Izmailov to F. A. Golovin). On Izmailov as later Russian ambassador in Berlin, see Helge Almquist, "Ivan Petrovitj Izmajlov, rysk diplomat i Preussen och krigsfånge i Sverige (1706–1710)," *Karolinska Förbundets Årsbok* (1937): 98–130.

[105] Berenger, *Léopold Ier*, 440–445. [106] Braubach, *Prinz Eugen*, vol. II, 128–151.

after the surrender of Augustus II at Altranstädt in October 1706.[107] Peter in turn was making overtures to Joseph about an alliance.[108] These overtures went nowhere, but the project for the marriage of the tsarevich was a success, though not in Vienna.

Vladimir Guerrier asserted, citing an unpublished letter, that it was Huyssen and Baron von Urbich who eventually decided on the Wolfenbüttel candidacy early in 1707.[109] Peter had sent Huyssen to Vienna right after the death of Emperor Leopold in 1705, bringing congratulations to his son and successor Joseph. There is no clear evidence that Huyssen was to look for a bride for Aleksei in the communications of that moment.[110] The only available record of his activity for the next year and a half involved his replies to Neugebauer's pamphlets and the recruitment of officers for Peter's army. He was also to explore an alliance of Russia with the anti-French coalition, the Empire, England and Holland.[111] Peter's letters to him through 1707 also say nothing of any marriage plans, they are all about international politics.[112] Huyssen, however, encountered Urbich sometime during that period and came to work with him. It was from this collaboration that the marriage plan arose.

Baron Johann Christoph von Urbich (1653–1715) was the son of an official in Thuringia and had spent the years 1691 to 1703 in the service of the kings of Denmark, mainly as ambassador in Vienna. He had also been a correspondent of Leibniz before 1689, and may have had other contacts with the court in Hannover. Leibniz wrote again to Urbich only in the autumn of 1705, and received a reply full of political information from

[107] Joseph and his government also had to fend off the demands placed on him by Charles XII in 1706–7: Charles W. Ingrao, *In Quest and Crisis: Emperor Joseph I and the Habsburg Monarchy* (West Lafayette, Indiana: Purdue University Press, 1979), 5–59.

[108] Mediger *Mecklenburg, Rußland und England-Hannover*, vol. I, 74–79. Peter was also trying out Prince Eugene for the Polish throne, as well as Ferenc Rákóczi. Peter had feelers out to Rákóczi until his surrender in 1711: Wittram, *Peter I Czar und Kaiser*, vol. I, 285.

[109] [Waldemar Guerrier], *Die Kronprinzessin Charlotte von Rußland* (Bonn: Max Cohen & Sohn, 1875), 2–6, quoting a conversation of Urbich and Huyssen on January 28, 1707. Guerrier stated that he found the relevant material for his book on Charlotte while working in the Wolfenbüttel archive on Leibniz.

[110] *PiB* 3, 363–364 (Peter to Joseph I, June 18, 1705). Huyssen remained in contact with Leibniz, exchanging both scholarly and political news, but nothing about a marriage for Aleksei: Leibniz, *Sämtliche Schriften und Briefe*, vol. 24, 724, 752–753, 799; vol. 25, 406–410.

[111] Korzun, *Heinrich von Huyssen*, 43–55, 156–163; *PiB* IV, pt. 1, 354–355; *PiB* IV, pt. 2, 1023–1024 (Instructions to – apparently – Huyssen, August 19, 1706). On December 26, 1706, Huyssen made a formal proposal of alliance to Vienna: Hassinger, *Brandenburg-Preussen*, 202, note 82.

[112] *PiB* V, 103, 127–130, 136–144, 157–163. The same is true of Huyssen's letters in early 1707: *PiB* V, 520, 551–556 [= RGADA, f. 32, op. 1, d. 4, 1707, ll. 83–92].

Vienna.[113] Urbich was no longer serving the king of Denmark, but he still was an important diplomat. He had been in regular correspondence on political matters with Duke Anton Ulrich of Braunschweig-Wolfenbüttel since 1696.[114] Their contacts continued through the negotiation for the marriage of Anton Ulrich's oldest granddaughter, Elisabeth Christine, to Archduke Karl, the Habsburg candidate for the Spanish throne as Carlos III. Anton Ulrich had proposed Elisabeth Christine in September 1704 through his privy councilor Baron Rudolf Christian von Imhoff, supported by Urbich. She became a serious candidate for the role of Karl's wife after August 1706. Imhoff seems to have been the primary agent, but Urbich had also played a role.[115] Whether it was Urbich or Huyssen who first thought of Anton Ulrich's second granddaughter, Charlotte Christine, born in 1694, and her younger sister Antonie Amalie, is unknown. The father of both girls was Anton Ulrich's son Ludwig Rudolf, a general in the Imperial army, but it was Anton Ulrich who was making the decisions on the Braunschweig side.

The first definite notice of the Russian marriage project with Braunschweig-Wolfenbüttel comes in Duke Anton Ulrich's letter to Urbich from Braunschweig on February 9, 1707, thanking him for his efforts. The duke commented that the Russian marriage might seem strange, but he approved of it in view of Peter's "Conduite und humeur." Also he thought that if the Russian heir came "in die Academie," as Patkul had earlier worked for, that would help, as well as leaving religion "free." The Russian religion was closer to "ours," that is, Lutheranism, than the Catholic religion, even if it was not among the officially tolerated religions in the Treaty of Westphalia. Finally, the alliance, in combination with the Spanish marriage,

113 The correspondence continued through 1706, with political news but nothing about a Russian marriage: Leibniz, *Sämtliche Schriften und Briefe*, vol. 25, 300–302; vol. 26, 103–106, 248–250, 355–358, 511–514. As librarian and Hofrat at the Hannover court, Leibniz was also in regular contact with the other branch of the house of Braunschweig at Wolfenbüttel, Duke Anton Ulrich in particular.

114 Wernigerode H82, no. 895, ff. 1–46v (correspondence, 1696). The only study of Anton Ulrich concentrates on his immense Baroque novels, for which he was then well known: Étienne Mazingue, *Anton Ulrich: Duc de Braunschweig-Wolfenbüttel (1633–1714), un prince romancier au XVIIème siècle*, 2 vols. (Bern, Frankfurt am Main, and Las Vegas, Nevada: Peter Lang, 1978).

115 On the marriage, see Wilhelm Hoeck, *Anton Ulrich und Elisabeth Christine von Braunschweig-Lüneburg-Wolfenbüttel* (Wolfenbüttel: Hollesche Buch-, Kunst- und Musikalienhandlung, 1845), 55–65; Marcus Landau, *Geschichte Karls VI. als König von Spanien* (Stuttgart: J. G. Cotta, 1889), 385–398, 481–487. On Charlotte Christine, see most recently Christian Helbig, "'Zum Nutzen der russischen Monarchie und größern Splendor des Hauses Braunschweig-Lüneburg' – Charlotte Christine Sophie von Braunschweig-Wolfenbüttel (1694–1715) als erste westeuropäische Kronprinzessin in Russland," in *Russlands Blick nach Nordwestdeutschland*, ed. Gerd Steinwascher. Veröffentlichungen des Niedersächsischen Landesarchivs 2 (Göttingen: Wallstein Verlag, 2018), 48–70.

would provide Braunschweig-Wolfenbüttel with support ("appuy") from both ends of Europe.[116] The mention of Patkul also offers a clue to the origins of the Wolfenbüttel candidacy. In it the duke noted that "der gute Patkul" had been occupied with the education of the tsarevich "for some time" (*vorlangst*). The first mention of Wolfenbüttel in Patkul's known correspondence came as early as July 9, 1704, in a report to Peter. The Livonian surveyed the German courts at that moment, noting that the house of Hannover was effectively pro-Swedish in spite of appearances. Wolfenbüttel, in contrast, was the mortal enemy of Hannover and in good understanding with the king of Poland, Prussia, and Denmark, and would join in an agreement if Russia could make one with Denmark and Prussia.[117] Duke Anton Ulrich was thus a potential ally on general political grounds.

Later in September that year Patkul gave Golovin a list of possible German recruits for the Russian diplomatic service. First on the list was Urbich. Then ambassador of Denmark to Vienna, Urbich was (in Patkul's view) inclined to the interest of the king of Poland and the tsar. He was a capable, honest man (*ein capabler, redlicher Mann*) and general Ogilvy gave him a good recommendation. Urbich had excellent connections in Vienna and at other courts.[118] It may have been Patkul who provided Huyssen with Urbich's name, the same Patkul who was already contemplating a Wolfenbüttel–Russia alliance. With the arrival of Huyssen in Vienna in 1705 and Patkul's imprisonment by August II in Saxony in December of the same year, the plan came into the hands of Huyssen and Urbich. The two were in contact in Vienna perhaps in January 1707, and by the spring of the same year at the latest, after Urbich had returned from travelling in Saxony.[119] Huyssen first mentioned the marriage proposal to Gavriil Ivanovich Golovkin, the deceased Fyodor Golovin's replacement at the head of Peter's foreign policy, in his letter of June 1, 1707. He did not yet know whether the tsar would agree, and he wanted to know whether the tsarevich was to see a portrait of the princess or actually meet her, if she had to change her religion (like her sister when she married

[116] Wernigerode H82, no. 895, ff. 232–233 (Anton Ulrich to Urbich, February 9, 1707).

[117] Johann Reinhold von Patkul, *Johann Reinhold von Patkuls ... Berichte an das zaarische Cabinet in Moscau* (Berlin: n.p., 1792), vol. I, 215–216 [= RGADA, f. 79, 1704, ll. 62–68ob. (German), ll. 73–86ob. (Russian translation)]. Guerrier also mentioned Patkul but with no source: [Guerrier], *Die Kronprinzessin Charlotte von Rußland*, 5.

[118] Patkul, *Patkuls Berichte*, vol. I, 296–297. Peter had just hired Baron Georg Ogilvy, a Scots-German mercenary, as his field marshal in early 1704. He came into conflict with Menshikov and departed late in 1706: Bushkovitch, *Peter the Great*, 239, 250–251.

[119] Erdmann, *Der livländische Staatsmann Johann Reinhold von Patkul*, 209–289; RGADA, f. 32, op. 1, d 4, 1707, ll. 169–172ob., Vienna, May 28, 1707, Huyssen to *tainyi sovetnik* (Golovkin).

Karl), and whether it would be considered safe for Aleksei to actually go to Hannover or other places in northern Germany.[120]

Urbich proposed the marriage of the seventeen-year-old tsarevich with Charlotte Christine to Peter on June 1/11, 1707. Judging by the documents, he had traveled to meet Peter in his camp at Stężyca near Lublin in Poland. Charlotte was, in his view, the most suitable German princess. He described the distinguished ancestry of the house of Braunschweig and the numerous ruling houses that the tsarevich would be related to: Spain, the Empire, England through the Elector of Hannover, and others. He noted that Anton Ulrich was in favor of the match but had certain conditions, primarily that his granddaughter would have freedom of religion and a German court. He also wanted Aleksei to make a journey to Wolfenbüttel to meet his future bride and his family. Peter's response on June 8/19 was favorable to all the conditions other than Aleksei's journey west. In a time of such uncertainty owing to the war with Sweden it was not advisable. Peter did not comment on Urbich's arguments for the match, nor did he provide any reasons of his own. The tsar also made Urbich his representative in Vienna, agreeing to his requirements for conditions of service and salary.[121]

Peter announced Urbich's mission to the emperor on June 28, 1707.[122] The diplomat's instructions for Vienna were not about marriage, but rather about Peter's attempts to make an alliance against Sweden.[123] On July 13, Huyssen reported that Urbich had gone to Wolfenbüttel.[124] In August, Peter wrote to Urbich that he approved of the choice of Charlotte over her sister and asked his representative to compose a marriage treaty. He warned that war conditions made it difficult to guarantee an annual subsidy to the duke, and hoped that portraits of the potential brides would soon arrive.[125] Urbich found in Wolfenbüttel that there was some opposition to the match, but in a letter of August 14/24 to Duchess Christine Luise, Charlotte's mother, he warned her that if the match did not find approval, the Viennese court would be glad to oblige the tsar with a candidate.[126] Anton-Ulrich, however, had written to

[120] RGADA, f. 32, op. 1, d. 4, 1707, ll. 174ob.–180, 184ob.–185, Vienna, June 1, 1707, Huyssen to *tainyi sovetnik* (Golovkin).

[121] Wernigerode H82, no. 1028, ff. 1–21v (Peter's response to Urbich: ff. 13–15v).

[122] *PiB* 5, 339–341.

[123] Wernigerode H82 no. 1029, ff. 11–14 (Peter to Urbich, Warsaw, August 23, 1707).

[124] RGADA, f. 32, op. 1, d. 4, 1707, ll. 242ob., Vienna, July 13, 1707, Huyssen to *tainyi sovetnik* (Golovkin). Huyssen received letters from Urbich (content unclear) RGADA, f. 32, op. 1, l. 4, 1707, ll. 254ob.–255, Vienna, July 30, 1707, Huyssen to Gavriil Ivanovich (Golovkin).

[125] Wernigerode H82, no. 1029, ff. 4–7 (Peter to Urbich, Warsaw, August 11, 1707).

[126] Manfred von Boetticher, ed., *Braunschweigische Fürsten in Rußland in der ersten Hälfte des 18. Jahrhunderts*. Veröffentlichungen der niedersächsischen Archivverwaltung 54

Peter on July 23, and on August 30, 1707, Peter gave his consent from Warsaw, where he was staying to watch the Swedes. The tsar agreed to an alliance with Braunschweig-Wolfenbüttel, to be strengthened by the marriage of his son to one of the princesses of that house.[127] In November, no final arrangement had yet been made public, for Urbich told the Mecklenburg ambassador to Vienna only that the tsar was looking for allies among the German princes and also for a wife for his son.[128] August II, in contrast, did know of the plans and approved of them.[129] The duke remained favorable to the understanding, but early in 1708 wrote to Peter suggesting that the marriage be put off because of the youth of the bride and groom, who also should meet before a final decision was reached.

The duke's adviser Baron Johann Christoph von Schleinitz was against the plan, believing Peter's position not secure enough. Charlotte's mother also opposed the marriage, and Anton Ulrich himself was not sure which of his granddaughters should be the bride. Certainly Russia's prospects at that moment did not look good, as Charles XII turned east, apparently bound for Moscow. To make things worse, the movements of the Swedish king, by early 1708 in Grodno with his army, coincided with the Bulavin rebellion on the Don. In any case, the letter did not reach Peter until the autumn of the year, and he agreed to a postponement but reiterated his desire for a family relationship (*svoistvo*) with the house of Braunschweig.[130] There seems to have been no more contact between Peter and the duke until after Poltava. After that Russian victory the way was clear, and the tsarevich moved on to Germany to work out the final details of the marriage agreement.

Why Peter agreed to the Braunschweig marriage is not clear from the published record. Charlotte was indeed the sister of Elizabeth Christine, who in 1708 would marry the future Emperor Karl VI, then the Habsburg

(Göttingen: Vandenhoeck & Ruprecht, 1998), 44–45. The Habsburg candidate was presumably Maria Magdalena (1689–1743), the sister of Emperors Joseph I and Karl VI.

[127] *PiB* VI, 65; [Guerrier], *Die Kronprinzessin Charlotte von Rußland*, 4–6; A. Brückner, *Der Zarewitsch Alexei (1690–1718)* (Heidelberg: Carl Winter's Universitätsbuchhandlung, 1880), 67–68; *PiB* 6, 65. Peter's letter was printed from the Wolffenbüttel archive, as no copy exists in the Russian archives. Wernigerode H82, no. 1029, ff. 21–21v (Peter to Herzog [Anton Ulrich], August 30, 1707).

[128] Mediger, *Mecklenburg, Rußland und England-Hannover*, vol. I, 43–44.

[129] Wernigerode H82, no. 895, ff. 253–53v (Anton Ulrich to Urbich, December 15, 1707).

[130] *PiB* 8, pt. 1, 141–142 (September 17, 1708), 8, pt. 2, 689–690; [Guerrier], *Die Kronprinzessin Charlotte von Rußland*, 10–14; Brückner, *Der Zarewitsch Alexei*, 68–69; Jill Bepler, "Marriage Markets and Risk Assessment: The Lure of the Russian Empire at the Turn of the Eighteenth Century," in *Frictions and Failures: Cultural Encounters in Crisis*, ed. Almut Bues. Deutsches Historisches Institut Warschau, Quellen und Studien 34 (Wiesbaden: Harrassowitz, 2017), 201–213.

contender for the Spanish throne. As Joseph I (1705–11) had no sons, Karl was the most likely heir to the Habsburg lands in central Europe and the Imperial crown, though how that would have played out if his fortunes in Spain had been better remains unknown. In addition, Charlotte was brought up at the court in Dresden of Peter's former ally, August II of Poland, staying with his estranged wife, Queen Christiane Eberhardine.[131] Peter's reasons for the choice remain obscure.[132] Anton Ulrich's reasons for wanting the marriage are not perfectly clear, but his February 1707 letter to Urbich stated that, with the marriage, his house would have support from both extremities of Europe, meaning Russia and Spain. Given the duke's previous political problems – in 1702 he had been nearly deposed by the Hannover branch of the dynasty for trying to ally with France – his desire for support and influential connections was understandable. At the same time, neither were absolutely secure. Karl had not landed in Spain until 1705, and in spite of English support ruled only in Catalonia. Peter was at the moment in better shape, but Charles XII had already deposed Peter's only ally, Augustus II of Poland, in the Treaty of Altranstädt (October 1706), a major loss for the tsar. The doubts on the Braunschweig side appeared only after the initial agreement and are understandable, but the reasons for Anton Ulrich's initial agreement remain obscure. Both sides kept the agreement secret. To complicate matters, the first credible accounts of opposition to Peter's policies among the Russian elite began to circulate

[131] Charlotte came to the Dresden court in 1701. By that point Christiane Eberhardine, the wife of King/Elector August, was already estranged over her husband's inability to provide a guarantee for her Protestant worship in Poland. Christiane even adduced the case of Poland's only non-Catholic queen, Helena, the Russian wife of King Alexander (1501–6), who had been permitted Orthodox worship, but in vain. She never visited Poland, and spent most of her time in her castle at Pretsch near Torgau. Christiane was close to the Lutheran court preacher, Samuel Benedikt Carpzov. See Paul Haake, *Christiane Eberhardine und August der Starke: Eine Ehetragödie* (Dresden: C. Heinrich, 1930), 66, 93–94, 99; Wolfgang Sommer, *Die lutherischen Hofprediger in Dresden: Grundzüge ihrer Geschichte und Verkündigung im Kurfürstlichen Sachsen* (Stuttgart: Steiner, 2006), 239–246. Charlotte probably had little experience of Dresden's quite magnificent court ceremonies and entertainments. See Helen Watanabe-O'Kelly, *Court Culture in Dresden: From Renaissance to Baroque* (Basingstoke and New York, New York: Palgrave, 2002); and Helen Watanabe-O'Kelly, "Religion and the Consort: Two Electresses of Saxony and Queens of Poland (1697–1757)," in *Queenship in Europe: The Role of the Consort*, ed. Clarissa Campbell Orr (Cambridge: Cambridge University Press, 2004), 252–265.

[132] Brückner cited an anonymous memorandum in the Russian foreign ministry archives which argued that, with this marriage, Aleksei might become the Holy Roman Emperor, since Joseph I had no sons (and presumably Joseph's brother Charles would be king of Spain), and otherwise the Austrians might help Russia to restore the Greek empire on the ruins of Turkey: Brückner, *Der Zarewitsch Alexei*, 67. Both ideas were extremely farfetched and also bore no relationship to Peter's foreign policy in 1707–8.

exactly in early 1707. The Austrian resident reported that a party had formed at the Russian court in opposition to the favorite Menshikov and in support of the tsarevich Aleksei. Menshikov was not quite as powerful as the reports stated, as the conflicts at the tsar's headquarters in Poland in that summer – just as Urbich arrived with the marriage proposal – demonstrated.[133] It is not clear how much of this Peter knew as yet, and neither Urbich nor Anton Ulrich had any sense of it. In any case, the duke kept the arrangements secret. Leibniz, who was in close touch with Wolfenbüttel, first heard of it in March 1709, not from Urbich but from a rumor at Anton Ulrich's court. Anton Ulrich admitted only that he was interested in an alliance, but denied the rumor of a marriage agreement. Urbich confirmed this fiction.[134] A few months later, in May, Leibniz told Urbich that the duke himself admitted the truth, but Urbich cautioned that there were intrigues on this subject both at Wolfenbüttel and around Charlotte.[135] If any doubt remained, Peter's victory over Charles XII at Poltava on June 27/July 8, 1709 removed it. Russia was now worth an alliance.

After Poltava, Tsarevich Aleksei made his first journey to Western Europe. The agreement with Wolfenbüttel was now moving ahead and becoming official. Charlotte had agreed to it, and the duke had informed the king of Poland, who wanted to play a role in the arrangements.[136] The main purpose of Aleksei's journey was to finalize the marriage treaty, but also to give the heir a conception of European courts and life. Already in 1707 there had been a project to send him to London to the court of Queen Anne. Peter's ambassador Andrei Matveev received a positive response from the duke of Marlborough, but cautioned that he hoped that the tsar would send experienced older people of solid character to supervise his son.[137] Nothing came of this proposal, and Aleksei stayed in Russia. The time for the journey came in 1709, when Aleksei was nineteen years old. Peter decided on the journey after talking to Menshikov and wrote on October 23 to his son that he was to go to Dresden and there study German and French, geometry and fortification, as well as partly

[133] Bushkovitch, *Peter the Great*, 256, 265–267. [134] Guerrier, *Leibniz*, 109–110, 112.
[135] Ibid., 114–115.
[136] Guerrier, *Leibniz*, 116–117 (Leibniz to Urbich, August 20, 1709), 118–120 (Leibniz to Urbich, August 27, 1709), 122.
[137] *PiB* 5, 425, 436–437; Henry L. Snyder, ed., *The Marlborough–Godolphin Correspondence* (Oxford: Clarendon Press, 1975), vol. 3, 747, Marlborough to Godolphin, April 9/20, 1707. See also Sir George Murray, *Letters and Despatches of John Churchill, First Duke of Marlborough from 1702–1712* (London: John Murray, 1845), vol. 3, 249, 277, 345–346. Peter was making overtures to Austria and England after the Treaty of Altranstädt. Marlborough and Prince Eugene were not willing to commit themselves to any particular course toward Russia since the outcome of the Russo-Swedish war was so uncertain: Murray, *Letters and Despatches of John Churchill*, vol. 4, 8–9 (note), 65.

political affairs (*takzhe otchasti i politicheskikh del*).[138] The next month Menshikov sent the tsarevich a memorandum on his behavior. He was to travel incognito and treat people honestly and politely. He was to learn the languages and other things that his father had ordered.[139] August II, in his role as Elector of Saxony, ordered his officials to find a house for Aleksei and the two noblemen accompanying him on the Old Market in Dresden.[140] Menshikov, however, soon heard that August II had gone to Saxony and was not sure what that meant. He told the boy to stay in Kraków until Peter sent him further orders. Aleksei arrived in Kraków by the end of 1709 and sent his father a letter in German.[141] With the tsarevich were two men to supervise his journey and education, Prince Iurii Iur'evich Trubetskoi and Aleksandr Gavrilovich Golovkin, the son of the chancellor.[142] Trubetskoi (1668–1739) was the descendant of boyars, and indeed his older brother Ivan was one of the last to hold that rank. Prince Iurii, however, had been a chamber *stol'nik* of Peter in the 1680s and became a captain in the Preobrazhenskii guards and participated in the Azov campaigns. Sent to Venice in 1697, he had also been briefly an envoy for Peter in Brandenburg.[143] Golovkin was much less aristocratic and also much younger. His father Gavriil (1660–1734) had also been a chamber *stol'nik* with Peter in the 1680s, and had accompanied the tsar on campaigns and the European trip. On the death of Golovin in 1706, he became the head of the Ambassadorial Office, serving as the chief of Russian foreign policy until Peter's death. His son Aleksandr Gavrilovich (1689–1760) was only a few years older than Tsarevich Aleksei. He had served as a German translator, and after his travels with the tsarevich was ambassador to Prussia, a senator, and then ambassador to Holland after 1731.[144]

Aleksei stayed over the winter, announcing his approaching move west to Saxony to Prince D. M. Golitsyn, then governor of Kiev, in March 1710. He thanked the prince for his letter and the books the prince had sent the heir. He also wrote to another Kiev friend, Ioannykii Seniutovych, the hegumen of the Zlatoverkhii Monastery of St. Michael, recommending a priest of his acquaintance for a parish in the city.[145] While Aleksei was

[138] *PiB* IX, pt. 1, 442–443.
[139] Ustrialov, *Istoriia tsarstvovaniia Petra Velikogo*, vol. VI, 311–312.
[140] *SRIO* XX, 33 (November 9, 1709). [141] *PiB* IX, pt. 1, 1326–1327.
[142] *PiB* X, 511–513.
[143] Later on he was also an important official and provincial governor. I. V. Babich and M. V. Babich, *Oblastnye praviteli Rossii 1719–1739 gg.* (Moscow: ROSSPEN, 2008), 642–43.
[144] *PiB* VIII, 1057–1058, "Golovkin, Aleksandr Gavrilovich," *Russkii biograficheskii slovar'* (Moscow: Aspekt Press, 1997), neopublikovannye materialy, 2, Gogol'–Giune, 261–264.
[145] Korzun, *Heinrich von Huyssen*, 39; Murzakevich, ed., *Pis'ma tsarevicha Alekseia Petrovicha*, 61; *Pis'ma russkikh gosudarei*, vol. III, 26–27.

moving west, his father celebrated the heir's birthday in St. Petersburg, as part of the emerging new and highly informal court ceremonial.[146] Aleksei went from Kraków to Dresden, arriving in May.[147] Again August II ordered his officials to provide food and other provisions for a suite of eight to ten people daily.[148] Charlotte, who does not seem to have yet met him, reported in August to her mother that the tsarevich spent his time improving his French and German and learning dancing and geography. He went out rarely, dining only with a few important officials and the wife of ambassador Matveev.[149] Peter wrote to his son warning him of a potential Swedish threat to Saxony, and informing him that he was awarding the Order of St. Andrew to Charlotte's father Ludwig Rudolf. He also wrote that he had heard that his son had actually met Charlotte in Karlsbad, but had not heard what the young man thought of her.[150] While these letters crossed Europe, Duke Anton Ulrich wrote to Urbich that he had heard that the entourage of the tsarevich was opposed to any foreign marriage. The one exception was the young count Golovkin, who was wiser and more honorable. Prince Trubetskoi, on the other hand, did everything he could to obstruct or delay the match.[151] In September and October, however, Aleksei wrote to Peter from Saxony, telling him that the princess was acceptable. Peter ordered Golovkin to inform her father and grandfather of the fact and that Peter gave his permission for the marriage. The old draft treaty that Urbich had sent, however, was unacceptable, and Peter wanted a new version.[152]

[146] Just Juel, *En Rejse til Rusland under Tsar Peter* (Copenhagen: Gyldendal (F Hegel & søn), 1893), 205–206.

[147] *Pis'ma russkikh gosudarei*, 1862, 28 (May 15, 1711, Aleksei to Ekaterina Alekseevna).

[148] *SRIO* XX, 34–35 (May 7, 1710). The suite consisted of Trubetskoi, Golovkin, Huyssen ("der Informator"), and their servants.

[149] Svetlana Romanovna Dolgova, "Das Heiratsprojekt zwischen dem Zarewitsch Aleksej und Prinzessin Charlotte," in *Braunschweigische Fürsten in Rußland in der ersten Hälfte des 18. Jahrhunderts*, ed. Manfred von Boetticher (Göttingen: Vandenhoeck & Ruprecht, 1998), 48–49 (August 1, 1710).

[150] *PiB* X, 280–281 (August 13, 1710), 303 (to Ludwig Rudolf, sending the order, August 21, 1710).

[151] *PiB* X, 694 (Russian translation of Anton Ulrich to Urbich, September 2, 1710). Matveev's wife also thought that Aleksei would never marry a foreigner. The Russian translation of Anton Ulrich's letter to Urbich in the Russian archives, among Peter's papers (not the correspondence with Russian ambassadors to foreign powers), is actually a composite of two letters to Urbich, one from Anton Ulrich on September 2 that expressed his concern that the entourage of the tsarevich was against foreign marriages but mentioned no names, and one from Schleinitz with the same date that stated that Golovkin was wiser and more honorable and that Matveev's wife thought Aleksei would not marry a foreigner. Neither mentioned Trubetskoi explicitly, though he was implied as the senior member of the entourage of the tsarevich. Wernigerode, H82, no. 895 (Anton Ulrich), 402–403; no. 957 (Schleinitz), 17–19v.

[152] *PiB* X, 422–423 (Peter to Aleksei Petrovich, December 5, 1710). Aleksei also wrote to Ignat'ev with the same favorable impression of Charlotte: G. V. Esipov, "Dokumenty po delu tsarevicha Alekseia Petrovicha," *ChOIDR* 3 (1861): 51.

In the spring of 1711, Peter sent more orders to Golovkin and asked his son to write more often.[153] Peter handled the negotiations for the final version of the treaty himself, and gave his final approval to the marriage treaty on April 29, 1711, at Jaworów in Poland, where Peter had been with the Russian army a few weeks earlier. Most of the text was taken up with the guarantee that Charlotte would be able to exercise her Lutheran faith freely and maintain her German household. She renounced all her rights of inheritance from the house of Braunschweig. In turn, Peter guaranteed that he would provide her with his protection and favor even in the case of the decease of his son, in his own name and in the name of those who would have the "right to inherit the Russian throne by natural inheritance." Both Peter and Aleksei signed the treaty.[154]

The tsarevich was in Dresden, leaving for Wolfenbüttel and arriving there in early May.[155] On May 23, 1711, Aleksei wrote from Anton Ulrich's estate at Salzdahlum to his father announcing the final conclusion of the treaty. The role of the tsarevich again was not merely symbolic. Peter ordered him to offer the duke 40,000 thalers in subsidy, with 50,000 as a maximum. The duke insisted on 50,000 and Aleksei, after some persuasion, wrote that figure into the space left blank on the treaty, as well as negotiating other details. Thus Aleksei finalized the marriage documents.[156]

While Aleksei was in Germany, Peter set out on his disastrous campaign against the Turks on the river Prut in Moldavia. There his army was surrounded, and he decided to cut his losses and make peace. The peace was costly, for he lost Azov, but otherwise he was able to return with his army largely intact. One of the consequences of the war was the reorganization of the state in Russia. Peter wanted a clear authority at home in his absence, so he established the Senate, composed of officials and aristocrats, to rule in his absence. After his return, the Senate quickly became the central organ of government, replacing both the old duma of boyars and the informal councils of the previous decade of Peter's rule.[157] It was the Senate that would be the scene of much of the drama of succession in the coming years.

While Peter was engaged in Moldavia, Duke Anton Ulrich took the tsarevich to see the sights of northwestern Germany, as he saw them. As

[153] *PiB* XI, pt. 1, 121 (Peter to Aleksei, March 4, 1711). The instructions to Golovkin and Aleksei were oral.

[154] *PiB* XI, pt. 1, 202–210, 484–485 (quotation 204); *PSZ* IV, no. 2354 (April 19/May 10, 1711), 669–673. "imenem tekh, kotorye Rossiiskii Prestol po natural'nomu naslediiu nasledstovat' pravo imet' mogut," Ibid., 670. German text: "Vermälungs-Tractat zwischen dem zarischen Kron-Prinzen Alexei Petrowitsch und der braunschweigischen Prinzessin Christina Sophia," *Magazin für die neue Historie und Geographie* XV (1781): 223–230.

[155] *Pis'ma russkikh gosudarei*, 1862, 31–32 (Aleksei to Peter, April 25 and May 4, 1711).

[156] Ibid., 1862, 33–34. [157] Bushkovitch, *Peter the Great*, 297–308.

the duke was increasingly inclined toward Catholicism, it is not surprising that one of the visits was to the monastery at Corvey, whose abbot, Florenz von dem Felde, was a friend of Anton Ulrich. Aleksei arrived for the feast of St. Vitus (one of the patrons of the monastery) on June 15 and spent several days there, attending church services and talking to the monks. He continued to observe the Orthodox fasts while he was there, however, even at dinners with the monks. Along with him were Trubetskoi, Huyssen, and an Orthodox priest who spoke Latin.[158] The tsarevich stayed in and around Wolfenbüttel through September. Peter had made his way back from the Prut campaign for a rest cure in Karlsbad, and at first wanted the wedding there. Then he changed his mind and settled on Torgau, the site of one of the residences of Christiane Eberhardine, Electress of Saxony and queen of Poland.[159] It was she who had brought up Charlotte at the Saxon court over the previous several years.

The wedding took place in Torgau, Saxony, on October, 14/25, 1711.[160] The ceremony was in the local palace of the electress and queen, in the main hall, rather than in a church. The service was Orthodox, with the crucial parts of the ceremony repeated in Greek, presumably for the Lutheran divines in the audience. Peter had a description composed and sent it to the dignitaries in St. Petersburg, but it was never printed.[161] Before they left Torgau, Peter and Anton Ulrich discussed the future. Anton Ulrich proposed that the young couple stay with him in Germany. Peter wanted Aleksei to spend more time abroad, but in Prussia or Poland, and Charlotte of course with him. He proposed that she could make a trip home in the spring. The duke also hoped for renewed friendship of Peter with the emperor, in this case the newly elected Karl VI, the husband of another of Anton Ulrich's granddaughters, Charlotte's sister. Peter assured him that he would be happy to renew that friendship if Vienna were interested.[162]

[158] H. Joachim Brüning, "Herzon Anton Ulrich von Brauschweig-Lüneburg zu Wolfenbüttel und Abt Florenz von Corvey," *Westfälische Zeitschrift* 126–127 (1976–7): 346–350. The priest was father Ioann Slonskii, for whose presence Aleksei thanked his spiritual father Iakov Ignat'ev from Dresden in February: G. V. Esipov, "Dokumenty po delu tsarevicha Alekseia Petrovicha," *ChOIDR* 3 (1861): 43, 45.

[159] *Pis'ma russkikh gosudarei*, vol. III, 1862, 28–37.

[160] G. V. Esipov, "Tsarevich Aleksei," *ChOIDR* 3 (1861): 65–67; *Pokhodnyi zhurnal 1711 goda* (St. Petersburg: n.p., 1854), 32–35.

[161] "Vedomost'," in *PiB* XI, pt. 2, 171–172. A German version closely based on the Russian description appeared in the Leipzig newspaper *Europäische Fama*, no. 123 (1711), 196–198.

[162] *PiB* XI, pt. 2, 177–182, 501–505. After the wedding Peter also had a meeting with Leibniz, where the latter made several proposals for the advancement of knowledge in Russia: Guerrier, *Leibniz*, 114–120.

The Heir's Maturity and Flight

Peter went on back to Russia, and Aleksei's next task was again to work for the supply of the Russian army. This task was much more extensive than the previous ones. He was now twenty-two, with a wife of eighteen. He was based in Toruń, in northern Poland, where he remained with his new bride for a year and a half.[163] He corresponded regularly not only with his father but also with Russian diplomats and the officers in charge of the collection of supplies in Poland. After spending the rest of 1712 with his father, who had gone to Pomerania and Mecklenburg with the Russian army, he returned to Poland only to find his wife gone. At the end of the year she had made a sudden trip back to Braunschweig to see her family, the first sign of discontent. Peter was annoyed that she went without telling him, and told her that he would have certainly agreed. Her relatives made various excuses, and she herself wrote to the tsar that she needed to see Anton Ulrich, given his age, and besides she had no money.[164] Aleksei returned to St. Petersburg with Peter's new wife, Ekaterina. They arrived early in 1713 without Charlotte.[165] Peter met with Charlotte briefly in March, and she went on to St. Petersburg, arriving at the beginning of the summer. The matter of succession seemed to be settled, for Aleksei was now married and could produce a son and heir himself. So far there was no serious friction between father and son.

Ekaterina was gradually moving to the center of the court, and the heir's relations with her until this point had not been contentious. She had been a fixture in Peter's life since at least 1704, but only as the tsar's mistress.[166] Her first child to live was Anna, born on January 27, 1708, while Peter was on campaign, and her second was Elisabeth, born on December 18, 1709. Peter was in Preobrazhenskoe, but the record of his movements and activity does not mention her birth.[167] As Peter was leaving for the Turkish campaign in March 1711, he declared, at least

[163] Peter's instructions: *PiB* XI, pt. 2, 191–193; Bushkovitch, *Peter the Great*, 340–341.

[164] *PiB* XIII, pt. 1, 31–32, 69–70, 218.

[165] *Pis'ma russkikh gosudarei*, vol. III, 38–54; Murzakevich, ed., *Pis'ma tsarevicha Alekseia Petrovicha*, 61–67.

[166] N. I. Pavlenko, *Ekaterina I* (Moscow: Molodaia gvardiia, 2004). Aleksei Petrovich exchanged formal greetings with Ekaterina in 1708–12 and asked for her help once with Peter in 1709: *Pis'ma russkikh gosudarei*, vol. III, 7–8, 17, 20–26, 29–30, 34, 44, 46, 51, 53, 56. In May 1713, he asked her to speed up the transfer of some villages she had given him: *Pis'ma russkikh gosudarei*, vol. III, 53–54. The exchange of greetings and other messages continued in 1714: *Pis'ma russkikh gosudarei*, vol. III, 56–57.

[167] *Pokhodnye zhurnaly 1706, 1707, 1708, i 1709 godov* (St. Petersburg: n.p., 1844), Iurnaly 1709 goda, 24. The omission may be the result of the very imperfect character of the early records of Peter's movements, which become detailed only after Poltava.

orally, that Ekaterina, the *gosudarynia tsaritsa*, was a true "sovereign" (*gosudarynia*) even though they were not yet married. It seems that some officials knew about this, for they did use the title.[168] Nevertheless, she kept out of sight: she did not attend Aleksei's wedding in Torgau, staying back in Poland to await Peter's return.[169] On February 19, 1712, Peter formally married Ekaterina, now officially and publicly titled tsaritsa. It was a quiet ceremony, without regal splendor.[170] From then on she was an acknowledged figure at court.[171] The marriage implied the legitimation of Peter's daughters by Ekaterina, but at the moment this was hardly an issue. The oldest two, Anna and Elisabeth, were only four and three years old at that moment, and Aleksei was the acknowledged heir. The only shadow on the succession was highly indirect, and came from Moscow. There Stefan Iavorskii, the locum tenens of the patriarchal throne and the effective head of the church, took the occasion of the name day of the tsarevich, March 17 (St. Alexius), 1712, to denounce Peter's use of *fiskaly* to enforce the payment of taxes and the honesty of officials, the lax observance of fasts, and to complain about Aleksei's having been cast among strangers. Perhaps the latter was a reference to the foreign marriage of the tsarevich, but in any case the senators then in Moscow came the next day to reproach him with inciting rebellion. He wrote to the tsar to defend himself and ask to be allowed to retire to a monastery.[172] Stefan did not directly raise any issue about succession, just as he had not in his earlier sermons on Peter's victories, his army, and his fleet, and nor did he later. Peter did not react to the sermon (as far as we know), but from this moment Stefan's relations with Peter deteriorated.

For the next two years we know little of the relations of father and son other than the tasks that Aleksei fulfilled as part of his duties to his father

168 Marker, *Imperial Saint*, 126; *Pokhodnyi zhurnal 1711*, 4 (March 7, 1711): "publichno obiavleno vsem o Gosudaryne Tsaritse Ekaterine Alekseevne, chto ona est' istinnaia Gosudarynia"; *PiB* XI, pt. 2, 370–371. Whitworth reported several months later that Peter had made this declaration to Tsarevna Natal'ia Alekseevna and his two half-sisters: *SRIO* 61, 143–144.

169 *Pokhodnyi zhurnal 1711*, 35.

170 *Pokhodnyi zhurnal 1712 goda* (St. Petersburg: n.p., 1854), 1–7: Bushkovitch, *Peter the Great*, 309; *SRIO* 61, 143–146 (Whitworth, February 20, 1712).

171 In 1714, she even became the head of a female order of chivalry, the Order of St. Catherine. Its aim was supposed to be the ransom of Christian captives in the Ottoman Empire: Marker, *Imperial Saint*, 125–144; *Pokhodnyi zhurnal 1714 goda* (St. Petersburg: n.p., 1854), 79.

172 For the sermon, see Viktor Zhivov, *Iz tserkovnoi istorii vremen Petra Velikogo* (Moscow: Novoe literaturnoe obozrenie, 2004), 262–281 and the letter in S. G. Runkevich, *Arkhierei petrovskoi epokhi v ikh perepiske s Petrom Velikim* (St. Petersburg: Tipografiia Montvida, 1906), 156–159. From Stefan's letter, it seems that the contentious issue was the part about the *fiskaly*. Bushkovitch, *Peter the Great*, 340; Zhivov, *Iz tserkovnoi istorii vremen Petra Velikogo*, 127–130.

and sovereign. From Saint Petersburg, he traveled on his father's orders to Novgorod and other interior Russian districts to collect timber for the construction of Peter's navy. Then he went back to Saint Petersburg.[173] It is at this time that the first news began to come through the diplomatic correspondence that the tsarevich was unhappy with his father and his reforms and spent most of his time with "Muscovite priests." Charlotte, who had arrived in the Russian capital in May, had come to realize that her husband did not love her, and indeed that she had no friends at the Russian court other than the tsar himself and Menshikov.[174] The tsarevich was still part of the court ceremonial: his birthday (February 19) and his name day a month later were the occasion of festivities in 1714, with Peter, Ekaterina, and the dignitaries in attendance. Peter also visited him every few weeks that spring until the tsarevich went to take the waters in Karlsbad in June, on Peter's orders.[175] There he read Cesario Baronio's Jesuit history of the church (taking notes on it) and other Western books, for he was in no sense a product of pre-Petrine Russian culture.[176] He also bought books in German, Catholic sermons, Lutheran devotional literature, histories, and Wolf Helmhardt von Hohberg's *Georgica curiosa*, a 1687 tract on household management for noblemen.[177] In that respect, Peter's upbringing of his son had succeeded, for his son read Western books as well as more traditional Russian devotional literature. Aleksei kept Peter informed of his cures, and congratulated his father as well as Ekaterina on the victory at Hangöudd.[178] While he was away, Charlotte gave birth to a daughter, Natal'ia Alekseevna.[179] The baptism was a great occasion, recorded by the Hanoverian ambassador Friedrich Christian

[173] *PiB* XIII, pt. 2, 48, 78, 328, 385; *Pokhodnyi zhurnal 1713*, 20, 57.

[174] Bushkovitch, *Peter the Great*, 341–342.

[175] *Pokhodnyi zhurnal 1713*, 88, 94, 96, 99, 101, 104: Esipov, "Dokumenty," 50.

[176] Ustrialov, *Istoriia tsarstvovaniia Petra Velikogo*, vol. VI, 324–326; Esipov, "Dokumenty," 144–163. Aleksei must have used a Russian manuscript translation, Piotr Skarga's Polish translation, or a Western edition in Latin or German, since the Russian text was published only in 1719: P. Pekarskii, *Nauka i literatura v Rossii pri Petre Velikom*, 2 vols. (St. Petersburg: Obshchestvennaia pol'za, 1862), vol. II, 446–447; T. A. Bykova and M. M. Gurevich, *Opisanie izdanii napechatannykh kirillitsei 1689–ianvar' 1725* (Moscow and Leningrad: Izdatel'stvo Akademii nauk SSSR, 1958), 208–211.

[177] Bushkovitch, *Peter the Great*, 339–340, 342; *Pokhodnyi zhurnal 1713 goda* (St. Petersburg, n.p., 1854), 58. Tsarevich Aleksei also bought books in Prague and Karlsbad and later in Nuremberg and Erfurt: Esipov, "Dokumenty," 89, 93, 95–96, 98. Some of them ended up as part of the library of the University of Helsinki in the nineteenth century: I. N. Lebedeva, "Biblioteka tsarevicha Alekseia Petrovicha," in *Kniga i knigotorgovlia v Rossii*, ed. S. P. Luppov (Leningrad: Biblioteka Akademii nauk SSSR, 1984), 56–64.

[178] Murzakevich, ed., *Pis'ma tsarevicha Alekseia Petrovicha*, 70–73, 76–77; *Pis'ma russkikh gosudarei* III, 56–57.

[179] On July 11, 1714: Ustrialov, *Istoriia tsarstvovaniia Petra Velikogo*, vol. VI, 322. Natal'ia lived until 1728.

Weber: the infant had no fewer than seven godfathers, Prince Ia. F. Dolgorukii, Prince M. V. Dolgorukii, Count I. A. Musin-Pushkin, T. N. Streshnev, N. M. Zotov, Prince F. Iu. Romodanovskii, and the senator Vasilii Andreevich Apukhtin.[180] Charlotte's husband returned to St. Petersburg in December, and largely disappeared from view for the next nine months.[181] He also seems to have acquired a mistress, Efrosin'ia Fyodorova, a serf of his former teacher and continuing confidant, Nikifor Viazemskii.[182] The only actual record of his activity during the first nine months of 1715 is a series of letters to Ioannykii Seniutovych in Kiev, the principal assistant to the aging metropolitan, Ioasaf. Aleksei congratulated him on his appointment as archimandrite of the Kiev Monastery of the Caves and thanked him for sending him some icons and one of his writings.[183]

The autumn brought momentous events for the family of the tsar. On October 12, Charlotte gave birth to a son, named Peter in honor of his grandfather, and then died ten days later. On October 29, Ekaterina too gave birth to a son, named Peter as well.[184] There were now two possible heirs as well as Aleksei himself, but the relations of father and son had now exploded. Peter greeted the birth of his grandson calmly, but that of his second son with tremendous rejoicing. According to Weber, the godfathers at the baptism were the kings of Denmark and Prussia (obviously by proxy), and at the banquet two dwarfs jumped nearly naked from cakes and made speeches in honor of the occasion. The whole party then went to the islands for fireworks.[185] Menshikov got so drunk he lost a valuable medal, a gift from the king of Prussia. Before the birth of the two boys, Peter had written a letter to his son, reproaching him for his lack of interest in military affairs and his unfitness to rule. He threatened to disinherit him. Aleksei did not respond until October 31, and agreed with his father. He asked Peter to remove him from the succession and said that now he had a brother, the new born Petr Petrovich. Peter did not respond.[186] Indeed, he had

180 F. C. Weber, *Das veränderte Russland* (Frankfurt and Leipzig: n.p., 1744) (originally Frankfurt: Nicolaus Förster, 1721), vol. I, 22–24. See also O. G. Ageeva, *Evropeizatsiia russkogo Dvora 1700–1796 gg.* (Moscow: Institut Rossiiskoi istorii RAN, 2006), 175–176.

181 Bushkovitch, *Peter the Great*, 342.

182 Ustrialov, *Istoriia tsarstvovaniia Petra Velikogo*, vol. VI, 40.

183 *Pis'ma russkikh gosudarei*, vol. III, 58–60.

184 Bushkovitch, *Peter the Great*, 343–345; *Pokhodnyi zhurnal 1715 goda* (St. Petersburg: n. p., 1855), 28.

185 Weber, *Das veränderte Russland*, vol. I, 121–122; Ageeva, *Evropeizatsiia russkogo Dvora*, 170–178.

186 Bushkovitch, *Peter the Great*, 344, 346; Ustrialov, *Istoriia tsarstvovaniia Petra Velikogo*, vol. VI, 348–349.

not named an alternative heir, since he had written before the birth of either his or Aleksei's son. It was Aleksei who suggested Peter's new son as the heir and commended his own children to Peter's care. In the meantime, the impasse did not prevent Aleksei Petrovich from participating in the baptism of Petr Petrovich on November 6, as one of the godfathers.[187] Peter answered Aleksei on January 19. He presented his son with an ultimatum: either change his ways and show some enthusiasm for his work as a future ruler or become a monk. Aleksei answered that he would become a monk. Peter gave him time to consider his decision.[188]

For the next nine months relations between Peter and Aleksei were at a standstill. At the end of January 1716, Peter and his wife went off to Danzig, where in April he celebrated the wedding of his niece Ekaterina Ivanovna to Karl-Leopold of Mecklenburg. In the summer, he continued on to northern Germany and Denmark. Plans were under discussion to invade southern Sweden from there, though after much preparation the idea was rejected. In October, Peter sent the Russian fleet back to Reval and went on south with Ekaterina toward Holland.[189] Peter did not know that his son had left St. Petersburg on September 26, ostensibly to join his father.

In fact, Aleksei was going to Vienna with his mistress Efrosin'ia, to the court of his brother-in-law, Karl VI. Long described by historians merely as the result of a family conflict, the flight to Vienna was in fact an attempt to find support abroad. The tsarevich was at the center of the hopes of all the grandees who were unhappy with Peter's policies and incidentally with the power of Menshikov.[190] The favorite had been under a cloud since Peter discovered the massive extent of his corruption in 1713, but had just made a comeback. During the summer of 1716, while Peter was with the fleet, the Russian army in Finland was running out of supplies. Faced with the passivity of the Senate, Menshikov commandeered enough food supplies and ships to rescue the army.[191] Perhaps Aleksei

[187] *Pokhodnyi zhurnal 1715*, 28–29. The others were Admiral Apraksin, standing in for Menshikov, and the Danish ambassador for the king of Denmark, Frederick IV.

[188] Ustrialov, *Istoriia tsarstvovaniia Petra Velikogo*, 349–351.

[189] *Pokhodnyi zhurnal 1716 goda* (St. Petersburg: n.p., 1855), 19–47.

[190] Bushkovitch, *Peter the Great*, 357–364; Iskra Schwarcz, "Die Flucht des Thronfolgers Aleksej und der Wiener Hof," in *Die Flucht des Thronfolgers Aleksej: Krise in der "Balance of Power" und den österreichischen-russischen Beziehungen am Anfang des 18. Jahrhunderts*, ed. Iskra Schwartz. Austria: Forschung und Wissenschaft: Geschichte 16 (Vienna and Berlin: Lit, 2019), 179–198; Ernst D. Petritsch, "Ein Bericht über den Aufenthalt des Zarewitsch Aleksej in den habsburgischen Ländern," in *Die Flucht des Thronfolgers Aleksej: Krise in der "Balance of Power" und den österreichischen-russischen Beziehungen am Anfang des 18. Jahrhunderts*, ed. Iskra Schwartz. Austria: Forschung und Wissenschaft: Geschichte 16 (Vienna and Berlin: Lit, 2019), 369–386.

[191] Bushkovitch, *Peter the Great*, 353–357. On this episode, see also Bushkovitch, *Petr Velikii: Bor'ba za vlast' (1671–1725)*, trans. N. L. Luzhitskaia (St. Petersburg: Dmitrii Bulanin, 2008), 359–364.

realized that Menshikov's return to favor would not help him, but even if he did not, the coincidence was not helpful to him and his supporters. Fortunately for Peter, Karl's ministers were skeptical. To be sure, they hid him from view, first in the Tirol and then in Naples (briefly an Austrian possession), but eventually Peter's agents found him. Petr Tolstoi, an experienced diplomat, was sent to convince him to return. His efforts succeeded in late 1717, and the tsarevich, with his mistress, made his way back to Russia. Peter followed all this from afar, spending several months in the Netherlands and making his first and only trip to France.[192] The return of father and son brought the crisis out into the open.

Peter returned to Russia in December 1717, and Aleksei, accompanied by Tolstoi, got to Moscow on the last day of January the next year. Peter immediately convened a meeting of the higher clergy, the senators, and other dignitaries in the Kremlin to witness his confrontation with his son. It was a dramatic moment: Aleksei was brought in as a prisoner, and Peter listed all the charges against him. In spite of his father's efforts to educate him and teach him how to be a monarch, he had shown his ingratitude by his flight to Vienna and his slander of his father. Is he not worthy of death? Peter concluded. At this point Aleksei fell on his knees, admitted his guilt, and begged for his life. Peter told him to stand up, to renounce the throne and name those who had advised him to flee. If he did that, he would be spared. The tsarevich agreed, and Peter took him into a small room where he named his associates. Shafirov read out the document with the renunciation of the throne and with the announcement of the new heir, Petr Petrovich. Everyone then proceeded to the palace church, where they signed the document and swore loyalty to the new heir. Many wept, even Peter's supporters such as Admiral Apraksin.[193] The next day Peter made public a manifesto that summarized Aleksei's misdeeds, very much as he had proclaimed at the meeting with the dignitaries, and announced the new heir.[194]

Peter devoted most of the next five months to the investigation of the affair. What he wanted to know was who had advised the tsarevich to flee to Vienna and, more generally, who had supported him. For years the

[192] Bushkovitch, *Peter the Great*, 364–382. [193] Ibid., 382–387.

[194] *PSZ* I, pt. 5, 534–539 (February 3, 1718); N. A. Voskresenskii, ed., *Zakonodatel'nye akty Petra I* (Moscow and Leningrad: Izadatel'stvo Akademii nauk SSSR, 1945), vol. I, 163–170; T. A. Bykova and M. M. Gurevich, *Opisanie izdanii grazhdanskoi pechati 1708–ianvar' 1725 g.* (Moscow: Izdatel'stvo Akademii nauk SSSR, 1955), 224–228. The manifesto included the statement that Peter had made his case to Aleksei at the funeral of Kronprintsessa Charlotte on October 27, 1715, two days before the birth of his son, and would deprive him of the throne "even though he was my only son" for he could not leave it to an heir who would lose what he had acquired with God's help and destroy the honor and glory of the Russian people (Voskresenskii, *Zakonodatel'nye akty Petra I*, vol. I, 165). This statement would seem to anticipate the succession decree of 1722.

resident diplomats had reported that the Russian elite was divided, some supporting Peter's innovations and some not. A complicating factor was Menshikov, whose overweening influence, at least until 1713, was widely disliked, and in 1716 he had come back to favor. Peter remained in Moscow with the court and his son until late March. In these weeks, the investigation was mainly into Aleksei's servants and also into his mother Evdokiia, for years a nun in Suzdal', who had maintained contacts with the outside world quite successfully. The result was the conviction and execution Major of Stepan Glebov, Evdokiia's main contact. In the case of the tsarevich, the main culprit was Aleksandr Kikin, a high official in the admiralty who had advised Aleksei to flee. He was executed on March 17. Prince V. V. Dolgorukii, since about 1710 an alternative favorite besides Menshikov, was also arrested but not yet fully investigated. At the end of March, Peter went to St. Petersburg, taking the court and his son with him.[195] There the investigation resumed, and grew wider and wider. By May it was clear that a large part of the Senate, the clergy, and the elite generally was sympathetic to Aleksei and had been for some time. This was the part of the investigation that the nineteenth-century historian of the case, N. G. Ustrialov, concealed, reducing the whole affair to a personal conflict of father and son. It presented Peter with a dilemma. Either he could follow it all up and execute or imprison the guilty, or he could forgive them and exile only the most important. Urged toward the latter course by his wife Ekaterina, Peter chose to muffle the affair. First, however, he brought the tsarevich on June 14 before the Senate and the officials and read out the charges and much of the results of the investigation. He did this in the main government building on St. Petersburg Island and left the windows open for the crowd (and the foreign diplomats) to hear. After that, the investigation continued, with Aleksei subjected to judicial torture and confessing more and more. On June 18, the clergy, headed by Stefan Iavorskii and Feofan Prokopovich, sent in its opinion. They cited the Biblical places that required obedience to the monarch, and then reviewed the Old and New Testaments. The Old pointed to punishment, in their view, and the New, the example of Christ, to mercy. In the end, they quoted that "the heart of the king is in the hand of the Lord" (Proverbs, 21). Finally, on June 24, Peter brought the full results to the Senate, and the officials and military officers met to consider the sentence. In all these proceedings, the testimony of Aleksei and others had implicated many of the judges, but nevertheless they voted for the death sentence and signed it.

[195] Bushkovitch, *Peter the Great*, 387–403. Aleksei arrived on March 22, Peter two days later: S. R. Dolgova and T. A. Lapteva, eds., *Trudy i dni Aleksandra Danilovicha Menshikova: Povsednevnye zapiski delam A. D. Menshikova 1716–1720, 1726–1727 gg.* (Moscow: Rossiiski fond kul'tury, 2004), 208.

An official manifesto appeared with the sentence and a detailed account of the testimony, but it was edited to leave out the names of most of the prominent supporters.[196] Before Peter could make a final determination, Tsarevich Aleksei died on June 26.[197] The case was closed.

Some remaining bits of the case lasted until the autumn, with the condemnation of Prince V. V. Dolgorukii to exile to his village and other punishments administered to lesser folk.[198] Peter had already declared his son Petr Petrovich the heir on February 3, so the succession seemed settled. In St. Petersburg the news had arrived by February 26, and the elite, both spiritual and lay, swore loyalty to the new heir in the Trinity church.[199] Russia's soldiers and diplomats, among others, were ordered to swear loyalty to the new heir and did so as the news reached them. Eleven regiments in Poland and elsewhere as well as the Reval garrison took the oath.[200] The diplomat Artemii Volynskii was then on a mission to Persia, and he and his staff swore the oath in a mobile church in Shemakha (in Azerbaidzhan) on June 8, 1718. The English surgeon traveling with him swore: "I John Bell acknowledge his Czarish Majesty's second son Prince Peter Petrovits for the very and true heir to the Russia Crown, and swearing upon the holy Gospel, I subscribe with my own hand. John Bell Ch[irurgus]." The Tatar Megmet "with the Russian name Aleksei" Tiavkelev added his oath on June 10.[201] From Paris, Peter's ambassador Baron Schleinitz sent in his own oath and those of his staff.[202]

All of the oaths were in vain, for Petr Petrovich died on April 25, 1719, only four and a half years old. He was buried in the Alexandr Nevskii Monastery near Peter's sister, Natal'ia Alekseevna.[203]

Succession in Court Culture and Religion

As the relations between Peter and his son Aleksei had worsened, especially after the birth of the two possible heirs in 1715, a new element

[196] Bushkovitch, *Peter the Great*, 403–421; Ustrialov, *Istoriia tsarstvovaniia Petra Velikogo*, vol. VI, 515–523, 529–536 (sentence); Bykova and Gurevich, *Opisanie*, 236–237 (Manifesto). The Manifesto, including many of the documents, eventually circulated in translation in Western Europe. See, for example, Weber, *Das veränderte Russland*, vol. I, 257–304; and *Manifest wegen der gerichtlichen Inquisition . . . über den Zarewitsch Alexium Petrowitsch* (Frankfurt and Leipzig: Johann Andreas Rüdigern, 1719).

[197] Dolgova and Lapteva, eds., *Trudy i dni Aleksandra Danilovicha Menshikova*, 234.

[198] Bushkovitch, *Peter the Great*, 421–424.

[199] Dolgova and Lapteva, eds., *Trudy i dni Aleksandra Danilovicha Menshikova*, 202.

[200] RGADA f. 140 (Prisiagi tsarevichu Petru Petrovichu), ll. 1–8, 16–26v, 75–224.

[201] RGADA f. 140, ll. 9–15 (Bell, l. 11, Tiavkelev: ll. 14–14v).

[202] RGADA, f. 140, ll. 41v–53.

[203] *Pokhodnyi zhurnal 1719 goda* (St. Petersburg, n.p., 1855), 119, 128; Dolgova and Lapteva, eds., *Trudy i dni Aleksandra Danilovicha Menshikova*, 304–305.

emerged in the person of Feofan Prokopovich, the Ukrainian bishop soon to become Peter's spokesman on succession as well as other political issues. His arrival at St. Petersburg in 1716 was part of the reconstruction of the court and the elaboration of a new and European court culture in the new capital and residence of the tsar. Feofan became the voice of the tsar, both in sermons preached in the main churches of the city and in print. Feofan had arrived at a critical time. Peter had been away since January 1716, and Tsarevich Aleksei had secretly left St. Petersburg for Vienna on September 26, but in October no one yet knew where he was.[204] Feofan's debut was his oration for the birthday of the infant tsarevich Petr Petrovich on October 29. This was an important event: Peter marked it with a feast ("they were rather merry") while traveling through Schleswig from Denmark.[205] According to the Menshikov diary, the prince himself, together with P. M. Apraksin, A. A. Matveev, and other senators, went to the Church of St. Isaac of Dalmatia and heard rector Prokopovich's "sufficient sermon" (*dovolno kazanie*). Afterward, they went to greet the baby along with the elite of St. Petersburg and dined merrily until two o'clock in the afternoon. Menshikov then continued the festivities in a smaller group.[206]

Feofan's 1716 sermon was devoted to the idea of monarchy. It was in two parts, the first on monarchy in general and the second on monarchy in Russia. The first was a spirited defense of monarchy, specifically hereditary monarchy. It was, he said, the most common form of government from ancient times to the present. It was the best to prevent internal discord and to repel external enemies. Hereditary monarchy was superior to elective monarchy, for the heir grew up learning the trade, so to speak, from his father. Elective monarchies led to internal strife and weakness, as he explained from the explicit example of Poland. Venice was able to manage to elect its doges only because it was a small state with unique conditions. Republics, other than the Venetian example, were also inferior to monarchies, as the example of the Roman republic demonstrated: its long history of internal discord, the Gracchi, Marius, and Sulla, led to the establishment of a monarchy under Augustus. Only then did Rome really prosper. Russia was fortunate in its monarchy. Peter had radically improved Russian administration, introduced new arts and sciences, and been victorious on land and sea. Previously Europe had despised the Russians as barbarians and now they treated them with respect. Feofan's rhetoric concealed, of course, some facts that did not fit very well with the picture. Peter had been effectively elected in

[204] Bushkovitch, *Peter the Great*, 339–358; *Pokhodnyi zhurnal* 1716, 19, 27–46.
[205] *Pokhodnyi ... 1716*, 49 (veselilis' dovol'no).
[206] Dolgova and Lapteva, eds., *Trudy i dni Aleksandra Danilovicha Menshikova*, 80.

1682, as his brother Ivan was the oldest surviving son of Tsar Aleksei. More seriously, who was the heir who was to continue the glorious work of Peter? The occasion was the birthday of Petr Petrovich, and the whereabouts of Tsarevich Aleksei were still unknown. Feofan simply praised the importance of heredity to the Russian monarchy without mentioning either of Peter's sons until the very end, when he listed the things that the audience had to be joyful about. Most important was Peter himself, then the tsar's son (for whom they also were to congratulate Tsaritsa Ekaterina), and finally Tsarevich Aleksei and the tsarevny (Anna and Elizabeth).[207]

Bishop Feofan went on to deliver a series of orations and sermons on important events and anniversaries in the court. When Peter returned from Europe in the fall of 1717, he composed a series of greetings in the personae of Peter's children, Petr, Anna, and Elisabeth, as well as a composition in the name of the Russian people. The children's greetings were simple expressions of joy at Peter's return, nothing more. The last greeting was full of praise for Peter and his accomplishments in war and peace, but said nothing about succession.[208]

He was not the only speaker. For the October 29 birthday of Petr Petrovich, now two years only, there was also a sermon at the church service on that day. This time the speaker was Gavriil Buzhinskii, another Ukrainian monk from the Kiev Academy who had come to St. Petersburg. The audience included Peter himself, Ekaterina, Menshikov, and various dignitaries, in the Trinity Church on the Peterburgskaia storona.[209] The theme was the happiness that the birth of children brought to their fathers. In this case, the birth of Petr Petrovich also brought happiness and benefits to Russia. He was the son of his father, and the virtues of fathers are passed on, he explained with numerous classical and Biblical examples, including that of Jesus the son of God(!).[210] "From these things know your well-being (*blagopoluchie*), O Russian state ... when you, Russia, have received the inheritance of such a monarch!"[211] He will be the inheritor of Peter's victories and other achievements, which he praised at some length. The second benefit of the boy's birth is that "the inheritance [of the ruling

[207] Feofan Prokopovich, *Slova i rechi* (St. Petersburg: Pri Sukhoputnom shliakhetnom kadetskom korpuse, 1760), vol. I, 99–119; Feofan Prokopovich, *Sochineniia* (Moscow and Leningrad: Izdatel'stvo Akademii nauk SSSR, 1961), 38–48.

[208] Prokopovich, *Slova i rechi*, vol. I, 167–194. All three greetings are dated October 21, but it is not clear what happened on that day. Peter returned on September 9: Dolgova and Lapteva, eds., *Trudy i dni Aleksandra Danilovicha Menshikova*, 165–166.

[209] Dolgova and Lapteva, eds., *Trudy i dni Aleksandra Danilovicha Menshikova*, 171–172. The diarist does not mention the sermon, only the church service and the celebration afterward. See Evgenii Petukhov, *Propovedi Gavriila Buzhinskogo (1717–1727)* (Iur'ev: Tipografiia K. Mattisena, 1901).

[210] Petukhov, *Propovedi Gavriila Buzhinskogo*, 84–92.

[211] Ibid., 92.

house] does not cease" (*nikogdazhe ne presekaetsia nasledie*).[212] Gavriil again illustrated the idea with classical and Biblical examples.[213] The throne would be safe, Russia a new Jerusalem. He concluded by congratulating both Peter and Ekaterina, the latter on her courage, which the son would inherit.[214] Gavriil nowhere said exactly that Petr Petrovich was the principal heir to the throne, but it was the implication throughout that he was at least a possible heir. A month later Feofan was the preacher again at the Trinity Church, this time for the name day of Tsaritsa Ekaterina (November 24).[215] Most of the sermon was on the love of God, true and false, and the martyr-saint Catherine was the example of that true love of God as well as her fellow men. At the end he adduced the example of Tsaritsa Ekaterina, whose love was exemplified in her behavior on the Prut campaign, where she showed her love for Peter and for Russia. Ekaterina's love appeared in her humility (*krotost'*) and justice, which made her a good ruler. She also showed her love of God and humanity in the establishment of the Order of St. Catherine.[216]

Feofan had become the main spokesman of the tsar in the Orthodox Church, and he did not omit the momentous occasion of the naming of Petr Petrovich as the heir. He spoke on February 3, 1718, the day of the proclamation, in Moscow. His speech was brief, celebrating the new heir with the now traditional words *otchich, dedich, i naslednik*, adding only the word *pravil'nyi* (correct) and repeating that he was chosen by God. He said nothing about Aleksei, exclaiming only on the bright future, a new dawn that awaited Russia with its future monarch.[217]

All of these events were the background to Feofan's next and major sermon, on the power and honor of the tsar, delivered on April 6, 1718 (Palm Sunday) in the Trinity Church in St. Petersburg before the tsar, Menshikov, and the senators.[218] The occasion was in the middle of the investigation of Tsarevich Aleksei. The text said nothing about succession, but defended the necessity of monarchy on the grounds of natural law and scripture. Everyone had to obey the ruler, including the clergy, and Feofan reminded the congregation of Peter's achievements and the evils brought about by disobedience (the Time of Troubles).[219] It was the

[212] Ibid., 92–97 (quotation 97). [213] Ibid., 97–101. [214] Ibid., 101–103.

[215] Dolgova and Lapteva, eds., *Trudy i dni Aleksandra Danilovicha Menshikova*, 177–178; Prokopovich, *Slova i rechi*, vol. I, 213–228; Prokopovich, *Sochineniia*, 68–76.

[216] Prokopovich, *Slova i rechi*, vol. I, 224–228; Prokopovich, *Sochineniia*, 74–76.

[217] Prokopovich, *Slova i rechi*, vol. I, 229–233.

[218] Dolgova and Lapteva, eds., *Trudy i dni Aleksandra Danilovicha Menshikova*, 212.

[219] Prokopovich, *Slova i rechi*, vol. I, 235–268; Prokopovich, *Sochineniia*, 76–93. I. P. Eremin thought that this sermon was a specific reaction to the February manifesto removing Aleksei from the succession, but the text does not support this conception:

last statement by Feofan on such themes before the death of Petr Petrovich early in 1719.

Feofan was an unusual and vivid speaker, and played a unique role in the last years of Peter's reign and beyond, but the church as a whole had to respond to the situation. As soon as the new heir was proclaimed in February 1718, archimandrite Feodosii (Ianovskii) of the Aleksandr Nevskii Monastery in St. Petersburg wrote to the tsar with a question: how was the new heir to be mentioned in the prayers during the liturgy? Was his name now to come first before that of Aleksei (all the members of the ruling family were usually mentioned), or was the name of Aleksei to be omitted?[220] For other churchmen, the situation was not easy. Stefan Iavorskii was clearly unhappy with the events, whether from sympathy for Aleksei or just despair at the tragedy is not clear.[221]

In any case, the resolution of the problem of succession achieved in 1718 was rendered moot by the death of the new heir the next year. His death left Russia with several possible heirs to the throne. There was Peter's grandson, Petr Alekseevich, not yet fully five years old but apparently healthy. There were also Peter's daughters, and even his nieces. The oldest of the daughters, Anna Petrovna, was herself only eleven years old in 1719. Peter, however, did not officially name an heir, leaving the issue unresolved over the next few years. While he considered the problem, he also issued a decree defining the procedure of succession, in the process opening the way to new possibilities and incidentally to new ideas.

Prokopovich, *Sochineniia*, 467. See also Bykova and Gurevich, *Opisanie*, 233, Prokopovich speech on Petr Petrovich, April 8, 1718 (for April 6?).

220 S. G. Runkevich, *Aleksandro-Nevskaia Lavra 1713–1913: Istoricheskoe issledovanie* (St. Petersburg: Sinodal'naia tipografiia, 1913), 23.

221 Bushkovitch, *Peter the Great*, 386–387, 407–409.

7 Peter's Heirs and Feofan Prokopovich 1719–1725

For Peter the Great, succession to the throne was not only a practical problem that required him to educate his eldest son, attempt to train him for the throne, and find him a suitable wife so as to secure the succession for yet another generation. It was also a theoretical problem, for Russian culture was changing rapidly, in large part because of Peter's own policies. Succession, as part of the mechanics of the state, had now to be understood and explained within the framework of European political thought and culture, both new to Russia. The succession crisis that broke with the flight of Tsarevich Aleksei to Vienna in 1716, and deepened with his trial and death two years later, brought the issue to a head. The presence of a possible heir in the person of the infant Petr Petrovich had provided an alternative to Aleksei's son, but only until April 25, 1719, when Petr Petrovich died. The story of the succession after that moment has not attracted attention from historians, yet it determined the future evolution of Russia and, not incidentally, formed the background for the principal Russian work of political theory from Peter's time, the *Pravda voli monarshei* of Feofan Prokopovich, then bishop of Pskov. Here was a new framework for succession in Russia, based for the first time on European thought.

The Succession Problem 1719–1725

The death of Petr Petrovich in April 1719 set off a whole series of rumors about the succession.[1] The French commercial agent Henri Lavie, who had recently acquired good informants in the Russian government and court, picked them up very quickly.[2] In June 1719, he reported that Peter

[1] S. M. Solov'ev, *Istoriia Rossii s drevneishikh vremen* (Moscow: Izdatel'stvo sotsial'no-ekonomicheskoi literatury, 1960–6), vol. IX, 532–537 (originally Moscow: Universitetskaia tipografiia, 1851–79); Igor' V. Kurukin, *Ekaterina I* (Moscow: Molodaia gvardiia, 2016), 133–146.

[2] Lavie had been sent in 1712 to improve Russian–French trade, especially in naval stores. Paul Bushkovitch, *Peter the Great: The Struggle for Power 1671–1725* (Cambridge: Cambridge University Press, 2001), 7; Samuel Baron, "Henri Lavie and the Failed Campaign to Expand Franco-Russian Commercial Relations (1712–1723),"

favored his eldest daughter, Anna Petrovna, for the throne, but that he did not want to openly express that wish since "les grands," who were calm only in appearance, might favor his grandson, and there were too many international complications.[3] The following month he wrote that he believed that Peter wanted to marry Anna to Karl Friedrich, Duke of Holstein, to provide her with a husband who could lead Russia in war if Peter died suddenly. The tsar had prepared an apartment in the Summer Palace for his grandson, possibly to prevent him from being seized by malcontents.[4] Later in the summer Lavie noted that Petr Alekseevich was well treated in his new lodgings, especially by his sisters, and that there was a rumor that he would be proclaimed heir in order to restore relations with the Holy Roman Emperor. The boy was handsome and healthy, interested in military affairs even at his tender age.[5] In the autumn Lavie reported Peter celebrated the birthday (October 12) of Petr Alekseevich, officially Grand Duke of Moscow.[6] The official court journal, however, reported that Peter was in Schlüsselburg that week to celebrate the anniversary of its capture.[7] Lavie was wrong about the object of the celebration. The first official celebration of the birthday of Petr

Forschungen zur osteuropäischen Geschichte 50 (1995): 29–50. Alfred Rambaud noted that Lavie's dispatches improved in 1719 with new informants: Alfred Rambaud, ed., *Recueil des instructions données aux ministers de France depuis les traités de la Westphalie jusqu'à la Révolution française VIII: Russie* (Paris: Félix Alcan, 1890), 132–134, esp. 132, note 1. The first of these new informants was the French sea captain de Collongues, serving in the Russian navy, who gave him better contacts, reporting his conversations with Admiral Apraksin: *SRIO* 40, 28, Lavie to Dubois, May 22, 1719 NS. Earlier on, Lavie said that Colongues could keep secrets: *SRIO* 34, 220, Lavie to Archbishop (later Cardinal) Guillaume Dubois, secretary of state for foreign affairs during the Regency, June 8, 1717 NS. The second and probably more important was the count Delonoy: "Je n'ai point encore eu l'honneur d'informer Votre Grandeur des soins que je me suis donnés de cultivar l'amitié de M-r le comte Delonoy, gentilhomme de la chamber de S. M. Czarienne dont l'épouse et la première dame des princesses, filles du Czar, et fort aimée et estimée de la Czarine, à cause de sa bonne conduite, sa sagesse et ses belles qualités. Ce gentilhomme, dont l'esprit est sublime et les connaissances infinies en beaucoup de choses, soit pour l'arrangement des intérêts d'un état, soit pour les finances et les arts, manufactures en general" had fallen afoul of "plusieurs gens en place" since he knew of their misdeeds and they were trying to ruin him and prevent him from getting a place in the administration of finances: Lavie to Dubois, July 25, 1719, *SRIO* 40, 38–39. Lavie reported earlier that Delonoy had been engaged by Peter in Paris and had arrived the day before to run a mirror and glass factory near St. Petersburg: *SRIO* 34, 259, Lavie to Dubois, October 29, 1717 NS.

[3] *SRIO* 40, 33, Lavie to Dubois, June 6, 1719 NS.
[4] *SRIO* 40, 40–41, Lavie to Dubois, July 25, 1719 NS.
[5] *SRIO* 40, 46, Lavie to Dubois, August 11, 1719 NS.
[6] *SRIO* 40, 62–63, Lavie to Dubois, October 26, 1719 NS. Lavie clearly never saw Petr Alekseevich, as he reported the four-year-old as being nine, if the number was correctly transcribed. He believed that if Petr Petrovich had lived, the tsar would have waited until both boys grew up and given the throne to the more worthy.
[7] *Pokhodnyi zhurnal . . . 1719* (St. Petersburg, n.p., 1855), 105–106, 123.

Alekseevich took place only on October 12, 1721, when the boy reached the age of six.[8]

Peter brought the Northern War to a victorious close with the Treaty of Nystad (August 30, 1721 OS). This was Peter's greatest moment of triumph, and the victorious end of the war transformed Russia's relations with Europe.[9] Russia moved toward an alliance with Sweden, and remained on good terms with Prussia. Peter sought friendship with France and Emperor Karl VI. For the latter, this was a change of front, for Karl had hardly been a friend of the tsar for some time. France had never had much of a relationship with Peter, having been preoccupied by the War of the Spanish Succession and weakened by the Regency during the first years of the reign of Louis XV (1715–23). Russia's main opponent was now England, in large part because of King George I's Hanoverian interests in Germany. Finally, Russia's longtime alliance with Denmark stumbled against the rapprochement with Sweden and Russian support for Karl Friedrich of Holstein, who had been in dispute with the king of Denmark over Schleswig since 1713. All of these changes reflected the new position of Russia in Europe. Peter had made his country into a major regional power, dominating the eastern coast of the Baltic and possessing a powerful navy. Russia's trade with Western Europe grew dramatically, though most of it was carried in English or Dutch ships. For all the unease in London and Hanover, Russia's aim was to maintain its position, not to try for further expansion in the north. Peter's aims were now in the east: after the Treaty of Nystad, Peter was already putting together an army to try to wrest from the Shah of Iran his northern provinces. He sailed down the Volga to this end in the summer of 1722, and did not return to St. Petersburg until the next year.[10] In these last years of the reign, a part of the tangled web of changing alliances was the possible marriages of Peter's daughters and Petr Alekseevich. The discussions and intrigues around the marriages were the result of European rulers and princes looking for Russian brides. They did not come on the initiative of the tsar or his advisers.

[8] *Pokhodnyi zhurnal . . . 1721*, 75.

[9] M. A. Polievktov, *Baltiiskii vopros v russkoi politike posle Nishtadskogo mira (1721–1725)*. Zapiski istoriko-filologicheskogo fakul'teta Sankt-Peterburgskogo universiteta 85 (St. Petersburg: Tipografiia M. A. Aleksandrova, 1907); James Frederick Chance, *George I and the Northern War: A Study of British-Hanoverian Policy in the North of Europe in the Years 1709 to 1721* (London: Smith, Elder, & Co., 1909); G. A. Nekrasov, *Russko-shvedskie otnosheniia i politika velikikh derzhav v 1721–1726 gg.* (Moscow: Nauka, 1964); Hans Bagger, *Ruslands alliancepolitik efter freden i Nystad: En studie i den slesvigske restitutionsspørgsmål indtil 1732* (Copenhagen: Rosenkilde og Bagger, 1974).

[10] I. V. Kurukin, *Persidskii pokhod Petra Velikogo: Nizovoi korpus na beregakh Kaspiia (1722–1735)* (Moscow: Kvadriga, 2010), 50–63.

The issue of succession remained open at the time of the Treaty of Nystad. Peter gave no hint of his intentions. Upon conclusion of the treaty the Senate, on the initiative of Feofan Prokopovich, proclaimed Peter *imperator*, the Latin word for emperor, in place of the traditional title of tsar, and Father of the Fatherland (*otets otechestva*).[11] At the end of December 1721, the Senate and Synod (including Feofan Prokopovich) also agreed to change the titles of his wife and daughters to match his new title *imperator*. His wife Catherine was henceforth to be titled *imperatritsa* or *tsesareva*, and his daughters *tsesarevny*. His grandson remained "grand prince" (*velikii kniaz'*) and Ivan V's daughters *tsarevny*.[12] None of these changes said anything about succession to the throne, but negotiations were afoot that potentially raised that issue.

As the war came to a close, Russia's dynastic relations with Europe had already expanded. The duke of Mecklenburg was Peter's nephew by marriage since 1716, and more connections were under discussion. Equally significant was the initiative from the court of Karl Friedrich, Duke of Holstein-Gottorp (1700–39). Besides his ducal inheritance, Karl Friedrich was the nephew of the late Charles XII, thus the king's closest male relative. At the death of Charles in 1718, the Swedish Riksdag chose his sister, Ulrika Eleonora, to be queen, and on her abdication it then chose her husband Friedrich of Hesse-Cassel as king in March 1720. The young duke of Holstein needed support for his claims to the throne of Sweden, an unlikely goal, but also to retain his inheritance in Holstein itself, which was repeatedly threatened by the king of Denmark. Russia was not the first choice of the duke's advisers, but it was the only one to show any interest. In spring 1720, Andreas Ernst von Stambke, the emissary of Karl Friedrich, arrived in St. Petersburg to solicit the hand of Anna Petrovna in marriage.[13] A year later, in May 1721, Karl Friedrich himself arrived in St. Petersburg with the tsar and tsaritsa themselves.[14]

[11] Paul Bushkovitch, "The Roman Empire in the Era of Peter the Great," in *Rude and Barbarous Kingdom Revisited: Essays in Russian History in Honor of Robert O. Crummey*, ed. Chester Dunning, Russell Martin, and Daniel Rowland (Bloomington, Indiana: Slavica, 2008), 155–172.

[12] *Polnoe sobranie postanovlenii i rasporiazhenii po vedomstvu pravoslavnogo ispovedaniia Rossiiskoi imperii*, 2nd ed. (St. Petersburg: Sinodal'naia tipografiia, 1879), vol. I, 400–401 (December 24, 1721); *PSZ* I, no. 3869, 467 (December 23, 1721); N. A. Voskresenskii, ed., *Zakonodatel'nye akty Petra I* (Moscow and Leningrad: Izadatel'stvo Akademii nauk SSSR, 1945), vol. I, 173–174. The decree was intended to provide correct titles for the traditional wish of many years (*mnogoletie*) in the Christmas Eve liturgies.

[13] *SRIO* 40, 94, Lavie to Dubois, May 27, 1720 NS; Bagger, *Ruslands alliancepolitik*, 99–100. The idea of a Holstein marriage with Tsarevna Anna Petrovna had come up in 1713–14: Polievktov, *Baltiiskii vopros*, 30, 73.

[14] *SRIO* 40, 253, Lavie to Dubois, June 30, 1721 NS; H. F. de Bassewitz, "Éclaircissements sur plusieurs faits arrivés sous le regne de Pierre le grand," *Magazin für die neue Historie*

At this point, the Holsteiners were still mainly concerned about the duke's claim to the Swedish throne, and their proposal of marriage was tied to Peter's support for that project. They rather naïvely thought that if Peter married one of his daughters to Karl Friedrich and the latter mounted the Swedish throne as Peter's son-in-law, the tsar would let him have Livonia. In reality, the Russians received the Baltic provinces in the Treaty of Nystad, and pledged not to interfere in Swedish politics. Karl Friedrich and his advisers had to start over. They decided that the marriage was still essential to maintain Holstein's position, even if the Swedish throne was not in sight.[15] The Russians asked the duke to remain in St. Petersburg, which he did as the discussions about his marriage to Anna Petrovna continued. For Peter, the duke of Holstein, with his pretensions to the Swedish throne and his claims to parts of Schleswig (ruled by the king of Denmark), was a useful element in his evolving relations with the northern kingdoms and therefore with Europe as a whole.

The Choice of the Heir

Soon after the peace, the imperial ambassador, Stefan Wilhelm Kinsky, tried to convince Peter to proclaim his grandson heir, but did not insist on it, according to the newly arrived French ambassador Jacques de Campredon writing in November 1721.[16] Kinsky, the Prussian envoy Gustav von Mardefeldt, and the duke of Holstein spent much time over the winter trying to arrange a marriage of the duke with Anna Petrovna and to encourage the succession of Petr Alekseevich. Mardefeldt told Campredon that the Russian people had a great affection for the young prince, but the French ambassador was skeptical.[17] Lavie shared his skepticism: to be sure Kinsky wanted Petr Alekseevich to be the heir, but the "party of the *tsarevny*" was too strong at the moment. It seemed, he thought, that the tsar wanted to establish the succession on Anna Petrovna.[18] Mardefeldt was working with General P. I. Iaguzhinskii, who was "in the interests of the emperor," that is to say, he supported

und Geographie IX (1775): 338–340. Russian translation: G. F. Bassevich, "Zapiski grafa Bassevicha," *Russkii arkhiv*, 1, 2, 5, 6 (1865–6).

15 Bagger, *Ruslands alliancepolitik*, 100–116.

16 *SRIO* 40, 302–302, Campredon to Cardinal Dubois, St. Petersburg, November 7, 1721 NS. For Cardinal Dubois's instructions to Campredon of August 25, 1721, see Rambaud, ed., *Recueil des instructions données aux ministers de France*, vol. VIII, pt. I, 233–247.

17 *SRIO* 40, 346–347, Campredon to Dubois, November 21, 1721 NS.

18 *SRIO* 40, 354–355, Lavie to Dubois, November 24, 1721 NS. Who was the "party of the tsarevny"? Surely it included their mother Ekaterina, but Lavie does not say.

the Habsburg plans.[19] Iaguzhinskii, however, could not accomplish much because the tsar was opposed to Kinsky's plans and even annoyed at the emperor for his entreaties on behalf of his grandson Petr Alekseevich.[20] P. P. Shafirov also assured Campredon, in November 1721, that Peter had not finally decided on the succession, but preferred Anna Petrovna. He would probably, Shafirov said, marry her to a foreign prince without a territory who would convert to Orthodoxy. The duke of Holstein was not the likeliest candidate, since Peter inclined at that point toward marrying him to his younger daughter Elizabeth.[21] At the end of 1721, Peter went to Moscow to prepare for the Persian campaign in the coming summer, and Karl Friedrich followed him with his suite.[22]

Whatever the diplomats were urging, Peter seems to have inclined toward Anna Petrovna as his heir. Besides Holstein, however, France also had plans for marriages with Anna. These schemes were part of the maneuvers of French foreign policy in the years after the death of Louis XIV in 1715, the years of the regency. Until 1723 the major figures in Paris were the regent, the duke of Orleans, and his adviser, Abbé Gulliaume Dubois. To make up for the weakness of France in those years, both of them cultivated an alliance with Britain, France's main rival for power. This was an unstable situation, and led to a variety of unrealized projects. One of them was the reconciliation of Russia and England, and marriage plans were part of that project. A Russo-French marriage also would cement friendship and give France leverage in the north of Europe. It took a while, however, for these plans to mature. Campredon pressed his government for an answer to the idea of a French marriage for Anna soon after he arrived in Moscow following the tsar. His conversations with Shafirov and other officials led him to believe that the tsar would probably favor a marriage to Louis, Duke of Chartres, both because Chartres was a prince of the blood in France and because he had no territory of his own. Louis (1703–52) was an interesting match; he was

[19] *SRIO* 40, 357, Campredon to Dubois, November 24, 1721 NS. Iaguzhinskii (1683–1736) was born in Lithuania (Belorussia), the son of a church organist. He came to Russia with his family as a child, and ended up in the Preobrazhenskii guards. From about 1701 he began to play a role in diplomacy and governments, and in January 1722, Peter named him General-Procurator of the Senate. He played a prominent role in Russian politics from then on until his death: V. Fursenko, "Iagushinskii (Iaguzhinskii), Pavel Ivanovich," in *Russkii biograficheskii slovar'*, Iablonovskii–Fomin (St. Petersburg: Izdanie Imperatorskogo Russkogo istoricheskogo obshchestva, 1913), 7–28. He appears in most histories of the later years of Peter's reign.

[20] *SRIO* 40, 396, Campredon to Dubois, December 4/15, 1721; Polievktov, *Baltiiskii vopros*, 187, following Kinsky's dispatches of October 1721.

[21] *SRIO* 40, 311–312, Campredon to Dubois, November 18, 1721 NS: 341–342, Campredon to Dubois, November 21, 1721 NS.

[22] *SRIO* 40, 401–402, Campredon to Dubois, December 19, 1721 NS.

the son of Philippe II of Orleans, then regent in France. The match could be important, because the French ambassador believed that Peter intended Anna to succeed him as empress, possibly even receiving the title while Peter was alive. If the French government, however, wanted to make the duke of Chartres king of Poland (a project then under consideration), it would have to abandon the idea of marrying him to Anna Petrovna. For Elizaveta, he thought, Prince Georg of Hesse-Cassel might be an appropriate husband, as the latter had pretensions to the throne of Sweden.[23] To all these plans, Peter introduced an unexpected element.

Peter introduced the new order of succession with his decree of February 5, 1722 from his old residence in Preobrazhenskoe near Moscow.[24] The decree declared that the succession to the Russian throne would henceforth be at the discretion of the reigning monarch. In European terminology, the decree established a form of testamentary succession. The decree did not merely assert the new law, it also justified it. Peter's son, it read, had been filled with the wickedness of Absalom, the son of King David who led a rebellion against his father [2 Kings/2 Samuel 13–18]. Aleksei's wickedness grew from the custom of succession to the eldest son. Since he was that eldest son, he saw no reason to obey his father. Such a form of succession was only a custom, Peter went on to proclaim, established "I do not know for what reason," and recounted the Biblical story of Isaac's wife. When her husband was old, she convinced him to give his inheritance to his younger son, and God's blessing followed. Peter referred here to the story of Esau and Jacob, the latter favored by their mother Rebecca.[25] The tsar then turned to the story of the sons of Ivan III. In Peter's words, Ivan had collected the dispersed lands of the descendants of Vladimir and then looked for a worthy heir. Twice he changed his mind, first giving the throne to his grandson Dmitrii and then later to his second son Vasilii. He explicitly cited the *Book of Degrees* as his source for the story, though the story he recounted, while accurate, did not follow the text of the *Book of Degrees*.[26] There were other

[23] *SRIO* 49, 53–60, Campredon to Dubois, February 20, 1722 NS.

[24] *PSZ* VI, no. 3893, 496–497; Voskresenskii, ed., *Zakondatel'nye akty Petra I*, vol. I, 174–176.

[25] Peter's version of the Bible story in Genesis 27 was not completely accurate. Rebecca told Jacob to deceive his father to get the blessing instead of his older twin brother Esau. The blessing was from Isaac, not from God.

[26] Gail Lenhoff and N. N. Pokrovskii, eds., *Stepennaia kniga tsarskogo rodosloviia po drevneishim spiskam* (Moscow: Iazyki slavianskikh kul'tur, 2008), vol. II, 273; N. N. Pokrovskii and A. V. Sirenov, *Latukhinskaia Stepennaia kniga 1676 goda* (Moscow: Iazyki slavianskoi kul'tury, 2012), 427–428. Peter gave precise dates for the events that are lacking in the *Book of Degrees* (either version) but are found in chronicles such as the Nikon Chronicle: *PSRL* 12, 246–247, 255.

examples, he said, but they would be put out in print. Finally, he cited the precedent of his own 1714 law of single inheritance that required fathers to leave their property to one son only, though they could choose which son and did not have to give it to the eldest. Peter asserted that this power in the hands of the monarch would keep his children from wickedness: it would be a bridle on them. Everyone was to swear an oath to obey this decree, on pain of death for treason and the curse of the church. Two days later, P. A. Tolstoi read the decree to the senators together with Archbishop Feodosii of Novgorod and Feofan Prokopovich, all of whom swore the required oath.[27]

The new law did not put an end to the intrigues. When he was reflecting on the various marriage possibilities, Campredon did not know that on February 5/16, Peter had already signed the new succession decree and presented it to Senate. On February 12/23, the French ambassador described the ceremony at which the decree was read in the square before the Kremlin (presumably Red Square) to the great approval of the crowd. He interpreted the decree to mean that Peter wanted to give the throne to one of the children of Tsaritsa Ekaterina, namely Anna or Elizaveta, though the tsar's grandson still had adherents.[28] The Saxon-Polish ambassador Jean Lefort reported as fact at the end of February that Peter wanted to leave the throne to Anna Petrovna.[29] Over the next three years, both Anna Petrovna and Petr Alekseevich were the objects of continuous rumors and intrigues. In Anna's case they revolved around her marriage to Karl Friedrich, Duke of Holstein.[30] Campredon still believed at the end of the year that Peter would give his throne to Anna and marry her to one of the Naryshkins. One of the reasons was the very great influence of the tsar's wife Ekaterina, who naturally favored her daughters over Peter's grandson.[31] The Holstein minister von Bassewitz believed as well that Peter wanted Anna as his heir, after his own death and that of his wife Ekaterina, and hoped for a marriage with his master, the duke.[32] So apparently did Shafirov.[33]

By the end of the summer of 1723, among long accounts of the Holstein intrigues in Sweden, the French ambassador reported that

[27] Voskresenskii, *Zakonodatel'nye akty Petra I*, vol. I, 176–177.
[28] *SRIO* 49, Campredon, February 23, 1722 NS, 65–66.
[29] Polievktov, *Baltiiskii vopros*, 181 (note).
[30] Polievktov, *Baltiiskii vopros*, 236, 281–283, 288–290; Nekrasov, *Russko-shvedskie otnosheniia*, 172–182; Bagger, *Ruslands alliancepolitik*, 113–115, 126.
[31] *SRIO* 49, 246–247, Campredon to Dubois, October 19, 1722 NS.
[32] After praising Anna's beauty, grace, and education, he commented: "C'était dans les mains de cette Princesse, que Pierre le Grand souhaitoit de voir passer son sceptre, après sa mort et celle de son épouse. Le mariage le plus convenable à cette vue étant celui de Charles-Frédéric [of Holstein]." De Bassewitz, "Éclaircissements sur plusieurs faits," 370–371.
[33] Polievktov, *Baltiiskii vopros*, 179.

Peter had decided to crown his wife as empress, to include her formally in government, and to establish the succession on Anna Petrovna.[34] Peter publicly announced the coming coronation only in November. In the brief manifesto, he alluded to the common European practice of coronation for a ruler's wife and cited several precedents of early Byzantine emperors who crowned their wives. He also asserted that her help to him, especially in the Prut campaign of 1711, made her worthy to be crowned.[35] The coronation took place on May 7/18, 1724 in the Dormition Cathedral in the Moscow Kremlin.[36]

The coronation of Peter's wife established her as co-ruler, with the implication that she would remain in power after his death. As we have seen in the cases of Irina Godunova and Tsaritsa Evdokiia in 1645, this was not entirely new, though there is no evidence that Peter knew of either precedent. The official description of the ceremony, published later in the year and again after Peter's death, made clear that she was being crowned not just as a consort. In the center of the Kremlin's Dormition Cathedral, where the ceremony took place, were two thrones of equal size and height from the ground. Even more important were the prayers of Fedosii, the archbishop of Novgorod, who conducted the ceremony. He called on God, who had anointed David as king over Israel, to look down on Ekaterina, "whom You have placed as ruler over your people ... give her strength from on high, place on her head the crown of honorable stone, and grant them long life. Give into her right hand the scepter of salvation, place her on the throne of justice." Then he switched again to the plural, meaning both Peter and Ekaterina, "guard them with all the weapons of Your holy spirit, strengthen their muscle, subject to them every barbarian tribe" and keep them in the

[34] *SRIO* 49, 363, Campredon to Louis XV, August 13, 1723 NS. Only two years earlier in 1721, after the Senate had given Peter the new title "imperator," it discussed a new title for Ekaterina, but this seems to have been only a discussion about the title, nothing more: Solov'ev, *Istoriia Rossii s drevneishikh vremen*, vol. IX, 538–539.

[35] *PSZ* I, 7, no. 4366 (November 15, 1723), 161–162. The Byzantines did crown their empresses, but Peter's Byzantine precedents were unexpected: Basiliscus (ruled 475–476) and his wife Zenonis, who was quickly overthrown and killed together with her; Justinian (which?) and "Lupicia," Heraclius (ruled 610–641) and his wife Martina, who was also his niece, and Leo the Wise (ruled 886–912) and Maria. Leo had four wives, none of them named Maria, but Peter seems to have confused him with Leo III the Isaurian (ruled 717–747) who did have a wife named Maria.

[36] *Opisanie koronatsii eia velichestva imperatritsy Ekateriny Alekseevny* (St. Petersburg and Moscow: Pri senate, 1724–5); N. I. Pavlenko, *Ekaterina I* (Moscow: Molodaia gvardiia, 2004), 24–27; Kurukin, *Ekaterina I*, 146–160. Gary Marker, *Imperial Saint: The Cult of St. Catherine and the Dawn of Female Rule in Russia* (DeKalb, Illinois: Northern Illinois University Press, 2007), 170–204, argues that the cult of St. Catherine as it developed in Russia from the seventeenth century provided a framework for the acceptance of a female empress and eventually female rule after Peter's death.

correct faith.[37] Then Peter placed the crown on her head, and the bishops anointed her with oil.[38] The ceremony crowned her in the image of King David, with explicit reference to God's choice of David as king of Israel. Campredon saw the significance of this element: "The most remarkable thing was the tsaritsa was anointed, contrary to the ordinary usage, so that by this ceremony she is recognized as ruling and sovereign after the death of the tsar her husband."[39] If the ceremony and Peter's earlier manifesto did not spell out in words that she was now a potential ruler, it was not necessary. The anointment made that clear, and also Peter was still alive and as yet showed no signs of serious illness. While he was alive he would always be the tsar, she only his helpmate. If he were to die, then the ceremony made her the obvious ruler, as was the case in Europe if the male successor was too young or there was none. There was no need to spell that out.

The coronation of Ekaterina did not remove the question of succession, for if Peter and Catherine both died, the potential heirs were still his grandson Petr and Anna Petrovna. The duke of Holstein's marriage project had not progressed much by the time Peter left for Persia in the spring of 1722, shortly after the succession decree. As he left, a plea for clarity from the duke produced an answer from Peter that only postponed the decision.[40] Even after returning from Persia, Peter waited for a clearer international situation, especially with Sweden. He settled on the Holstein marriage in May 1724, right after the coronation of Catherine I.[41] The context was the earlier treaty of Stockholm (February 22, 1724) that established an alliance between Russia and Sweden that lasted only until 1727.[42] The Holstein marriage treaty was not concluded until

[37] "Gospodi ... izhe chrez Samuil proroka izbravyi raba tvoego Davida i pomaza ego vo Tsari nad liudom tvoim Israilem ... prizri ot Sviatago zhlishcha tvoego, i vernuiu tvoiu rabu ... imperatritsu Ekaterinu ... iuzhe blagovolil esi postaviti Polelitel'nitsu nad iazykom tvoim ... odei iu silu s vysoty, nalozhi na glavu ee venets ot kamene chestnago i darui im dolgotu dni. Dazhd' v desnitus eia Skeptr Spaseniia, Posadi iu na Prestol pravdy, ogradi ikh vseoruzhiem svatogo tvoego dukkha, ukrepi ikh myshtsu, podchini im vsia varvarskii iazyk ...," *Opisanie koronatsii*, 34–36.

[38] *Opisanie koronatsii*, 37–38, 42–43.

[39] "Ce qu'il y a de plus remarquable, c'est que la Czarine a été ointe, contre l'usage ordinaire, en sorte que par cette cérémonie elle est reconnue régente et souveraine après la mort du Czar, son époux." *SRIO* 52, 220, Campredon to count de Morville, May 26, 1724. The "ordinary usage" presumably meant the Russian usage, though erroneously, as there had been no coronations of tsaritsy in Russia. In France and much of Western Europe, the queens were anointed at their coronation: Nicolas Menin, *Traité historique et chronologique du sacre et couronnement des rois et des reines de France* (Paris: Jean van Septeren, 1723), 401.

[40] Bagger, *Ruslands alliancepolitik*, 115–116.

[41] Nekrasov, *Russko-shvedskie otnosheniia*, 172

[42] Ibid., 96–130. Text of the treaty: *PSZ* I, VII, 254–259, and the secret articles in P. Shchebal'skii, *Politicheskaia sistema Petra III* (Moscow: Universitetskaia tipografiia,

November 24/December 5, 1724. The public articles of the Holstein treaty mostly consisted of the usual detailed arrangements about the household and income of Anna as Duchess of Holstein as well as her renunciation of her rights to the Russian throne for herself and her descendants. The first secret article, however, contradicted the public text and reserved to Peter the right to name one of her descendants as his successor.[43] Thus Anna still figured one way or another in the succession to the Russian throne two months before Peter's death. At the time of the final agreement for Anna Petrovna to marry the duke of Holstein, Mardefeldt was convinced that Peter still favored her over his grandson to take the throne after his death.[44] The marriage of Anna and the duke, however, did not take place until May 21, 1725, after Peter's death.

Her younger sister Elizaveta did not play a major role in the succession schemes, but she was not wholly absent.[45] She figured most often in schemes for a French marriage.[46] The first mention seems to have been early in 1721. Campredon reported that Tsar Peter might make a French son-in-law the king of Poland, but it was not clear which daughter was intended.[47] A few months later he spoke of marrying Elizaveta to Prince Georg of Hesse-Cassel (as there were other plans for Anna), whom the French at that moment thought a suitable candidate for the throne of

Katkov i ko., 1870), prilozheniia, 1–2. In the first secret article Peter promised to use his "good offices" to help him with Schleswig. In 1727, Sweden joined the Hanoverian alliance of France and England against the Vienna alliance of Russia and Austria: Nekrasov, *Russko-shvedskie otnosheniia*, 158–170; Gunnar Wetterberg, *Från tolv till ett: Arvid Horn (1664–1742)* (Stockholm: Atlantis, 2006), 449–459. See also Bagger, *Ruslands alliancepolitik*, 124–132.

[43] F. Martens, ed., *Sobranie traktatov traktatov i konventsii zakliuchennykh Rossiei s inostrannymi derzhavami*, 15 vols. (St. Petersburg: Tipografiia ministerstva putei soobshcheniia, 1874–1909), vol. V, 215–232; Bagger, *Ruslands alliancepolitik*, 133–140. Another secret article bound Russia to help the duke recover his part of Schleswig from the king of Denmark.

[44] *SRIO* 15, 237–244, Memorandum of Mardefeldt, 1724, undated but around the time of the Holstein marriage.

[45] The marriage plans for Elizaveta scarcely figure in any of the standard biographies, which are generally thin on her youth: Kazimierz Waliszewski, *La dernière des Romanovs: Élisabeth 1re impératrice de Russie 1741–1762* (Paris: Plon-Nourrit, 1902); Francine-Dominique Liechtenhan, *Élisabeth 1re de Russie: L'autre impératrice* (Paris: Fayard, 2007), 15–23, 32–37; Konstantin Pisarenko, *Elizaveta Petrovna* (Moscow: Molodaia gvardiia, 2014), 14–23.

[46] *SRIO* 40, 268, Lavie to Dubois, September 5, 1721 NS ; 304, Campredon to Dubois, November 8, 1721 NS, reporting that "a friend" told him that Peter wanted leave the throne to Anna Petrovna and marry her to one of the Naryshkins, so it would be best for France to marry Elizaveta to some French prince.

[47] *SRIO* 40, 350–351, Campredon to Dubois, November 24, 1721 NS. It is not clear from Campredon's text whether he believed this or was reporting the words of Henning Friedrich, Count Bassewitz, the Holstein minister.

Sweden.[48] During these weeks the Russian court celebrated the end of the Swedish war, with Peter distributing gold medals. He also celebrated the maturity of Elizaveta (at age thirteen, on January 28, 1722), cutting off the guiding strings of her dress symbolic of her childhood and giving them to her governess.[49] The idea of the Hesse-Cassel marriage came to nothing, in part because Campredon recommended to the French government the option of marrying her to the duke of Chartres (who was also a candidate for Anna).[50] During this time, rumors even floated around that she might be married to one of the sons of the king of Spain.[51] Insofar as the French government was serious about this project, it began to discuss it only in autumn 1722. By early 1723, Dubois had decided Russia and France needed to be allies. The alliance was to be cemented by a marriage and a Russo-French condominium in Poland ruled by the duke of Chartres and his wife, one of Peter's daughters, unspecified but in fact Elizaveta.[52] Dubois died, however, in August, and the regent, Philippe of Orleans, died in December. In the event the young duke of Chartres, now duke of Orleans, married a German princess early in 1724.[53] There were hints of another French marriage scheme late in the year, but the French plan for a reconciliation of Russia and Britain came to naught. That was the end of the marriage plans as well.[54] In none of these ultimately unsuccessful ideas for a French marriage did succession to the Russian throne play any role. Neither Peter nor the European courts seem to have considered Elizaveta a possible heir.

If the succession by Anna Petrovna was still a possibility in 1722 and after, it did not mean that maneuvers on the part of Peter's grandson went away. Meanwhile the Austrian ambassador Kinsky continued to lobby to

[48] *SRIO* 49, 36, Campredon to Dubois, February 2, 1722 NS; 60, Campredon to Dubois, February 20, 1722 NS.

[49] *SRIO* 49, 44, Campredon to Dubois, February 9, 1722 NS. Campredon described the ceremony for Elizaveta as "coupes les ailes," the end of her childhood. See also de Bassewitz, "Éclaircissements sur plusieurs faits," 345; and *Pokhodnyi zhurnal 1722 goda* (St. Petersburg, 1855), 26 (mentioning only the celebration of the peace).

[50] *SRIO* 48, 122, Campredon to Dubois, July 24, 1722 NS.

[51] *SRIO* 49, 90, Campredon to Dubois, April 3, 1722 NS.

[52] *SRIO* 52, 22 (French memorandum, February 10, 1723 NS); 62–68, Dubois to Campredon, August 1, 1723 NS.

[53] *SRIO* 49, 166, 185, Dubois to Campredon, Versailles, October 14, 1722 NS; 316, 319, Campredon to Louis XV, March 13, 1723 NS; Albert Vandal, *Louis XV et Élisabeth de Russie: Étude sur les rélations de la France et de la Russie au dix-huitième siècle* (Paris: Plon, Nourrit, 1896), 53–57, 62–63, 68; Jean Dureng, *Le Duc de Bourbon et l'Angleterre* (Paris: Hachette, 1911), 38. Cf. P. P. Cherkasov, *Dvuglavyi Orel i korolevskie lilii* (Moscow: Nauka, 1995).

[54] Vandal, *Louis XV et Élisabeth de Russie*, 77; Dureng, *Le Duc de Bourbon*, 208–211, 231–234 ; Sergei Mezin, *Petr I vo Frantsii* (St. Petersburg: Evropeiskii dom, 2015), 106 (Peter to Kurakin, January 1724).

secure the succession on Petr Alekseevich. As the nephew of Karl VI, the boy would secure a favorable attitude to the Habsburgs, but Kinsky and his allies, including Iaguzhinskii, went farther: they wanted the boy married to one of his half-sisters, Anna or Elizaveta. Peter had such authority over the church that he could secure this arrangement, they thought, and it would reconcile his desire for a daughter on the throne with the alleged desire of the Russians to have Petr Alekseevich as their ruler rather than Peter's daughters.[55] The proposed wife in this scheme was Elizaveta.[56] Nothing came of these fantastic plans, given the influence of Ekaterina and Peter's reported dislike of his grandson.[57]

The intrigues and rumors about the marriages of Peter's daughters and his grandson occupied the minds of the diplomats and presumably the Russian court. The reality of the family of the tsar was more prosaic. Peter ordered the Synod on September 2, 1720 to convey to the clergy that they were to mention the names of the ruling house during the Great Entrance (part of the mass) in the following order: Tsar Peter naturally first, then Tsaritsa Ekaterina, then Tsaritsa Praskov'ia (the widow of Tsar Ivan Alekseevich), then "the noble Grand Duke Petr Alekseevich and the noble tsarevny." On September 22, 1721 the Synod got around to sending the order out to the clergy throughout the land.[58] Peter's grandson was to be named first among the children, ahead of Peter's daughters. This was to be expected for a male child or grandchild, but it meant that everyone in Russia who went to church heard his name first, among the offspring of the tsar.

All of the children and grandchildren of the tsar seem to have lived more or less together under the supervision of Ekaterina and her court. Petr Alekseevich was now seven years old and a healthy child, and Peter treated him as part of the family. Before he went to the Caspian, he appointed a teacher for the boy, one Ivan Zeiken or Zeiker, a Hungarian German who seems to have succeeded in teaching him Latin. The tutor came from the household of Aleksandr L'vovich Naryshkin, Peter's cousin and the son of Lev Kirillovich Naryshkin, Peter's uncle and a major figure at the court in the 1690s.[59] Peter treated Petr Alekseevich as his grandson, if not as the heir. Judging by the surviving

[55] *SRIO* 49, 128–132, Campredon to Dubois, July 30, 1722 NS; 146, Dubois to Campredon, September 11, 1722 NS.

[56] *SRIO* 49, 247, Campredon to Dubois, October 19, 1722 NS.

[57] *SRIO* 49, 285–286. Campredon to Dubois, January 6, 1723 NS.

[58] *Polnoe sobranie postanovlenii i rasporiazhenii*, vol. I, 282.

[59] From 1718 to 1722 Tsaritsa Ekaterina looked after the boy. N. I. Pavlenko, *Petr II* (Moscow: Molodaia gvardiia, 2006), 27–29, 172–174. Naryshkin (1694–1745) had spent the years 1708, 1713, and 1718 in Holland, England, and France learning the skills of a naval officer. Peter kept the upbringing of his grandson in the family: *PiB* X,

correspondence of the tsar's children and grandchildren in those years, he lived in close contact with Anna and Elizaveta.[60] During these years, perhaps even a bit earlier, Peter ordered portraits of all of his children and grandchildren as well as his wife Ekaterina. Portraits of the tsar and some members of his family were not completely new, since some are extent from the later seventeenth century. Peter, however, had begun to hire West European painters to come to Russia to serve the needs of the court and elite. One of the first was Johann Gottfried Tannauer (1680–1737?), hired by Urbich in 1710. Indeed, Tannauer painted portraits of Tsarevich Aleksei Petrovich and his bride Charlotte around the time of the wedding or soon after.[61] Besides Tannauer, Peter's agents in Paris had engaged Louis Caravaque (1684–1754) in 1715 to come to St. Petersburg, and it was he who painted the children and Peter's grandson Petr Alekseevich. These were among the first portraits of children in Russia, and the portrait of Petr Petrovich as the naked Cupid with a bow was certainly unique. Caravaque painted Anna and Elizaveta, the latter also separately as a nude goddess, probably when she was about ten years old. Petr Alekseevich, the future Tsar Peter II, was also among the set, portrayed with his sister Natal'ia as Apollo and Diana. The dates of all of these works are conjectural, but they seem to date mostly from about 1716 or 1717, except for those of Petr Alekseevich and his sister, which must come from about 1722, judging in part from the subjects' apparent ages.[62] As all of the children and

694–695; A. B. Lobanov-Rostovskii, *Russkaia rodoslovnaia kniga* (St. Petersburg: Izdatel'stvo A. S. Suvorina, 1895), vol. 2, 6–8; [Anon.] "Naryshkin, Aleskandr L'vovich," *Russkii biograficheskii slovar'*, Naake-Nakenskii–Nikolai Nikolaevich Starshii (St. Petersburg: Izdanie Imperatorskogo Russkogo istoricheskogo obshchestva, 1914), 80–82.

[60] N. Iu. Bolotina, ed., "Epistoliarnoe nasledie zhenshchin tsarskoi sem'i (pervaia tret' XVIII veka)," *Rossiiskii arkhiv* XX (2011): 11–69.

[61] Larissa Vasser, *Europäische Hofkünstler in St. Petersburg in der ersten Hälfte des 18. Jahrhunderts: Bildhauer Bartolomeo Carlo Rastrelli, Maler Johann Gottfried Tannauer und Louis Caravaque: Ein Beitrag zur "Europäisierung" Russlands* (Berlin: Logos Verlag, 2015), 45–46, 51–52, 69–70, 217–220; T. A. Lebedeva, *Ivan Nikitin* (Moscow: Iskusstvo, 1975), 18–19 (Tannauer's contract: October 1, 1710), 143. Tannauer was the teacher and mentor of the Russian painter Ivan Nikitin. See also O. S. Evangulova, *Izobrazitel'noe iskusstvo v Rossii pervoi chetverti XVIII veka* (Moscow: Izdatel'stvo Moskovskogo universiteta, 1987), 156–163.

[62] Vasser, *Europäische Hofkünstler in St. Petersburg*, 50–51, 73–82, 228–242, 263–269; A. Dorozhkin, "Portrety kisti Karavaka," in *Zolotoi os'mnadtsatyi: Russkoe iskusstvo 18 veka v otechestvennom iskusstvoznanii* (St. Petersburg: Izdatel'stvo Sankt-Peterburgskogo universiteta, 2006), 37–62, esp. 38–42. The portrait of Elizaveta as a nude goddess also shows her holding a medallion with a picture of Peter himself. This element has caused some art historians to date it to a later period, interpreting it as her claim to legitimacy when empress. This interpretation does not explain why she would have wanted a picture of herself as a child or why she later(?) had herself portrayed nude as Flora as a young woman by Georg Christoph Grooth. The medallion may not be a claim to legitimacy of

grandchildren were still minors, Peter must have made the decision to have them all painted and at that time by Caravaque. Also about 1722, Peter had Tannauer's Russian student Ivan Nikitin (recently returned from Italy) paint not just himself and Ekaterina but also his daughters Anna and Elizaveta as well as his grandson Petr Aleksevich.[63] For portraits Peter made no distinction among his descendants, ordering Petr Petrovich, Petr Alekseevich, and all of his daughters to be portrayed. Indeed if we assume that Peter favored Petr Petrovich while he was alive, Cupid does not seem to convey the notion of a hereditary prince. What the pictures do convey is a radically new phenomenon in Russian culture, the secular portrayal of children. They also reinforced the notion of the imperial family as a unit.

Finally, the record of court ceremonies shows that Peter celebrated the birthdays and name days of all of his children as well as of his grandson Petr Aleksevich. The court records are not always complete, but they show the celebrations for Anna, Elizaveta, Petr Alekseevich, and the other, mostly short-lived, children. Peter was in Schlüsselburg on October 10–11 of 1719 and 1720 to celebrate the anniversary of its capture, but in 1721 he returned to the capital in time to participate in the celebration of his grandson's birthday on the twelfth. Petr Alekseevich on that day was six years old, no longer an infant.[64] The next year Peter and Ekaterina were away for the Persian campaign, but in 1723 and 1724 he did as he had done in 1721: he celebrated the anniversary of the capture of Schlüsselburg but returned for this grandson's birthday.[65] Furthermore, Petr Alekseevich, in spite of his age, was present with the rest of the family for many important public ceremonies. He was not present at the celebration of the Treaty of Nystad in October 1721 because of illness, but he did join the family for the reception at Easter

rule, since all it does is indicate her paternity, which was neither controversial nor unique to her among her sisters. See also E. Beliutin and N. Moleva, *Zhivopisnykh del mastera: Kantseliariia ot stroenii i russkaia zhivopis' pervoi poloviny XVIII veka* (Moscow: Iskusstvo, 1965); and L. A. Markina, *Portretist Georg Khristof Groot i nemetskie zhivopistsy v Rossii serediny XVIII veka* (Moscow: Pamiatniki istoricheskoi mysli, 1999).

63 S. O. Androsov, *Zhivopisets Ivan Nikitin* (St. Petersburg: Dmitrii Bulanin, 1998), 70, 75, 191, 194.

64 *Pokhodnyi zhurnal 1721 goda* (St. Petersburg: n.p., 1855), 75; Friedrich Wilhelm von Bergholz, "Tagebuch," *Magazin für die neue Historie und Geographie* XIX (1785), 3–202; XX (1786), 331–592; XXI (1787), 178–360; XXII (1788), 425–506. Russian translation: F. V. Bergholtz, *Dnevnik*, trans. I. F. Ammon, vols. I–IV (St. Petersburg: Universitetskaia tipografiia, 1902). See in particular Bergholz, "Tagebuch," XIX (1785), 139; Bergholtz, *Dnevnik*, vol. I, 131.

65 *Pokhodnyi zhurnal 1722 goda*, 46; *Pokhodnyi zhurnal 1723 goda* (St. Petersburg: n.p., 1855), 28, 38–39; *Pokhodnyi zhurnal 1724 goda* (St. Petersburg: n.p., 1855), 21; Bergholz, "Tagebuch," XXI (1787), 334; XXII (1788), 494; Bergholtz, *Dnevnik* vol. III, 162–163; vol. IV, 69.

(April 14), in 1723.[66] Anna and Elizaveta's birthdays were also the cause of celebration for the family, and Petr Alekseevich participated. Anna's birthday was January 27 and her name day February 3. As was the case with Petr Alekseevich, there is no record of either celebration for 1719 and 1720, but 1721 began the series. There was a celebration of Anna Petrovna's birthday in 1722, not in 1723 (again owing to the Persian campaign), but in 1724 there were celebrations both for her birthday and for her name day.[67] For Elizaveta there were birthday (December 18) and name day (September 5) events, again not in 1719. In 1720 and 1721 there is no record of any court events for her in December, but both years her name day was celebrated, and in 1722 Peter was on the Persian campaign.[68] In 1722, the Synod also officially regularized the public celebration of the name days of Elizaveta, Anna, and Natal'ia Alekseevna, requiring the printing of the services for Sts. Zacharias and Elizaveta, besides those for the patron saints of the other two tsarevny.[69] The next year, however, the family celebrated both Elizaveta's name day and her birthday (the latter including Petr Alekseevich), but for September 5, 1724 her name day was omitted as the tsar was ill. In December Peter was still not well, and the birthday celebration seems to have been omitted.[70] The coronation of Ekaterina in May 1724, the first coronation of the wife of a Russian tsar, was a special event of great magnificence, and the tsar's family was mostly present: not Petr Alekseevich, but Anna and Elizaveta as well as the duchesses of Kurland (Anna Ivanovna) and Mecklenburg (Ekaterina Ivanovna). They came to the cathedral, but did not march in the procession.[71] In contrast to the coronation and other public ceremonies, the birthday and name day celebrations were small. They included the whole ruling family, but the number of other guests was limited. The public part was often only the inevitable fireworks.[72] Peter maintained the ruling family intact and functioning as a group before the court and the country, whatever internal fissures may have existed.

[66] Bergholz, "Tagebuch," XIX (1785), 144; XXI (1787), 226; Bergholtz, *Dnevnik*, vol. I, 135; vol. III, 53.

[67] *Pokhodnyi zhurnal 1721 goda*, 19; *Pokhodnyi zhurnal 1724 goda*, 1–2; Bergholz, "Tagebuch," XX (1786), 384; XXII (1788), 436–437; Bergholtz, *Dnevnik*, vol. II, 55; vol. IV, 14. Petr Alekseevich participated in the dancing for Anna's name day in 1724.

[68] *Pokhodnyi zhurnal 1720* (St. Petersburg: n.p., 1855), 36; *Pokhodnyi zhurnal 1721*, 59.

[69] *Polnoe sobranie postanovlenii i rasporiazhenii*, vol. II, 1872, 583–584.

[70] *Pokhodnyi zhurnal 1723*, 21, 37, 41; Bergholz, "Tagebuch," XXI (1787), 318–320; XXII (1788), 487–488; Bergholtz, *Dnevnik*, vol. III, 146, 184–185; vol. IV 63–64.

[71] Bergholz, "Tagebuch," XXII (1788), 459; Bergholtz, *Dnevnik*, vol. IV, 36. *Opisanie koronatsii* does not mention them.

[72] For example, February 3, 1722 (Anna's name day), Bergholz, "Tagebuch," XX (1786), 384; Bergholtz, *Dnevnik*, vol. II, 55.

Feofan Prokopovich

Peter was not bluffing when he said that other examples supporting his new law would be published. By 1722 Russia had entered into a new world of culture, political and otherwise, and the old forms were no longer valid. Not only were the sixteenth-century modes of argument, revolving as they did around the piety of the monarch, now insufficient, but even the new court culture of the late seventeenth century was not enough. Indeed, Peter continued to sponsor sermons that provided panegyrics on his rule and celebration of his accomplishments, but the succession law demanded something more. The task of defending Peter's decree according to the new emerging cultural values fell to Feofan Prokopovich, bishop of Pskov and already the principal figure in the Russian Orthodox Church. This text was not only one of the first official statements that relied mostly on secular legal and political thought, but has also provided a proof text for the idea that Peter the Great's reign was the moment of creation of "absolutism" in Russia. Thus the problem of succession to the throne was intimately tied to the conception of the monarchy in Russia in the eighteenth century and also to twentieth-century debates on the nature of the Russian state.

Prokopovich was a colorful figure. Born Elisei in 1681 in Kiev to a humble family, he spent some years studying at the Kiev Academy, then (probably) in Poland, finishing off in the College of St. Athanasius in Rome. This was the typical education of the Kiev clergy of that time, and produced men who were theologically and confessionally loyal to Orthodoxy to be sure, but steeped in the Catholic culture of the Counter-Reformation. Feofan, however, took a different path. Either in Rome or on his way home through Germany, he developed a fascination with Lutheran theology and religious culture. It seems that he never learned German, but most Lutheran writings of the time were available in Latin, if not composed in that tongue, and he assembled a giant library of Lutheran and Protestant theology. He returned to Kiev Orthodox, and from 1705 taught the course in poetics and later rhetoric at the academy, becoming a monk under the name Feofan. He wrote verses in Latin and Polish, as well as sermons and secular orations. Already as a prefect at the Academy he came to the attention of Tsar Peter during his visits to Kiev and cemented his reputation with an oration in celebration of Peter's victory at Poltava only a few days afterward. In 1711, he received the office of Rector of the Academy, spending the succeeding years teaching philosophy and writing occasional theological works. In 1715, at the time that Peter's relations with Stefan Iavorskii and the church authorities were deteriorating, the tsar called Feofan to St. Petersburg, promising him a bishopric. Feofan was not enthusiastic about the latter, but arrived in the new capital in October 1716.[73] There he delivered the sermons that complimented and lionized Peter and his family over the next few years. He became Peter's right-hand man in the church, but also a spokesman for the church and the state. It was he who proposed the new title, imperator, with its Roman associations, for the tsar on the conclusion of the war with Sweden in 1721.

The book he wrote to defend the succession decree was called *Pravda voli monarshei* and appeared soon after the decree itself.[74] Feofan's text was in two parts, one a long discussion of Biblical precedents and the other a defense of the decree founded on the writings of the legal theorists of Western Europe, though he explicitly named only Hugo Grotius. The book was an important witness to the Westernization of Russian political thought, but also found a fundamental misinterpretation in twentieth-century historiography. This was the 1915 work of Georgii Gurvich (1894–1965), then a student in the Law Faculty at Iur'ev (Dorpat, Tartu) University.[75] Gurvich went on to Petrograd University, where he received a doctorate in law for a dissertation on Rousseau, and then emigrated.[76] In Paris, as Georges Gurvitch, he had a long and distinguished career as a sociologist. Gurvich's student work was a remarkable performance, based on careful reading of the text, but also relying on then authoritative works in legal history. He argued that the bishop had imported into Russia Western theories of absolutism, as expounded by Hugo Grotius and Samuel Pufendorf (borrowing from Grotius), to support Peter's reforms. To make matters worse, historians have regularly misquoted Gurvich to the effect that he also believed that Hobbes had influenced Prokopovich.[77] In fact, Gurvich

[73] Iu. F. Samarin, *Stefan Iavorskii i Feofan Prokopovich* (Moscow: D. Samarin, 1880); I. Chistovich, *Feofan Prokopovich i ego vremia* (St. Petersburg: Tipografiia Imperatorskoi Akademii nauk, 1868); V. M. Nichik, *Feofan Prokopovich* (Moscow: Mysl', 1977); T. V. Avtukhovich, "Prokopovich Elisei (Eleazar)," *Slovar' russkikh pisatelei XVIII v.* (St. Petersburg: Nauka, 1999), vol. II, 488–496; Andrey Ivanov, "Reforming Orthodoxy: Russian Bishops and Their Church 1721–1801," PhD dissertation, Yale University, 2012, 26–93.

[74] A. Lentin, ed. and trans., *Peter the Great: His Law on the Imperial Succession in Russia 1722 – the Official Commentary (Pravda Voli Monarshei)* (Oxford: Headstart History, 1996); *PSZ* VII, 602–643.

[75] Georgii Gurvich, *"Pravda voli monarshei" Feofana Prokopovicha i ee zapadnoevropeiskie istochniki.* Uchenye zapiski Imperatorskogo Iur'evskogo universiteta 11 (Iur'ev: Tipografiia K. Mattisena, 1915), 1–112. On Gurvich, see M. V. Antonov, *Pravo i obshchestvo v kontseptsii Georgiia Davidovicha Gurvicha* (Moscow: Izdatel'skii dom Vysshei shkoly ekonomiki, 2013).

[76] G. D. Gurvich, *Russo i deklaratsiia prav: Idea neot"emlemykh prav individa v politicheskoi doctrine Russo* (Petrograd: Tipografiia M. V. Vol'fa, 1918) (at e-heritage.ru).

[77] N. I. Pavlenko, "Idei absoliutizma v zakonodatel'stve XVIII veka," in *Absolutizm v Rossii*, ed. N. M. Druzhinin (Moscow: Nauka, 1964), 390–391; E. V. Anisimov, *Gosudarstvennye preobrazovaniia i samoderzhavie Petra Velikogo* (St. Petersburg: Dmitrii

explicitly stated that he found no evidence of the influence of Hobbes. It was his adviser, F. V. Taranovskii, who chided his pupil in the preface and asserted without adducing any proof that Hobbes had influenced the bishop.[78] Gurvich did believe, without dragging in Hobbes, that Prokopovich was an exponent of absolutism. In this belief, Gurvich was wrong.[79]

The basic problem with the analysis of Gurvich and later scholars who followed him lay in the conception of Grotius as a proponent of absolutism. Today, this may seem a strange view of a jurist who spent most of his life as a spokesman for the Dutch republic, and left for Paris in 1621 not because he preferred the French monarchy but because of the fall from power of Johan van Oldenbarnevelt and his political–religious party in the Netherlands. Yet, to the generation of Gurvich, the main authorities in the history of law, especially Otto von Gierke (1841–1921) and other German legal historians, saw Grotius as an absolutist, for reasons that are not perfectly clear.[80] The irony is that later in emigration Gurvich changed his mind on Grotius and came to criticize Gierke in his French work on the sociology of law.[81] That later work seems to have remained unknown to historians. Perhaps if Gurvich had also returned to Feofan he might have seen him differently, but in 1915 he was convinced by all the authorities in the field that Grotius, and hence Feofan Prokopovich, was an absolutist.

Bulanin, 1997), 274; Lindsey Hughes, *Russia in the Age of Peter the Great* (New Haven, Connecticut: Yale University Press, 1998), 95; Bushkovitch, *Peter the Great*, 440–441, corrected in Paul Bushkovitch, *Petr Velikii: Bor'ba za vlast' (1671–1725)*, trans. N. L. Luzhitskaia (St. Petersburg: Dmitrii Bulanin, 2008); Cynthia Whittaker, *Russian Monarchy: Eighteenth-Century Rulers and Writers in Political Dialogue* (DeKalb, Illinois: Northern Illinois University Press, 2003), 52–58.

78 Gurvich, "*Pravda voli monarshei*," vols. VIII–IX, 109–110. Antonov correctly noted Gurvich's rejection of the influence of Hobbes and Taranovskii's criticism of his student: Antonov, *Pravo i obshchestvo*, 23.

79 Paul Bushkovitch, "Political Ideology in the Reign of Peter I: Feofan Prokopovich, Succession to the Throne and the West," in *ГИИМ: Доклады по истории* 18 и 19 вв./ *DHI Moskau: Vorträge zum 18. und 19. Jahrhundert*, ed. Ingrid Schierle and Denis Anatol'evič Sdvižkov (2012), 1–16, www.perspectivia.net/content/publikationen/vortraege-moskau/bushkovitch_ideology.

80 Gierke was quite hostile to Jean Bodin and Grotius, whom he saw as absolutists, and promoted the cause of the otherwise rather obscure German jurist Johann Althusius, in his view a proponent of a specifically German form of the Rechtsstaat: Otto von Gierke, *Johannes Althusius und die Entwicklung der naturrechtlichen Staatstheorie* (Berlin: W. Koebner, 1880). From him and his contemporary Georg Jellinek (1851–1911), Gurvich got the idea that Grotius identified the state with monarchy: Gurvich, "*Pravda voli monarshei*," 40. Here Gurvich cited Gierke, *Johannes Althusius*, 172–174; and Georg Jellinek, *Allgemeine Staatslehre*, 2nd ed. (Berlin: O. Häring, 1905), 446–447.

81 Georges Gurvitch, *Éléments de sociologie juridique* (Paris: Aubier, Éditions Montaigne, 1940), 61–64. Gurvich based these revised judgements on his earlier work, *L'idée du Droit social* (Paris: Librairie du Recueil Sirey, 1931), 171–567.

Prokopovich was the principal spokesman and propagandist for Peter in the last years of his reign, but he was also the first person in Russia to write a political tract based on Western ideas of politics, not the traditional Orthodox conception of the just and pious tsar. His life, his specific Ukrainian experience, and his culture prepared him for the central role in the story of succession as reformulated by Peter. Feofan was a supporter of the tsar in Kiev long before he moved to St. Petersburg and began to command the Orthodox Church in the Russian Empire. Feofan's position came out of the extremely complex politics of the Orthodox church in his native Ukraine. after the legalization of the Kiev metropolitanate in Poland in 1632 with Metropolitan Peter Mohyla (1633–47), the Orthodox clergy had a complex relation with the Cossack leadership from the 1630s onward, for the higher clergy supported the king and was supported by him as well as by the local Orthodox Ruthenian nobility. Metropolitan Syl'vestr Kosov (1647–57) was uncomfortable with Khmel'nyts'kyi's Cossack revolt and with the Russian tsar, and after his death internal disputes left the metropolitanate effectively vacant until 1685. Petro Doroshenko, the hetman of the right-bank Ukraine under Ottoman protection from about 1668 to his defeat in 1675, supported his candidate for the metropolitanate, Iosif (Neliubovych-Tukal'skyi), but he never made it to Kiev.[82] In those years the de facto leader of the Orthodox in the Ukrainian hetmanate was usually Lazar Baranovych, the archbishop of Chernigov, who was generally favorable to the tsar and had good connections in Moscow. Church politics in the Ukrainian hetmanate, however, were multi-directional. The clergy wanted to affirm its position against the hetmanate and the tsar as well, without completely alienating either. Baranovych, for example, supported the tsar against Hetman Demian Mnohohrishnyi in 1672. Thus the clergy often supported the tsar, and the tsar the clergy, but the clergy was not united. The clergy was also by family origin usually part of the Cossack elite, and to some extent shared its political divisions and evolution. Thus the election of Gedeon Chetvertyns'kyi as metropolitan of Kiev in 1685 seems to have had the support of the clergy as well as Hetman Samoilovych and the tsar, but certainly Baranovych and the Kiev Monastery of the Caves were not happy when the tsar agreed to place them under Metropolitan Gedeon's direct authority, not that of the Moscow patriarch (earlier they had both been under Constantinople). The clergy was unhappy with the transfer of jurisdiction over the Kiev metropolitanate from Constantinople to Moscow in 1686, but did not

[82] Serhii Plokhy, *The Cossacks and Religion in Early Modern Ukraine* (Oxford: Oxford University Press, 2001), 236–273, 318–333.

rebel. The fall of Samoilovych and the appointment of Ivan Mazepa by Prince V. V. Golitsyn in the managed election of 1687 diminished Gedeon's position: in 1688 the tsars restored the autonomy of the Kiev monasteries and the archbishop of Chernigov.[83] Nevertheless, the Kiev metropolitans sent to Moscow for protection from their opponents and for grants of privilege and money for Ukrainian institutions such as the Kiev Academy.[84] The tsar also served as a court of last resort, resolving disputes in various directions as the local struggles evolved.

Many of the Ukrainian clergy had good reasons to support the tsar. Not surprisingly, it was common for the books published in Kiev to have dedications to the tsar. In these dedications, the authors followed European precedent. Ioannykii Galiatovs'kyi, for example, dedicated some of the versions of his 1669 edition of his *Messiia pravdivyi* to Tsar Aleksei and his 1683 *Alkoran Machometow* to Tsars Ivan and Peter.[85] The sermon collections *Mech dukhovnyi* (1666) and *Truby sloves propovednykh* (1674–79) of Lazar' Barnovych featured dedications to Tsar Aleksei, who provided paper for the editions.[86]

During the time of this tangled web of conflicts the most influential historical work to come out of Kiev was the *Sinopsis* of 1674/81, a publication of the Kiev Monastery of the Caves, the center of Ukrainian Orthodoxy and very likely the work of its archimandrite, Innokentii Gizel'. The book was a history of the East Slavs, now all described as Russians (*Rossiiane*), that centered on the ruling dynasties. It presented a legendary account of the Slavs that portrayed all the eastern Slavs as one people and chronicled the history of Kiev, Novgorod, and Moscow, including a long description of the victory of Dmitrii Donskoi, the prince of Moscow, at the battle of Kulikovo in 1380. In the *Sinopsis* Lithuania conquered Kiev and reduced it from a principality to a *voevodstvo*, and Tsar Aleksei, as the inheritor of the Riurikovich dynasty,

[83] *AIuZR* vol. 5, pt. 1; Nikolai Kostomarov, *Ruina*. Istoricheskie monografii i issledovaniia 15 (St. Petersburg and Moscow: Izdatel'stvo M. O. Vol'fa, 1882), 643–646; F. I. Titov, *Russkaia pravoslavnaia tserkov' v Pol'sko-litovskom gosudarstve*, vol. 2. *Kievskaia mitropoliia-eparkhiia v XVII–XVIII vv. (1686-1797)* (Kiev: Tipografiia I. I. Chokolova, 1905), 1–51, 213–305. More recent work includes K. A. Kochegarov, *Rech' Pospolitaia i Rossiia v 1680–1686 godakh: Zakliuchenie dogovora o vechnom mire* (Moscow: Indrik, 2008); A. S. Almazov, *Politicheskii portret ukrainskogo getmana Ivana Samoilovicha v kontekste russko-ukrainskikh otnoshenii* (Moscow: MGU, 2012); and V. G. Chentsova, "Sinodal'noe reshenie 1686 g. o Kievskoi mitropolii," *Drevniaia Rus': voprosy medievistiki* 68, 2 (2017): 89–110.

[84] Titov, *Kievskaia mitropoliia-eparkhiia*, 411 (1691 conflict with Józef Szumliański, Uniate archbishop of Lwów), 428–433, 436–437 (requests on behalf of the Kiev Academy).

[85] Natalia Iakovenko, *U poshukakh Novoho neba: Zhyttia i teksty Ioannykiia Galiatov'skoho* (Kyiv: Laurus Kritika, 2017), 68, 73.

[86] N. F. Sumtsov, *K istorii iuzhnorusskoi literatury semnadtsago stoletiia*, vol. I. *Lazar' Baranovich* (Khar'kov: Tipografiia M. F. Zil'berberga, 1885), 53–55.

was only reclaiming his own patrimony in 1654. By this act, the tsar restored Kiev and the Monastery of the Caves to their ancient dignity lost under Lithuanian–Polish rule. The text said nothing about the Cossack revolt or Hetman Khmel'nyts'kyi, and the Ukrainian Cossacks appeared only in a short account of the siege of Chigirin in 1677–8 as part of the Russian army.[87] The story it presented was dynastic. One Riurikovich succeeded another, interrupted in Kiev only by the Mongol invasion and the Lithuanian conquest. The text does not explicitly reject elected kingship (as in Poland), but assumes dynastic succession, and that succession was in the branch of the Riurikovich dynasty ruling in Moscow.

In this context, the Ukrainian church's support of Peter against Mazepa was not unexpected. In November 1708, after Hetman Ivan Mazepa had gone over to Charles XII, Stefan Iavors'kyi, at that point metropolitan of Riazan', anathematized Mazepa in a sermon that elaborated on his betrayal of Peter and Orthodoxy. Feofan Prokopovich supported Peter against Mazepa as well.[88] In most respects he was a typical product of the intellectual milieu of the Kiev church and Academy, but he very soon began to move in different directions.

Feofan's education was acquired partly in Rome, but more fundamentally in Kiev at the academy, the same academy that had produced Simeon Polotskii fifty years before and was one of the main sources of the culture of the Kiev clergy that had such an impact on the Russian court. To be sure, the Cossack revolt had not been without consequences for the Academy. The political battles among the Ukrainian Cossacks after 1657 not only involved the clergy to a greater or lesser extent, but also undermined the material resources of the Academy, which had so carefully been built up in Mohyla's time. After 1665, it was in terrible shape, but through the efforts of its rector Varlaam Iasyns'kyi (later metropolitan of Kiev 1690–1707) it managed to restore the full course

[87] Hans Rothe, ed., *Sinopsis, Kiev 1681*. Bausteine zur Geschichte der Literatur bei den Slaven 17 (Cologne and Vienna: Böhlau, 1983); Zenon Kohut, "Servant of the Tsar, Defender of Ukrainian Church Autonomy and Promoter of the Kyivan Caves Monastery: The Political World of Innokentii Gizel' (1650s–1670s)," *Harvard Ukrainian Studies* 32–33 (2011–2014): 437–454; and Zenon Kohut, "Vplyv polityky na Innokentiia Gizelia ta vydannia kyivs'koho 'Synopsysu': Nove osmyslennia," in Innokentii Gizel', *Vybrani tvory* (Kyiv and Lviv: Svichado, 2010), vol. 3, 9–30.

[88] Stefan Iavorskii, "Slovo pred prokliatiem Mazepy," *Trudy Kievskoi dukhovnoi akademii* 3, 12 (1865): 499–512; Giovanna Brogi Bercoff, "Poltava: A Turning Point in the History of Preaching," in *Poltava 1709: The Battle and the Myth*, ed. Serhii Plokhy (Cambridge, Massachusetts: Harvard University Press, 2012), 205–226; Giovanna Brogi Bercoff, "Mazepa, lo zar e il diavolo. Un inedito di Stefan Javorskij," *Russica Romana* VII (2000): 167–188; T. G. Tairova-Iakovleva, *Ivan Mazepa i Rossiiskaia imperiia: Istoriia "predatel'stva"* (Moscow and St. Petersburg: Tsentropoligraf, 2011).

of instruction by 1672.[89] In these years, the Russian government was not sure that the Academy was worth supporting, and in 1666 the Russian *voevoda* in Kiev, the boyar V. P. Sheremetev, had to defend it.[90] Petitions for financial support were referred to the hetman. Still, the number of students rose to about 240 by the middle of the 1680s.[91] It was only in 1694 that the requests of Metropolitan Varlaam and the Academy met with success: the tsars provided it with an extensive privilege that granted it autonomy from other authorities, ecclesiastical and civil. Hetman Mazepa provided money for new buildings.[92] At the same time, the Academy managed to expand its offerings and for the first time it offered a theology course to crown its curriculum in 1689.[93]

While the Academy struggled to maintain itself, its distinguished graduates produced a whole series of books of sermons, accounts of icons and saints, and occasional polemics. Ioannykii Galiatovs'kyi, Innokentii Gizel', Lazar Baranovych, and some lesser lights formed a generation. They had gone to the academy in Mohyla's time or shortly after, and started publishing around 1660. They continued into the 1680s, and gradually ceased writing or died by the early 1690s. Most of their work got to Moscow, if not without occasional controversy, and reinforced the impact of Simeon Polotskii and other Kiev-trained scholars on the culture of the Russian church and court. All of them reflected the interest in Catholic spirituality that their education and languages (Slavonic, Latin, Polish) made possible, even if they remained true to Orthodoxy in their fundamental beliefs. With the recovery of the Academy at the end of the century, younger men took over. Dmitrii Tuptalo (St. Dmitrii Rostovskii, 1651–1709) had studied in the Academy, as best he could in that time, in the 1660s. He began his great work of compilation of a new and fuller version of the lives of the saints in 1684. He wrote the work as a monk in the Kiev Monastery of the Caves, which was then, even more than earlier, the center of religious life in Kiev. The first volume appeared in 1698, the

89 N. I. Petrov, *Kievskaia akademiia vo vtoroi polovine XVII veka* (Kiev: Tipografiia G. T. Korchak-Novitskogo, 1895) (originally in *Trudy Kievskoi dukhovnoi Akademii*, 1895), 18, 30–34; Fedor Titov, *Imperatorskaia kievskaia dukhovnaia Akademiia 1615–1915* (Kiev: Gopak, 2003), 85–159 (originally 1915).

90 Titov, *Imperatorskaia kievskaia dukhovnaia Akademiia*, 100; *AIuZR* VI, 93–96.

91 Petrov, *Kievskaia akademiia*, 88. In Mohyla's time there were about 160 students, and presumably fewer in the 1660s–70s. S. Golubev, *Kievskaia akademiia v kontse XVII i v nachale XVIII stoletii* (Kiev: Tipografiia I. I. Gorbukova, 1901), 2–3.

92 Petrov, *Kievskaia akademiia*, 51–52; Titov, *Kievskaia mitropoliia-eparkhiia*, 428–433; D. Vishnevskii, *Kievskaia akademiia v pervoi polovine XVIII stoletiia* (Kiev: Tipografiia I. I. Gorbunova, 1903).

93 Petrov, *Kievskaia akademiia*, 47–48. The teacher was Ioasaf Krokovs'kyi, later metropolitan of Kiev (1707–18).

last in 1705.[94] Stefan Iavorskii was slightly younger, born in 1658, he was prefect of the Academy in the 1690s, and was a major figure as an instructor there as well as a preacher.[95] Both of them continued the absorption with Catholic culture inherited from their predecessors. St. Dmitrii's sources included the Polish Jesuit Piotr Skarga's lives of the saints, and Stefan followed the Jesuit Cardinal Robert Bellarmine for most of his later famous *Kamen' very* of 1713–17, published only after his death in 1722.[96] Stefan was also the first of the Ukrainians who not only sent his books to Moscow, but also came to Russia to lead the Orthodox Church. Peter placed him as the locum tenens of the patriarchal throne in 1701, a position he held until the establishment of the Holy Synod in 1721.

Before his departure for Rome, Feofan attended the academy and lived in the religious and political culture of his native town. He does not seem to have been very concerned with the various jurisdictional issues that absorbed the Kiev clergy, and he lacked their fascination with Catholic spirituality. Though he had studied in Rome in the 1690s, his admiration was for the Protestant writers of the seventeenth century, and he would come to see the Lutheran consistories as an appropriate structure for the Orthodox Church. He returned from Rome in 1702 to teach in the Kiev Academy, where he taught poetics in 1705–6 and rhetoric the next year.[97] He moved on to philosophy about 1707 and continued with it until 1710, followed by theology.[98] He first came to Peter's notice in the course of the Poltava campaign, pronouncing a panegyric on the Russian victory, followed by a poem on the same subject. The Academy quickly put out a Latin version, with the poem translated into both Latin and Polish. The Poltava sermon certainly exalted Peter in the most dramatic terms possible, but as a great victor in battle, not as a ruler over his subjects. He defeated rebellion in the form of Mazepa, but that was something every monarch was supposed to do and had nothing to do with "absolutism."[99] The positive response to the defeat of rebellion was a cliché of European political thought outside the few republican traditions.[100]

[94] I. A. Shliapkin, *Sv. Dmitrii Rostovskii i ego vremia (1654–1709 g.)*. Zapiski istoriko-filologicheskogo fakul'teta imperatorskogo Sankt-Peterburgskogo universiteta 24 (St. Petersburg: Tipografiia i khromolitografiia A. Transhel', 1891).

[95] Stefan taught theology in 1693–7: Petrov, *Kievskaia akademiia*, 53–54.

[96] Ioann Morev, *"Kamen' very" Mitropolita Stefana Iavorskogo* (St. Petersburg: Tipografiia Artilleriiskogo zhurnala, 1904).

[97] Chistovich, *Feofan Prokopovich i ego vremia*, 1–23; D. Vishnevskii, *Kievskaia akademiia*, 132–133, 152; Ivanov, "Reforming Orthodoxy"; Feofan Prokopovič, *De arte rhetorica libri X, Kijoviae 1706*, ed. Renate Lachmann (Cologne and Vienna: Böhlau, 1982).

[98] Vishnevskii, *Kievskaia akademiia*, 192, 246–248.

[99] Prokopovich, *Sochineniia*, 23–38, 459–463.

[100] Laura Manzano Baena, *Conflicting Words: The Peace Treaty of Münster (1648) and the Political Culture of the Dutch Republic and the Spanish Monarchy* (Leuven: Leuven University Press, 2011), 33–66.

Prokopovich had served as the prefect of the Kiev Academy from 1707 and then as rector from 1711, remaining at his post until his move to St. Petersburg in 1716.[101] At the behest of Peter, he also translated by 1716 the work of the Spanish diplomat Diego de Saavedra Fajardo (1584–1648). Saavedra was then quite famous as the author of *Idea de un principe politico christiano en cien empresas* (1640), usually known as *Empresas políticas*, a book of emblems explained to provide political advice to rulers. The Spanish diplomat's book was translated into Latin in 1649 as *Idea principis Christiano-politica centum symbolis expressa*, and in that form acquired a European audience that extended to Russia.[102] Feofan's translation remained unpublished, perhaps because of the problem of reproducing the engravings of the emblems. The St. Petersburg copy has empty spaces left for them.[103] In the preface to his translation, Feofan briefly surveyed the political literature which he knew. It was, he said, of three types. First, Aristotle and his followers had written about the state, but they mostly talked about virtue in a philosophical manner and said little about actual practice. Second, others, Plato being his example, analyzed politics according to their intelligence (*po umyshlenii svoem*), but came up only with an abstract scheme not concordant with popular customs (*narodnye obychai*). Still others tried to make their difficult teaching acceptable by writing history – this was Tacitus – or in the form of stories. His other examples of writings that used stories were Xenophon's *Cyropaedia* and two early modern best sellers. One was the sixteenth-century Spanish bishop Antonio de Guevara's 1529 *Reloj de principes* on Marcus Aurelius (Feofan mistakenly said Marcus Antonius), widely read in Latin as *Horologium principis*.[104] The other was John Barclay's Latin novel allegorizing the French Wars of Religion, *Argenis* (1621).[105] Their works, said Feofan, were clever and pleasing, but incomplete. He rejected entirely the Jesuit writers Robert Bellarmine and Juan de

[101] Vishnevskii, *Kievskaia akademiia*, 22–23, 31–32.

[102] José Antonio Maravall, "Saavedra Fajardo: Moral de acomodación y carácter conflictivo de la libertad," in José Antonio Maravall, *Estudios de Historia del Pensamiento Español. Serie tercera: El siglo del Barocco* (Madrid: Ediciones Cultura Hispánica, 2001), 203–230, originally in *Cuadernos Hispanoamericanos* (May–June 1971): 257–258; Christian Romanoski, *Tacitus Emblematicus: Diego de Saavedra Fajardo und seine "Empresas Políticas"* (Berlin: Weidler Buchverlag, 2006).

[103] RNB, Osnovnoe sobranie, F II 67.

[104] Augustin Redondo, *Antonio de Guevara (1480?–1545) et l'Espagne de son temps: De la carrière officielle aux œuvres politico-morales* (Geneva: Droz, 1976); Simon A. Vosters, *Antonio de Guevara y Europa* (Salamanca: Ediciones Universidad de Salamanca, 2009).

[105] Susanne Siegl-Mocavini, *John Barclays "Argenis" und ihr staatspolitischer Kontext: Untersuchungen zum politischen Denken der frühen Neuzeit* (Tübingen: M. Niemeyer, 1999).

Mariana, for they placed kings under the power of the Pope and advocated regicide. The only writer who discussed all the important tasks for monarchs without the defects of the others was Saavedra Fajardo. He had practical experience as an advisor to kings and provided advice for every occasion, person, or customs that the monarch might encounter. His only defect was that he was occasionally obscure, and Feofan had tried his best to rectify this in his translation.

What is striking about Feofan's description of European political thought is that there are no writers here that are normally understood to be advocates of absolutism. Guevara and Barclay were certainly advocates of strong royal power. Guevara, however, was mainly concerned with the moral personality of the king, while Barclay's main enemy was disorder and aristocratic faction. Though a Catholic, he opposed the claims of the Pope to superiority over the king of France. Barclay certainly advocated a strong monarchy, but the closest he came to "absolutism" was the defense of the royal prerogative to tax the subjects without asking them,[106] which was the norm in France in any case, but he did not advocate the suppression of assemblies and insisted that the king should rule according to law. Feofan did not cite any "absolutist" authors, such as Jean Bodin or Thomas Hobbes, but he also did not approve or reject any writers on the basis of "absolutist" views. Neither "absolutism" nor even the degree of royal power was his criterion.

Feofan preferred Saavedra. In the commentary to emblem forty-one, "Ne quid nimis" ("Nothing in excess"), the Spaniard advised kings to avoid ambition: "Inordinate ambition encourages the oppression of the liberty of the people, the humbling of the nobility, the weakening of the powerful, and the reduction of all to royal authority, thinking that the more absolute it is and the lower the people are reduced, the more secure it is. An illusion which by flattery gains the will of princes and puts them in great danger. It is modesty that preserves empires, correcting the prince's ambition and maintaining within the bounds of reason the power of his dignity, the rank of the nobility and the liberty of the people, for a monarchy is not durable which is not mixed and is composed of aristocracy and democracy. Absolute power is tyranny. He who seeks it,

[106] John Barclay, *Argenis*, 2 vols., ed. and trans. Mark Riley and Dorothy Pritchard. Huber, Medieval and Renaissance Texts and Studies 273 (Tempe, Arizona: Arizona Center for Medieval and Renaissance Studies, 2004), vol. 1, 202–217 [Book I, 18], vol. 2, 732–749 [book IV, 18]. Siegel-Mocavini interpreted Barclay as an "absolutist," but in the sense that the monarch was still to be bound by "fundamental laws": Siegl-Mocavini, *John Barclays Argenis*, 177–180, 311–360. Barclay's enemy was anarchy caused by powerful aristocrats, so his main concern was state sovereignty, and that state should be a monarchy. What kind of monarchy was a question he did not discuss.

seeks his own ruin." ("El poder absoluto es tiranía. Quien le procura, procura su ruina.")[107]

These are not the words of an ideologist of absolutism, and modern scholars recognize that, like the natural law theorists, Saavedra Fajardo was not an absolutist.[108] He was not a legal theorist, like Bodin or Grotius, reflecting on the sovereignty of the state, nor did he present an argument for any particular form of government. His advice to kings was a mixture of the traditional moral advice calling for moderation and prudence, such as had made Guevara and so many others so famous, and more practical suggestions, such as the passage on ambition and absolute power. This combination seems to have been what attracted Prokopovich, but the learned bishop had a great deal of difficulty understanding this passage and particularly the phrase "absolute power."

Prokopovich made the following translation of the passage from emblem forty-one in Saavedra's text:

Понуждает к тому излишнее властолюбие отяти свободу лю [sic] людем, покорити старейшину, велможамъ сломити силы, и все к единовластелству оустроевати. Разумѣет бо властолюбец яко безбѣднѣиший будетъ, егда самъ все одержитъ, и людей болшою работою отяготитъ. Но се великое заблуждение, в не же ласкатели срдца княжие въводятъ и купно ихъ въ великие бѣды ъвергаютъ, яко и достоинства своего власть и честь Велможъ своихъ и свободу народа в добромъ разума определении содержитъ. Не можетъ же долго пребывать Монархия, аще что от Аристократии и Демократии примѣшенного себѣ не имеетъ. Совершенное и самоволное единовластителство есть мучителство, его же аще кто ищетъ, ищетъ погибели своея. Вся убо якоже глаголетъ Аритотелем тако оустроевати подобаетъ, да Царя людие не мучителемъ но Государемъ

[107] "Suadet porro ambitio nimia Populi libertatem opprimere, subigere Nobilitatem, potentiorum vires infringet, et ad auctoritatem Regiam reducere omnia: existimat enim tum securiorem se fore, cum fuerit absoluta, et subditos magis in servitutem redegerit; grandis error, quo adulatio animos occupat Principum, eosque gravibus periculis objicit. Modestia est, quae conservat Imperia, nimirum Princeps suam dominandi cupiditatem ita corrigit, ut dignitatis suae potestatem, Nobilitatis amplitudinem, et populi libertatem intra rationis limites coerceat; neque enim diu stare poterit Monarchia, cui de Aristocratia et Democratia aliquid admixtum non fuerit. Potestas absoluta tyrannis est; qui illam quaerit, exitium suum quaerit. *Huc* denique *Principi sunt omnia reducenda, ut iis, qui sub imperio sunt non tyrannum, sed Patremfamilias, aut Regem agere videatur, et rem non quasi Dominus, sed quasi Procurator et Praefectus administrare ac moderate vivere, nec quod nimium est, sectari.* [in italics: supposedly Aristotle, *Politica*, 5. 11]" Diego de Saavedra Fajardo, *Idea principis Christiano-politica centum symbolis expressa* (Brussels: Ioannes Mommartius and Francisco Vivieni, 1649), 270; Diego de Saavedra Fajardo, *Empresas políticas*, ed. Sagrario López Poza (Madrid: Cátedra, 1999), 512–513. Saavedra did not quote Aristotle accurately, apparently following his own notes and comments rather than the original text: López Poza in Saavedra Fajardo, *Empresas políticas*, 73.

[108] Romanoski, *Tacitus Emblematicus*, 277–289; Manzano Baena, *Conflicting Words*, 105–132.

нарицаютъ: и да вся говоритъ не тако Господьствующий, но яко домовитъ и Икономъ да живетъ в мѣрности, и всего еже излишнее есть да хранится.[109]

Prokopovich left out the phrase "[auctoritas] absoluta" in the first sentence. His attempt to translate "Potestas absoluta tyrannis est" was a mixture of periphrasis and the traditional terminology of Old Rus' literature. For the single phrase "absolute power" he put "*sovershennoe i samovolnoe edinovlastitelstvo*," roughly "complete and self-willed [free] single-rulership," a locution as awkward in English as it was in Slavonic. What gave Prokopovich trouble was the notion of power. For the abstract latin "potestas" he used a much more specific neologism that really meant "monarchy." For tyranny he used the word found in translations of "tyrannis" in Greek texts from the Middle Ages, "*muchitel'stvo*," from "*muchitel'*," that is, "tormentor," which hardly conveyed the force of the Greek word.[110] The word *muchitel'* was the normal term for the person responsible for the death of a Christian martyr, and to the Russian reader thus had religious implications that "tyrant" did not. Saavedra's pseudo-quotation from Aristotle fared no better, with *muchitel'* again for *tyrannus* but *paterfamilias aut rex* became *gosudar'* and *dominus* turned into *gospod'stviiushchii.* In a general way Prokopovich was faithful to Saavedra: he conveyed clearly that a monarch with "complete and self-willed" power was bad, a "tormentor" in the traditional Russian terminology. He could not, however, fully render the whole notion of absolute power, in part because "power" was too abstract a concept. He was well along the road to contemporary European political thought by 1716, but not quite there.

Prokopovich was not alone in having difficulties with European political terminology. Two years after he moved to St. Petersburg, a Russian translation of Samuel Pufendorf's pioneering introduction to European history of 1681 appeared.[111] The translator was Gavriil Buzhinskii, another

[109] RNB, Otdel rukopisei, F II 67: "Izobrazhenie Khristianopoliticheskogo vlastelina simvolami obiasnenno ot Didaka Savedry Faksarda, nyne zhe s latinskogo na dialect russkii perevedenoe," [l. 1], "Vashego Tsarskogo S[via]shchenneishago Velichestva Nizhaishii rab i nedostoinyi bogomolets Feofan Prokopovich uchilishch kievskikh prefekt" [l. 3], l. 41.

[110] I. I. Sreznevskii, *Materialy dlia slovaria drevnerusskogo iazyka* (Moscow: Kniga, 1989), vol. II, pt. 1, 199 (originally St. Petersburg: Otdeleniia russkogo iazyka i slovesnosti Imperatorskoi akademii nauk, 1902).

[111] Samuel Pufendorf, *Einleitung zu der Historie der vornehmsten Reiche und Staaten, so itziger Zeit in Europa befinden*, 2nd ed. (Frankfurt am Main: Knoch, 1684). On Pufendorf, see Leonard Krieger, *The Politics of Discretion: Pufendorf and the Acceptance of Natural Law* (Chicago, Illinois: University of Chicago Press, 1965); Thomas Behme, *Samuel von Pufendorf: Naturrecht und Staat: Eine Analyse und Interpretation seiner Theorie*, ihrer Grundlagen und Probleme (Göttingen: Vandenhoeck & Ruprecht, 1995); Ian Hunter, *Rival Enlightenments: Civil and Metaphysical Philosophy in Early Modern Germany* (Cambridge: Cambridge University Press, 2001), 170–218; and

Ukrainian monk who had come to live and work in the Russian capital, who worked from the Latin translation of Pufendorf's German.[112] At the beginning of the book he placed an "interpretation of difficult words" (*tolkovanie nekikh rechenii trudnykh*) which included monarchy, aristocracy, and democracy. His definitions were simple: "monarchy or a monarchical government is where one person rules and has the highest power over everyone. Aristocracy is where the most select or very first nobles hold the rule over society. Democracy is where the people govern."[113] Pufendorf's description of Russian history, like that of other countries, included an account of Russia's government. In the German original Pufendorf said that Muscovy was headed by an "absoluter Monarch," but in Cramer's Latin translation, from which Buzhinskii worked, the phrase was "despoticum imperium."[114] Buzhinskii rendered it as "*povelitelstvo vladychestvennoe*," but placed an asterisk by "*vladychestvennoe*" and in the margin had "*samoderzhavnoe*." What "*vladychestvennoe*" was supposed to mean is perfectly unclear: mostly he seems to have used the word and other terms coming from "*vladyka*" just to mean "ruler" or "rule" (*vladychestvuet*).[115] Russia was not the only problem. For King Frederik III of Denmark's proclamation of absolutism (1660), Pufendorf put "absolute Souverainetät," which Cramer rendered as "absoluta potestas" and Buzhinskii "sovershennaia vlast'," echoing Prokopovich's translation of Saavedra.[116] For Buzhinskii,

T. J. Hochstrasser, *Natural Law Theories in the Early Enlightenment* (Cambridge: Cambridge University Press, 2000). Unfortunately, none of these authors devotes much space to his history of Europe.

[112] Samuel Pufendorf, *Introductio ad historiam europaeam*, trans. Johann Friedrich Cramer (Frankfurt am Main: Knoch, 1704). On Buzhinskii, see Iu. K. Begunov, "Buzhinskii, Gavriil Fedorovich," in *Slovar' russkikh pisatelei XVIII veka* (Leningrad: Nauka, 1988), vol. 1, 128–129.

[113] "Monarkhiia, ili monarkhicheskoe pravlenie toe est, idezhe edin vladychestvuet, i nad vsemi vysochaishuiu vlast' imat'. Aristokratiia, idezhe izbranneishii ili blagorodnii perveishii soderzhat pravlenie obshchestva. Dimokratiia, idezhe narod pravitel'stvuet," Samuel Pufendorf, *Vvedenie v gistoriiu evropeiskuiu* (St. Petersburg: n.p., 1718), 10. The note was to explain his account of ancient Rome's government on page 19.

[114] Pufendorf, *Introductio ad historiam europaeam*, 541. Cf. Pufendorf, *Einleitung zu der Historie der vornehmsten Reiche und Staaten*, 718.

[115] Pufendorf, *Vvedenie v gistoriiu evropeiskuiu*, 409.

[116] Pufendorf, *Einleitung zu der Historie der vornehmsten Reiche und Staaten*, 648; Pufendorf, *Introductio ad historiam europaeam*, 485; Pufendorf, *Vvedenie v gistoriiu evropeiskuiu*, 367. On the proclamation of absolutism and the Danish royal law of 1665, see Adolf Ditlef Jørgensen, ed., *Kongeloven og dens forhistorie* (Copenhagen: C. A. Reitzel, 1886); Knud F. K. Fabricius, *Kongeloven: Dens tilblivelse og plads i samtidens natur- og arveretlige udvikling* (Copenhagen: H. Hagerups Forlag, 1920). The Danish Royal Law created translation problems as well even in Western Europe. The Danish "*ubundene Eenevoldsmagt*" ("unlimited power of one ruler") in article 15 was translated in an anonymous English version of 1731 as "an Hereditary Despotick or Absolute King": "Kongeloven 1665" on Danmarkshistorien.dk (Aarhus Universitet); *Lex Regia* (London: n.p., 1731), 12. *Eenevold* (modern Danish *enevælde*) literally means "rule of

sovereignty and power were interchangeable, and were equivalent to the ability to give orders (*povelitel'stvo*). It was the concept of power that was difficult. He had no trouble with the concrete forms of government, though he believed that his audience would not understand them, if only because of the alien (non-Slavic) words. Like Prokopovich, he had mastered a great deal of the conceptual apparatus of European political thought, but not all of it. The distinctions among different sorts of monarchs with different degrees of power were as yet beyond the powers of the Ukrainian clergy to translate into Russian. Their translations obscured the differences between "absolute" kings and others.

Prokopovich's knowledge of Western political thought stood him in good stead when he arrived in St. Petersburg in 1716, but, as we have seen, his public role was mainly as preacher and orator at court ceremonies and church festivals. Peter made him archbishop of Pskov and Narva in 1718, which gave him an ecclesiastical role near the new capital, and then in 1721 Peter changed the whole structure of the church. He abolished the patriarchate and established the Holy Synod, which ruled the Orthodox Church in Russia until 1917. At the head of the Synod were Stefan Iavorskii and Prokopovich, but it was clear who had the tsar's favor. Further, Stefan died in November 1722, leaving Feofan as by far the most important figure in the church.[117] Prokopovich was centrally placed at the side of the tsar to explain his decisions when necessary.

Feofan's Tract

Prokopovich's principal source, Hugo Grotius, had nothing to do with absolutism.[118] The bishop founded his tract on the works of a republican jurist. To Feofan, Grotius was the most relevant author because the bishop was not writing a tract on political thought, absolutist or otherwise. Grotius was a jurist, and the subject of Feofan's tract was a specific

one," but was already used to mean "absolute ruler." The English translator saw that as equivalent to "despotic," as did Cramer in translating Pufendorf's "absolute monarch."

[117] P. V. Verkhovskii, *Uchrezhdenie Dukhovnoi kollegii i dukhovnyii reglament: K voprosu ob otnosheniii tserkvi i gosudarstva v Rossii*, 2 vols. (Rostov: n.p., 1916); James Cracraft, *The Church Reform of Peter the Great* (Stanford, California: Stanford University Press, 1971).

[118] Bushkovitch, "Political Ideology in the Reign of Peter I"; Richard Tuck, *Philosophy and Government 1572–1651* (Cambridge: Cambridge University Press, 1993), 154–201; Martin van Gelderen, "Aristotelians, Monarchomachs and Republicans: Sovereignty and *respublica mixta* in Dutch and German Political Thought 1580–1650," in *Republicanism: A Shared European Heritage*, vol. 1, ed. Martin van Gelderen and Quinten Skinner (Cambridge: Cambridge University Press, 2002), 199–204; Henk Nellen, *Hugo de Groot: Een leven in strijd om de vrede, 1583–1645* (Amsterdam: Balans, 2007); English translation by J. G. Grayson, *Hugo Grotius: A Lifelong Struggle for Peace in Church and State, 1583–1645* (Leiden: Brill, 2015).

law, not the nature of the state, political power, or the virtues of one or other sort of monarchy. Prokopovich produced a defense of a specific law, Peter's inheritance law of 1722, so the most relevant authors were naturally jurists. The first half of the text (chapters 1–9) is a discussion, based on Biblical precedent, historical examples, and law, of the legal power of parents over their children. The second half (chapters 10–16) concerns the power of monarchs over their children. It repeats the earlier arguments, applying them to monarchs. In chapters 10–12 he noted the duty of parents, including monarchs, to bring up their sons as best they can, though he saw no obligation to make them exactly resemble themselves, citing Biblical and classical examples.[119] Only in chapter 13 does he discuss the power of monarchs in general, and then he finishes (chapters 14–16) with a discussion of the application of the preceding chapters to the issue of succession.[120] In that connection, the first part of chapter 15 contains a brief discussion of the forms of government and monarchy. In other words, only a chapter and a half out of the entire Prokopovich text formed the object of analysis in the work of Gurvich, the analysis that has informed all subsequent discussion.

Feofan stuck closely to his task, devoting most of the text to the issue of parental power. This was a legal, not a political issue, as he made clear in chapter 3, calling on the reader to examine the 300 law books that can be found in St. Petersburg and going on to cite the Code of Justinian for the right of a parent to disinherit his son.[121] He then quoted Grotius[122] in describing the power of parents to sell and even kill their children in various societies, though he adds that these customs "are not very praiseworthy" (*ne ves'ma dostokhval'ny sut'*). His summation, that it is natural for parents to provide for their children, including by inheritance, and that therefore the children receive it not by right, but by the good will of the parents, closely followed Grotius.[123] So far Feofan produced essentially a legal thesis, though he noted (ch. 8) that "political philosophers" agree with the relevant laws and traditions.

Only in chapter 13, after the long discourse on parental right and duties, did Prokopovich take up the nature of supreme power. In this he followed Grotius's exposition in book 1, chapter 3 of *De jure belli et pacis*.

[119] Lentin, ed. and trans., *Peter the Great*, 138–184. [120] Ibid., 184–244.

[121] Ibid., 144–146.

[122] Hugo Grotius, *De iure belli et pacis*, ed. P. C. Molhuysen (Leiden: A. W. Sijthoff, 1919) (originally Paris: Apud Nicolavm Bvon, 1625); Hugo Grotius, *The Law of War and Peace*, trans. Francis W. Kelsey, vol. 2 of Grotius, *De iure belli et pacis*, 1913–1925 (Washington, D.C.: Carnegie Foundation, 1925; Indianapolis, Indiana: Bobbs-Merrill, 1925). See Grotius, *De iure belli et pacis*, vol. II, ch. 5, 147; Grotius, *The Law of War and Peace*, 233–234.

[123] Lentin, ed. and trans., *Peter the Great*, 152.

For Grotius "supreme power" (*summum imperium*) meant sovereignty. Any sort of state, a monarchy, aristocracy, or democracy, possessed sovereignty in most conditions.[124] His own theme, Feofan declared, was "*velichestvo*," or, in Latin, "*majestas*." Prokopovich says that it has two meanings, one a superior dignity and the other supreme power subject to no laws.[125] *Maiestas*, of course, was the Latin word Bodin used for "*souverainté*."[126] Feofan never referred to Bodin, however, and went on to quote Grotius: "That power is called supreme whose actions are not subject to the legal control of another, so that they cannot be rendered void by the operation of another human will" (*Summa autem illa [potestas] dicitur, cuius actus alterius iuri non subsunt, ita ut alterius voluntatis humanae arbitrio irriti possint reddi*).[127] He interpreted the Dutchman's expression "*summa potestas*" as *vysochaishaia vlast'* and inserted into the quotation in parentheses the explanation of that phrase: "which is called majesty" (*velichestvo naritsaemaia*), thus equating *majestas* and *potestas*. Generally Grotius used the term *imperium* or *potestas*, not *majestas*, to speak of the sovereignty of kings or other types of ruler over subjects.[128] Feofan was adding his own interpretation here: he understood Grotius correctly, however, that this supreme power, sovereignty, is not subject to the will of another, and its actions cannot be annulled by any other besides God himself. The justification for this notion, Prokopovich continued, is natural reason: if a power is called supreme, it cannot be subject to another's will. Therefore, no one can judge or scrutinize (*istiazati*) the monarch.[129] A long series of statements from scripture and various church fathers demonstrated the same conclusion: the monarch must be obeyed and not judged or scrutinized. He is therefore free from human law, though not from God's law.[130] This section is the heart of the argument by Gurvich and all others ever after that the text reflects an absolutist doctrine. Prokopovich, like Grotius, however, was writing not about the power of the monarch but about the sovereignty of the state, in the Russian case, a monarchy.

[124] Grotius, *De iure belli et pacis*, vol. I, ch. 3, 45–137; Grotius, *The Law of War and Peace*, 45–79.

[125] Lentin, ed. and trans., *Peter the Great*, 184.

[126] "La souveraineté est la puissance absolue et perpetuelle d'une République, que les Latins appellent majestatem." Jean Bodin, *Les six livres de la république 1576*, ed. Christiane Frémont, Marie-Dominque Couzinet, and Henri Rochais, 6 vols. (Paris: Fayard, 1986), vol. I, ch. 8, 179.

[127] Lentin, ed. and trans., *Peter the Great*, 186; Grotius, *De iure belli et pacis*, vol. I, ch. 3, 52; Grotius, *The Law of War and Peace*, 102.

[128] Grotius, *De iure belli et pacis*, vol. I, ch. 3, 59–60; Grotius, *The Law of War and Peace*, 115–119. Grotius seems to have used *majestas* only in the sense of dignity, for example, Grotius, *De iure belli et pacis*, vol. I, ch. 3, 66; Grotius, *The Law of War and Peace*, 130.

[129] Lentin, ed. and trans., *Peter the Great*, 186–188.

[130] Ibid., 188–196.

The second part of Feofan's argument in section 13, that the monarch is not subject to human law, looks very absolutist. The idea is more or less the same as that found in the ancient maxim from the Code of Justinian (Ulpian, *Digest*, I, 3, 31), "princeps legibus solutus est."[131] This maxim had a long history in medieval and early modern Europe, but in the Middle Ages it was not taken by jurists to imply absolutism. In the early modern era it appeared more frequently as a defense of royal power, for example, in France as a justification for extraordinary measures such as the *lettres de cachet* rather than of normal legislation.[132] The problem with this conception is that it was irrelevant to Russian conditions. The idea in Western Europe was that the monarch was free to ignore existing laws, whether written law or legal fictions like the French "fundamental laws" (one of which was the law of succession), under certain circumstances. Russia, however, had no such laws or legal fictions on succession. The succession practices of the Kievan and Moscow princes were entirely based on custom, and the content of that custom is to this day a matter of debate among historians. The Romanov dynasty came to power by an election, and Peter himself was chosen in 1682 by the boyars and the church over an elder brother. In 1713, Louis XIV tried to alter the law of succession, thus overturning one of the fundamental laws of France. In 1722, Peter's law of succession did not overturn an existing law; it created a written law of succession for the first time in Russian history. The tsar himself in the preface to that law stated that it was to supersede a harmful custom (*obychai*), not a law.

Why, then, should Feofan want to argue that Peter could make such a law because the sovereign did not have to obey human law? A closer examination of his text in the second part of chapter 13, however, shows that he, like many interpreters of the maxim of Ulpian, meant something quite different from the original intent. All of his scriptural examples in the chapter are about obeying the king's commands, not about the king's actions in relationship to law. The emphasis is that no one, least of all subjects, may oppose or particularly may judge the king or call him to account for his actions. The idea that the monarch did not have to obey human law had to have a new meaning in a country without a learned legal profession and which was defining the powers of various state institutions

[131] Paul Krueger and Theodor Mommsen, eds., *Corpus iuris civilis*, vol. 1. Digesta (Berlin: Weidmann, 1889), 6; Alan Watson, ed. and trans., *Digest of Justinian* (Philadelphia, Pennsylvania: University of Pennsylvania Press, 1985), vol. 1, 13.

[132] Kenneth Pennington, *The Prince and the Law, 1200–1600: Sovereignty and Rights in the Western Legal Tradition* (Berkeley, California: University of California Press, 1993); Fanney Cosandey and Robert Descimon, *L'absolutisme en France: Histoire et historiographie* (Paris: Éditions du Seuil, 2002).

in written law for the first time. Either Feofan did not understand the function of the idea in European law or he realized that in Russian conditions it had different implications. For him, the issue was obedience.

Prokopovich took the idea of sovereignty, an idea that was new to the Russians, but used it to buttress very traditional arguments for obedience to the monarch. The notion of sovereignty as the intellectual basis of the analysis of the state was an innovation, not the political conclusions that called for obedience to the monarch. Feofan borrowed more from the natural law school than the definition of state sovereignty, even if on a rather theoretical level. All governments, he continued, derive their origin from an original agreement among the people. Once again he asserted a general principle, one held by most of the European lawyers and theorists of the time. This agreement, in the case of hereditary monarchy, implied a desire on the part of the people that the ruler should leave an heir in some fashion: that is the meaning of hereditary monarchy. As the Bible teaches that all power is from God, then God has willed the agreement and its details. In a monarchy then, the exercise of sovereignty means that the people must obey the monarch and can neither depose nor judge him (he was thinking of Charles I, as he states), unless conditions were laid down in the initial agreement. Thus the Polish constitution was perfectly legitimate, but in Russia there were no such conditions. In Russia there were no such prior conditions, so no one could dispute the Russian monarch's choice of an heir. He also argued that it is a mistake to assume that in making a hereditary monarchy the people intended that the king not have the power to name a successor. The only case in which the people can have any role in determining the succession is the case in which the ruler dies without making his wishes known. In this situation they are to try to determine his opinion of his children or any other persons, so as to enthrone someone whom the king had preferred. Feofan's idea of hereditary monarchy implied not just primogeniture but also the option of testamentary succession, a practice known also in the West, as in the case of the Spanish monarchy before the Bourbon accession.

The final chapter, chapter 16, of the *Pravda* was an argument for hereditary (in this sense) monarchy against elective monarchy. The reasoning here was political rather than legal or Biblical, with contemporary examples. Elective monarchies, Feofan argued, led to all sorts of disputes over succession that could even be violent, as the history of Poland demonstrated. Monarchs in a hereditary system could even assign part of the state as a hereditary possession to get around the custom of election (this was apparently a reference to the Habsburgs and the Pragmatic Sanction of 1713). Elective monarchy was even harmful culturally, as the practice encouraged kings to keep the nobility ignorant so as not to provide rivals.[133] As a sort of appendix, Feofan provided forty-one examples from secular history of rulers appointing their successors, concluding with the case of Ivan III, cited also in Peter's law, and five from sacred history as well. He concluded the work by ridiculing the idea that Peter's succession law was bad because it was an innovation, and noted once again that the example of Ivan III shows that in fact it was not an innovation. If Russia's lack of learning did not prevent the composition of a complete history, he suggested, there would be more examples.

Absolutism

Prokopovich did not advocate "absolutism," because it did not exist in either theory or practice in Western Europe for Russia to borrow. Political writers of the time used the word "absolute" occasionally, but they did not elaborate a theory of absolute monarchy or its virtues.

Whatever the views of legal scholars, the growth of royal power, at least in some European states, was real, and its "enemies" identified by the past historians of "absolutism" were also real. In Catholic countries, the Pope remained a rival to the kings. The kings also did contend with aristocracies, local and "central," but they dealt with them not by wholesale suppression or by "taming" them but by making arrangements, giving them offices and rewards and suppressing the few who remained recalcitrant or rebelled. Power was in fact shared. The kings did try to expand the central administration, but in limited ways and not eliminating the older structures, merely supplementing them.[134] They also did not suppress assemblies of estates: in France, the Estates General may not have met after 1614, but nearly half the country remained *pays d'états* until 1789. The ongoing effort of French and other kings to establish permanent taxes and a standing army was only partially successful, even in countries later labeled "absolutist." The absence of "absolutist" theory is even more striking. The political and legal theorists of the time, a few royalist pamphleteers aside, did not advocate unlimited power of the monarch. They believed that the state possessed absolute sovereignty, but were neutral about the type of state: republics or limited monarchies were sovereign as well as "unlimited" monarchies. Political leaders proclaimed "absolute" power for the kings in certain situations, not as generalities. The Third Estate in the 1614 Estates General of France

[133] Lentin, ed. and trans., *Peter the Great*, 227–245, 286.

[134] William Beik, *Absolutism and Society in Seventeenth Century France: State Power and Provincial Aristocracy in Languedoc* (Cambridge: Cambridge University Press, 1985).

asserted that the king's sovereignty implied that no one could judge or oppose him, but they meant the Pope, not themselves or the parlements.[135] King Frederick III of Denmark proclaimed "absolute power" in 1660–5, meaning that the throne was henceforth hereditary and the succession did not need to be confirmed or asserted by the estates, mainly the nobility.[136] After the proclamation of royal sovereignty in Sweden in 1682, the riksdag continued to meet.

Prokopovich, as a more careful examination of his writings demonstrates, understood all this. In any case, Russia's situation differed considerably from that of France or the Western monarchies. However powerful the last patriarchs of the Orthodox Church in Russia may have been, they were not the local representatives of a large and powerful international church. The Russian boyars in the seventeenth century (and perhaps before) were not the representatives of any local noble community or territory. They had always acted in concert with the tsar even if they fought with one another for influence on him. Russia also had no rebellious princes of the blood. If the tsar's power had no legal limit, neither did that of the boyars in the duma. Both followed custom, and custom could change. Only in Peter's time did a short-lived opposition to monarchical power emerge among the aristocracy, but, as the events of 1730 demonstrated, it was too small and too limited in aims to gain much support among the elite. The Zemskii sobor was not trivial, but it did not deal with taxation or the army. What it did do was name the tsar (in 1598 and 1613), and that function was inherited after 1725 by the guards regiments, through which the Russian elite continued to name its rulers until 1801. The centralized administration certainly grew in the seventeenth century, and more from Peter's time onward, but seventeenth-century offices were headed by aristocrats. In Peter's time and after, the new composite elite soon saw itself as equally aristocratic to the old boyars. The provinces remained notoriously undergoverned, and the weakness of local administration in Russia had no parallel in the major European states. Russia had no *intendants*.

In the Russian situation, the natural law theorists and other political writers in the West did have an audience, but not because of "absolutist" theory, which they did not represent. It may have been their very neutrality about forms of government, combined with the assertion of state sovereignty and insistence on written law, which gave rise to their appeal

[135] J. Russell Major, *From Renaissance Monarchy to Absolutism: French Nobles, Kings, and Estates* (Baltimore, Maryland: Johns Hopkins University Press, 1994), 186–187; J. Michael Hayden, *France and the Estates General of 1614* (London: Cambridge University Press, 1974), 131–148.

[136] Fabricius, *Kongeloven.*

to the Russians. Peter (and Prokopovich) wanted to create a stronger state and base its actions on written law. Prokopovich as well as the tsar could rely on Western writers for arguments about the state in general, but for particular forms of administration they had to find models in Western practice (such as the Swedish colleges), not in political or legal theory.

Power and Succession

The misinterpretation by Gurvich and later scholars of the political thought of Prokopovich inevitably entangled "absolutism" with the conceptions of succession to the throne and the evolving measures of Peter the Great to secure the future of the throne after his death. Peter and his spokesman did not ensure the absolute power of the tsar, but they did ensure that he would have the last word about his successor. The reasons for this were contingent. Until 1718, the successor to the throne was Tsarevich Aleksei Petrovich. Peter prepared him for the future by all the methods available in Russian and European tradition. He had the boy brought up first under the supervision of the women of the family, then of male tutors. Aleksei was given a Western education, and the result was visible in his library. He knew German and some Latin. He was also expected to be a pious Orthodox Christian, and became one. That his adherence to some of the practices such as fasting was greater than that of his father was a detail. His private behavior, with at least one mistress, was no more rigorous than Peter's. As soon as he was old enough, the tsar set him to work at governance, learning administrative tasks such as supplying the army with recruits and provisions. Peter married him off to Charlotte at the usual age, but the marriage was not a great success. It produced children, but not a united couple. It is after the marriage that the heir's relations with the tsar began to spoil. By 1716, they had come to a crisis point, ending in the flight, return, deposition, and death of Aleksei. It was only at this moment, in 1718, that Peter had to think about the future more seriously. He had several possible heirs, but the two boys were infants and even the girls were not out of childhood. The result was the succession decree of 1722, which declared that the tsar was free to appoint whomever he pleased as his heir. How large the circle of possibilities really was in Peter's mind is unknown. In crowning his wife Ekaterina he in effect created a sort of co-ruler who could take over the state immediately after his death. That solution, however, only put off the problem. What Peter did do by inaction, however, was in a sense a continuation of Russian tradition. The only heirs under discussion were the Romanov family, his children and grandson, but also his nieces and their descendants. The secret clause of the marriage treaty with

Holstein is testimony: Peter was thinking that his daughter Anna and the duke might produce a suitable heir.

Peter the Great's succession law of February 5, 1722 is supposed to have wrought a radical change in the manner of succession to the throne. It stated that the ruling emperor (the new title since the previous autumn) could choose anyone whom he pleased to inherit the throne, not just his eldest son. As we have seen, in context that was not a complete break. Previous tsars had in fact chosen successors other than the eldest son and the law adduced the example of Ivan III's choice of Vasilii III. What the law did not state, however, is that the choices had all been within the ruling family, and Peter's law did not make that qualification. The importance of the law, however, was in another area: for the first time, the succession practices were encoded in written law, not merely in custom. The law also eliminated the possibility of election by any section of the elite or the people. In that sense it reinforced the power of the ruler, but it did not establish or reinforce absolutism. The law was another example of the Westernization of Russian political thought and culture, especially when Feofan Prokopovich defended it relying on Hugo Grotius for his conception of state sovereignty. Custom had become law, and that law was framed in European terms.

Epilogue and Conclusion

Peter the Great died on January 28, 1725. In spite of the provisions of his 1722 law on succession, he left no testament and did not indicate his choice of heir. The Princes D. M. Golitsyn and V. L. Dolgorukii wanted a regency with Ekaterina and the Senate. Menshikov and his allies defeated that plan together with the guards and placed Ekaterina on the throne. Their argument was that her coronation signified that she was clearly the heir to her husband.[1] Though contentious, the transition was peaceful. Ekaterina ruled in her own name, but she also appointed a Supreme Privy Council, where Menshikov was the leader but worked with Golitsyn and the other dignitaries. Unlike Peter, Ekaterina did write a testament, specifying that Petr Alekseevich, Peter's grandson, should inherit the throne. With Ekaterina's death at age forty-three in 1727, the throne passed peacefully to Petr II, then only twelve years old.[2] The real power came into the hands of the Supreme Privy Council. That institution quickly became the preserve of the Princes D. M. Golitsyn and V. V. Dolgorukii, who sent Menshikov into Siberian exile. It was these oligarchs who decided, on the sudden death of the young tsar from smallpox in 1730, to call on Anna, the duchess of Kurland and the daughter of Peter's brother Tsar Ivan. The Supreme Privy Council envisioned her rule as subordinate to themselves. The reaction was the "restoration of autocracy," engineered by aristocrats left out of power by the oligarchy and the ordinary nobles, including the guards officers. In

[1] Konstantin Arsen'ev, *Tsarstvovanie Ekateriny I* (St. Petersburg: Tipografiia Imperatorskoi akademii nauk, 1856); S. M. Solov'ev, *Istoriia Rossii s drevneishikh vremen* (Moscow: Izdatel'stvo sotsial'no-ekonomicheskoi literatury, 1960–6), vol. IX (= 18), 555–570; N. I. Pavlenko, *Ekaterina I* (Moscow: Molodaia gvardiia, 2004), 46–58; Igor' V. Kurukin, *Epokha "dvortsovykh bur'": Ocherki politicheskoi istorii poslepetrovskoi Rossii* (Riazan': NRIID, 2003), 85–97.

[2] Ekaterina also specified that if Peter II had no heirs, her daughters Anna and then Elizaveta would inherit the throne, excluding Peter's nieces (such as Anna Ivanovna). Arsen'ev, *Tsarstovanie Ekateriny I*, 83–84 (text of Ekaterina's testament); *PSZ* VII, 788–790 (5070: Manifesto with testament); Kurukin, *Epokha "dvortsovykh bur'*,*"* 120–129.

fact it was a coup d'état.[3] It was not the last. Empress Anna soon decided that her heir would be Anna Leopol'dovna (1718–46), the daughter of Peter's niece Ekaterina Ivanovna and Karl-Leopold of Mecklenburg. Anna Leopol'dovna was thus Empress Anna's niece as well, and had lived in Russia with her mother since her parents separated in 1722. For much of the 1730s intrigue followed intrigue about the young woman's marriage, and finally in 1739 the empress succeeded in giving her in marriage to Anton Ulrich, Duke of Braunschweig-Bevern.[4] In 1740, Anna Leopol'dovna gave birth to Ivan Antonovich, proclaimed by the manifesto of Empress Anna (shortly before her death in October) the heir to the throne.[5] The baby became the tsar as Ivan VI, with his mother, father, and at first Anna Ivanovna's favorite Ernst Johann von Biron as regents. In spite of Biron's rapid fall, the rule of Anna Leopol'dovna's mostly German entourage was not popular.[6]

Empress Elizaveta, Peter's daughter, came to the throne in 1741 on the shoulders of the guards, who allegedly carried her into the Winter Palace.[7] Catherine II took the same path: she arrived in St. Petersburg at the head of the guards to overthrow her unpopular husband, Peter III, himself the fruit of Peter's marriage schemes in Holstein.[8] The first peaceful succession was on Catherine's death in 1796, when her son Paul took her place. It was he who proclaimed Russia's first hereditary succession law in 1797. Henceforth the rulers were to be the sons of the monarch in descending order of birth, and the daughters were to have the throne only if the whole male line failed. Paul's attempt to put order into the system failed: the

[3] Kurukin, *Epokha "dvortsovykh bur',"* 164–224; I. V. Kurukin and A. B. Plotnikov, *19 ianvaria–25 fevralia 1730 goda: Sobytiia, liudi, dokumenty* (Moscow: Kvadriga, 2010); N. N. Petrukhintsev, *Tsarstvovanie Anny Ioannovny: Formirovanie vnutrennopoliticheskogo kursa i sud'ba armii i flota 1730–1735 gg.* (St. Petersburg: Aleteiia, 2001); Lorenz Erren, *Der russische Hof nach Peter dem Grossen 1725–1730: Eine Kulturgeschichte des Politischen*, Habilitation Thesis, Universität Mainz, 2018.

[4] Anton Ulrich was the son of Ferdinand Albrecht II, the duke of Braunschweig-Wolfenbüttel after 1735. He inherited the Wolfenbüttel duchy on the death of Ludwig Rudolf (ruled 1731–5), who was the father of Charlotte, the wife of Tsarevich Aleksei Petrovich. Ludwig Rudolf had no sons, so the duchy went to the Braunschweig-Bevern line in the person of Ferdinand Albrecht II. On his death only a few months after taking the duchy, it went to his eldest son Karl I, the older brother of Anton Ulrich, the husband of Anna Leopol'dovna. Karl I ruled in Wolfenbüttel until his death in 1780.

[5] Kurukin, *Epokha "dvortsovykh bur',"* 276–281.

[6] During all this time there was another candidate to the throne whom Empress Anna rejected: the son of Peter's own oldest daughter Anna Petrovna and Karl-Friedrich of Holstein. He would be the future Peter III of Russia.

[7] *Kurukin, Epokha "dvortsovykh bur',"* 326–337; *Francine-Dominique* Liechtenhan, *Élisabeth Ire de Russie: L'autre impératrice* (Paris: Fayard, 2007), 79–86.

[8] Isabel de Madariaga, *Russia in the Age of Catherine the Great* (New Haven, Connecticut and London: Yale University Press, 1981), 21–37; Kurukin, *Epokha "dvortsovykh bur',"* 370–413.

guards overthrew and murdered him on March 11, 1801. After that, his son Alexander took the throne, and succession from then on until the end of the Romanov dynasty proceeded according to law, if with an attendant revolt in 1825.

*

Succession to the throne, like everything else in the Russian state after Peter, was now understood in the framework of Western political theory, as adapted in Russia. Peter's whole reign meant the introduction of Western culture, and indeed one of Peter's last acts was to order the translation into Russian of Samuel Pufendorf's tract of 1673, *De officio hominis et civis juxta legem naturalem* (*On the Duty of Man and the Citizen According to Natural Law*).[9] Pufendorf and other European legal and political writers argued that the state grew out of the state of nature, that the state was sovereign, and that it should be based on law.[10] Concrete institutions, like succession, were to be couched in the terms that Western political theory provided.[11] Pufendorf was not an absolutist. His task was in any case mainly analysis, not the advocacy of a particular form of government. His *De officio hominis et civis* made that very clear. He dealt with the term absolute in his chapter on the "Qualifications" of civil government (*De affectionibus imperii civilis*) in book II, chapter 9 of the work. The chapter is about *summum imperium* (supreme authority), and in it he expounds the characteristics of authority called "supreme."[12] Then he notes that in some monarchies *and aristocracies* (my emphasis) the

[9] Samuel Pufendorf, *O dolzhnosti cheloveka i grazhdanina po zakonu estestvennomu* (St. Petersburg: Sankt-Peterburgskaia tipografiia, 1726).

[10] On Russian political thought, see Marc Raeff, *The Well-Ordered Police State: Social and Institutional Change through Law in the Germanies and Russia 1600–1800* (New Haven, Connecticut and London: Yale University Press, 1983); Cynthia Whittaker, *Russian Monarchy: Eighteenth-Century Rulers and Writers in Political Dialogue* (DeKalb, Illinois: Northern Illinois University Press, 2003); K. D. Bugrov and M. A. Kiselev, *Estestvennoe pravo i dobrodetel': Integratsiia evropeiskogo vliianiia v rossiiskuiu politicheskuiu kul'turu XVIII veka* (Ekaterinburg: Izdatel'stvo Ural'skogo universiteta, 2016); Gary Hamburg, *Russia's Path toward Enlightenment: Faith, Politics, and Reason 1500–1801* (New Haven, Connecticut: Yale University Press, 2016); E. N. Marasinova, *"Zakon" i "grazhdanin" v Rossii vtoroi poloviny XVIII veka: Ocherki istorii obshchestvennogo soznaniia* (Moscow: Novoe literaturnoe obozrenie, 2017).

[11] Pufendorf divided monarchies into "patrimonial" and those established by popular consent. In the former case, the monarch was free to convey his lands to whomever he wished, though the assumption was that the successor would be his son, normally the eldest: Samuel Pufendorf, *De officio hominis et civis*, 6th ed. (Cambridge and London: Typis Academicis. Impensis Edvardi Hall, Bibliopolæ, 1701), 133–134 (Book II, chapter X); Samuel von Pufendorf, *De officio hominis et civis*, trans. Frank Gardner Moore, 2 vols. (Oxford and New York: Oxford University Press, 1927), vol. 2, 119.

[12] Pufendorf, *De officio hominis et civis*, 130–132. Pufendorf, *De officio hominis et civis*, trans. Moore, vol. 2, 116.

government may be either absolute or limited. "Absolute authority is said to belong to the monarch who can administer it according to his own judgement, not according to the norm of definite and permanent statutes, but as the present exigency seems to demand; and who provides for the safety of the state at his own discretion, according as its circumstances require." In some states, the power of the monarch is limited, and he must have the agreement of the people or their representatives.[13] Pufendorf does not recommend either form of government; he simply states that both exist. Peter ordered the book to be translated into Russian in November 1721 and then to be published in December 1724. His death intervened, and it appeared only in 1726.[14] In practice, Russians did not adopt every detail of the theories they examined, and they ignored some parts of the edifice being constructed by Western theorists. After the publication of Prokopovich's tract, succession did not attract much attention, if only because the law remained in theory Peter's decree. The state of nature, the social contract, natural law, virtue, and the citizen came to be subjects of discussion throughout the eighteenth century in Russia.

The evolution of the Russian state and its succession practices up to Peter's time was not a straightforward story of the triumph of primogeniture over collateral succession. Rather it was the story of the rulers' efforts to secure the succession of their chosen heirs. In most cases that was the eldest son, but not always, and in all cases the rulers made a show of designating and presenting the heir once he was of age. Tsar Aleksei devised a new ceremony to present the heir once he came of age. All the rulers blessed their sons with the throne on their deathbeds if they were physically and mentally able and had time in their final illnesses. They did not assume that custom would simply ensure the succession of the designated heir.

Russia's rulers contended with the possibility that someone, mostly but not exclusively among the elite, would prefer a different ruler than the designated heir. This was the case in 1682. The other problem the rulers faced was the consequences of genetic fate and early modern medicine. There were many times when the rulers had no children, no sons, or sons with some sort of disability that made it difficult or impossible to rule. This outcome of a marriage was common, and the rulers had to keep this

[13] "Absolutum imperium monarcha habere dicitur, qui illud administrare potest proprio ex judicio, non ad normam certorum ac perpetuorum statutorum, sed prout praesens rerum conditio videtur exigere, quique adeo proprium ad arbitrium salutem rei publicae prout ejusdem tempora postulaverint, procurat." Pufendorf, *De officio hominis et civis*, 131.

[14] Pekarskii, *Nauka i literatura v Rossii pri Petre Velikom*, 2 vols. (St. Petersburg: Obshchestvennaia pol'za, 1862), vol. I, 213; Paul Bushkovitch, *Peter the Great: The Struggle for Power 1671–1725* (Cambridge: Cambridge University Press, 2001), 444.

in mind. At the same time, identical consequences meant that there might be no obvious contenders for the throne outside the immediate family of the ruler. Juggling all these balls in the air was an important part of the monarch's task.

Succession practices also reflected and perhaps influenced conceptions of the monarchy and the culture of the court. Succession to the throne took place against the background of the customs of inheritance of aristocratic property. In Russia, landed property was always divided among the sons, with a portion (usually moveable property) for all the daughters. The inheritance of an entire estate by the eldest son did not exist until Peter's 1714 law of single inheritance, and it was repealed as early as in 1731. The rulers also had to provide land for all their sons, as they did in the testaments from the fourteenth century to the sixteenth, but they also left the throne to just one of them. Several sons of a boyar might attain boyar rank, but only one son would be grand prince or tsar. At the same time, the rulers tried to expand the loyalty of the people from just the ruler to his whole family, his wife and all his children, including the daughters, in the oaths of service as well as other occasions for the ruling family to demonstrate its identity.

Succession in the ruling family was different from the inheritance of property in one other respect: land with no heirs returned to the crown. For the throne the solution had to be different. If the Russian throne was completely vacant, as happened four times between 1598 and 1613, the result was the election of the tsar by the Assembly of the Land. This result was perhaps not so unexpected, considering the appearance of the practice of calling an assembly from 1566 until at least 1653. The Russians may have used this assembly (besides electing the tsars, mainly over foreign policy) to manage political affairs, but they did not theorize about it. It is not possible to detect in any of the writings of the period, bureaucratic or literary, a conception of the advantages of either inherited or elected monarchy. The problem here is that Russian culture remained until roughly the 1660s entirely within a religious framework. They argued about whether the ruler was a pious and just Orthodox Christian, not about monarchy or aristocracy, inheritance or election.

When that religious culture began to change in the reign of Tsar Aleksei Mikhailovich, the impact of that change on the framing of succession was profound. Tsar Aleksei from 1667 presented his heir to the assembled elite and people on September 1, and that presentation was accompanied by speeches and poetry composed by Simeon Polotskii and others. Speeches and poetry from then on accompanied all the events in the life of the ruling family, births, deaths, and other events. The practice continued into Peter's time, with speeches and sermons by major churchmen, fireworks, and other festivities. Feofan Prokopovich's tract on Peter's succession law was the first example in Russia of the full impact of Western legal and political thinking.

Russian succession practices at first glance look a bit peculiar in a Western context, but only if the assumption is that the norm in early modern Western Europe was primogeniture. That rule was certainly widespread, but much of Europe was an elective monarchy by law (the Empire, Poland, Denmark until 1660) and also de facto. The English parliament ultimately decided who was king, in the sixteenth century and after, even if it tried to follow the male line in the royal family. When that was not possible in 1688, it just chose a new ruler. Succession by designation cohabited with inheritance in Spain, Sweden, and elsewhere.

The practices of succession to the throne also illuminate the long discussions among historians and publicists of autocracy as well as its modern cousin, absolutism. In the context of Western Europe, primogeniture has appeared as a natural feature of absolutism or at least of a strong monarchy as it removed the transfer of power from any parliament, oligarchy, or assembly of estates. Since Russia has been described as an autocracy, it would seem that primogeniture was a natural part of that regime. In reality it was not, and Peter's succession law combined with the biological fate of his family only led to another sort of designation, the choice of the monarch by the elite and the guards officers for the seventy years after his death. These chosen monarchs were all women. Russia was ruled for almost all of the seventy years after Peter's death by women, all of them put on the throne by the elite and the guards, one of the many paradoxes of Russian history. This was an outcome no one could have predicted.

Succession in the monarchies of early modern Europe was not a matter of the private life of the kings to be left to historical novelists and popular biographers. It was the fundamental mechanism of the transfer of power, and as such was just as important as the relations of monarchs with ruling elites, estate institutions, and the development of state administration. In Russia the monarchy was neither elective nor was it founded on primogeniture. The tsars had to demonstrate their choice of heir in practice and in ritual, inner court rituals and ones that presented the heir to the larger public, at least in Moscow. The transfer of power was based in part on custom, in part on display and the acquiescence of the elite, sometimes of wider groups of the population. Russia's rulers were able to maintain an evolving practice that contributed as much as the administrative offices or the boyar and aristocratic elite to the stability of the state and to the growing power of Russia. In the Darwinian world of early modern relations between states, that stability and power was essential for survival.

References

Abbreviations

AI	*Akty istoricheskie*
AAE	*Akty . . . sobrannye arkheograficheskoi kommissieiu imperatorskoi Akademii nauk*
AIuZR	*Akty otnosiashchiesia k istorii Iuzhnoi i Zapadnoi Rossii*
ChOIDR	*Chteniia v Obshchestve istorii i drevnostei rossiiskikh pri Moskovskom universtitete*
DAI	*Dopolneniia k aktam istoricheskim*
DR	*Dvortsovye razriady*
DRV	*Dreniaia rossiiskaia vifliofika*
KR	*Knigi razriadnye*
PDS	*Pamiatniki diplomaticheskikh snoshenii drevnei Rossii s dervazhami inostrannymi*
PSRL	*Polnoe sobranie russkikh letopisei*
PSZ	*Polnoe sobranie zakonov Rossiskoi imperii*
SGGD	*Sobranie gosudarstvennykh gramot i dogovorov*
SKKDR	*Slovar' knizhnikov i knizhnosti Drevnei Rusi*
SRIO	*Sbornik Russkogo istoricheskogo obshchestva*
TODRL	*Trudy Otdela drevnerusskoi literatury Pushkinskogo doma*
PiB	*Pis'ma i bumagi Petra Velikogo*

Manuscript Sources

Danske Rigsarkiv, Tyske Kancelli, Udenrigske Avdelning [hereafter TKUA], Rusland A II.

Gennadius Library, Athens, MS 260 (Paisios Ligarides, *Report of the Council against Nikon*).

Gosudarstvennei istoricheskii muzei, Moscow, Otdel Rukopisei, Sinodal'noe sobranie 229 (Simeon Polotskii, collection of speeches and greetings).

Landesarchiv Sachsen-Anhalt, Standort Wernigerode: Nachlass Johann Christian von Urbichs, Gutsarchiv Goseck, Familienarchiv 03.09, Korrespondenz Johann Christoph von Urbichs mit Menschikow, Golowkin, Schaphirof,

Herzog Anton Ulrich von Wolffenbüttel; H82, no. 420 (Urbich), no. 895 (Anton Ulrich), no. 1029 (Peter).
RGADA:
f. 32 (Snosheniia s Avstriei)
f. 53 (Snosheniia s Daniei)
f. 79 (Snosheniia s Pol'shei)
f. 140 (Prisiagi tsarevichu Petru Petrovichu)
f. 210 (Razriad)
Rossiiskaia Natsional'naia Biblitoteka (RNB), St. Petersburg, Otdel rukopisei, Osnovnoe sobranie F XVII 83 (Simeon Polotskii, collection of works); F II 67 (Feofan Prokopovich).
Svenska Riksarkiv (SR), Muscovitica 33.

Primary Sources

Abramovich, D. I. *Das Paterikon des Kiever Höhlenklosters*, edited by Dmitrij Tschizewskij. Munich: Eidos Verlag, 1964.
Zhitiia sviatykh muchennikov Borisa i Gleba i sluzhby im. Petrograd: Otdelenie russkogo iazyka i slovesnosti Imperatorskoi akademii nauk, 1916.
Acta Tomiciana 18 vols. Poznań, Sumptibus Bibliothecae Kornicensis, 1852–1999.
Adrianova-Peretts, V. P. *Zhitie Alekseia cheloveka Bozhiia v drevnei russkoi literature i narodnoi slovestnosti*. Petrograd, n.p., 1917.
Adrianova-Peretts, V. P., and O. A. Derzhavina, eds. *Vremennik Ivana Timofeeva*. St. Petersburg: Nauka, 2004.
Adrianova-Peretts, V. P., and D. S. Likhachev, eds. *Povest' vremennykh let*, 2nd ed. St. Petersburg: Nauka, 1999.
Adrianova-Peretts, V. P., D. S. Likhachev, and Ia. S. Lur'e, eds. *Poslaniia Ivana Groznogo*. Moscow and Leningrad: Izdatel'stvo Akademii nauk SSSR, 1951.
Akty istoricheskie, 5 vols., St. Petersburg: Tipografiia ekspeditsii zagotovleniia gosudarstvennykh bumag, 1841–1842.
Akty otnosiashchiesia k istorii Iuzhnoi i Zapadnoi Rossii, 15 vols. St. Petersburg: Eduard Prats, 1863–92.
Akty, sobrannye v bibliotekakh i arkhivakh Rossiiskoi Imperii Arkheograficheskoi͡u ekspeditisieiu Imperatorskoĭ Akademii Nauk, 5 vols., St. Petersburg: V Tipografii vtorogo otdeleniia Sobstvennoi E. I. V. Kan͡tseli͡arii, 1836–1858.
Alekseev, A. I. ed., "Sinodik Chudova Monastyria v Moskovskom Kremle." *Vestnik tserkovnoi istorii*, 3, 4 (55/56) (2019): 5–239.
Ammann, Albert M., ed. "Ein russischer Reisebericht aus dem Jahre 1581."*Ostkirchliche Studien* X, 2–3 (September 1961): 156–193; X, 4 (December 1961): 283–300.
"I. P. Campani Relatio de itinere Moscovitico." *Antemurale* VI (1960–1): 1–87.
Anfologion [Arsenii Grek]. Moscow: Pechatnyi dvor, 1660.
Anon., ed. "Rodoslovnaia kniga." *Vremennik OIDR* 10, 3rd pagination, I–IV (1851), 1–286.

Anon., ed. "Rodoslovnaia keleinaia kniga sviateishego gosudaria Filareta patriarkha vseia Rossii." In *Iubileinyi sbornik S.-Peterburgskogo Arkheologicheskogo Instituta 1613–1913*, i–xxvii, 1–106. St. Petersburg: Sinodalnaia Tipografiia, 1913.

Anon. *Wahrhaftige Relation der Reussischen und Muscowitischen Reyse . . . des Herren Herzog Johansen des Jüngern . . .* Lübeck: Johann Balhorn, 1603; Hamburg: Phillip von Ohr, 1604; Magdeburg: Bey Johan Francken, 1604. Reprinted in *Magazin für die neue Historie und Geographie* VII (1773).

Archiwum domu Radziwiłłów. Scriptores rerum polonicarum VIII. Kraków: Nakład Księcia Antoniego Radziwiłła, 1885.

Archiwum Jana Zamoyskiego, 4 vols. Warsaw: Komisja Historyczna Akademii Umiejętności w Krakowie, 1904–48.

Arkhimandrit Iosif. *Podrobnoe Oglavlenie Velikikh chetiikh minei vserossiiskogo mitropolita Makariia*. Moscow: Sinodal'naia tipografiia, 1892.

Arkhiv Iugo-Zapadnoi Rossii, 32 vols. in 8 parts. Kiev: Kommisiia dlia razbora drevnikh aktov, 1859–1914.

Baranovich, Lazar'. *Truby sloves propovednykh*. Kiev: Tipografiia lavry, 1674.

Barclay, John. *Argenis*, 2 vols., edited and translated by Mark Riley and Dorothy Pritchard Huber. Medieval and Renaissance Texts and Studies 273. Tempe, Arizona: Arizona Center for Medieval and Renaissance Studies, 2004.

Barsov, P. P., and O. M. Bodianskii, eds. and trans. *Puteshestvie cherez Moskoviiu Korneliia de Bruina*. Moscow: Imperatorskoe obshchestvo istorii i drevnostei rossiskikh pri Moskovskom universitete, 1873. First published 1872–3 in *ChOIDR*.

Barsov, V. "Drevnerusskie pamiatniki sviashchennogo venchaniia tsarei na tsarstvo." *ChOIDR* I (1883): 25–31.

Basilii Romanorum Imp. exhortationum capita LXVI. ad Leonem filium. Paris: Apud F. Morellum, 1584.

Bassevich, G. F. "Zapiski grafa Bassevicha." *Russkii arkhiv* 1, 2, 5, 6 (1865–6).

Bassewitz, H. F. de. "Éclaircissements sur plusieurs faits arrivés sous le regne de Pierre le grand." *Magazin für die neue Historie und Geographie* IX (1775): 281–380.

Batalov, A. L., and I. A. Vorotnikova, eds. *Kniga ob izbranii na prevysochaishii prestol Velikogo Rossiiskogo Tsarstviia velikogo gosudaria tsaria i velikogo kniazia Mikhaila Fyodorovicha vseia Velikiia Rossii samoderzhtsa: Rukopis', kommentarii, tekst*. Moscow: Federal'noe gosudarstvennoe biudzhetnoe uchrezhdenie kul'tury – Gosudarstvennyi istoricheskii kul'turnyi muzei-zapovednik Moskovskii kreml', 2014.

Begunov, Iu. K., and A. N. Kirpichnikova, eds. *Aleksandr Nevskii i ego epokha: Issledovaniia i materialy*. St. Petersburg: Izdatel'stvo Dmitrii Bulanin, 1995.

Bell, Peter N., ed. and trans. *Three Political Voices from the Age of Justinian*. Translated Texts for the Historian 52. Liverpool: Liverpool University Press, 2009.

Belokurov, S. A. "*Dneval'nye zapiski Prikaza tainykh del 7165–7183 gg.*" *ChOIDR* 1 (1908): i–x, 1–224; 2 (1908) 225–346.

Razriadnye zapisi za Smutnoe vremia, 7113–7121 gg. Moscow: Izdatel'stvo Imperatorskogo obshestva istorii drevnostei rossiiskikh pri Moskovskom universiteta, 1907. First published *ChOIDR* 2–3 (1907).

Snosheniia Rossii s Kavkazom. Moscow: Universitetskaia tipografiia, 1889.

Belokurov, S. A., ed. *Utverzhennaia gramota ob izbranii na Moskovskoe gosudarstvo Mikhaila Fedorovicha Romanova*. Moscow: Tipografiia Obshchestva rasprostraneniia poleznykh knig, 1906.

Bergholtz, F. V. *Dnevnik*. Translated by I. F. Ammon. pts. I–IV. St. Petersburg: Universitetskaia tipografiia, 1902.

Bergholz, Friedrich Wilhelm von. "Tagebuch." *Magazin für die neue Historie und Geographie* XIX (1785): 3–202; XX (1786): 331–592; XXI (1787): 178–360; XXII (1788): 425–506.

Bernard, Auguste, ed. *Procès-Verbaux des États Généraux de 1593*. Collection de documents inédits sur l'histoire de France. Paris: Imprimerie royale, 1842.

Bielski, Marcin. *Kronika*, 3 vols. Sanok: Karol Pollak, 1856. First published Kraków: Drukarnia Jakuba Sibeneychera, 1597.

Biliarski, Ivan. *Paleologoviiat Sinodik v slavianski prevod*. Sofiia: Universitetsko izdatelstvo Sv. Kliment Ochridski, 2013.

Biliarski, Ivan, Ivan Bozhikov, and A. Totomanova. *Borilov Sinodik: Izdanie i prevod*. Sofiia: PAM Publishing Company, 2010.

Birgegård, Ulla, ed. *J. G. Sparwenfeld's Diary of a Journey to Russia 1684–87*. Kungliga Vitterhets Historie och Antikvitets Akademien, Slavica Suecana, Series A, vol. 1. Stockholm: Almquist & Wiksell, 2002.

Blümcke, Otto. *Berichte und Akten der hansischen Gesandtschaft nach Moskau im Jahre 1603*. Hansische Geschichtsquellen VII. Halle: Verlag der Buchhandlung des Waisenhauses, 1894.

Bodemann, Eduard, ed. *Briefe der Kurfürstin Sophie von Hannover an die Raugräfinnen und Raugrafen zu Pfalz*. Publikationen aus den preußischen Archiven 37. Leipzig: S. Hirzel, 1888.

Bodin, Jean. *Les six livres de la république 1576*, edited by Christiane Frémont, Marie-Dominque Couzinet, and Henri Rochais, 6 vols. Paris: Fayard, 1986.

Bogdanov, A. P. *Pamiatniki obshchestvenno-politicheskoi mysli v Rossii kontsa XVII veka: Literaturnye panegiriki*. Moscow: Institut istorii SSSR, 1983.

—— *Stikh torzhestva: Rozhdenie russkoi ody posledniaia chetvert' XVII–nachalo XVIII veka*, 2 vols. Moscow: Rossiiskaia akademiia nauk, Institut rossiskoi istorii, 2012.

Boor, Carolus de, ed. *Georgii monachi chronicon*, 2 vols. Leipzig: Teubner, 1904.

Bolotina, N. Iu., ed. "Epistoliarnoe nasledie zhenshchin tsarskoi sem'i (pervaia tret' XVIII veka)." *Rossiiskii arkhiv* XX (2011): 11–69.

Bowes, Sir Jerome. "The Ambassage of Sir Hierome Bowes to the Emperour of Muscovie 1583." In *The Principall Navigations, Voiages and Discoveries of the English Nation*, edited by Richard Hakluyt, vol. 1, 487–500. London: George Bishop and Ralph Newberie, deputies to Christopher Barker, printer to the Queenes most excellent Maiestie, 1589.

Bruijn, Cornelis de. *Reizen over Moskovie door Persie en Indie*. Amsterdam: Willem en David Goeree, 1711.

Buganov, V. I., ed. *Razriadnaia kniga 1475–1598*. Moscow: Nauka, 1966.

—— *Razriadnaia kniga 1550–1636 gg*. Moscow: Nauka, 1975.

—— *Razriadnye knigi poslednei chetverti XV–nachala XVII v*. Moscow: Izdatel'stvo Akademii nauk SSSR, 1962.

Bushkovitch, Paul. "Shvedskie istochniki o Rossii 1624–26 gg." *Arkhiv russkoi istorii* 8 (2007): 359–381.

Bushkovitch, Paul, Maija Jansson, and Nikolai Rogozhin. *England and the North: The Russian Embassy of 1613–1614*. Memoirs of the American Philosophical Society 210. Philadelphia, Pennsylvania: American Philosophical Society, 1994.

Caussin, Nicolas, and Denis Pétau. *Pompa regia*. La Fleche: Flexiae, 1615.

Cherepnin, L. V., ed. *Dukhovnye i dogovornye gramoty velikikh i udel'nykh kniazei XIV–XVI vv.* Moscow and Leningrad: Izdatel'stvo Akademii nauk SSSR, 1950.

Cherepnin, L. V., O. A. Derzhavina, and E. V. Kolosova, eds. *Skazanie Avraamiia Palitsyna*. Moscow and Leningrad: Izdatel'stvo Akademii nauk SSSR, 1955.

"Chin postavlenie ... 1498 goda." In *Russkii feodal'nyi arkhiv*, edited by A. I. Pliguzov, vol. 3, 608–621. Moscow: Iazyski slavianskikh kul'tur, 2008.

Chistovich, I. "Neizdannye propovedi Stefana Iavorskogo." *Khristianskoe chtenie* 1 (1867): 259–279, 414–429, 814–837.

Coyet, B. *Posol'stvo Kunraada fan-Klenka*, ed. A. M. Loviagin. St. Petersburg: Izdatel'stvo Arkheograficheskoi Komisii, 1900.

Daniel, Samuel. "A Panegyric Congratulatorie to the King's Most Excellent Majestie." In *The Complete Works in Verse and Prose*, vol. 1, 144. London: Hazell, Watson and Viney, 1885.

Danilovich, I., and M. Obolenskii, eds. *Kniga Posol'skaia Metriki Velikogo Kniazhestva Litovskogo*, vol. I. Moscow: Universitetskaia tipografiia, 1843.

Dan, Pierre. *Le trésor des merveilles de la maison royale de Fontainebleau*. Paris: Sébastien Cramoisy, 1642.

Dantiscus, Ioannes [Jan Dantyszek]. *Sylvula de victoria inclyti Sigismundi regis Polonie contra Moschos*. Kraków: Grachovie per Florianum Unglerium XXIII, 1514.

Demkova, N. S. "Gramoty Ivana Groznogo shvedskim koroliam Eriku XIV i Iogannu III (po rukopisiam Shvedskogo gosudarstvennogo arkhiva)." *TODRL* 50 (1996): 488–500.

Dergacheva, I. V. *Drevnerusskii Sinodik: Issledovaniia i teksty*. Moscow: Izdatel'stvo Krug, 2011.

Derzhavina, O. A., ed. *Vremennik Ivana Timofeeva*. St. Petersburg: Nauka, 2004.

Długosz, Jan. *Historia Polonica*. Opera omnia X–XIV. Kraków: Tipographia Czas F. Klurzycki, 1873–8.

Dmitrieva, R. P. *Skazanie o kniaziakh vladimirskikh*. Moscow and Leningrad: Izdatel'stvo Akademii nauk SSSR, 1955.

Dopolneniia k aktam istoricheskim, otnosiashchimsia k Rossii, 12 vols. St. Petersburg: Tipografiia Vtorogo otdeleniia sobstvennoi E.I.V. Kantseliarii, 1846–72.

Drevniaia rossiiskaia vivliofika ili sobranie raznykh drevnikh sochinenii, 20 vols., 2nd ed. Moscow: Kompaniia tipograficheskaia, 1788–91.

Droblenkova, N. F., and L. S. Shepeleva, eds. "Zhitie Aleksiia cheloveka Bozhiia." *BLDR*, vol. 2. St. Petersburg: Nauka, 1999.

Dubenskii, D., and M. Pogodin, eds. *Kniga Posol'skaia Metriki Velikogo Kniazhestva Litovskogo*, vol. II. Moscow: Universitetskaia tipografiia, 1843.

Durnovo, N. N. "'Privetstvo brachnoe' Sil'vestra Medvedeva." *Izvestiia Otdeleniia russkogo iazyka i slovesnosti Akademii nauk*, new series, 9, 2 (1904): 303–350.

Du Bellay, Joachim. *L'Olive*. Paris: Arnoul L'Angelier, 1549–50.

Œuvres complètes, edited by Olivier Millet, vol. 2. .Paris: Honoré Champion, 2003.

Emchenko, E. B. *Stoglav: Issledovanie i tekst.* Moscow: Izdatel'stvo Indrik, 2000.

Engelstoft, L. "Udtog af Rigsraad Axel Gyldenstiernes Dagbog holden paa hans reise til og under hans Ophold i Moskow 1602–1603." *Historisk Calender* I (1814): 73–212.

Eskin, Iu. M., ed., *Tsarskii tituliarnik*, 2 vols. Moscow: Fond Stoliarova, 2007.

Esipov, G. V. "Dokumenty po delu tsarevicha Alekseia Petrovicha." *ChOIDR* 3 (1861): 1–369.

Sbornik vypisok iz arkhivnykh bumag o Petre Velikom, 2 vols. Moscow: Universitetskaia tipografiia, 1872.

Fajardo, Diego de Saavedra. *Empresas políticas*, edited by Sagrario López Poza. Madrid: Cátedra, 1999.

Idea principis Christiano-politica centum symbolis expressa. Brussels:Ioannes Mommartius & Francisco Vivieni, 1649.

Fedosov, Dmitry, ed. *The Diary of General Patrick Gordon of Auchleuchries 1635–1699*, 6 vols. Aberdeen: AHRC Centre for Irish and Scottish Studies, University of Aberdeen, 2009–16.

Fleurance, David Rivault de. *Remonstrances de Basile, empereur des Romains, à Leon son fils.* Paris: A. Estiene, 1612, 1646.

Forsten, G. V. *Akty i pis'ma k istorii Baltiiskogo voprosa v XVI i XVII stoletiiakh.* Zapiski istoriko-filologicheskogo fakul'teta Sankt-Peterburgskogo universiteta XXI. Moscow: Tipografiia I. N. Skorokhodova, 1889.

Froianov, I. Ia., ed. *Sudebnik Ivana III: Stanovlenie samoderzhavnogo gosudarstva na Rusi.* St. Petersburg: Izdatel'stvo Sankt-Peterburgskogo universiteta, 2004.

Fuchte, Johann von, ed. *Basilii imperatoris constantinopolitani capita sexaginta sex.* Helmstedt: Lucius, 1616.

Gazette de France. Paris: 1631 onward.

Gerd, A. S., ed. *Zhitie Antoniia Siiskogo.* St. Petersburg: Izdatel'stvo Sankt-Peterburgskogo Universiteta, 2003.

Gibbenet, N. *Istoricheskoe issledovanie dela Patriarkha Nikona*, 2 vols. St. Petersburg, Tipografiia Ministerstva vnutrennikh del, 1882–4.

Goar, Jacobus, ed. *Euchologion.* Venice: Typographia Bartholomei Javarina, 1730.

Golubtsov, Aleksandr, ed. "Pamiatniki prenii o vere." *ChOIDR* 2, 2 (1892): 1–350.

Gordon, Alexander. *History of Peter the Great.* Aberdeen: F. Douglass and W. Murray, 1755.

Goślicki, Wawrzyniec Grzymała. *The Counsellor.* London: Richard Bradocke, 1598.

De optimo senatore. Venice: Apud Iordanum Zilettum, 1568.

Gouillard, Jean, ed. *Le Synodikon de l'orthodoxie. Édition et commentaire.* Travaux et Mémoires du Centre de recherche d'histoire et civilisation byzantines, vol. 2. Paris: E. de Boccard, 1967.

Grotius, Hugo. *De iure belli et pacis*, edited by P. C. Molhuysen. Leiden: A. W. Sijthoff, 1919. First published Paris: Apud Nicolavm Bvon, 1625.

The Law of War and Peace. Translated by Francis W. Kelsey. *De iure belli et pacis*, 1913–1925, vol. 2. Washington, D.C.: Carnegie Foundation, 1925; Indianapolis, Indiana: Bobbs-Merrill, 1925.

Hanhart, Robert, and Alfred Rahlfs, eds. *Septuaginta*, 2 vols., 2nd ed. Stuttgart: Deutsche Bibelgesellschaft, 2006.

Herberstein, Sigismund von. *Rerum Moscoviticarum Comentarii*, edited by Frank Kämpfer, Eva Maurer, Andreas Fülberth, and Hermann Beyer-Thoma. Munich: Osteuropa-Institut Regensburg, 2007.

Holinshed, Raphael. *Chronicles of England, Scotland, and Ireland*. London: Iohn Harrison, 1587.

Howe, Robert Craig, ed. and trans. *The Testaments of the Grand Princes of Moscow*. Ithaca, NY: Cornell University Press, 1967.

Iavorskii, Stefan. "Slovo pred prokliatiem Mazepy." *Trudy Kievskoi dukhovnoi akademii* 3, 12 (1865): 499–512.

Istomin, Karion. *Kniga liubvi znak v chestne brake*, edited by L. I. Sazonova. Moscow: Izdatel'stvo Kniga, 1989.

James I. *Basilikon Doron*. London: Felix Kyngston, 1603.

Jonson, Ben. "A Panegyre on the Happy Entrance of James, Our Sovereign" (1603). In *Workes*, 87–90 (second count). London: Richard Bishop, 1640.

Juel, Just. *En Rejse til Rusland under Tsar Peter*. Copenhagen: Gyldendal (F. Hegel & søn), 1893.

Kamchatnov, Aleksandr, ed. *Paleia tolkovaia*. Moscow: Soglasie, 2002.

Kashtanov, S. M., ed. *Rossiia i grecheskii mir v XVI veke*, vol. 1. Moscow: Nauka, 2004.

Knigi razriadnye, 2 vols. St. Petersburg: Tipografiia II otdeleniia sobstvennoi Ego Imperatorskogo Vysochestva Kantseliarii, 1853–5.

Kochanowski, Jan. *Carmina latina*, edited by Józef Przyborowski. Warsaw: Officina Fratrum Jezynsciorum, 1884.

Korb, Johannes Georg. *Diarium itineris in Moscoviam*. Vienna: Typis Leopoldi Voigt, 1700.

Korb, Iogann Georg. *Dnevnik puteshestviia v Moskoviiu (1698 i 1699 gg.)*, edited and translated by A. I. Malein. St. Petersburg: A. S. Suvorin, 1906.

Kotoshikhin, G. K. *O Rossii v tsarstvovanie Alekseia Mikhailovicha*. Moscow: Rosspen, 2000.

Krueger,Paul, and Theodor Mommsen, eds. *Corpus iuris civilis*, 3 vols. Berlin: Weidmann, 1889–95.

Krzycki, Andrzej. *Andreae Cricii Carmina*. Corpus antiquissimorum poetarum Poloniae latinorum III. Edited by Kazimierz Morawski. Kraków: Typis Universitatis Jagellonicae, 1888.

Kruse, Elert, and Iohann Taube. "Zar' Iwan der Grausame." In *Beyträge zur Kenntnis Rußlands und seiner Geschichte*, vol. I, edited by Gustav Ewers and Moritz von Engelhardt, 187–240. Dorpat: n.p., 1816.

Kurbskii, Andrei. *Istoriia o delakh velikogo kniazia Moskovskogo*, ed. K. Iu. Erusalimskii. Moscow: Nauka, 2015.

Leibniz, Gottfried Wilhem. *Sämtliche Schriften und Briefe*. Series I. Allgemeiner, Politischer und Historischer Briefwechsel, 25 vols. Berlin: Brandenburgische Akademie der Wissenschaften; Göttingen: Akademie der Wissenschaften zu Göttingen, 1923–2017.

Lenhoff, Gail, and N. N. Pokrovskii, eds. *Stepennaia kniga tsarskogo rodosloviia po drevneishim spiskam*, vols. 1–3. Moscow: Iazyki slavianskikh kul'tur, 2007–12.

Lentin, A., ed. and trans. *Peter the Great: His Law on the Imperial Succession in Russia 1722 – the Official Commentary (Pravda Voli Monarshei)*. Oxford: Headstart History, 1996.

Leonid, ed. *Chin postavleniia na tsarstvo tsaria Alekseia Mikhailovicha*. Pamiatniki drevnei pis'mennosti 16. St. Petersburg: I. Voshchinskii, 1882.

Lex Regia, or the Royal Law of Denmark. London: n.p., 1731.

L[ohenstein], J. H. von. *Des grossen Herrens Czaars und Gross-Fürsten von Moscau Petri Alexiewitz ... Leben und Thaten*. Frankfurt and Leipzig: Johann Leonhard Buggeln, 1710.

Lyseck, Adolph. *Relatio, eorum quae ... ad Magnum Moscorum Czarum, ... 1675 gesta sunt*. Salzburg: Aulico-Academici, 1676.

Majeska, George P. *Russian Travellers to Constantinople in the Fourteenth and Fifteenth Centuries*. Dumbarton Oaks Studies, vol. XIX. Washington, D.C.: Dumbarton Oaks Research Library and Collection, 1984.

Maksim Grek. *Sochineniia*, 3 vols. Kazan': Tipografiia gubernskogo pravleniia, 1860.

Malein, A. I., ed. *Novoe izvestie o Rossii vremeni Ivana Groznogo: Skazanie Al'berta Shlikhtinga*. Leningrad: Izdatel'stvo Akademii nauk SSSR, 1934.

Malherbe, François de. "Prière pour le roi Henri le Grand allant en Limousin" (1605–07). In *Les Poésies*, 27–32. Paris: Société des textes français modernes, 1999. First published in *Recueil des plus beaux vers de messieurs de Malherbe, Racan* .... 8–13. Paris: Pierre Mettayer, 1638.

Manifest wegen der gerichtlichen Inquisition ... über den Zarewitsch Alexium Petrowitsch. Frankfurt and Leipzig: Johann Andreas Rüdigern, 1719.

Mansikka, V. *Zhitie Aleksandra Nevskogo: Razbor redaktsii i tekst*. Pamiatniki drevnei pis'mennosti i iskusstva 180. St. Petersburg: OLDP 1913.

Martens, F. *Sobranie traktatov i konventsii zakliuchennykh Rossiei s inostrannymi derzhavami*, 15 vols. St. Petersburg: Tipografiia ministerstva putei soobshcheniia, 1874–1909.

Massa, Isaac. *Histoire des guerres de la Moscovie*, 2 vols. Brussels: Fr. J. Olivier, 1866.

A Short History of the Beginnings and Origins of These Present Wars in Moscow. Translated by G. Edward Orchard. Toronto: University of Toronto Press, 1982.

Matveev, A. A. "Zapiski Andreia Artamonovicha Matveeva." In *Zapiski russkikh liudei*, edited by I. Sakharov, 1–94. St. Petersburg: Tipografiia Sakharova, 1841.

"Mnenie Iosafa patriarkha i vsego osviashchennogo sobora." In *Zapiski otdeleniia russkoi i slavianskoi arkheologii imperatorskogo Russkogo arkheologicheskogo obshchestva*, edited by Vladimir Lamanskii, vol. II, 372–373. St. Petersburg: Russkoe arkheologicheskoe obshchestvo Otdeleniia russkoi i slavianskoi arkheologii, 1861.

Murray, Sir George. *Letters and Despatches of John Churchill, First Duke of Marlborough from 1702–1712*. London: John Murray, 1845.

Murzakevich, N., ed. *Pis'ma tsarevicha Alekseia Petrovicha*. Odessa: n.p., 1849.

"Nachricht von Woldemar Christian Guldenlöwe, Grafen von Schleswig-Holstein ... Reise nach Russland." *Magazin für die neue Historie und Geographie* X (1776): 211–276.

Novikov, N. I., ed., *Rodoslovnaia kniga kiazei i dvorian rossiiskikh i vyezzhikh*, 2 vols. Moscow: Universitetskaia Tipografiia u N. Novikova, 1787.

Olearius, Adam. *Vermehrte Newe Beschreibung Der Muscowitischen und Persischen Reyse*, edited by Dieter Lohmeier. Tübingen: Niemeyer, 1971. First published Schleswig: Johann Holwein, 1656.

Olszewski, Jakub. *Kazania*. Wilno: Drukarnia Akademicka, 1645.

Opisanie koronatsii eia velichestva imperatritsy Ekateriny Alekseevny. St. Petersburg and Moscow: Pri senate, 1724–5.

Paleia tolkovaia po spisku sdelannomu v g. Kolomne v 1406 g., trud uchenikov N. S. Tikhonravova, 2 vols. Moscow: Tipografiia i slovolitnia O. Gerbska, 1892–6.

Palmer, William. *The Patriarch and the Tsar*, 6 vols. London: Trubner and Co., 1871–6.

Pasquier, Étienne. *Les recherches de la France*. Paris: L. Sonnivs, 1607.

Patkul, Johann Reinhold von. *Johann Reinhold von Patkuls*... *Berichte an das zaarische Cabinet in Moscau*, 3 vols. Berlin: Karl Matzdorffs Buchhandlung, 1792–7.

P[evnitskii], V. "Slova mitropolita Stefana Iavorskogo," *Trudy Kievskoi dukhovnoi akademii* (1874): (7), 72–121; (10), 123–154; (12), 505–520; 1875 (1), 118–128; (3), 631–647; (5), 486–505; (9), 463–492; (10), 124–145.

Pierling, Paul, ed. *Antonii Possevinii Missio Moscovitica*. Paris: Apud Ernestum Leroux, 1882.

Pielgrzymowski, Eliasz. *Poselstwo i krótkie spisanie rozprawy z Moskwą. Poselstwo do Zygmunta Trzeciego*, edited by Roman Krzywy. Humanizm: Polonika IV. Warsaw: Neriton, 2010.

Pilgrimovius, Elias [Eliasz Pielgrzymowski]. *Didžioji Leono Sapiegos pasiuntinybė i Moskvą 1600–1601 m.*, edited by Jūratė Kiaupienė. Historiae Lituaniae Fontes Minores IV. Vilnius: Žara, 2002.

Pis'ma russkikh gosudarei i drugikh osob tsarskogo semeistva, 4 vols. Moscow: n.p., 1861–2.

Platonov, S. F., ed., *Inoe skazanie*. RIB 13 (St. Petersburg: Tovarishchestvo Pechatnia S. P. Iakovleva, 1893)

Pliguzov, A. I., ed., *Russkii feodal'nyi arkhiv*, 5 vols. Moscow: Institut Istorii SSSR AN SSSR, 1986–92.

Pokhodnye zhurnaly 1706, 1707, 1708, i 1709 godov. St. Petersburg: n.p., 1844.

Pokhodnyi zhurnal 1711 goda. St. Petersburg: n.p., 1854.

Pokhodnyi zhurnal 1712 goda. St. Petersburg: n.p., 1854.

Pokhodnyi zhurnal 1713 goda. St. Petersburg, n.p., 1854.

Pokhodnyi zhurnal 1714 goda. St. Petersburg: n.p., 1854.

Pokhodnyi zhurnal 1715 goda. St. Petersburg: n.p., 1855.

Pokhodnyi zhurnal 1716 goda. St. Petersburg: n.p., 1855.

Pokhodnyi zhurnal 1719 goda. St. Petersburg, n.p., 1855.

Pokhodnyi zhurnal 1720 goda. St. Petersburg, n.p., 1855.

Pokhodnyi zhurnal 1721 goda. St. Petersburg, n.p., 1855.

Pokhodnyi zhurnal 1722 goda. St. Petersburg: n.p., 1855.

Pokhodnyi zhurnal 1723 goda. St. Petersburg: n.p., 1855.

Pokhodnyi zhurnal 1724 goda. St. Petersburg: n.p., 1855.

Pokrovskii, N. N., and A. V. Sirenov, eds. *Latukhinskaia Stepennaia kniga 1676 goda*. Moscow: Iazyki slavianskoi kul'tury, 2012.

Polnoe sobranie postanovlenii i rasporiazhenii po vedomstvu pravoslavnogo ispovedaniia Rossiiskoi imperii, 2nd ed., 10 vols. St. Petersburg: Sinodal'naia tipografiia, 1869–1911.

Polockij, Simeon. *Rifmologion: Eine Sammlung höfisch-zeremonieller Gedichte*, 2 vols. Vienna, Cologne, and Weimar: Böhlau, 2017.

Polotskii, Simeon. *Izbrannye sochinennia*. St. Petersburg: Nauka, 2004. First published Moscow: Izdatel'stvo Akademii nauk SSSR, 1953.

Orel Rossiiskii, edited by L. I. Sazonova. Moscow: Indrik, 2015.

Virshi, edited by V. K. Bylinin and L. U. Zvonareva. Minsk: Mastatskaia literatura, 1990.

Povsiadnevnykh dvortsovykh vremen gosudarei tsarei Mikhaila Fedorovicha i Alekseia Mikhailovicha zapisok, chast' 1 i 2. Moscow: Pechatana pri Imperatorskom Moskovskom universiteta, 1769.

"Povest' izvestno o ezhe sluchisia byti v nashei rustei zemle . . ." In *Pamiatniki prenii o vere, voznikshikh po delu korolevicha Val'demara i tsarevny Iriny*, edited by A. Golubtsov. *ChOIDR*, 2, 2 (1892): 1–22.

Pozdeeva, I. V., A. V. Dadykin, and V. P. Pushkov. *Moskovskii pechatnyi dvor – fakt i faktor russkoi kul'tury 1652–1700 gody*, 2 vols. Moscow: Nauka, 2007–11.

Pozdeeva, I. V., V. P. Pushkov, and A. V. Dadykin. *Moskovskii pechatnyi dvor – fakt i faktor russkoi kul'tury 1618–1652 gg*. Moscow: Mosgorarkhiv, 2001.

Preobrazhenskii, A. A., and T. E. Novitskaia, eds. *Zakonodatel'stvo Petra I*. Moscow: Iuridicheskaia literatura, 1997.

Priselkov, M. D., ed. *Troitskaia letopis'*. Moscow and Leningrad: Izdatel'stvo Akademii nauk SSSR, 1950.

Prokopovič, Feofan. *De arte rhetorica libri X, Kijoviae 1706*, edited by Renate Lachmann. Cologne and Vienna: Böhlau, 1982.

Prokopovich, Feofan. *Slova i rechi*. St. Petersburg: Pri Sukhoputnom shliakhetnom kadetskom korpuse, 1760.

Sochineniia. Moscow and Leningrad: Izdatel'stvo Akademii nauk SSSR, 1961.

Prozorovskii, Aleksandr. *Sil'vestr Medvedev, ego zhizni i deiatel'nost'*, *ChOIDR* 2, 4 (1896): 1–148; 3, 6 (1896): 149–378; 4, 3 (1896): 379–606.

ed. *Sil'vestra Medvedeva sozertsanie kratkoe let 7190, 91, i 92, v nikh chto sodeiasia v grazhdanstve*. *ChOIDR* 4, 2 (1894), i–lii, 1–198.

Pudalov, B. M., ed. *Sinodik Nizhegorodskogo Voznesenskogo Pecherskogo monastyria 1552 goda. Sinodik opal'nykh tsaria Ivana Groznogo*. Nizhnii Novgorod: Izdatel'stvo Otdeleniia Nizhegorodskoi Eparkhii i Vosnesenskii Pecherskii muzhskoi monastir', 2009.

Pufendorf, Samuel. *De officio hominis et civis*, 6th ed. Cambridge and London: Typis Academicis. Impensis Edvardi Hall, Bibliopolæ, 1701.

De officio hominis et civis, 2 vols. Translated by Frank Gardner Moore. Oxford and New York, New York: Oxford University Press, 1927.

Einleitung zu der Historie der vornehmsten Reiche und Staaten, so itziger Zeit in Europa befinden, 2nd. ed. Frankfurt am Main: Knoch, 1684.

Introductio ad historiam europaeam. Translated by Johann Friedrich Cramer. Frankfurt am Main: Knoch, 1704.

O dolzhnosti cheloveka i grazhdanina po zakonu estestvennomu. St. Petersburg: Sankt-Peterburgskaia tipografiia, 1726.

Vvedenie v gistoriiu evropeiskuiu. St. Petersburg: n.p., 1718.

Rambaud, Alfred, ed. *Recueil des instructions données aux ministres de France depuis les traités de Westphalie jusqu'à la Révolution française VIII: Russie*, 2 vols. Paris: Félix Alcan,1890.

Recueil des plus beaux vers de messieurs de Malherbe, Racan .... Paris: Pierre Mettayer, 1638.

"Relation wegen der jungsten Anno 98 von der Röm. Kay. Mayt. unsers allergn. Herrn Hofdiener Michael Spielen [sic] anbefohlenen Rais in die Moscaw." In *Sammlung bisher noch ungedruckten kleiner Schriften*, vol. I, edited by B. von Wichmann, 423–464. Berlin: Georg Reimer, 1820.

"Relationer til K. Christian den Femte fra den danske envoyé i Moskov Hildebrand von Horrn November 1682–Juni 1684," *Aarsberetninger fra det Kongelige Geheimearchiv* 6 (1876–82): 138–198.

"Responsus legati Mosci in negotio secreto matrimoniali." In V. N. Aleksandrenko, ed., "Materialy po Smutnomu vremeni na Rusi XVII v.," *Starina i Novizna* XIV (1911): 304–308.

Resen, Peder Hansen. *Kong Fredericks den andens Krønicke*. Copenhagen: S. M. Jørgensøn, 1680.

Roginskii, M. G., trans. "Poslanie Ioganna Taube i Elerta Kruze kak istoricheskii istochnik." *Russkii istoricheskii zhurnal* 8 (1922): 10–59.

Rogozhin, N. M., ed. *Posol'skaia kniga po sviaizam Rossii s Angliei 1613–1614 gg.* Moscow: Institut istorii SSSR, 1979.

Ronsard, Pierre de. *Œuvres*, 6 vols. Paris: Alphonse Lemerre, 1887–93.

Rothe, Hans, ed. *Sinopsis, Kiev 1681*. Bausteine zur Geschichte der Literatur bei den Slaven 17. Cologne and Vienna: Böhlau, 1983.

Rychalovskii, E. E., ed. *Perepiska getmanov levoberezhnoi Ukrainy s Moskvoi i Sankt-Peterburgom 1654–1764 gg.*, vol. 1, *Getmanstvo Bogdana Khmel'nitskogo 1654–1657 gg.* Moscow: Drevlekhranilishche, 2017.

Ryden, Lennart. "The Andreas Salos Apocalypse: Greek Text, Translation and Commentary." *Dumbarton Oaks Papers* 28 (1974): 197–261.

Rymer, Thomas. *Foedera*, vol. 16, 2nd ed. London: A. and J. Churchill, 1727.

Rywocki, Jan SJ. *Monumentum gratae testificationis invictissimo et potentissimo Poloniae et Sueciae regi Vladislao IV*. Wilno: Vilnae Typis Akademicis, 1639.

Salmina, M. A., ed., "Slovo o zhitii i o prestavlenii velikogo kniazia Dmitriia Ivanovicha, tsaria russkogo." In *Biblioteka literatury Drevnei Rusi*, vol. 6. St. Petersburg: Nauka, 1999, 206–227.

Sakharov, N., ed. *Zapiski russkikh liudei*. St. Petersburg: Tipografiia I. Sakharova, 1841.

Sarbievius, Matthias Casimirus [Maciej Kazimierz Sarbiewski]. *Lyricorum libri IV*. Antwerp: Ex officina Plantinia Balthasaris Moreti, 1634.

Scudamore, James, trans. *The Sixty-Six Admonitory Chapters of Basilius, King of the Romans, to His Sonne Leo*. Paris: n.p., 1638.

Scultetus, Joachim, "Beschreibung der zwoten Gesandschaft," *Magazin für die neue Historie und Geographie* IX (1775): 1–76.

Sevast'ianova, A. S., ed. *Dzherom Gorsei: Zapiski o Rossii kontsa XVI–nachala XVII veka.* Moscow: Izdatel'stvo MGU, 1990.

Ševčenko, Ihor. "A New Greek Source Concerning the Nikon Affair." *Palaeoslavica* 7 (1999): 80–83.

Seyssel, Claude de. *La grant monarchie de France.* Paris: Regnault Chaudière, 1519.

Shablova, T. I., ed. *Sinodik Iosifo-volokolamskogo monastyria.* St. Petersburg: Dmitrii Bulanin, 2004.

Shemiakin, A. N. , trans. "Dva svatovstva inozemnykh printsev k russkim velikim kniazhnam v XVII stoletii: Izvestie o puteshestvii v Rossiiu i Moskvu gertsoga Gansa mladshego datskogo." *ChOIDR* 4, 4 (1867): 1–56.

Shemiakin, A. N., ed. and trans. "Poezdka v Rossiu Vol'demara Khristiana Gil'denleve." *ChOIDR* 4 (1867): i–ii, 1–72.

Shcherbachev, Iu. N. "Datskii arkhiv: Materialy po istorii Drevnei Rossii, khraniashchiesia v Kopengagene 1326–1690 gg." *ChOIDR* 1 (1893): 150–175.

"Iz donesenii pervogo datskogo rezidenta v Moskve (1672–1676 gg.)." *ChOIDR* 2 (1917): smes' 32–42.

"Kopengagenskie akty, otnosiashchiesia do russkoi istorii I (1326–1569)." *ChOIDR* 255, 4 (1915): 284–288

"Kopengagenskie akty, otnosiashchiesia do russkoi istorii II (1570–1575)." *ChOIDR* 257, 2 (1916): 1–224.

ed. *Russkie akty Kopengagenskogo gosudarstvennogo arkhiva.* RIB 16. St. Petersburg: Tovarishchestvo Pechatnia S. P. Iakovleva, 1897.

Shcherbachev, Iu. N. , trans. "Puteshestvie ego kniazheskoi svetlosti Gertsoga Gansa Shlezvig-Golshtinskogo v Rossiiu 1602 goda." *ChOIDR* 238, 3 (1911): 1–64.

Shcherbatov, M. M. *Istoriia Rossiiskaia.* St. Petersburg: Imperatorskaia Akademiia nauk, 1790.

Shemiakin, A. "Donesenie o poezdke v Moskvu pridvornogo rimskogo imperatora Mikhaila Shilia v 1598 godu," *ChOIDR* 2 (1875): i–ii, 1–22.

ed. and trans. "Opisanie puteshestviia v Moskvu posla Rimskogo Imperatora Nikolaia Varkocha s 22 iiulia 1593 g." *ChOIDR* 4 (1874): i–xii, 1–36.

Sinodik Nizhegorodskogo Voznesenskogo Pecherskogo monastyria 1595 goda: Sinodik arkhimandrita Trifona. Nizhnii Novgorod: Izdatel'skii otdel Nizhegorodskoi eparkhii pri Voznesenskom Pecherskom monastyre, 2010.

Sluzhebnik. Moscow: Pechatnyi dvor, 1627, 1633, 1640.

Smirnov, N. A., ed. *Orel Rossiiskii: Tvorenie Simeona Polotskogo.* Obshchestvo liubitelei drevnei pis'mennosti 133. St. Petersburg: Tipografiia M. A. Aleksandrova, 1915.

Snyder, Henry L., ed. *The Marlborough–Godolphin Correspondence.* Oxford: Clarendon Press, 1975.

Statutes of the Realm, 11 vols. London: Record Commission, 1810–28.

"Stolovaia kniga patriarkha Filareta Nikiticha." *Starina i novizna* 6 (1911): 67–163.

Stroev, Pavel, ed. *Vykhody gosudarei tsarei i velikikh kniazei Mikhaila Fedorovicha, Aleksiia Mikhailovicha, Fedora Aleksievicha vseia Rusi samoderzhtsev s 1632 po 1682 god.* Moscow: Tipografiia A. Semena, 1844.

Stryjkowski, Maciej. *Kronika Polska, Litewska, Żmódzka, i wszystkiej Rusi*, 2 vols. Warsaw: Gustaw Leon Glücksberg, 1846.

Sudebniki XV–XVI vv. Moscow and Leningrad: Izdatel'stvo Akademii nauk SSSR, 1952.

Sveriges ridderskaps och adels Riksdags-Protokoll, vols. 13–14. Stockholm: P. A. Norstedt, 1896–8.

Svod zakonov Rossiiskoi Imperii, 15 vols. St. Petersburg: Tipografiia Vtorogo otdeleniia sobstvennoi E.I.V. Kantseliarii, 1857–68.

Szujski, Józef, ed. *Diariusze sejmów koronnych 1548, 1553, 1570 r.* Scriptores rerum polonicarum I. Kraków:Komisja Historyczna Towarzystwa Naukowego Krakowskiego, 1872.

Tarnava-Borichevskii, I. "Skazanie Adol'fa Lizeka." *Zhurnal Ministerstva narodnogo prosveshcheniia* 16 (November, 1837): 327–394.

Tatishchev, V. N. *Istoriia Rossiiskaia*, 7 vols. Moscow: Izdatel'lstvo Akademii nauk SSSR, 1962–8. First published Moscow: Imperatorskii moskovskii universitet, 1768.

Theiner, Augustin, ed. *Monuments historiques relatifs aux règnes d'Alexis Michaélowitch, Féodor III, et Pierre le Grand, czars de Russie, extraits des Archives du Vatican et de Naples.* Rome: Imprimerie du Vatican, 1859.

Tolstoi, Iurii. *Pervye sorok let snoshenii mezhdu Rossiei i Anglieiu 1553–1593.* St. Petersburg: Tipografiia i khromolitografiia A. Transhelia, 1875.

Traktaty pokojowe pomiędzy Rzeczpospolitą a Rosją w XVII wieku/Mirnye dogovory mezhdu Rech'iu Pospolitoi i Rossiei v XVII veke. Świadectwa minionych wieków. Kraków: Platan, 2002.

Trebnik. Moscow: Pechatnyi dvor, 1658.

Trebnik inocheskii. Moscow: Pechatnyi dvor, 1639.

Trefologion, I (sentiabr'–noiabr'). Moscow: Pechatnyi dvor, 1637.

Turgenev, A. I., ed., *Historica Russiae monumenta.* St. Petersburg: Eduard Prats, 1842.

Tvorogov, O. V., ed. *Letopisets ellinskii i rimskii*, 2 vols. St. Petersburg: Dmitrii Bulanin, 1999–2001.

Twardowski, Samuel. *Władysław IV, król polski i szwedzki*, edited by Roman Krzywy. Warsaw: PAN, 2012. First published 1649 (Lezno).

Tzoumerkas, Panagiotis. *Ho Kodiks arithm. 393 tes Alexandrines Patriarkhikes Vivliothekes ho legomenos tou Patriarkhou Paisiou.* Alexandria: Ekdose Patriarkhikes Bibliothekes tou Patrikarkheiou Alexandreias, 2010.

Ul'feldt, Iakov. *Puteshestvie v Rossiiu.* Translated by L. N. Godovikova (Moscow: Iazyki slavianskoi kul'tury 2002).

Ulfeldt, Jakob. *Hodoeporicon Ruthenicum.* Frankfurt:Matthias Becker, Ioannis Theodoris, and Ioannis Israelis de Bry, 1608.

Undol'skii, V. ed. "Biblioteka Pavla, mitropolita sarskogo i podonskogo." *Vremennik OIDR* 5 (1850): 65–73.

"Urkunden von der Vermälung des Herzogs zu Curland Friedrich Wilhelm mit der rußischen Prinzessin Anna." *Magazin für die neue Historie und Geographie* 15 (1781): 199–220.

Vedel, Anders Sørenson. *En sørgelig Ligpredicken ... Frederich den anden.* Copenhagen: Aff Laurentz Benedicht, 1588.

Oratio panegyrica oblata ... Frederico II. Copenhagen: Andreas Gutterwitz, 1580.
Vergil, Polydore. *Historia anglica*. Oxford: Clarendon Press, 1952.
"Vermälungs-Tractat zwischen dem zarischen Kron-Prinzen Alexei Petrowitsch und der braunschweigischen Prinzessin Christina Sophia." *Magazin für die neue Historie und Geographie* XV (1781): 223–230.
Verzhbovskii, Fedor [Theodor Wierzbowski]. *Donesenie Ioanna Kobentselia*. Materialy k istorii Moskovskogo gosudarstva v XVI i XVII stoletiiakh IV. Warsaw: Tipografiia Varshavskogo uchebnogo okruga, 1901.
Vitsen, Nikolaas. *Puteshestvie v Moskoviiu 1664–1665*. Translated by V. G. Trisman. St. Petersburg: Simpozium, 1996.
Vodolazkin, E. G. "Kratkaia khronograficheskaia Paleia (tekst), vypusk I." *TODRL* 57 (2006): 891–915.
"Kratkaia khronograficheskaia Paleia (tekst), vypusk II." *TODRL* 58 (2008): 534–556.
"Kratkaia khronograficheskaia Paleia (tekst), vypusk III." *TODRL* 61 (2010): 345–374.
"Redaktsii kratkoi khronograficheskoi Palei." *TODRL* 56 (2004): 164–180.
Volumina Legum, 10 vols. St. Petersburg: J. Ohryzk; Kraków: Akademia Umiejętności; Poznań: Poznańskie Towarzystwo Przyjaciół Nauk, 1859–1952.
"'Vypiska iz posol'skikh knig' o snosheniikh Rossiiskogo gosudarstva s Pol'sko-Litovskim za 1547 [sic: 1487]–1572 gg.," edited by B. N. Morozov. In *Pamiatniki istorii Vostochnoi Evropy*, vol. II, 272–273. Moscow and Warsaw: Arkheograficheskii tsentr, 1997.
Wapowski, Bernard. *Chronicorum pars posterior*. Scriptores rerum polonicarum II. Kraków: Akademia Umiejętności, 1874.
Watson, Alan, ed. and trans., *The Digest of Justinian*, 2 vols. Philadelphia, Pennsylvania: University of Pennsylvania Press, 1985.
Weber, F. C. *Das veränderte Russland*, 3 vols. Frankfurt and Leipzig: Nicolaus Förster, 1739–44. First published Frankfurt: Nicolaus Förster, 1721.
Wichmann, B. von, ed. *Sammlung bisher noch ungedruckten kleiner Schriften zur ältern Geschichte und Kenntniss des russischen Reiches*, vol. 1. Berlin: Reimer, 1820.
Witsen, Nicolaas. *Moscovische Reyse 1664–1665*. Werken uitgeven door de Linschoten-Vereeniging 67. The Hague: Martinus Nijhoff, 1966.
Zabelin, Ivan, ed. *Materialy dlia istorii, arkheologii i statistiki goroda Moskvy*, 2 vols. Moscow: Moskovskaia gorodskaia duma, 1884–91.
Zapiski otdeleniia russkoi i slavianskoi arkheologii Imperatorskogo Russkogo arkheologicheskogo obshchestva, 9 vols. St. Petersburg: Russkoe arkheologicheskoe obshchestvo, Otdeleniia russkoi i slavianskoi arkheologii, 1851–1913.

Secondary Sources

1594: Le sacre d'Henri IV à Chartres. Chartres: Le musée, 1994.
Abramovich, G. V. *Kniazia Shuiskie i Rossiiskii tron*. Leningrad: Izdatel'stvo Leningradskogo universiteta, 1991.
Ageeva, O. G. *Evropeizatsiia russkogo Dvora 1700–1796 gg*. Moscow: Institut Rossiiskoi istorii RAN, 2006.

Alef, Gustave. "The Adoption of the Muscovite Two-Headed Eagle: A Discordant View." *Speculum* 41 (1966): 1–21.

The Origins of Muscovite Autocracy: the Age of Ivan III. Forschungen zur osteuropäischen Geschichte 39. Berlin: Osteuropa-Institut; Wiesbaden: Harrassowitz, 1986.

Alekseev, A. A. *Tekstologiia slavianskoi Biblii.* Moscow: Dmitrii Bulanin; Cologne: Böhlau, 1999.

Alekseev, Iu. G. *'K Moskve khotim': Zakat boiarskoi respublike v Novgorode.* St. Petersburg: Lenizdat, 1991.

U Kormila Rossiiskogo gosudarstva: Ocherk razvitiia apparata upravleniia v XIV–XV vv. St. Petersburg: Izdatel'stvo Sankt-Peterburgskogo universiteta, 1998.

Allen, W. E. D. "The Georgian Marriage Projects of Boris Godunov." *Oxford Slavonic Papers* 12 (1965): 69–79.

Almazov, A. S. *Istoriia chinoposledovanii kreshcheniia i miropomazaniia.* Kazan': n.p., 1884.

Almazov, A. S. *Politicheskii portret ukrainskogo getmana Ivana Samoilovicha v kontekste russko-ukrainskikh otnoshenii.* Moscow: MGU, 2012.

Almquist, Helge. "Ivan Petrovitj Izmajlov, rysk diplomat i Preussen och krigsfånge i Sverige (1706–1710)." *Karolinska Förbundets Årsbok* (1937): 98–130.

Sverge och Ryssland 1595–1911. Uppsala: Almquist & Wiksell, 1907.

Al'shits, D. N. "Krestotseloval'nye zapisi Vladimira Andreevicha Staritskogo i nedoshedshee zaveshchanie Ivana Groznogo." *Istoriia SSSR* 4 (1959): 147–155.

Althoff, Gerd. *Kontrolle der Macht: Formen und Regeln politischer Beratung im Mittelalter.* Darmstadt: WBG, 2016.

Amburger, Erik. *Die Familie Marselis: Studien zur russischen Wirtschaftsgeschichte.* Osteuropastudien der Hochschulen des Landes Hessen; Reihe 1: Gießener Abhandlungen zur Agrar- und Wirtschaftsforschung des europäischen Ostens, vol. 4. Gießen: W. Schmitz, 1957.

Androsov, S. O. *Zhivopisets Ivan Nikitin.* St. Petersburg: Dmitrii Bulanin, 1998.

Angelov, Dimiter. *Imperial Ideology and Political Thought in Byzantium 1204–1330.* Cambridge: Cambridge University Press, 2006.

Angelov, Dimiter, J. A. Munitiz, and Ruth Macrides. *Pseudo-Kodinos and the Constantinopolitan Court: Offices and Ceremonies.* Farnham: Ashgate, 2013.

Anisimov, E. V. *Gosudarstvennye preobrazovaniia i samoderzhavie Petra Velikogo.* St. Petersburg: Dmitrii Bulanin, 1997.

Anisimova, T. V. *Khronika Georgiia Amartola v drevnerusskikh spiskakh.* Moscow: Indrik, 2009.

Antonov, D. I. *Smuta v kul'ture srednevekovoi Rusi.* Moscow: RGGU, 2009.

Antonov, M. V. *Pravo i obshchestvo v kontseptsii Georgiia Davidovicha Gurvicha.* Moscow: Izdatel'skii dom Vysshei shkoly ekonomiki, 2013.

Argyriou, Asterios *Les exégèses grecques de l'Apocalypse à l'époque turque (1453–1821): Esquisse d'une histoire des courants idéologiques au sein du peuple grec asservi.* Thessaloniki: Hetaireia makedonikon spoudon, 1982.

Arianzi, Despoina. *Kindheit in Byzanz.* Boston, Massachusetts and Berlin: De Gruyter, 2012.

Arsen'ev, Konstantin. *Tsarstvovanie Ekateriny I.* St. Petersburg: Tipografiia Imperatorskoi akademii nauk, 1856.
Asch, Roland G., and Heinz Duchhardt, eds. *Der Absolutismus – ein Mythos? Strukturwandel monarchischer Herrschaft in West- und Mitteleuropa (ca. 1550–1700)*. Münstersche historische Forschungen 9. Cologne, Weimar, and Vienna: Böhlau, 1996.
Avtukhovich, T. V. "Prokopovich Elisei (Eleazar)." In *Slovar' russkikh pisatelei XVIII v.*, vol. II, 488–496. St. Petersburg: Nauka, 1999.
Babelon, Jean-Pierre. *Henri IV.* Paris: Fayard 1982.
Babich, I. V., and M. V. Babich. *Oblastnye praviteli Rossii 1719–1739 gg.* Moscow: ROSSPEN, 2008.
Baena, Laura Manzano. *Conflicting Words: The Peace Treaty of Münster (1648) and the Political Culture of the Dutch Republic and the Spanish Monarchy.* Leuven: Leuven University Press, 2011.
Bagger, Hans. *Ruslands alliancepolitik efter freden i Nystad: En studie i den slesvigske restitutionsspørgsmål indtil 1732.* Copenhagen: Rosenkilde og Bagger, 1974.
Barbey, Jean. *Être roi: Le roi et son gouvernement en France de Clovis à Louis XVI.* Paris: Fayard, 1992.
Barbiche, Bernard. *Institutions de la monarchie française à l'époque moderne, XVIe–XVIIIe siècles.* Paris: Presses universitaires de France, 2001.
Baron, Samuel. "Henri Lavie and the Failed Campaign to Expand Franco-Russian Commercial Relations (1712–1723)." *Forschungen zur osteuropäischen Geschichte* 50 (1995): 29–50.
Barsukov, Aleskandr. *Spiski gorodovykh voevod i drugikh lits voevodskogo upravleniia Moskovskogo gosudarstva XVII stoletiia.* St. Petersburg: Tipografiia M. M. Stasiulevicha, 1902.
Beaune, Colette. *Naissance de la nation française.* Paris: Gallimard, 1985.
Begunov, Iu. K. "Buzhinskii, Gavriil Fedorovich." In *Slovar' russkikh pisatelei XVIII veka*, vol. 1, 128–129. Leningrad:Nauka, 1988.
"Povest' o vtorom brake Vasiliia III." *TODRL* 25 (1970): 105–118.
Behme, Thomas. *Samuel von Pufendorf: Naturrecht und Staat: Eine Analyse und Interpretation seiner Theorie, ihrer Grundlagen und Probleme.* Göttingen: Vandenhoeck & Ruprecht, 1995.
Beihammer, Alexander D. "Comnenian Imperial Succession and the Ritual World of Niketas Choniates's Chronike Diegesis." In *Court Ceremonies and Rituals of Power in Byzantium and the Medieval Mediterranean: Comparative Perspectives*, edited by Alexander Beihammer, Stavroula Constantinou, and Maria Parani. Leiden and Boston, MA: Brill, 2013.
Beik, William. *Absolutism and Society in Seventeenth Century France: State Power and Provincial Aristocracy in Languedoc.* Cambridge: Cambridge University Press, 1985.
Beliakov, A. V. *Chingisidy v Rossii XV–XVII vekov: Prosopograficheskoe issledovanie.* Riazan': Mir, 2011.
Beliakova, E. V., L. V. Moshkova, and T. A. Oparina. *Kormchaia kniga: Ot rukopisnoi traditsii k pervomu pechatnomu izdaniiu.* Moscow and St. Petersburg: Tsentr gumanitarnikh initsiativ, 2017.

Beliutin, E., and N. Moleva. *Zhivopisnykh del mastera: Kantseliariia ot stroenii i russkaia zhivopis' pervoi poloviny XVIII veka*. Moscow: Iskusstvo, 1965.

Belokurov, S. A., and A. N. Zertsalov, eds. "O nemetskikh shkolakh v Moskve v pervoi chetverti XVIII v. (1701–1715 gg.): Dokumenty moskovskikh arkhivov." *ChIODR* I (1907): i–xli, 1–244.

Bentsianov, M. M. "Dvor Kniazia Andreia Staritskogo i problema 'staritskogo miatezha 1537 g.'" *Drevniaia Rus': Voprosy medievistiki* 50, 4 (2012): 64–76; 51, 1 (2013): 17–26.

"Sluzhilye liudi kniazia Iuriia dmitrovskogo." *Drevniaia Rus': Voprosy medievistiki* 40, 2 (2010): 41–55; 41, 3 (2010): 55–68.

Bepler, Jill. "Marriage Markets and Risk Assessment: The Lure of the Russian Empire at the Turn of the Eighteenth Century." In *Frictions and Failures: Cultural Encounters in Crisis*. Deutsches Historisches Institut Warschau, Quellen und Studien 34, edited by Almut Bues. Wiesbaden: Harrassowitz, 2017.

Bercé, Yves-Marie. *Le roi absolu: Idées reçues sur Louis XIV*. Paris: Cavalier bleu, 2013.

Bérenger, Jean. *Léopold Ier (1640–1705): Fondateur de la puissance autrichienne*. Paris: Presses universitaires de France, 2004.

Bernadskii, V. N. *Novgorod i novgorodskaia zemlia v XV veke*. Leningrad: Izdatel'stvo Akademii nauk SSSR, 1961.

Bercoff, Giovanna Brogi. "Mazepa, lo zar e il diavolo. Un inedito di Stefan Javorskij." *Russica Romana* VII (2000): 167–188.

"Poltava: A Turning Point in the History of Preaching." In *Poltava 1709: The Battle and the Myth*, edited by Serhii Plokhy, 205–226. Cambridge, Massachusetts: Harvard University Press, 2012.

Biaudet, Henri. *Gustaf Eriksson Vasa, Prince de Suède: Une énigme historique du XVIe siècle*. Suomalaisen Tiedeakatemian Toimituksia Series B, vol. 8, no. 5. Geneva: Expédition historique finlandaise à Rome, 1913.

Bluche, François. *Louis XIV*. Paris: Fayard, 1986.

Boetticher, Manfred von, ed. *Braunschweigische Fürsten in Rußland in der ersten Hälfte des 18. Jahrhunderts*. Veröffentlichungen der niedersächsischen Archivverwaltung 54. Göttingen: Vandenhoeck & Ruprecht, 1998.

Bogatyrev, Sergei. "The Battle for Divine Wisdom: The Rhetoric of Ivan IV's Campaign against Polotsk." In *The Military and Society in Russia 1450–1917*, edited by Eric Lohr and Marshall Poe, 325–363. Leiden and Boston, MA: Brill, 2002.

"Ivan the Terrible Discovers the West: The Cultural Transformation of Autocracy during the Early Northern Wars." *Russian History* 34, 1–4 (2007): 161–188.

"Reinventing the Russian Monarchy in the 1550s: Ivan the Terrible, the Dynasty, and the Church." *Slavonic and East European Review* 85, 2 (2007): 271–293.

"Shapka Monomakha i shlem naslednika: Vlasti i dinasticheskaia politika pri Vasilie III i Ivane Groznom." *Studia Slavica et Balcanica Petropolitana* 9, 1 (2011): 171–200.

The Sovereign and His Counsellors: Ritualized Consultations in Muscovite Political Culture 1350s–1570s. Suomalaisen Tiedeakatemian Toimituksia, Sarja Humaniora 307. Helsinki: Academia Scientiarum Fennica, 2000.

Bogoiavlenskii, S. K. *Moskovskii prikaznyi apparat i deloproizvodstvo XVI–XVII vekov*. Moscow: Izdatel'stvo Moskovskogo universiteta, 2006.

Bogoslovskii, M. M. *Petr I: Materialy dlia bibliografii*, 5 vols. Moscow: OGIZ, 1940–8.

Bolotina, N. Iu. "Domashnii byt iunogo tsarevicha Alekseia Petrovicha (po materialam F. 396, Arkhiva Oruzheinoi palaty RGADA)." In *Petrovskoe vremia v litsakh 2013*. Trudy gosudarstvennogo Ermitazha 70, 96–101. St. Petersburg: Izdatel'stvo Gosudarstvennogo Ermitazha, 2013.

Borisova, Tamara. "Bor'ba za russkoe 'natsional'noe' pravo v pervoi chetverti 19 veka: Izobretenie novykh smyslov starykh slov." In *Istoricheskie poniatiia i politicheskie idei v Rossii*, edited by Nikolai Koposov, 123–151. St. Petersburg: Izdatel'stvo Evropeiskogo universiteta v Sankt-Peterburge Aleteia, 2006.

"Russian National Legal Tradition: Svod versus Ulozhenie in Nineteenth Century Russia." *Review of Central and East European Law* 33 (2008): 295–341.

Brailovskii, S. N. *Odin iz 'pestrykh' XVII stoletiia: Istoriko-literaturnoe issledovanie*. Zapiski Imperatorskoi Akademii nauk, series 8, Istoriko-filologicheskoe otdelenie 5. St. Petersburg: Tipografiia Akademii nauk, 1902.

Brandes, Wolfram. "Oracula Leonis." In *Christian–Muslim Relations: A Bibliographical History*, vol. 4, edited by David Thomas and Alex Mallett. Leiden: Brill, 2012.

Braubach, Max. *Prinz Eugen von Savoyen*, vol. 1. Munich: R. Oldenbourg, 1963.

Brückner, A. *Der Zarewitsch Alexei (1690–1718)*. Heidelberg: Carl Winter's Universitätsbuchhandlung, 1880.

Brulin, Herman. "Österrike och det stora nordiske kriget före Karl XII:s infall i Sachsen (1700–1706)." *Historisk tidskrift* 29 (1909): 141–166, 197–242.

Brüning, H. Joachim. "Herzog Anton Ulrich von Brauschweig-Lüneburg zu Wolfenbüttel und Abt Florenz von Corvey." *Westfälische Zeitschrift* 126–127 (1976–7): 329–371.

Buganov, V. I. *Moskovskoe vosstanie 1662 goda*. Moscow: Nauka, 1964.

Moskovskie vosstaniia kontsa XVII veka. Moscow: Nauka, 1969.

"Skazanie o smerti tsaria Fyodora Ivanovicha i votsarenii Borisa Godunova (Zapiski v Razriadnoi knige)." In *Zapiski Otdela rukopisei GBL* 19, 167–186. Moscow: Kniga, 1957.

Vosstanie moskovskikh strel'tsov: 1698 god. Moscow: Nauka, 1980.

Bugrov, K. D., and M. A. Kiselev. *Estestvennoe pravo i dobrodetel': Integratsiia evropeiskogo vliianiia v rossiiskuiu politicheskuiu kul'turu XVIII veka*. Ekaterinburg: Izdatel'stvo Ural'skogo universiteta, 2016.

Bulychev, A. A. *Istoriia odnoi politicheskoi kampanii XVII veka*. Moscow: Iazyki slavianskoi kul'tury, 2004.

Burdowicz-Nowicki, Jacek. *Piotr I, August II, i Rzeczpospolita 1697–1706*. Kraków: Arcana, 2010.

Burke, Peter. *The Fabrication of Louis XIV*. New Haven, Connecticut: Yale University Press, 1992.

Buseva-Davydova, I. A. *Kul'tura i iskusstvo v epokhu peremen: Rossiia semnadtsatogo stoletiia*. Moscow: Indrik, 2008.

Bushkovitch, Paul. "The Church and Russian Foreign Policy, 1480–1725." *Canadian–American Slavic Studies* 54, 1–3 (2020): 7–50.

"The Court of Tsar Michael in Swedish Sources." *Forschungen zur osteuropäischen Geschichte* 58 (2001): 235–242.

"Cultural Change among the Russian Boyars 1650–1680: New Sources and Old Problems." *Forschungen zur osteuropäischen Geschichte* 56 (2000): 91–111.

"The Epiphany Ceremony of the Russian Court in the Sixteenth and Seventeenth Centuries." *Russian Review* 49, 1 (1990): 1–17.

"Latinskie politicheskie knigi v Rossii 17-go veka," In *Sbornik statei i publikatsii posviachchennyi Andreiu Alekseevichu Bulychevu*, 38–55. Moscow: Drevlekhranilishche, 2019.

"The *Life of Saint Filipp*: Tsar and Metropolitan in the Late Sixteenth Century." In *Medieval Russian Culture*, vol. 2, edited by Michael S. Flier and Daniel Rowland. California Slavic Studies 19, 29–46. Berkeley, California, Los Angeles, California, and London: University of California Press, 1994.

Peter the Great: The Struggle for Power 1671–1725. Cambridge: Cambridge University Press, 2001.

Petr Velikii: Bor'ba za vlast' (1671–1725). Translated by N. L. Luzhitskaia. St. Petersburg: Dmitrii Bulanin, 2008.

"Political Ideology in the Reign of Peter I: Feofan Prokopovich, Succession to the Throne and the West." In *ГИИМ: Доклады по истории 18 и 19 вв./DHI Moskau: Vorträge zum 18. und 19. Jahrhundert*, edited by Ingrid Schierle and Denis Anatol'evič Sdvižkov, 1–16. Moscow: DHI Moskau, 2012, www.perspectivia.net/content/publikationen/vortraege-moskau/bushkovitch_ideology.

"Possevino and the Death of Tsarevich Ivan Ivanovich." *Cahiers du monde russe* 55, 1–2 (2014): 119–134.

Religion and Society in Russia: The Sixteenth and Seventeenth Centuries. New York, New York: Oxford University Press, 1992.

"The Roman Empire in the Era of Peter the Great." In *Rude and Barbarous Kingdom Revisited: Essays in Russian History in Honor of Robert O. Crummey*, edited by Chester Dunning, Russell Martin, and Daniel Rowland, 155–172. Bloomington, Indiana: Slavica, 2008.

"Russian Boyars and the Ukrainian Hetmanate." *Journal of Ukrainian Studies* 29, 1–2 (Summer–Winter 2004): 47–63.

"Sofia Palaiologina in Life and Legend." *Canadian–American Slavic Studies* 52 (2018): 158–180.

"The Tsar and the Sobor: 1613–53." In *The State in Early Modern Russia: New Directions*, edited by Paul Bushkovitch, 133–162. Bloomington, Indiana: Slavica, 2019.

"The *Vasiliologion* of Nikolai Spafarii Milescu." *Russian History* 36 (2009): 1–15.

Bychkova, M. E. *Sostav klassa feodalov Rossii v XVI v.* Moscow: Nauka, 1986.

Rodoslovnye knigi XVI–XVII vv. Moscow: Nauka, 1975.

Bykova, T. A., and M. M. Gurevich. *Opisanie izdanii napechatannykh kirillitsei 1689–ianvar' 1725.* Moscow and Leningrad: Izdatel'stvo Akademii nauk SSSR, 1958.

Opisanie izdanii grazhdanskoi pechati 1708–ianvar' 1725 g. Moscow: Izdatel'stvo Akademii nauk SSSR, 1955.

Chance, James Frederick. *George I and the Northern War: A Study of British-Hanoverian Policy in the North of Europe in the Years 1709 to 1721.* London: Smith, Elder, & Co., 1909.

Chentsova, V. G. "Eschatologie byzantine et pensée historique à la cour d'Alexis Romanov: Paisios Ligaridès, Nicolas le Spathaire et Francesco Barozzi aux origines du messianisme russe (1656–1673)." In *Écrire et réécrire l'histoire russe d'Ivan le Terrible à Vasilij Ključevskij (1547–1917)*, edited by Pierre Gonneau and Ecatherina Rai. Collection historique de l'Insitut des études slaves 51, 41–51. Paris: Institut d'études slaves, 2013.

"Paisii Ligarid, Nikolai Spafarii i Franchesko Barotstsi: Eskhatoligicheskie idei pri dvore tsaria Alekseia Mikhailovicha." *Drevniaia Rus': Voprosy medievistiki* 55, 1 (2014): 69–82.

"Sinodal'noe reshenie 1686 g. o Kievskoi mitropolii." *Drevniaia Rus': Voprosy medievistiki* 68, 2 (2017): 89–110.

Cherepnin, L. V. *Obrazovanie russkogo tsentralizovannogo gosudarstva v XIV–XV vv.: Ocherki sotsial'no-ekonomicheskoi i politicheskoi istorii Rusi.* Moscow: Izdatel'stvo sotsial'no-ekonomicheskoi literatury, 1960.

Russkie feodal'nye arkhivy XIV–XV vekov, 2 vols. Moscow and Leningrad: Izdatel'stvo Akademii nauk SSSR, 1948–51.

Zemskie sobory Russkogo gosudarstva v XVI–XVII vv. Moscow: Iazyki slavianskoi kul'tury, 1978.

Cherkasov, P. P. *Dvuglavyi Orel i korolevskie lilii.* Moscow: Nauka, 1995.

Chernaia, L. A. "Verkhniaia tipografiia Simeona Polotskogo." In *Simeon Polotskii i ego knigoizdatel'skaia deiatel'nost': Russkaia staropechatnaia literatura: XVI–pervaia chetvert' XVIII v.*, edited by A. N. Robinson, 46–59. Moscow: Nauka, 1982.

Cherniavsky, Michael. "Khan or Basileus: An Aspect of Russian Medieval Political Theory." *Journal of the History of Ideas* 20 (1959): 3–28.

Cheynet, Jean-Claude. *Pouvoir et contestations à Byzance (963–1210).* Paris: Publications de la Sorbonne, 1990.

Chichurov, I. S. *Politicheskaia ideologiia Srednevekov'ia: Vizantiia i Rus'.* Moscow: Nauka, 1990.

Chistiakova, E. V. "Boiarskaia biblioteka." In *Problemy istorii, russkoi knizhnosti, kul'tury i obshchestvennogo soznaniia*, edited by E. V. Romodanovskaia, 252–258. Novosibirsk: Sibirskii khronograf, 2000.

Gorodskie vosstaniia v Rossii v pervoi polovine XVII veka: 30–40-e gody. Voronezh: Izdatel'stvo Voronezhskogo universiteta, 1975.

Chistovich, I. *Feofan Prokopovich i ego vremia*. St. Petersburg: Tipografiia Imperatorskoi Akademii nauk, 1868.

Chrissidis, Nikolaos. "Whoever Does Not Drink to the End, He Wishes Evil: Ritual Drinking and Politics in Early Modern Russia." In *The New Muscovite Cultural History: A Collection in Honor of Daniel B. Rowland*, edited by Valerie Kivelson, Karen Petrone, Nancy Shields Kollmann, and Michael S. Flier, 107–124. Bloomington, Indiana: Slavica, 2009.

Chrissidis, Nikolaos A. *An Academy at the Court of the Tsars: Greek Scholars and Jesuit Education in Early Modern Russia*. DeKalb, Illinois: Northern Illinois University Press, 2016.

Christophilopoulou, Aikaterini. *Ekloge, anagoreusis kai stepsis tou Byzantinou autokratoros*. Pragmateiai tes akademias Athenon 22/2. Athens: Akademia Athenon, 1956.

Collins, James B. *The State in Early Modern France*. Cambridge: Cambridge University Press, 2009.

Coogan, Michael D., ed. *Oxford Encyclopedia of the Books of the Bible*. New York, New York: Oxford University Press, 2011.

Cosandey, Fanney and Robert Descimon. *L'absolutisme en France: Histoire et historiographie*. Paris: Éditions du Seuil, 2002.

Cracraft, James. *The Church Reform of Peter the Great*. Stanford, California: Stanford University Press, 1971.

The Petrine Revolution in Russian Culture. Cambridge, Massachusetts: The Belknap Press of Harvard University Press, 2004.

Croft, Pauline. "The Parliamentary Installation of Henry, Prince of Wales." *Bulletin of the Institute of Historical Research* 65, 157 (1992), 177–193.

Croskey, Robert M. "Byzantine Greeks in Late Fifteenth- and Early Sixteenth-Century Russia'." In *The Byzantine Legacy in Eastern Europe*, edited by Lowell Clucas, 33–56. New York, New York: Columbia University Press, 1988.

Cross, Claire. *The Puritan Earl: The Life of Henry Hastings, Third Earl of Huntingdon 1536–1595*. London: Macmillan, 1966.

Crummey, Robert O. *Aristocrats and Servitors: The Boyar Elite in Russia 1613–1689*. Princeton, New Jersey: Princeton University Press, 1983.

"Court Spectacles in Seventeenth Century Russia: Illusion and Reality." In *Essays in Honor of A. A. Zimin*, edited by Daniel Clarke Waugh, 130–158. Columbus, Ohio: Slavica, 1985.

Czapliński, Władysław. *Władysław IV i jego czasy*. Warsaw, Wiedza Powszechna, 1976.

Czwołek, Arkadiusz. *Piórem i Buławą: Działalność polityczna Lwa Sapiehy kanclerza litewskiego, wojewody wileńskiego*. Toruń: Wydawnictwo Naukowe Uniwersytetu Mikołaja Kopernika, 2012.

Dagron, Gilbert. *Empereur et prêtre: Étude sur le "césaropapisme" byzantin*. Paris: Gallimard, 1996.

Dansk undenrigspolitiks historie, vol. I. Copenhagen: Danmarks Nationalleksikon, 2001.

Demidova, N. F., *Sluzhilaia biurokratiia v Rossii XVII veka; biograficheskii spravochnik*. Moscow: Pamiatniki istoricheskoi mysli, 2011.

Dergachev, V. V. "Vselenskii sinodik v drevnei i srednevekovoi Rossii." *Drevniaia Rus': Voprosy medievistiki* 1, 3 (2001): 18–29.

Dewey, Horace W. "Political Poruka in Muscovite Rus'." *Russian Review* 46, 2 (1987): 117–133.

D'iakonov, M. *Vlast' Moskovskikh gosudarei: Ocherki iz istorii politicheskikh idei drevnei Rusi do kontsa XVI veka.* St. Petersburg: I. N. Skorokhodov, 1889.

Dolgorukov, Petr. *Rossiiskaia Rodoslovnaia kniga*, vol. 1. St. Petersburg: Tipografiia Karla Vingebera, 1854.

Dolgova, Svetlana Romanovna. "Das Heiratsprojekt zwischen dem Zarewitsch Aleksej und Prinzessin Charlotte." In *Braunschweigische Fürsten in Rußland in der ersten Hälfte des 18. Jahrhunderts*, edited by Manfred von Boetticher, 24–91. Göttingen: Vandenhoeck & Ruprecht, 1998.

Dolgova, S. R. and T. A. Lapteva, eds. *Trudy i dni Aleksandra Danilovicha Menshikova: Povsednevnye zapiski delam A. D. Menshikova 1716–1720, 1726–1727 gg.* Moscow: Rossiiski fond kul'tury, 2004.

Dorozhkin, A. "Portrety kisti Karavaka." In *Zolotoi os'mnadtsatyi: Russkoe iskusstvo 18 veka v otechestvennom iskusstvoznanii*, 37–62. St. Petersburg: Izdatel'stvo Sankt-Peterburgskogo universiteta, 2006.

Dreitzel, Horst. *Monarchiebegriffe in der Fürstengesellschaft: Semantik und Theoretik der Einherrschaft in Deutschland von der Reformation bis zum Vormärz*, 2 vols. Cologne, Weimar, and Vienna: Böhlau, 1991.

Dubrovskii, I. V. "Issledovaniia o diplomaticheskoi perepiske Ivana Groznogo." *Russkii sbornik* 24 (2018): 30–98.

"Latinskie rukopisi sochineniia Al'berta Shlikhtinga." *Russkii sbornik* 18 (2016): 74–217.

Dukes, Paul, Graeme P. Herd, and Jarmo Kotilaine. *Stuarts and Romanovs: The Rise and Fall of a Special Relationship.* Dundee: Dundee University Press, 2009.

Dukmeyer, Friedrich. *Korbs Diarium itineris in Moscoviam und die Quellen die es ergänzen: Beiträge zur moskowitisch-russischen, österreichisch-kaiserlichen und brandenburgisch-preußischen Geschichte aus der Zeit Peters des Großen*, 2 vols. Historische Studien 70, 80. Berlin: Emil Ebering, 1909–10.

Dumschat, Sabine. *Ausländische Mediziner im Moskauer Russland.* Quellen und Studien zur Geschichte des östlichen Europas 67. Stuttgart: Franz Steiner, 2006.

Dunning, Chester S. L. *Russia's First Civil War: The Time of Troubles and the Founding of the Romanov Dynasty.* University Park, Pennsylvania: Pennsylvania State University Press, 2001.

Dureng, Jean. *Le Duc de Bourbon et l'Angleterre.* Paris: Hachette, 1911.

Ebbinghaus, Andreas. *Die altrussischen Marienikonen-Legenden.* Slavistische Veröffentlichungen 770. Berlin: Harrassowitz, 1990.

Eingorn, V. O. "O snosheniiakh Malorossiiskogo dukhovenstva s Moskovskim pravitel'stvom v tsarstvovanie Alekseia Mikhailovicha." *ChOIDR* 2, 4 (1893): 1–370; 3, 3 (1894): 371–570; 4, 3 (1898): 571–794; 1, 4 (1899): 795–932; 2, 4 (1899): 933–1104.

Ekzempliarskii, A. V. *Velikie i udel'nye kniazia.* Moscow: Tera-Knizhnyi klub, 1998.

Eleonskaia, A. S. *Russkaia oratorskaia proza v literaturnom protsesse XVII veka.* Moscow: Nauka, 1990.

"En svensk beskickning til Ryssland under Erik XIV:s regering." *Historisk tidskrift* VII (1887): 325–341.

Emminger, Kurt, *Studien zu den griechischen Fürstenspiegeln.* Munich: Lindl, 1913.

Erdmann, Yella. *Der livländische Staatsmann Johann Reinhold von Patkul.* Berlin: Haude & Spener, 1970.

Erren, Lorenz. *Der russische Hof nach Peter dem Grossen 1725–1730: Eine Kulturgeschichte des Politischen*, Habilitation Thesis, Universität Mainz, 2018.

Erusalimskii, K. Iu., and I. Shvarts [Iskra Schwarcz]. "Missiia Zhdana Kvashnina v Sviashchennoi Rimskoi Imperii: K istorii rossiisko-imperskikh otnoshenii XVI veka." *Peterburgskie slaviankie i balkanskie issledovaniia* 1, 23 (2018): 71–104.

Eskin, Iu. M. *Dmitrii Mikhailovich Pozharskii.* Moscow: Kvadriga, 2013.

Esipov, G. V. "Zhizneopisanie kniazia A. D. Menshikova po novootkrytym bumagam." *Russkii arkhiv* 13, 7 (1875): 233–247; 13, 9 (1875): 47–74; 13, 10 (1875): 198–211; 13, 12 (1875): 477–481.

Evangulova, O. S. *Izobrazitel'noe iskusstvo v Rossii pervoi chetverti XVIII veka.* Moscow: Izdatel'stvo Moskovskogo universiteta, 1987.

Evans, Norman. "The Anglo-Russian Royal Marriage Negotiations of 1600–1603." *Slavonic and East European Review* 61, 3 (1983): 363–387.

Fabricius, Knud F. K. *Kongeloven: Dens tilblivelse og plads i samtidens natur- og arveretlige udvikling.* Copenhagen: H. Hagerups Forlag, 1920.

Feldbrugge, Ferdinand. *A History of Russian Law: From Ancient Times to the Council Code (Ulozhenie) of Tsar Aleksei Mikhailovich of 1649.* Leiden and Boston, Massachusetts: Brill, 2017.

Fennell, J. L. I. *The Crisis of Medieval Russia 1200–1304.* London and New York, New York: Longman, 1983.

The Emergence of Moscow 1304–1359. Berkeley, California: University of California Press, 1968.

Ivan the Great of Moscow. London: Macmillan, 1963.

ed. and trans. *Prince A. M. Kurbsky's History of Ivan IV.* Cambridge: Cambridge University Press, 1965.

Fiedler, Joseph. "Die Beziehungen Österreichs zu Russland in den Jahren 1584–1598." *Almanach der kaiserlichen Akademie der Wissenschaften* 16 (1866): 253–278.

Filina, E. I. *"V poiskakh al'ternativy": "Pridvornye partii" v politicheskoi bor'be v Rossii 30–50-gg. XVII v.* Moscow: Izdatel'stvo Prometei, 2011.

Filiushkin, A. I. *Istoriia odnoi mistifikatsii: Ivan Groznyi i "Izbrannaia Rada."* Moscow: VGU, 1998.

"Ivan the Terrible's Struggle for Recognition in the Latter Half of the Sixteenth Century." *Russian Studies in History* 53, 1 (2014): 28–41.

Izobretaia pervuiu voinu Rossii i Evropy: Baltiiskie voiny vtoroi poloviny XVI v. glazami sovremennikov i potomkov. St. Petersburg: Izdatel'stvo Dmitrii Bulanin, 2013.

Tituly russkikh gosudarei. Moscow and St. Petersburg: Al'ians-Arkheo, 2006.

Vasilii III. Moscow: Molodaia gvardiia, 2010.

Flier, Michael S. "Court Ceremony in an Age of Reform: Patriarch Nikon and the Palm Sunday Ritual." In *Religion and Culture in Early Modern Russia and Ukraine*, edited by Samuel H. Baron and Nancy Shields Kollmann, 73–95. DeKalb, Illinois: Northern Illinois University Press, 1997.

"Political Ideas and Rituals." In *The Cambridge History of Russia*, edited by Maureen Perrie, vol. 1, 387–408. Cambridge: Cambridge University Press.

Floria, B. N. "Izbranie tsaria Mikhaila," *Istoricheskii vestnik* 3, 150 (2013): 6–23.

Pol'sko-litovskaia interventsiia v Rossii i russkoe obshchestvo. Moscow: Indrik, 2005.

Russko-pol'skie otnosheniia i baltiiskii vopros v kontse shestnadtsatogo–nachale semnadtsatogo v. Moscow: Nauka, 1973.

Russko-pol'skie otnosheniia i politicheskoe razvitie Vostochnoi Evropy vo vtoroi polovine XVI–nachale XVII v. Moscow: Nauka, 1978.

Rossiia i cheshskoe vosstanie protiv Gabsburgov. Moscow: Nauka, 1986.

Vneshnepoliticheskaia program A. L. Ordina-Nashchokina i popytki ee osushchestvleniia. Moscow: Indrik, 2013.

Forsten, G. V. *Baltiiskii vopros v XVI i XVII stoletiiakh (1544–1648)*, 2 vols. Zapiski istoriko-filologicheskogo fakul'teta Sankt-Peterburgskogo universiteta 33, 34. St. Petersburg: Tipografiia V. S. Balasheva, 1893–4.

"Snosheniia Danii s Rossiei v tsarstvovanie Khristiana IV." *Zhurnal Ministerstva narodnogo prosveshcheniia* 280 (1892): 281–335.

"Snosheniia Shvetsii s Rossiei v tsarstvovaniia Khristiny." *Zhurnal Ministerstva narodnogo prosveshcheniia*, 275 (1891): 347–375.

Forstreuter, Kurt. *Preußen und Rußland von den Anfängen des Deutschen Ordens bis zu Peter dem Großen*. Göttinger Bausteine zur Geschichtswissenschaft 23. Göttingen: Musterschmidt, 1955.

Franklin, Simon. "The Empire of the Rhomaioi as Viewed from Kievan Russia: Aspects of Byzantino-Russian Cultural Relations." *Byzantion* 53, 2 (1983): 507–537.

"Literacy and Documentation in Early Medieval Russia." *Speculum* 60, 1 (1985): 1–38.

Writing, Society, and Culture in Early Rus'. Cambridge: Cambridge University Press, 2002.

Frey, Linda, and Marsha Frey. *A Question of Empire: Leopold I and the War of Spanish Succession 1701–1705*. Boulder, Colorado: East European Monographs, 1983.

Friedeburg, Robert von, and Michael Seidler. "The Holy Roman Empire of the German Nation." In *European Political Thought 1500–1700: Religion, Law and Philosophy*, edited by Howell A. Lloyd, Glenn Burgess, and Simon Hodson, 102–175. New Haven, Connecticut and London: Yale University Press, 2007.

Friedrich, Karin. "Poland-Lithuania." In *European Political Thought 1500–1700: Religion, Law and Philosophy*, edited by Howell A. Lloyd, Glenn Burgess, and Simon Hodson, 208–242. New Haven, Connecticut and London: Yale University Press, 2007.

Frost, Robert. *The Oxford History of Poland-Lithuania. Volume I: The Making of the Polish-Lithuanian Union, 1385–1569*. Oxford: Oxford University Press, 2015.

Frost, Robert I. "'Ut unusquisque qui vellet, ad illum venire possit': Nobility, Citizenship, and Corporate Decision-Making in the Polish-Lithuanian Commonwealth 1454–1795." In *What Makes the Nobility Noble? Comparative Perspectives from the Sixteenth to the Twentieth Centuries*, edited by Jörn Leonhard and Christian Wieland, 146–150. Schriftenreihe der FRIAS School of History 2. Göttingen: Vandenhoeck & Ruprecht, 2011.

Fursenko, V. "Iagushinskii (Iaguzhinskii), Pavel Ivanovich." In *Russkii biograficheskii slovar'*. Iablonovskii–Fomin, 7–28. St. Petersburg: Izdanie Imperatorskogo Russkogo istoricheskogo obshchestva, 1913.

Gelderen, Martin van. "Aristotelians, Monarchomachs and Republicans: Sovereignty and *respublica mixta* in Dutch and German Political Thought 1580–1650." In *Republicanism: A Shared European Heritage*, vol. 1, edited by Martin van Gelderen and Quinten Skinner, 195–218. Cambridge: Cambridge University Press, 2002.

Georgievskii, V. *Florishcheva Pustyn'*. Viazniki: Izdatel'stvo Arkhimandrita Antoniia, nastoiatelia Florishchevoi pustyni, 1896.

Gierke, Otto von. *Johannes Althusius und die Entwicklung der naturrechtlichen Staatstheorie*. Berlin: W. Koebner, 1880.

Glück, Helmut, and Ineta Polanska. *Johann Ernst Glück (1654–1705): Pastor, Philologe, Volksaufklärer im Baltikum und in Russland.* Wiesbaden: Harrassowitz, 2005.

"Golovkin, Aleksandr Gavrilovich." In *Russkii biograficheskii slovar'*. Moscow: Aspekt Press, 1997.

Golubev, S. *Kievskaia akademiia v kontse XVII i v nachale XVIII stoletii.* Kiev: Tipografiia I. I. Gorbukova, 1901.

Gömöri, George. "Drama in Poland," "Opera in Poland," and "Ballet in Poland." In *Spectaculum Europaeum*, edited by Pierre Béhar and Helen Watanabe-O'Kelly, 309–320, 477–481, and 585–590. Wiesbaden: Harrassowitz, 1999.

Gorskii, A. A. *Moskva i Orda*. Moscow: Nauka, 2000.

"Zaveshchaniia Vasiliia I Dmitrievicha: Problemy posledovatel'nosti i datirovki." *Drevniaia Rus': Voprosy medievistiki* 67, 1 (2017): 20–34.

Gorskii, A. A., V. A. Kuchkin, P. V. Lukin, and P. S. Stefanovich. *Drevniaia Rus': Ocherki politicheskogo i sotsial'nogo stroia.* Moscow: Indrik, 2008.

Gorskii, A. V., and K. I. Nevostruev. *Opisanie slavianskikh rukopisei Moskovskoi sinodal'noi biblioteki.* Wiesbaden: Harrassowitz, 1964.

Grebeniuk, V. P. "'Rifmologion' Simeona Polotskogo (Istoriia sozdaniia, struktura, idei)." In *Simeon Polotskii i ego knigoizdatel'skaia deiatel'nost': Russkaia staropechatnaia literatura: XVI–pervaia chetvert' XVIII v.*, edited by A. N. Robinson, 259–308. Moscow: Nauka, 1982.

Grekov, B. D. *Kievskaia Rus'*. Moscow: Gosudarstvennoe uchebno-pedagogicheskoe izdatel'stvo, 1949.

Grekov, B. D., and A. Iu. Iakubovskii. *Zolotaia Orda i ee padenie*. Moscow and Leningrad: Izdatel'stvo Akademii nauk SSSR, 1950.

Gruber, Isaiah. *Orthodox Russia in Crisis: Church and Nation in the Time of Troubles*. DeKalb, Illinois, Northern Illinois University Press, 2012.

Gruszecki, Stefan. *Walka o władzę w Rzeczypospolitej polskiej po wygaśnięciu dynastii Jagiellonów (1572–1573)*. Warsaw: Państwowe Wydawnictwo Naukowe, 1969.
Guerrier, W. *Die Kronprinzessin Charlotte von Rußland*. Bonn: Max Cohen & Sohn, 1875.
Leibniz in seinen Beziehungen zu Rußland und Peter dem Großen. St. Petersburg and Leipzig: Kaiserliche Akademie der Wissenschaften, 1873.
Guran, Petre. "Historical Prophecies from Late Antique Apocalypticism to Secular Eschatology," *Revue des études sud-est européennes* 52 (2014): 47–62.
Gurliand, I. Ia. *Ivan Gebdon: Kommissarius i resident*. Iaroslavl': Tipografiia Gubernskogo pravleniia, 1903.
Gurvich, Georgii. *"Pravda voli monarshei" Feofana Prokopovicha i ee zapadnoevropeiskie istochniki*. Uchenye zapiski Imperatorskogo Iur'evskogo universiteta 11. Iur'ev: Tipografiia K. Mattisena, 1915.
Russo i deklaratsiia prav: Idea neot"emlemykh prav individa v politicheskoi doctrine Russo. Petrograd: Tipografiia M. V. Vol'fa, 1918.
Gurvitch, Georges. *Éléments de sociologie juridique*. Paris: Aubier, Éditions Montaigne, 1940.
L'idée du Droit social. Paris: Librairie du Recueil Sirey, 1931.
Haake, Paul. *Christiane Eberhardine und August der Starke: Eine Ehetragödie*. Dresden: C. Heinrich, 1930.
Halperin, Charles J. "Ivan IV as Autocrat (samoderzhets)." *Cahiers du monde russe* 55, 3–4 (2014): 1–18.
Ivan the Terrible: Free to Reward and Free to Punish. Pittsburgh, Pennsylvania: Pittsburgh University Press, 2019.
"Ivan the Terrible's Younger Brother: Prince Iury Vasil'evich (1533–63)." *The Court Historian* 22, 1 (2017): 1–16.
"Metropolitan Makarii and Muscovite Court Politics in the Reign of Ivan IV." *Russian Review* 73 (July 2014): 447–464.
"The Minority of Ivan IV." In *Rude and Barbarous Kingdom Revisited: Essays in Russian History in Honor of Robert O. Crummey*, edited by Chester Dunning, Russell Martin, and Daniel Rowland, 41–52. Bloomington, Indiana: Slavica, 2008.
Russia and the Golden Horde: The Mongol Impact on Russian History. Bloomington, Indiana: Indiana University Press, 1985.
"Simeon Bekbulatovich and Mongol Influence on Ivan IV's Muscovy." *Russian History* 39, 3 (2012): 306–330.
The Tatar Yoke: The Image of the Mongols in Medieval Russia, 2nd ed. Bloomington, Indiana: Slavica, 2009.
"What is an 'Official' Muscovite Source for the Reign of Ivan IV?" In *The Book of Royal Degrees and the Genesis of Russian Historical Consciousness*, edited by Gail Lenhoff and Ann Kleimola (Bloomington, Indiana: Slavica, 2011), 81–93.
Hamburg, Gary. *Russia's Path toward Enlightenment: Faith, Politics, and Reason 1500–1801*. New Haven, Connecticut: Yale University Press, 2016.
Harris, Jonathan "A Worthless Prince? Andreas Palaeologus in Rome, 1465–1502." *Orientalia Christiana Periodica* 61 (1995): 537–554.

Hartung, Fritz, and Roland Mousnier. "Quelques problèmes concernant la monarchie absolue." In *Relazioni del X Congresso Internazionale di Scienze Storiche: Storia moderna*, vol IV. Florence: G. C. Sansoni, 1955.

Hassinger, Erich. *Brandenburg-Preußen, Rußland und Schweden, 1700–1713.* Munich: Isar Verlag, 1953.

Hautecœur, Louis. *Louis XIV: Roi soleil.* Paris: Plon, 1953.

Hayden, J. Michael. *France and the Estates General of 1614.* London: Cambridge University Press, 1974.

Helbig, Christian. "'Zum Nutzen der russischen Monarchie und größern Splendor des Hauses Braunschweig-Lüneburg' – Charlotte Christine Sophie von Braunschweig-Wolfenbüttel (1694–1715) als erste westeuropäische Kronprinzessin in Russland." In *Russlands Blick nach Nordwestdeutschland: Politisch-dynastische Beziehungen vom 16. bis frühen 20. Jahrhundert im Spiegel von Dokumenten aus dem Niedersächsischen Landesarchiv*, edited by Gerd Steinwascher. Veröffentlichungen des Niedersächsischen Landesarchivs 2, 48–70. Göttingen: Wallstein Verlag, 2018.

Hellie, Richard "Early Modern Russian Law: The Ulozhenie of 1649." *Russian History* 15, 2–4 (1988): 181–224.

"Ulozhenie-Preamble." *Russian History* 15, 2–4 (1988): 155–179.

Henshall, Nicholas. *The Myth of Absolutism: Change and Continuity in Early Modern Monarchy.* London: Longman, 1992.

Hildebrand, Emil. *Svenska statsförfattningens historiska utveckling.* Stockholm: P. A. Norstedt 1896.

Hionides, Harry T. *Paisius Ligarides.* New York, New York: Twayne Publishers, 1972.

Hippisley, Anthony, and Evgenija Luk'janova. *Simeon Polockij's Library: A Catalogue.* Bausteine zur slavischen Philologie und Kulturgeschichte. Series B, Editions, new sequence, vol. 22. Cologne, Weimar, and Vienna: Böhlau, 2004.

Hjärne, Harald. "Ur brefvexlingen mellan konung Johan III och tsar Ivan Vasilevitj." *Historiskt Bibliotek* 7 (1880): 530–554.

Hochstrasser, T. J. *Natural Law Theories in the Early Enlightenment.* Cambridge: Cambridge University Press, 2000.

Hoeck, Wilhelm. *Anton Ulrich und Elisabeth Christine von Braunschweig-Lüneburg-Wolfenbüttel.* Wolfenbüttel: Hollesche Buch-, Kunst- und Musikalienhandlung, 1845.

Hoffman, Martha K. *Raised to Rule: Educating Royalty at the Court of the Spanish Habsburgs 1601–1634.* Baton Rouge, Louisiana: Louisiana State University Press, 2011.

Horsey, Sir Jerome. "Travels." In *Rude and Barbarous Kingdom: Russia in the Accounts of Sixteenth-Century English Voyagers*, edited by Lloyd E. Berry and Robert O. Crummey. Madison, Wisconsin: University of Wisconsin Press, 1969.

"The Most Solemn and Magnificent Coronation of Pheodore Ivanowiche, Emperour of Russia," in *The Principall Navigations, Voiages and Discoveries of the English Nation*, edited by Richard Hakluyt, vol. 1, 819–825. London: George Bishop and Ralph Newberie, deputies to Christopher Barker, printer to the Queenes most excellent Maiestie, 1589. (Also in the 1599 edition, vol. 1, 466–470.)

Hübner, Eckhard. "Zwischen aller Fronten: Magnus von Holstein als König von Livland." In *Zwischen Christianisierung und Europäisierung: Beiträge zur Geschichte Osteuropas in Mittelalter und Früher Neuzeit*, edited by Eckhard Hübner, Ekkehard Klug, and Jan Kusber. Quellen und Studien zur Geschichte des Östlichen Europa 51, 313–334. Stuttgart: Franz Steiner, 1998.

Hughes, Lindsey. *Russia in the Age of Peter the Great.* New Haven, Connecticut: Yale University Press, 1998.

Sophia, Regent of Russia 1657–1704. New Haven, Connecticut: Yale University Press, 1990.

Hunger, Herbert, ed. *Das byzantinische Herrscherbild.* Darmstadt: Wissenschaftliche Buchgesellschaft, 1975.

Hunter, Ian. *Rival Enlightenments: Civil and Metaphysical Philosophy in Early Modern Germany.* Cambridge: Cambridge University Press, 2001.

Iakovenko, Natalia. *U poshukakh Novoho neba: Zhyttia i teksty Ioannykiia Galiatov'skoho.* Kyiv: Laurus Kritika, 2017.

Ianushkevich A. N., *Livonskaia voina: Vil'no protiv Moskvy 1558–1570.* Moscow: Kvadriga, 2015.

Iglesias, R. F. "K voprosu o predpolagaemom naslednike Vasiliia III mezhdu 1505 i 1530 gg." *Kapterevskie chteniia* 14 (2016): 246–296; 15 (2017): 235–306.

Ikonnikov, V. S. *Maksim Grek i ego vremia.* Kiev: Tipografiia Imperatorskogo universiteta Sv. Vladimira, 1915.

Ingrao, Charles W. *In Quest and Crisis: Emperor Joseph I and the Habsburg Monarchy.* West Lafayette, Indiana: Purdue University Press 1979.

Isachenko, T. A. *Perevodnaia moskovskaia knizhnost': Metropolichii i patriarshii skriptorii XV–XVII vv.* Moscow: Pashkov dom, 2009.

Isoaho, Mari. *The Image of Alexander Nevskiy in Medieval Russia.* Leiden and Boston, Massachusetts: Brill, 2006.

Istomin, Karion. *Kniga liubvi znak v chestne brake*, edited by L. I. Sazonova. Moscow: Izdatel'stvo Kniga, 1989.

Istrin, V. M. *Knigi vremennye i obraznye Georgiia Mnikha*, 3 vols. Petrograd–Leningrad: Izdanie Otdeleniia Russkogo iazyka i slovesnosti Rossiiskoi Akademii nauk, 1920–30.

Iurganov, A. L. "O date napisaniia zaveshchaniia Ivana Groznogo." *Otechestvennaia istoriia* 6 (1993): 125–141.

Iushko, A. A. *Moskovskaia zemlia IX–XIV vekov.* Moscow: Nauka, 1991.

Ivanov, Andrey. "Reforming Orthodoxy: Russian Bishops and Their Church 1721–1801." PhD dissertation, Yale University, 2012.

Ivanov, Andrey, *A Spiritual Revolution: The Impact of the Reformation and Enlightenment in Orthodox Russia.* Madison, Wisconsin: University of Wisconsin Press, 2020.

[Ivanov, P. I.] *Alfavitnyi ukazatel' familii i lits upominaemykh v boiarskikh knigakh.* Moscow: S. Selivanovskii, 1853.

Izvekov, N. D. *Moskovskie kremlevskie dvortsovye tserkvi i sluzhivshie pri nikh litsa v XVII veke*. Moscow: Pechat' A. I. Snegirevoi, 1906.

Jackson, Richard A. *Vive le Roi! A History of the French Coronation from Charles V to Charles X*. Chapel Hill, North Carolina and London: University of North Carolina Press,1984.

Jellinek, Georg. *Allgemeine Staatslehre*, 2nd ed. Berlin: O. Häring, 1905.

Jensen, Claudia, and Ingrid Maier. "Orpheus and Pickelherring in the Kremlin: The 'Ballet' for the Tsar of February, 1672." *Scando-Slavica* 59, 2 (2013): 145–184.

"Pickelherring Returns: More New Sources on the Prehistory of the Russian Court Theater." *Scando-Slavica* 61, 1 (2015): 7–56.

Pridvornyi teater v Rossii XVII veka. Moscow: Indrik, 2016.

Jensen, Frede P. "Hertug Magnus af Holstens forsvarsskrift af 1579 om hans forhold til tsar Ivan den Grusomme." *Danske Magazin* series 8, 5 (1976): 54–83

Jespersen, Knud J. V. *Danmarks historie*, vol. 3. Copenhagen: Gyldendal, 1989.

Jespersen, Leon, ed. *A Revolution from Above? The Power State of Sixteenth and Seventeenth Century Scandinavia*. Odense: Odense University Press, 2000.

Jespersen, Leon. "Teokrati og kontraktlære: Et aspekt af de statsretlige brydninger ved Frederik 3.s kroning." In *Struktur og funktion: Festskrift til Erling Ladewig Petersen*, edited by Carsten Due-Nielsen, Knud J. V. Jespersen, Leon Jespersen, and Anders Monrad Møller, 169–186. Odense: Odense universitetsforlag, 1994.

Johannesson, Kurt. *Renaissance of the Goths in Sixteenth-Century Sweden*. Berkeley, California: University of California Press, 1991.

Jørgensen, Adolf Ditlev, ed. *Kongeloven og dens forhistorie*. Copenhagen: C. A. Reitzel, 1886.

Kain, Kevin M. "Before New Jerusalem: Patriarch Nikon's Iverskii and Krestnyi Monasteries." *Russian History* 39 (2012): 173–231.

Kaldellis, Anthony. *The Byzantine Republic: People and Power in New Rome*. Cambridge, Massachusetts: Harvard University Press, 2015.

Kallash, V. V. ed. *Tri veka: Rossiia ot Smuty do nashego vremeni*, vol. 1. Moscow: I. D. Sytin, 1912.

Kämpfer, Frank. "'Rußland an der Schwelle zur Neuzeit': Kunst, Ideologie und historisches Bewußtsein unter Ivan Groznyj." *Jahrbücher für Geschichte Osteuropas* Neue Folge 23, 4 (1975): 504–524.

Kantorowicz, Ernst. *The King's Two Bodies: A Study in Medieval Political Theology*. Princeton, New Jersey: Princeton University Press, 1957.

Kapterev, N. F. *Kharakter otnoshenii Rossii k pravoslavnomu vostoku v XVI i XVII stoletiiakh*, 2nd ed. Sergiev Posad: Izdanie knizhnogo magazina M. S. Elova,1914.

Patriarkh Nikon i tsar' Aleksei Mikhailovich, 2 vols. Sergiev Posad: Izdatel'stvo Spaso-Priobrazhenskogo Valaamskogo monastyria, 1909–12.

Karamzin, N. M. *Istoriia gosudarstva Rossiiskogo*, 4 vols. St. Petersburg: Eduard Prats, 1842–4; 4 vols., Moscow: Izdatel'stvo Kniga, 1988–9.

Kashtanov, S. M. *Sotsial'no-politicheskaia istoriia Rossii kontsa pervoi poloviny XVI veka*. Moscow: Nauka, 1967.

Kern, Fritz. *Gottesgnadentum und Widerstandsrecht im früheren Mittelalter*, 3rd ed. Darmstadt: Wissenschaftliche Buchgesellschaft, 1962. First published Leipzig: R. F. Roehler, 1914.

Khoroshkevich, A. L. *Rossiia v sisteme mezhdunarodnykh otnoshenii XVI veka*. Moscow: Drevlekhranilishche, 2003.

Russkoe gosudarstvo v sisteme mezhdunarodnykh otnoshenii kontsa XV–nachala XVI vv. Moscow: Nauka, 1980.

Kivelson, Valerie. "The Devil Stole His Mind: The Tsar and the 1648 Moscow Uprising." *American Historical Review* 98, 3 (1993): 733–756.

Kliuchevskii, V. O. *Sochineniia*, 8 vols. Moscow: Izdatel'stvo sotsial'no-ekonomicheskoi literatury, 1956–9.

Kloss, B. M. *Nikonovskii svod i russkie letopisi XVI–XVII vekov*. Moscow: Nauka,1980.

Kobzareva, E. I. *Shvedskaia okkupatsiia Novgoroda v period Smuty XVII veka*. Moscow: Institut rossiskoi istorii RAN, 2005.

Kochegarov, K. A. "Bor'ba boiarskikh gruppirovok vokrug planov zhenit'by tsaria Petra i russko-pol'skie otnosheniia v 1684–89 gg." In *Rossiia, Pol'sha, Germaniia v evropeiskoi politike: Istoricheskii opyt vzaimodeistviia i imperativy sotrudnichestva*, edited by B. V. Nosov, 45–88. Moscow: Indrik, 2012.

Rech' Pospolitaia i Rossiia v 1680–1686 godakh: Zakliuchenie dogovora o vechnom mire. Moscow: Indrik, 2008.

Kochetkov, I. A. *Slovar' russkikh ikonopistev XI–XVII vekov*. Moscow: Indrik, 2003.

Köhler, Joachim. "Lüdingshausen genannt Wolff, Friedrich von." *Neue Deutsche Biographie*, vol. 15, 457–459, www.deutsche-biographie.de/sfz54923.html #ndbcontent.

Kohut, Zenon. "Servant of the Tsar, Defender of Ukrainian Church Autonomy and Promoter of the Kyivan Caves Monastery: The Political World of Innokentii Gizel' (1650s–1670s)," *Harvard Ukrainian Studies* 32–33 (2011–2014): 437–454.

"Vplyv polityky na Innokentiia Gizelia ta vydannia kyivs'koho 'Synopsysu': Nove osmyslennia." In Innokentii Gizel', *Vybrani tvory*, vol. 3, 9–30. Kyiv and Lviv: Svichado, 2011.

Kolankowski, Ludwik. *Dzieje Wielkiego Księstwa Litewskiego za Jagiellonów*. Warsaw: Kasa im. Mianowskiego, 1930.

Zygmunt August Wielki Książę Litwy do roku 1548. Lwów: Towarzystwo dla Popierania Nauki Polskiej, 1913.

Kollmann, Nancy Shields. *Kinship and Politics: The Making of the Muscovite Political System 1345–1547*. Stanford, California: Stanford University Press, 1987.

Kondrat'ev, S. V., and Kondrat'eva T. N. *"Nauka ubezhdat'" ili Spory sovetskikh istorikov o frantsuzkom absoliutizme i klassovoi bor'be: 20-e–nachalo 50-kh godov*. Tiumen', Mandr i ko., 2003.

Konovalov, S. "England and Russia: Two Missions, 1666–1668." *Oxford Slavonic Papers* XIII (1967): 47–71.

"Patrick Gordon's Dispatches from Russia 1667." *Oxford Slavonic Papers* XI (1964): 11–12.

Kontler, László, and Balázs Trencsényi. "Hungary." In *European Political Thought 1500–1700: Religion, Law and Philosophy*, edited by Howell A. Lloyd, Glenn Burgess, and Simon Hodson, 176–207. New Haven, Connecticut and London: Yale University Press, 2007.

Korczak, Lidia. *Monarcha i poddani: System władzy w Wielkim Księstwie Litewskim w okresie wczesnojagiellońskim*. Kraków: Towarzystwo Wydawnicze Historia Iagellonica, 2008.

Korsakova, V. "Romanov, Ivan Nikitich." In *Russkii biograficheskii slovar'*, vol. 17 (Romanova–Riasovskii). Petrograd: Izdanie Imperatorskogo Russkogo istoricheskogo obshchestva, 1918.

Korzo, Margarita A. *Nravstvennoe bogoslovie Simeona Polotskogo: Osvoenie katolicheskoi traditsii Moskovskimi knizhnikami vtoroi poloviny XVII veka*. Moscow: IFRAN, 2011.

Ukrainskaia i belorusskaia katekheticheskaia traditsiia kontsa XVI–XVIII vv.: Stanovlenie, evoliutsiia i problema zaimstvovanii. Moscow: KANON+, 2007.

Korzun, Svetlana. *Heinrich von Huyssen (1666–1739): Prinzenerzieher, Diplomat und Publizist in den Diensten Zar Peters I., des Großen*. Jabloniana 3: Quellen und Forschungen zur europäischen Kulturgeschichte der Frühen Neuzeit. Wiesbaden: Harrassowitz, 2013.

Kosheleva, Ol'ga E. "Leto 1645 goda: Smena lits na Rossiiskom prestole." In *Kazus: Individual'nie i unikal'nie v istorii*, edited by Iu. L. Bessmertnyi and M. A. Boitsov, 148–170. Moscow: Izdatel'skii tsentr Rossiiskogo gosudarstvennogo gumanitarnogo universiteta, 1999.

Kostomarov, Nikolai. *Ruina*. Istoricheskie monografii i issledovaniia 15. St. Petersburg and Moscow: Izdatel'stvo M. O. Vol'fa, 1882.

Koukoules, Phaidon. "Ta kata ten gennesin kai ten baptisin ethima ton Vyzantinon." *Epiteris etaireias Vyzantinon spoudon* 14 (1938): 87–146.

Kovrigina, V. A. *Nemetskaia sloboda Moskvy i ee zhiteli v kontse XVII–pervoi polovine XVIII veka*. Moscow: Arkheograficheskii tsentr, 1998.

Kozliakov, Viacheslav. *Mikhail Fedorovich*. Moscow: Molodaia gvardiia, 2004.

Kozlovskii, I. *F. M. Rtishchev: Istoriko-biograficheskoe issledovanie*. Kiev: n.p., 1906. First published 1906 in *Kievskie universitetskie izvestiia* 46 (January 1906): 1–52; (February 1906): 53–100; (June 1906): 101–132; (November 1906): 133–152; (December 1906): 153–201.

Kozlovskii, I. P. *Sil'vestr Medvedev: Ocherk iz istorii russkogo prosveshcheniia i obshchestvennoi zhizni v kontse XVII veka*. Kiev: Tipografiia universiteta Sv. Vladimira, 1895. First published 1895 in *Kievskie universitetskie izvestiia* 35.

Krasnosel'tsev, N. *K istorii pravoslavnogo bogosluzheniia*. Kazan': Tipografiia Imperatorskogo universiteta, 1889.

Krieger, Leonard. *The Politics of Discretion: Pufendorf and the Acceptance of Natural Law*. Chicago, Illinois: University of Chicago Press, 1965.

Krom, M. M. *"Vdovstvuiushchee tsarstvo": Politicheskii krizis v Rossii 30–40-kh godakh XVI veka*. St. Petersburg: Novoe literaturnoe obozrenie, 2010.

Krzyżaniakowa, Jadwiga, and Jerzy Ochmański. *Władysław II Jagiełło*. Wrocław: Zakład Narodowy im. Ossolińskich, 1990.

Kuchkin, V. A. "Poslednee zaveshchanie Dmitriia Donskogo." *Srednevkovaia Rus'* 3 (2001): 106–183.
"Tri zaveshchaniia Vasiliia I." *Drevniaia Rus': Voprosy medievistiki* 64, 2 (2016): 33–54.
Kunisch, Johannes, and Helmut Neuhaus, eds. *Der dynastische Fürstenstaat: Zur Bedeutung von Sukzessionsordungen für die Entstehung des frühmodernen Staates*, Historische Forschungen 21. Berlin: Duncker & Humblot, 1982.
Kurukin, Igor' V. *Ekaterina I.* Moscow: Molodaia gvardiia, 2016.
Epokha "dvortsovykh bur'": Ocherki politicheskoi istorii poslepetrovskoi Rossii. Riazan': NRIID, 2003.
Persidskii pokhod Petra Velikogo: Nizovoi korpus na beregakh Kaspiia (1722–1735). Moscow: Kvadriga, 2010.
Kurukin, I. V., and A. B. Plotnikov. *19 ianvaria–25 fevralia 1730 goda: Sobytiia, liudi, dokumenty.* Moscow: Kvadriga, 2010.
Lachaud, Frédérique, and Michael Penman, eds. *Making and Breaking the Rules: Succession in Medieval Europe c. 1000–c. 1600.* Turnhout: Brepols, 2008.
Lahaye, Matthieu. *Le fils de Louis XIV: Monseigneur le Grand Dauphin (1661–1711).* Seyssel: Champ Vallon, 2013.
Landau, Marcus. *Geschichte Karls VI. als König von Spanien.* Stuttgart: J. G. Cotta, 1889.
Lavrent'ev, A. V. *Tsarevich – tsar' – tsesar': Lzhedmitrii I, ego gosudarstvennaia pechat', nagradnye znaki i medali 1604–1606 gg.* St. Petersburg: Dmitrii Bulanin, 2001.
Lavrov, A. S. *Regenstvo tsarevny Sofii Alekseevna.* Moscow: Arkheologicheskii tsentr, 1999.
Lebedeva, I. N. "Biblioteka tsarevicha Alekseia Petrovicha." In *Kniga i knigotorgovlia v Rossii*, edited by S. P. Luppov. Leningrad: Biblioteka Akademii nauk SSSR, 1984.
"Lichnaia biblioteka tsaria Fedora Alekseevicha." In *Kniga v Rossii XVIII–pervoi polovine XIX v.* Leningrad: Biblioteka Akademii nauk SSSR, 1989.
Lebedeva, T. A. *Ivan Nikitin.* Moscow: Iskusstvo, 1975.
LeDonne, John. *Absolutism and Ruling Class: The Formation of the Russian Political Order 1700–1825.* New York, New York and Oxford: Oxford University Press, 1991.
Le Fur, Didier. *Henri II.* Paris: Talandier, 2009.
Leitsch, Walter. *Moskau und die Politik des Kaiserhofes im XVII. Jahrhundert.* Wiener Archiv für die Geschichte des Slawentums und Osteuropas IV. Graz and Cologne:Böhlau, 1960.
Lenhoff, Gail. *The Martyred Princes Boris and Gleb: A Socio-cultural Study of the Cult and Its Texts.* UCLA Slavic Studies 19. Columbus, Ohio: Slavica, 1989.
Lenhoff, Gail, and Ann Kleimola, eds. *The Book of Royal Degrees and the Genesis of Russian Historical Consciousness.* Bloomington, Indiana: Slavica, 2011.
Liechtenhan, Francine-Dominique. *Élisabeth 1re de Russie: L'autre impératrice.* Paris: Fayard, 2007.
Likhachev, D. S. *Russkie letopisi i ikh kul'turno-istoricheskoe znachenie.* Moscow and Leningrad: Izdatel'stvo Akademii nauk SSSR, 1947.
Likhachev, N. P. *Razriadnye d'iaki XVI veka.* St. Petersburg: Tipografiia V. S. Balashova, 1887.

Limon, Jerzy. *Gentlemen of a Company: English Players in Central and Eastern Europe 1590–1660*. Cambridge: Cambridge University Press, 1985.

Liseitsev, D. M. "Legitimnost' verkhonvnoi vlasti v Rossii v epokhu Smuty: K voprosu o statuse 'vybornykh liudei.'" *Rossiiskaia istoriia* 4 (2014): 146–154.

Prikaznaia sistema Moskovskogo gosudarstva v epokhu Smuty. Moscow and Tula: Institut rossiiskoi istorii RAN and Grif i K, 2009.

Lisitsyn, M. *Pervonachal'nyi slaviano-russkii tipikon*. St. Petersburg: Tipografiia V. D. Smirnova, 1911.

Liubomirov P. G., *Ocherk istorii nizhegorodskogo opolcheniia 1611–1613 gg.* Moscow: Izdatel'stvo sotsial'no-ekonomicheskoi literatury, 1939.

Loades, D. M. *Princes of Wales: Royal Heirs in Waiting*. Richmond: National Archives, 2008.

Lobachev, S. V. *Patriarkh Nikon*. St. Petersburg: Iskusstvo-SPB, 2003.

Lobakova, I. A. *Zhitie mitropolita Filippa*. St. Petersburg: Dmitrii Bulanin, 2006.

Lobanov-Rostovskii, A. B. *Russkaia rodoslovnaia kniga*. St. Petersburg: Izdatel'stvo A. S. Suvorina, 1895.

Longworth, Philip. *Alexis, Tsar of All the Russias*. New York, New York: F. Watts, 1984.

Loseva, O. V. *Russkie mesiatseslovy XI–XIV vekov*. Moscow: Pamiatniki istoricheskoi mysli, 2001.

Łowmiański, Henryk. *Polityka Jagiellonów*. Poznań: Wydawnictwo Poznańskie, 1999.

Lulewicz, Henryk. *Gniewów o unię ciąg dalszy: Stosunki polsko-litewskie w latach 1569–1588*. Warsaw: Instytut Historii Polskiej Akademii Nauk, 2002.

Lur'e, Ia. S. *Dve istorii Rusi XV veka*. St. Petersburg: Tipografiia D. Bulanin; Paris: Institut d'études slaves, 1994.

Ideologicheskaia bor'ba v russkoi publitsistike kontsa XV–nachala XVI veka. Moscow and Leningrad: Izdatel'stvo Akademii nauk, 1960.

Obshcherusskie letopisi XIV–XV vv. Leningrad: Nauka, 1976.

Lur'e, Ia. S., and Iu. D. Rykov, eds. *Perepiska Ivana Groznogo s Andreem Kurbskim*. Leningrad: Nauka, 1979.

Madariaga, Isabel de. *Ivan the Terrible: First Tsar of Russia*. New Haven, Connecticut: Yale University Press, 2005.

Russia in the Age of Catherine the Great. New Haven, Connecticut and London: Yale University Press, 1981.

Majeska, George P. "The Moscow Coronation of 1498 Reconsidered." *Jahrbücher für Geschichte Osteuropas*, Neue Folge 26, 3 (1978): 353–361.

Major, J. Russell. *From Renaissance Monarchy to Absolutism: French Nobles, Kings, and Estates*. Baltimore, Maryland: Johns Hopkins University Press, 1994.

Makarii, *Istoriia Russkoi tserkvi*, 9 vols. Moscow: Izdatel'stvo Spaso-Priobrazhenskogo Valaamskogo monastyria, 1996.

Marasinova, E. N. *"Zakon" i "grazhdanin" v Rossii vtoroi poloviny XVIII veka: Ocherki istorii obshchestvennogo soznaniia*. Moscow: Novoe literaturnoe obozrenie, 2017.

Maravall, José Antonio . "Saavedra Fajardo: Moral de acomodación y carácter conflictivo de la libertad." In José Antonio Maravall, *Estudios de Historia del*

Pensamiento Español. Serie tercera: El siglo del Barocco, 203–230. Madrid: Ediciones Cultura Hispánica, 2001. First published in *Cuadernos Hispanoamericanos* 257–258 (May–June 1971), 663–693.

Marinis, Vasilieos. *Death and the Afterlife in Byzantium: The Fate of the Soul in Theology, Liturgy, and Art*. New York, New York: Cambridge University Press, 2017.

Marker, Gary. *Imperial Saint: The Cult of St. Catherine and the Dawn of Female Rule in Russia*. DeKalb, Illinois: Northern Illinois University Press, 2007.

Markina, L. A. *Portretist Georg Khristof Groot i nemetskie zhivopistsy v Rossii serediny XVIII veka*. Moscow: Pamiatniki istoricheskoi mysli, 1999.

Martin, Russell E. *A Bride for the Tsar: Bride Shows and Marriage Politics in Early Modern Russia*. DeKalb, Illinois: Northern Illinois University Press, 2012.

"Anticipatory Association of the Heir in Early Modern Russia: Primogeniture and Succession in Russia's Ruling Dynasties." In *The Routledge History of Monarchy*, edited by Elena Woodacre, Lucinda H. S. Dean, Chris Jones, Russell E. Martin, and Zita Eva Rohr, 420–444. Abingdon and New York, New York: Routledge, 2019.

"Familial Order, Dynasty, and Succession in Early Modern Russia: Towards a Gendered History of the Muscovite Dynasty." In *The State in Early Modern Russia: New Directions*, edited by Paul Bushkovitch, 29–58. Bloomington, Indiana: Slavica, 2019.

"Praying for the Dead in Muscovy: Kinship Awareness and Orthodox Belief in the Commemorations of Muscovite Royalty." In *The Tapestry of Russian Christianity*, edited by Nickolas Lupinin, Donald Ostrowski, and Jennifer B. Spock. Ohio Slavic Papers 10/Eastern Christian Studies 2, 189–228. Columbus, Ohio: Ohio State University, 2016.

Matasova, Tat'iana. *Sof'ia Paleolog*. Moscow: Molodaia gvardiia, 2016.

Matveev, P. A. "Baturinskii perevorot 13-go marta 1672 goda (Delo Dem'iana Mnogogreshnogo)." *Russkaia starina* 11 (1903): 459–470.

Mazingue, Étienne. *Anton Ulrich: Duc de Braunschweig-Wolfenbüttel (1633–1714), un prince romancier au XVIIème siècle*, 2 vols., Bern, Frankfurt am Main, and Las Vegas, Nevada: Peter Lang, 1978.

Mediger, Walther. *Mecklenburg, Rußland und England-Hannover 1706–1721: Ein Betrag zur Geschichte des Nordischen Krieges*. Quellen und Darstellungen zur Geschichte Niedersachsens 70. Hildesheim: Lax, 1967.

Mel'nikov, S. A. *Pravovyi rezhim nasledovaniia prestola v drevnei Rusi IX–nachala XVI vv.: Istoriko-pravovoe issledovanie*. Moscow: Inform-Znanie, 2009.

Mikhailova, Yulia. *Property, Power, and Authority in Rus and Latin Europe, ca. 1000–1236*. Leeds: ARC Humanities Press, 2018.

Miller, David B. "Another Sort of Genealogy: The Culture of Commemoration at the Trinity-Sergius Monastery and Trinity's First *Sinodik*." In *"The Book of Royal Degrees" and the Genesis of Russian Historical Consciousness*, edited by Gail Lenhoff and Ann Kleimola, 271–286. Bloomington, Indiana: Slavica, 2011.

"The Velikie Minei Chet'i and the Stepennaia Kniga of Metropolitian Makarii and the Origins of Russian National Consciousness." *Forschungen zur osteuropäischen Geschichte* 26 (1979): 263–382.

Menin, Nicolas. *Traité historique et chronologique du sacre et couronnement des rois et des reines de France*. Paris: Jean van Septeren, 1723.

Meyendorff, Paul. *Russia, Ritual and Reform: The Liturgical Reforms of Nikon in the Seventeenth Century*. Crestwood, New York: St. Vladimir's Press, 1991.

Mezin, Sergei. *Petr I vo Frantsii*. St. Petersburg: Evropeiskii dom, 2015.

Mohler, Ludwig. *Kardinal Bessarion als Theologe, Humanist und Staatsman: Funde und Forschungen*, 3 vols. Quellen und Forschungen aus dem Gebiete der Geschichte, herausgegeben von der Görres-Gesellschaft 20, 22, 24. Paderborn: F. Schöningh, 1923–1942.

Moiseeva, G. N. "Pergamennyi sinodik Gosudarstvennogo Istoricheskogo Muzeia v izdanii N. I. Novikova." *TODRL* 26 (1971): 100–108.

Monumenta Poloniae vaticana, 8 vols., Wydawnictwa nos. 71–74, 82, 83, 85. Warsaw: Komisja Historyczna Akademii Umiejętności w Krakowie, 1908–48.

Morev, Ioann. *"Kamen' very" Mitropolita Stefana Iavorskogo*. St. Petersburg: Tipografiia Artilleriiskogo zhurnala, 1904.

Morris, Rosemary. *Monks and Laymen in Byzantium, 843–1118*. Cambridge and New York, New York: Cambridge University Press, 1995.

Mordovina, S. P. "K istorii utverzhdennoi gramoty 1598 g." In *Arkheograficheskii ezhegodnik za 1968 god*, 127–141. Moscow: Izdatel'stvo Akademii, 1970.

Mordovina, S. P., and A. L. Stanislavskii, *Boiarskie spiski poslednei chetverti XVI–nachala XVII v.* Moscow: TSGADA, 1979.

Mormiche, Pascale. *Devenir prince: L'école du pouvoir en France XVIIe–XVIIIe siècles*. Paris: Éditions CNRS, 2009.

Morozova, L. E. *Dva tsaria: Fyodor i Boris*. Moscow: Russkaia slovo 2001.

Rossiia na puti iz Smuty: Izbranie na tsarstvo Mikhaila Romanova. Moscow: Nauka, 2005.

Moshin, V. A. "Serbskaia redaktsiia Sinodika v Nedeliu Pravoslaviia: Analiz tekstov." *Vizantiiskii vremennik* 16 (1959): 317–394.

"Serbskaia redaktsiia Sinodika v Nedeliu Pravoslaviia: Teksty." *Vizantiiskii vremennik* 17 (1960): 278–353.

Mote, Frederick W., and Dennis Twitchett, eds. *The Cambridge History of China*, vol. 7. Cambridge: Cambridge University Press, 1988.

Mousnier, Roland. *Les institutions de la France sous la monarchie absolue*, 2 vols. Paris: Presses universitaires de France, 1974–80.

Les XVIe et XVIIe siècles: Les progrès de la civilisation européenne et le déclin de l'Orient (1492–1715), 2nd ed. Paris: Presses universitaires de France, 1956.

Nekrasov, G. A. *Russko-shvedskie otnosheniia i politika velikikh derzhav v 1721–1726 gg.* Moscow: Nauka, 1964.

Nellen, Henk. *Hugo de Groot: Een leven in strijd om de vrede, 1583–1645*. Amsterdam: Balans, 2007.

Hugo Grotius: A Lifelong Struggle for Peace in Church and State, 1583–1645. Translated by J. G. Grayson. Leiden: Brill, 2015.

Nenner, Howard. *The Right to be King: The Succession in the Crown of England 1603*–1714. Houndsmill and London: Macmillan Press, 1995.

Neubauer, Helmut. *Car und Selbstherrscher: Beiträge zur Geschichte der Autokratie in Rußland*. Veröffentlichungen der Osteuropa-Institut München 22. Wiesbaden:Harrassowitz, 1964.

Nichik, V. M. *Feofan Prokopovich*. Moscow: Mysl', 1977.

Nicol, Donald M. *The Immortal Emperor: The Life and Legend of Constantine Palaiologos, Last Emperor of the Romans*. Cambridge: Cambridge University Press, 1992.

The Last Centuries of Byzantium 1261–1453. Cambridge: Cambridge University Press, 1993.

Nikitina, T. L. *Russkie tserkovnye stennye rospisi 1670–1680-kh godov*. Moscow: Indrik, 2015.

Nikodem, Jarosław. *Witołd Wielki Książe Litewski (1354 lub 1355–27 października 1430)*. Kraków: Avalon, 2013.

Nikolaev, S. I. "Iavorskii, Stefan." In *Slovar' russkikh pisatelei XVIII veka*, vol. III, 456–458. St. Petersburg: Nauka, 2010.

Nikolov, Angel. "Srednevekovyi slavianskii perevod 'Uchitel'nykh glav' imperatora Vasiliia I: Problemy izucheniia rukopisnoi traditsii i rannikh pechatnykh izdanii." In *XIX Ezhegodnaia bogoslovskaia konferentsiia*, vol. I, 41–47. Moscow: Sviato-Tikhvinskii bogoslovskii institut, 2009.

Nikol'skii, Konstantin, *O sluzhbakh russkoi tservki byvshikh v prezhnikh pechatnykh bogosluzhebnykh knigakh*. St. Petersburg: Tipografiia tovarishchestva Obshchestvennaia pol'za, 1885.

Nimchuk, V. V. *Leksykon latyns'kyi E. Slavynets'koho. Leksykon sloveno-latyns'kyi E. Slavynets'koho ta A. Korets'koho-Satanovs'koho*. Kiev: Naukova dumka, 1973.

Nitsche, Peter. *Großfürst und Thronfolger: Die Nachfolgepolitik der Moskauer Herrscher bis zum Ende des Rjurikidenhauses*. Kölner historische Abhandlungen 21. Cologne and Vienna: Böhlau, 1972.

Noflatscher, Heinz. *Maximilian der Deutschmeister (1558–1618): Glaube, Reich und Dynastie*. Quellen und Studien zur Geschichte des Deutschen Ordens 11. Marburg: N. G. Elwert, 1987.

Novodvorskii, V. [Witold Nowodworski]. *Bor'ba za Livoniiu mezhdu Moskvoiu i Rech'iu Pospolitoiu (1570–1582)*. Zapiski istoriko-filologicheskogo fakul'teta imperatorskogo Sankt-Peterburgskogo universiteta 72. St. Petersburg: Tipografiia I. N. Skorokhodova, 1904.

Novokhatko, O. V. *Zapisnye knigi Moskovskogo stola Razriadnogo prikaza XVII veka*. Moscow: Pamiatniki istoricheskoi mysli, 2000.

Nyrop, C. "Nogle oplysninger om Grev Valdemar Christians Ruslandsfærd 1643–45." *Historisk Tidsskrift*, series 6, 3 (1891–2): 237–338.

Odesskii, M. P. *Poetika russkoi dramy: Posledniaia tret' XVII–pervaia tret' XVIII v.* Moscow: Rossiiskii gosudarstvennyi gumanitarnyi universitet, 2004.

Olden-Jørgensen, Sebastian. "Scandinavia." In *European Political Thought 1450–1700: Religion, Law and Philosophy*, edited by Howell A. Lloyd, Glenn Burgess, and Simon Hodson, 300–331. New Haven, Connecticut and London: Yale University Press, 2007.

Oparina, T. A. *Inozemtsy v Rossii XVI–XVII vv.* Moscow: Progress–Traditsiia, 2007.

Ivan Nasedka i polemicheskoe bogoslovie kievskoi mitropolii. Novosibirsk: Nauka, 1998.

Orchard, G. Edward. "The Election of Michael Romanov." *Slavonic and East European Review* 67 (July 1989): 378–402.

Ostrowski, Donald G. *Muscovy and the Mongols: Cross-Cultural Influences on the Steppe Frontier 1304–1589*. Cambridge: Cambridge University Press, 1998.

"Simeon Bekbulatovich's Remarkable Career as Tatar Khan, Grand Prince of Rus', and Monastic Elder." *Russian History* 39, 3 (2012): 269–299.

Paidas, Konstantinos D. S. *Vasileios A' Makedōn: Dyo parainetika keimena pros ton autokratora Leonta 6. ton Sopho*. Athens: Ekdoseis Kanake, 2009.

Ta Vizantina "Katoptra hegemonos" tes hysteres periodou (1251–1403). Athens: Ekdoseis Gregore, 2006.

Panchenko, O. V. "Iz istorii kul'turnykh sviazei Solovetskogo i Troitse-Sergieva Monastyrei v pervoi polovine XVII v.: Troitskii kelar' Aleksandr Bulatnikov." *TODRL* 55 (2004): 488–507.

Panek, Jaroslav. "Königswahl oder Königsannahme? (Thronwechsel im Königreich Böhmen an der Schwelle der Neuzeit)." *Historica: Historical Sciences in the Czech Republic* 3–4 (1996–7): 51–67.

Papée, Fryderik. *Aleksander Jagiellończyk*. Kraków: n.p., 1949.

Jan Olbracht. Kraków: Gebethner i Wolff, 1936.

Pavlenko, N. I. *Ekaterina I*. Moscow: Molodaia gvardiia, 2004.

"Idei absoliutizma v zakonodatel'stve XVIII veka." In *Absolutizm v Rossii*, edited by N. M. Druzhinin. Moscow: Nauka, 1964.

Petr II. Moscow: Molodaia gvardiia, 2006.

Petr Velikii. Moscow: Mysl', 1994.

Pavlov, A. *Nomokanon pri Bol'shom Trebnike*. Odessa: Tipografiia Ul'rikha i Shul'tse, 1872.

Pavlov, A. P. *Dumnye i komnatnye liudi tsaria Mikhaila Romanova: Prosopograficheskoe issledovanie*, 2 vols., St. Petersburg: Dmitrii Bulanin, 2019.

Gosudarev dvor i politicheskaia bor'ba pri Borise Godunove, 1584–1604. St. Petersburg: Nauka, 1992.

"Les Strešnev et les Miloslavskij dans la première moitié du XVIIe siècle: Liens de famille et liens sociaux, carrière à la cour, voies d'accès à l'élite dirigeante." *Cahiers du monde russe* 57, 2–3 (2016): 276–292.

"Ob odnom episode pridvornoi bor'by vremeni tsarstvovaniia Mikhaila Romanova v rasskaze V. N. Tatishcheva." *Canadian–American Slavic Studies* 48 (2014): 146–156.

"Sobornaia utverzhdennaia gramota ob izbranii Borisa Godunova na prestol." *Vspomogatel'nye istoricheskie distsipliny* 10 (1978): 206–225.

Pavlov, Andrey, and Maureen Perrie. *Ivan the Terrible*. London: Pearson/Longman, 2003.

Pekarskii, P. *Nauka i literatura v Rossii pri Petre Velikom*, 2 vols. St. Petersburg: Obshchestvennaia pol'za, 1862.

Pelc, Janusz. *Barok: Epoka przeciwieństw*. Warsaw: Czytelnik, 1993.

Pelenski, Jaroslaw. *The Contest for the Legacy of Kievan Rus*. Boulder, Colorado: East European Monographs, 1998.

Pelenskyj, Jaroslav Z. *Russia and Kazan': Conquest and Imperial Ideology (1438–1560s)*. The Hague: De Gruyter Mouton, 1974.

Péneau, Corinne, ed. *Élections et pouvoirs politiques du VIIe au XVIIe siècle*. Paris: Éditions Bière, 2008.

Pennington, Kenneth. *The Prince and the Law, 1200–1600: Sovereignty and Rights in the Western Legal Tradition*. Berkeley, California: University of California Press, 1993.

Perrie, Maureen. *Pretenders and Popular Monarchism in Early Modern Russia: The False Tsars of the Time of Troubles*. Cambridge: Cambridge University Press, 1995.

Pesenson, Michael. "Nicolae Milescu Spafarii's 'Khrismologion' and 'Skazanie o Sivillakh': Prophecies of Power in Late Seventeenth Century Russia." In *Religion and Identity in Russia and the Soviet Union: A Festschrift for Paul Bushkovitch*, edited by Nikolaos A. Chrissidis, Cathy J. Potter, David Schimmelpenninck van der Oye, and Jennifer Spock, 59–76. Bloomington, Indiana: Slavica, 2011.

Peters, Marion. *De wijze koopman: Het wereldwijde onderzoek van Nicolaes Witsen (1641–1717), burgemeester en VOC-bewindhebber van Amserdam*. Amsterdam: Bakker, 2010.

Petrikeev, D. I. *Krupnoe krepostnoe khoziaistvo XVII v.: Po materialam votchiny B. I. Morozova*. Leningrad: Nauka, 1967.

Petritsch, Ernst D. "Ein Bericht über den Aufenthalt des Zarewitsch Aleksej in den habsburgischen Ländern." In *Die Flucht des Thronfolgers Aleksej: Krise in der "Balance of Power" und den österreichischen-russischen Beziehungen am Anfang des 18. Jahrhunderts*, edited by Iskra Schwartz. Austria: Forschung und Wissenschaft: Geschichte 16, 369–386. Vienna and Berlin: Lit, 2019.

Petrov, N. I. *Kievskaia akademiia vo vtoroi polovine XVII veka*. Kiev: Tipografiia G. T. Korchak-Novitskogo, 1895.

Petrukhintsev, Nikolai "The Duration of Integration as a Factor in Russian History and Its Impact on Social and Political Development in Sixteenth-Century Russia." In *The State in Early Modern Russia: New Directions*, edited by Paul Bushkovitch, 97–132. Bloomington, Indiana: Slavica, 2019.

Tsarstvovanie Anny Ioannovny: Formirovanie vnutrennopoliticheskogo kursa i sud'ba armii i flota 1730–1735 gg. St. Petersburg: Aleteiia, 2001.

Petukhov, Evgenii. *Propovedi Gavriila Buzhinskogo (1717–1727)*. Iur'ev: Tipografiia K. Mattisena, 1901.

Picot, Georges. *Histoire des États généraux*, 2nd ed., 5 vols. Paris: Hachette, 1888.

Pierling, Paul. *La Russie et la Sainte-Siège*, 5 vols. Paris: Plon-Nourrit, 1896–1912.

La Russie et l'Orient: Mariage d'un Tsar au Vatican: Ivan III et Sophie Paléologue. Paris: Leroux, 1891.

Pisarenko, Konstantin. *Elizaveta Petrovna*. Moscow: Molodaia gvardiia, 2014.

Platonov, S. F. *Boris Godunov*. Petrograd: Knigoizdatel'stvo Ogni, 1921.

Ocherki po istorii Smuty v Moskovskom gosudarstve, 3rd ed. St. Petersburg: Ia. Bashmakov i ko., 1910.

Pliukhanova, M. B. "'Poslanie na Ugru' i vopros o proiskhozhdenii moskovskoi imperskoi ideologii." *TODRL* 61 (2010): 452–488.

Siuzhety i simvoly Moskovskogo tsarstva. St. Petersburg: Akropol, 1995.

Plokhy, Serhii. *The Cossacks and Religion in Early Modern Ukraine*. Oxford: Oxford University Press, 2001.

Podobedova, O. I. *Moskovskaia shkola zhivopisi pri Ivane IV: Rabota v moskovskoi Kremle 40kh–70kh godov XVI veka*. Moscow: Nauka, 1972.

Podtergera, Irina A. "Reconstructing the Life of Simeon Polotskii on the Basis of Manuscripts." *Canadian Slavonic Papers* 49, 3–4 (2007): 293–306.

Poe, Marshall. *The Russian Elite in the Seventeenth Century*. Helsinki: Academia Scientarium Fennica, 2004.

Polekhov, Sergei. *Nasledniki Vitovta: Dinasticheskaia voina v Velikom kniazhestve Litovskom v 30-e gody XV veka*. Moscow: Indrik, 2015.

"Poslednie zaveshchaniia Vasiliia I i pechati Vitovta." *Srednevekovaia Rus'* 12 (2016): 183–200.

Polievktov, M. A. *Baltiiskii vopros v russkoi politike posle Nishtadskogo mira (1721–1725)*. Zapiski istoriko-filologicheskogo fakul'teta Sankt-Peterburgskogo universiteta 85. St. Petersburg: Tipografiia M. A. Aleksandrova, 1907.

Poljakov, Fedor B. "Paisios Ligarides und die ostslavische Barockliteratur in Moskau." *Wiener Slavistisches Jahrbuch* 49 (2003): 143–156.

Ponomareva, I. G. "Boiarskoe okruzhenie moskovskogo velikog kniazia Vasiliia Vasil'evicha v 1425–1432 gg." *Rossiiskaia Istoriia* I (2011): 96–107.

"Kto upravlial Moskovskim velikim kniazhestvom v 1425–1432 gg.?" *Srednevekovaia Rus'* 9 (2011): 167–196.

Presniakov, A. E. *Kniazhoe pravo v drevnei Rusi*. St. Petersburg: Nauka, 1909.

Obrazovanie velikorusskogo gosudarstva. Petrograd: Tipografiia Ia. Bashmakov i ko., 1918.

Prozorovskii, Aleksandr. "Sil'vestr Medvedev, ego zhizni i deiatel'nost'."*ChOIDR* 2, 4 (1896): 1–148; 3, 6 (1896): 149–378; 4, 3 (1896): 379–606.

Puech, Vincent. "Élections et enjeux politiques à Byzance: Patriarcat et régence imperial au milieu du XIIIe siècle," In *Élections et pouvoirs politiques du VIIe au XVIIe siècle*, edited by Corinne Péneau, 311–324. Paris: Éditions Bière, 2008.

Raba, Joel. "Moscow – the Third Rome or the New Jerusalem?" *Forschungen zur osteuropäischen Geschichte* 50 (1995): 297–308.

Rady, Martyn. "'They Brought in an Ox as King, They Elected and Installed Him': The Royal Succession in Later Medieval Hungary." In *Making and Breaking the Rules: Succession in Medieval Europe c. 1000–1600*, edited by Frédérique Lachaud and Michael Penman. Turnhout: Brepols, 2008.

Raeff, Marc. *Michael Speransky, Statesman of Imperial Russia, 1772–1839*, 2nd rev. ed. The Hague: Martinus Nijhoff, 1969.

The Well-Ordered Police State: Social and Institutional Change through Law in the Germanies and Russia 1600–1800. New Haven, Connecticut and London: Yale University Press, 1983.

Ram, Harsha. *Imperial Sublime: A Russian Poetics of Empire*. Madison, Wisconsin: University of Wisconsin Press, 2003.

Ramazanova, D. N. "Bukharestskii spisok 'Khrismologiona' Paisiia Ligarida: Paleograficheskoe i kodikologicheskoe issledovanie." *Vestnik RGGU* (50) 10, 7 (2010): 178–191.

Ransel, David. *The Politics of Catherinian Russia: The Panin Party*. New Haven, Connecticut: Yale University Press, 1975.

Redin, D. A. *Administrativnye struktury i biurokratiia Urala v epokhu Petrovskikh reform*. Ekaterinburg: Volot, 2007.
Redondo, Augustin. *Antonio de Guevara (1480?–1545) et l'Espagne de son temps: De la carrière officielle aux œuvres politico-morales*. Geneva: Droz, 1976.
Rees, Roger, ed. *Latin Panegyric*. Oxford: Oxford University Press, 2011.
Rendtorff, Rolf. *Das alte Testament: Eine Einführung*. Neukirchen-Vluyn: Neukirchener Verlag, 1983.
Revelli, Giorgetta. *Monumenti letterari su Boris e Gleb* Genoa: La Quercia, 1993.
Roberts, Michael *The Early Vasas: A History of Sweden 1623–1611*. Cambridge: Cambridge University Press, 1968.
Gustavus Adolphus, 2 vols. London and New York, New York: Longmans, Green and Co., 1953–8.
The Swedish Imperial Experience. Cambridge: Cambridge University Press, 1979.
Robinson, A. N. *Bor'ba idei v russkoi literature XVII veka*. Moscow: Nauka, 1974.
Robinson, A. N., ed. *Simeon Polotskii i ego knigoizdatel'skaia deiatel'nost': Russkaia staropechatnaia literatura: XVI–pervaia chetvert' XVIII v*. Moscow: Nauka, 1982.
Robinson, A. N., O. M. Derzhavina, A. S. Demin, and E. K. Romodanovskaia, eds. *Ranniaia russkaia dramaturgiia*, vols. 1–2. Moscow: Nauka, 1972.
Roche, Paul, ed. *Pliny's Praise: The Panegyricus in the Roman World*. Cambridge: Cambridge University Press, 2011.
Rogov, A. I. *Russko-pol'skie kul'turnye sviazi v epokhu Vozrozhdeniia: Stryikovskii i ego Khronika*. Moscow: Nauka, 1966.
Rolland, Peter. "'Nie skoro prawi monsztuk do tych trąb otrzymacie': On Lazar' Baranovyč's 'Truby sloves propovidnyx' and Their Non-publication in Moscow." *Journal of Ukrainian Studies* 17, 1–2 (1992): 205–216.
Romanoski, Christian. *Tacitus Emblematicus: Diego de Saavedra Fajardo und seine "Empresas Políticas."* Berlin: Weidler Buchverlag, 2006.
Rost, Leonhart. *Die Überlieferung von der Thronnachfolge Davids*. Stuttgart: W. Kohlhammer, 1926.
Rowland, Daniel. "Did Muscovite Literary Ideology Place Limits on the Power of the Tsar (1540s–1660s)?" *Russian Review* 49 (1990): 125–155.
"Moscow – the Third Rome or the New Israel?" *Russian Review* 55 (1996): 591–614.
"Muscovy" in *European Political Thought 1500–1700: Religion, Law and Philosophy*, edited by Howell A. Lloyd, Glenn Burgess, and Simon Hodson, 267–99. New Haven, Connecticut and London: Yale University Press, 2007.
"The Problem of Advice in Muscovite Tales about the Time of Troubles." *Russian History* 6, 2 (1979): 259–283.
Rozov, N. N. "Pokhval'noe slovo velikomu kniaziu Vasiliiu III." In *Arkheograficheskii ezhegodnik za 1964 god*, 278–289. Moscow: Izdatel'stvo Akademii, 1965.
Rummel', V. "Viazemskie." In *Entsiklopediia Brokgauz-Efron*, vol. 7A. St. Petersburg: Semenovskaia tipo litografiia, I. A. Efrona, 1892.
Runkevich, S. G. *Aleksandro-Nevskaia Lavra 1713–1913: Istoricheskoe issledovanie*. St. Petersburg: Sinodal'naia tipografiia, 1913.

Arkhierei petrovskoi epokhi v ikh perepiske s Petrom Velikim. St. Petersburg: Tipografiia Montvida, 1906.

Salmina, M. A. "Slovo o zhitii i prestavlenii velikogo kniazia Dmitriia Ivanovicha, tsaria Rus'skogo." *TODRL* 25 (1970): 81–104.

Samarin, Iu. F. *Stefan Iavorskii i Feofan Prokopovich*. Moscow: D. Samarin, 1880.

Sapiega, L. "Diplomaticheskoe donesenie Sigizmundu III, koroliu pol'skomu o delakh Moskovskikh," *ChOIDR* 1858, book 2, pt. 4, 1–24

Sapozhnikova, O. S. *Russkii knizhnik XVII veka Sergei Shelonin*. Moscow and St. Petersburg: Al'ians-Arkheo, 2010.

Savel'eva, E. A. *Katalog knig iz sobraniia Aptekarskogo prikaza*. St. Petersburg, Alfaret, 2006.

Savva, V. I. *Moskovskie tsari i vizantiiskie vasilevsy: K voprosu o vliianii Vizantii na obrazovanie idei tsarskoi vlasti moskovskikh gosudarei*. Khar'kov: Tipografiia M. Zil'bergerg, 1901.

Sazonova, L. I. *Literaturnaia kul'tura Rossii: Rannee Novoe vremia*. Moscow: Iazyki slavianskikh kul'tur, 2006.

Schaub, Marie-Karine. "Les élections des tsars russes durant les Temps des Troubles (1598–1613). In *Élections et pouvoirs politiques du VIIe au XVIIe siècle*, edited by Corinne Péneau, 325–338. Paris: Éditions Bière, 2008.

Scheliha, Wolfram von. *Russland und die orthdoxe Universalkirche in der Patriarchsperiode (1589–1721)*. Forschungen zur Geschichte Osteuropas 62. Wiesbaden: Harrassowitz, 2004.

Schenk, Frithjof Benjamin. *Aleksandr Nevskij, Heiliger, Fürst, Nationalheld: Eine Erinnerungsfigur im russischen kulturellen Gedächtnis*. Cologne: Böhlau, 2004.

Schilling, Lothar, ed. *Absolutismus, ein unersetzliches Forschungskonzept? Eine deutsch-französische Bilanz/L'absolutisme, un concept irremplaçable? Une mise au point franco-allemande*. Munich: Oldenbourg, 2008.

Schnath, Georg. *Geschichte Hannovers im Zeitalter der neunten Kur und der englischen Sukzession 1674–1714*, vol. III. Hildesheim: August Lax Verlagsbuchhandlung, 1978.

Schreiner, Peter. *Byzanz 565–1453*, 4th ed. Munich: Oldenbourg, 2011.

Schwarcz, Iskra, ed., *Die Flucht des Thronfolgers Aleksej: Krise in der "Balance of Power" und den österreichisch-russischen Beziehungen am Anfang des 18. Jahrhunderts*. Austria: Forschung und Wissenschaft: Geschichte 16. Vienna and Berlin: Lit, 2019.

"Die Flucht des Thronfolgers Aleksej und der Wiener Hof." In *Die Flucht des Thronfolgers Aleksej: Krise in der "Balance of Power" und den österreichischen-russischen Beziehungen am Anfang des 18. Jahrhunderts*, edited by Iskra Schwartz. Austria: Forschung und Wissenschaft: Geschichte 16, 179–198. Vienna and Berlin: Lit, 2019.

Sedov, P. V. *Zakat moskovskogo tsarstva: Tsarskii dvor kontsa XVII veka*. St. Petersburg: Dmitrii Bulanin, 2007.

Seleznev, Iu V. *"A peremenit Bog Ordu": Russko-ordynskie otnosheniia v kontse XIV–pervoi treti XV vv*. Voronezh: Voronezhskii gosudarstvennii universitet, 2006.

Semevskii, M. I. *Tsaritsa Praskov'ia 1664–1723*, 2nd ed. St. Petersburg: Russkaia starina, 1883.

Serov, D. O. *Sudebnaia reforma Petra I: Istoriko-pravovoe issledovanie.* Moscow: Zerkalo-M, 2008.

Setin, F. I. "'Testament' v izdanii Simeon Polotskogo." In *Simeon Polotskii i ego knigoizdatel'skaia deiatel'nost': Russkaia staropechatnaia literatura: XVI–pervaia chetvert' XVIII v.*, edited by A. N. Robinson, 105–115. Moscow: Nauka, 1982.

Shablova, T. I. *Kormovoe pominovanie v Uspenskom Kirillo-belozerskom Monastyre v XVI–XVII vekakh.* St. Petersburg: Renome, 2012.

Shakhmatov, A. A. *Razyskaniia o drevneishikh russkikh letopisnykh svodov.* St. Petersburg: Tipografiia M. A. Aleksandrova, 1908.

Shamin, S. M. "Tsirk tsarevicha Alekseia Mikhailovicha." *Peterburgskie slavianskie i balkanskie issledovaniia*, 2, 20 (2016): 136–151.

Shaposhnik, V. V. "Miatezh Andreia Staritskogo (osen' 1536–iun' 1537 g.)." *Studia Slavica et Balcanica Petropolitana*, 1 (2013): 174–212.

Sharpe, Kevin. *Image Wars: Kings and Commonwealths in England 1603–1660.* New Haven, Connecticut: Yale University Press, 2010.

Selling the Tudor Monarchy: Authority and Image in Sixteenth-Century England. New Haven, Connecticut: Yale University Press, 2009.

Shchebal'skii, P. *Politicheskaia sistema Petra III.* Moscow: Universitetskaia tipografiia, Katkov i ko., 1870.

Shliapkin, I. A. *Sv. Dmitrii Rostovskii i ego vremia (1654–1709 g.).* Zapiski istoriko-filologicheskogo fakul'teta imperatorskogo Sankt-Peterburgskogo universiteta 24. St. Petersburg: Tipografiia i khromolitografiia A. Transhel', 1891.

Shmurlo, E. F. "Kriticheskie zametki po istorii Petra Velikogo." *Zhurnal Ministerstva narodnogo prosveshcheniia* 329 (May 1900): 54–95; 330 (August 1900): 193–234; 331 (October 1900): 335–366; 338 (December 1901): 237–249; 340 (April 1902): 421–439; 341 (June 1902): 233–256.

Shustova, Iu. E. "Prazdnik Novogo Goda v Rossii XVII vv." In *Kalendar': Khronologicheskaia kul'tura i problemy ee izucheniia*, 192–201. Moscow: Rossiiskii gosudarstvennyi gumanitarnyi universitet, 2006.

"Prazdnik Novoletiia v epokhu tsaria Alekseia Mikhailovicha: Zarozhdenie novoi prazdnichnoi kul'tury." *Kolomenskoe: Materialy i issledovaniia* 13 (2011): 31–48.

Siegl-Mocavini, Susanne. *John Barclays "Argenis" und ihr staatspolitischer Kontext: Untersuchungen zum politischen Denken der frühen Neuzeit.* Tübingen: M. Niemeyer, 1999.

Simonin, Michel. *Charles IX.* Paris: Fayard, 1995.

Sinitsyna, N. V. *Maksim Grek v Rossii.* Moscow: Nauka, 1977.

Tretii Rim: Istoki i evoliutsiia russkoi srednevekovoi kontseptsii, XV–XVII vv. Moscow: Indrik, 1998.

Sirenov, A. V. *Stepennaia kniga: Istoriia teksta.* Moscow: Iazyki Slaviaskikh kul'tur, 2007.

Skovgaard-Petersen, Karen. "'... By the Direction of the Most Noble and Distinguished Christen Friis': The Influence of the Chancellor Christen Friis (1581–1639) on the Histories of Denmark by Johannes Pontanus (1571–1639) and Johannes Meursius (1579–1639)." In *Pomp, Power, and*

Politics: Essays on German and Scandinavian Court Culture and Their Context, edited by Mara R. Wade, special issue. *Daphnis: Zeitschrift für mittlere deutsche Literatur und Kultur der frühen Neuzeit (1400–1750)* 32, 1–2 (2003): 199–229.

Skrynnikov, R. G. "Dukhovnoe zaveshchaniia tsaria Ivana Groznogo. *TODRL* 21 (1965): 309–318.

Rossiia nakanune "Smutnogo vremeni." Moscow: Mysl', 1980.

Rossiia posle Oprichniny. Leningrad: Izdatel'stvo Leningradskogo universiteta, 1975.

Tsarstvo terrora. St. Petersburg: Nauka, 1992.

Skrzhinskaia, E. Ch. *Rus', Italiia, i Vizantiia v Srednevekov'e*. St. Petersburg: Aleteiia, 2000.

Smirnov, I. I. *Ocherki politicheskoi istorii Russkogo gosudarstva 30–50-kh godov*. Moscow and Leningrad: Izdatel'stvo Akademii nauk SSSR, 1958.

Smirnov, P. P. *Posadskie liudi i ikh klassovaia bor'ba do serediny XVII veka*, 2 vols. Moscow: Izdatel'stvo Akademii nauk SSSR, 1947–8.

Soldat, Cornelia *Das Testament Ivans des Schrecklichen von 1572: Eine kritische Aufklärung*. Lewiston, New York, Queenston, and Lampeter: Edwin Mellen Press, 2013.

Solnon, Jean-François. *Henri III: Un désir de majesté*. Paris: Perrin, 2001.

Solodkin, Ia. G. "Prisiagi moskovskim gosudariam po dannym sibirskogo letopisnogo svoda," *Vestnik All'ians-Arkheo* 17 (2016): 90–102.

Zemskie sobory Moskovskoi Rusi kontsa XVI veka: Spornye problemy istorii i istoriografii. Nizhnevartovsk: Izdatel'stvo Nizhnevartovskogo gosudarstvennogo gumanitarnogo universiteta, 2010.

Solov'ev, S. M. *Istoriia Rossii s drevneishikh vremen*, 15 vols. Moscow: Izdatel'stvo sotsial'no-ekonomicheskoi literatury, 1960–6. First published 29 vols., Moscow: Universitetskaia tipografiia, 1851–79.

Sommer, Wolfgang. *Die lutherischen Hofprediger in Dresden: Grundzüge ihrer Geschichte und Verkündigung im Kurfürstlichen Sachsen*. Stuttgart: Steiner, 2006.

Spuler, Bertold. *Die goldene Horde: Die Mongolen in Rußland 1223–1502*, 2nd ed. Wiesbaden: Harrassowitz 1965.

Sreznevskii, I. I. *Materialy dlia slovaria drevnerusskogo iazyka*, 3 vols. Moscow: Kniga, 1989. First published 3 vols. St. Petersburg: Otdelenie russkogo iazyka i slovesnosti Imperatorskoi akademii nauk, 1902.

Stanislavskii, A. L. *Grazhdanskaia voina v Rossii XVII v.: Kazachestvo na perelome istorii*. Moscow: Mysl', 1990.

Stashevskii, E. *Ocherki po istorii tsarstvovaniia Mikhaila Fyodorovicha*. Kiev: Tipografiia vtoroi Arteli, 1913.

Smolenskaia voina 1632–1634 gg.: Organizatsiia i sostoianie Moskovskoi armii. Kiev: Universitetskaia tipografiia N. T. Korchak-Novitskogo, 1919.

Stefanovič, Petr S. "Expressing Loyalty in Medieval Russia: Oath vs. Oral Formulas." In *Oralité et lien social au Moyen Âge (Occident, Byzance, Islam)*, edited by Marie-France Auzépy and Guillaume Saint-Guillain. Paris: Association des amis du Centre d'histoire et civilisation de Byzance, 2008.

Stefanovich, Petr S. "Kniaz' i boiare: Kliatva vernosti i pravo ot"ezda." In *Drevniaia Rus': Ocherki politicheskogo i sotsial'nogo stroia*, edited by A. A. Gorskii, V. A. Kuchkin, P. V. Lukin, and P. S. Stefanovich, 148–269. Moscow: Indrik, 2008.

Steindorff, Ludwig. "Desirable Ubiquity? Family Strategies of Donation and Commemoration in Muscovy." *Cahiers du monde russe* 57, 2–3 (2016): 641–665.

Memoria in Altrußland: Untersuchungen zu den Formen christlicher Totensorge, Quellen und Studien zur Geschichte des östlichen Europa 38. Stuttgart: F. Steiner, 1994.

"Wer sind die Meinen? Individuum und Memorialkultur in frühneuzeitlichen Russland." In *Das Individuum und die Seinen: Individualität in der okzidentalen und in der russischen Kultur in Mittelalter und früher Neuzeit*, edited by Yuri L. Bessmertny and Otto Gerhard Oexle, 231–258. Veröffentllichungen des Max-Planck-Instituts für Geschichte 163. Göttingen: Vandenhoeck & Ruprecht, 2001.

Stökl, Günter. *Testament und Siegel Ivans IV.* Wiesbaden: Westdeutscher Verlag, 1972.

Strakhov, Olga B. *The Byzantine Culture in Muscovite Rus': The Case of Evfimii Chudovskii (1620–1705)*. Bausteine zur slavischen Philologie und Kulturgeschichte. Series A, Slavistische Forschungen; New sequence, vol. 26. Cologne: Böhlau, 1998.

Strong, Roy. *Henry, Prince of Wales and England's Lost Renaissance.* London: Thames and Hudson, 1986.

Sumtsov, N. F. *K istorii iuzhnorusskoi literatury semnadtsago stoletiia*, vol. I. *Lazar' Baranovich.* Khar'kov: Tipografiia M. F. Zil'berberga, 1885.

Svalenius, Ivan. *Gustav Vasa.* Stockholm: Wahlstrom & Widstrand, 1963.

Sverdlov, M. B. *Domongol'skaia Rus'.* St. Petersburg: Akademicheskii proekt, 2003.

Svetova, E. A. *Dvor Alekseia Mikhailovicha v kontekste absoliutizatsii tsarskoi vlasti.* Moscow: Moskovskii pedagogicheskii gosudarstvennyi universitet, 2013.

Svoronos, Nicolas. "Le serment de fidélité à l'empereur byzantin et sa signification constitutionelle." *Revue des études byzantines* 9 (1951): 106–142.

Szeftel, Marc. "The Title of the Muscovite Monarch." *Canadian–American Slavic Studies* 13, 1–2 (1979): 59–81.

Taimasova, L. Iu. "Diplomaticheskii etiud vremen Livonskoi voiny: Skandal'naia svad'ba v Novgorode." *Novyi istoricheskii vestnik* 3, 45 (2015): 79–126; 4, 46 (2015): 40–76.

Tairova-Iakovleva, T. G. *Ivan Mazepa i Rossiiskaia imperiia: Istoriia "predatel'stva."* Moscow and St. Petersburg: Tsentropoligraf, 2011.

Targosz-Kretowa, Karolina. *Teatr dworski Władysława IV, 1635–1648.* Kraków: Wydawnictwo Literackie, 1965.

Tatarskii, I. *Simeon Polotskii (ego zhizn' i deiatel'nost').* Moscow: M. G. Volchaninov, 1886.

Tęgowski, Jan. "O następstwie tronu na Litwie po śmierci Olgierda." *Przegląd Historyczny* 84, 2 (1993): 127–134.

Ternovskii, Filipp. *Izuchenie vizantiiskoi istorii i ee tendentsioznoe prilozhenie v drevnei Rusi*, 2 vols. Kiev: Universitetskaia tipografiia, 1875–6.

"Stefan Iavorskii (Biograficheskii ocherk)," *Trudy Kievskoi dukhovnoi akademii* (1864): (1), 36–70; (3), 237–290; (6), 137–186.

Thomson, Francis. *The Reception of Byzantine Culture in Medieval Russia*. Farnham: Ashgate, 1999.

Thyrêt, Isolde. *Between God and Tsar: Religious Symbolism and the Royal Women of Muscovite Russia*. DeKalb, Illinois: Northern Illinois University Press, 2001.

"The Cultural Politics of the Grand Princesses of Moscow and the Emergence of the Muscovite Dynasty." *Russian History/Histoire Russe* 33, 2–4 (2006): 333–352.

"Marfa Ivanovna and the Expansion of the Role of the Tsar's Mother in the 17th Century." In *Rude and Barbarous Kingdom Revisited: Essays in Russian History in Honor of Robert O. Crummey*, edited by Chester Dunning, Russell Martin, and Daniel Rowland, 109–130. Bloomington, Indiana: Slavica, 2008.

"The *Tale of the Death of Vasilii Ivanovich* and the Evolution of the Muscovite Tsaritsa's Role in 16th Century Russia." In *Dubitando: Studies in History and Culture in Honor of Donald Ostrowski*, edited by Brian J. Boeck, Russell E. Martin, and Daniel Rowland. Bloomington, Indiana: Slavica, 2012.

Tikhomirov, M. N. "Maloizvestnye letopisnye istochniki XVI v." *Istoricheskie zapiski* 10 (1941): 84–94.

Titov, F. I. *Imperatorskaia kievskaia dukhovnaia Akademiia 1615–1915*. Kiev: Gopak, 2003. First published 1915.

Russkaia pravoslavnaia tserkov' v Pol'sko-litovskom gosudarstve, vol. 2. *Kievskaia mitropoliia-eparkhiia v XVII–XVIII vv. (1686–1797)*. Kiev: Tipografiia I. I. Chokolova, 1905.

Tiumentsev, I. O. *Smutnoe vremia v Rossii v nachale XVII veka: Dvizhenzie Lzhedmitriia II*. Moscow: Nauka, 2008.

Tolstikov, A. V. "'Reliatsiia o Gustave, syne korolia Erika' i Petr Petrei." In *Grani sotrudnichestva: Rossiia i Severnaia Evropa*, edited by I. R. Takal and I. M. Solomeshch, 104–121. Petrozavodsk: Izdatel'stvo PetrGU, 2012.

Tougher, Shaun. "Macedonian Mirrors: The Advice of Basil I for His Son Leo VI." In *Concepts of Ideal Rulership from Antiquity to the Renaissance*, edited by G. Roskam and S. Schorn. Turnhout: Brepols, 2018.

Trachevskii, Aleksandr. *Pols'koe beskorolev'e po prekrashchenii dinastii Iagiellonov*. Moscow: K. Soldatenkov, Tipografiia Gracheva i ko., 1869.

Treadgold, Warren. *The Middle Byzantine Historians*. London: Palgrave Macmillan, 2013.

Treitinger, Otto. *Die oströmische Kaiser- und Reichsidee*, 2nd ed. Darmstadt: Hermann Gentner Verlag, 1956. First published Jena: W. Biedermann, 1938.

Trepavlov, V. V. *Stepnye imperii Evrazii: Mongoly i tatary*. Moscow: Kvadriga, 2015.

Zolotaia Orda v XIV stoletii. Moscow: Kvadriga, 2010.

Tsereteli, E. *Elena Ioannovna Velikaia Kniaginia Litovskaia, russkaia, koroleva pol'skaia*. St. Petersburg: Tipografiia I. N. Skorokhodova, 1898.

Tsvetaev, D. "Mariia Vladimirovna i Magnus Datskii." *Zhurnal Ministerstvo narodnogo prosveshcheniia* 196, 3 (1878): 57–85.

"Protestantstvo i protestanty v Rossii do epokhi preobrazovanii." *ChOIDR*, 4 (1889): 1–328; 1 (1890): 329–782.

Tuck, Richard. *Philosophy and Government 1572–1651*. Cambridge: Cambridge University Press, 1993.

Tupikov, N. "Literaturnaia deiatel'nost' tsarevicha Ivana Ivanovicha," *Zhurnal Ministerstva Narodnago Prosveshcheniia* 296 (December 1894): 358–374.

Tvorogov, O. V. *Drevnerusskie khronografy*. Leningrad: Nauka, 1975.

Tyszkowski, Kazimierz. *Poselstwo Lwa Sapiehy w Moskwie 1600 r.* Archiwum Towarzystwa Naukowego we Lwowie. Lwów: Towarzystwo Naukowe, 1927.

Uebersberger, Hans. *Österreich und Russland seit dem Ende des 15. Jahrhunderts*. Veröffentlichungen der Kommission für neuere Geschichte Österreichs. Vienna: W. Braumüller, 1906.

Ulewicz, Tadeusz. *Sarmacja: Studium z problematyki słowiańskiej XV i XVI w.* Kraków: Studium Słowiańskiego Uniwersytetu Jagiellońskiego, 1950.

Ulianovs'kyi, V. I. *Mytropolyt Kyivs'kyi Spyrydon: Obraz kriz' epokhu, epokha kriz' obraz*. Kyiv: Lybid, 2004.

Upton, A. F. *Charles XI and Swedish Absolutism*. Cambridge: Cambridge University Press, 1998.

Usachev, A. S. *Stepennaia kniga i drevnerusskaia knizhnost' vremeni mitropolita Makariia*. Moscow and St. Petersburg: Al'ians-Arkheo, 2009.

Uspenskii, B. A. *Izbrannye trudy*, 3 vols. Moscow: Gnozis, 1994–7.

Tsar' i patriarkh: Kharizma vlasti v Rossii. Moscow: Shkola iazyki russkoi kul'tury, 1998.

"Vospriiatiia istorii v Drevnei Rusi i doktrina 'Moskva – Tretii Rim'." In *Russkoe podvizhnichestvo*, edited by T. B. Kniazevskaia. Moscow: Nauka 1996.

Ustinova, I. A. *Knigi patriarshikh prikazov 1620–1649 gg. kak istoricheskii istochnik*. Moscow: Institut rossiskoi istorii RAN, 2011.

Ustrialov, N. G. *Istoriia tsarstvovaniia Petra Velikogo*, 5 vols. St. Petersburg: Tipografiia Vtorogo otdelenie sobstvennoi E.I.V. Kantseliarii, 1858–63.

Val'denberg, Vladimir. *Drevnerusskie ucheniia o predelakh tsarskoi vlasti*. Petrograd: n.p., 1916.

Vandal, Albert. *Louis XV et Élisabeth de Russie: Étude sur les rélations de la France et de la Russie au dix-huitième siècle*. Paris: Plon-Nourrit, 1896.

Vasser, Larissa. *Europäische Hofkünstler in St. Petersburg in der ersten Hälfte des 18. Jahrhunderts: Bildhauer Bartolomeo Carlo Rastrelli, Maler Johann Gottfried Tannauer und Louis Caravaque: Ein Beitrag zur "Europäisierung" Russlands*. Berlin: Logos Verlag, 2015.

Vatin, Nicholas and Gilles Veinstein. *Le sérail ébranlé: Essai sur les morts, dépositions et avènements des sultans ottomans, XIVe–XIXe siècle*. Paris: Fayard, 2003.

Verkhovskii, P. V. *Uchrezhdenie Dukhovnoi kollegii i dukhovnyii reglament: K voprosu ob otnosheniii tserkvi i gosudarstva v Rossii*, 2 vols. Rostov: n.p., 1916.

Vernadsky, George. *Kievan Russia*. New Haven, Connecticut: Yale University Press, 1948.

The Mongols and Russia. New Haven, Connecticut: Yale University Press, 1953.

Veselovskii, S. B. *D'iaki i pod'iachie XV–XVII vv.* Moscow: Nauka, 1975.

"Dukhovnoe zaveshchanie Ivana Groznogo kak istoricheskii istochnik." In S. B. Veselovskii, *Issledovaniia po istorii Oprichniny*, 302–322. Moscow: Akademiia nauk SSSR, 1963.

Vilkul, T. L. *Liudi i kniaz' v drevnerusskikh letopisiakh serediny XI–XIII vv.* Moscow: Kvadriga, 2009.

Vishnevskii, D. *Kievskaia akademiia v pervoi polovine XVIII stoletiia*. Kiev: Tipografiia I. I. Gorbunova, 1903.

Vladimirskii-Budanov M. F. *Obzor istorii russkogo prava*. St. Petersburg: Izdatel'stvo N. Ia. Obolgina, 1905.

Vodoff, Vladimir. "Remarques sur la valeur du terme 'tsar' appliqué aux princes russes avant le milieu du XVe siècle." *Oxford Slavonic Papers* XI (1978): 1–41.

Vodolazkin, E. G. *Vsemirnaia istoriia v literature drevnei Rusi*, 2nd ed. St. Petersburg: Pushkinskii dom, 2008.

Voskresenskii, N. A., ed. *Zakonodatel'nye akty Petra I*, vol. I. Moscow and Leningrad: Izadatel'stvo Akademii nauk SSSR, 1945.

Vosters, Simon A. *Antonio de Guevara y Europa*. Salamanca: Ediciones Universidad de Salamanca, 2009.

Vovina-Lebedeva, V. G. *Novyi letopisets: Istoriia teksta*. St. Petersburg: Dmitrii Bulanin, 2004.

Vsevolodskii-Gerngross, V. N. *Russkii teatr ot istokov do serediny XVIII veka*. Moscow: Izdatel'stvo Akademii nauk SSSR, 1957.

Waliszewski, Kazimierz. *La dernière des Romanovs: Élisabeth 1re impératrice de Russie 1741–1762*. Paris: Plon-Nourrit, 1902.

Watanabe-O'Kelly, Helen. *Court Culture in Dresden: From Renaissance to Baroque*. Basingstoke and New York, New York: Palgrave, 2002.

"Religion and the Consort: Two Electresses of Saxony and Queens of Poland (1697–1757)." In *Queenship in Europe: The Role of the Consort*, edited by Clarissa Campbell Orr. Cambridge: Cambridge University Press, 2004.

Watson, Christine. *Tradition and Translation: Maciej Stryjkowski's Polish Chronicle in Seventeenth-Century Russian Manuscripts*. Studia Slavica Upsaliensia 46. Uppsala: Uppsala University, 2012.

Wetterberg, Gunnar. *Från tolv till ett: Arvid Horn (1664–1742)*. Stockholm: Atlantis, 2006.

Whittaker, Cynthia. *Russian Monarchy: Eighteenth-Century Rulers and Writers in Political Dialogue*. DeKalb, Illinois: Northern Illinois University Press, 2003.

Willson, Justin "Virtue Idealized in the Palace Frescoes of Ivan the Terrible." Slavic Review, 2021.

Wittram, Reinhard. *Peter I Czar und Kaiser*, 2 vols. Göttingen, Vandenhoeck & Ruprecht, 1964.

Wójcik, Zbigniew. *Traktat andruszowski 1667 roku i jego geneza*. Warsaw: Państwowe Wydawnictwo Naukowe, 1959.

Rzeczpospolita wobec Turcji i Rosji, 1674–1679: Studium z dziejów polskiej polityki zagranicznej. Wrocław: Zakład Narodowy im. Ossolińskich, 1976.

Woodworth, C. K. "Sophia and the Golden Belt: What Caused Moscow's Civil Wars of 1425–1450." *Russian Review* 68 (April, 2009): 187–198.

Woodworth, Cherie. "The Tsar's Descent from Caesar." PhD dissertation, Yale University, 2001.

Wortman, Richard S. "The 'Fundamental State Laws' of 1832 as Symbolic Act." In *Miscellanea Slavica: Sbornik statei k 70-letiiu Borisa Andreevicha Uspenskogo*. Moscow: Indrik, 2008.

Zabelin, Ivan. *Domashnii byt russkogo naroda v XVI i XVII st.*, vols. 1–2: *Domashnii byt russkikh tsarei v XVI–XVII stoletiiakh*, vol. 3: *Domashnii byt russkikh tsarits v XVI i XVII st.* Moscow: Kniga, 2000–3.

"Opisanie novgorodskoi sviatyni v 1634 godu." *ChOIDR* 4 (1862): smes', 50–56.

Zamiatin, G. A. "K istorii zemskogo sobora 1613 g." *Trudy Voronezhskogo gosudarstvennogo universiteta* III (1926): 1–74.

Rossiia i Shvetsiia v nachale XVII veka: Ocherki politicheskoi i voennoi istorii. St. Petersburg: RGGU, 2008.

Zawitkowska, Wioletta. *Walka polityczno-prawna o następstwo tronu po Władysławie Jagielle w latach 1424–1434.* Rzeszów: Wydawnictwo Uniwersytetu Rzeszowskiego, 2015.

Zernova, A. S. "Belorusskii pechatnik S. Sobol'." *Kniga: Issledovaniia i materialy* 10 (1965): 126–145.

Knigi kirillovskoi pechati izdannye v Moskve v XVI–XVII vekakh. Moscow: Tipografiia Biblioteki SSSR imeni V. I. Lenina, 1958.

Zhivov, Viktor. *Iz tserkovnoi istorii vremen Petra Velikogo.* Moscow: Novoe literaturnoe obozrenie, 2004.

Zimin, A. A., *Formirovanie boiarskoi aristokratii v Rossii vo vtoroi polovine XV–pervoi terti XVI v.* Moscow: Nauka, 1988.

Krupnaia feodal'naia votchina i sotsial'no-politicheskaia bor'ba v Rossii (konets XV–XVI v.). Moscow: Nauka, 1977.

Oprichnina, 2nd ed. Moscow: Territoriia, 2001.

Oprichnina Ivana Groznogo. Moscow: Mysl', 1964.

Reformy Ivana Groznogo. Moscow: Izdatel'stvo sotsial'no-ekonomicheskoi literatury, 1960.

Rossiia na poroge novogo vremeni. Moscow: Mysl', 1972.

Rossiia na rubezhe XV–XVI stoletii. Moscow: Mysl', 1982.

"Udel'nye kniazia i ikh dvory vo vtoroi polovine XV i pervoi polovine XVI veka." In *Istoriia i genealogiia*, edited by N. I. Pavlenko,161–188. Moscow: Nauka, 1977.

V kanun groznykh potriasenii. Moscow: Mysl', 1986.

Vitiaz' na rasput'e: Feodal'naia voina v Rossii XV v. Moscow: Mysl', 1991.

Zitser, Ernest A. *The Transfigured Kingdom: Sacred Parody and Charismatic Authority at the Court of Peter the Great.* Ithaca, New York and London: Cornell University Press, 2004.

Zoberman, Pierre. *Les panégyriques du roi prononcés dans l'Académie française.* Paris: Presses de l'Université de Paris-Sorbonne, 1991.

Index

Lightning Source UK Ltd.
Milton Keynes UK
UKHW022308080321
380022UK00003B/59

9 781108 479349